7TH EDITION

MACROECONOMICS
for Today

IRVIN B. TUCKER
UNIVERSITY OF NORTH CAROLINA CHARLOTTE

SOUTH-WESTERN
CENGAGE Learning™

Australia • Brazil • Japan • Korea • Mexico • Singapore • Spain • United Kingdom • United States

SOUTH-WESTERN
CENGAGE Learning

Macroeconomics for Today,
Seventh Edition
Irvin B. Tucker

Vice President, Editorial Director:
Jack W. Calhoun

Publisher: Joe Sabatino

Senior Acquisitions Editor: Steven Scoble

Developmental Editor: Michael
Guendelsberger

Senior Marketing Manager: John Carey

Senior MarCom Manager: Sarah Greber

Content Project Manager: Kelly Hillerich

Editorial Assistant: Allyn Bissmeyer

Marketing Coordinator: Suellen Ruttkay

Media Editor: Deepak Kumar

Senior Frontlist Buyer, Manufacturing:
Sandra Milewski

Production Service: PreMediaGlobal

Senior Art Director: Michele Kunkler

Cover and Internal Designer: Kim Torbeck/
Imbue Design

Cover Image: © Media Bakery;
© IMAGEMORE Co, Ltd.

For product information and technology assistance, contact us at
Cengage Learning Customer & Sales Support, 1-800-354-9706

For permission to use material from this text or product,
submit all requests online at **cengage.com/permissions**
Further permissions questions can be emailed to
permissionrequest@cengage.com

Library of Congress Control Number: 2010934778

ISBN 13: 978-0-538-46944-9

ISBN 10: 0-538-46944-7

South-Western Cengage Learning
5191 Natorp Boulevard
Mason, OH 45040
USA

Cengage Learning is a leading provider of customized learning solutions with office locations around the globe, including Singapore, the United Kingdom, Australia, Mexico, Brazil, and Japan. Locate your local office at:
international.cengage.com/region

Cengage Learning products are represented in Canada by
Nelson Education, Ltd.

For your course and learning solutions, visit **academic.cengage.com**

Purchase any of our products at your local college store or at our preferred online store **www.cengagebrain.com**

Printed in Canada
1 2 3 4 5 6 7 14 13 12 11 10

Irvin B. Tucker

Irvin B. Tucker has over thirty years of experience teaching introductory economics at the University of North Carolina Charlotte. He earned his B.S. in economics at N.C. State University and his M.A. and Ph.D. in economics from the University of South Carolina. Dr. Tucker is former director of the Center for Economic Education at the University of North Carolina Charlotte and a longtime member of the National Council on Economic Education. He is recognized for his ability to relate basic principles to economic issues and public policy. His work has received national recognition by being awarded the Meritorious Levy Award for Excellence in Private Enterprise Education, the Federation of Independent Business Award for Postsecondary Educator of the Year in Entrepreneurship and Economic Education, and the Freedom Foundation's George Washington Medal for Excellence in Economic Education. In addition, his research has been published in numerous professional journal articles on a wide range of topics including industrial organization, entrepreneurship, and economics of education. Dr. Tucker is also the author of the highly successful *Survey of Economics*, seventh edition, a text for the one-semester principles of economics courses, published by Cengage South-Western Publishing.

Brief Contents

Contents

2

PART 2

Microeconomic Fundamentals 57

CHAPTER 3

Market Demand and Supply 58

APPENDIX TO CHAPTER 3
Consumer Surplus, Producer Surplus, and Market Efficiency 91

CHAPTER 4

Markets in Action 100

APPENDIX TO CHAPTER 4
Applying Supply and Demand Analysis to Health Care 125

PART 4

Macroeconomic Theory and Policy   209

CHAPTER 8

The Keynesian Model   210

CHAPTER 9

The Keynesian Model in Action   237

CHAPTER 10

Aggregate Demand and Supply   258

Conversion Table for the Four Versions of this Text

Economics for Today	Economics for Today	Macroeconomics for Today	Microeconomics for Today	Survey of Economics
1 Introducing the Economic Way of Thinking	X	X	X	X
2 Production Possibilities, Opportunity Cost, and Economic Growth	X	X	X	X
3 Market Supply and Demand	X	X	X	X
4 Markets in Action	X	X	X	X
5 Price Elasticity of Demand and Supply	X		X	X
6 Consumer Choice Theory	X		X	
7 Production Costs	X		X	X
8 Perfect Competition	X		X	X
9 Monopoly	X		X	X
10 Monopolistic Competition and Oligopoly	X		X	X
11 Labor Markets	X		X	X
12 Income Distribution, Poverty, and Discrimination	X		X	X
13 Antitrust and Regulation	X		X	
14 Environmental Economics	X		X	
15 Gross Domestic Product	X	X		X
16 Business Cycles and Unemployment	X	X		X
17 Inflation	X	X		X
18 The Keynesian Model	X	X		
19 The Keynesian Model in Action	X	X		
20 Aggregate Demand and Supply	X	X		X
21 Fiscal Policy	X	X		X
22 The Public Sector	X	X		X
23 Federal Deficits, Surpluses, and the National Debt	X	X		X
24 Money and the Federal Reserve System	X	X		X
25 Money Creation	X	X		X
26 Monetary Policy	X	X		X
27 The Phillips Curve and Expectations Theory	X	X		
28 International Trade and Finance	X	X	X	X
29 Economies in Transition	X	X	X	X
30 Growth and the Less-Developed Countries	X	X	X	X

Note: Chapter numbers refer to the complete book, Economics for Today

Preface

TEXT WITH A MISSION

The purpose of *Economics for Today*, Seventh Edition, is to teach, in an engaging style, the basic operations of the U.S. economy to students who will take a two-term economics course. Rather than taking an encyclopedic approach to economic concepts, *Economics for Today* focuses on the most important tool in economics—supply and demand analysis—and applies it to clearly explain real-world economic issues.

Every effort has been made to make *Economics for Today* the most "student friendly" text on the market. This text was written because so many others expose students to a confusing array of economic analyses that force students to simply memorize in order to pass the course. Instead, *Economics for Today* presents a straightforward and unbiased approach that effectively teaches the application of basic economic principles. After reading this text, the student should be able to say "now that economics stuff in the news makes sense."

HOW IT FITS TOGETHER

The text presents the core principles of microeconomics, macroeconomics, and international economics. The first 14 chapters introduce the logic of economic analysis and develop the core of microeconomic analysis. Here students learn the role of demand and supply in determining prices in competitive versus monopolistic markets. This part of the book explores such issues as minimum wage laws, rent control, and pollution. The next 13 chapters develop the macroeconomics part of the text. Using the modern, yet simple, aggregate demand and aggregate supply model, the text explains measurement of and changes in the price level, national output, and employment in the economy. The study of macroeconomics also includes how the supply of money and the demand for money influence the economy. Finally, the text concludes with three chapters devoted entirely to global issues. For example, students will learn how the supply of and demand for currencies determine exchange rates and what the complications of a strong or a weak dollar are.

TEXT FLEXIBILITY

The full version of *Economics for Today* is easily adapted to an instructor's preference for the sequencing of microeconomics and macroeconomics topics. The text can be used in a macroeconomic–microeconomic sequence by teaching the first four chapters and then Parts 5 through 7. Next, microeconomics is covered in Parts 2 through 4. Finally, the course can be completed with Part 8, consisting of three chapters devoted to international economics.

An important design of this text is that it accommodates the two camps for teaching principles of macroeconomics: (1) those who cover both the Keynesian Cross and *AD/AS* models and (2) those who skip the Keynesian model and cover only the *AD/AS* model. For instructors who prefer the former model sequence, *Economics for Today* moves smoothly in Chapters 18–19 (8–9) from the Keynesian model (based on the Great Depression) to the *AD/AS* model in Chapter 20 (10). For instructors using the latter approach, this text is written so that instructors can skip the Keynesian model in Chapters 18–19 (8–9) and proceed from Chapter 17 (7) to Chapter 20 (10) without losing anything. For example, the spending multiplier is completely covered both in the Keynesian and *AD/AS* model chapters.

For instructors who wish to teach the self-correcting *AD/AS* model, emphasis can be placed on the appendixes to Chapters 20 (10) and 26 (16). Instructors who choose not to cover this model can simply skip these appendixes. In short, *Economics for Today* provides more comprehensive and flexible coverage of macroeconomics models than is available in other texts. Also, a customized text might meet your needs. If so, contact your South-Western/Cengage Learning sales representative for information.

HOW NOT TO STUDY ECONOMICS

To some students, studying economics is a little frightening because many chapters are full of graphs. Students often make the mistake of preparing for tests by trying to memorize the lines of graphs. When their graded tests are returned, the students using this strategy will probably exclaim, "What happened?" The answer to this query is that the students should have learned the economic concepts *first*; then they would understand the graphs as *illustrations* of these underlying concepts. Stated simply, superficial cramming for economics quizzes does not work.

For students who are anxious about using graphs, the appendix to Chapter 1 provides a brief review of graphical analysis. In addition, the *Graphing Workshop* and *Study Guide* contain step-by-step features on how to interpret graphs.

CHANGES TO THE SEVENTH EDITION

The basic layout of the seventh edition remains the same. The following are changes:

- Chapter 1 recognizes that students taking introductory college-level economics courses are considering their major. One reason to select economics is that the average starting salary for an undergraduate economics major is higher compared to many other majors. To aid their decision, current average starting salary figures for selected majors have been provided.

- Chapter 9 on Monopoly presents a new concept, network good, which updates this chapter by linking economies of scale and monopoly power to the popular Facebook and Match.com Web sites.

- Chapter 12 on Income Distribution, Poverty, and Discrimination has been updated with the latest figures on family income distribution and poverty rates. In addition, the feature articles on Social Security and fair pay for females have been updated. These are all timely features that generate great interest for students.

- Chapter 14 on Environmental Economics is among today's highly controversial issues. This issue is addressed by new Global Economics features titled "How Should Carbon Emissions Be Reduced: Cap and Trade or Carbon Taxes?" and "Why Is the Climate Change Problem So Hard to Solve?" The Analyze the Issue sections that accompany these features give students an opportunity to participate in this important environmental debate.

- Chapter 17 on Inflation updates data on inflation and the You're the Economist feature on "How Much More Does It Cost to Laugh?" In addition, a new Checkpoint titled "What Is the Real Price of Gasoline?" is added that provides an application for adjusting the price of gasoline for inflation over time. And here students enjoy learning how to convert Babe Ruth's 1932 salary into today's dollars.

- Chapter 20(10) on Aggregate Demand and Supply has been revised to provide a unique, complete, unbiased, and realistic comparison of the Keynesian and self-correction macroeconomic models in contrast to texts that present only or primarily the self-correction model. To enhance student understanding and interest, updated actual CPI and real GDP numbers are used throughout rather than generic P_s and Q_s. For example, a new exhibit is added that explains with actual data how decreases in aggregate demand during the current recession caused a movement along the flat Keynesian range of the aggregate supply curve with the CPI constant. Here students can clearly visualize and comprehend the Keynesian argument against the classical school that prices and wages are inflexible downward.

- The appendix to Chapter 20(10) fully develops and explains the opposing self-correction model based on downward flexibility of prices and wages and a downward shifting short-run aggregate supply curve. Only by providing a complete presentation of both the Keynesian and self-correction models can the student understand the current macroeconomic public policy debate.

- Chapter 21(11) on Fiscal Policy also uses realism as its hallmark by explaining the stimulus package and the spending multiplier process with real-world updated numbers.

- Chapter 22(12) on The Public Sector highlights the important current issue of the changing economic character of the United States with global comparisons to other countries. Here, for example, updated data traces the growth of U.S. government expenditures and taxes since the Great Depression. And U.S. spending and taxation are compared to other countries. An explanation of the Value Added Tax (VAT) has been added to the You're the Economist feature discussion of the flat tax and national sales tax.

- Chapter 23(13) on Federal Deficits, Surpluses, and the National Debt focuses on the current "hot button" issue of federal deficits and the national debt using updated data and exhibits. This chapter now includes a discussion of the "PayGo" rule and a new exhibit giving a global comparison of the national debt as a percentage of GDP. The current financial crisis in Greece is included in the chapter debate over the consequences of the U.S. national debt.

- Chapter 26(16) on Monetary Policy has been updated using actual data in the model that link changes in the money supply and changes in the aggregate demand curve required to restore the economy to full employment. Students' interest is enhanced by adding a set of exhibits comparing monetary policy during the Great Depression to monetary policy during the current Great Recession.

• The final three chapters of the text are the international chapters, and each has been updated. For example, the chapter on International Trade and Finance explains the recent sharp decline in the U.S. balance of trade. The chapter on Economies in Transition contrasts privatization in Cuba, Russia, and China to recent nationalization in the United States. And the chapter on Growth and the Less-Developed Countries presents updated data used to explain, for example, the link between economic freedom and quality-of-life indicators.

• New lecture PowerPoint® slides have been developed by the author and tested in his classroom.

ALTERNATE VERSIONS OF THE BOOK

For instructors who wish to spend various amounts of time for their courses and offer different topics of this text:

• *Economics for Today.* This complete version of the book contains all 30 chapters. It is designed for two-semester introductory courses that cover both microeconomics and macroeconomics.

• *Microeconomics for Today.* This version contains 17 chapters and is designed for one-semester courses in introductory microeconomics.

• *Macroeconomics for Today.* This version contains 20 chapters and is designed for one-semester courses in introductory macroeconomics.

• *Survey of Economics.* This version of the book contains 23 chapters. It is designed for one-semester courses that cover the basics of both microeconomics and macroeconomics.

The accompanying table shows precisely which chapters are included in each book.

Instructors who wish more information about these alternative versions should contact their local South-Western/Cengage Learning representative.

MOTIVATIONAL PEDAGOGICAL FEATURES

Economics for Today strives to motivate and advance the boundaries of pedagogy with the following features:

Part Openers

Each part begins with a statement of the overall mission of the chapters in the part. In addition, there is a nutshell introduction of each chapter in relation to the part's learning objective.

Chapter Previews

Each chapter begins with a preview designed to pique the student's interest and reinforce how the chapter fits into the overall scheme of the book. Each preview appeals to the student's "Sherlock Holmes" impulses by posing several economics puzzles that can be solved by understanding the material presented in the chapter.

Margin Definitions and Flashcards

Key concepts introduced in the chapter are highlighted in bold type and then defined with the definitions again in the margins. This feature therefore serves as a quick reference. Key terms are also defined on the Tucker Web site with a Flashcard feature that is great for learning terms.

You're the Economist

Each chapter includes boxed inserts that provide the acid test of "relevance to everyday life." This feature gives the student an opportunity to encounter timely, real-world extensions of economic theory. For example, students read about Fred Smith as he writes an economics term paper explaining his plan to create FedEx. To ensure that the student wastes no time figuring out which concepts apply to the article, applicable concepts are listed after each title. Many of these boxed features include quotes from newspaper articles over a period of years demonstrating that economic concepts remain relevant over time.

Conclusion Statements

Throughout the chapters, highlighted conclusion statements of key concepts appear at the ends of sections and tie together the material just presented. Students will be able to see quickly if they have understood the main points of the section. A summary of these conclusion statements is provided at the end of each chapter.

Global Economics

Today's economic environment is global. *Economics for Today* carefully integrates international topics throughout the text and presents the material using a highly readable and accessible approach designed for students with no training in international economics. All sections of the text that present global economics are identified by a special global icon in the text margin and in the Global Economics boxes. In addition, the final three chapters of the book are devoted entirely to international economics.

Analyze the Issue

This feature follows each *You're the Economist* and *Global Economics* feature and asks specific questions that require students to test their knowledge of how the material in the boxed insert is relevant to the applicable concept. To allow these questions to be used in classroom discussions or homework assignments, answers are provided in the Instructor's Manual rather than the text.

Checkpoint

Watch for these! Who said learning economics can't be fun? This feature is a unique approach to generating interest and critical thinking. These questions spark students to check their progress by asking challenging economics puzzles in game-like style. Students enjoy thinking through and answering the questions, and then checking the answers at the end of the chapter. Students who answer correctly earn the satisfaction of knowing they have mastered the concepts.

Illustrations

Attractive large graphical presentations with grid lines and real-world numbers are essential for any successful economics textbook. Each exhibit has been carefully analyzed to ensure that the key concepts being represented stand out clearly. Brief descriptions are included with graphs to provide guidance for students as they study the graph. When actual data are used, the Web site reference is provided so that students can easily locate the data source.

Causation Chains Game

This will be one of your favorites. The highly successful causation chains are included under many graphs throughout the text. This pedagogical device helps students visualize complex economic relationships in terms of simple box diagrams that illustrate how one change causes another change. Each exhibit having a causation chain in the text is included in the Animated Causation Chains game on the Tucker Web site (www.cengage.com/economics/tucker). This game makes it fun to learn. Arrange the blocks correctly and hear the cheers.

Key Concepts

Key concepts introduced in the chapter are listed at the end of each chapter and on the Tucker Web site (www.cengage.com/economics/tucker). As a study aid, you can use the key concepts as flashcards to test your knowledge. First state the definition and then click on the term to check for correctness.

Visual Summaries

Each chapter ends with a brief point-by-point summary of the key concepts. Many of these summarized points include miniaturized versions of the important graphs and causation chains that illustrate many of the key concepts. These are intended to serve as visual reminders for students as they finish the chapters and are also useful in reviewing and studying for quizzes and exams.

Study Questions and Problems

The end-of-chapter questions and problems offer a variety of levels ranging from straightforward recall to deeply thought-provoking applications. The answers to odd questions and problems are in the back of the text. This feature gives students immediate feedback without requiring the instructor to check their work.

End-of-Chapter Practice Quizzes

A great help before quizzes. Many instructors test students using multiple-choice questions. For this reason, the final section of each chapter provides the type of multiple-choice questions given in the instructor's Test Bank. The answers to all of these questions are given in the back of the text. In addition, students may visit the Tucker Web site (www.cengage.com/economics/tucker) and answer these questions online where an explanation of each correct answer is given.

Part Road Map

This feature concludes each part with review questions listed by chapter from the previous part. To reinforce the concepts, each set of questions relates to the interactive causation chain game. Click on the Tucker Web site (www.cengage.com/economics/tucker) and make learning fun listening to the cheers when correct and jeers for a wrong answer. Answers to the questions are in the back of the text.

Interactive Quizzes

In addition to the end-of-chapter practice quizzes, there are additional multiple-choice questions written by the author on the Tucker Web site (www.cengage.com/economics/tucker). Each quiz contains multiple questions like those found on a typical exam. Feedback is included for each answer so that you may know instantly why you have answered correctly or incorrectly. In addition, you may email yourself and/or your instructor the quiz results with a listing of correct and incorrect answers. Between this feature and the end-of-chapter practice quizzes, students are well prepared for tests.

Online Exercises

These exercises for each chapter are designed to spark students' excitement about researching on the Internet by asking them to access online economic data and then answer questions related to the content of the chapter. All Internet exercises are on the Tucker Web site (www.cengage.com/economics/tucker) with direct links to the addresses so that students will not have the tedious and error-prone task of entering long Web site addresses.

Learning Objectives

Learning objectives link sections in the text and steps to achieve learning objectives. The steps include reference to "Ask the Instructor Video Clips" and the "Graphing Workshop" available through the CourseMate Web site.

A SUPPLEMENTS PACKAGE DESIGNED FOR SUCCESS

To learn more about the supplements for *Economics for Today*, visit the Tucker Web site, www.cengage.com/economics/tucker. For additional information, contact your South-Western/Cengage sales representative.

INSTRUCTOR RESOURCES

Aplia

Aplia, www.aplia.com, has joined forces with South-Western, the leading publisher for principles of economics and finance, to create the Aplia Integrated Textbook Solution. More students are currently using an Aplia product for principles of economics than those who are using all other Web-based learning programs combined. Because the homework in Aplia is automatically graded, you can assign homework more frequently to ensure your students are putting forth full effort and getting the most out of your class.

Instructor's Manual

This manual, prepared by Douglas Copeland of Johnson County Community College, provides valuable course assistance to instructors. It includes chapter outlines, instructional objectives, critical thinking/group discussion questions, hints for effective teaching, answers to the Analyze the Issue questions, answers to even-numbered questions and problems, summary quizzes with answers, and classroom games. Instructor's Manual ISBN: 1111222452.

Test Bank

Too often, Test Banks are not written by the author and the questions do not really fit the text. Not so here. The Test Bank is prepared by the text author to match the text. The Test Bank includes over 7,000 multiple-choice, true-false, and short essay questions arranged by the order presented in the chapter and grouped with concept headings that make it easy to select questions. Most questions have been thoroughly tested in the classroom by the author and are classified by topic and degree of difficulty. Text page references help locate pages where material related to questions is explained.

Macro Test Bank ISBN: 1111222495
Micro Test Bank ISBN: 1111222509

ExamView

ExamView Computerized Testing Software contains all of the questions in the printed *Test Bank*. ExamView is an easy-to-use test creation software compatible with both Windows and Macintosh. Instructors can add or edit questions, instructions, and answers; select questions by previewing them on the screen; or select questions randomly or by number. Instructors can also create and administer quizzes online, whether over the Internet, a local area network (LAN), or a wide area network (WAN). ExamView is available on the Instructor's Resource CD ISBN: 1111222525.

PowerPoint® Lecture Slides

This state-of-the-art slide presentation developed by the text author provides instructors with visual support in the classroom for each chapter. Lecture slides contain vivid automated highlights of important concepts and exhibits. Instructors can edit the PowerPoint® presentations or create their own exciting in-class presentations. These slides are available on the Instructor's Resource CD (ISBN: 1111222525) as well as for downloading from the Tucker Web site at www.cengage.com/economics/tucker.

PowerPoint® Exhibit Slides

These slides contain the figures, charts, and tables from the text. Instructors can easily incorporate them into their own PowerPoint® presentations by downloading from the Tucker Web site at www.cengage.com/economics/tucker. They are also available on the Instructor's Resource CD ISBN: 1111222525.

Instructor's Resource CD-ROM

Get quick access to all instructor ancillaries from your desktop. This easy-to-use CD lets you review, edit, and copy exactly what you need in the format you want. This supplement contains the Instructor's Manual, Test Bank, ExamView Testing software, and the PowerPoint® Lecture and Exhibit slides. IRCD ISBN: 1111222525.

JoinIn TurningPoint CD JoinIn is a response system that allows you to transform your classroom and assess your students' progress with instant in-class quizzes and polls. Our exclusive agreement to offer TurningPoint software lets you pose book-specific questions and display students' answers seamlessly within the Microsoft PowerPoint® slides of your own lecture, in conjunction with the "clicker" hardware of your choice. Enhance how your students interact with you, your lecture, and each other. For college and university adopters only. Contact your local South-Western representative to learn more.

Complete Online Tomlinson Videos Course The Tomlinson videos are online multimedia video lecture series that provide students with instructional assistance 24/7. Students can watch these segments over and over as they prepare for class, review topics, and study for exams. Lecture notes and quizzes for each segment are also available. Professors may require students to view the videos before class to leave the class time free for activities or further explanation. www.cengage.com/economics/tomlinson

STUDENT RESOURCES

Study Guide

The Study Guide is recommended for each student using the text. It is perhaps the best way to prepare for quizzes. The Study Guide was prepared by the text author to prepare students before they take tests in class. The Study Guide contains student-friendly features such as the chapter in a nutshell, key concepts review, learning objectives, fill-in-the-blank questions, step-by-step interpretation of the graph boxes, multiple-choice questions, true-false questions, and crossword puzzles.

    Full Study Guide ISBN: 1111222460
    Macro Study Guide ISBN: 1111222487
    Micro Study Guide ISBN: 1111222479

The Tucker CourseMate Web site

Available for purchase, the CourseMate Web site: (www.cengagebrain.com) features a content-rich, robust set of multimedia learning tools. These Web features have been specifically developed with the student in mind:

- **ABC News Videos.** This supplement consists of high-interest clips from current news events as well as historic raw footage going back forty years. Perfect for discussion starters or to enrich your lectures and spark interest in the material in the text, these brief videos provide students with a new lens through which to view the past and present, one that will greatly enhance their knowledge and understanding of significant events and open up new dimensions in learning. Clips are drawn from such programs as *World News Tonight*, *Good Morning America*, *This Week*, *Primetime Live*, *20/20*, and *Nightline*, as well as numerous ABC News specials and material from the Associated Press Television News and British Movietone News collections. Your South-Western Publishing representative will be happy to provide a complete listing of the videos and policies addressed.

- **The Graphing Workshop.** The Graphing Workshop is a one-stop learning resource for help in mastering the language of graphs, one of the more difficult aspects of an economics course for many students. It enables students to explore important economic concepts through a unique learning system made up of tutorials, interactive drawing tools, and exercises that teach how to interpret, reproduce, and explain graphs.

- **Ask the Instructor Video Clips.** Via streaming video, difficult concepts are explained and illustrated. These video clips are extremely helpful review and clarification tools if a student has trouble understanding an in-class lecture or is a visual learner.

- **Economic Applications** *(EconApps)*. EconNews Online, EconDebates, and EconData features help to deepen students' understanding of the theoretical concepts through hands-on exploration and analysis of the latest economic news stories, policy debates, and data.

FOR STUDENTS AND INSTRUCTORS

The Wall Street Journal

The *Wall Street Journal* is synonymous with the latest word on business, economics, and public policy. *Economics for Today* makes it easy for students to apply economic concepts to this authoritative publication, and for you to bring the most up-to-date, real-world events into your classroom. For a nominal additional cost, *Economics for Today* can be packaged with a card entitling students to a 15-week subscription to both the print and online versions of the *Wall Street Journal*. Instructors with at least seven students who activate their subscriptions will automatically receive their own free subscription. Contact your South-Western/Cengage Learning sales representative for package pricing and ordering information.

CENGAGE LEARNING'S GLOBAL ECONOMIC WATCH

Lessons from real life right now

The credit collapse. Tumbling markets. Bailouts and bankruptcies. Surging unemployment. Political debate. Today's financial turmoil transforms academic theory into intense real-life challenges that affect every family and business sector—making it one of the most teachable moments in modern history.

Cengage Learning's Global Economic Watch helps instructors bring these pivotal current events into the classroom—through a powerful, continuously updated online suite of content, discussion forums, testing tools, and more.

The Watch, a first-of-its-kind resource, stimulates discussion and understanding of the global downturn with easy-to-integrate teaching solutions:

- A content-rich blog of breaking news, expert analysis, and commentary—updated multiple times daily—plus links to many other blogs

- A powerful real-time database of hundreds of relevant and vetted journal, newspaper, and periodical articles, videos, and podcasts—updated four times every day

- A thorough overview and timeline of events leading up to the global economic crisis

- Discussion and testing content, PowerPoint® slides on key topics, sample syllabi, and other teaching resources

- Instructor and student forums for sharing questions, ideas, and opinions

- History is happening now. Bring it into your classroom. For more information on how you can enrich your course with The Watch, please visit www.cengage.com/thewatch.

TextChoice: Economic Issues and Activities

TextChoice is the home of Cengage Learning's online digital content. TextChoice provides the fastest, easiest way for you to create your own learning materials. South-Western's Economic Issues and Activities content database includes a wide variety of high-interest, current event/policy applications as well as classroom activities that are designed specifically to enhance introductory economics courses. Choose just one reading, or many—even add your own material—to create an accompaniment to the textbook that is perfectly customized to your course. Contact your South-Western/Cengage Learning sales representative for more information.

Tucker Web Site

The Tucker Web site at www.cengage.com/economics/tucker provides access to: Animated Causation Chains, practice quizzes, interactive quizzing, and other downloadable teaching and learning resources.

ACKNOWLEDGMENTS

A deep debt of gratitude is owed to the reviewers for their expert assistance. All comments and suggestions were carefully evaluated and served to improve the final product. To each of the reviewers of all seven editions, I give my sincerest thanks.

Jack E. Adams
University of Arkansas-Little Rock

John W. Alderson, III
East Arkansas Community College

Irma Alonso
Florida International University

Hasaan Aly
The Ohio State University

James Q. Aylsworth
Lakeland Community College

Randy Barnes
Mirimar College

Atin Basu
Virginia Military Institute

Klaus G. Becker
Texas Tech University

Randall W. Bennett
Gonazaga University

John P. Blair
Wright State University

Orn B. Bodvarsson
St. Cloud State University

Tantatape Brahmasrene
Purdue University North Central

Joyce Bremer
Oakton Community College

Anne Bresnock
California State University, Pomona

Stacey Brook
University of Sioux Falls

Stephanie Campbell
Mineral Area College

Juan Castro
ETX Baptist University

Dell Champlin
Eastern Illinois University

Doug Copeland
Johnson County Community College

John P. Dahlquist
College of Alameda

James P. D'Angelo
University of Cincinnati

Jan L. Dauve
University of Missouri

Gregory J. Delemeester
Marietta College

Robert C. Dolan
University of Richmond

William Dougherty
Carroll County Community College

James W. Eden
Portland Community College

Ronald Elkins
Central Washington University

Tommy Eshleman
University of Nebraska, Kearney

John L. Ewing-Smith
Burlington County College

Chris Fawson
Utah State University

Arthur A. Fleisher, III
Metropolitan State College of Denver

Kaya Ford
Northern Virginia Community College

Arthur Friedberg
Mohawk Valley Community College

Scott Gabeheart
Mesa Community College

Linda Ghent
Eastern Illinois University

Cindy Gibson
Keuka College

J. P. Gilbert
Mira Costa College

Deborah Goldsmith
City College of San Francisco

Sanford D. Gordon
University of South Florida

Gary Green
Manatee Community College

Serge S. Grushchin
ASA College of Advanced Technology

Steven Hackett
Humbolt State University

Gail A. Hawks
Miami Dade Community College

Michael G. Heslop
Northern Virginia Community College

Yu-Mong Hsiao
Campbell University

R. Jack Inch
Oakland Community College

Hans R. Isakson
University of Northern Iowa

Barbara H. John
University of Dayton

Petur O. Jonsson
Fayetteville State University

Paul Jorgensen
*Linn-Benton Community
College*

Louise Keely
University of Wisconsin

Randall G. Kesselring
Arkansas State University

Harry T. Kolendrianos
Danville Community College

William F. Kordsmeier
University of Central Arkansas

Margaret Landman
Bridgewater State College

David Latzko
Pennsylvania State University, York

Ralph F. Lewis
Orange Coast College

Stephen E. Lile
Western Kentucky University

Dandan Liu
Bowling Green State University

Melody Lo
University of Southern Mississippi

Thomas Maloy
Muskegon Community College

Dayle Mandelson
University of Wisconsin-Stout

Robert A. Margo
Vanderbilt University

Melanie Marks
Longwood College

Michael Marlow
Cal Polytechnic State U-SLO

Fred May
Trident Technical College

James C. McBrearty
University of Arizona

Diana L. McCoy
*Truckee Meadows Community
College*

Donald P. McDowell
Florida Community College

Fazlul Miah
Fayetteville State University

David S. Moewes
Concordia College

Margaret Moore
Franklin University

Marie Mora
New Mexico State University

Kevin J. Murphy
Oakland University

Jack Muryn
*University of Wisconsin-
Washington County*

Lee Nordgren
Indiana University

Peter K. Olson
Indiana University

Patrick B. O'Neill
University of North Dakota

Jan Palmer
Ohio University

Michael L. Palmer
*Maple Woods Community
College*

Elliott Parker
University of Nevada in Reno

Kathy Parkison
Indiana University-Kokomo

Donald W. Pearson
Eastern Michigan University

Martin Perline
Wichita State University

Elaine Peterson
*California State University,
Stanislaus*

Maurice Pfannestiel
Wichita State University

Michael J. Pisani
Texas A&M University

L. Wayne Plumly, Jr.
Valdosta State University

Ray Polchow
*Muskingum Area Technical
College*

Renee Prim
*Central Piedmont Community
College*

Fernando Quijano
Dickinson State University

R. Larry Reynolds
Boise State University

Kathryn Roberts
Chipola Junior College

Steve Robinson
*University of North Carolina
at Wilmington*

Craig Rogers
Canisius College

Daniel A. Talley
Dakota State University

Harold Warren
East Tennessee State University

Lawrence P. Schrenk
University of Baltimore

Daryl Thorne
Valencia Community College

Leo M. Weeks
Northwestern University

Kurt A. Schwabe
Ohio University

Larry Towle
Eastern Nazarene College

Robert G. Welch
Midwestern State University

Lisa Simon
*California Polytechnic State
University*

Greg Trandel
University of Georgia

Herbert D. Werner
University of Missouri

Richard Trieff
*Des Moines Area Community
College*

Michael D. White
St. Cloud State University

Larry Singell
University of Oregon

Gwen Williams
Alvernia College

Alden W. Smith
Anne Arundel Community College

Tracy M. Turner
Kansas State University

Virginia S. York
Gulf Coast Community College

Tricia Snyder
William Patterson University

Lee Van Scyok
University of Wisconsin-Oshkosh

Paul Young
Dodge City Community College

Angela M. Sparkman
Itawamba Community College

Roy van Til
University of Maine-Farmington

Michael J. Youngblood
Rock Valley College

Larry Spizman
SUNY-Oswego

Darlene Voeltz
*Rochester Community and
Technical College*

Rebecca Summary
*Southeast Missouri State
University*

Rosemary Walker
Washburn University

SPECIAL THANKS

My appreciation goes to Steve Scoble, Sr. Acquisitions Editor for South-Western/
Cengage Learning. My thanks also to Michael Guendelsberger, Developmental Editor, Kelly Hillerich, Content Project Manager; Allyn Bissmeyer, Editorial
Assistant; and Suellen Ruttkay, Marketing Coordinator, who put all the pieces of
the puzzle together and brought their creative talent to this text, and Sharon Tripp
for the copyediting of the manuscript. I am also grateful to John Carey for his
skillful marketing. I especially wish to express my deepest appreciation to Douglas
Copeland of Johnson County Community College for preparing the Instructor's
Manual. Finally, I give my sincere thanks for a job well done to the entire team at
Cengage South-Western.

Introduction to Economics

© Getty Images

The first two chapters introduce you to a foundation of economic knowledge vital to understanding the other chapters in the text. In these introductory chapters, you will begin to learn a valuable reasoning approach to solving economics puzzles that economists call "the economic way of thinking." Part 1 develops the cornerstone of this type of logical analysis by presenting basic economic models that explain such important topics as scarcity, opportunity cost, production possibilities, and economic growth.

chapter

1

Introducing the Economic Way of Thinking

Welcome to an exciting and useful subject economists call "the economic way of thinking." As you learn this reasoning technique, it will become infectious. You will discover that the world is full of economics problems requiring more powerful tools than just common sense. As you master the methods explained in this book, you will appreciate economics as a valuable reasoning approach to solving economics puzzles. Stated differently, the economic way of thinking is important because it provides a logical framework for organizing your thoughts and understanding an economic issue or event. Just to give a sneak preview, in later chapters you will study the perils of government price fixing for gasoline and health care. You will also find out why colleges and universities charge students different tuitions for the same education. You will investigate whether you should worry if the federal government fails to balance its budget. You will learn that the island of

Yap uses large stones with holes in the center as money. In the final chapter, you will study why some countries grow rich while others remain poor and less developed. And the list of fascinating and relevant topics continues throughout each chapter. As you read these pages, your efforts will be rewarded by an understanding of just how economic theories and policies affect our daily lives—past, present, and future.

Chapter 1 acquaints you with the foundation of the economic way of thinking. The first building blocks joined are the concepts of scarcity and choice. The next building blocks are the steps in the model-building process that economists use to study the choices people make. Then we look at some pitfalls of economic reasoning and explain why economists might disagree with one another. The chapter concludes with a discussion of why you may wish to be an economics major.

In this chapter, you will learn to solve these economics puzzles:

- Can you prove there is no person worth a trillion dollars?

- Why would you purchase more Coca-Cola when the price increases?

- How can we explain the relationship between the Super Bowl winner and changes in the stock market?

THE PROBLEM OF SCARCITY

Our world is a finite place where people, both individually and collectively, face the problem of scarcity. Scarcity is the condition in which human wants are forever greater than the available supply of time, goods, and resources. Because of scarcity, it is impossible to satisfy every desire. Pause for a moment to list some of your unsatisfied wants. Perhaps you would like a big home, gourmet meals, designer clothes, clean air, better health care, shelter for the homeless, more leisure time, and so on. Unfortunately, nature does not offer the Garden of Eden, where every desire is fulfilled. Instead, there are always limits on the economy's ability to satisfy unlimited wants. Alas, scarcity is pervasive, so "You can't have it all."

You may think your scarcity problem would disappear if you were rich, but wealth does not solve the problem. No matter how affluent an individual is, the wish list continues to grow. We are familiar with the "rich and famous" who never seem to have enough. Although they live well, they still desire finer homes, faster planes, and larger yachts. In short, the condition of scarcity means all individuals, whether rich or poor, are dissatisfied with their material well-being and would like more. What is true for individuals also applies to society. Even Uncle Sam can't escape the problem of scarcity because the federal government never has enough money to spend for the poor, education, highways, police, national defense, Social Security, and all the other programs it wishes to fund.

Scarcity is a fact of life throughout the world. In much of South America, Africa, and Asia, the problem of scarcity is often life threatening. On the other hand, North America, Western Europe, and some parts of Asia have achieved substantial economic growth and development. Although life is much less grueling in the more developed countries, the problem of scarcity still exists because individuals and countries never have as much of all the goods and services as they would like to have.

SCARCE RESOURCES AND PRODUCTION

Because of the economic problem of scarcity, no society has enough resources to produce all the goods and services necessary to satisfy all human wants. Resources are the basic categories of inputs used to produce goods and services. Resources are also called *factors of production*. Economists divide resources into three categories: *land*, *labor*, and *capital* (see Exhibit 1).

Scarcity

The condition in which human wants are forever greater than the available supply of time, goods, and resources.

Resources

The basic categories of inputs used to produce goods and services. Resources are also called *factors of production*. Economists divide resources into three categories: land, labor, and capital.

Exhibit 1   **Three Categories of Resources**

Resources are the basic categories of inputs organized by entrepreneurship (a special type of labor) to produce goods and services. Economists divide resources into the three categories of land, labor, and capital.

Land   Labor   Capital

Entrepreneurship organizes resources to produce goods and services

Land

Land

A shorthand expression for any natural resource provided by nature.

Land is a shorthand expression for any natural resource provided by nature. *Land* includes those resources that are gifts of nature available for use in the production process. Farming, building factories, and constructing oil refineries would be impossible without land. Land includes anything natural above or below the ground, such as forests, gold, diamonds, oil, coal, wind, and the ocean. Two broad categories of natural resources are *renewable resources* and *nonrenewable resources*. Renewable resources are basic inputs that nature can automatically replace. Examples include lakes, crops, and clean air. Nonrenewable resources are basic inputs that nature cannot automatically replace. There is only so much coal, oil, and natural gas in the world. If these fossil fuels disappear, we must use substitutes.

Labor

Labor

The mental and physical capacity of workers to produce goods and services.

Entrepreneurship

The creative ability of individuals to seek profits by taking risks and combining resources to produce innovative products.

Labor is the mental and physical capacity of workers to produce goods and services. The services of farmers, assembly-line workers, lawyers, professional football players, and economists are all *labor*. The labor resource is measured both by the number of people available for work and by the skills or quality of workers. One reason nations differ in their ability to produce is that human characteristics, such as the education, experience, health, and motivation of workers, differ among nations.

Entrepreneurship is a special type of labor. Entrepreneurship is the creative ability of individuals to seek profits by taking risks and combining resources to produce innovative products. An *entrepreneur* is a motivated person who seeks profits by undertaking such risky activities as starting new businesses, creating new products, or inventing new ways of accomplishing tasks. Entrepreneurship is a scarce human resource because relatively few people are willing or able to innovate and make decisions involving greater-than-normal chances for failure.

Entrepreneurs are the agents of change who bring material progress to society. The birth of the Levi Strauss Company is a classic entrepreneurial success story. In 1853, at the age of 24, Levi Strauss, who was born in Bavaria, sailed from New York to join the California Gold Rush. His intent was not to dig for gold, but to sell cloth. By the time he arrived in San Francisco, he had sold most of his cloth to other people on the ship. The only cloth he had left was a roll of canvas for tents and covered wagons. On the dock, he met a miner who wanted sturdy pants that would last while digging for gold, so Levi made a pair from the canvas. Later, a customer gave Levi the idea of using little copper rivets to strengthen the seams. Presto! Strauss knew a good thing when he saw it, so he hired workers, built factories, and became one of the largest pants makers in the world. As a reward for taking business risks, organizing production, and introducing a product, the Levi Strauss Company earned profits, and Strauss became rich and famous.

Capital

Capital is the physical plants, machinery, and equipment used to produce other goods. Capital goods are human-made goods that do not directly satisfy human wants. Before the Industrial Revolution, *capital* meant a tool, such as a hoe, an axe, or a bow and arrow. In those days, these items served as capital to build a house or provide food for the dinner table. Today, capital also consists of factories, office buildings, warehouses, robots, trucks, and distribution facilities. College buildings, the printing presses used to produce this textbook, and iPhones are also examples of capital.

The term *capital* as it is used in the study of economics can be confusing. Economists know that capital in everyday conversations means money or the money value of paper assets, such as stocks, bonds, or a deed to a house. This is actually *financial* capital. In the study of economics, capital does not refer to money assets. Instead, capital in economics means a factor of production, such as a factory or machinery. Stated simply, you must pay special attention to this point: Money is not capital and is therefore not a resource.

> **CONCLUSION** *Financial capital by itself is not productive; instead, it is only a paper claim on economic capital.*

ECONOMICS: THE STUDY OF SCARCITY AND CHOICE

The perpetual problem of scarcity forcing people to make choices is the basis for the definition of economics. Economics is the study of how society chooses to allocate its scarce resources to the production of goods and services in order to satisfy

Capital

The physical plants, machinery, and equipment used to produce other goods. Capital goods are human-made goods that do not directly satisfy human wants.

Economics

The study of how society chooses to allocate its scarce resources to the production of goods and services in order to satisfy unlimited wants.

unlimited wants. You may be surprised by this definition. People often think economics means studying supply and demand, the stock market, money, and banking. In fact, there are many ways one could define *economics*, but economists accept the definition given here because it includes the link between *scarcity* and *choices*.

Society makes two kinds of choices: economywide, or macro choices, and individual, or micro, choices. The prefixes *macro* and *micro* come from the Greek words meaning "large" and "small," respectively. Reflecting the macro and micro perspectives, economics consists of two main branches: *macroeconomics* and *microeconomics*.

Macroeconomics

Macroeconomics

The branch of economics that studies decision making for the economy as a whole.

The old saying "Looking at the forest rather than the trees" describes macroeconomics. Macroeconomics is the branch of economics that studies decision making for the economy as a whole. Macroeconomics applies an overview perspective to an economy by examining economywide variables, such as inflation, unemployment, growth of the economy, the money supply, and the national incomes of developing countries. Macroeconomic decision making considers such "big picture" policies as the effect that federal tax cuts will have on unemployment and the effect that changing the money supply will have on prices.

Microeconomics

Microeconomics

The branch of economics that studies decision making by a single individual, household, firm, industry, or level of government.

Examining individual trees, leaves, and pieces of bark, rather than surveying the forest, illustrates microeconomics. Microeconomics is the branch of economics that studies decision making by a single individual, household, firm, industry, or level of government. Microeconomics applies a microscope to study specific parts of an economy, as one would examine cells in the body. The focus is on small economic units, such as economic decisions of particular groups of consumers and businesses. An example of microeconomic analysis would be to study economic units involved in the market for ostrich eggs. Will suppliers decide to supply more, less, or the same quantity of ostrich eggs to the market in response to price changes? Will individual consumers of these eggs decide to buy more, less, or the same quantity at a new price?

We have described macroeconomics and microeconomics as two separate branches, but they are related. Because the overall economy is the sum, or aggregation, of its parts, micro changes affect the macro economy, and macro changes produce micro changes.

THE METHODOLOGY OF ECONOMICS

As used by other disciplines, such as criminology, biology, chemistry, and physics, economists employ a step-by-step procedure for solving problems by developing a theory, gathering data, and testing whether the data are consistent with the theory. Based on this analysis, economists formulate a conclusion. Exhibit 2 summarizes the model-building process.

Exhibit 2 | **The Steps in the Model-Building Process**

The first step in developing a model is to identify the problem. The second step is to select the critical variables necessary to formulate a model that explains the problem under study. Eliminating other variables that complicate the analysis requires simplifying assumptions. In the third step, the researcher collects data and tests the model. If the evidence supports the model, the conclusion is to accept the model. If not, the model is rejected.

Identify the problem

Develop a model based on simplified assumptions

Collect data, test the model, and formulate a conclusion

Problem Identification

The first step in applying the economic method is to define the issue. Suppose an economist wishes to investigate the microeconomic problem of why U.S. motorists cut back on gasoline consumption in a given year from, for example, 400 million gallons per day in May to 300 million gallons per day in December.

Model Development

The second step in our hypothetical example toward finding an explanation is for the economist to build a **model**. A model is a simplified description of reality used to understand and predict the relationship between variables. The terms

Model

A simplified description of reality used to understand and predict the relationship between variables.

model and *theory* are interchangeable. A model emphasizes only those variables that are most important to explaining an event. As Albert Einstein said, "Theories should be as simple as possible, but not more so." The purpose of a model is to construct an abstraction from real-world complexities and make events understandable. Consider a model airplane that is placed in a wind tunnel to test the aerodynamics of a new design. For this purpose, the model must represent only the shapes of the wings and fuselage, but it does not need to include tiny seats, electrical wiring, or other interior design details. A highway map is another example. To find the best route to drive between two distant cities, you do not want extraneous information on the location of all roads, streets, potholes, telephone lines, trees, stoplights, schools, hospitals, and firehouses. This would be too much detail, and the complexity would make it difficult to choose the best route.

A map is a model because it is an abstraction from reality.

To be useful, a model requires simplified assumptions. Someone must decide, for example, whether a map will include only symbols for the major highways or the details of hiking trails through mountains. In our gasoline consumption example, several variables might be related to the quantity of gasoline consumed, including consumer incomes, the prices of substitutes for gasoline, the price of gasoline, the fuel economy of cars, and weather conditions. Because a theory focuses only on the main or critical variables, the economist must be a Sherlock Holmes and use a keen sense of observation to form a model. Using his or her expertise, the economist must select the variables that are related to gasoline consumption and reject variables that have only slight or no relationship to gasoline consumption. In this simple case, the economist removes the cloud of complexity by formulating the theory that increases in the price of gasoline *cause* the quantity of gasoline consumed to decrease during the time period.

Testing a Theory

An economic model can be stated as a verbal argument, numerical table, graph, or mathematical equation. You will soon discover that a major part of this book is devoted to building and using economic models. The purpose of an economic model is to *forecast* or *predict* the results of various changes in variables. Note that the appendix to this chapter provides a review of graphical analysis. An economic theory can be expressed in the form "If *A*, then *B*, other things held constant." An economic model is useful only if it yields accurate predictions. When the evidence is consistent with the theory that *A* causes outcome *B*, there is confidence in the theory's validity. When the evidence is inconsistent with the theory that *A* causes outcome *B*, the researcher rejects this theory.

In the third step, the economist gathers data to test the theory that if the price of gasoline rises, then gasoline purchases fall—all other relevant factors held constant. Suppose the investigation reveals that the price of gasoline rose sharply between September and December of the given year. The data are therefore consistent with the theory that the quantity of gasoline consumed per month falls when its price rises, assuming no other relevant factors change. Thus, the conclusion is that the theory is valid if, for example, consumer incomes or population size do not change at the same time that gasoline prices rise.

CHECKPOINT

Can You Prove There Is No Trillion-Dollar Person?

Suppose a theory says no U.S. citizen is worth $1 trillion. You decide to test this theory and send researchers to all corners of the nation to check financial records to see whether someone qualifies by owning assets valued at $1 trillion or more. After years of checking, the researchers return and report that not a single person is worth at least $1 trillion. Do you conclude that the evidence proves the theory?

HAZARDS OF THE ECONOMIC WAY OF THINKING

Models help us understand and predict the impact of changes in economic variables. A model is an important tool in the economist's toolkit, but it must be handled with care. The economic way of thinking seeks to avoid reasoning mistakes. Two of the most common pitfalls to clear thinking are (1) failing to understand the *ceteris paribus assumption* and (2) confusing *association* and *causation*.

The Ceteris Paribus Assumption

As you work through a model, try to think of a host of relevant variables assumed to be "standing still," or "held constant." **Ceteris paribus** is a Latin phrase that means while certain variables change, "all other things remain unchanged." In short, the ceteris paribus assumption allows us to isolate or focus attention on selected variables. In the gasoline example discussed earlier, a key simplifying assumption of the model is that changes in consumer incomes and certain other variables do not occur and complicate the analysis. The ceteris paribus assumption holds everything else constant and therefore allows us to concentrate on the relationship between two key variables: changes in the price of gasoline and the quantity of gasoline purchased per month.

Now suppose an economist examines a model explaining the relationship between the price and quantity purchased of Coca-Cola. The theory is "If the price increases, then the quantity of Coca-Cola purchased decreases, ceteris paribus." Now assume you observe that the price of Coca-Cola increased one summer and some people actually bought more, not less. Based on this real-world observation, you declare the theory is incorrect. Think again! The economist responds that this is a reasoning pitfall because the model is valid based on the assumption of ceteris paribus, and your observation gives us no reason to reject the model. The reason the model appeared flawed is because another factor, a sharp rise in the temperature, *caused* people to buy more Coca-Cola in spite of its higher price. If the temperature and all other factors are held constant as the price of Coca-Cola rises, then people will indeed buy less Coca-Cola, as the model predicts.

Ceteris paribus

A Latin phrase that means while certain variables change, "all other things remain unchanged."

> **CONCLUSION** *A theory cannot be tested legitimately unless its ceteris paribus assumption is satisfied.*

Association versus Causation

Another common error in reasoning is confusing *association* (or correlation) and *causation* between variables. Stated differently, you err when you read more into a relationship between variables than is actually there. A model is valid only when a cause-and-effect relationship is stable or dependable over time, rather than being an association that occurs by chance and eventually disappears. Suppose a witch doctor performs a voodoo dance during three different months and stock market prices skyrocket during each of these months. The voodoo dance is *associated* with the increase in stock prices, but this does not mean the dance *caused* the event. Even though there is a statistical relationship between these two variables in a number of observations, eventually the voodoo dance will be performed, and stock prices will fall or remain unchanged. The reason is that there is no true systematic economic relationship between voodoo dances and stock prices.

Further investigation may reveal that stock prices actually responded to changes in interest rates during the months that the voodoo dances were performed. Changes in interest rates affect borrowing and, in turn, profits and stock prices. In contrast, there is no real economic relationship between voodoo dances and stock prices, and, therefore, the voodoo model is not valid.

> **CONCLUSION** *The fact that one event follows another does not necessarily mean that the first event caused the second event.*

CHECKPOINT

Should Nebraska State Join a Big-Time Athletic Conference?

Nebraska State (a mythical university) stood by while Penn State, Florida State, the University of Miami, and the University of South Carolina joined big-time athletic conferences. Now Nebraska State officials are pondering whether to remain independent or to pursue membership in a conference noted for high-quality football and basketball programs. An editorial in the newspaper advocates joining and cites a study showing that universities belonging to major athletic conferences have higher graduation rates than nonmembers. Because educating its students is the number one goal of Nebraska State, will this evidence persuade Nebraska State officials to join a big-time conference?

You're The Economist Mops and Brooms, the Boston Snow Index, the Super Bowl, and Other Economic Indicators *Applicable*

Concepts: association versus causation

Although the Commerce Department, the Wharton School, the Federal Reserve Board, and other organizations publish economic forecasts and data on key economic indicators, they are not without armchair competition. For example, the chief executive of Standex International Corporation, Daniel E. Hogan, reported that his company can predict economic downturns and recoveries from sales reports of its National Metal Industries subsidiary in Springfield, Massachusetts. National makes metal parts for about 300 U.S. manufacturers of mops and brooms. A drop in National's sales always precedes a proportional fall in consumer spending. The company's sales always pick up slightly before consumer spending does.[1]

The Boston Snow Index (BSI) is the brainchild of a vice president of a New York securities firm. It predicts a rising economy for the next year if there is snow on the ground in Boston on Christmas Day. The BSI predicted correctly about 73 percent of the time over a

30-year period. However, its creator, David L. Upshaw, did not take it too seriously and views it as a spoof of other forecasters' methods.

Greeting card sales are another tried and true indicator, according to a vice president of American Greetings. Before a recession sets in, sales of higher-priced greeting cards rise. It seems that people substitute the cards for gifts, and since there is no gift, the card must be fancier.

A Super Bowl win by an NFC team predicts that in the following December the stock market will be higher than the year before. A win by an old AFL team predicts a dip in the stock market.

Several other less well-known indicators have also been proposed. For example, one economist suggested that the surliness of waiters is a countercyclical indicator. If they are nice, expect that bad times are coming, but if they are rude, expect an upturn. Waiters, on the other hand, counter that a fall in the average tip usually precedes a downturn in the economy.

© iStockphoto.com/Sean Locke

Finally, Anthony Chan, chief economist for Bank One Investment Advisors, studied marriage trends over a 34-year period. He discovered that when the number of marriages increases, the economy rises significantly, and a slowdown in marriages is followed by a decline in the economy. Chan explains that there is usually about a one-year lag between a change in the marriage rate and the economy.[2]

ANALYZE THE ISSUE

Which of the above indicators are examples of causation? Explain.

1. "Economic Indicators, Turtles, Butterflies, Monks, and Waiters," *The Wall Street Journal*, Aug. 27, 1979, pp. 1, 16.
2. Sandra Block, "Worried? Look at Wedding Bell Indicator," *The Charlotte Observer*, Apr. 15, 1995, p. 8A.

Throughout this book, you will study economic models or theories that include variables linked by stable cause-and-effect relationships. For example, the theory that a change in the price of a good *causes* a change in the quantity purchased is a valid microeconomic model. The theory that a change in the money supply *causes* a change in interest rates is an example of a valid macroeconomic model. The You're the Economist gives some amusing examples of the "association means causation" reasoning pitfall.

WHY DO ECONOMISTS DISAGREE?

Why might one economist say a clean environment should be our most important priority and another economist say economic growth should be our most important goal? If economists share the economic way of thinking and carefully avoid reasoning pitfalls, then why do they disagree? Why are economists known for giving advice by saying, "On the one hand, if you do this, then *A* results, and, on the other hand, doing this causes result *B*?" In fact, President Harry Truman once jokingly exclaimed, "Find me an economist with only one hand." George Bernard Shaw offered another famous line in the same vein: "If you took all the economists in the world and laid them end to end, they would never reach a conclusion." These famous quotes imply that economists should agree, but they ignore the fact that physicists, doctors, business executives, lawyers, and other professionals often disagree.

Economists may appear to disagree more than other professionals partly because it is more interesting to report disagreements than agreements. Actually, economists agree on a wide range of issues. Many economists, for example, agree on free trade among nations, the elimination of farm subsidies and rent ceilings, government deficit spending to recover from a recession, and many other issues. When disagreements do exist, the reason can often be explained by the difference between *positive economics* and *normative economics*.

Positive Economics

Positive economics

An analysis limited to statements that are verifiable.

Positive economics deals with facts and therefore addresses "what is" or "verifiable" questions. Positive economics is an analysis limited to statements that are verifiable. Positive statements can be proven either true or false. Often a positive statement is expressed: "If *A*, then *B*." For example, if the national unemployment rate rises to 9 percent, then teenage unemployment exceeds 80 percent. This is a positive "if-then" prediction, which may or may not be correct. Accuracy is not the criterion for being a positive statement. The key consideration is whether the statement is *testable* and not whether it is true or false. Suppose the data show that when the nation's overall unemployment rate is close to 9 percent, the unemployment rate for teenagers never reaches 80 percent. For example, the overall unemployment rate was 9.3 percent in 2009, and the rate for teenagers was 24.3 percent—far short of 80 percent. Based on the facts, we would conclude that this positive statement is false.

Now, we can explain one reason why economists' forecasts can diverge. The statement "If event *A* occurs, then event *B* follows" can be thought of as a *conditional* positive statement. For example, two economists may agree that if the federal government cuts spending by 10 percent this year, prices will fall about 2 percent next year. However, their predictions about the fall in prices may differ because one economist assumes Congress will not cut spending, while the other economist assumes Congress will cut spending by 10 percent.

CONCLUSION *Economists' forecasts can differ because, using the same methodology, economists can agree that event A causes event B, but disagree over the assumption that event A will occur.*

Normative Economics

Instead of using objective statements, an argument can be phrased subjectively. **Normative economics** attempts to determine "what should be." Normative economics is an analysis based on value judgments. Normative statements express an individual or collective opinion on a subject and cannot be proven by facts to be true or false. Certain words or phrases, such as *good, bad, need, should,* and *ought to,* tell us clearly that we have entered the realm of normative economics.

The point here is that people wearing different-colored glasses see the same facts differently. Each of us has individual subjective preferences that we apply to a particular subject. An animal rights activist says that no one *should* purchase a fur coat. Or one senator argues, "We *ought to* see that every teenager who wants a job has one." Another senator counters by saying, "Maintaining the purchasing power of the dollar is *more important* than teenage unemployment."

> **CONCLUSION** *When opinions or points of view are not based on facts, they are scientifically untestable.*

When considering a debate, make sure to separate the arguments into their positive and normative components. This distinction allows you to determine if you are choosing a course of action based on factual evidence or on opinion. The material presented in this textbook, like most of economics, takes pains to stay within the boundaries of positive economic analysis. In our everyday lives, however, politicians, business executives, relatives, and friends use mostly normative statements to discuss economic issues. Economists also may associate themselves with a political position and use normative arguments for or against some economic policy. When using value judgments, an economist's normative arguments may have no greater validity than those of others. Biases or preconceptions can cloud an economist's thinking about deficit spending or whether to increase taxes on gasoline. Like beginning economics students, economists are human.

CAREERS IN ECONOMICS

The author of this text entered college more years ago than I would like to admit. In those days, economics was not taught in high school, so I knew nothing of the subject. Like many students taking this course, I was uncertain about which major to pursue, but selected electrical engineering because I was an amateur radio operator and enjoyed building radio receivers and transmitters. My engineering curriculum required a course in economics. I signed up thinking that "econ is boring." Instead, it was an eye-opening experience that inspired me to change my major to economics and pursue an economics teaching career.

The study of economics has attracted a number of well-known people. For example, the Rolling Stones' Mick Jagger attended the London School of Economics, and other famous people who majored in economics include former Supreme Court Justice Sandra Day O'Connor, California Governor Arnold Schwarzenegger, and three former presidents—George H. W. Bush, Ronald Reagan, and Gerald Ford.

An economics major can choose many career paths. Most economics majors work for business firms. Because economists are trained in analyzing financial matters, they find good jobs in management, sales, or as a market analyst interpreting

Normative economics

An analysis based on value judgment.

You're The Economist Does Raising the Minimum Wage Help the Working Poor? *Applicable Concepts: positive and normative analyses*

Minimum wages exist in more than one hundred countries. In 1938, Congress enacted the federal Fair Labor Standards Act, commonly known as the "minimum-wage law." Today, a minimum-wage worker who works full time still earns a deplorably low annual income. One approach to help the working poor earn a living wage might be to raise the minimum wage.

The dilemma for Congress is that a higher minimum wage for the employed is enacted at the expense of jobs for unskilled workers. Opponents forecast that the increased labor cost from a large minimum-wage hike would jeopardize hundreds of thousands of unskilled jobs. For example, employers may opt to purchase more capital and less expensive labor. The fear of such sizable job losses forces Congress to perform a difficult balancing act to ensure that a minimum-wage increase is large enough to help the working poor, but not so large as to threaten their jobs.

Some politicians claim that raising the minimum wage is a way to help the working poor without cost to taxpayers. Others believe the cost is hidden in inflation and lost employment opportunities for marginal workers, such as teenagers, the elderly, and minorities. One study by economists, for example, examined sixty years of data and concluded that minimum wage increases resulted in reduced employment and hours of work for low-skilled workers.[1]

Another problem with raising the minimum wage to aid the working poor is that minimum wage is a blunt weapon for redistributing wealth. Studies show that only a small percentage of minimum-wage earners are full-time workers whose family income falls below the poverty line. This means that most increases in the minimum wage go to workers who are not poor. For example, many minimum-wage workers are students living at home or workers whose spouse earns a much higher income. To help only the working poor, some economists argue that the government should target only those who need assistance, rather than using the "shotgun" approach of raising the minimum wage.

Supporters of raising the minimum wage are not convinced by these arguments. They say it is outrageous that a worker can work full time and still live in poverty. Moreover, people on this side of the debate believe that opponents exaggerate the dangers to the economy from a higher minimum wage. For example, one could argue that a higher minimum wage will force employers to upgrade the skills and productivity of their workers. Increasing the minimum wage may therefore be a win-win proposition, rather than a win-lose proposition. Finally, across the United States, thirty-two states and numerous localities have implemented living-wage laws. Note that we return to this issue in Chapter 4 as an application of supply and demand analysis.

ANALYZE THE ISSUE

1. Identify two positive and two normative statements given above concerning raising the minimum wage. List other minimum-wage arguments not discussed in this You're the Economist, and classify them as either positive or normative economics.
2. Give a positive and a normative argument why a business leader would oppose raising the minimum wage. Give a positive and a normative argument why a labor leader would favor raising the minimum wage.
3. Explain your position on this issue. Identify positive and normative reasons for your decision. Are there alternative ways to aid the working poor?

1. David Neumark and William Wascher, *Minimum Wages* (Cambridge, MA: The MIT Press, 2008).

economic conditions relevant to a firm's market. For those with an undergraduate degree, private sector job opportunities exist in banking, securities brokering, management consulting, computer and data processing firms, the power industry, market research, finance, health care, and many other industries. Other economics majors work for government agencies and in colleges and universities.

Government economists work for federal, state, and local governments. For example, a government economist might compile and report national statistics for economic growth or work on projects such as how to improve indexes to measure trends in consumer prices. Economists in academe not only enjoy the challenge of teaching economics, but have great freedom in selecting research projects.

Studying economics is also an essential preparation for other careers. Those preparing for law school, for example, find economics an excellent major because of its emphasis on a logical approach to problem solving. Economics is also great preparation for an MBA. In fact, students majoring in any field will benefit throughout their lives from learning how to apply the economic way of thinking to analyze real-world economic issues.

Finally, economics majors shine in salary offers upon graduation. Exhibit 3 shows average yearly salary offers for bachelor's degree candidates for January 2009.

Exhibit 3   Average Yearly Salary Offers for Selected Majors

Undergraduate major	Average offer, January 2009
Computer engineering	$59,803
Computer science	58,419
Electrical engineering	57,404
Management information systems	52,817
Economics	50,343
Accounting	48,334
Nursing	46,655
Business administration	45,887
Mathematics	45,853
Marketing	43,334
Visual and performing arts	37,545
Political science	36,745
Environmental science	36,736
Journalism	36,333
Liberal arts and sciences	36,154
Foreign language	35,783
Psychology	35,005
Sociology	34,319
Animal science	31,349
Criminal Justice	30,570
Social work	30,025

SOURCE: National Association of Colleges and Employers, *Salary Survey*, Spring 2009.

Key Concepts

Scarcity

Resources

Land

Labor

Entrepreneurship

Capital

Economics

Macroeconomics

Microeconomics

Model

Ceteris paribus

Positive economics

Normative economics

Summary

- *Scarcity* is the fundamental economic problem that human wants exceed the availability of time, goods, and resources. Individuals and society therefore can never have everything they desire.

- *Resources* are factors of production classified as land, labor, and capital. Entrepreneurship is a special type of labor. An entrepreneur seeks profits by taking risks and combining resources to produce innovative products.

- *Economics* is the study of how individuals and society choose to allocate scarce resources in order to satisfy unlimited wants. Faced with unlimited wants and scarce resources, we must make choices among alternatives.

- *Macroeconomics* applies an economywide perspective that focuses on such issues as inflation, unemployment, and the growth rate of the economy.

- *Microeconomics* examines individual decision-making units within an economy, such as a consumer's response to changes in the price

of coffee and the reasons for changes in the market price of personal computers.

- *Models* are simplified descriptions of reality used to understand and predict economic events. An economic model can be stated verbally or in a table, a graph, or an equation. If the evidence is not consistent with the model, the model is rejected.

- *Ceteris paribus* holds "all other factors unchanged" that might affect a particular relationship. If this assumption is violated, a model cannot be tested. Another reasoning pitfall is to think that *association* means *causation*.

- Use of **positive versus normative economic analysis** is a major reason for disagreements among economists. *Positive economics* uses testable statements. Often a positive argument is expressed as an *if-then* statement. *Normative economics* is based on value judgments or opinions and uses words such as *good, bad, ought to,* and *should.*

Summary of Conclusion Statements

- Financial capital by itself is not productive; instead, it is only a paper claim on economic capital.
- A theory cannot be tested legitimately unless its ceteris paribus assumption is satisfied.
- The fact that one event follows another does not necessarily mean that the first event caused the second event.

- Economists' forecasts can differ because, using the same methodology, economists can agree that event *A* causes event *B*, but disagree over the assumption that event *A* will occur.
- When opinions or points of view are not based on facts, they are scientifically untestable.

Study Questions and Problems

1. Explain why both nations with high living standards and nations with low living standards face the problem of scarcity. If you won $1 million in a lottery, would you escape the scarcity problem?

2. Why isn't money considered capital in economics?

3. Computer software programs are an example of
   a. capital.
   b. labor.
   c. a natural resource.
   d. none of the above.

4. Explain the difference between macroeconomics and microeconomics. Give examples of the areas of concern to each branch of economics.

5. Which of the following are microeconomic issues? Which are macroeconomic issues?
   a. How will an increase in the price of Coca-Cola affect the quantity of Pepsi-Cola sold?
   b. What will cause the nation's inflation rate to fall?
   c. How does a quota on textile imports affect the textile industry?
   d. Does a large federal budget deficit reduce the rate of unemployment in the economy?

6. A model is defined as a
   a. value judgment of the relationship between variables.
   b. presentation of all relevant aspects of real-world events.

   c. simplified description of reality used to understand the way variables are related.
   d. data set adjusted for irrational actions of people.

7. Explain why it is important for an economic model to be an abstraction from the real world.

8. Explain the importance of the ceteris paribus assumption for an economic model.

9. Suppose Congress cuts spending for the military, and then unemployment rises in the U.S. defense industry. Is there causation in this situation, or are we observing an association between events?

10. Which of the following is an example of a proposition from positive economics?
    a. If Candidate X had been elected president, taxpayers would have been treated more fairly than under President Y.
    b. The average rate of inflation was higher during President X's presidency than during Presdient Y's presidency.
    c. In economic terms, President X is better than President Y.
    d. President X's policies were more just toward poor people than President Y.

11. "The government should collect higher taxes from the rich and use the additional revenues to provide greater benefits to the poor." This statement is an illustration of a
    a. testable statement.
    b. basic principle of economics.

c.   statement of positive economics.

d.   statement of normative economics.

12. Analyze the positive versus normative arguments in the following case. What statements of positive economics are used to support requiring air bags? What normative reasoning is used?

Should the Government Require Air Bags?

Air bag advocates say air bags will save lives and the government should require them in all cars. Air bags add an estimated $600 to the cost of a car, compared to about $100 for a set of regular seat belts. Opponents argue that air bags are electronic devices subject to failure and have produced injuries and death. For example, air bags have killed both adults and children whose heads were within the inflation zone at the time of deployment. Opponents therefore believe the government should leave the decision of whether to spend an extra $600 or so for an air bag to the consumer. The role of the government should be limited to providing information on the risks of having versus not having air bags.

For Online Exercises, go the Tucker Web site at www.cengage.com/economics/tucker.

CHECKPOINT ANSWERS

Can You Prove There Is No Trillion-Dollar Person?

How can researchers ever be certain they have seen all the rich people in the United States? There is always the possibility that somewhere there is a person who qualifies. If the researchers had found one, you could have rejected the theory. Because they did not, you cannot reject the theory. If you said that the evidence can support, but never prove, the theory, **YOU ARE CORRECT.**

Should Nebraska State Join a Big-Time Athletic Conference?

Suppose universities that belong to big-time athletic conferences do indeed have higher graduation rates than nonmembers. This is not the only possible explanation for the statistical correlation (or association) between the graduation rate and membership in a big-time athletic conference. A more plausible explanation is that improving academic variables, such as tuition, quality of faculty, and student-faculty ratios, and not athletic conference membership, increase the graduation rate. If you said correlation does not mean causation, and therefore Nebraska State officials will not necessarily accept the graduation rate evidence, **YOU ARE CORRECT.**

Practice Quiz

For an explanation of the correct answers, visit the Tucker Web site at www.cengage.com/economics/tucker.

1. Scarcity exists
   a.   when people consume beyond their needs.
   b.   only in rich nations.
   c.   in all countries of the world.
   d.   only in poor nations.

2. Which of the following would eliminate scarcity as an economic problem?
   a.   Moderation of people's competitive instincts
   b.   Discovery of sufficiently large new energy reserves
   c.   Resumption of steady productivity growth
   d.   None of the above because scarcity cannot be eliminated

Practice Quiz Continued

3. Which of the following is *not* a resource?
   a. Land
   b. Labor
   c. Money
   d. Capital

4. Economics is the study of
   a. how to make money.
   b. how to operate a business.
   c. people making choices because of the problem of scarcity.
   d. the government decision-making process.

5. Microeconomics approaches the study of economics from the viewpoint of
   a. individual or specific markets.
   b. the operation of the Federal Reserve.
   c. economywide effects.
   d. the national economy.

6. A review of the performance of the U.S. economy during the 1990s is primarily the concern of
   a. macroeconomics.
   b. microeconomics.
   c. both macroeconomics and microeconomics.
   d. neither macroeconomics nor microeconomics.

7. An economic theory claims that a rise in gasoline prices will cause gasoline purchases to fall, ceteris paribus. The phrase *ceteris paribus* means that
   a. other relevant factors like consumer incomes must be held constant.
   b. gasoline prices must first be adjusted for inflation.
   c. the theory is widely accepted but cannot be accurately tested.
   d. consumers' need for gasoline remains the same regardless of price.

8. An economist notices that sunspot activity is high just prior to recessions and concludes that sunspots cause recessions. The economist has
   a. confused association and causation.
   b. misunderstood the ceteris paribus assumption.

   c. used normative economics to answer a positive question.
   d. built an untestable model.

9. Which of the following is a statement of positive economics?
   a. The income tax system collects a lower percentage of the incomes of the poor
   b. A reduction in tax rates of the rich makes the tax system more fair
   c. Tax rates ought to be raised to finance health care
   d. All of the above are primarily statements of positive economics

10. Which of the following is a statement of positive economics?
    a. An unemployment rate greater than 8 percent is good because prices will fall.
    b. An unemployment rate of 7 percent is a serious problem.
    c. If the overall unemployment rate is 7 percent, unemployment rates among African Americans will average 15 percent.
    d. Unemployment is a more severe problem than inflation.

11. Which of the following is a statement of normative economics?
    a. The minimum wage is good because it raises wages for the working poor.
    b. The minimum wage is supported by unions.
    c. The minimum wage reduces the number of jobs for less-skilled workers.
    d. The minimum wage encourages firms to substitute capital for labor.

12. Select the normative statement that completes the following sentence: If the minimum wage is raised rapidly, then
    a. inflation will increase.
    b. workers will gain their rightful share of total income.
    c. profits will fall.
    d. unemployment will rise.

Practice Quiz Continued

13. Computer programs, or software, are an example of
    a. land.
    b. labor.
    c. capital.
    d. none of the above.

14. Which of the following would *not* be classified as a capital resource?
    a. The Empire State Building.
    b. A Caterpillar bulldozer.
    c. A Macintosh computer.
    d. 100 shares of stock in General Motors.

15. A model (or theory)
    a. is a general statement about the causal relationship between variables based on facts.
    b. helps explain and predict the relationship between variables.
    c. when expressed as a downward (negatively) sloping graph implies an inverse relationship between the variables.
    d. all of the above.

1

Applying Graphs to Economics

Economists are famous for their use of graphs. The reason is "a picture is worth a thousand words." Graphs are used throughout this text to present economics models. By drawing a line, you can use a two-dimensional illustration to analyze the effects of a change in one variable on another. You could describe the same information using other model forms, such as verbal statements, tables, or equations, but a graph is the simplest way to present and understand the relationship between economic variables.

Don't be worried that graphs will "throw you for a loop." Relax! This appendix explains all the basic graphical language you will need. The following illustrates the simplest use of graphs for economic analysis.

A DIRECT RELATIONSHIP

Basic economic analysis typically concerns the relationship between two variables, both having positive values. Hence, we can confine our graphs to the upper-right (northeast) quadrant of the coordinate number system. In Exhibit A-1, notice that the scales on the horizontal axis (*x*-axis) and the vertical axis (*y*-axis) do not necessarily measure the same numerical values.

The horizontal axis in Exhibit A-1 measures annual income, and the vertical axis shows the amount spent per year for a personal computer (PC). In the absence of any established traditions, we could decide to measure income on the vertical axis and expenditure on the horizontal axis. The intersection of the horizontal and vertical axes is the *origin*, and the point at which both income and expenditure are zero. In Exhibit A-1, each point is a coordinate that matches the dollar value of income and the corresponding expenditure for a PC. For example, point *A* on the graph shows that people with an annual income of $10,000 spent $1,000 per year for a PC. Other incomes are associated with different expenditure levels. For example, at $30,000 per year (point *C*), $3,000 will be spent annually for a PC.

The straight line in Exhibit A-1 allows us to determine the direction of change in PC expenditure as annual income changes. This relationship is *positive* because PC expenditure, measured along the vertical axis, and annual income, measured along the horizontal axis, move in the same direction. PC expenditure increases as annual income increases. As income declines, so does the amount spent on a PC. Thus, the straight line representing the relationship between income and PC expenditure is a **direct relationship**. A direct relationship is a positive association between two variables. When one variable

Direct relationship

A positive association between two variables. When one variable increases, the other variable increases, and when one variable decreases, the other variable decreases.

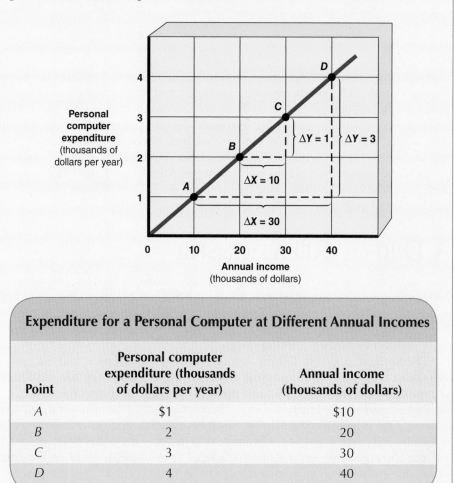

Exhibit A-1   **A Direct Relationship between Variables**

The line with a positive slope shows that the expenditure per year for a personal computer has a direct relationship to annual income, ceteris paribus. As annual income increases along the horizontal axis, the amount spent on a PC also increases, as measured by the vertical axis. Along the line, each 10-unit increase in annual income results in a 1-unit increase in expenditure for a PC. Because the slope is constant along a straight line, we can measure the same slope between any two points. Between points *B* and *C* or between points *A* and *D*, the slope = $\Delta Y/\Delta X$ = +3/+30 = +1/+10 = 1/10.

Expenditure for a Personal Computer at Different Annual Incomes

Point	Personal computer expenditure (thousands of dollars per year)	Annual income (thousands of dollars)
A	$1	$10
B	2	20
C	3	30
D	4	40

increases, the other variable increases, and when one variable decreases, the other variable decreases. In short, both variables change in the *same* direction.

Finally, an important point to remember: A two-variable graph, like any model, isolates the relationship between two variables and holds all other variables constant under the ceteris paribus assumption. In Exhibit A-1, for example, such factors as the prices of PCs and education are held constant by assumption. In Chapter 3, you will learn that allowing variables not shown in the graph to change can shift the position of the curve.

AN INVERSE RELATIONSHIP

Now consider the relationship between the price of compact discs (CDs) and the quantity consumers will buy per year, shown in Exhibit A-2. These data indicate a *negative* relationship between the price and quantity variables. When the price is low, consumers purchase a greater quantity of CDs than when the price is high.

Exhibit A-2 **An Inverse Relationship between Variables**

The line with a negative slope shows an inverse relationship between the price per compact disc and the quantity of CDs consumers purchase, ceteris paribus. As the price of a CD rises, the quantity of CDs purchased falls. A lower price for CDs is associated with more CDs purchased by consumers. Along the line, with each $5 decrease in the price of CDs, consumers increase the quantity purchased by 25 units. The slope = $\Delta Y / \Delta X = -5/+25 = -1/5$.

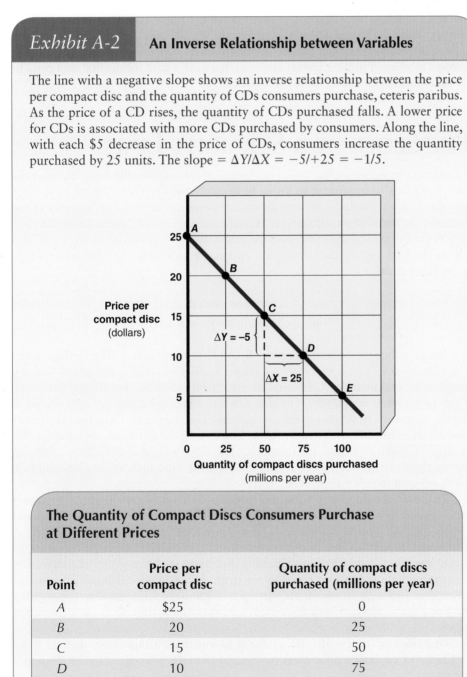

The Quantity of Compact Discs Consumers Purchase at Different Prices

Point	Price per compact disc	Quantity of compact discs purchased (millions per year)
A	$25	0
B	20	25
C	15	50
D	10	75
E	5	100

Inverse relationship

A negative association between two variables. When one variable increases, the other decreases, and when one variable decreases, the other variable increases.

In Exhibit A-2, there is an **inverse relationship** between the price per CD and the quantity consumers buy. An inverse relationship is a negative association between two variables. When one variable increases, the other variable decreases, and when one variable decreases, the other variable increases. Stated simply, the variables move in *opposite* directions.

The line drawn in Exhibit A-2 is an inverse relationship. By long-established tradition, economists put price on the vertical axis and quantity on the horizontal axis. In Chapter 3, we will study in more detail the relationship between price and quantity called the *law of demand*.

In addition to observing the inverse relationship (slope), you must interpret the *intercept* at point A in the exhibit. The intercept in this case means that at a price of $25 no consumer is willing to buy a single CD.

THE SLOPE OF A STRAIGHT LINE

Slope

The ratio of the change in the variable on the vertical axis (the rise or fall) to the change in the variable on the horizontal axis (the run).

Plotting numbers gives a clear visual expression of the relationship between two variables, but it is also important to know how much one variable changes as another variable changes. To find out, we calculate the **slope**. The slope is the ratio of the change in the variable on the vertical axis (the rise or fall) to the change in the variable on the horizontal axis (the run). Algebraically, if Y is on the vertical axis and X is on the horizontal axis, the slope is expressed as follows (the delta symbol, Δ, means "change in"):

$$\text{Slope} = \frac{\text{rise}}{\text{run}} = \frac{\text{change in vertical axis}}{\text{change in horizontal axis}} = \frac{\Delta Y}{\Delta X}$$

Consider the slope between points B and C in Exhibit A-1. The change in expenditure for a PC, Y, is equal to $+1$ (from $2,000 to $3,000 per year), and the change in annual income, X, is equal to $+10$ (from $20,000 to $30,000 per year). The slope is therefore $+1/+10$. The sign is positive because computer expenditure is directly, or positively, related to annual income. The steeper the line, the greater the slope because the ratio of ΔY to ΔX rises. Conversely, the flatter the line, the smaller the slope. Exhibit A-1 also illustrates that the slope of a straight line is constant. That is, the slope between any two points along the line, such as between points A and D, is equal to $+3/+30 = 1/10$.

What does the slope of 1/10 mean? It tells you that a $1,000 increase (decrease) in PC expenditure each year occurs for each $10,000 increase (decrease) in annual income. The line plotted in Exhibit A-1 has a *positive slope*, and we describe the line as "upward sloping."

On the other hand, the line in Exhibit A-2 has a *negative slope*. The change in Y between points C and D is equal to -5 (from $15 down to $10), and the change in X is equal to $+25$ (from 50 million up to 75 million CDs purchased per year). The slope is therefore $-5/+25 = -1/5$, and this line is described as "downward sloping."

What does this slope of $-1/5$ mean? It means that raising (lowering) the price per CD by $1 decreases (increases) the quantity of CDs purchased by 5 million per year.

Suppose we calculate the slope between any two points on a flat line—say, points B and C in Exhibit A-3. In this case, there is no change in Y (expenditure for toothpaste) as X (annual income) increases. Consumers spend $20 per year on toothpaste regardless of annual income. It follows that $\Delta Y = 0$ for any ΔX, so the slope is equal to 0. The two variables along a flat line (horizontal or vertical) have an independent relationship. An independent relationship is a zero association between two variables. When one variable changes, the other variable remains unchanged.

Independent relationship

A zero association between two variables. When one variable changes, the other variable remains unchanged.

Exhibit A-3   **An Independent Relationship between Variables**

The flat line with a zero slope shows that the expenditure per year for toothpaste is unrelated to annual income. As annual income increases along the horizontal axis, the amount spent each year for toothpaste remains unchanged at 20 units. If annual income increases 10 units, the corresponding change in expenditure is zero. The slope = $\Delta Y/\Delta X = 0/+10 = 0$.

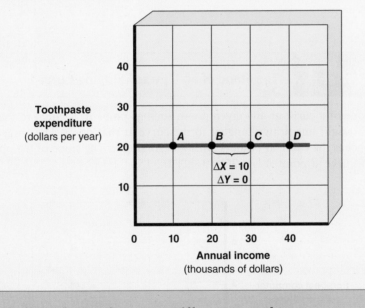

Expenditure for Toothpaste at Different Annual Incomes

Point	Toothpaste expenditure (dollars per year)	Annual income (thousands of dollars)
A	$20	$10
B	20	20
C	20	30
D	20	40

THE SLOPE OF A CURVE

The slope of a curve changes from one point to another. Suppose the relationship between the expenditure for a PC per year and annual income is not a straight line, but an upward-sloping curve, as drawn in Exhibit A-4. This means the slope of the curve is *positive* as we move along the curve. To calculate the slope of a given point on the curve requires two steps. For example, at point A, the first step is to draw a tangent line that just touches the curve at this point without crossing it. The second step is to determine the slope of the tangent line. In Exhibit A-4, the slope of the tangent line, and therefore the slope of the curve at point A, is $+2/+30 = 1/15$. What does this slope of 1/15 mean? It means that at point A there will be a $1,000 increase (decrease) in PC expenditure each year for each $15,000 increase (decrease) in annual income.

Now consider that the relationship between the price per CD and the quantity demanded by consumers per year is the downward-sloping curve shown in Exhibit A-5. In this case, the slope of the curve is *negative* as we move along the curve. To calculate the slope at point A, draw a line tangent to the curve at point A. Thus, the slope of the curve at point A is $-10/+50 = -1/+5 = -1/5$.

Exhibit A-4   The Slope of an Upward-Sloping Curve

The slope of a curve at any given point, such as point A, is equal to the slope of the straight line drawn tangent to the curve at that point. The tangent line just touches the curve at point A without crossing it. The slope of the upward-sloping curve at point A is $+2/+30 = +1/+15 = 1/15$.

Exhibit A-5	The Slope of a Downward-Sloping Curve

In this exhibit, the negative slope changes as one moves from point to point along the curve. The slope at any given point, such as point *A*, can be determined by the slope of the straight line tangent to that point. The slope of the downward-sloping curve at point *A* is $-10/+50 = -1/+5 = -1/5$.

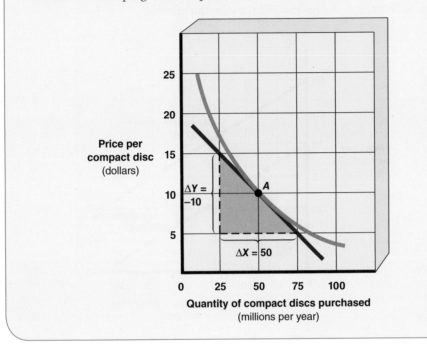

A THREE-VARIABLE RELATIONSHIP IN ONE GRAPH

The two-variable relationships drawn so far conform to a two-dimensional flat piece of paper. For example, the vertical axis measures the price per CD variable, and the horizontal axis measures the quantity of CDs purchased variable. All other factors, such as consumer income, that may affect the relationship between the price and quantity variables are held constant by the ceteris paribus assumption. But reality is frequently not so accommodating. Often a model must take into account the impact of changes in a third variable (consumer income) drawn on a two-dimensional piece of graph paper.

Economists' favorite method of depicting a three-variable relationship is shown in Exhibit A-6. As explained earlier, the cause-and-effect relationship between price and quantity of CDs determines the downward-sloping curve. A change in the price per CD causes a movement downward along either of the two separate curves.

| Exhibit A-6 | Changes in Price, Quantity, and Income in Two Dimensions |

Economists use a multicurve graph to represent a three-variable relationship in a two-dimensional graph. A decrease in the price per CD causes a movement downward along each curve. As the annual income of consumers rises, there is a shift rightward in the position of the demand curve.

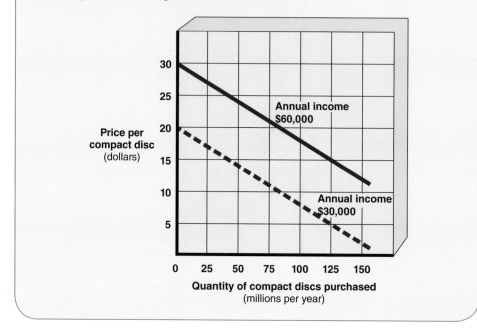

As the price falls, consumers increase the quantity of CDs demanded. The location of each curve on the graph, however, depends on the annual income of consumers. As the annual income variable increases from $30,000 to $60,000 and consumers can afford to pay more, the price-quantity demanded curve shifts rightward. Conversely, as the annual income variable decreases and consumers have less to spend, the price-quantity demanded curve shifts leftward.

This is an extremely important concept that you must understand: Throughout this book, you must distinguish between *movements along* and *shifts in* a curve. Here's how to tell the difference. A change in one of the variables shown on either of the coordinate axes of the graph causes *movement along* a curve. On the other hand, a change in a variable not shown on one of the coordinate axes of the graph causes a *shift in* a curve's position on the graph.

CONCLUSION *A shift in a curve occurs only when the ceteris paribus assumption is relaxed and a third variable not shown on either axis of the graph is allowed to change.*

A Helpful Study Hint for Using Graphs

To some students, studying economics is a little frightening because many chapters are full of graphs. An often-repeated mistake is to prepare for tests by trying to memorize the lines of graphs. When their graded tests are returned, the students using this strategy will probably exclaim, "What happened?" The answer is that if you learn the economic concepts first, then you will understand the graphs as illustrations of these underlying concepts. Stated simply, superficial cramming for economics quizzes does not work. For students who are anxious about using graphs, in addition to the brief review of graphical analysis in this appendix, the Graphing Workshop on the CourseMate link of the Tucker Web site and the Study Guide contain step-by-step features on how to interpret graphs.

Key Concepts

Direct relationship
Inverse relationship

Slope
Independent relationship

Summary

- *Graphs* provide a means to clearly show economic relationships in two-dimensional space. Economic analysis is often concerned with two variables confined to the upper-right (northeast) quadrant of the coordinate number system.
- A *direct relationship* occurs when two variables change in the *same* direction.

Direct Relationship

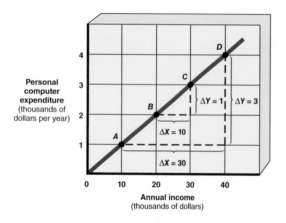

- An *inverse relationship* occurs when two variables change in *opposite* directions.

Inverse Relationship

- An *independent relationship* occurs when two variables are unrelated.

Independent Relationship

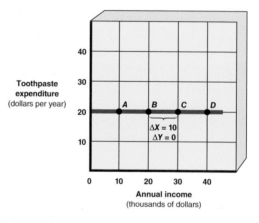

- *Slope* is the ratio of the vertical change (the rise or fall) to the horizontal change (the run). The slope of an *upward-sloping* line is *positive*, and the slope of a *downward-sloping* line is *negative*.

Positive Slope of an Upward-Sloping Curve

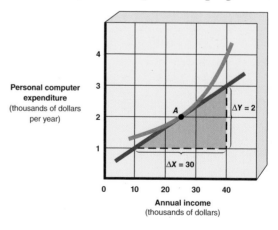

Negative Slope of a Downward-Sloping Curve

- A *three-variable relationship* is depicted by a graph showing a shift in a curve when the ceteris paribus assumption is relaxed and a third variable (such as annual income) not on either axis of the graph is allowed to change.

Three-Variable Relationship

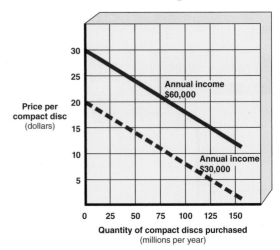

Summary of Conclusion Statement

- A shift in a curve occurs only when the ceteris paribus assumption is relaxed and a third variable not shown on either axis of the graph is allowed to change.

Study Questions and Problems

1. Draw a graph without specific data for the expected relationship between the following variables
   a. The probability of living and age
   b. Annual income and years of education
   c. Inches of snow and sales of bathing suits
   d. The number of football games won and the athletic budget
   In each case, state whether the expected relationship is *direct* or *inverse*. Explain an additional factor that would be included in the *ceteris paribus* assumption because it might change and influence your theory.

2. Assume a research firm collects survey sales data that reveal the relationship between the possible selling prices of hamburgers and the quantity of hamburgers consumers would purchase per year at alternative prices. The report states that if the price of a hamburger is $4, 20,000 will be bought. However, at a price of $3, 40,000 hamburgers will be bought. At $2, 60,000 hamburgers will be bought, and at $1, 80,000 hamburgers will be purchased.

   Based on these data, describe the relevant relationship between the price of a hamburger and the quantity consumers are willing to purchase, using a verbal statement, a numerical table, and a graph. Which model do you prefer and why?

Practice Quiz

For an explanation of the correct answers, visit the Tucker Web site at www.cengage.com/economics/tucker.

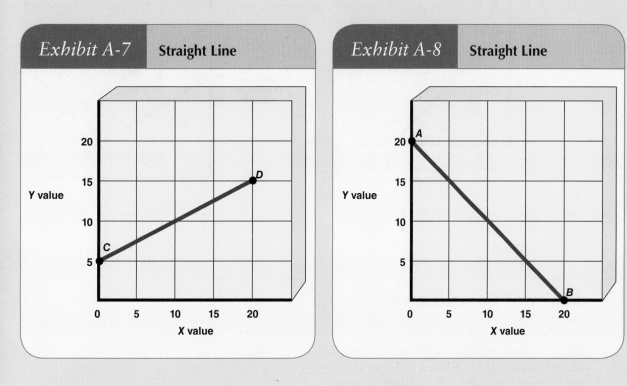

| Exhibit A-7 | Straight Line |
| Exhibit A-8 | Straight Line |

1. Straight line *CD* in Exhibit A-7 shows that
   a. increasing the value of *X* will increase the value of *Y*.
   b. decreasing the value of *X* will decrease the value of *Y*.
   c. there is a direct relationship between *X* and *Y*.
   d. all of the above are true.

2. In Exhibit A-7, the slope of straight line *CD* is
   a. 3.
   b. 1.
   c. −1.
   d. 1/2.

3. In Exhibit A-7, the slope of straight line *CD* is
   a. positive.
   b. zero.
   c. negative.
   d. variable.

4. Straight line *AB* in Exhibit A-8 shows that
   a. increasing the value of *X* reduces the value of *Y*.
   b. decreasing the value of *X* increases the value of *Y*.
   c. there is an inverse relationship between *X* and *Y*.
   d. all of the above are true.

5. As shown in Exhibit A-8, the slope of straight line *AB*
   a. decreases with increases in *X*.
   b. increases with increases in *X*.
   c. increases with decreases in *X*.
   d. remains constant with changes in *X*.

6. In Exhibit A-8, the slope of straight line *AB* is
   a. 3.
   b. 1.

Practice Quiz Continued

   c. −1.
   d. −5.

7. A shift in a curve represents a change in
   a. the variable on the horizontal axis.
   b. the variable on the vertical axis.
   c. a third variable that is not on either axis.
   d. any variable that is relevant to the relationship being graphed.

8. A change in a third variable *not* on either axis of a graph is illustrated by a
   a. horizontal or vertical line.
   b. movement along a curve.
   c. shift of a curve.
   d. point of intersection.

9. What is used to illustrate an independent relationship between two variables?
   a. An upward-sloping curve
   b. A downward-sloping curve
   c. A hill-shaped curve
   d. A horizontal or vertical line

10. When an inverse relationship is graphed, the resulting line or curve is
   a. horizontal.
   b. vertical.

   c. upward sloping.
   d. downward sloping.

11. Which of the following pairs is the *most* likely to exhibit an inverse relationship?
   a. The amount of time you study and your grade point average
   b. People's annual income and their expenditure on personal computers
   c. Baseball players' salaries and their batting averages
   d. The price of a concert and the number of tickets people purchase

12. Which of the following pairs is the *most* likely to exhibit a direct relationship?
   a. The price of gasoline and the amount of gasoline that people purchase
   b. Cholesterol levels and the likelihood of developing heart disease
   c. Outdoor temperature and heating oil sales
   d. Annual income and weekly pawn shop visits

Production Possibilities, Opportunity Cost, and Economic Growth

This chapter continues building on the foundation laid in the preceding chapter. Having learned that *scarcity* forces *choices*, here you will study the choices people make in more detail. This chapter begins by examining the three basic choices: *What, How,* and *For Whom* to produce. The process of answering these basic questions introduces two other key building blocks in the economic way of thinking: *opportunity cost* and *marginal analysis*. Once you understand these important concepts stated in words, it will be easier to interpret our first formal economic model, the *production possibilities curve*. This model illustrates how economists use graphs as a powerful tool to supplement words and develop an understanding of basic economic principles. You will discover that the production possibilities model teaches many of the most important concepts in economics, including scarcity, the law of increasing opportunity costs, efficiency, investment, and economic growth. For example, the chapter concludes by using the production possibilities curve to explain why underdeveloped countries do not achieve economic growth and thereby improve their standard of living.

In this chapter, you will learn to solve these economics puzzles:

• Why do so few rock stars and movie stars go to college?

• Why would you spend an extra hour reading this text rather than going to a movie or sleeping?

• Why are investment and economic growth so important?

THREE FUNDAMENTAL ECONOMIC QUESTIONS

Whether rich or poor, every nation must answer the same three fundamental economic questions: (1) *What* products will be produced? (2) *How* will they be produced? (3) *For Whom* will they be produced? Later, the chapter on economies in transition introduces various types of economic systems and describes how each deals with these three economic choices.

What to Produce?

Should society devote its limited resources to producing more health care and fewer military goods? Should society produce more iPods and fewer CDs? Should more capital goods be produced instead of consumer goods, or should small hybrid cars and fewer SUVs be produced? The problem of scarcity restricts our ability to produce everything we want during a given period, so the choice to produce "more" of one good requires producing "less" of another good.

How to Produce?

After deciding which products to make, the second question for society to decide is how to mix technology and scarce resources in order to produce these goods. For instance, a towel can be sewn primarily by hand (labor), partially by hand and partially by machine (labor and capital), or primarily by machine (capital). In short, the *How* question asks whether a production technique will be more or less capital-intensive.

Education plays an important role in answering the *How* question. Education improves the ability of workers to perform their work. Variation in the quality and quantity of education among nations is one reason economies differ in their capacities to apply resources and technology to answer the *How* question. For example, the United States is striving to catch up with Japan in the use of robotics. Answering the question *How do we improve our robotics?* requires engineers and employees with the proper training in the installation and operation of robots.

For Whom to Produce?

Once the *What* and *How* questions are resolved, the third question is *For Whom*. Among all those desiring the produced goods, who actually receives them? Who is fed well? Who drives a Mercedes? Who receives organ transplants? Should economics professors earn a salary of $1 million a year and others pay higher taxes to support economists? The *For Whom* question means that society must have a method to decide who will be "rich and famous" and who will be "poor and unknown."

OPPORTUNITY COST

Because of scarcity, the three basic questions cannot be answered without sacrifice or cost. But what does the term *cost* really mean? The common response would be to say that the purchase price is the cost. A movie ticket *costs* $8, or a shirt *costs* $50. Applying the economic way of thinking, however, *cost* is defined differently. A well-known phrase from Nobel Prize-winning economist Milton Friedman says, "There is no such thing as a free lunch." This expression captures the links among the concepts of scarcity, choice, and cost. Because of scarcity, people must make choices, and each choice incurs a cost (sacrifice). Once one option is chosen, another option is given up. The money you spend on a movie ticket cannot also buy a DVD. A business may purchase a new textile machine to manufacture towels, but this same money cannot be used to buy a new recreation facility for employees.

The DVD and recreation facility examples illustrate that the true cost of these decisions is the **opportunity cost** of a choice, not the purchase price. Opportunity cost is the best alternative sacrificed for a chosen alternative. Stated differently, it is the cost of not choosing the next best alternative. This principle states that some highly valued opportunity must be forgone in all economic decisions. The actual good or use of time given up for the chosen good or use of time measures the opportunity cost. We may omit the word *opportunity* before the word *cost*, but the concept remains the same. Exhibit 1 illustrates the causation chain linking scarcity, choice, and opportunity cost.

Opportunity cost

The best alternative sacrificed for a chosen alternative.

Exhibit 1 — The Links between Scarcity, Choice, and Opportunity Cost

Scarcity means no society has enough resources to produce all the goods and services necessary to satisfy all human wants. As a result, society is always confronted with the problem of making choices. This concept is captured in Milton Friedman's famous phrase, "There is no such thing as a free lunch." This means that each decision has a sacrifice in terms of an alternative not chosen.

Examples are endless, but let's consider a few. Suppose your economics professor decides to become a rock star in the Rolling in Dough band. Now all his or her working hours are devoted to creating hit music, and the opportunity cost is the educational services no longer provided. Now a personal example: The opportunity cost of dating a famous model or movie star (name your favorite) might be the loss of your current girlfriend or boyfriend. Opportunity cost also applies to national economic decisions. Suppose the federal government decides to spend tax revenues on a space station. The opportunity cost depends on the next best program *not* funded. Assume roads and bridges are the highest-valued projects not built as a result of the decision to construct the space station. Then the opportunity cost of the decision to devote resources to the space station is the forgone roads and bridges and not the money actually spent to build the space station.

To personalize the relationship between time and opportunity cost, ask yourself what you would be doing if you were not reading this book. Your answer might be watching television or sleeping. If sleeping is your choice, the opportunity cost of studying this text is the sleep you sacrifice. Rock stars and movie stars, on the other hand, must forfeit a large amount of income to attend college. Now you know why you see so few of these stars in class.

Decisions often involve sacrifice of *both* goods and time. Suppose you decide to see a movie at a theater located 15 minutes from campus. If you had not spent the money at the movie theater, you could have purchased a DVD and watched a movie at home. And the time spent traveling to and from the movie and sitting through it could have been devoted to studying for your economics exam. The opportunity cost of the movie consists of giving up (1) a DVD and (2) study time needed to score higher on the economics exam.

MARGINAL ANALYSIS

At the heart of many important decision-making techniques used throughout this text is **marginal analysis**. Marginal analysis examines the effects of additions to or subtractions from a current situation. This is a very valuable tool in the economic-way-of-thinking toolkit because it considers the "marginal" effects of change. The rational decision maker decides on an option only if the marginal benefit exceeds the marginal cost. For example, you must decide how to use your scarce time. Should you devote an extra hour to reading this book, going to a movie, watching television, talking on the phone, or sleeping? Which of your many options do you choose? The answer depends on marginal analysis. If you decide the benefit of a higher grade in economics exceeds the opportunity cost of, say, sleep, then you allocate the extra hour to studying economics. Excellent choice!

Businesses use marginal analysis. Hotels, for example, rent space to student groups for dances and other events. Assume you are the hotel manager and a student group offers to pay $400 to use the ballroom for a party. To decide whether to accept the offer requires marginal analysis. The marginal benefit of renting otherwise vacant space is $400, and the marginal cost is $300 for extra electricity and cleaning services. Since the marginal benefit exceeds the marginal cost, the manager sensibly accepts the offer.

> **Marginal analysis**
>
> An examination of the effects of additions to or subtractions from a current situation.

Similarly, farmers use marginal analysis. For example, a farmer must decide whether to add fertilizer when planting corn. Using marginal analysis, the farmer estimates that the corn revenue yield will be about $75 per acre without fertilizer and about $100 per acre using fertilizer. If the cost of fertilizer is $20 per acre, marginal analysis tells the farmer to fertilize. The addition of fertilizer will increase profit by $5 per acre because fertilizing adds $25 to the value of each acre at a cost of $20 per acre.

Marginal analysis is an important concept when the government considers changes in various programs. For example, as demonstrated in the next section, it is useful to know that an increase in the production of military goods will result in an opportunity cost of fewer consumer goods produced.

THE PRODUCTION POSSIBILITIES CURVE

The economic problem of scarcity means that society's capacity to produce combinations of goods is constrained by its limited resources. This condition can be represented in a model called the **production possibilities curve**. The production possibilities curve shows the maximum combinations of two outputs that an economy can produce in a given period of time with its available resources and technology. Three basic assumptions underlie the production possibilities curve model:

Production possibilities curve

A curve that shows the maximum combinations of two outputs an economy can produce in a given period of time with its available resources and technology.

1. **Fixed Resources.** The quantities and qualities of all resource inputs remain unchanged during the time period. But the "rules of the game" do allow an economy to shift any resource from the production of one output to the production of another output. For example, an economy might shift workers from producing consumer goods to producing capital goods. Although the number of workers remains unchanged, this transfer of labor will produce fewer consumer goods and more capital goods.
2. **Fully Employed Resources.** The economy operates with all its factors of production fully employed and producing the greatest output possible without waste or mismanagement.
3. **Technology Unchanged.** Holding existing technology fixed creates limits, or constraints, on the amounts and types of goods any economy can produce. Technology is the body of knowledge applied to how goods are produced.

Technology

The body of knowledge applied to how goods are produced.

Exhibit 2 shows a hypothetical economy that has the capacity to manufacture any combination of military goods ("guns") and consumer goods ("butter") per year along its production possibilities curve (*PPC*), including points *A, B, C,* and *D*. For example, if this economy uses all its resources to make military goods, it can produce a *maximum* of 160 billion units of military goods and zero units of consumer goods (combination *A*). Another possibility is for the economy to use all its resources to produce a *maximum* of 100 billion units of consumer goods and zero units of military goods (point *D*). Between the extremes of points *A* and *D* lie other production possibilities for combinations of military and consumer goods. If combination *B* is chosen, the economy will produce 140 billion units of military goods and 40 billion units of consumer goods. Another possibility (point *C*) is to produce 80 billion units of military goods and 80 billion units of consumer goods.

Exhibit 2	The Production Possibilities Curve for Military Goods and Consumer Goods

All points along the production possibilities curve (*PPC*) are maximum possible combinations of military goods and consumer goods. One possibility, point *A*, would be to produce 160 billion units of military goods and zero units of consumer goods each year. At the other extreme, point *D*, the economy uses all its resources to produce 100 billion units of consumer goods and zero units of military goods each year. Points *B* and *C* are obtained by using some resources to produce each of the two outputs. If the economy fails to utilize its resources fully, the result is the inefficient point *U*. Point *Z* lies beyond the economy's present production capabilities and is unattainable.

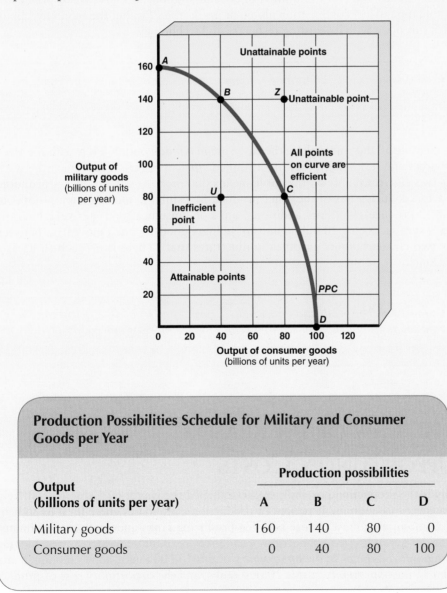

Production Possibilities Schedule for Military and Consumer Goods per Year

Output	Production possibilities			
(billions of units per year)	**A**	**B**	**C**	**D**
Military goods	160	140	80	0
Consumer goods	0	40	80	100

What happens if the economy does not use all its resources to their capacity? For example, some workers may not find work, or plants and equipment may be idle for any number of reasons. The result is that our hypothetical economy fails to reach any of the combinations along the *PPC*. In Exhibit 2, point *U* illustrates an *inefficient* output level for any economy operating without all its resources fully employed. At point *U*, our model economy is producing 80 billion units of military goods and 40 billion units of consumer goods per year. Such an economy is underproducing because it could satisfy more of society's wants if it were producing at some point along *PPC*.

Even if an economy fully employs all its resources, it is impossible to produce certain output quantities. Any point outside the production possibilities curve is *unattainable* because it is beyond the economy's present production capabilities. Point *Z*, for example, represents an unattainable output of 140 billion units of military goods and 80 billion units of consumer goods. Society would prefer this combination to any combination along, or inside, the *PPC*, but the economy cannot reach this point with its existing resources and technology.

> **CONCLUSION** *Scarcity limits an economy to points on or below its production possibilities curve.*

Because all the points along the curve are *maximum* output levels with the given resources and technology, they are all called *efficient* points. A movement between any two efficient points on the curve means that *more* of one product is produced only by producing *less* of the other product. In Exhibit 2, moving from point *A* to point *B* produces 40 billion additional units of consumer goods per year, but only at a cost of sacrificing 20 billion units of military goods. Thus, a movement between any two efficient points graphically illustrates that "There is no such thing as a free lunch."

> **CONCLUSION** *The production possibilities curve consists of all efficient output combinations at which an economy can produce more of one good only by producing less of the other good.*

THE LAW OF INCREASING OPPORTUNITY COSTS

Why is the production possibilities curve shaped the way it is? Exhibit 3 will help us answer this question. It presents a production possibilities curve for a hypothetical economy that must choose between producing tanks and producing sailboats. Consider expanding the production of sailboats in 20,000-unit increments. Moving from point *A* to point *B*, the *opportunity cost* is 10,000 tanks; between point *B* and point *C*, the *opportunity cost* is 20,000 tanks; and the *opportunity cost* of producing at point *D*, rather than point *C*, is 50,000 tanks.

Exhibit 3   The Law of Increasing Opportunity Costs

A hypothetical economy produces equal increments of 20,000 sailboats per year as we move from point *A* through point *D* on the production possibilities curve (*PPC*). If the economy moves from point *A* to point *B*, the opportunity cost of 20,000 sailboats is a reduction in tank output of 10,000 per year. This opportunity cost rises to 20,000 tanks if the economy moves from point *B* to point *C*. Finally, production at point *D*, rather than point *C*, results in an opportunity cost of 50,000 tanks per year. The opportunity cost rises because workers are not equally suited to making tanks and sailboats.

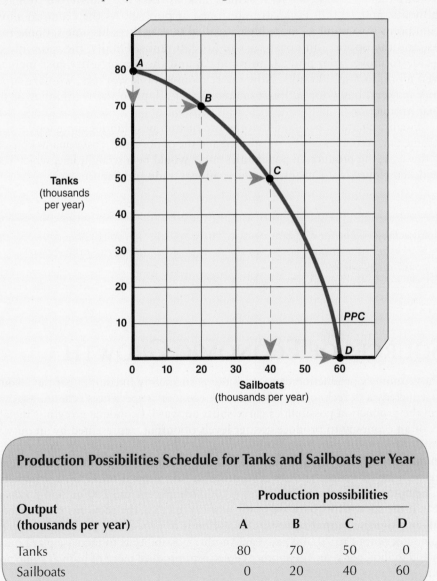

Production Possibilities Schedule for Tanks and Sailboats per Year

Output (thousands per year)	Production possibilities			
	A	**B**	**C**	**D**
Tanks	80	70	50	0
Sailboats	0	20	40	60

Law of increasing opportunity costs

The principle that the opportunity cost increases as production of one output expands.

Exhibit 3 illustrates the **law of increasing opportunity costs**, which states that the opportunity cost increases as production of one output expands. Holding the stock of resources and technology constant (ceteris paribus), the law of increasing opportunity costs causes the production possibilities curve to display a *bowed-out* shape.

Why must our hypothetical economy sacrifice larger and larger amounts of tank output in order to produce each additional 20,000 sailboats? The reason is that all workers are not equally suited to producing one good, compared to another good. Expanding the output of sailboats requires the use of workers who are less suited to producing sailboats than producing tanks. Suppose our hypothetical economy produces no sailboats (point A) and then decides to produce them. At first, the least-skilled tank workers are transferred to making sailboats, and 10,000 tanks are sacrificed at point B. As the economy moves from point B to point C, more highly skilled tank makers become sailboat makers, and the opportunity cost rises to 20,000 tanks. Finally, the economy can decide to move from point C to point D, and the opportunity cost increases even more, to 50,000 tanks. Now the remaining tank workers, who are superb tank makers, but poor sailboat makers, must adapt to the techniques of sailboat production.

Finally, it should be noted that the production possibilities curve model could assume that resources can be substituted and the opportunity cost remains constant. In this case, the production possibilities curve would be a straight line, which is the model employed in the chapter on international trade and finance.

CONCLUSION *The lack of interchangeability between workers is the cause of increasing opportunity costs and the bowed-out shape of the production possibilities curve.*

SOURCES OF ECONOMIC GROWTH

Economic growth

The ability of an economy to produce greater levels of output, represented by an outward shift of its production possibilities curve.

The economy's production capacity is not permanently fixed. If either the resource base increases or technology advances, the economy experiences **economic growth**, and the production possibilities curve shifts outward. Economic growth is the ability of an economy to produce greater levels of output, represented by an outward shift of its production possibilities curve. Exhibit 4 illustrates the importance of an outward shift. (Note the causation chain, which is often used in this text to focus on a model's cause-and-effect relationship.) At point A on PPC_1, a hypothetical full-employment economy produces 40,000 computers and 200 million pizzas per year. If the curve shifts outward to the new curve PPC_2, the economy can expand its full-employment output options. One option is to produce at point B and increase computer output to 70,000 per year. Another possibility is to increase pizza output to 400 million per year. Yet another choice is to produce more of both at some point between points B and C.

Exhibit 4	An Outward Shift of the Production Possibilities Curve for Computers and Pizzas

The economy begins with the capacity to produce combinations along the first production possibilities curve PPC_1. Growth in the resource base or technological advances can shift the production possibilities curve outward from PPC_1 to PPC_2. Points along PPC_2 represent new production possibilities that were previously impossible. This outward shift permits the economy to produce greater quantities of output. Instead of producing combination A, the economy can produce, for example, more computers at point B or more pizzas at point C. If the economy produces at a point between B and C, more of both pizzas and computers can be produced, compared to point A.

Changes in Resources

One way to accelerate economic growth is to gain additional resources. Any increase in resources—for example, more natural resources, a "baby boom," or more factories—will shift the production possibilities curve outward. In Exhibit 4, assume curve PPC_1 represents Japan's production possibilities for clothing and food in a given year. Suddenly, Japan discovers within its borders new sources of labor and other resources. As a result of the new resources, Japan will have an expanded capacity to produce any combination along an expanded curve, such as curve PPC_2.

Reductions in resources will cause the production possibilities curve to shift inward. Assume curve PPC_2 describes Japan's economy before World War II and the destruction of its factors of production during the war caused Japan's curve to shift leftward to curve PPC_1. Over the years, Japan trained its workforce, built new factories and equipment, and used new technology to shift its curve outward and surpass its original production capacity at curve PPC_2.

Technological Change

Another way to achieve economic growth is through research and development of new technologies. The knowledge of how to transform a stone into a wheel vastly improved the prehistoric standard of living. Technological change also makes it possible to shift the production possibilities curve outward by producing more from the same resources base. One source of technological change is *invention*. Computer chips, satellites, and the Internet are all examples of technological advances resulting from the use of science and engineering knowledge.

Technological change also results from the innovations of entrepreneurship, introduced in the previous chapter. Innovation involves creating and developing new products or productive processes. Seeking profits, entrepreneurs create new, better, or less expensive products. This requires organizing an improved mix of resources, which expands the production possibilities curve.

One entrepreneur, Henry Ford, changed auto industry technology by pioneering the use of the assembly line for making cars. Another entrepreneur, Chester Carlson, a law student, became so frustrated copying documents that he worked on his own to develop photocopying. After years of disappointment, a small firm named Xerox Corporation accepted Carlson's invention and transformed a good idea into a revolutionary product. These, and a myriad of other business success stories, illustrate that entrepreneurs are important because they transform their new ideas into production and practical use.

The phrase "new economy" refers to economic growth resulting from technological advances that make businesses and workers more productive. Success stories in the new economy are endless. The dizzying array of technological changes marches on cutting costs, boosting productivity and profits. Dairy farmers, for example, use new computer technology to milk their cows 24/7. New technology is even saving tropical fish at pet stores. Computer-controlled monitors that track water temperatures, acidity, and chlorine levels are resulting in fewer fish deaths per store. Such widespread technological gains mean real progress in the way we work and live.

It can be argued that there is nothing really "new" in the new economy concept. Throughout history, technological advances have fostered economic growth by increasing our nation's productive power. Today, the Internet and computers are "new" technologies, but railroads, electricity, and automobiles, for example, were also "new" technologies in their time.

You're The Economist FedEx Wasn't an Overnight
Success *Applicable Concept: entrepreneurship*

Frederick W. Smith is a classic entrepreneurial success story. Young Fred went to Yale University, had a good new idea, secured venture capital, worked like crazy, made a fortune, and the Smithsonian Institution rendered its ultimate accolade. It snapped up an early Federal Express jet for its collection, displaying it for a time in the Air and Space Museum in Washington, D.C., not far from the Wright brothers' first airplane.

Smith's saga began with a college economics term paper that spelled out a nationwide overnight parcel delivery system that would be guaranteed to "absolutely, positively" beat the pants off the U.S. Postal Service. People, he said, would pay much more if their packages would arrive at their destination the next morning. To accomplish his plan, planes would converge nightly on Memphis, Tennessee, carrying packages accepted at any location throughout the nation. Smith chose this city for its central U.S. location and because its airport has little bad weather to cause landing delays. In the morning hours, all items would be unloaded, sorted, and rerouted to other airports, where vans would battle rush-hour traffic to make deliveries before the noon deadline.

Smith's college term paper got a C grade. Perhaps the professor thought the idea was too risky, and lots of others certainly agreed. In 1969, after college and a tour as a Marine pilot in Vietnam, the 24-year-old Smith began pitching his parcel delivery plan to mostly skeptical financiers. Nevertheless, with $4 million of his family's money, he persuaded a few venture capitalists to put up $80 million. At this time, this was the largest venture capital package ever assembled. In 1973, delivery service began with 33 jets connecting 25 cities, but on the first night only 86 packages showed up.

It was years before Smith looked like a genius. The company posted a $27 million loss the first year, turned the corner in 1976, and then took off, helped by a 1981 decision to add letters to its basic package delivery service. Today, Smith's basic strategy hasn't changed, but the scale of the operation has exploded. FedEx is the world's largest express transportation company, serving over 200 countries.

ANALYZE THE ISSUE

Draw a production possibilities curve for an economy producing only pizzas and computers. Explain how Fred Smith and other entrepreneurs affect the curve.

CHECKPOINT
What Does a War on Terrorism Really Mean?

With the disappearance of the former Soviet Union and the end of the Cold War, the United States became the world's only superpower and no longer engaged in an intense competition to build up its military. As a result, in the 1990s Congress and the White House had the opportunity to reduce the military's share of the budget and spend more funds for nondefense goods. This situation was referred to as the "peace dividend." Now consider that the need to combat terrorism diverts resources back to military and security output. Does the peace dividend or a reversal to more military spending represent a possible shift of the production possibilities curve or a movement along it?

Exhibit 5   **Alpha's and Beta's Present and Future Production Possibilities Curves**

In part (a), each year Alpha produces only enough capital (K_a) to replace existing capital being worn out. Without greater capital and assuming other resources remain fixed, Alpha is unable to shift its production possibilities curve outward. In part (b), each year Beta produces K_b capital, which is more than the amount required to replenish its depreciated capital. In 2010, this expanded capital provides Beta with the extra production capacity to shift its production possibilities curve to the right (outward). If Beta chooses point *B* on its curve, it has the production capacity to increase the amount of consumer goods from C_b to C_c without producing fewer capital goods.

PRESENT INVESTMENT AND THE FUTURE PRODUCTION POSSIBILITIES CURVE

Global Economics

When the decision for an economy involves choosing between capital goods and consumer goods, the output combination for the present period can determine future production capacity.

Exhibit 5 compares two countries producing different combinations of capital and consumer goods. Part (a) shows the production possibilities curve for the low-investment economy of Alpha. This economy was producing combination *A* in 2000, which is an output of C_a of consumer goods and an output of K_a of capital goods per year. Let's assume K_a is just enough capital output to replace the capital being worn out each year (depreciation). As a result, Alpha fails to accumulate the net gain of factories and equipment required to expand its production possibilities curve outward in future years.[1] Why wouldn't Alpha simply move up along its

---

1. Recall from the Appendix to Chapter 1 that a third variable can affect the variables measured on the vertical and horizontal axes. In this case, the third variable is the quantity of capital worn out per year.

Global Economics How Does Public Capital Affect a Nation's Curve? *Applicable Concept: economic growth*

The discussion of low-investment country Alpha versus high-investment country Beta explained that sacrificing production of consumer goods for an increase in capital goods output can result in economic growth and a higher standard of living. Stated differently, there was a long-run benefit from the accumulation of capital that offset the short-run opportunity cost in terms of consumer goods. Here the analysis was in terms of investment in private capital such as factories, machines, and inventories. However, public or government capital can also influence the production of both capital goods and consumption goods. For example, the government provides infrastructure such as roads, schools, bridges, ports, dams, and sanitation that makes the accumulation process for private capital more efficient, and in turn, an economy grows at a greater rate.

Using data from 21 high-investment countries, a recent study by economists investigated how government investment policy affected the productivity of new private capital goods.[1] Countries included in the research were, for example, Canada, Japan, New Zealand, Spain, and the United States. A key finding was that a 1 percent increase in public investment increased the productivity of private investment by 27 percent. As a result, public capital caused the stock of private capital to rise more quickly over time.

Finally, economic growth and development is a major goal of countries throughout the world, and there are numerous factors that cause some countries to experience greater economic growth compared to other countries. Note that this topic is discussed in more depth in the last chapter of the text.

ANALYZE THE ISSUE

Construct a production possibilities curve for a hypothetical country. Put public capital goods per year on the vertical axis and consumer goods per year on the horizontal axis. Not shown directly in your graph, assume that this country produces just enough private capital per year to replace its depreciated capital. Assume further that this country is without public capital and is operating at point *A* where consumer goods are at a maximum. Based on the above research and using a production possibilities curve, show and explain what happens to this country's private capital, production possibilities curve, and standard of living if it increases its output of public capital.

---

1. Stuart Fowler and Bichaka Fayissa, "Public Capital Spending Shocks and the Price of Investment: Evidence from a Panel of Countries," The 2007 Missouri Economics Conference, http://www.mtsu.edu/~sfowler/research/fs1.pdf.

production curve by shifting more resources to capital goods production? The problem is that sacrificing consumer goods for capital formation causes the standard of living to fall.

Comparing Alpha to Beta illustrates the importance of being able to do more than just replace worn-out capital. Beta operated in 2000 at point *A* in part (b), which is an output of C_b of consumer goods and K_b of capital goods. Assuming K_b is more than enough to replenish worn-out capital, Beta is a high-investment economy, adding to its capital stock and creating extra production capacity. This process of accumulating capital *(capital formation)* is **investment**. Investment is the accumulation of capital, such as factories, machines, and inventories, used to produce goods

Investment

The accumulation of capital, such as factories, machines, and inventories, that is used to produce goods and services.

and services. Newly built factories and machines in the present provide an economy with the capacity to expand its production options in the future. For example, the outward shift of its curve allows Beta to produce C_c consumer goods at point *B* in 2010. This means Beta will be able to improve its standard of living by producing $C_c - C_b$ extra consumer goods, while Alpha's standard of living remains unchanged because the production of consumer goods remains unchanged.

> **CONCLUSION** *A nation can accelerate economic growth by increasing its production of capital goods in excess of the capital being worn out in the production process.*

Key Concepts

What, How, and *For Whom*
  questions
Opportunity cost
Marginal analysis

Production possibilities curve
Technology
Law of increasing
  opportunity costs

Economic growth
Investment

Summary

- *Three fundamental economic questions* facing any economy are *What, How,* and *For Whom* to produce goods. The *What* question asks exactly which goods are to be produced and in what quantities. The *How* question requires society to decide the resource mix used to produce goods. The *For Whom* problem concerns the division of output among society's citizens.
- *Opportunity cost* is the best alternative forgone for a chosen option. This means no decision can be made without cost.

- *Marginal analysis* examines the impact of changes from a current situation and is a technique used extensively in economics. The basic approach is to compare the additional benefits of a change with the additional costs of the change.
- A *production possibilities* **curve** illustrates an economy's capacity to produce goods, subject to the constraint of scarcity. The production possibilities curve is a graph of the maximum possible combinations of two outputs that can be produced in a given period of time, subject to three conditions: (1) All resources are fully employed. (2) The resource base is not allowed to vary during the time period. (3) **Technology**, which is the body of knowledge applied to the production of goods, remains constant. **Inefficient** production occurs at any point inside the production possibilities curve. All points along the curve are **efficient** points because each point represents a maximum output possibility.

Production Possibilities Curve

- The **law of increasing opportunity costs** states that the opportunity cost increases as the production of an output expands. The explanation for this law is that the suitability of resources declines sharply as greater amounts are transferred from producing one output to producing another output.
- *Economic growth* is represented by the production possibilities curve shifting outward as the result of an increase in resources or an advance in technology.

Economic Growth

CAUSATION CHAIN

Increase in resources or technological advances ⇒ Economic growth

- *Investment* means that an economy is producing and accumulating capital. Investment consists of factories, machines, and inventories (capital) produced in the present that are used to shift the production possibilities curve outward in the future.

Summary of Conclusion Statements

- Scarcity limits an economy to points on or below its production possibilities curve.
- The production possibilities curve consists of all efficient output combinations at which an economy can produce more of one good only by producing less of the other good.
- The lack of perfect interchangeability between workers is the cause of increasing opportunity costs and the bowed-out shape of the production possibilities curve.
- A nation can accelerate economic growth by increasing its production of capital goods in excess of the capital being worn out in the production process.

Study Questions and Problems

1. Explain why scarcity forces individuals and society to incur opportunity costs. Give specific examples.

2. Suppose a retailer promotes its store by advertising a drawing for a "free car." Is this car *free* because the winner pays *zero* for it?

3. Explain verbally the statement "There is no such thing as a free lunch" in relation to scarce resources.

4. Which of the following decisions has the greater opportunity cost? Why?
   a. A decision to use an undeveloped lot in Tokyo's financial district for an apartment building.
   b. A decision to use a square mile in the desert for a gas station.

5. Attending college is expensive, time consuming, and it requires effort. So why do people decide to attend college?

6. The following is a set of hypothetical production possibilities for a nation.

Combination	Automobiles (thousands)	Beef (thousands of tons)
A	0	10
B	2	9
C	4	7
D	6	4
E	8	0

   a. Plot these production possibilities data. What is the opportunity cost of the first 2,000 automobiles produced? Between which points is the opportunity cost per thousand automobiles highest? Between which points is the opportunity cost per thousand tons of beef highest?
   b. Label a point *F* inside the curve. Why is this an inefficient point? Label a point *G* outside the curve. Why is this point unattainable? Why are points *A* through *E* all efficient points?
   c. Does this production possibilities curve reflect the law of increasing opportunity costs? Explain.
   d. What assumptions could be changed to shift the production possibilities curve?

7. The following table shows the production possibilities for pies and flowerboxes. Fill in the opportunity cost (pies forgone) of producing the first through the fifth flowerbox.

Combination	Pies	Flowerboxes	Opportunity cost
A	30	0	_____
B	26	1	_____
C	21	2	_____
D	15	3	_____
E	8	4	_____
F	0	5	_____

8. Why does a production possibilities curve have a bowed-out shape?

9. Interpret the phrases "There is no such thing as a free lunch" and "A free lunch is possible" in terms of the production possibilities curve.

10. Suppose, unfortunately, your mathematics and economics professors have decided to give tests two days from now and you can spend a total of only twelve hours studying for both exams. After some thought, you conclude that dividing your study time equally between each subject will give you an expected grade of C in each course. For each additional three hours of study time for one of the subjects, your grade will increase one letter for that subject, and your grade will fall one letter for the other subject.
   a. Construct a table for the production possibilities and corresponding number of hours of study in this case.
   b. Plot these production possibilities data in a graph.
   c. Does this production possibilities curve reflect the law of increasing opportunity costs? Explain.

11. Draw a production possibilities curve for a hypothetical economy producing capital goods and consumer goods. Suppose a major technological breakthrough occurs in the capital goods industry and the new technology is widely adopted only in this industry. Draw the new production possibilities curve. Now assume that a technological advance occurs in consumer goods production, but not in capital goods production. Draw the new production possibilities curve.

12. The present choice between investing in capital goods and producing consumer goods now affects the ability of an economy to produce in the future. Explain.

For Online Exercises, go to the Tucker Web site at www.cengage.com/economics/tucker.

CHECKPOINT ANSWER

What Does a War on Terrorism Really Mean?

A "peace dividend" suggests resources are allocated away from military production and used for greater nonmilitary production. The war on terrorism arguably shifts resources in the opposite direction.

If you said that this phrase represents a movement along the production possibilities curve, **YOU ARE CORRECT.**

Practice Quiz

For an explanation of the correct answers, visit the Tucker Web site at www.cengage.com/economics/tucker.

1. Which of the following decisions must be made by all economies?
   a. How much to produce? When to produce? How much does it cost?
   b. What is the price? Who will produce it? Who will consume it?
   c. What to produce? How to produce it? For whom to produce?
   d. None of the above.

2. A student who has one evening to prepare for two exams on the following day has the following two alternatives:

Possibility	Score in Economics	Score in Accounting
A	95	80
B	80	90

   The opportunity cost of receiving a 90, rather than an 80, on the accounting exam is represented by how many points on the economics exam?
   a. 15 points
   b. 80 points
   c. 90 points
   d. 10 points

3. Opportunity cost is the
   a. purchase price of a good or service.
   b. value of leisure time plus out-of-pocket costs.

   c. best option given up as a result of choosing an alternative.
   d. undesirable sacrifice required to purchase a good.

4. On a production possibilities curve, the opportunity cost of good *X* in terms of good *Y* is represented by
   a. the distance to the curve from the vertical axis.
   b. the distance to the curve from the horizontal axis.
   c. the movement along the curve.
   d. all of the above.

5. If a farmer adds 1 pound of fertilizer per acre, the value of the resulting crops rises from $80 to $100 per acre. According to marginal analysis, the farmer should add fertilizer if it costs less than
   a. $12.50 per pound.
   b. $20 per pound.
   c. $80 per pound.
   d. $100 per pound.

6. On a production possibilities curve, a change from economic inefficiency to economic efficiency is obtained by
   a. movement along the curve.
   b. movement from a point outside the curve to a point on the curve.
   c. movement from a point inside the curve to a point on the curve.
   d. a change in the slope of the curve.

Practice Quiz Continued

7. Any point inside the production possibilities curve is a (an)
   a. efficient point.
   b. unfeasible point.
   c. inefficient point.
   d. maximum output combination.

8. Using a production possibilities curve, unemployment is represented by a point located
   a. near the middle of the curve.
   b. at the top corner of the curve.
   c. at the bottom corner of the curve.
   d. outside the curve.
   e. inside the curve.

9. Along a production possibilities curve, an increase in the production of one good can be accomplished only by
   a. decreasing the production of another good.
   b. increasing the production of another good.
   c. holding constant the production of another good.
   d. producing at a point on a corner of the curve.

10. Education and training that improve the skill of the labor force are represented on the production possibilities curve by a (an)
    a. movement along the curve.
    b. inward shift of the curve.
    c. outward shift of the curve.
    d. movement toward the curve from an exterior point.

11. A nation can accelerate its economic growth by
    a. reducing the number of immigrants allowed into the country.
    b. adding to its stock of capital.
    c. printing more money.
    d. imposing tariffs and quotas on imported goods.

12. From the information in Exhibit 6, which of the following points on the production possibilities curve are attainable with the resources and technology currently available?
    a. A, B, C, E, U
    b. A, B, C, D, W
    c. E, U, W
    d. B, C, D, U
    e. A, B, C, E

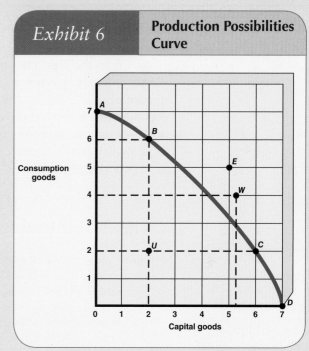

Exhibit 6   **Production Possibilities Curve**

13. In Exhibit 6, which of the following points on the production possibilities curve are efficient production points?
    a. A, B, C, U
    b. A, B, C, D, U
    c. E, U, W
    d. B, C, D, U
    e. A, B, C, D

14. In Exhibit 6, to move from U to B, the opportunity cost
    a. would be 4 units of consumption goods.
    b. would be 2 units of capital goods.
    c. would be zero.
    d. would be 5 units of capital goods.
    e. cannot be estimated.

15. In Exhibit 6, which of the following points on the production possibilities curve are full-employment production points?
    a. A, B, C, D
    b. A, B, C, D, U
    c. E, U, W
    d. B, C, D, U
    e. A, B, C, U

Road Map Introduction to Economics

This road map feature helps you tie material in the part together as you travel the Economic Way of Thinking Highway. The following are review questions listed by chapter from the previous part. The key concept in each question is given for emphasis, and each question or set of questions concludes with an interactive game to reinforce the concepts. Click on the Tucker Web site at www.cengage.com/economics/tucker, select the chapter, and play the visual causation chain game designed to make learning fun. Enjoy the cheers when correct and suffer the jeers if you miss. The correct answers to the multiple-choice questions are given in Appendix C of the text.

part

1

Chapter 1. Introducing the Economic Way of Thinking

1. **Key Concept: Scarcity**
    Economists believe that scarcity forces everyone to
    a. satisfy all their wants.
    b. abandon consumer sovereignty.
    c. lie about their wants.
    d. create unlimited resources.
    e. make choices.

2. **Key Concept: Economics**
    The subject of economics is primarily the study of
    a. the government decision-making process.
    b. how to operate a business successfully.
    c. decision making because of the problem of scarcity.
    d. how to make money in the stock market.

    Causation Chain Game
    The Relationship Between Scarcity and Decision Making

3. **Key Concept: Model**
    When building a model, an economist must
    a. adjust for exceptional situations.
    b. provide a complete description of reality.
    c. make simplifying assumptions.
    d. develop a set of behavioral equations.

4. **Key Concept: Ceteris paribus**
    If the price of a textbook rises and then students purchase fewer textbooks, an economic model can show a cause-and-effect relationship only if which of the following conditions hold?
    a. Students' incomes fall.
    b. Tuition decreases.

   c.   The number of students increases.
   d.   Everything else is constant.
   e.   The bookstore no longer accepts used book trade-ins.

5. **Key Concept: Association vs. causation**
   Someone notices that sunspot activity is high just prior to recessions and concludes that sunspots cause recessions. This person has
   a.   confused association and causation.
   b.   misunderstood the ceteris paribus assumption.
   c.   used normative economics to answer a positive question.
   d.   built an untestable model.

   Causation Chain Game
   The Steps in the Model-Building Process—Exhibit 2

Chapter 2. Production Possibilities, Opportunity Cost, and Economic Growth

6. **Key Concept: Production possibilities curve**
   Which of the following is *not true* about a production possibilities curve? The curve
   a.   indicates the combinations of goods and services that can be produced with a given technology.
   b.   indicates the efficient production points.
   c.   indicates the non-efficient production points.
   d.   indicates the feasible (attainable) and non-feasible production points.
   e.   indicates which production point will be chosen.

7. **Key Concept: Production possibilities curve**
   Which of the following is *true* about the production possibilities curve when a technological progress occurs?
   a.   Shifts inward to the left.
   b.   Becomes flatter on one end and steeper at the other end.
   c.   Becomes steeper.
   d.   Shifts outward to the right.
   e.   Does not change.

8. **Key Concept: Shifting the production possibilities curve**
   An outward shift of an economy's production possibilities curve is caused by
   a.   entrepreneurship.
   b.   an increase in labor.
   c.   an advance in technology.
   d.   all of the above.

9. **Key Concept: Shifting the production possibilities curve**
   Which would be *least likely* to cause the production possibilities curve to shift to the right?
   a.   An increase in the labor force
   b.   Improved methods of production

    c.   An increase in the education and training of the labor force

    d.   A decrease in unemployment

10. Key Concept: Investment

A nation can accelerate its economic growth by

    a.   reducing the number of immigrants allowed into the country.

    b.   adding to its stock of capital.

    c.   printing more money.

    d.   imposing tariffs and quotas on imported goods.

Causation Chain Game

Economic Growth and Technology—Exhibit 4

Microeconomic Fundamentals

© Getty Images

In order to study the microeconomy, the chapters in Part 2 build on the basic concepts learned in Part 1. Chapters 3 and 4 explain the market demand and supply model, which has a wide range of real-world applications. Chapter 5 takes a closer look at movements along the demand curve introduced in Chapter 3. Chapter 6 returns to the law of demand and explores in more detail exactly why consumers make their choices among goods and services. Part 2 concludes in Chapter 7 with an extension of the concept of supply that explains how various costs of production change as output varies.

3

Market Demand and Supply

A cornerstone of the U.S. economy is the use of markets to answer the basic economic questions discussed in the previous chapter. Consider baseball cards, DVDs, physical fitness, gasoline, soft drinks, alligators, and sneakers. In a *market economy*, each is bought and sold by individuals coming together as buyers and sellers in markets. This chapter is extremely important because it introduces basic supply and demand analysis. This technique will prove to be valuable because it is applicable to a multitude of real-world choices of buyers and sellers facing the problem of scarcity. For example, the Global Economics feature asks you to consider the highly controversial issue of international trade in human organs.

Demand represents the choice-making behavior of consumers, while supply represents the choices of producers. The chapter begins by looking closely at demand and then supply. Finally, it combines these forces to see how prices and quantities are determined in the marketplace. Market demand and supply analysis is the basic tool of microeconomic analysis.

In this chapter, you will learn to solve these economics puzzles:

- What is the difference between a "change in quantity demanded" and a "change in demand"?

- Can Congress repeal the law of supply to control oil prices?

- Does the price system eliminate scarcity?

THE LAW OF DEMAND

Economics might be referred to as "graphs and laughs" because economists are so fond of using graphs to illustrate demand, supply, and many other economic concepts. Unfortunately, some students taking economics courses say they miss the laughs.

Exhibit 1 reveals an important "law" in economics called the law of demand. The law of demand states there is an inverse relationship between the price of a good and the quantity buyers are willing to purchase in a defined time period, ceteris paribus. The law of demand makes good sense. At a "sale," consumers buy more when the price of merchandise is cut.

In Exhibit 1, the *demand curve* is formed by the line connecting the possible price and quantity purchased responses of an individual consumer. The demand curve therefore allows you to find the quantity demanded by a buyer at any possible selling price by moving along the curve. For example, Bob, a sophomore at Marketplace College, loves watching movies on DVDs. Bob's demand curve shows that at a price of $15 per DVD his quantity demanded is 6 DVDs purchased annually (point *B*). At the lower price of $10, Bob's quantity demanded increases to 10 DVDs per year (point *C*). Following this procedure, other price and quantity possibilities for Bob are read along the demand curve.

Note that until we know the actual price determined by both demand and supply, we do not know how many DVDs Bob will actually purchase annually. The demand curve is simply a summary of Bob's buying intentions. Once we know the market price, a quick look at the demand curve tells us how many DVDs Bob will buy.

> **CONCLUSION** *Demand is a curve or schedule showing the various quantities of a product consumers are willing to purchase at possible prices during a specified period of time, ceteris paribus.*

Market Demand

To make the transition from an *individual* demand curve to a *market* demand curve, we total, or sum, the individual demand schedules. Suppose the owner of Zap Mart, a small retail chain of stores serving a few states, tries to decide what to charge for DVDs

---

Law of demand

The principle that there is an inverse relationship between the price of a good and the quantity buyers are willing to purchase in a defined time period, ceteris paribus.

Demand

A curve or schedule showing the various quantities of a product consumers are willing to purchase at possible prices during a specified period of time, ceteris paribus.

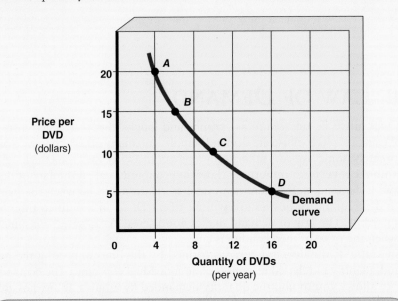

Exhibit 1 — An Individual Buyer's Demand Curve for DVDs

Bob's demand curve shows how many DVDs he is willing to purchase at different possible prices. As the price of DVDs declines, the quantity demanded increases, and Bob purchases more DVDs. The inverse relationship between price and quantity demanded conforms to the law of demand.

An Individual Buyer's Demand Schedule for DVDs

Point	Price per DVD	Quantity demanded (per year)
A	$20	4
B	15	6
C	10	10
D	5	16

and hires a consumer research firm. For simplicity, we assume Fred and Mary are the only two buyers in Zap Mart's market, and they are sent a questionnaire that asks how many DVDs each would be willing to purchase at several possible prices. Exhibit 2 reports their price–quantity demanded responses in tabular and graphical form.

The market demand curve, D_{total}, in Exhibit 2 is derived by summing *horizontally* the two individual demand curves, D_1 and D_2, for each possible price. At a price of $20, for example, we sum Fred's 2 DVDs demanded per year and Mary's 1 DVD demanded per year to find that the total quantity demanded at $20 is 3 DVDs per year. Repeating the same process for other prices generates the market demand curve, D_{total}. For example, at a price of $5, the total quantity demanded is 12 DVDs.

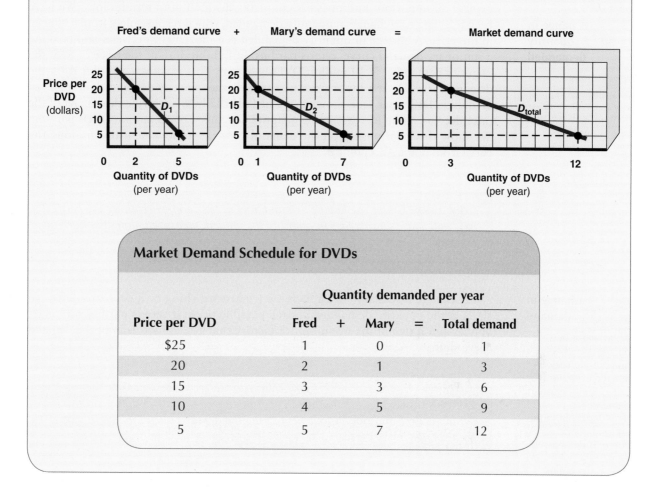

Exhibit 2 **The Market Demand Curve for DVDs**

Individual demand curves differ for consumers Fred and Mary. Assuming they are the only buyers in the market, the market demand curve, D_{total}, is derived by summing horizontally the individual demand curves, D_1 and D_2.

Market Demand Schedule for DVDs

Price per DVD	Fred	+	Mary	=	Total demand
$25	1		0		1
20	2		1		3
15	3		3		6
10	4		5		9
5	5		7		12

THE DISTINCTION BETWEEN CHANGES IN QUANTITY DEMANDED AND CHANGES IN DEMAND

Price is not the only variable that determines how much of a good or service consumers will buy. Recall from Exhibit A-6 of Appendix 1 that the price and quantity variables in our model are subject to the ceteris paribus assumption. If we relax this assumption and allow other variables held constant to change, a variety of factors can influence the position of the demand curve. Because these factors are not the price of the good itself, these variables are called *nonprice determinants,* or simply, *demand shifters.* The major nonprice determinants include (1) the number of buyers; (2) tastes and preferences; (3) income; (4) expectations of future changes in prices, income, and availability of goods; and (5) prices of related goods.

Before discussing these nonprice determinants of demand, we must pause to explain an important and possibly confusing distinction in terminology. We have been referring to a change in quantity demanded, which results solely from a change in the price. A change in quantity demanded is a movement between points along a stationary demand curve, ceteris paribus. In Exhibit 3(a), at the price of $15, the quantity demanded is 20 million DVDs per year. This is shown as point A on the demand curve, D. At a lower price of, say, $10, the quantity demanded increases to 30 million DVDs per year, shown as point B. Verbally, we describe the impact of the price decrease as an increase in the quantity demanded of 10 million DVDs per year. We show this relationship on the demand curve as a movement down along the curve from point A to point B.

Change in quantity demanded

A movement between points along a stationary demand curve, ceteris paribus.

CONCLUSION *Under the law of demand, any decrease in price along the vertical axis will cause an increase in quantity demanded, measured along the horizontal axis.*

Change in demand

An increase or a decrease in the quantity demanded at each possible price. An increase in demand is a rightward shift in the entire demand curve. A decrease in demand is a leftward shift in the entire demand curve.

A change in demand is an increase (rightward shift) or a decrease (leftward shift) in the quantity demanded at each possible price. If ceteris paribus no longer applies and if one of the five nonprice factors changes, the location of the demand curve shifts.

CONCLUSION *Changes in nonprice determinants can produce only a shift in the demand curve and not a movement along the demand curve, which is caused by a change in the price.*

Comparing parts (a) and (b) of Exhibit 3 is helpful in distinguishing between a change in quantity demanded and a change in demand. In part (b), suppose the market demand curve for DVDs is initially at D_1 and there is a shift to the right (an increase in demand) from D_1 to D_2. This means that at *all* possible prices consumers wish to purchase a larger quantity than before the shift occurred. At $15 per DVD, for example, 30 million DVDs (point B) will be purchased each year, rather than 20 million DVDs (point A).

Now suppose a change in some nonprice factor causes demand curve D_1 to shift leftward (a decrease in demand). The interpretation in this case is that at *all* possible prices consumers will buy a smaller quantity than before the shift occurred.

Exhibit 4 summarizes the terminology for the effects of changes in price and nonprice determinants on the demand curve.

| Exhibit 3 | Movement along a Demand Curve versus a Shift in Demand |

Part (a) shows the demand curve, *D*, for DVDs per year. If the price is $15 at point *A*, the quantity demanded by consumers is 20 million DVDs. If the price decreases to $10 at point *B*, the quantity demanded increases from 20 million to 30 million DVDs.

Part (b) illustrates an increase in demand. A change in some nonprice determinant can cause an increase in demand from D_1 to D_2. At a price of $15 on D_1 (point *A*), 20 million DVDs is the quantity demanded per year. At this same price on D_2 (point *B*), the quantity demanded increases to 30 million.

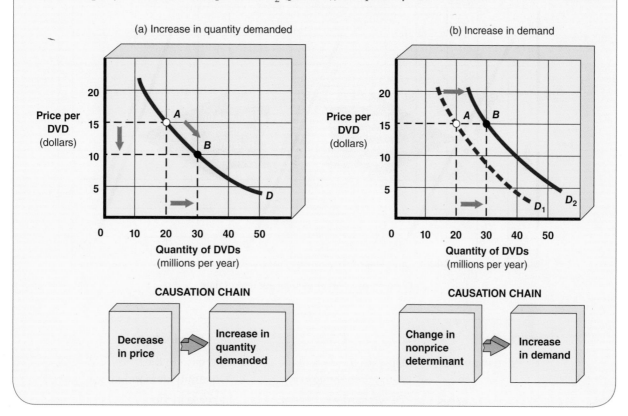

NONPRICE DETERMINANTS OF DEMAND

Distinguishing between a change in quantity demanded and a change in demand requires some patience and practice. The following discussion of specific changes in nonprice factors or demand shifters will clarify how each nonprice variable affects demand.

Number of Buyers

Look back at Exhibit 2, and imagine the impact of adding more individual demand curves to the individual demand curves of Fred and Mary. At all possible prices, there is extra quantity demanded by the new customers, and the market demand curve for DVDs shifts rightward (an increase in demand). Population growth

---

Exhibit 4   **Terminology for Changes in Price and Nonprice Determinants of Demand**

Caution! It is important to distinguish between a change in quantity demanded, which is a movement along a demand curve (D_1) caused by a change in price, and a change in demand, which is a shift in the demand curve. An increase in demand (shift to D_2) or decrease in demand (shift to D_3) is not caused by a change in price. Instead, a shift is caused by a change in one of the nonprice determinants.

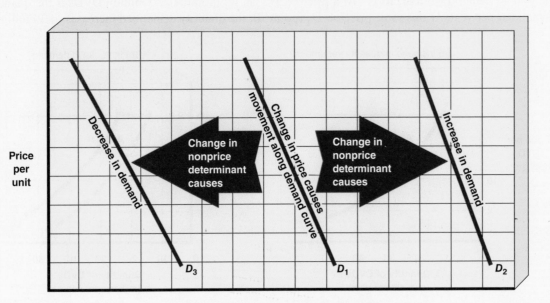

Quantity of good or service per unit of time

Change	Effect	Terminology
Price increases	Upward movement along the demand curve	Decrease in the quantity demanded
Price decreases	Downward movement along the demand curve	Increase in the quantity demanded
Nonprice determinant	Leftward or rightward shift in the demand curve	Decrease or increase in demand

---

therefore tends to increase the number of buyers, which shifts the market demand curve for a good or service rightward. Conversely, a population decline shifts most market demand curves leftward (a decrease in demand).

The number of buyers can be specified to include both foreign and domestic buyers. Suppose the market demand curve D_1 in Exhibit 3(b) is for DVDs purchased in the United States by customers at home and abroad. Also assume Japan restricts the import of DVDs into Japan. What would be the effect of Japan removing this trade restriction? The answer is that the demand curve shifts rightward from D_1 to

D_2 when Japanese consumers add their individual demand curves to the U.S. market demand for DVDs.

Tastes and Preferences

A favorable or unfavorable change in consumer tastes or preferences means more or less of a product is demanded at each possible price. Fads, fashions, advertising, and new products can influence consumer preferences to buy a particular good or service. Beanie Babies, for example, became the rage in the 1990s, and the demand curve for these products shifted to the right. When people tire of a product, the demand curve will shift leftward. The physical fitness trend has increased the demand for health clubs and exercise equipment. On the other hand, have you noticed many stores selling hula hoops? Advertising can also influence consumers' taste for a product. As a result, consumers are more likely to buy more at every price, and the demand curve for the product will shift to the right. Concern for global climate change has increased the demand for hybrid cars and recycling.

Income

Most students are all too familiar with how changes in income affect demand. There are two possible categories for the relationship between changes in income and changes in demand: (1) **normal goods** and (2) **inferior goods**.

A normal good is any good for which there is a direct relationship between changes in income and its demand curve. For many goods and services, an increase in income causes buyers to purchase more at any possible price. As buyers receive higher incomes, the demand curve shifts rightward for such *normal goods* as cars, steaks, vintage wine, cleaning services, and DVDs. A decline in income has the opposite effect, and the demand curve shifts leftward.

An inferior good is any good for which there is an inverse relationship between changes in income and its demand curve. A rise in income can result in reduced purchases of a good or service at any possible price. This might happen with such *inferior* goods as generic brands, Spam, discount clothing, and used cars. Instead of buying these inferior goods, higher incomes allow consumers to buy brand-name products, steaks, designer clothes, or new cars. Conversely, a fall in income causes the demand curve for inferior goods to shift rightward.

Normal good

Any good for which there is a direct relationship between changes in income and its demand curve.

Inferior good

Any good for which there is an inverse relationship between changes in income and its demand curve.

Expectations of Buyers

What is the effect on demand in the present when consumers anticipate future changes in prices, incomes, or availability? What happens when a war breaks out in the Middle East? Expectations that there will be a shortage of gasoline induce consumers to say "fill-'er-up" at every opportunity, and demand increases. Suppose students learn that the prices of the textbooks for several courses they plan to take next semester will double soon. Their likely response is to buy now, which causes an increase in the demand curve for these textbooks. Another example is a change in the weather, which can indirectly cause expectations to shift demand for some products. Suppose a hailstorm destroys a substantial portion of the peach crop.

Consumers reason that the reduction in available supply will soon drive up prices, and they dash to stock up before it is too late. This change in expectations causes the demand curve for peaches to increase. Prior to Hurricane Katrina hitting New Orleans, sales of batteries and flashlights soared.

Prices of Related Goods

Possibly the most confusing nonprice factor is the influence of other prices on the demand for a particular good or service. The term *nonprice* seems to forbid any shift in demand resulting from a change in the price of *any* product. This confusion exists when one fails to distinguish between changes in quantity demanded and changes in demand. Remember that ceteris paribus holds all prices of other goods constant. Therefore, movement along a demand curve occurs solely in response to changes in the price of a product, that is, its "own" price. When we draw the demand curve for Coca-Cola, for example, we assume the prices of Pepsi-Cola and other colas remain unchanged. What happens if we relax the ceteris paribus assumption and the price of Pepsi rises? Many Pepsi buyers switch to Coca-Cola, and the demand curve for Coca-Cola shifts rightward (an increase in demand). Coca-Cola and Pepsi-Cola are one type of related goods called **substitute goods**. A substitute good competes with another good for consumer purchases. As a result, there is a direct relationship between a price change for one good and the demand for its "competitor" good. Other examples of substitutes include margarine and butter, domestic cars and foreign cars, email and the U.S. Postal Service, and Internet movie downloads and DVDs.

DVDs and DVD players illustrate a second type of related goods called **complementary goods**. A complementary good is jointly consumed with another good. As a result, there is an inverse relationship between a price change for one good and the demand for its "go together" good. Although buying a DVD and buying a DVD player can be separate decisions, these two purchases are related. The more DVD players consumers buy, the greater the demand for DVDs. What happens when the price of DVD players falls sharply? The market demand curve for DVDs shifts rightward (an increase in demand) because new owners of players add their individual demand curves to those of persons already owning players and buying DVDs. Conversely, a sharp rise in the price of Hewlett-Packard (HP) Deskjet color printers would decrease the demand for color ink cartridges.

Exhibit 5 summarizes the relationship between changes in the nonprice determinants of demand and the demand curve, accompanied by examples for each type of nonprice factor change.

Substitute good

A good that competes with another good for consumer purchases. As a result, there is a direct relationship between a price change for one good and the demand for its "competitor" good.

Complementary good

A good that is jointly consumed with another good. As a result, there is an inverse relationship between a price change for one good and the demand for its "go together" good.

CHECKPOINT

Can Gasoline Become an Exception to the Law of Demand?

Suppose war in the Middle East threatened oil supplies and gasoline prices began rising. Consumers feared future oil shortages, and so they rushed to fill up their gas tanks. In this case, as the price of gas increased, consumers bought more, not less. Is this an exception to the law of demand?

Exhibit 5	Summary of the Impact of Changes in Nonprice Determinants of Demand on the Demand Curve

Nonprice Determinant of Demand	Relationship to Changes in Demand Curve	Shift in the Demand Curve	Examples
1. Number of buyers	Direct	Price / Quantity (D_1 → D_2)	• Immigration from Mexico increases the demand for Mexican food products in grocery stores.
		Price / Quantity (D_2 ← D_1)	• A decline in the birthrate reduces the demand for baby clothes.
2. Tastes and preferences	Direct	Price / Quantity (D_1 → D_2)	• For no apparent reason, consumers want Beanie Babies and demand increases.
		Price / Quantity (D_2 ← D_1)	• After a while, the fad dies and demand declines.
3. Income a. Normal goods	Direct	Price / Quantity (D_1 → D_2)	• Consumers' incomes increase, and the demand for steaks increases.
		Price / Quantity (D_2 ← D_1)	• A decline in income decreases the demand for air travel.
b. Inferior goods	Inverse	Price / Quantity (D_1 → D_2)	• Consumers' incomes increase, and the demand for hamburger decreases.
		Price / Quantity (D_2 ← D_1)	• A decline in income increases the demand for bus service.
4. Expectations of buyers	Direct	Price / Quantity (D_1 → D_2)	• Consumers expect that gasoline will be in short supply next month and that prices will rise sharply. Consequently, consumers fill the tanks in their cars this month, and there is an increase in demand for gasoline.

Continued

Continued from previous page

Nonprice Determinant of Demand	Relationship to Changes in Demand Curve	Shift in the Demand Curve	Examples
			• Months later consumers expect the price of gasoline to fall soon, and the demand for gasoline decreases.
5. Prices of related Goods a. Substitute goods	Direct		• A reduction in the price of tea decreases the demand for coffee.
			• An increase in the price of airfares causes higher demand for train transportation.
b. Complementary goods	Inverse		• A decline in the price of cellular service increases the demand for cell phones.
			• A higher price for peanut butter decreases the demand for jelly.

THE LAW OF SUPPLY

Law of supply

The principle that there is a direct relationship between the price of a good and the quantity sellers are willing to offer for sale in a defined time period, ceteris paribus.

Supply

A curve or schedule showing the various quantities of a product sellers are willing to produce and offer for sale at possible prices during a specified period of time, ceteris paribus.

In everyday conversations, the term *supply* refers to a specific quantity. A "limited supply" of golf clubs at a sporting goods store means there are only so many for sale and that's all. This interpretation of supply is *not* the economist's definition. To economists, supply is the relationship between ranges of possible prices and quantities supplied, which is stated as the **law of supply**. The law of supply states there is a direct relationship between the price of a good and the quantity sellers are willing to offer for sale in a defined time period, ceteris paribus. Interpreting the individual *supply curve* for Entertain City shown in Exhibit 6 is basically the same as interpreting Bob's demand curve shown in Exhibit 1. Each point on the curve represents a quantity supplied (measured along the horizontal axis) at a particular price (measured along the vertical axis). For example, at a price of $10 per disc (point C), the quantity supplied by the seller, Entertain City, is 35,000 DVDs per year. At the higher price of $15, the quantity supplied increases to 45,000 DVDs per year (point B).

CONCLUSION *Supply is a curve or schedule showing the various quantities of a product sellers are willing to produce and offer for sale at possible prices during a specified period of time, ceteris paribus.*

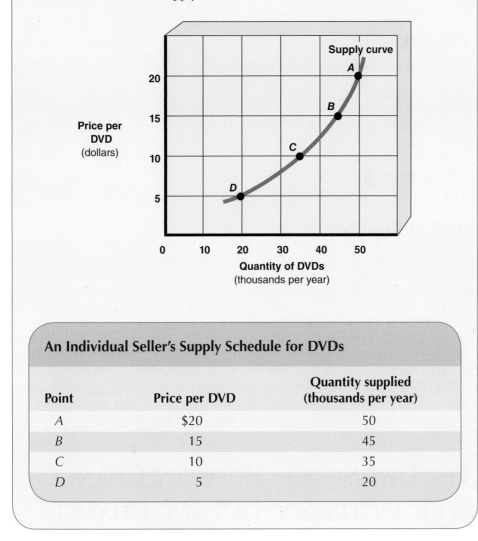

Exhibit 6 **An Individual Seller's Supply Curve for DVDs**

The supply curve for an individual seller, such as Entertain City, shows the quantity of DVDs offered for sale at different possible prices. As the price of DVDs rises, a retail store has an incentive to increase the quantity of DVDs supplied per year. The direct relationship between price and quantity supplied conforms to the law of supply.

An Individual Seller's Supply Schedule for DVDs

Point	Price per DVD	Quantity supplied (thousands per year)
A	$20	50
B	15	45
C	10	35
D	5	20

Why are sellers willing to sell more at a higher price? Suppose Farmer Brown is trying to decide whether to devote more of his land, labor, and barn space to the production of soybeans. Recall from Chapter 2 the production possibilities curve and the concept of increasing opportunity cost developed in Exhibit 3. If Farmer Brown devotes few of his resources to producing soybeans, the opportunity cost of, say, producing milk is small. But increasing soybean production means a higher opportunity cost, measured by the quantity of milk not produced. The logical question is: What would induce Farmer Brown to produce more soybeans for sale and overcome the higher opportunity cost of producing less milk? You guessed it! There must be the *incentive* of a higher price for soybeans.

> **CONCLUSION** *Only at a higher price will it be profitable for sellers to incur the higher opportunity cost associated with producing and supplying a larger quantity.*

CHECKPOINT

Can the Law of Supply Be Repealed for the Oil Market?

The United States experienced two oil shocks during the 1970s in the aftermath of Middle East tensions. Congress said no to high oil prices by passing a law prohibiting prices above a legal limit. Supporters of such price controls said this was a way to ensure adequate supply without allowing oil producers to earn excess profits. Did price controls increase, decrease, or have no effect on U.S. oil production during the 1970s?

Market Supply

To construct a *market* supply curve, we follow the same procedure used to derive a market demand curve. That is, we *horizontally* sum all the quantities supplied at various prices that might prevail in the market.

Let's assume Entertain City and High Vibes Company are the only two firms selling DVDs in a given market. As you can see in Exhibit 7, the market supply curve, S_{total}, slopes upward to the right. At a price of $25, Entertain City will supply 25,000 DVDs per year, and High Vibes will supply 35,000 DVDs per year. Thus, summing the two individual supply curves, S_1 and S_2, *horizontally*, the total of 60,000 DVDs is plotted at this price on the market supply curve, S_{total}. Similar calculations at other prices along the price axis generate a market supply curve, telling us the total amount of DVDs these businesses offer for sale at different selling prices.

Change in quantity supplied

A movement between points along a stationary supply curve, ceteris paribus.

Change in supply

An increase or a decrease in the quantity supplied at each possible price. An increase in supply is a rightward shift in the entire supply curve. A decrease in supply is a leftward shift in the entire supply curve.

THE DISTINCTION BETWEEN CHANGES IN QUANTITY SUPPLIED AND CHANGES IN SUPPLY

As in demand theory, the price of a product is not the only factor that influences how much sellers offer for sale. Once we relax the ceteris paribus assumption, there are six principal *nonprice determinants* (or simply, *supply shifters*) that can shift the supply curve's position: (1) the number of sellers, (2) technology, (3) resource prices, (4) taxes and subsidies, (5) expectations, and (6) prices of other goods. We will discuss these nonprice determinants in more detail momentarily, but first we must distinguish between a **change in quantity supplied** and a **change in supply**.

Exhibit 7   **The Market Supply Curve for DVDs**

Entertain City and High Vibes are two individual businesses selling DVDs. If these are the only two firms in the DVD market, the market supply curve, S_{total}, can be derived by summing horizontally the individual supply curves, S_1 and S_2.

The Market Supply Schedule for DVDs

| | Quantity supplied per year | | | |
Price per DVD	Entertain City	+	High Vibes	=	Total supply
$25	25		35		60
20	20		30		50
15	15		25		40
10	10		20		30
5	5		15		20

A change in quantity supplied is a movement between points along a stationary supply curve, ceteris paribus. In Exhibit 8(a), at the price of $10, the quantity supplied is 30 million DVDs per year (point *A*). At the higher price of $15, sellers offer a larger "quantity supplied" of 40 million DVDs per year (point *B*). Economists describe the effect of the rise in price as an increase in the quantity supplied of 10 million DVDs per year.

CONCLUSION *Under the law of supply, any increase in price along the vertical axis will cause an increase in the quantity supplied, measured along the horizontal axis.*

A change in supply is an increase (rightward shift) or a decrease (leftward shift) in the quantity supplied at each possible price. If ceteris paribus no longer applies and if one of the six nonprice factors changes, the impact is to alter the supply curve's location.

> **CONCLUSION** *Changes in nonprice determinants can produce only a shift in the supply curve and not a movement along the supply curve.*

In Exhibit 8(b), the rightward shift (an increase in supply) from S_1 to S_2 means that at all possible prices sellers offer a greater quantity for sale. At $15 per DVD, for instance, sellers provide 40 million for sale annually (point B), rather than 30 million (point A).

Exhibit 8   Movement along a Supply Curve versus a Shift in Supply

Part (a) presents the market supply curve, S, for DVDs per year. If the price is $10 at point A, the quantity supplied by firms will be 30 million DVDs. If the price increases to $15 at point B, the quantity supplied will increase from 30 million to 40 million DVDs.

Part (b) illustrates an increase in supply. A change in some nonprice determinant can cause an increase in supply from S_1 to S_2. At a price of $15 on S_1 (point A), the quantity supplied per year is 30 million DVDs. At this price on S_2 (point B), the quantity supplied increases to 40 million.

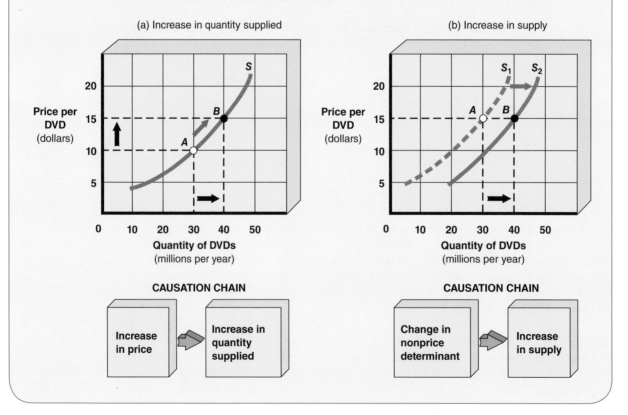

Another case is that some nonprice factor changes and causes a leftward shift (a decrease in supply) from supply curve S_1. As a result, a smaller quantity will be offered for sale at any price.

Exhibit 9 summarizes the terminology for the effects of changes in price and nonprice determinants on the supply curve.

Exhibit 9	**Terminology for Changes in Price and Nonprice Determinants of Supply**

Caution! As with demand curves, you must distinguish between a change in quantity supplied, which is a movement along a supply curve (S_1) in response to a change in price, and a shift in the supply curve. An increase in supply (shift to S_2) or decrease in supply (shift to S_3) is caused by a change in some nonprice determinant and not by a change in the price.

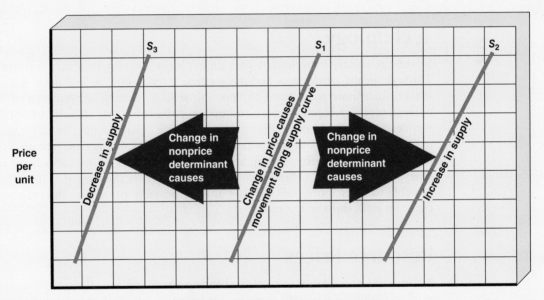

Quantity of good or service per unit of time

Change	Effect	Terminology
Price increases	Upward movement along the supply curve	Increase in the quantity supplied
Price decreases	Downward movement along the supply curve	Decrease in the quantity supplied
Nonprice determinant	Leftward or rightward shift in the supply curve	Decrease or increase in supply

NONPRICE DETERMINANTS OF SUPPLY

Now we turn to how each of the six basic nonprice factors affects supply.

Number of Sellers

What happens when a severe drought destroys wheat or a frost ruins the orange crop? The damaging effect of the weather may force orange growers out of business, and supply decreases. When the government eases restrictions on hunting alligators, the number of alligator hunters increases, and the supply curve for alligator meat and skins increases. Internationally, the United States may decide to lower trade barriers on textile imports, and this action increases supply by allowing new foreign firms to add their individual supply curves to the U.S. market supply curve for textiles. Conversely, higher U.S. trade barriers on textile imports shift the U.S. market supply curve for textiles leftward.

Technology

Never has society experienced such an explosion of new production techniques. Throughout the world, new and more efficient technology is making it possible to manufacture more products at any possible selling price. New, more powerful computers reduce production costs and increase the supply of all sorts of goods and services. For example, computers are now milking cows. Computers admit the cows into the milking area and then activate lasers to guide milking cups into place. Dairy farmers no longer must wake up at 5:30 a.m., and cows get milked whenever they fancy, day or night. As this technology spreads across the United States, it will be possible to offer more milk for sale at each possible price, and the entire supply curve for milk shifts to the right.

Resource Prices

Natural resources, labor, capital, and entrepreneurship are all required to produce products, and the prices of these resources affect supply. Suppose many firms are competing for computer programmers to design their software, and the salaries of these highly skilled workers increase. This increase in the price of labor adds to the cost of production. As a result, the supply of computer software decreases because sellers must charge more than before for any quantity supplied. Any reduction in production cost caused by a decline in the price of resources will have an opposite effect and increase supply.

Taxes and Subsidies

Certain taxes, such as sales taxes, have the same effect on supply as an increase in the price of a resource. The impact of an increase in the sales tax is similar to a rise in the salaries of computer programmers. The higher sales tax imposes an additional production cost on, for example, DVDs, and the supply curve shifts leftward. Conversely, a payment from the government for each DVD produced (an unlikely

You're The Economist PC Prices: How Low Can They Go?

Applicable Concepts: nonprice determinants of demand and supply

Radio was in existence for 38 years before 50 million people tuned in. Television took 13 years to reach that benchmark. Sixteen years after the first PC kit came out, 50 million people were using one. Once opened to the public, the Internet crossed that line in four years.[1]

An Associated Press article reported in 1998:

Personal computers, which tumbled below the $1,000-price barrier just 18 months ago, now are breaking through the $400 price mark—putting them within reach of the average U.S. family. The plunge in PC prices reflects declining wholesale prices for computer parts, such as microprocessors, memory chips, and hard drives. "We've seen a massive transformation in the PC business," said Andrew Peck, an analyst with Cowen & Co., based in Boston. Today's computers costing below $1,000 are equal or greater in power than PCs costing $1,500 and more just a few years ago—working well for word processing, spreadsheet applications, and Internet access, the most popular computer uses.[2]

In 1999, a *Wall Street Journal* article reported that PC makers and distributors were bypassing their industry's time-honored sales channels. PC makers such as Compaq and Hewlett-Packard are now using the Internet to sell directly to consumers. In doing so, they are following the successful strategy of Dell, which for years has bypassed storefront retailers and the PC distributors who traditionally keep them stocked, going instead straight to the consumer with catalogs, an 800 number, and Web sites.[3]

In 2001, a *New York Times* article described a computer price war:

We reached a situation where the market was saturated in 2000. People who needed computers had them. Vendors are living on sales of replacements, at least in the United States. But that doesn't give you the kind of growth these companies were used to. In the past, most price cuts came from falling prices for processors and other components. In addition, manufacturers have been narrowing profit margins for the last couple years. But when demand dried up

last fall, the more aggressive manufacturers decided to try to gain market share by cutting prices to the bone. This is an all-out battle for market share.[4]

In 2006, an analyst in *USA Today* observed that users could pick up good deals on desktop and notebook PCs following computer chip price cuts. Chipmakers Intel and AMD reduced the cost of computer chips in a price war. This article concluded that prices were falling at the right time and users will get good specification for their investment.[5] And in 2009, Dell, Gateway, and Asus sold computers for less than $300 that outperformed most middle-of-the-road PCs from only a few years previously.

ANALYZE THE ISSUE

Identify changes in quantity demanded, changes in demand, changes in quantity supplied, and changes in supply described in the article. For any change in demand or supply, also identify the nonprice determinant causing the change.

1. The Emerging Digital Economy (U.S. Department of Commerce, 1998), Chap. 1, p. 1.
2. David E. Kalish, "PC Prices Fall Below $400, Luring Bargain-Hunters," Associated Press/*Charlotte Observer*, Aug. 25, 1998, p. 3D.
3. George Anders, "Online Web Seller Asks: How Low Can PC Prices Go?" *The Wall Street Journal*, Jan. 19, 1999, p. B1.
4. Barnaby J. Feder, "Five Questions for Martin Reynolds: A Computer Price War Leaves Buyers Smiling," *New York Times*, May 13, 2001.
5. Michelle Kessler, "School Shoppers See PC Prices Fall," *USA Today*, Aug. 14, 2006, p. B1.

subsidy) would have the same effect as lower prices for resources or a technological advance. That is, the supply curve for DVDs shifts rightward.

Expectations of Producers

Expectations affect both current demand and current supply. Suppose a war in the Middle East causes oil producers to believe that oil prices will rise dramatically. Their initial response could be to hold back a portion of the oil in their storage tanks so they can sell more and make greater profits later when oil prices rise. One approach used by the major oil companies might be to limit the amount of gasoline delivered to independent distributors. This response by the oil industry shifts the current supply curve to the left. Now suppose farmers anticipate the price of wheat will soon fall sharply. The reaction is to sell their inventories stored in silos today before the price declines tomorrow. Such a response shifts the supply curve for wheat to the right.

Prices of Other Goods the Firm Could Produce

Businesses are always considering shifting resources from producing one good to producing another good. A rise in the price of one product relative to the prices of other products signals to suppliers that switching production to the product with the higher relative price yields higher profit. Suppose the price of corn rises because of government incentives to grow corn for ethanol, while the price of wheat remains the same; then many farmers will divert more of their land to corn and less to wheat. The result is an increase in the supply of corn and a decrease in the supply of wheat. This happens because the opportunity cost of growing corn, measured in forgone corn profits, increases.

Exhibit 10 summarizes the relationship between changes in the nonprice determinants of supply and the supply curve, accompanied by examples for each type of nonprice factor change.

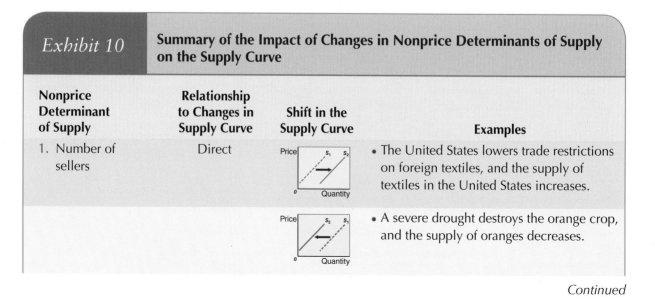

Exhibit 10	Summary of the Impact of Changes in Nonprice Determinants of Supply on the Supply Curve			
Nonprice Determinant of Supply	**Relationship to Changes in Supply Curve**	**Shift in the Supply Curve**		**Examples**
1. Number of sellers	Direct			• The United States lowers trade restrictions on foreign textiles, and the supply of textiles in the United States increases.
				• A severe drought destroys the orange crop, and the supply of oranges decreases.

Continued

Continued from previous page

Nonprice Determinant of Supply	Relationship to Changes in Supply Curve	Shift in the Supply Curve	Examples
2. Technology	Direct	Price / S_1 S_2 / 0 Quantity	• New methods of producing automobiles reduce production costs, and the supply of automobiles increases.
		Price / S_2 S_1 / 0 Quantity	• Technology is destroyed in war, and production costs increase; the result is a decrease in the supply of good *X*.
3. Resource prices	Direct	Price / S_1 S_2 / 0 Quantity	• A decline in the price of computer chips increases the supply of computers.
		Price / S_2 S_1 / 0 Quantity	• An increase in the cost of farm equipment decreases the supply of soybeans.
4. Taxes and subsidies	Inverse and direct	Price / S_2 S_1 / 0 Quantity	• An increase in the per-pack tax on cigarettes reduces the supply of cigarettes.
		Price / S_1 S_2 / 0 Quantity	• Government payments to ethanol refineries based on the number of gallons produced increases the supply of ethanol.
5. Expectations	Inverse	Price / S_2 S_1 / 0 Quantity	• Oil companies anticipate a substantial rise in future oil prices, and this expectation causes these companies to decrease their current supply of oil.
		Price / S_1 S_2 / 0 Quantity	• Farmers expect the future price of wheat to decline, so they increase the present supply of wheat.
6. Prices of other goods and services	Inverse	Price / S_2 S_1 / 0 Quantity	• A rise in the price of brand-name drugs causes drug companies to decrease the supply of generic drugs.
		Price / S_1 S_2 / 0 Quantity	• A decline in the price of tomatoes causes farmers to increase the supply of cucumbers.

There is a global market in human organs in spite of attempts to prevent these transactions. For example, China banned organ sales in 2006, and India did the same in 1994.

The National Transplant Organ Act of 1984 made sale of organs illegal in the United States. Economist James R. Rinehart wrote the following on this subject:

> *If you were in charge of a kidney transplant program with more potential recipients than donors, how would you allocate the organs under your control? Life and death decisions cannot be avoided. Some individuals are not going to get kidneys regardless of how the organs are distributed because there simply are not enough to go around. Persons who run such programs are influenced in a variety of ways. It would be difficult not to favor friends, relatives, influential people, and those who are championed by the press. Dr. John la Puma,*

> *at the Center for Clinical Medical Ethics, University of Chicago, suggested that we use a lottery system for selecting transplant patients. He feels that the present rationing system is unfair.*

> *The selection process frequently takes the form of having the patient wait at home until a suitable donor is found. What this means is that, at any given point in time, many potential recipients are just waiting for an organ to be made available. In essence, the organs are rationed to those who are able to survive the wait. In many situations, patients are simply screened out because they are not considered to be suitable candidates for a transplant. For instance, patients with heart disease and overt psychosis often are excluded. Others with end-stage liver disorders are denied new organs on the grounds that the habits that produced the disease may remain to jeopardize recovery. . . .*

A MARKET SUPPLY AND DEMAND ANALYSIS

Market

Any arrangement in which buyers and sellers interact to determine the price and quantity of goods and services exchanged.

A drumroll please! Buyer and seller actors are on center stage to perform a balancing act in a **market**. A market is any arrangement in which buyers and sellers interact to determine the price and quantity of goods and services exchanged. Let's consider the retail market for sneakers. Exhibit 11 displays hypothetical market demand and supply data for this product. Notice in column 1 of the exhibit that price serves as a common variable for both supply and demand relationships. Columns 2 and 3 list the quantity demanded and the quantity supplied for pairs of sneakers per year.

The important question for market supply and demand analysis is: Which selling price and quantity will prevail in the market? Let's start by asking what will happen if retail stores supply 75,000 pairs of sneakers and charge $105 a pair. At this relatively high price for sneakers, consumers are willing and able to purchase only 25,000 pairs. As a result, 50,000 pairs of sneakers remain as unsold inventory on the shelves of sellers (column 4), and the market condition is a **surplus** (column 5). A surplus is a market condition existing at any price where the quantity supplied is greater than the quantity demanded.

Surplus

A market condition existing at any price where the quantity supplied is greater than the quantity demanded.

How will retailers react to a surplus? Competition forces sellers to bid down their selling price to attract more sales (column 6). If they cut the selling price to $90, there will still be a surplus of 40,000 pairs of sneakers, and pressure on sellers

Under the present arrangements, owners receive no monetary compensation; therefore, suppliers are willing to supply fewer organs than potential recipients want. Compensating a supplier monetarily would encourage more people to offer their organs for sale. It also would be an excellent incentive for us to take better care of our organs. After all, who would want an enlarged liver or a weak heart. . .?[1]

The following excerpt from a newspaper article illustrates the controversy:

Mickey Mantle's temporary deliverance from death, thanks to a liver transplant, illustrated how the organ-donations system is heavily weighted against poor potential recipients who cannot pass what University of Pennsylvania medical ethicist Arthur Caplan calls the "wallet biopsy.". . . Thus, affluent patients like Mickey Mantle may get evaluated and listed simultaneously in different regions to increase their odds of finding a donor. The New Yorker found his organ donor in Texas' Region 4. Such a system is not only highly unfair, but it leads to other kinds of abuses.[2]

Based on altruism, the organ donor distribution system continues to result in shortages. In 2009, the United Network for Organ Sharing (UNOS) reported that there were over 100,000 patients waiting on the list for organs. To address the shortage of organ donation, some European countries such as Spain, Belgium, and Austria have implemented an "opt-out" organ donation system. In the "opt-out" system, people are automatically considered to be organ donors unless they officially declare that they do not wish to be donors.

ANALYZE THE ISSUE

1. Draw supply and demand curves for the U.S. organ market and compare the U.S. market to the market in a country where selling organs is legal.
2. What are some arguments against using the price system to allocate organs?
3. Should foreigners have the right to buy U.S. organs and U.S. citizens have the right to buy foreign organs?

---

1. James R. Rinehart, "The Market Approach to Organ Shortages," *Journal of Health Care Marketing* 8, no. 1 (March 1988): 72–75.
2. Carl Senna, "The Wallet Biopsy," *Providence Journal*, June 13, 1995, p. B-7.

to cut their selling price will continue. If the price falls to $75, there will still be an unwanted surplus of 20,000 pairs of sneakers remaining as inventory, and pressure to charge a lower price will persist.

Exhibit 11	Demand, Supply, and Equilibrium for Sneakers (pairs per year)				
(1) Price per pair	(2) Quantity demanded	(3) Quantity supplied	(4) Difference (3) − (2)	(5) Market condition	(6) Pressure on price
$105	25,000	75,000	+50,000	Surplus	Downward
90	30,000	70,000	+40,000	Surplus	Downward
75	40,000	60,000	+20,000	Surplus	Downward
60	50,000	50,000	0	Equilibrium	Stationary
45	60,000	35,000	−25,000	Shortage	Upward
30	80,000	20,000	−60,000	Shortage	Upward
15	100,000	5,000	−95,000	Shortage	Upward

Now let's assume sellers slash the price of sneakers to $15 per pair. This price is very attractive to consumers, and the quantity demanded is 100,000 pairs of sneakers each year. However, sellers are willing and able to provide only 5,000 pairs at this price. The good news is that some consumers buy these 5,000 pairs of sneakers at $15. The bad news is that potential buyers are willing to purchase 95,000 more pairs at that price but cannot, because the shoes are not on the shelves for sale. This out-of-stock condition signals the existence of a **shortage**. A shortage is a market condition existing at any price where the quantity supplied is less than the quantity demanded.

In the case of a shortage, unsatisfied consumers compete to obtain the product by bidding to pay a higher price. Because sellers are seeking the higher profits that higher prices make possible, they gladly respond by setting a higher price of, say, $30 and increasing the quantity supplied to 20,000 pairs annually. At the price of $30, the shortage persists because the quantity demanded still exceeds the quantity supplied. Thus, a price of $30 will also be temporary because the unfulfilled quantity demanded provides an incentive for sellers to raise their selling price further and offer more sneakers for sale. Suppose the price of sneakers rises to $45 a pair. At this price, the shortage falls to 25,000 pairs, and the market still gives sellers the message to move upward along their market supply curve and sell for a higher price.

Shortage
A market condition existing at any price where the quantity supplied is less than the quantity demanded.

Equilibrium Price and Quantity

Assuming sellers are free to sell their products at any price, trial and error will make all possible price-quantity combinations unstable except at **equilibrium**. Equilibrium occurs at any price and quantity where the quantity demanded and the quantity supplied are equal. Economists also refer to *equilibrium* as *market clearing*.

In Exhibit 11, $60 is the *equilibrium* price, and 50,000 pairs of sneakers is the *equilibrium* quantity per year. Equilibrium means that the forces of supply and demand are "in balance" or "at risk" and there is no reason for price or quantity to change, ceteris paribus. In short, all prices and quantities except a unique equilibrium price and quantity are temporary. Once the price of sneakers is $60, this price will not change unless a nonprice factor changes demand or supply.

English economist Alfred Marshall (1842–1924) compared supply and demand to a pair of scissor blades. He wrote, "We might as reasonably dispute whether it is the upper or the under blade of a pair of scissors that cuts a piece of paper, as whether value is governed by utility [demand] or cost of production [supply]."[1] Joining market supply and market demand in Exhibit 12 allows us to clearly see the "two blades," that is, the demand curve, *D*, and the supply curve, *S*. We can measure the amount of any surplus or shortage by the horizontal distance between the demand and supply curves. At any price *above* equilibrium—say, $90—there is an *excess quantity supplied* (surplus) of 40,000 pairs of sneakers. For any price *below* equilibrium—$30, for example—the horizontal distance between the curves tells us there is an *excess quantity demanded* (shortage) of 60,000 pairs. When the price per pair is $60, the market supply curve and the market demand curve intersect at point *E*, and the quantity demanded equals the quantity supplied at 50,000 pairs per year.

Equilibrium
A market condition that occurs at any price and quantity where the quantity demanded and the quantity supplied are equal.

CONCLUSION *Graphically, the intersection of the supply curve and the demand curve is the market equilibrium price-quantity point. When all other nonprice factors are held constant, this is the only stable coordinate on the graph.*

1. Alfred Marshall, *Principles of Economics*, 8th ed. (New York: Macmillan, 1982), p. 348.

Exhibit 12   **The Supply and Demand for Sneakers**

The supply and demand curves represent a market for sneakers. The intersection of the demand curve, *D*, and the supply curve, *S*, at point *E* indicates the equilibrium price of $60 and the equilibrium quantity of 50,000 pairs bought and sold per year. At any price above $60, a surplus prevails, and pressure exists to push the price downward. At $90, for example, the excess quantity supplied of 40,000 pairs remains unsold. At any price below $60, a shortage provides pressure to push the price upward. At $30, for example, the excess quantity demanded of 60,000 pairs encourages consumers to bid up the price.

RATIONING FUNCTION OF THE PRICE SYSTEM

Our analysis leads to an important conclusion. The predictable or stable outcome in the sneakers example is that the price will eventually come to rest at $60 per pair. All other factors held constant, the price may be above or below $60, but the forces of surplus or shortage guarantee that any price other than the equilibrium price is temporary. This is the theory of how the price system operates, and it is the cornerstone of microeconomic analysis. The price system is a mechanism that uses the forces of supply and demand to create an equilibrium through rising and falling prices. Stated simply, price plays a *rationing* role. The price system is important because it is a mechanism for distributing scarce goods and services. At the equilibrium price of $60, only those consumers willing to pay $60 per pair get sneakers, and there are no shoes for buyers unwilling to pay that price.

Price system

A mechanism that uses the forces of supply and demand to create an equilibrium through rising and falling prices.

CHECKPOINT

Can the Price System Eliminate Scarcity?

You visit Cuba and observe that at "official" prices there is a constant shortage of consumer goods in government stores. People explain that in Cuba scarcity is caused by low prices combined with low production quotas set by the government. Many Cuban citizens say that the condition of scarcity would be eliminated if the government would allow markets to respond to supply and demand. Can the price system eliminate scarcity?

Key Concepts

Law of demand
Demand
Change in quantity
  demanded
Change in demand
Normal good

Inferior good
Substitute good
Complementary good
Law of supply
Supply
Change in quantity supplied

Change in supply
Market
Surplus
Shortage
Equilibrium
Price system

Summary

- The *law of demand* states there is an inverse relationship between the price and the quantity demanded, ceteris paribus. A market demand curve is the horizontal summation of individual demand curves.

- A *change in quantity demanded* is a movement along a stationary demand curve caused by a change in price. When any of the nonprice determinants of demand changes, the demand curve responds by shifting. An *increase in demand* (rightward shift) or a *decrease in demand* (leftward shift) is caused by a change in one of the nonprice determinants.

Change in Quantity Demanded

(a) Increase in quantity demanded

Change in Demand

(b) Increase in demand

- *Nonprice determinants of demand* are as follows:
  a. Number of buyers
  b. Tastes and preferences
  c. Income (normal and inferior goods)
  d. Expectations of future price and income changes
  e. Prices of related goods (substitutes and complements)

- The *law of supply* states there is a direct relationship between the price and the quantity supplied, ceteris paribus. The market supply curve is the horizontal summation of individual supply curves.

- A *change in quantity supplied* is a movement along a stationary supply curve caused by a change in price. When any of the nonprice determinants of supply changes, the supply curve responds by shifting. An *increase in supply* (rightward shift) or a *decrease in supply* (leftward shift) is caused by a change in one of the nonprice determinants.

Change in Quantity Supplied

(a) Increase in quantity supplied

Change in Supply

(b) Increase in supply

- *Nonprice determinants of supply* are as follows:
  a. Number of sellers
  b. Technology
  c. Resource prices
  d. Taxes and subsidies
  e. Expectations of future price changes
  f. Prices of other goods and services
- A *surplus* or *shortage* exists at any price where the quantity demanded and the quantity supplied are not equal. When the price of a good is higher than the equilibrium price, there is an excess quantity supplied, or a *surplus*. When the price is less than the equilibrium price, there is an excess quantity demanded, or a *shortage*.
- *Equilibrium* is the unique price and quantity established at the intersection of the supply and demand curves. Only at equilibrium does quantity demanded equal quantity supplied.

Equilibrium

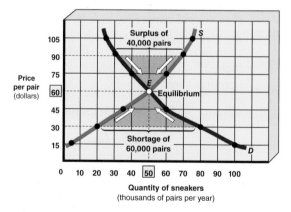

- The *price system* is the supply and demand mechanism that establishes equilibrium through the ability of prices to rise and fall.

Summary of Conclusion Statements

- Demand is a curve or schedule showing the various quantities of a product consumers are willing to purchase at possible prices during a specified period of time, ceteris paribus.
- Under the law of demand, any decrease in price along the vertical axis will cause an increase in quantity demanded, measured along the horizontal axis.
- Changes in nonprice determinants can produce only a shift in the demand curve and not a movement along the demand curve, which is caused by a change in price.
- Supply is a curve or schedule showing the various quantities of a product sellers are willing to produce and offer for sale at possible prices during a specified period of time, ceteris paribus.

- Only at a higher price will it be profitable for sellers to incur the higher opportunity cost associated with producing and supplying a larger quantity.
- Under the law of supply, any increase in price along the vertical axis will cause an increase in quantity supplied, measured along the horizontal axis.
- Changes in nonprice determinants can only produce a shift in the supply curve and not a movement along the supply curve.
- Graphically, the intersection of the supply curve and the demand curve is the market equilibrium price-quantity point. When all other nonprice factors are held constant, this is the only stable coordinate on the graph.

Study Questions and Problems

1. Some people will pay a higher price for brand-name goods. For example, some people buy Rolls Royces and Rolex watches to impress others. Does knowingly paying higher prices for certain items just to be a "snob" violate the law of demand?

2. Draw graphs to illustrate the difference between a decrease in the quantity demanded and a decrease in demand for Mickey Mantle baseball cards. Give a possible reason for change in each graph.

3. Suppose oil prices rise sharply for years as a result of a war in the Persian Gulf region. What happens and why to the demand for
   a. cars.
   b. home insulation.
   c. coal.
   d. tires.

4. Draw graphs to illustrate the difference between a decrease in quantity supplied and a decrease in supply for condominiums. Give a possible reason for change in each graph.

5. Use supply and demand analysis to explain why the quantity of word processing software exchanged increases from one year to the next.

6. Predict the direction of change for either supply or demand in the following situations:
   a. Several new companies enter the cell phone industry.
   b. Consumers suddenly decide SUVs are unfashionable.
   c. The U.S. Surgeon General issues a report stating that tomatoes prevent colds.
   d. Frost threatens to damage the coffee crop, and consumers expect the price to rise sharply in the future.
   e. The price of tea falls. What is the effect on the coffee market?
   f. The price of sugar rises. What is the effect on the coffee market?
   g. Tobacco lobbyists convince Congress to remove the tax paid by sellers on each carton of cigarettes sold.

h. A new type of robot is invented that will pick peaches.
i. A computer game company anticipates that the future price of its games will fall much lower than the current price.

7. Explain the effect of the following situations:
   a. Population growth surges rapidly.
   b. The prices of resources used in the production of good *X* increase.
   c. The government is paying a $1-per-unit subsidy for each unit of a good produced.
   d. The incomes of consumers of normal good *X* increase.
   e. The incomes of consumers of inferior good *Y* decrease.
   f. Farmers are deciding what crop to plant and learn that the price of corn has fallen relative to the price of cotton.

8. Explain why the market price may not be the same as the equilibrium price.

9. If a new breakthrough in manufacturing technology reduces the cost of producing DVD players by half, what will happen to the

   a. supply of DVD players?
   b. demand for DVD players?
   c. equilibrium price and quantity of DVD players?
   d. demand for DVDs?

10. The U.S. Postal Service is facing increased competition from firms providing overnight delivery of packages and letters. Additional competition has emerged because communications can be sent by email, fax machines, and text messaging. What will be the effect of this competition on the market demand for mail delivered by the post office?

11. There is a shortage of college basketball and football tickets for some games, and a surplus occurs for other games. Why do shortages and surpluses exist for different games?

12. Explain the statement "People respond to incentives and disincentives" in relation to the demand curve and supply curve for good *X*.

For Online Exercises, go to the Tucker Web site at www.cengage.com/economics/tucker.

CHECKPOINT ANSWERS

Can Gasoline Become an Exception to the Law of Demand?

As the price of gasoline began to rise, the expectation of still higher prices caused buyers to buy more now, and therefore, demand increased. As shown in Exhibit 13, suppose the price per gallon of gasoline was initially at P_1 and the quantity demanded was Q_1 on demand curve D_1 (point A). Then the war in the Middle East caused the demand curve to shift rightward to D_2. Along the new demand curve, D_2, consumers increased their quantity demanded to Q_2 at the higher price of P_2 per gallon of gasoline (point B).

The expectation of rising gasoline prices in the future caused "an increase in demand," rather than "an increase in quantity demanded" in response to a higher price. If you said there are no exceptions to the law of demand, **YOU ARE CORRECT.**

Exhibit 13

Can the Law of Supply Be Repealed for the Oil Market?

There is not a single quantity of oil—say, 3 million barrels—for sale in the world on a given day. The supply curve for oil is not vertical. As the law of supply states, higher oil prices will cause greater quantities of oil to be offered for sale. At lower prices, oil producers have less incentive to drill deeper for oil that is more expensive to discover.

The government cannot repeal the law of supply. Price controls discourage producers from oil exploration and production, which causes a reduction in the quantity supplied. If you said U.S. oil production decreased in the 1970s when the government put a lid on oil prices, **YOU ARE CORRECT.**

Can the Price System Eliminate Scarcity?

Recall from Chapter 1 that scarcity is the condition in which human wants are forever greater than the resources available to satisfy those wants. Using markets free from government interference will not solve the scarcity problem. Scarcity exists at any price for a good or service. This means scarcity occurs at any disequilibrium price at which a shortage or surplus exists, and scarcity remains at any equilibrium price at which no shortage or surplus exists.

Although the price system can eliminate shortages (or surpluses), if you said it cannot eliminate scarcity, **YOU ARE CORRECT.**

exceeds the $1.00 price at which firms are willing to supply this additional quantity of ground beef. Note that producer surplus is lower at point *B* compared to point *A*, and marginal producer surplus continues to fall at point *C* until it reaches zero at the equilibrium point *E*.

The total value of producer surplus is represented in Exhibit A-2(b). Start at point *X*, where none of the product will be supplied at the price of zero. Now consider the quantities of ground beef producers are willing to offer for sale at each possible price upward along the supply curve until the equilibrium price of $2.00 is reached at point *E*. The result is that the entire red triangular area between the horizontal line at the equilibrium price and the supply curve represents total producer surplus.

> **CONCLUSION** *Total producer surplus measured in dollars is represented by the total area under the equilibrium price and above the supply curve.*

Market Efficiency

In this section, the equilibrium price and quantity will be shown to achieve market efficiency because at any other market price the total net benefits to consumers and producers will be less. Stated differently, competitive markets are efficient when they maximize the sum of consumer and producer surplus. The analysis continues in Exhibit A-3(a), which combines parts (b) from the two previous exhibits. The green triangle represents consumer surplus earned in excess of the $2.00 equilibrium price consumers pay for ground beef. The red triangle represents producer surplus producers receive by selling ground beef at $2.00 per pound in excess of the minimum price at which they are willing to supply it. The total net benefit (total surplus) is therefore the entire triangular area consisting of both the green consumer surplus and red producer surplus triangles.

Now consider in Exhibit A-3(b) the consequences to market efficiency of producers devoting fewer resources to ground beef production and only 2 million pounds being bought and sold per year compared with 4 million pounds at the equilibrium price of $2.00. The result is a deadweight loss. Deadweight loss is the net loss of consumer and producer surplus from underproduction or overproduction of a product. In Exhibit A-3(b), the deadweight loss is equal to the gray triangle *ABE*, which represents the total surplus of green and red triangles in part (a) that is not obtained because the market is operating below equilibrium point *E*.

Exhibit A-3(c) illustrates that a deadweight loss of consumer and producer surplus can also result from overproduction. Now suppose more resources are devoted to production and 6 million pounds of ground beef are bought and sold at the equilibrium price. However, from the producers' side of the market, the equilibrium selling price is only $2.00 and below any possible selling price on the supply curve between points *E* and *C*. Therefore, firms have a net loss for each pound sold, represented by the area under the supply curve and bounded below by the horizontal equilibrium price line. Similarly, consumers pay the equilibrium price of $2.00, but this price exceeds any price consumers are willing to pay between points *E* and *D* on the demand curve. This means consumers experience a total net benefit loss for each pound purchased, represented by the rectangular area between

Deadweight loss

The net loss of consumer and producer surplus for underproduction or overproduction of a product.

Key Concepts

Consumer surplus   Producer surplus   Deadweight loss

Summary

- *Consumer surplus* measures the value between the price consumers are willing to pay for a product along the demand curve and the price they actually pay.
- *Producer surplus* measures the value between the actual selling price of a product and the price along the supply curve at which sellers are

willing to sell the product. Total surplus is the sum of consumer surplus and producer surplus.
- *Deadweight loss* is the result of a market that operates in disequilibrium. It is the net loss of both consumer and producer surplus resulting from underproduction or overproduction of a product.

Summary of Conclusion Statements

- Total consumer surplus measured in dollars is represented by the total area under the market demand curve and above the equilibrium price.
- Total producer surplus measured in dollars is represented by the total area under the equilibrium price and above the supply curve.

- The total dollar value of potential benefits not achieved is the deadweight loss resulting from too few or too many resources used in a given market.

Study Questions and Problems

1. Consider the market for used textbooks. Use Exhibit A-4 to calculate the total consumer surplus.

2. Consider the market for used textbooks. Use Exhibit A-5 to calculate the total producer surplus.

Exhibit A-4	Used Textbook Market	
Potential buyer	Willingness to pay	Market price
Brad	$60	$30
Juan	45	30
Sue	35	30
Jamie	25	30
Frank	10	30

Exhibit A-5	Used Textbook Market	
Potential buyer	Willingness to pay	Market price
Forest	$60	$30
Betty	45	30
Alan	35	30
Paul	25	30
Alice	10	30

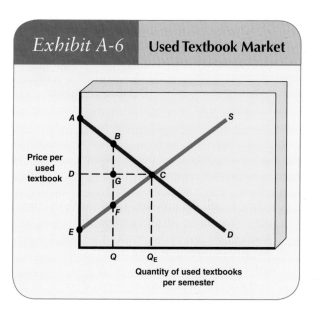

Exhibit A-6 | **Used Textbook Market**

Price per used textbook (vertical axis); Quantity of used textbooks per semester (horizontal axis)

3. Using Exhibits A-4 and A-5 above, calculate the total surplus. Now calculate the effect on consumer surplus, producer surplus, and total surplus of a fall in the equilibrium price of textbooks from $30 to $15 each. Explain the meaning of your calculations.

4. Using Exhibit A-6, and assuming the market is in equilibrium at Q_E, identify areas *ACD*, *DCE*, and *ACE*. Now explain the result of underproduction at *Q* in terms of areas *BCG*, *GCF*, and *BCF*.

Practice Quiz

For an explanation of the correct answers, visit the Tucker Web site at www.cengage.com/economics/tucker.

1. If Bill is willing to pay $10 for one good X, $8 for a second, and $6 for a third, and the market price is $5, then Bill's consumer surplus is
   a. $24.
   b. $18.
   c. $9.
   d. $6.

2. Suppose Gizmo Inc. is willing to sell one gizmo for $10, a second gizmo for $12, a third for $14, and a fourth for $20, and the market price is $20. What is Gizmo Inc.'s producer surplus?
   a. $56.
   b. $24.
   c. $20.
   d. $10.

3. In an efficient market, deadweight loss is
   a. maximum.
   b. minimum.
   c. constant.
   d. zero.

4. Deadweight loss results from
   a. equilibrium.
   b. underproduction.
   c. overproduction.
   d. none of the above are correct.
   e. Either (b) or (c).

5. Total surplus equals
   a. consumer surplus + producer surplus − deadweight loss.
   b. consumer surplus − producer surplus − deadweight loss.
   c. consumer surplus − producer surplus + deadweight loss.
   d. consumer surplus + producer surplus.

6. Which of the following statements is *correct*?
   a. Total surplus is the sum of consumer and producer surplus.
   b. Deadweight loss is the net loss of both consumer and producer surplus.
   c. Deadweight loss is a measure of market inefficiency.
   d. All of the above.

Practice Quiz Continued

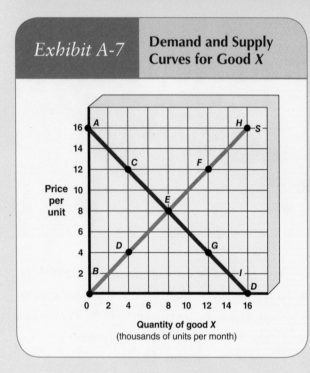

Exhibit A-7 — **Demand and Supply Curves for Good X**

7. In Exhibit A-7, suppose firms devote resources sufficient to produce 4,000 units of good *X* per month. The result is a deadweight loss of triangle:
a. *ABE.*
b. *CDE.*
c. *EGE.*
d. *EDE.*

8. Suppose in Exhibit A-7 that exchange in the market for good *X* yields triangle *ABE*. This means that which of the following conditions exists in the market?
a. Only consumer surplus
b. Only producer surplus
c. Deadweight loss
d. Maximum consumer plus producer surplus

9. As shown in Exhibit A-7, assume that the quantity of good *X* exchanged results in triangle *EIH*. This would be caused by _____ resources being used by producers to produce good *X*.
a. too many
b. too few
c. an optimal amount of
d. asymmetric

10. As shown in Exhibit A-7, assume that the quantity of good *X* exchanged results in triangle *CDE*. This would be caused by _____ resources being used by producers to produce good *X*.
a. too many
b. too few
c. an optimal amount of
d. asymmetric

4

Markets in Action

Once you understand how buyers and sellers respond to changes in equilibrium prices, you are progressing well in your quest to understand the economic way of thinking. This chapter begins by showing that changes in supply and demand influence the equilibrium price and quantity of goods and services exchanged around you every day. For example, you will study the impact of changes in supply and demand curves on the markets for Caribbean cruises, new homes, and AIDS vaccinations. Then you will see why the laws of supply and demand cannot be repealed. Using market supply and demand analysis, you will learn that government policies to control markets

have predictable consequences. For example, you will understand what happens when the government limits the maximum rent landlords can charge and who benefits and who loses from the federal minimum-wage law.

In this chapter, you will also study situations in which the market mechanism fails. Have you visited a city and lamented the smog that blankets the beautiful surroundings? Or have you ever wanted to swim or fish in a stream, but could not because of industrial waste? These are obvious cases in which market-system magic failed and the government must consider cures to reach socially desirable results.

100

In this chapter, you will learn to solve these economics puzzles:

- How can a spotted owl affect the price of homes?

- How do demand and supply affect the price of ethanol fuel?

- Why might government warehouses overflow with cheese and milk?

- What do ticket scalping and rent controls have in common?

Changes in Market Equilibrium

Using market supply and demand analysis is like putting on glasses if you are nearsighted. Suddenly, the fuzzy world around you comes into clear focus. In the following examples, you will open your eyes and see that economic theory has something important to say about so many things in the real world.

Changes in Demand

The Caribbean cruise market shown in Exhibit 1(a) assumes market supply, S, is constant and market demand increases from D_1 to D_2. Why has the demand curve shifted rightward in the figure? We will assume the popularity of cruises to these vacation islands has suddenly risen sharply due to extensive advertising that influenced tastes and preferences. Given supply curve S and demand curve D_1, the initial equilibrium price is $600 per cruise, and the initial equilibrium quantity is 8,000 cruises per year, shown as point E_1. After the impact of advertising, the new equilibrium point, E_2, becomes 12,000 cruises per year at a price of $900 each. Thus, the increase in demand causes both the equilibrium price and the equilibrium quantity to increase.

It is important to understand the force that caused the equilibrium to shift from E_1 to E_2. When demand initially increased from D_1 to D_2, there was a temporary shortage of 8,000 cruises at $600 per cruise. Firms in the cruise business responded to the excess demand by hiring more workers, offering more cruises to the Caribbean, and raising the price. The cruise lines therefore move upward along the supply curve (increasing quantity supplied, but not changing supply). During some period of trial and error, Caribbean cruise sellers increase their price and quantity supplied until a shortage no longer exists at point E_2. Therefore, the increase in demand causes both the equilibrium price and the equilibrium quantity to increase.

What will happen to the demand for gas-guzzling automobiles (for example, SUVs) if the price of gasoline triples? Because gasoline and automobiles are complements, a rise in the price of gasoline decreases the demand for gas guzzlers from D_1 to D_2 in Exhibit 1(b). At the initial equilibrium price of $30,000 per gas guzzler ($E_1$), the quantity supplied now exceeds the quantity demanded by 20,000 automobiles per month. This unwanted inventory forces automakers to reduce the price and quantity supplied. As a result of this movement downward on the supply curve, market equilibrium changes from E_1 to E_2. The equilibrium price falls from

Exhibit 1 — The Effects of Shifts in Demand on Market Equilibrium

In Part (a), demand for Caribbean cruises increases because of extensive advertising, and the demand curve shifts rightward from D_1 to D_2. This shift in demand causes a temporary shortage of 8,000 cruises per year at the initial equilibrium of E_1. This disequilibrium condition encourages firms in the cruise business to move upward along the supply curve to a new equilibrium at E_2.

Part (b) illustrates a decrease in the demand for gas-guzzling automobiles (SUVs) caused by a sharp rise in the price of gasoline (a complement). This leftward shift in demand from D_1 to D_2 results in a temporary surplus of 20,000 gas guzzlers per month at the initial equilibrium of E_1. This disequilibrium condition forces sellers of these cars to move downward along the supply curve to a new equilibrium at E_2.

(a) Increase in demand

(b) Decrease in demand

$30,000 to $20,000, and the equilibrium quantity falls from 30,000 to 20,000 gas guzzlers per month.

Changes in Supply

Now reverse the analysis by assuming demand remains constant and allow some nonprice determinant to shift the supply curve. In Exhibit 2(a), begin at point E_1 in a market for babysitting services at an equilibrium price of $9 per hour and

Exhibit 2   **The Effects of Shifts in Supply on Market Equilibrium**

In Part (a), begin at equilibrium E_1 in the market for babysitters, and assume an increase in the number of babysitters shifts the supply curve rightward from S_1 to S_2. This shift in supply causes a temporary surplus of 4,000 unemployed babysitters per month. This disequilibrium condition causes a movement downward along the demand curve to a new equilibrium at E_2. At E_2, the equilibrium price declines, and the equilibrium quantity rises.

In Part (b), steps to protect the environment cause the supply curve for lumber to shift leftward from S_1 to S_2. This shift in supply results in a temporary shortage of 4 billion board feet per year. Customer bidding for the available lumber raises the price. As a result, the market moves upward along the demand curve to a new equilibrium at E_2, and the quantity demanded falls.

4,000 babysitters hired per month. Then assume there is a population shift and the number of people available to babysit rises. This increase in the number of sellers shifts the market supply curve rightward from S_1 to S_2 and creates a temporary surplus of 4,000 babysitters at point E_1 who offer their services but are not hired. The unemployed babysitters respond by reducing the price and the number of babysitters available for hire, which is a movement downward along S_2. As the price falls, buyers move down along their demand curve and hire more babysitters per month. When the price falls to $6 per hour, the market is in equilibrium again at point E_2, instead of E_1, and consumers hire 6,000 babysitters per month.

Exhibit 3	Effect of Shifts in Demand or Supply on Market Equilibrium	
Change	**Effect on equilibrium price**	**Effect on equilibrium quantity**
Demand increases	Increases	Increases
Demand decreases	Decreases	Decreases
Supply increases	Decreases	Increases
Supply decreases	Increases	Decreases

Exhibit 2(b) illustrates the market for lumber. Suppose this market is at equilibrium at point E_1, where the going price is $400 per thousand board feet, and 8 billion board feet are bought and sold per year. Now suppose a new Endangered Species Act is passed, and the federal government sets aside huge forest resources to protect the spotted owl and other wildlife. This means the market supply curve shifts leftward from S_1 to S_2, and a temporary shortage of 4 billion board feet of lumber exists at point E_1. Suppliers respond by hiking their price from $400 to $600 per thousand board feet, and a new equilibrium is established at E_2, where the quantity is 6 billion board feet per year. This higher cost of lumber, in turn, raises the price of a new 1,800-square-foot home by $4,000, compared to the price of an identical home the previous year.

Exhibit 3 gives a concise summary of the impact of changes in demand or supply on market equilibrium.

CHECKPOINT

Why the Higher Price for Ethanol Fuel?

Suppose more consumers purchased ethanol fuel for their cars, and at the same time, producers switched over to ethanol fuel production. Within a year period, the price of ethanol fuel shot up $2.00 per gallon. During this year period, which increased more—demand, supply, or neither?

Trend of Equilibrium Prices over Time

Basic demand and supply analysis allows us to explain a trend in prices over a number of years. Exhibit 4 shows the effect of changes in nonprice determinants that increase both the demand and supply curves for good X between 2000, 2005, and 2010. A line connects the equilibrium prices for each year in order to summarize the trend of equilibrium price and quantity changes over this time period. In this case, the observed prices trace an upward-sloping trend line.

Exhibit 4 | **Trend of Equilibrium Prices over Time**

Nonprice determinants of demand and supply for good X have caused both the demand and supply curves to shift rightward between 2000 and 2010. As a result, the equilibrium price and quantity in this example rise along the upward-sloping trend line connecting each observed equilbrium price.

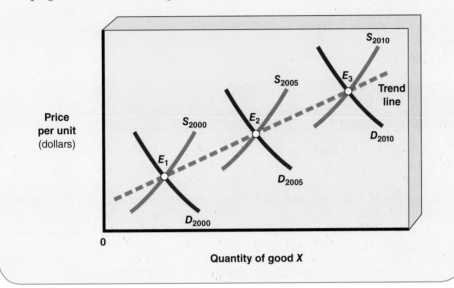

CAN THE LAWS OF SUPPLY AND DEMAND BE REPEALED?

The government intervenes in some markets with the objective of preventing prices from rising to the equilibrium price. In other markets, the government's goal is to intervene and maintain a price higher than the equilibrium price. Market supply and demand analysis is a valuable tool for understanding what happens when the government fixes prices. There are two types of price controls: *price ceilings* and *price floors.*

Price Ceilings

Case 1: Rent Controls What happens if the government prevents the price system from setting a market price "too high" by mandating a **price ceiling**? A price ceiling is a legally established maximum price a seller can charge. Rent controls are an example of the imposition of a price ceiling in the market for rental units. New York City, Washington, D.C., Los Angeles, San Francisco, and other communities in the United States have some form of rent control. Since World War I, rent controls have been widely used in Europe. The rationale for rent controls is to provide an "essential service" that would otherwise be unaffordable by many people at the equilibrium rental price. Let's see why most economists believe that rent controls are counterproductive.

Price ceiling

A legally established maximum price a seller can charge.

Exhibit 5 is a supply and demand diagram for the quantity of rental units demanded and supplied per month in a hypothetical city. We begin the analysis by assuming no rent controls exist and equilibrium is at point E, with a monthly rent of $1,200 per month and 6 million units occupied. Next, assume the city council imposes a rent control (ceiling price) that by law forbids any landlord from renting a unit for more than $800 per month. What does market supply and demand theory predict will happen? At the low rent ceiling of $800, the quantity demanded of rental units will be 8 million, but the quantity supplied will be only 4 million. Consequently, the price ceiling creates a persistent market shortage of 4 million rental units because suppliers cannot raise the rental price without being subjected to legal penalties.

Exhibit 5   **Rent Control Results in a Shortage of Rental Units**

If no rent controls exist, the equilibrium rent for a hypothetical apartment is $1,200 per month at point E. However, if the government imposes a rent ceiling of $800 per month, a shortage of 4 million rental units occurs. Because rent cannot rise by law, one outcome is that consumers must search for available units instead of paying a higher rent. Other outcomes include a black market, bribes, discrimination, and other illegal methods of dealing with a shortage of 4 million rental units per month.

Note that a rent ceiling at or above $1,200 per month would have no effect. If the ceiling is set at the equilibrium rent of $1,200, the quantity of rental units demanded and the quantity of rental units supplied are equal regardless of the rent control. If the rent ceiling is set above the equilibrium rent, the quantity of rental units supplied exceeds the quantity of rental units demanded, and this surplus will cause the market to adjust to the equilibrium rent of $1,200.

What is the impact of rent controls on consumers? First, as a substitute for paying higher prices, consumers must spend more time on waiting lists and searching for housing. This means consumers incur an *opportunity cost* added to the $800 rent set by the government. Second, an illegal market, or *black market*, can arise because of the excess quantity demanded. Because the price of rental units is artificially low, the profit motive encourages tenants to risk breaking the law by subletting their unit to the highest bidder over $800 per month.

From the seller's perspective, rent control encourages two undesirable effects. First, faced with a mandated low rent, landlords may cut maintenance expenses, and housing deterioration will reduce the stock of rental units in the long run. Second, landlords may use discriminatory practices to replace the price system. Once owners realize there is an excess quantity demanded for rentals at the controlled price, they may resort to preferences based on pet ownership or family size to determine how to allocate scarce rental space.

Case 2: Gasoline Price Ceiling The government placed ceilings on most nonfarm prices during World War II and, to a lesser extent, during the Korean War. In 1971, President Nixon "froze" virtually all wages, prices, and rents for 90 days in an attempt to control inflation. As a result of an oil embargo in late 1973, the government imposed a price ceiling of 55 cents per gallon of gasoline. To deal with the shortage, nonprice rationing schemes were introduced in 1974. Some states used a first-come, first-served system, while other states allowed consumers with even-numbered license plates to buy gas on even-numbered days and those with odd-numbered license plates to buy on odd-numbered days. Gas stations were required to close on Friday night and not open until Monday morning. Regardless of the scheme, long waiting lines for gasoline formed, just as the supply and demand model predicts. Finally, in the past, legally imposed price ceilings have been placed on such items as natural gas shipped in interstate commerce and on interest rates for loans. Maximum interest rate laws are called *usury laws*, and state governments have adopted these ceilings in the past to regulate home mortgages and other types of loans. Internationally, as discussed later in the chapter on economies in transition, price ceilings on food and rent were common in the former Soviet Union. Soviet sociologists estimated that members of a typical urban household spent a combined total of 40 hours per week standing in lines to obtain various goods and services.

Price Floors

The other side of the price-control coin is a **price floor** set by government because it fears that the price system might establish a price viewed as "too low." A price floor is a legally established minimum price a seller can be paid. We now turn to two examples of price floors. The first is the minimum wage, and the second is agricultural price supports.

Price floor

A legally established minimum price a seller can be paid.

Case 1: The Minimum-Wage Law In the first chapter, the second You're the Economist applied *normative* and *positive* reasoning to the issue of the minimum wage. Now you are prepared to apply market supply and demand analysis (positive reasoning) to this debate. Begin by noting that the demand for unskilled labor is the downward-sloping curve shown in Exhibit 6. The wage rate on the vertical axis is the price of unskilled labor, and the amount of unskilled labor employers are willing to hire varies inversely with the wage rate. At a higher wage rate, businesses will hire fewer workers. At a lower wage rate, they will employ a larger quantity of workers.

Exhibit 6	**A Minimum Wage Results in a Surplus of Labor**

When the federal or state government sets a wage-rate floor above the equilibrium wage, a surplus of unskilled labor develops. The supply curve is the number of workers offering their labor services per year at possible wage rates. The demand curve is the number of workers employers are willing and able to hire at various wage rates. Equilibrium wage, W_e, will result if the price system is allowed to operate without government interference. At the minimum wage of W_m, there is a surplus of unemployed workers, $Q_s - Q_d$.

CAUSATION CHAIN

Minimum wage ⇨ Unemployment (surplus)

On the supply side, the wage rate determines the number of unskilled workers willing and able to work per year. At higher wages, workers will give up leisure or schooling to work, and at lower wages, fewer workers will be available for hire. The upward-sloping curve in Exhibit 6 is the supply of labor.

Assuming the freedom to bargain, the price system will establish an equilibrium wage rate of W_e and an equilibrium quantity of labor employed of Q_e. But suppose the government enacts a minimum wage, W_m, which is a price floor above the equilibrium wage, W_e. The intent of the legislation is to "wave a carrot" in front of people who will not work at W_e and to make lower-paid workers better off with a higher wage rate. But consider the undesirable consequences. One result of an artificially high minimum wage is that the number of workers willing to offer their labor increases upward along the supply curve to Q_s, but there are fewer jobs because the number of workers firms are willing to hire decreases to Q_d on the demand curve. The predicted outcome is a labor surplus of unskilled workers, $Q_s - Q_d$, who are unemployed. Moreover, employers are encouraged to substitute machines and skilled labor for the unskilled labor previously employed at equilibrium wage W_e. The minimum wage is therefore considered counterproductive because employers lay off the lowest-skilled workers, who ironically are the type of workers minimum wage legislation intends to help. Also, loss of minimum wage jobs represents a loss of entry-level jobs to those who seek to enter the workforce.

Supporters of the minimum wage are quick to point out that those employed (Q_d) are better off. Even though the minimum wage causes a reduction in employment, some economists argue that a more equal or fairer income distribution is worth the loss of some jobs. Moreover, the shape of the labor demand curve may be much more vertical than shown in Exhibit 6. If this is the case, the unemployment effect of a rise in the minimum wage would be small. In addition, they claim opponents ignore the possibility that unskilled workers lack bargaining power versus employers.

Finally, a minimum wage set at or below the equilibrium wage rate is ineffective. If the minimum wage is set at the equilibrium wage rate of W_e, the quantity of labor demanded and the quantity of labor supplied are equal regardless of the minimum wage. If the minimum wage is set below the equilibrium wage, the forces of supply of and demand for labor establish the equilibrium wage regardless of the minimum wage rate.

Case 2: Agricultural Price Supports A farm price support is a well-known example of a price floor, which results in government purchases of surplus food and in higher food prices. Agricultural price support programs began in the 1930s as a means of raising the income of farmers, who were suffering from low market prices during the Great Depression. Under these programs, the government guarantees a minimum price above the equilibrium price and agrees to purchase any quantity the farmer is unable to sell at the legal price.

A few of the crops that have received price supports are corn, peanuts, soybeans, wheat, cotton, rice, tobacco, and dairy products. As predicted by market supply and demand analysis, a price support above the equilibrium price causes surpluses. Government warehouses therefore often overflow with such perishable products as butter, cheese, and dry milk purchased with taxpayers' money. The following You're the

You're The Economist Rigging the Market for Milk

Applicable Concept: price supports

Each year the milk industry faces an important question: What does the federal government plan to do about its dairy price support program, which has helped boost farmers' income since 1949? Under the price support program, the federal government agrees to buy storable milk products, such as cheese, butter, and dry milk. If the farmers cannot sell all their products to consumers at a price exceeding the price support level, the federal government will purchase any unsold grade A milk production. Although state-run dairy commissions set their own minimum prices for milk, state price supports closely follow federal levels and are kept within 3 percent of levels in bordering states to reduce interstate milk price competition.

Members of Congress who advocate changes in the price support programs worry that milk surpluses are costing taxpayers too much. Each year the federal government pays billions of dollars to dairy farmers for milk products held in storage at a huge cost. Moreover, the problem is getting worse because the federal government encourages dairy farmers to use ultramodern farming techniques to increase the production per cow. Another concern is that the biggest government price support checks go to the largest

farmers, while the number of dairy farmers continues to decline.

Congress is constantly seeking a solution to the milk price support problem. The following are some of the ideas that have been considered:

1. Freeze the current price support level. This prospect dismays farmers, who are subject to increasing expenses for feed, electricity, and other resources.
2. Eliminate the price supports gradually in yearly increments over the next five years. This would subject the milk market to the price fluctuations of the free market, and farmers would suffer some bad years from low milk prices.
3. Have the Department of Agriculture charge dairy farmers a tax of 50 cents for every 100 pounds of milk they produce. The farmers oppose this approach because it would discourage production and run small farmers out of business.
4. Have the federal government implement a "whole herd buyout" program. The problem is that using taxpayers' money to get farmers out of the dairy business pushes up milk product prices and rewards dairy farmers who own a lot of cows. Besides, what does the government do with the cows after it purchases them?

Finally, opponents of the dairy price support program argue that the market for milk is inherently a competitive industry and that consumers and taxpayers would be better served without government price supports for milk.

ANALYZE THE ISSUE

1. Draw a supply and demand graph to illustrate the problem described in the case study, and prescribe your own solution.
2. Which proposal do you think best serves the interests of small dairy farmers? Why?
3. Which proposal do you think best serves the interests of consumers? Why?
4. Which proposal do you think best serves the interest of a member of Congress? Why?

Economist on the dairy industry examines one of the best-known examples of U.S. government interference with agricultural market prices.

> **CONCLUSION** *A price ceiling or price floor prevents market adjustment in which competition among buyers and sellers bids the price upward or downward to the equilibrium price.*

CHECKPOINT

Is There Price-Fixing at the Ticket Window?

At sold-out concerts, sports contests, and other events, some ticket holders try to resell their tickets for more than they paid—a practice known as scalping. For scalping to occur, must the original ticket price be legally set by a price floor, at the equilibrium price, or by a price ceiling?

Market Failure

In this chapter and the previous chapter, you have gained an understanding of how markets operate. Through the price system, society coordinates economic activity, but markets are not always "Prince Charmings" that achieve *market efficiency* without a misallocation of resources. It is now time to step back with a critical eye and consider markets that become "ugly frogs" by allocating resources inefficiently. **Market failure** occurs when market equilibrium results in too few or too many resources being used in the production of a good or service. In this section, you will study four important cases of market failure: lack of competition, externalities, public goods, and income inequality. Market failure is discussed in more detail in the chapter on environmental economics, except for the macroeconomics version of the text.

Market failure

A situation in which market equilibrium results in too few or too many resources used in the production of a good or service. This inefficiency may justify government intervention.

Adam Smith (1723–1790). The father of modern economics, who wrote *The Wealth of Nations*, published in 1776.

Lack of Competition

There must be competition among both producers and consumers for markets to function properly. But what happens if the producers fail to compete? In *The Wealth of Nations*, Adam Smith stated, "People of the same trade seldom meet together, even for merriment and diversion, but the conversation ends in a conspiracy against the public, or in some diversion to raise prices."[1] This famous quotation clearly underscores the fact that in the real world businesses seek ways to replace consumer sovereignty with "big business sovereignty." What happens when a few firms rig the market and they become the market's boss? By restricting supply through artificial limits on the output of a good, firms can enjoy higher prices and profits. As a result, firms may waste resources and retard technology and innovation.

---

1. Adam Smith, *An Inquiry into the Nature and Causes of the Wealth of Nations* (1776; reprint, New York: Random House, The Modern Library, 1937), p. 128.

Exhibit 7 illustrates how IBM, Apple, Gateway, Dell, and other suppliers of personal computers (PCs) could benefit from rigging the market. Without collusive action, the competitive price for PCs is $1,500, the quantity of 200,000 per month is sold, and efficient equilibrium prevails at point E_1. It is in the best interest of sellers, however, to take steps that would make PCs artificially scarce and raise the price. Graphically, the sellers wish to shift the competitive supply curve, S_1, leftward to the restricted supply curve, S_2. This could happen for a number of reasons, including an agreement among sellers to restrict supply (collusion) and government action. For example, the sellers could lobby the government to pass a law allowing an association of PC suppliers to set production quotas. The proponents might argue this action raises prices and, in turn, profits. Higher profits enable the industry to invest in new capital and become more competitive in world markets.

Exhibit 7   Rigging the PC Market

At efficient equilibrium point E_1, sellers compete. As a result, the price charged per PC is $1,500, and the quantity of PCs exchanged is 200,000. Suppose suppliers use collusion, government intervention, or other means to restrict the supply of this product. The decrease in supply from S_1 to S_2 establishes inefficient market equilibrium E_2. At E_2, firms charge the higher price of $2,000, and the equilibrium quantity of PCs falls to 150,000. Thus, the outcome of restricted supply is that the market fails because firms use too few resources to produce PCs at an artificially higher price.

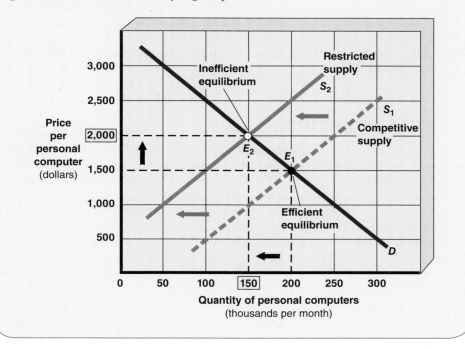

Opponents of artificially restricted supply argue that, although the producers benefit, the lack of competition means the economy loses. The result of restricting supply is that the efficient equilibrium point, E_1, changes to the inefficient equilibrium point, E_2. At point E_2, the higher price of $2,000 is charged, and the lower equilibrium quantity means that firms devote too few resources to producing PCs and charge an artificially high price. Note that under U.S. antitrust laws, the Justice Department is responsible for prosecuting firms that collude to restrict supply to force higher prices.

Externalities

Even when markets are competitive, some markets may still fail because they suffer from the presence of side effects economists call **externalities**. An externality is a cost or benefit imposed on people other than the consumers and producers of a good or service. Externalities are also called *spillover effects* or *neighborhood effects*. People other than consumers and producers who are affected by these side effects of market exchanges are called *third parties*. Externalities may be either negative or positive; that is, they may be detrimental or beneficial. Suppose you are trying to study and your roommate is listening to Steel Porcupines at full blast on the stereo. The action of your roommate is imposing an unwanted *external cost* or *negative externality* on you and other third parties who are trying to study or sleep. Externalities can also result in an *external benefit* or *positive externality* to nonparticipating parties. When a community proudly displays its neat lawns, gorgeous flowers, and freshly painted homes, visitors are third parties who did none of the work, but enjoy the benefit of the pleasant scenery.

Externality

A cost or benefit imposed on people other than the consumers and producers of a good or service.

A Graphical Analysis of Pollution   Exhibit 8 provides a graphical analysis of two markets that fail to include externalities in their market prices unless the government takes corrective action. Exhibit 8(a) shows a market for steel in which steel firms burn high-sulfur coal and pollute the environment. Demand curve D and supply curve S_1 establish the inefficient equilibrium, E_1, in the steel market. Not included in S_1 are the *external costs* to the public because the steel firms are not paying for the damage from smoke emissions. If steel firms discharge smoke and ash into the atmosphere, foul air reduces property values, raises health care costs, and, in general, erodes the quality of life. Because supply curve S_1 does not include these external costs, they are also not included in the price of steel, P_1. In short, the absence of the cost of pollution in the price of steel means the firms produce more steel and pollution than is socially desirable.

S_2 is the supply curve that would exist if the external costs of respiratory illnesses, dirty homes, and other undesirable side effects were included. Once S_2 includes the charges for environmental damage, the equilibrium price rises to P_2, and the equilibrium quantity becomes Q_2. At the efficient equilibrium point, E_2, the steel market achieves allocative efficiency. At E_2, steel firms are paying the full cost and using fewer resources to produce the lower quantity of steel at Q_2.

> **CONCLUSION** *When the supply curve fails to include external costs, the equilibrium price is artificially low, and the equilibrium quantity is artificially high.*

Exhibit 8   Externalities in the Steel and AIDS Vaccination Markets

In part (a), resources are overallocated at inefficient market equilibrium E_1 because steel firms do not include the cost per ton of pollution in the cost per ton of steel. Supply curve S_2 includes the external costs of pollution. If firms are required to purchase equipment to remove the pollution or to pay a tax on pollution, the economy achieves the efficient equilibrium of E_2.

Part (b) demonstrates that external benefits cause an underallocation of resources. The efficient output at equilibrium point E_2 is obtained if people are required to purchase AIDS shots or if the government pays a subsidy equal to the external benefit per shot.

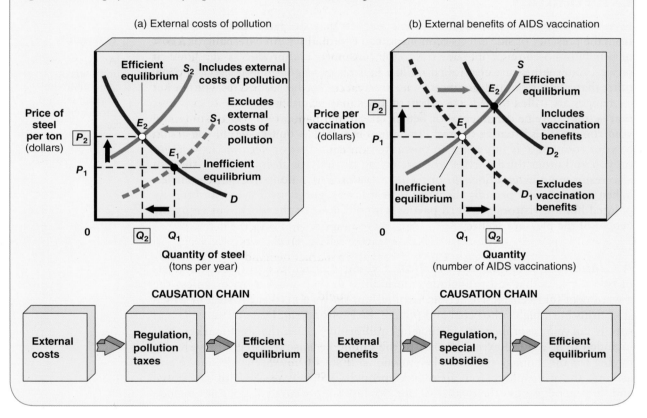

(a) External costs of pollution

(b) External benefits of AIDS vaccination

CAUSATION CHAIN

External costs → Regulation, pollution taxes → Efficient equilibrium

CAUSATION CHAIN

External benefits → Regulation, special subsidies → Efficient equilibrium

Regulation and pollution taxes are two ways society can correct the market failure of pollution:

1. **Regulation.** Legislation can set standards that force firms to clean up their emissions as a condition of remaining in business. This means firms must buy, install, and maintain pollution-control equipment. When the extra cost of the pollution equipment is added to the production cost per ton of steel, the initial supply curve, S_1, shifts leftward to supply curve S_2. This means regulation has forced the market equilibrium to change from E_1 to E_2. At point E_2, the firms use fewer resources to produce Q_2 compared to Q_1 output of steel per year, and, therefore, the firms operate efficiently.

2. **Pollution Taxes.** Another approach would be for the government to levy a tax per ton of steel equal to the external cost imposed on society when the firm

emits pollution into the air. This action inhibits production by imposing an additional production cost per ton of steel from the pollution taxes and shifts the supply curve leftward from S_1 to S_2. Again, the objective is to change the equilibrium from E_1 to E_2 and eliminate the overuse of resources devoted to steel production and its pollution. The tax revenue could be used to compensate those damaged by the pollution.

A Graphical Analysis of AIDS Vaccinations   As explained above, the supply curve can understate the *external costs* of a product. Now you will see that the demand curve can understate the *external benefits* of a product. Suppose a vaccination is discovered that prevents AIDS. Exhibit 8(b) illustrates the market for immunization against AIDS. Demand curve D_1 reflects the price consumers would pay for shots to receive the benefit of a reduced probability of infection by AIDS. Supply curve S shows the quantities of shots suppliers offer for sale at different prices. At equilibrium point E_1, the market fails to achieve an efficient allocation of resources. The reason is that when buyers are vaccinated, other people who do not purchase AIDS shots (called *free riders*) also benefit because this disease is less likely to spread. Once demand curve D_2 includes external benefits to nonconsumers of AIDS vaccinations (increase in the number of buyers), the efficient equilibrium of E_2 is established. At Q_2, sellers devote greater resources to AIDS vaccinations, and the underallocation of resources is eliminated.

How can society prevent the market failure of AIDS vaccinations? Two approaches follow:

1. **Regulation.** The government can boost consumption and shift the demand curve rightward by requiring all citizens to purchase AIDS shots each year. This approach to capturing external benefits in market demand explains why all school-age children must have polio and other shots before entering school.

2. **Special Subsidies.** Another possible solution would be for the government to increase consumer income by paying consumers for each AIDS vaccination. This would mean the government pays each citizen a dollar payment equal to the amount of external benefits per shot purchased. Because the subsidy amount is payable at any price along the demand curve, the demand curve shifts rightward until the efficient equilibrium price and quantity are reached.

CONCLUSION *When externalities are present, market failure gives incorrect price and quantity signals, and as a result, resources are misallocated. External costs cause the market to overallocate resources, and external benefits cause the market to underallocate resources.*

Public Goods

Private goods are produced through the price system. In contrast, national defense is an example of a **public good** provided by the government because of its special characteristics. A public good is a good or service that, once produced, has two properties: (1) users collectively consume benefits, and (2) there is no way to bar people who do not pay (free riders) from consuming the good or service.

Public good

A good or service with two properties: (1) users collectively consume benefits, and (2) there is no way to bar people who do not pay (free riders) from consuming the good or service.

You're The Economist   Can Vouchers Fix Our Schools?

Applicable Concepts: public goods versus private goods

In their book, *Free to Choose*, published in 1980, economists Milton Friedman and his wife Rose Friedman proposed a voucher plan for schools.[1] The objective of their proposal was to retain government financing, but give parents greater freedom to choose the schools their children attend. The Friedmans pointed out that under the current system parents face a strong incentive not to remove their children from the public schools. This is because, if parents decide to withdraw their children from a public school and send them to a private school, they must pay private tuition in addition to the taxes that finance children enrolled in the public schools.

To remove the financial penalty that limits the freedom of parents to choose schools, the government could give parents a voucher, which is a piece of paper redeemable for a sum of money payable to any approved school. For example, if the government spends $8,000 per year to educate a student, then the voucher could be for this amount. The voucher plan embodies exactly the same principle as the GI Bill that provides educational benefits to military veterans. The veteran receives a voucher good only for educational expenses and is completely free to choose the school where it is used, provided the school satisfies certain standards.

The Friedmans argue that parents could, and should, be permitted to use the vouchers not only at private schools but also at other public schools—and not only at schools in their own district, city, or state, but at any school that is willing to accept their child. That would give every parent a greater opportunity to choose and at the same time would require public schools to charge tuition. The tuition would be competitive because public schools must compete for students both with other public schools and with private schools. It is important to note that this plan relieves no one of the burden of taxation to pay for schooling. It simply gives parents a wider choice as to which competing schools their children attend, given the amount of funding per student that the community has obligated itself to provide. The plan also does not affect the present standards imposed on private schools to ensure that students attending them satisfy the compulsory attendance laws.

1. Milton Friedman and Rose Friedman, *Free to Choose: A Personal Statement* (New York: Harcourt Brace Jovanovich, 1980), pp. 160–161.

To see why the marketplace fails, imagine that Patriot Missiles Inc. offers to sell missile defense systems to people who want private protection against attacks from incoming missiles. First, once the system is operational, everyone in the defense area benefits from increased safety. Second, the *nonexclusive* nature of a public good means it is impossible or very costly for any owner of a Patriot missile defense system to prevent nonowners, the free riders, from reaping the benefits of its protection.

Given the two properties of a public good, why would any private individual purchase a Patriot missile defense system? Why not take a free ride and wait until someone else buys a missile system? Thus, each person wants a Patriot system, but does not want to bear the cost of the system when everyone shares in the benefits. As a result, the market fails to provide Patriot missile defense systems, and everyone hopes no missile attacks occur before someone finally decides to purchase one. Government can solve this public goods problem by producing Patriot missiles and taxing the public to pay. Unlike a private citizen, the government can use force to collect payments and prevent the free-rider problem. Other examples of

In 1990, Milwaukee began an experiment with school vouchers. The program gave selected children from low-income families taxpayer-funded vouchers to allow them to attend private schools. There has been a continuing heated debate among parents, politicians, and educators over the results. In 1998, Wisconsin's highest court ruled in a 4–2 decision that Milwaukee could use public money for vouchers for students who attend religious schools without violating the constitutional separation of church and state.

A 2002 article in *USA Today* reported:

Opponents of vouchers have repeatedly argued that they would damage the public schools, draining them of resources and better students. A recent study of the Milwaukee voucher program by Caroline Hoxby, a Harvard economist, suggests just the opposite. She wrote that "*schools that faced the most potential competition from vouchers had the best productivity response.*" *No doubt, the nation's experience with vouchers is limited, yet the evidence cited in a recent Brookings Institution report shows that they do seem to benefit African-American youngsters.*[2]

The controversy continues: For example, in a 2002 landmark case, the U.S. Supreme Court ruled that government vouchers for private or parochial schools are constitutional. In 2003, however, a Denver judge struck down Colorado's new school voucher law, ruling that it violated the state's constitution by stripping local school boards of their control over education. And in 2006, the Florida Supreme Court ruled that Florida's voucher program for students in the lowest-rated public schools was unconstitutional. Finally, in the 2008–2009 school year, over 20 percent of Milwaukee students received publicly funded vouchers to attend private schools.[3]

Analyze the Issue

1. In recent years, school choice has been a hotly debated issue. Explain whether education is a public good. If education is not a public good, why should the government provide it?
2. The Friedmans present a very one-sided view of the benefits of a voucher system. Other economists disagree about the potential effectiveness of vouchers. Do you support a voucher system for education? Explain your reasoning.

---

2. Robert J. Bresler, "Vouchers and the Constitution," *USA Today,* May 2002, p. 15.
3. Data available at http://dpi.state.wi.us/sms/geninfo.html.

public goods include global agreements to reduce emissions, the judicial system, the national emergency warning system, air traffic control, prisons, and traffic lights.

Conclusion *If public goods are available only in the marketplace, people wait for someone else to pay, and the result is an underproduction or zero production of public goods.*

Income Inequality

In the cases of insufficient competition, externalities, and public goods, the marketplace allocates too few or too many resources to producing output. The market may also result in a very unequal distribution of income, thereby raising a very

controversial issue. Under the impersonal price system, movie stars earn huge incomes for acting in movies, while homeless people roam the streets penniless. The controversy is therefore over how equal the distribution of income should be and how much government intervention is required to achieve this goal. Some people wish to remove most inequality of income. Others argue for the government to provide a "safety net" minimum income level for all citizens. Still others see high income as an incentive and a "fair" reward for productive resources.

To create a more equal distribution of income, the government uses various programs to transfer money from people with high incomes to those with low incomes. Unemployment compensation and food stamps are examples of such programs. The federal minimum wage is another example of a government attempt to raise the earnings of low-income workers.

CHECKPOINT

Should There Be a War on Drugs?

The U.S. government fights the use of drugs, such as marijuana and cocaine, in a variety of ways, including spraying crops with poisonous chemicals; imposing jail sentences for dealers and users; and confiscating drug-transporting cars, boats, and planes. Which market failure motivates the government to interfere with the market for drugs: lack of competition, externalities, public goods, or income inequality?

Key Concepts

Price ceiling
Price floor

Market failure
Externality

Public good

Summary

- *Price ceilings* and *price floors* are maximum and minimum prices enacted by law, rather than allowing the forces of supply and demand to determine prices. A *price ceiling* is a maximum price mandated by government, and a *price floor,* or *support price* for agricultural products, is a minimum legal price. If a price ceiling is set below the equilibrium price, a shortage will persist. If a price floor is set above the equilibrium price, a surplus will persist.

Price Ceiling

Price Floor

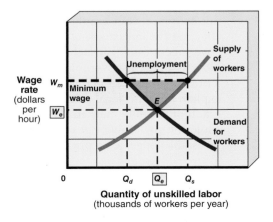

- *Market failure* occurs when the market mechanism does not achieve an efficient allocation of resources. Sources of market failure include lack of competition, externalities, public goods, and income inequality. Although controversial, government intervention is a possible way to correct market failure.

- An *externality* is a cost or benefit of a good imposed on people who are not buyers or sellers of that good. Pollution is an example of an *external cost*, which means too many resources are used to produce the product responsible for the pollution. Two basic approaches to solve this market failure are regulation and pollution taxes. Vaccinations provide *external benefits*, which means sellers devote too few resources to produce this product. Two basic solutions to this type of market failure are laws to require consumption of shots and special subsidies.

Externalities

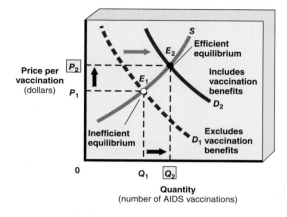

(b) External benefits of AIDS vaccination

- **Public goods** are goods that are consumed by all people in a society regardless of whether they pay or not. National defense, air traffic control, and other public goods can benefit many individuals simultaneously and are provided by the government.

Summary of Conclusion Statements

- A price ceiling or price floor prevents market adjustment in which competition among buyers and sellers bids the price upward or downward to the equilibrium price.
- When the supply curve fails to include external costs, the equilibrium price is artificially low, and the equilibrium quantity is artificially high.
- When externalities are present, market failure gives incorrect price and quantity signals,

and as a result, resources are misallocated. External costs cause the market to overallocate resources, and external benefits cause the market to underallocate resources.

- If public goods are available only in the marketplace, people wait for someone else to pay, and the result is an underproduction or zero production of public goods.

Study Questions and Problems

1. Market researchers have studied the market for milk, and their estimates for the supply of and the demand for milk per month are as follows:

Price per gallon	Quantity demanded (millions of gallons)	Quantity supplied (millions of gallons)
$10.00	100	500
8.00	200	400
6.00	300	300
4.00	400	200
2.00	500	100

   a. Using the above data, graph the demand for and the supply of milk. Identify the equilibrium point as *E*, and use dotted lines to connect *E* to the equilibrium price

on the price axis and the equilibrium quantity on the quantity axis.

   b. Suppose the government enacts a milk price support of $8 per gallon. Indicate this action on your graph, and explain the effect on the milk market. Why would the government establish such a price support?

   c. Now assume the government decides to set a price ceiling of $4 per gallon. Show and explain how this legal price affects your graph of the milk market. What objective could the government be trying to achieve by establishing such a price ceiling?

2. Use a graph to show the impact on the price of Japanese cars sold in the United States if

the United States imposes import quotas on Japanese cars. Now draw another graph to show how the change in the price of Japanese cars affects the price of American-made cars in the United States. Explain the market outcome in each graph and the link between the two graphs.

3. Using market supply and demand analysis, explain why labor union leaders are strong advocates of raising the minimum wage above the equilibrium wage.

4. What are the advantages and disadvantages of the price system?

5. Suppose a market is in equilibrium and both demand and supply curves increase. What happens to the equilibrium price if demand increases more than supply?

6. Consider this statement: "Government involvement in markets is inherently inefficient." Do you agree or disagree? Explain.

7. Suppose coal-burning firms are emitting excessive pollution into the air. Suggest two ways the government can deal with this market failure.

8. Explain the impact of external costs and external benefits on resource allocation.

9. Why are public goods not produced in sufficient quantities by private markets?

10. Which of the following are public goods?
    a. Air bags
    b. Pencils
    c. Cycle helmets
    d. City streetlights
    e. Contact lenses

For Online Exercises, go to the Tucker Web site at www.cengage.com/economics/tucker.

CHECKPOINT ANSWERS

Why the Higher Price for Ethanol Fuel?

As shown in Exhibit 9, an increase in demand leads to higher ethanol prices, while an increase in supply leads to lower prices. Because the overall direction of price in the ethanol market was up, the demand increase must have been larger than the supply increase. If you said demand increased by more than supply because consumers reacted more quickly than producers, **YOU ARE CORRECT.**

Is There Price-Fixing at the Ticket Window?

Scalpers are evidence of a shortage whereby buyers are unable to find tickets at the official price. As shown in Exhibit 10, scalpers (often illegally) profit from the shortage by selling tickets above the official price. Shortages result when prices are restricted below equilibrium, as is the case when there is a price ceiling. If you said scalping occurs when there is a price ceiling because scalpers charge more than the official maximum price, **YOU ARE CORRECT.**

Exhibit 9

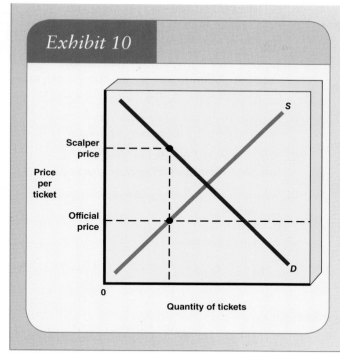

Exhibit 10

Should There Be a War on Drugs?

Drug use often affects not only the person using the drugs, but other members of society as well. For example, higher crime rates are largely attributable to increased drug usage, and AIDS is often spread when users inject drugs with nonsterile needles. When one person's actions affect others not involved in the decision to buy or sell, the market fails to operate efficiently. If you said the market failure motivating government intervention in the drug market is externalities because drug users impose costs on nonusers, **YOU ARE CORRECT.**

Practice Quiz

For an explanation of the correct answers, visit the Tucker Web site at www.cengage.com/economics/tucker.

1. Suppose prices for new homes have risen, yet the number of homes sold has also risen. We can conclude that
   a. the demand for new homes has risen.
   b. the law of demand has been violated.
   c. new firms have entered the construction industry.
   d. construction firms must be facing higher costs.

2. Which of the following statements is *true*?
   a. An increase in demand, with no change in supply, will increase the equilibrium price and quantity.
   b. An increase in supply, with no change in demand, will decrease the equilibrium price and the equilibrium quantity.

   c. A decrease in supply, with no change in demand, will decrease the equilibrium price and increase the equilibrium quantity.
   d. All of the above are true.

3. Consider the market for chicken. An increase in the price of beef will
   a. decrease the demand for chicken, resulting in a lower price and a smaller amount of chicken purchased in the market.
   b. decrease the supply of chicken, resulting in a higher price and a smaller amount of chicken purchased in the market.
   c. increase the demand for chicken, resulting in a higher price and a greater amount of chicken purchased in the market.
   d. increase the supply of chicken, resulting in a lower price and a greater amount of chicken purchased in the market.

Practice Quiz Continued

4. An increase in consumers' incomes increases the demand for oranges. As a result of the adjustment to a new equilibrium, there is a (an)
   a. leftward shift of the supply curve.
   b. downward movement along the supply curve.
   c. rightward shift of the supply curve.
   d. upward movement along the supply curve.

5. An increase in the wage paid to grape pickers will cause the
   a. demand curve for grapes to shift to the right, resulting in higher prices for grapes.
   b. demand curve for grapes to shift to the left, resulting in lower prices for grapes.
   c. supply curve for grapes to shift to the left, resulting in lower prices for grapes.
   d. supply curve for grapes to shift to the left, resulting in higher prices for grapes.

6. If the federal government wants to raise the price of cheese, it will
   a. take cheese from government storage and sell it.
   b. encourage farmers to research ways to produce more cheese.
   c. subsidize purchases of farm equipment.
   d. encourage farmers to produce less cheese.

7. Which of the following is *least* likely to result from rent controls set below the equilibrium price for rental housing?
   a. Shortages and black markets will result.
   b. The existing rental housing will deteriorate.
   c. The supply of rental housing will increase rapidly.
   d. People will demand more apartments than are available.

8. Suppose the equilibrium price set by supply and demand is lower than the price ceiling set by the government. The eventual result will be
   a. a shortage.
   b. that quantity demanded is equal to quantity supplied.
   c. a surplus.
   d. a black market.

9. A good that provides external benefits to society has
   a. too few resources devoted to its production.
   b. too many resources devoted to its production.

   c. the optimal resources devoted to its production.
   d. not provided profits to producers of the good.

10. Pollution from cars is an example of
    a. a harmful opportunity cost.
    b. a negative externality.
    c. a production dislocation.
    d. none of the above.

11. Which of the following is the *best* example of a public good?
    a. Pencils
    b. Education
    c. Defense
    d. Trucks

12. A public good may be defined as any good or service that
    a. allows users to collectively consume benefits.
    b. must be distributed to all citizens in equal shares.
    c. is never produced by government.
    d. is described by answers (a) and (c) above.

13. In Exhibit 11, which of the following might cause a shift from S_1 to S_2?
    a. A decrease in input prices
    b. An improvement in technology
    c. An increase in input prices
    d. An increase in consumer income

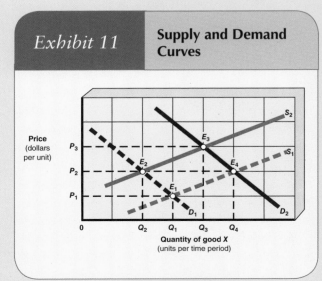

Exhibit 11 — **Supply and Demand Curves**

Practice Quiz Continued

14. In Exhibit 11, an increase in supply would cause a move from which equilibrium point to another, other things being equal?
  a. E_1 to E_2
  b. E_1 to E_3
  c. E_4 to E_1
  d. E_3 to E_4

15. Beginning from an equilibrium at point E_1 in Exhibit 11, an increase in demand for good X, other things being equal, would move the equilibrium point to
  a. E_1 (no change).
  b. E_2.
  c. E_3.
  d. E_4.

Applying Supply and Demand Analysis to Health Care

4

One out of every seven dollars spent in the United States is spent for health care services. This is a greater percentage than in any other industrialized country. And in 2010, historic health care legislation was enacted to dramatically reform the U.S. system.[1] The topic of health care arouses deep emotions and generates intense media coverage. How can we understand many of the important health care issues? One approach is to listen to the normative statements made by politicians and other concerned citizens. Another approach is to use supply and demand theory to analyze the issue. Here again the objective is to bring textbook theory to life and use it to provide you with a deeper understanding of third-party health service markets.

THE IMPACT OF HEALTH INSURANCE

There is a downward-sloping demand curve for health care services just as there is for other goods and services. Following the same law of demand that applies to cars, clothing, entertainment, and other goods and services, movements along the demand curve for health care occur because consumers respond to changes in the price of health care. As shown in Exhibit A-1, we assume that health care, including doctor visits, medicine, hospital bills, and other medical services, can be measured in units of health care. Without health insurance, consumers buy Q_1 units of health care services per year at a price of P_1 per unit. Assuming supply curve S represents the quantity supplied, the market is in equilibrium at point A. At this point, the total cost of health care can be computed by the price of health care (P_1) times the quantity demanded (Q_1) or represented geometrically by the rectangle $0P_1 AQ_1$.

Analysis of the demand curve for health care is complicated by the way health care is financed. About 80 percent of all health care is paid for by *third parties*, including private insurance companies and government programs, such as Medicare and Medicaid. The price of health care services therefore depends on the *copayment rate*, which is the percentage of the cost of services consumers pay out-of-pocket. To understand the impact, it is more realistic to assume consumers are insured and extend the analysis represented in Exhibit A-1. Because patients pay only 20 percent of the bill, the quantity of health care demanded in the figure increases to Q_2 at

---

1. U.S. Census Bureau, *Statistical Abstract of the United States, 2010*, http://www.census.gov/compendia/statab/, Table 1301.

Exhibit A-1   The Impact of Insurance on the Health Care Market

Without health insurance, the market is in equilibrium at point A, with a price of P_1 and a quantity demanded of Q_1. Total spending is $0P_1AQ_1$. With copayment health insurance, consumers pay the lower price of P_2, and the quantity demanded increases to Q_2. Total health care costs rise to $0P_3CQ_2$, with $0P_2BQ_2$ paid by consumers and P_2P_3CB paid by insurers. As a result, the quantity supplied increases from point A to point C, where it equals the quantity demanded of Q_2.

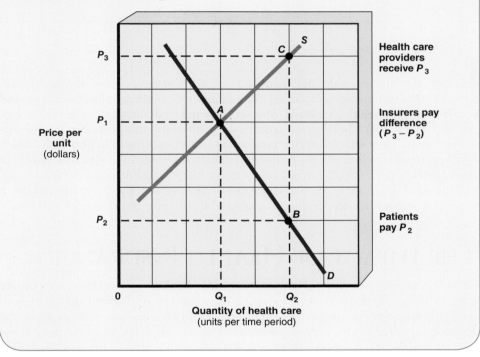

a lower price of P_2. At point B on the demand curve, insured consumers pay an amount equal to rectangle $0P_2BQ_2$, and insurers pay an amount represented by rectangle P_2P_3CB. Health care providers respond by increasing the quantity supplied from point A to point C on the supply curve S, where the quantity supplied equals the quantity demanded of Q_2. The reason that there is no shortage in the health care market is that the combined payments from the insured consumers and insurers equal the total payment required for the movement upward along the supply curve. Stated in terms of rectangles, the total health care payment of $0P_3CQ_2$ equals $0P_2BQ_2$ paid by consumers plus P_2P_3CB paid by insurers.

CONCLUSION *Compared to a health care market without insurance, the quantity demanded, the quantity supplied, and the total cost of health care are increased by copayment health care insurance.*

Finally, note that Exhibit A-1 represents an overall or general model of the health care market. Individual health care markets are subject to *market failure*. For example, there would be a lack of competition if hospitals, doctors, health maintenance organizations (HMOs), or drug companies conspired to fix prices. Externalities provide another source of market failure, as illustrated previously for vaccinations in Exhibit 8(b). We are also concerned that health care be distributed in a fair way. This concern explains why the government Medicare and Medicaid programs help the elderly and poor afford health care.

SHIFTS IN THE DEMAND FOR HEALTH CARE

While changes in the price of health care cause movements along the demand curve, other factors can cause the demand curve to shift. The following are some of the nonprice determinants that can change the demand for health care.

Number of Buyers

As the population increases, the demand for health care increases. In addition to the total number of people, the distribution of older people in the population is important. As more people move into the 65-and-older age group, the demand for health care services becomes greater because older people have more frequent and prolonged spells of illness. An increase in substance abuse involving alcohol, tobacco, or drugs also increases the demand for health care. For example, if the percentage of babies born into drug-prone families increases, the demand for health care will shift rightward.

Tastes and Preferences

Changes in consumer attitudes toward health care can also change demand. For example, television, movies, magazines, and advertising may be responsible for changes in people's preferences for cosmetic surgery. Moreover, medical science has improved so much that we believe there must be a cure for most ailments. As a result, consumers are willing to buy larger quantities of medical services at each possible price.

Doctors also influence consumer preferences by prescribing treatment. It is often argued that some doctors guard against malpractice suits or boost their incomes by ordering more tests or office visits than are really needed. Some estimates suggest that fraud and abuse account for about 10 percent of total health care spending. These studies reveal that as many as one-third of some procedures are inappropriate.

Income

Health care is a normal good. Rising inflation-adjusted incomes of consumers in the United States cause the demand curve for health care services to shift to the right. On the other hand, if real median family income remains unchanged, there is no influence on the demand curve.

Prices of Substitutes

The prices of medical goods and services that are substitutes can change and, in turn, influence the demand for other medical services. For example, treatment of a back problem by a chiropractor is an alternative for many of the treatments provided by orthopedic doctors. If the price of orthopedic therapy rises, then some people will switch to treatment by a chiropractor. As a result, the demand curve for chiropractic therapy shifts rightward.

SHIFTS IN THE SUPPLY OF HEALTH CARE

Changes in the following nonprice factors change the supply of health care.

Number of Sellers

Sellers of health care include hospitals, nursing homes, physicians in private practice, HMOs, drug companies, chiropractors, psychologists, and a host of other suppliers. To ensure the quality and safety of health care, virtually every facet of the industry is regulated and licensed by the government or controlled by the American Medical Association (AMA). The AMA limits the number of persons practicing medicine primarily through medical school accreditation and licensing requirements. The federal Food and Drug Administration (FDA) requires testing that delays the introduction of new drugs. Tighter restrictions on the number of sellers shift the health care supply curve leftward, and reduced restrictions shift the supply curve rightward.

Resource Prices

An increase in the costs of resources underlying the supply of health care shifts the supply curve leftward. By far the single most important factor behind increasing health care spending has been technological change. New diagnostic, surgical, and therapeutic equipment is used extensively in the health care industry, and the result is higher costs. Wages, salaries, and other costs, such as the costs of malpractice suits, also influence the supply curve. If hospitals, for example, are paying higher prices for inputs used to produce health care, the supply curve shifts to the left because the same quantities may be supplied only at higher prices.

Macroeconomic Fundamentals

3

© Getty Images

T he three chapters in this part explain key measures of how well the macroeconomy is performing. Knowledge of this material is vital to the discussion of macro theory and policy in the next part. The first chapter in this part explains GDP computation. The next chapter begins by teaching how to measure business cycles and concludes with an examination of unemployment. The final chapter in this part explores the measurement and consequences of inflation.

Gross Domestic Product

Measuring the performance of the economy is an important part of life. Suppose one candidate for president of the United States proclaims that the economy's performance is the best in a generation, and the opposing presidential candidate argues that the economy could perform better. Which statistics would you seek to tell how well the economy is doing? The answer requires understanding some of the nuts and bolts of *national income accounting*. National income accounting is the system used to measure the aggregate income and expenditures for a nation. Despite certain limitations, the national income accounting system provides a valuable indicator of an economy's performance. For example, you can visit the Internet and check the annual Economic Report of the President to compare the size or growth of the U.S. economy between years.

Prior to the Great Depression, there were no national accounting procedures for estimating the data required to assess the economy's performance. To provide accounting methodologies for macro data, the late economist Simon Kuznets published a small report in 1934 titled *National Income, 1929–32*. For his pioneering work, Kuznets, the "father of GDP," earned the 1971 Nobel Prize in Economics. Today, thanks in large part to Kuznets, most countries use common national accounting methods. National income accounting serves a nation similar to the manner in which accounting serves a business or household. In each case, accounting methodology is vital for identifying economic problems and formulating plans for achieving goals.

In this chapter, you will learn to solve these economics puzzles:

• Why doesn't economic growth include increases in spending for welfare, Social Security, and unemployment programs?

• Can one newscaster report that the economy grew, while another reports that for the same year the economy declined, and both reports be correct?

• How is the calculation of national output affected by environmental damage?

GROSS DOMESTIC PRODUCT

The most widely reported measure throughout the world of a nation's economic performance is **gross domestic product (GDP)**, which is the market value of all final goods and services produced in a nation during a period of time, usually a year. GDP therefore excludes production abroad by U.S. businesses. For example, GDP excludes Microsoft's earnings on its foreign operations. On the other hand, GDP includes Toyota's profits from its car plants in the United States. Why is GDP important? One advantage of GDP is that it avoids the "apples and oranges" measurement problem. If an economy produces 10 apples one year and 10 oranges the next, can we say that the value of output has changed in any way? To answer this question, we must attach price tags in order to evaluate the relative monetary value of apples and oranges to society. This is the reason GDP measures value using dollars, rather than listing the number of cars, heart transplants, legal cases, toothbrushes, and tanks produced. Instead, the market-determined dollar value establishes the monetary importance of production. In GDP calculations, "money talks." That is, GDP relies on markets to establish the relative value of goods and services.

GDP is compiled by the Bureau of Economic Analysis (BEA), which is an agency of the Department of Commerce. GDP requires that the following two points receive special attention: (1) GDP counts only new domestic production, and (2) it counts only final goods.

GDP Counts Only New Domestic Production

National income accountants calculating GDP carefully exclude transactions in two major areas: secondhand transactions and nonproductive financial transactions.

Secondhand Transactions GDP includes only current transactions. It does not include the sale of a used car or the sale of a home constructed some years ago. Such transactions are merely exchanges of previously produced goods and not *current* production of new goods that add to the existing stock of cars and homes. However, the sales commission on a used car or a home produced in another GDP period counts in current GDP because the salesperson performed a service during the present period of time.

Nonproductive Financial Transactions GDP does not count purely private or public financial transactions, such as giving private gifts, buying and selling stocks and bonds, and making **transfer payments**. A transfer payment is a government

Gross domestic product (GDP)

The market value of all final goods and services produced in a nation during a period of time, usually a year.

Transfer payment

A government payment to individuals not in exchange for goods or services currently produced.

payment to individuals not in exchange for goods or services currently produced. Welfare, Social Security, veterans' benefits, and unemployment benefits are transfer payments. These transactions are considered nonproductive because they do not represent production of any new or *current* output. Similarly, stock market transactions represent only the exchange of certificates of ownership (stocks) or indebtedness (bonds) and not actual new production.

GDP Counts Only Final Goods

Final goods

Finished goods and services produced for the ultimate user.

Intermediate goods

Goods and services used as inputs for the production of final goods.

The popular press usually defines GDP as simply "the value of all goods and services produced." This is technically incorrect because GDP counts only **final goods**, which are finished goods and services produced for the ultimate user. Including all goods and services produced would inflate GDP by *double counting* (counting many items more than once). In order to count only final goods and avoid overstating GDP, national income accountants must take care not to include **intermediate goods**. Intermediate goods are goods and services used as inputs for the production of final goods. Stated differently, intermediate goods are not produced for consumption by the ultimate user.

Suppose a wholesale distributor sells glass to an automaker. This transaction is not included in GDP. The glass is an intermediate good used in the production of cars. When a customer buys a new car from the car dealer, the value of the glass is included in the car's selling price, which is the value of a final good counted in GDP. Let's consider another example. A wholesale distributor sells glass to a hardware store. GDP does not include this transaction because the hardware store is not the final user. When a customer buys the glass from the hardware store to repair a broken window, the final purchase price of the glass is added to GDP as a consumer expenditure.

MEASURING GDP

GDP is like an enormous puzzle with many pieces to fit together, including markets for products, markets for resources, consumers spending and earning money, and businesses spending and earning money. How can one fit all these puzzle pieces together? One way to understand how all these concepts fit together is to use a simple macroeconomic model called the **circular flow model**. The circular flow model shows the flow of products from businesses to households and the flow of resources from households to businesses. In exchange for these resources, money payments flow between businesses and households. Exhibit 1 shows the circular flow in a hypothetical economy with no government, no financial markets, and no foreign trade. In this ultra simple pure market economy, only the households and the businesses make decisions.

Circular flow model

A diagram showing the flow of products from businesses to households and the flow of resources from households to businesses. In exchange for these resources, money payments flow between businesses and households.

The Circular Flow Model

The upper half of the diagram in Exhibit 1 represents *product markets,* in which households exchange money for goods and services produced by firms. The *supply* arrow in the top loop represents all finished products and the value of services produced, sold, and delivered to consumers. The *demand* arrow in the top loop shows

Exhibit 1	The Basic Circular Flow Model

In this simple economy, households spend all their income in the upper loop and demand consumer goods and services from businesses. Businesses seek profits by supplying goods and services to households through the product markets. Prices and quantities in individual markets are determined by the market supply and demand model. In the factor markets in the lower loop, resources (land, labor, and capital) are owned by households and supplied to businesses that demand these factors in return for money payments. The forces of supply and demand determine the returns to the factors, for example, wages and the quantity of labor supplied. Overall, goods and services flow clockwise, and the corresponding payments flow counterclockwise.

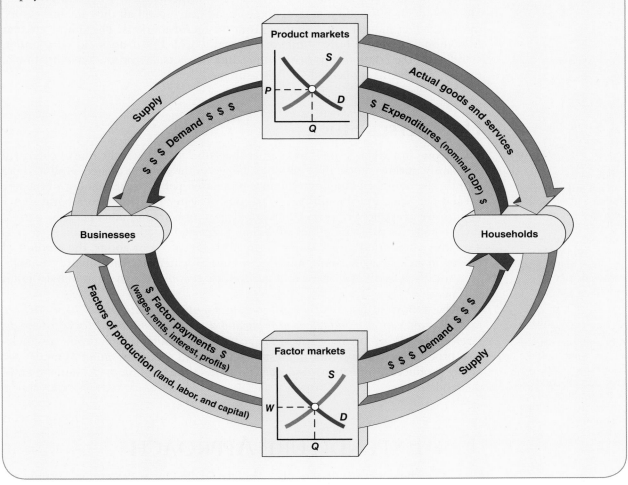

why the businesses make this effort to satisfy the consuming households. When consumers decide to buy products, they are actually voting with their dollars. This flow of consumption expenditures from households is sales revenues to businesses and expenses from the viewpoint of households. Notice that the box labeled *product markets* contains a supply and demand graph. This means the forces of supply and demand in individual markets determine the price and quantity of each product exchanged without government interference.

The bottom half of the circular flow diagram consists of the *factor markets*, in which firms *demand* the natural resources, labor, capital, and entrepreneurship needed to produce the goods and services sold in the product markets. Our hypothetical economy is capitalistic, and the model assumes for simplicity that households own the factors of production. Businesses therefore must purchase all their resources from the households. The *supply* arrow in the bottom loop represents this flow of resources from households to firms, and the *demand* arrow is the flow of money payments for these resources. These payments are also income earned by households in the form of wages, rents, interest, and profits. As in the product markets, market supply and demand determine the price and quantity of factor payments.

This simple model also assumes all households live from hand to mouth. That is, households spend all the income they earn in the factor markets on products. Households therefore do not save. Likewise, all firms spend all their income earned in the product markets on resources from the factor markets. The simple circular flow model therefore fails to mirror the real world. But it does aid your understanding of the relationships between product markets, factor markets, the flow of money, and the theory behind GDP measurement.

Flow versus Stock

Flow

A flow is the rate of change in a quantity during a given time period, such as dollars per year. For example, income and consumption are flows that occur per week, per month, or per year.

Stock

A quantity measured at one point in time. For example, an inventory of goods or the amount of money in a checking account.

The arrows in Exhibit 1 are **flows**, rather than **stocks**. A flow is the rate of change in a quantity during a given time period. Changes in the amount of steel produced per month, the number of computer games purchased per day, the amount of income earned per year, and the number of gallons of water pouring into a bathtub per minute are examples of flows. Flows are always measured in units per time period, such as tons per month, billions of dollars per year, or gallons per hour. A stock is a quantity measured at one point in time. An inventory of goods, the amount of money in a checking account, and the amount of water in a bathtub are examples of stocks. Stocks are measured in tons, dollars, gallons, and so on at a given point in time.

The important point is this: *All measurements in the circular flow model are rates of change (flows) and tell us nothing about the total amounts (stocks) of goods, services, money, or anything else in the economy.* Consumption expenditures, business production, wages, rents, interest payments, and profits are *flows* of money for newly produced products or resources that affect the level of *stocks* not shown in the model.

THE EXPENDITURE APPROACH

Expenditure approach

The national income accounting method that measures GDP by adding all the spending for final goods during a period of time.

How does the government actually calculate GDP? One way national income accountants calculate GDP is to use the **expenditure approach** to measure total spending flowing through product markets in the circular flow diagram. The expenditure approach measures GDP by adding all the spending for final goods during a period of time. Exhibit 2 shows 2009 GDP using the expenditure approach, which breaks down expenditures into four components. The data in this exhibit show that all production in the U.S. economy is ultimately purchased by spending from households, businesses, government, or foreigners. Let's discuss each of these expenditure categories.

Exhibit 2	Gross Domestic Product Using the Expenditure Approach, 2009		
National income account		**Amount (billions of dollars)**	**Percentage of GDP**
Personal consumption expenditures (**C**)		$10,089	71%
Durable goods	$1,035		
Nondurable goods	2,220		
Services	6,834		
Gross private domestic investment (**I**)		1,629	12
Fixed investment	1,750		
Change in business inventories	−121		
Government consumption expenditures and gross investment (**G**)		2,930	20
Federal	1,144		
State and local	1,786		
Net exports of goods and services (**X − M**)		−392	−3
Exports (X)	1,564		
Imports (M)	1,956		
Gross domestic product (**GDP**)		$14,256	100%

SOURCE: Bureau of Economic Analysis, *National Economic Accounts*, http://www.bea.gov/national/nipaweb/SelectTable.asp?Selected=Y, Table 1.1.5.

Personal Consumption Expenditures (C)

The largest component of GDP in 2009 was $10,089 billion for the category national income accountants call *personal consumption expenditures*, represented by the letter C. Personal consumption expenditures comprise total spending by households for durable goods, nondurable goods, and services. Durable goods include items such as automobiles, appliances, and furniture because they last longer than three years. Food, clothing, soap, and gasoline are examples of nondurables, because they are considered used up or consumed in less than these years. Services, which is the largest category, include recreation, legal advice, medical treatment, education, and any transaction not in the form of a tangible object.

Gross Private Domestic Investment (I)

In 2009, $1,629 billion was spent for what is officially called *gross private domestic investment* (I). This national income account includes "gross" (all) "private" (not government) "domestic" (not foreign) spending by businesses for investment in assets that are expected to earn profits in the future. Gross private domestic investment is the sum of two components: (1) *fixed investment* expenditures for newly produced capital goods, such as commercial and residential structures, machinery, equipment, tools, and computers; and (2) change in *business inventories*, which is the net change in spending for unsold finished goods. Note that gross private domestic investment is simply the national income accounting category for "investment," defined in Chapter 2. The only difference is that investment in Exhibit 5 in Chapter 2 was in physical capital such as manufacturing plants, oil wells, or fast food restaurants, rather than the dollar value of capital used here.

Now we will take a closer look at gross private domestic investment. Note that national income accountants include the rental value of newly constructed residential housing in the $1,629 billion spent for fixed investment. A new factory, warehouse, or robot is surely a form of investment, but why include residential housing as business investment rather than consumption by households? The debatable answer is that a new home is considered investment because it provides services in the future that the owner can rent for financial return. For this reason, all newly produced housing is considered investment whether the owner rents or occupies the property.

Finally, the −$121 billion change in business inventories means this amount of net dollar value of unsold finished goods and raw materials was subtracted from the stock of inventories during 2009. A decline in inventories would reduce GDP because households consumed more output than firms produced during this year. When businesses have more on their shelves this year than last, more new production has taken place than has been consumed during this year.

Government Consumption Expenditures and Gross Investment (*G*)

This official category simply called *government spending* includes the value of goods and services government at all levels purchased measured by their costs. For example, spending for police and state university professors enters the GDP accounts at the prices the government pays for them. In addition, the government spends for investment additions to its stock of capital, such as tanks, schools, highways, bridges, and government buildings. In 2009, federal, state, and local government spending (*G*) were totaled $2,930 billion. As the figures in Exhibit 2 reveal, government purchases of state and local governments far exceeded those of the federal government. It is important to understand that consumption expenditures and gross investment exclude *transfer payments* because, as explained at the beginning of the chapter, they do not represent newly produced goods and services. Instead, transfer payments are paid to those entitled to Social Security benefits, veterans' benefits, welfare, unemployment compensation, and benefits from other programs.

Net Exports (*X* − *M*)

The last GDP expenditure account is *net exports*, expressed in the formula (*X* − *M*). *Exports* (*X*) are expenditures by foreigners for U.S. domestically produced goods. *Imports* (*M*) are the dollar amount of U.S. purchases of Japanese automobiles, French wine, clothes from China, and other goods produced abroad. Because we are using expenditures for U.S. output to measure GDP, one might ask why imports are subtracted from exports. The answer is the result of how the government actually collects data from which GDP is computed. Spending for imports is not subtracted when spending data for consumption, investment, and government spending are reported. These three components of GDP therefore overstate the value of expenditures for U.S.-produced products.

Consider the data collected to compute consumption (C). In reality, personal consumption expenditures reported to the U.S. Department of Commerce include expenditures for both domestically produced and imported goods and services. For example, automobile dealers report to the government that consumers purchased a given dollar amount of new cars during 2009, but they are not required to separate their figures between sales of U.S. cars and sales of foreign cars. Because GDP measures only domestic economic activity, foreign sales must be removed. Subtracting imports in the net exports category removes all sales of foreign goods, including new foreign cars, from consumption (C) and likewise from investment (I) and government spending (G).

The overstatement of 2009 GDP expenditures is corrected by subtracting $1,956 billion in imports from $1,564 billion in exports to obtain net exports of −$392 billion. The negative sign indicates that the United States is spending more dollars to purchase foreign products than it is receiving from the rest of the world for U.S. goods. The effect of a negative net exports figure is to reduce U.S. GDP when it is subtracted from the consumption, investment, and government components. Prior to the early 1980s, the United States was a consistent net exporter, selling more goods and services to the rest of the world than we purchased from abroad. Since 1983, the United States has been a net importer. International trade is discussed in more detail in the last section of the text.

A Formula for GDP

Using the expenditure approach, GDP is expressed mathematically in billions of dollars as

$$GDP = C + I + G + (X - M)$$

For 2009 (see Exhibit 2),

$$\$14,256 = \$10,089 + \$1,629 + \$2,930 + (\$1,564 - \$1,956)$$

This simple equation plays a central role in macroeconomics. It is the basis for analyzing macro problems and formulating macro policy. When economists study the macro economy, they can apply this equation to predict the behavior of the major sectors of the economy: consumption (C) is spending by households, investment (I) is spending by firms, government spending (G) is spending by the government, and net exports (X − M) is net spending by foreigners.

THE INCOME APPROACH

The second, somewhat more complex approach to measuring GDP is the **income approach**. The income approach measures GDP by adding all the incomes earned by households in exchange for the factors of production during a period of time. Both the expenditure approach and the income approach yield identical GDP

Income approach

The national income accounting method that measures GDP by adding all incomes, including compensation of employees, rents, net interest, and profits.

Exhibit 3	**Gross Domestic Product Using the Income Approach, 2009**	
National income account	**Amount (billions of dollars)**	**Percentage of GDP**
Compensation of employees	$ 7,791	55%
Rental income	268	2
Profits	2,350	16
Proprietors' income 1,041		
Corporate profits 1,309		
Net interest	788	5
Indirect business taxes	1,091	8
Depreciation	1,968	14
Gross domestic product (GDP)	$14,256	100%

SOURCE: Bureau of Economic Analysis, *National Income Accounts,* http://www.bea.doc/bea.gov/national/nipaweb/SelectTable.asp?Selected=Y, Table 1.7.5.

calculations. As shown in the basic circular flow model, each dollar of expenditure paid by households to businesses in the product markets means a dollar of income flows to households through the factor markets as a payment for the land, labor, and capital required to produce the product. Using the income approach, GDP is expressed as follows:

$$\text{GDP} = \text{compensation of employees} + \text{rents} + \text{profits} \\ + \text{net interest} + \text{indirect taxes} + \text{depreciation}$$

In practice, it is necessary to add depreciation (capital consumption allowance) to factor payments so that national income equals GDP. Exhibit 3 presents actual 2009 GDP calculated following the income approach, and then each component is discussed in turn.

COMPENSATION OF EMPLOYEES

Employees' compensation is the largest of the national income accounts. About 55 percent of GDP in 2009 ($7,791 billion) was income earned from wages, salaries, and certain supplements paid by firms and government to suppliers of labor. Since labor services play such an important role in production, it is not surprising that employee compensation represents the largest share of the GDP income pie. The supplements consist of employer taxes for Social Security and unemployment insurance. Also included are fringe benefits from a variety of private health insurance and pension plans.

Rental Income

The smallest source of income is from rent and royalties received by property owners who permit others to use their assets during a time period. For example, this category includes house and apartment rents received by landlords. In 2009, $268 billion was earned in rental income.

Profits

Proprietors' Income All forms of income earned by unincorporated businesses totaled $1,041 billion in 2009. Self-employed proprietorships and partnerships simultaneously own their businesses and pay themselves for labor services to their firms.

Corporate Profits This income category includes all income earned by the stockholders of corporations regardless of whether stockholders receive it. The $1,309 billion of corporate profits in 2009 was the sum of three sources: (1) dividends, (2) undistributed corporate profits (retained earnings for expanding plant and equipment), and (3) corporate income taxes. Thus, corporate profits using the income approach are "before taxes."

Net Interest

Households both receive and pay interest. Persons who make loans to businesses earn interest income. Suppose you purchase a bond issued by General Motors. When General Motors pays interest on its bonds, the interest payments are included in the national income accounts. Households also received interest from savings accounts and certificates of deposits (CDs). On the other hand, households borrow money and pay interest on, for example, credit cards, installment loans, and mortgage loans. The net interest of $788 billion in 2009 is the difference between interest income earned and interest payments.

Indirect Business Taxes

As reported in Exhibit 3, $1,091 billion was collected by government in the form of **indirect business taxes**. Why do national income accountants include business taxes in the income approach to GDP competition? Indirect business taxes are levied as a percentage of the prices of goods sold and therefore become part of the revenue received by firms. These taxes include sales taxes, federal excise taxes, license fees, business property taxes, and customs duties. Indirect taxes are not income payments to suppliers of resources. Instead, firms collect indirect taxes and send these funds to the government. Suppose you purchased a new automobile for $20,000, including a $1,000 federal excise tax and state sales tax. These taxes are included in the price, but are income for the government, which represents the public interest of households.

Indirect business taxes

Taxes levied as a percentage of the prices of goods sold and therefore collected as part of the firm's revenue. Firms treat such taxes as production costs. Examples include general sales taxes, excise taxes, and customs duties.

Depreciation

To reconcile the above income accounts with GDP requires adding the category labeled *consumption of fixed capital*. Consumption of fixed capital is an estimate of the depreciation of capital. This somewhat imposing term is simply an allowance

Exhibit 4   **Expenditure and Income Approaches to GDP**

Expenditure approach	Income approach
Consumption (C) expenditures by households	Compensation of employees
plus	plus
Investment (I) expenditures by businesses	Rents
plus	plus
Government consumption expenditures and gross investment (G)	Profits
plus	plus
Net exports (X − M) expenditures by foreign economies	Net Interest
	plus
	Indirect business taxes
	plus
	Depreciation

= GDP =

for the portion of capital worn out producing GDP. Over time, capital goods, such as buildings, machines, and equipment wear out and become less valuable. Depreciation (capital consumption allowance) is therefore a portion of GDP that is not available for income payments. Because it is impossible to measure depreciation accurately, an estimate is entered. In 2009, $1,968 billion was the estimated amount of GDP attributable to depreciation during the year.

Exhibit 4 presents the conceptual frameworks of the expenditure and income approaches to computing GDP.

CHECKPOINT

How Much Does Mario Add to GDP?

Mario works part-time at Pizza Hut and earns an annual wage plus tips of $15,000. He sold 4,000 pizzas at $15 per pizza during the year. He was unemployed part of the year, so he received unemployment compensation of $3,000. During the past year, Mario bought a used car for $5,000. Using the expenditure approach, how much has Mario contributed to GDP?

Global Economics

GDP IN OTHER COUNTRIES

Exhibit 5 compares GDP for selected countries in 2009. The United States had the world's highest GDP. U.S. GDP, for example, was about three times Japan's and China's GDP.

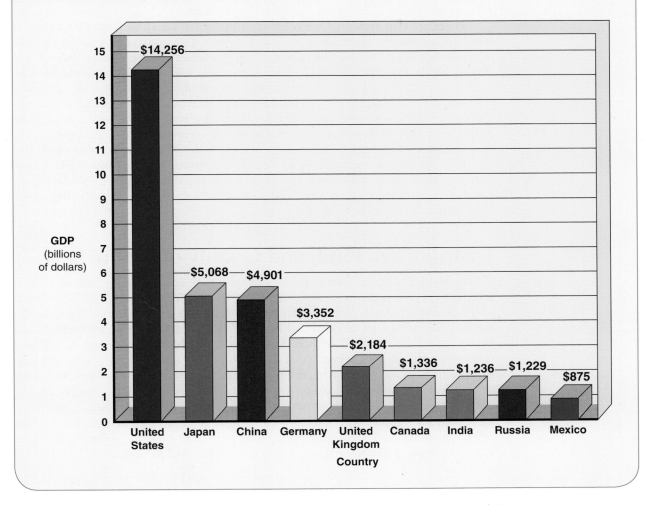

Exhibit 5   An International Comparison of GDPs, 2009 (billions of dollars)

This exhibit shows GDPs in 2009 for selected countries. The United States had the world's highest GDP. U.S. GDP, for example, is about three times the size of Japan's and China's GDP.

SOURCE: International Monetary Fund, *World Economic Outlook Database,* http://www.imf.org/external/ns/cs.aspx?id=28.

GDP SHORTCOMINGS

For various reasons, GDP omits certain measures of overall economic well-being. Because GDP is the basis of government economic policies, there is concern that GDP may be giving us a false impression of the nation's material well-being. GDP is a less-than-perfect measure of the nation's economic pulse because it excludes the following factors.

Nonmarket Transactions

Because GDP counts only market transactions, it excludes certain unpaid activities, such as homemaker production, child rearing, and do-it-yourself home repairs and services. For example, if you take your dirty clothes to the laundry, GDP increases by the amount of the cleaning bill paid. But GDP ignores the value of laundering these same clothes if you wash them yourself at home.

There are two reasons for excluding nonmarket activities from GDP. First, it would be extremely imprecise to attempt to collect data and assign a dollar value to services people provide for themselves or others without compensation. Second, it is difficult to decide which nonmarket activities to exclude and which ones to include. Perhaps repairing your own roof, painting your own house, and repairing your own car should be included. Now consider the value of washing your car. GDP does include the price of cleaning your car if you purchase it at a car wash, so it could be argued that GDP should include the value of you washing your car at home.

The issue of unpaid, do-it-yourself activities affects comparisons of the GDPs of different nations. One reason some less-developed nations have lower GDPs than major industrialized nations is that a greater proportion of people in less-developed nations farm, clean, make repairs, and perform other tasks for their families rather than hiring someone else to do the work.

Distribution, Kind, and Quality of Products

GDP is blind to whether a small fraction of the population consumes most of a country's GDP or consumption is evenly divided. GDP also wears a blindfold with respect to the quality and kinds of goods and services that make up a nation's GDP. Consider the fictional economies of Zuba and Econa. Zuba has a GDP of $2,000 billion, and Econa has a GDP of $1,000 billion. At first glance, Zuba appears to possess superior economic well-being. However, Zuba's GDP consists of only military goods, and Econa's products include computers, cell phones, tractors, wheat, milk, houses, and other consumer items. Moreover, assume the majority of the people of Zuba could care less about the output of military goods and would be happier if the country produced more consumer goods. Now consider for example the difference in quality between a cell phone purchased today and a cell phone with only a few capabilities purchased years ago. Such qualitative improvements are not reflected in GDP.

> **CONCLUSION** *GDP is a quantitative, rather than a qualitative, measure of the output of goods and services.*

Neglect of Leisure Time

In general, the wealthier a nation becomes the more leisure time its citizens can afford. Rather than working longer hours, workers often choose to increase their time for recreation and travel. Since 1900, the length of the typical workweek in the United States declined steadily from about 50 hours to about 34 hours in 2009.[1]

---

1. *Economic Report of the President, 2010,* http://www.gpoaccess.gov/eop/, Table B-47.

CONCLUSION *It can be argued that GDP understates national well-being because no allowance is made for people working fewer hours than they once did.*

The Underground Economy

Illegal gambling, prostitution, loan-sharking, illegal guns, and illegal drugs are goods and services that meet all the requirements for GDP. They are final products with a value determined in markets, but GDP does not include unreported criminal activities. The "underground" economy also includes tax evasion. One way to avoid paying taxes on a legal activity is to trade or barter goods and services rather than selling them. One person fixes a neighbor's car in return for baby-sitting services, and the value of the exchange is unreported. Other individuals and businesses make legal sales for cash and do not report the income earned to the Internal Revenue Service.

Estimates of the size of this subterranean economy vary. Some studies by economists estimate the size of the underground sector is about 9 percent of GDP.[2] This range of estimates is slightly less than the estimated size of the underground economy in most European countries.

CONCLUSION *If the underground economy is sizable, GDP will understate an economy's performance.*

Economic Bads

More production means a larger GDP, regardless of the level of pollution created in the process. Recall from Chapter 4 the discussion of *negative externalities*, such as pollution caused by steel mills, chemical plants, and cigarettes. Air, water, and noise pollution are *economic bads* that impose costs on society not reflected in private market prices and quantities bought and sold. When a polluting company sells its product, this transaction increases GDP. However, critics of GDP argue that it fails to account for the diminished quality of life from the "bads" not reported in GDP.

Stated another way, if production results in pollution and environmental damage, GDP overstates the nation's well-being.

CONCLUSION *Since the costs of negative by-products are not deducted, GDP overstates the national well-being.*

OTHER NATIONAL INCOME ACCOUNTS

In addition to GDP, the media often report several other national income accounts because they are necessary for studying the macro economy. We now take a brief look at each.

---

2. Jim McTague, "Going Underground: America's Shadow Economy," *Frontpagemag.com*, Jan. 6, 2005, http://www.frontpagemag.com/Default.aspx.

You're The Economist Is GDP a False Beacon Steering Us into the Rocks? *Applicable Concept: national income accounting "goods" and "bads"*

Suppose a factory in your community has been dumping hazardous wastes into the local water supply and people develop cancer and other illnesses from drinking polluted water. The Environmental Protection Agency (EPA) discovers this pollution and under the federal "Superfund" law, orders a cleanup and imposes a fine for the damages. The company defends itself against the EPA by hiring lawyers and experts to take the case to court. After years of trial, the company loses the case and has to pay for the cleanup and damages.

In terms of GDP, an amazing "good" result occurs: The primary measure of national economic output, GDP, increases. GDP counts the millions of dollars spent to clean up the water supply. GDP even includes the health care expenses of anyone who develops cancer or other illnesses caused by drinking polluted water. GDP also includes the money spent by the company on lawyers and experts to defend itself against the EPA. And GDP includes the money spent by the EPA to regulate the polluting company.

Now consider what happens when trees are cut down and oil and minerals are used to produce houses, cars, and other goods. The value of the wood, oil, and minerals is an intermediate good

implicitly computed in GDP because the value of the final goods is explicitly computed in GDP. Using scarce resources to produce goods and services therefore raises GDP and is considered a "good" result. On the other hand, don't we lose the value of trees, oil, and minerals in the production process, so isn't this a "bad" result?

The Bureau of Economic Analysis (BEA) is an agency of the U.S. Department of Commerce. The BEA is the nation's economic accountant, and it publishes the Survey of Current Business, which is the source of GDP data cited throughout this text. Critics have called for a new measure designed to estimate the kinds of damage described above. These new accounts would adjust for changes in air and water quality and depletion of oil and minerals. These accounts would also adjust for changes in the stock of renewable natural resources, such as forests and fish stocks. In addition, accounts should be created to measure global warming and destruction of the ozone layer.

As explained in this chapter, a dollar estimate of capital depreciation is subtracted from GDP to compute national income (NI). The argument here is that a dollar estimate of the damage to the environment should also be subtracted.

© Image copyright haak78, 2009. Used under license from Shutterstock.com

To ignore measuring such environmental problems, critics argue, threatens future generations. In short, conventional GDP perpetuates a false dichotomy between economic growth and environmental protection.

Critics of this approach argue that assigning a dollar value to environmental damage and resource depletion requires a methodology that is extremely subjective and complex. Nevertheless, national income accountants have not ignored these criticisms, and the National Academy of Sciences has reviewed BEA proposals for ways to account for interactions between the environment and the economy.

ANALYZE THE ISSUE

Suppose a nuclear power plant disaster occurs. How could GDP be a "false beacon" in this case?

Exhibit 6	National Income Calculated from Gross Domestic Product, 2009	
		Amount (billions of dollars)
Gross domestic product (GDP)		$14,256
Depreciation		−1,968
National income (NI)		$12,288

SOURCE: Bureau of Economic Analysis, *National Economic Accounts*, http://www.bea.gov/national/nipaweb/SelectTable. asp?Selected=Y, Table 1.7.5.

National Income (NI)

It can be argued that depreciation should be subtracted from GDP. Recall that GDP is not entirely a measure of newly produced output because it includes an estimated value of capital goods required to replace those worn out in the production process. The measurement designed to correct this deficiency is **national income (NI)**, which is the gross domestic product minus depreciation of the capital worn out in producing output. Stated as a formula:

$$NI = GDP - depreciation \text{ (consumption of fixed capital)}$$

In 2009, $1,968 billion was the estimated amount of GDP attributable to depreciation during the year. Exhibit 6 shows the actual calculation of NI from GDP in 2009. NI measures how much income is *earned* by households who own and supply resources. It includes the total flow of payments to the owners of the factors of production, including wages, rents, interest, and profits. Another way to compute national income is to add compensation of employees, rents, profits, net interest, and indirect business taxes using the income approach demonstrated in Exhibit 3. Exhibit 7 illustrates the transition from GDP to NI and two other measures of the macro economy.[3]

Personal Income (PI)

National income measures the total amount of money *earned*, but determining the amount of income actually *received* by households (not businesses) requires a measurement of **personal income (PI)**. Personal income is the total income received by households that is available for consumption, saving, and payment of personal taxes. Suppose we want to measure the total amount of money individuals receive that they can use to consume products, save, and pay taxes. National income is not the appropriate measure for two reasons. First, NI excludes transfer payments, which constitute unearned income that can be spent, saved, or used to pay taxes. Second, NI includes corporate profits, but stockholders do not receive all these profits.

National income (NI)

The total income earned by resource owners, including wages, rents, interest, and profits. NI is calculated as gross domestic product minus depreciation of the capital worn out in producing output.

Personal income (PI)

The total income received by households that is available for consumption, saving, and payment of personal taxes.

---

3. As a result of a revision in national income accounting, the only difference between net domestic product (NDP) and national income (NI) is a statistical discrepancy. Since NI is more widely reported in the media, and to simplify, NDP is not calculated here.

Exhibit 7   Four Measures of the Macro Economy

The four bars show major measurements of the U.S. macro economy in 2009 in billions of dollars. Beginning with gross domestic product, depreciation is subtracted to obtain national income. Next, personal income equals national income minus corporate profits and contributions for Social Security insurance (FICA payments) plus transfer payments and other income. Subtracting personal taxes from personal income yields disposable personal income.

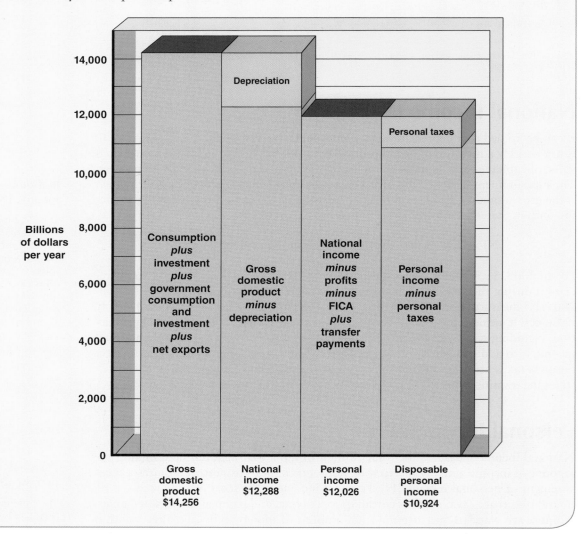

A portion of corporate profits is paid in corporate taxes. Also, retained earnings are not distributed to stockholders, but are channeled back into business operations.

Exhibit 7 illustrates the relationship between personal income and national income, and Exhibit 8 gives the figures for 2009. National income accountants adjust national income by subtracting corporate profits and payroll taxes for Social Security (FICA deductions). Next, *transfer payments* and other income individuals receive from net interest and dividends are added. The net result is the personal income received by households, which in 2009 amounted to $12,026 billion.

Exhibit 8	Personal Income Calculated from National Income, 2009
	Amount (billions of dollars)
National income (NI)	$12,288
Corporate profits	−1,309
Contributions for Social Security (FICA)	−967
Transfer payments and other income	2,014
Personal income (PI)	$12,026

SOURCE: Bureau of Economic Analysis, National Economic Accounts, http://www.bea.gov/national/nipaweb/SelectTable.asp?Selected=Y, Table 1.7.5.

Exhibit 9	Disposable Personal Income Calculated from Personal Income, 2009
	Amount (billions of dollars)
Personal income (PI)	$12,026
Personal taxes	−1,102
Disposable personal income (DI)	$10,924

SOURCE: Bureau of Economic Analysis, National Economic Accounts, http://www.bea.gov/national/nipaweb/SelectTable.asp?Selected=Y, Table 2.1.

Disposable Personal Income (DI)

One final measure of national income is shown at the far right of Exhibit 7. Disposable personal income (DI) is the amount of income that households actually have to spend or save after payment of personal taxes. Disposable, or *after-tax*, income is equal to personal income minus personal taxes paid to federal, state, and local governments. Personal taxes consist of personal income taxes, personal property taxes, and inheritance taxes. As tabulated in Exhibit 9, disposable personal income in 2009 was $10,924 billion.

CHANGING NOMINAL GDP TO REAL GDP

So far, GDP has been expressed as **nominal GDP**. Nominal GDP is the value of all final goods based on the prices existing during the time period of production. Nominal GDP is also referred to as *current-dollar* or *money GDP*. Nominal GDP grows in three ways: First, output rises, and prices remain unchanged. Second, prices rise

Disposable personal income (DI)

The amount of income that households actually have to spend or save after payment of personal taxes.

Nominal GDP

The value of all final goods based on the prices existing during the time period of production.

and output is constant. Third, in the typical case, both output and prices rise. The problem, then, is how to adjust GDP so it reflects only changes in output and not changes in prices. This adjusted GDP allows meaningful comparisons over time when prices are changing.

Changing prices can have a huge impact on how we compare dollar figures. Suppose a newspaper headline reports that a film entitled *The History of Economic Thought* is the most popular movie of all time. You ask, How could this be? What about *Gone with the Wind*? Reading the article reveals that this claim is based on the nominal measure of gross box-office receipts. This gives a recent movie with higher ticket prices an advantage over a movie released in 1939 when the average ticket price was only 25 cents. A better measure of popularity would be to compare "real" box office receipts by multiplying actual attendance figures for each movie by a base year movie price.

Measuring the difference between changes in output and changes in the price level involves making an important distinction between nominal GDP and **real GDP**. Real GDP is the value of all final goods produced during a given time period based on the prices existing in a selected base year. The U.S. Department of Commerce currently uses 2005 as the base year. Real GDP is also referred to as *constant dollar GDP*.

The GDP Chain Price Index

The most broadly based measure used to take the changes-in-the-price-level "air" out of the nominal GDP "balloon" and compute real GDP is officially called the **GDP chain price index**. The GDP chain price index is a measure that compares changes in the prices of all final goods produced during a given time period relative to the prices of those goods in a base year. The GDP chain price index is a broad "deflator" index calculated by a complex chain-weighted geometric series (you are spared the details). It is highly inclusive because it measures not only price changes of consumer goods, but also price changes of business investment, government purchases, exports, and imports. Do not confuse the GDP chain price index with the *consumer price index* (CPI), which is widely reported in the news media. The CPI is a different index, measuring only consumer prices, which we will discuss in the chapter on inflation.

Now it's time to see how it works. We begin with the following conversion equation:

$$\text{Real GDP} = \frac{\text{nominal GDP}}{\text{GDP chain price index}} \times 100$$

Using 2005 as the base year, suppose you are given the 2009 nominal GDP of $14,256 billion and the 2009 GDP chain price index of 109.77. To calculate 2009 real GDP, use the above formula as follows:

$$\$12,987 \text{ billion} = \frac{\$14,256 \text{ billion}}{109.77} \times 100$$

Exhibit 10 shows actual U.S. nominal GDP, real GDP, and the GDP chain price index computations for selected years. Column 1 reports nominal GDP, column 2 gives real GDP figures for these years, and column 3 lists corresponding GDP chain price indexes. Notice that the GDP chain price index exceeds 100 in years beyond 2005. This means that prices, on average, have risen since 2005, causing the real

Real GDP

The value of all final goods produced during a given time period based on the prices existing in a selected base year.

GDP chain price index

A measure that compares changes in the prices of all final goods during a given year to the prices of those goods in a base year.

Exhibit 10	Nominal GDP, Real GDP, and the GDP Chain Price Index for Selected Years

Real GDP reflects output valued at 2005 base-year prices, but nominal GDP is annual output valued at prices prevailing during the current year. The intersection of real and nominal GDP occurs in 2005 because in the base year both nominal GDP and real GDP measure the same output at 2005 prices. Note that the nominal GDP curve has risen more sharply than the real GDP curve as a result of inflation included in the nominal figures.

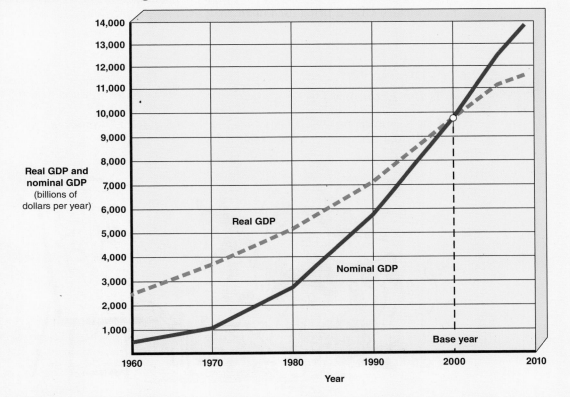

Year	(1) Nominal GDP (billions of dollars)	(2) Real GDP (billions of 2005 dollars)	(3) GDP chain price index (2005 = 100)
1960	$ 526	$ 2,831	18.60
1970	1,038	4,270	24.31
1980	2,788	5,839	47.77
1990	5,800	8,034	72.20
2000	9,951	11,226	88.64
2005	12,638	12,638	100.00
2009	14,256	12,987	109.77

SOURCES: Bureau of Economic Analysis, *National Economic Accounts,* http://www.bea.gov/national/nipaweb/SelectTable.asp?Selected=Y, Tables 1.1.5, 1.1.6, and *Economic Report of the President,* http://www.gpoaccess.gov/eop/, Table B-7.

purchasing power of the dollar to fall. In years before 2005, the GDP chain price index was less than 100, which means the real purchasing power of the dollar was higher relative to the 2005 base year. At the base year of 2005, nominal and real GDP are identical, and the GDP price index equals 100.

The graph in Exhibit 10 traces real GDP and nominal GDP for the U.S. economy since 1960. Note that nominal GDP usually grows faster than real GDP because inflation is included in the nominal figures. For example, if we calculate the economy's average growth rate in nominal GDP between 1990 and 2000, we find it was 7.2 percent. If instead we calculate average real GDP growth between the same years, we find the growth rate was 4.0 percent. You must, therefore, was pay attention to which GDP is being used in an analysis.

CHECKPOINT

Is the Economy Up or Down?

One person reports, "GDP rose this year by 8.5 percent." Another says, "GDP fell by 0.5 percent." Can both reports be right?

Drawing by Lorenz; © 1972 *The New Yorker Magazine, Inc.*

"And so, extrapolating from the best figures available, we see that current trends, unless dramatically reversed, will inevitably lead to a situation in which the sky will fall."

Key Concepts

Gross domestic product (GDP)
Transfer payment
Final goods
Intermediate goods
Circular flow model
Flow

Stock
Expenditure approach
Income approach
Indirect business taxes
National income (NI)
Personal income (PI)

Disposable personal
  income (DI)
Nominal GDP
Real GDP
GDP chain price index

Summary

- *Gross domestic product (GDP)* is the most widely used measure of a nation's economic performance. GDP is the market value of all *final goods* produced in the United States during a period of time, regardless of who owns the factors of production. Secondhand and financial transactions are not counted in GDP. To avoid double counting, GDP also does not include *intermediate goods*. GDP is calculated by either the expenditure approach or the income approach.

- The *circular flow model* is a diagram representing the flow of products and resources between businesses and households in exchange for money payments. *Flows* must be distinguished from *stocks*. Flows are measured in units per time period—for example, dollars per year. Stocks are quantities that exist at a given point in time measured in dollars.

Circular Flow Model

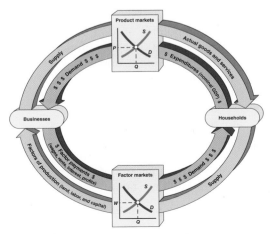

- The *expenditure approach* sums the four major spending components of GDP: consumption, investment, government spending, and net exports. Algebraically, $GDP = C + I + G + (X - M)$, where X equals foreign spending for domestic exports and M equals domestic spending for foreign products.

- The *income approach* sums the major income components of GDP, consisting of compensation of employees, rents, profits, net interest, *indirect business taxes*, and depreciation. Indirect business taxes are levied as a percentage of product prices and include sales taxes, excise taxes, and customs duties.

- *National income (NI)* is total income *earned* by households who own and supply resources. It is calculated as GDP minus depreciation.

- *Personal income (PI)* is the total income *received* by households and is calculated as NI minus corporate taxes and Social Security taxes plus transfer payments and other income.

- *Disposable personal income (DI)* is personal income minus personal taxes. DI is the amount of income a household has available to consume or save.

Measures of the Macro Economy

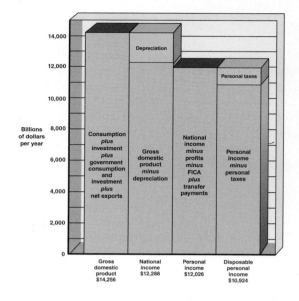

- *Nominal GDP* measures all final goods and services produced in a given time period, valued at the prices existing during the time period of production.
- *Real GDP* measures all final goods and services produced in a given time period, valued at the prices existing in a base year.
- The *GDP chain price index* is a broad price index used to convert nominal GDP to real GDP. The GDP chain price index measures changes in the prices of consumer goods, business investment, government spending, exports, and imports. Real GDP is computed by dividing nominal GDP for year X by year X's GDP chain price index and then multiplying the result by 100.

Summary of Conclusion Statements

- GDP is a quantitative, rather than a qualitative measure of the output of goods and services.
- It can be argued that GDP understates national well-being because no allowance is made for people working fewer hours than they once did.

- If the underground economy is sizable, GDP will understate an economy's performance.
- Since the costs of negative by-products are not deducted, GDP overstates the national well-being.

Study Questions and Problems

1. Which of the following are final goods or services, and which are intermediate goods or services?
   a. A haircut purchased from a hair salon
   b. A new automobile
   c. An oil filter purchased in a new automobile
   d. Crude oil

2. Using the basic circular flow model, explain why the value of businesses' output of goods and services equals the income of households.

3. A small economy produced the following final goods and services during a given month:

3 million pounds of food, 50,000 shirts, 20 houses, 50,000 hours of medical services, 1 automobile plant, and 2 tanks. Calculate the value of this output at the following market prices:
- $1 per pound of food
- $20 per shirt
- $50,000 per house
- $20 per hour of medical services
- $1 million per automobile plant
- $500,000 per tank

4. An economy produces final goods and services with a market value of $5,000 billion in a

given year, but only $4,500 billion worth of goods and services is sold to domestic or foreign buyers. Is this nation's GDP $5,000 billion or $4,500 billion? Explain your answer.

5. Explain why a new forklift sold for use in a warehouse is a final good even though it is fixed investment (capital) used to produce other goods. Is there a double-counting problem if this sale is added to GDP?

6. Explain why the government spending (*G*) component of GDP falls short of actual government expenditures.

7. Explain how net exports affect the U.S. economy. Describe both positive and negative impacts on GDP. Why do national income accountants use net exports to compute GDP, rather than simply adding exports to the other expenditure components of GDP?

8. Suppose the data in Exhibit 11 are for a given year from the annual Economic Report of the President. Calculate GDP, using the expenditure and the income approaches.

9. Using the data in Exhibit 11, compute national income (NI) by making the required subtraction from GDP. Explain why NI might be a better measure of economic performance than GDP.

10. Again using the data from Exhibit 11, derive personal income (PI) from national income (NI). Then make the required adjustments to PI to obtain disposable personal income (DI).

11. Suppose U.S. nominal GDP increases from one year to the next year. Can you conclude that these figures present a misleading measure of economic growth? What alternative method would provide a more accurate measure of the rate of growth?

12. Which of the following are counted in this year's GDP? Explain your answer in each case.
    a. Flashy Car Company sold a used car.
    b. Juanita Jones cooked meals for her family.

Exhibit 11	National Income Data

	Amount (billions of dollars)
Corporate profits	$ 305
Depreciation	479
Gross private domestic investment	716
Personal taxes	565
Personal saving	120
Government spending	924
Imports	547
Net interest	337
Compensation of employees	2,648
Rental income	19
Exports	427
Personal consumption expenditures	2,966
Indirect business taxes	370
Contributions for Social Security (FICA)	394
Transfer payments and other income	967
Proprietors' income	328

c. IBM paid interest on its bonds.
d. José Suarez purchased 100 shares of IBM stock.
e. Bob Smith received a welfare payment.
f. Carriage Realty earned a brokerage commission for selling a previously owned house.
g. The government makes interest payments to persons holding government bonds.
h. Air and water pollution increase.
i. Gambling is legalized in all states.
j. A retired worker receives a Social Security payment.

13. Explain why comparing the GDPs of various nations might not tell you which nations are better off.

For Online Exercises, go to the Tucker Web site at www.cengage.com/economics/tucker.

CHECKPOINT ANSWERS

How Much Does Mario Add to GDP?

Measuring GDP by the expenditure approach, Mario's output production is worth $60,000 because consumers purchased 4,000 pizzas at $15 each. Transfer payments and purchases of goods produced in other years are excluded from GDP. The $3,000 in unemployment compensation received and the $5,000 spent for a used car are therefore not counted in GDP. Mario's income of $15,000 is also not counted using the expenditure approach. If you said, using the expenditure approach to measure GDP, Mario contributed $60,000 to GDP, **YOU ARE CORRECT.**

Is the Economy Up or Down?

Between 1973 and 1974, for example, nominal GDP rose from $1,382 to $1,500 billion—an 8.5 percent increase. During the same period, real GDP fell from $4,917 to $4,890 billion—a 0.5 percent decrease. If you said both reports can be correct because of the difference between nominal and real GDP, **YOU ARE CORRECT.**

Practice Quiz

For an explanation of the correct answers, visit the Tucker Web site at www.cengage.com/economics/tucker.

1. The dollar value of all final goods and services produced within the borders of a nation is
   a. GNP deflator.
   b. gross national product.
   c. net domestic product.
   d. gross domestic product.

2. Based on the circular flow model, money flows from businesses to households in
   a. factor markets.
   b. product markets.
   c. neither factor nor product markets.
   d. both factor and product markets.

3. The circular flow model does not include which of the following?
   a. The quantity of shoes in inventory on January 1.
   b. The total wages paid per month.
   c. The percentage of profits paid out as dividends each year.
   d. The total profits earned per year in the U.S. economy.

4. The expenditure approach measures GDP by adding all the expenditures for final goods made by
   a. households.
   b. businesses.
   c. government.
   d. foreigners.
   e. all of the above.

5. GDP is a less-than-perfect measure of the nation's economic pulse because it
   a. excludes nonmarket transactions.
   b. does not measure the quality of goods and services.
   c. does not report illegal transactions.
   d. all of the above are true.

6. Subtracting an allowance for depreciation of fixed capital from gross domestic product yields
   a. real GDP.
   b. nominal GDP.
   c. personal income.
   d. national income.

Practice Quiz Continued

7. Adding all incomes earned by households from the sale of resources yields
   a. intermediate goods.
   b. indirect business taxes.
   c. national income.
   d. personal income.

8. Personal income equals disposable income plus
   a. personal savings.
   b. transfer payments.
   c. dividend payments.
   d. personal taxes.

9. Disposable personal income
   a. is the income people spend for personal items, such as homes and cars.
   b. includes transfer payments.
   c. excludes transfer payments.
   d. includes personal taxes.

10. Which of the following statements is *true*?
    a. National income is total income *earned* by households whereas personal income is total income *received* by households.
    b. Disposable personal income equals personal income minus personal taxes.
    c. The expenditure approach and the income approach yield the same GDP figure.
    d. All of the above are true.

11. Gross domestic product data that reflect actual prices as they exist in a given year are expressed in terms of
    a. fixed dollars.
    b. current dollars.
    c. constant dollars.
    d. real dollars.

12. The GDP chain price index is
    a. widely reported in the news.
    b. broadly based.
    c. adjusted for government spending.
    d. a measure of changes in consumer prices.

13. Which of the following statements is *true*?
    a. The inclusion of intermediate goods and services in GDP calculations would underestimate our nation's production level.
    b. The expenditure approach sums the compensation of employees, rents, profits, net interest, and nonincome expenses for depreciation and indirect business taxes.
    c. Real GDP has been adjusted for changes in the general level of prices due to inflation or deflation.
    d. Real GDP equals nominal GDP multiplied by the GDP deflator.

14. Which of the following is a shortcoming of GDP?
    a. GDP measures nonmarket transactions.
    b. GDP includes an estimate of illegal transactions.
    c. GDP includes an estimate of the value of household services.
    d. None of the above are true.

15. Which of the following items is included in the calculation of GDP?
    a. Purchase of 100 shares of General Motors stock
    b. Purchase of a used car
    c. The value of a homemaker's services
    d. Sale of Gulf War military surplus
    e. None of the above would be included.

appendix to chapter

5

A Four-Sector Circular Flow Model

Sound the trumpets! This exhibit is going to put all the puzzle pieces together. Exhibit A-1 presents a more complex circular flow model by adding three sectors: financial markets, government, and foreign markets. In addition to the spending of households for the output of firms shown in the simplified model in Exhibit 1, these additions add three *leakages* from the amount of income paid to households. First, part of households' income is saved. Second, part of it is taxed. Third, part of the income is spent on imports. On the other hand, this model includes three sources of spending *injections* for firms' output other than from households. First, firms purchase new plants, equipment, and inventories (investment) from other firms. Second, government consumption purchases are for goods and services from firms. Third, foreigners purchase exports from the firms.

Exhibit A-1	**The Circular Flow Model of an Open Economy**

This exhibit presents a circular flow model for an economy, such as the United States, that engages in international trade. The theoretical model includes links between the product and factor markets in the domestic economy and the financial markets, government, and foreign economies. To simplify the model, only dollar payments are shown for the foreign sector.

Business Cycles and Unemployment

The headline in the morning newspaper reads, "The Economy is in Deep Recession." Later in the day, a radio announcer begins the news by saying, "The unemployment rate rose for the tenth consecutive month." On television, the evening news broadcasts an interview with several economists who predict that the slump will last for another year. Next, a presidential candidate appears on the screen and says, "It's time for change," and the media are abuzz with speculation on the political implications. The growth rate of the economy and the unemployment rate are headline-catching news. Indeed, these measures of macroeconomic instability are important because they affect your future. When real GDP rises and the economy

"booms," jobs are more plentiful. A fall in real GDP means a "bust" because the economy forces some firms into bankruptcy and workers lose their jobs. Not being able to find a job when you want one is a painful experience not easily forgotten.

This chapter looks behind the macro economy at a story that touches each of us. It begins by discussing the business cycle. How are the expansions and contractions of business cycles measured? And what causes the business cycle roller coaster? Finally, you will learn what the types of unemployment are, what "full employment" is, and what the monetary, nonmonetary, and demographic costs of unemployment are.

In this chapter, you will learn to solve these economics puzzles:

* What is the difference between a recession and a depression?

* Is a worker who has given up searching for work counted as unemployed?

* Can an economy produce more output than its potential?

THE BUSINESS-CYCLE ROLLER COASTER

A central concern of macroeconomics is the upswings and downswings in the level of real output called the **business cycle**. The business cycle consists of alternating periods of economic growth and contraction. Business cycles are inherent in market economies. A key measure of cycles is the rise and fall in real GDP, which mirrors changes in employment and other key measures of the macro economy. Recall from the previous chapter that changes in real GDP measure changes in the value of national output, while ignoring changes in the price level.

The Four Phases of the Business Cycle

Exhibit 1(a) illustrates a theoretical business cycle. Although business cycles vary in duration and intensity, each cycle is divided into four phases: **peak, recession, trough,** and **recovery**. The business cycle looks like a roller coaster. It begins at a peak, drops to a bottom, climbs steeply, and then reaches another peak. Once the trough is reached, the upswing starts again. Although forecasters cannot precisely predict the phases of a cycle, the economy is always operating along one of these phases. Over time, there has been a long-term upward trend with shorter-term cyclical fluctuations around the long-run trend.

Two *peaks* are illustrated in Exhibit 1(a). At each of these peaks, the economy is close to or at full employment. That is, as explained in Chapter 2, the economy is operating near its production possibilities curve, and real GDP is at its highest level relative to recent years. A macro setback called a *recession* or *contraction* follows each peak. A recession is a downturn in the business cycle during which real GDP declines, business profits fall, the percentage of the workforce without jobs rises, and production capacity is underutilized. A general rule is that a recession consists of at least two consecutive quarters (six months) in which there is a decline in real GDP. Stated differently, during a recession, the economy is functioning inside and farther away from its production possibilities curve.

What is the difference between a *recession* and a *depression*? According to the old saying: "A recession is when your neighbor loses his or her job, and a depression is when you also lose your job!" This one-liner is close to the true distinction between these two concepts. The answer is: Because no subsequent recession has

---

Business cycle

Alternating periods of economic growth and contraction, which can be measured by changes in real GDP.

Peak

The phase of the business cycle in which real GDP reaches its maximum after rising during a recovery.

Recession

A downturn in the business cycle during which real GDP declines and the unemployment rate rises. Also called a *contraction*.

Trough

The phase of the business cycle in which real GDP reaches its minimum after falling during a recession.

Recovery

An upturn in the business cycle during which real GDP rises. Also called an *expansion*.

Exhibit 1   Hypothetical and Actual Business Cycles

Part (a) illustrates a hypothetical business cycle consisting of four phases: peak, recession, trough, and recovery. These fluctuations of real GDP can be measured by a growth trend line, which shows that over time real GDP has trended upward. In reality, the fluctuations are not so clearly defined as those in this graph.

Part (b) illustrates actual ups and downs of the business cycle. After a recession during 2001, an upswing continued until another recession began in 2007.

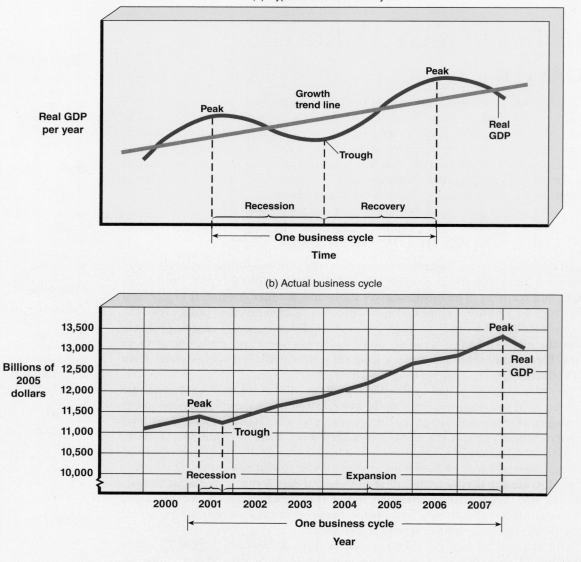

(a) Hypothetical business cycle

(b) Actual business cycle

SOURCE: Bureau of Economic Analysis, National Income Accounts, http://www.bea.gov/national/nipaweb/SelectTable.asp?Selected=Y, Table 1.1.6.

Exhibit 2	**Severity of Post-World War II Recessions**		
Recession dates	**Duration (months)**	**Percentage decline in real GDP**	**Peak unemployment rate**
Nov. 1948–Oct. 1949	11	−1.7%	7.9%
July 1953–May 1954	10	−2.7	5.9
Aug. 1957–Apr. 1958	8	−1.2	7.4
Apr. 1960–Feb. 1961	10	−1.6	6.9
Dec. 1969–Nov. 1970	11	−0.6	5.9
Nov. 1973–Mar. 1975	16	−3.1	8.6
Jan. 1980–July 1980	6	−2.2	7.8
July 1981–Nov. 1982	16	−2.9	10.8
July 1990–Mar. 1991	8	−1.3	6.8
Mar. 2001–Nov. 2001	8	−0.5	5.6
Dec. 2007–	—	—	—
Average	**10**	**−1.8**	**7.4**

SOURCE: National Bureau of Economic Research, Business Cycle Expansion and Contractions, http://www.nber.org/cycles/cyclesmain.html. Real GDP and unemployment rate data added by author.

approached the prolonged severity of the Great Depression from 1929 to 1933, the term *depression* is primarily a historical reference to this extremely deep and long recession. The Great Depression is discussed at the end of this chapter, the chapter on aggregate demand and supply, and the chapter on monetary policy.

The *trough* is where the level of real GDP "bottoms out." At the trough, unemployment and idle productive capacity are at their highest levels relative to recent years. The length of time between the peak and the trough is the duration of the recession. Since the end of World War II, recessions in the United States have averaged 10 months. As shown in Exhibit 2, the previous recession lasted eight months from March 2001 to November 2001. The percentage decline in real GDP was 0.5 percent, and the national unemployment rate hit a high of 5.6 percent. Compared to the averages for previous recessions, the 2001 recession was mild. The latest recession began in December 2007 and it is the longest recession since the Great Depression, which lasted 43 months.

The trough is both bad news and good news. It is simultaneously the bottom of the "valley" of the downturn and the foot of the "hill" of improving economic conditions called a *recovery* or *expansion*. A recovery is an upturn in the business cycle during which real GDP rises. During the recovery phase of the cycle, profits generally improve, real GDP increases, and employment moves toward full employment.

Exhibit 1(b) illustrates an actual business cycle by plotting the movement of real GDP in the United States from 2000 to 2007. The economy's initial peak, recession, and trough occurred in 2001 and a strong recovery phase lasted until a second peak in 2007. The National Bureau of Economic Research's Business Cycle Dating Committee determined that the U.S. economy entered a recession in March 2001 and the recession ended in November 2001. This committee is composed of six economists who decide on the beginning and ending dates for a recession based on monthly data rather than real GDP because real GDP is measured quarterly and subject to large revisions. Factors that the committee considers in defining a recession include decline in employment, industrial production, income, and sales. This committee will also determine when the recession beginning in December 2007 ends.

Finally, we will now expand the definition of **economic growth** given in Chapter 2. Economic growth is an expansion in national output measured by the annual percentage increase in a nation's real GDP. The growth trend line in the hypothetical model in Exhibit 1(a) illustrates that over time our real GDP tends to rise. This general, long-term upward trend in real GDP persists in spite of the peaks, recessions, troughs, and recoveries. As shown by the dashed line in Exhibit 3, since 1930 real GDP in the United States has grown at an average annual rate of 3.5 percent. This annual change may seem small, but about 3 percent annual growth will lead to a doubling of real GDP in only 24 years. One of our challenging policy goals is to maintain or increase that growth rate.

Economic growth

An expansion in national output measured by the annual percentage increase in a nation's real GDP.

Exhibit 3 — A Historical Record of Business Cycles in the United States, 1929–2009

Real GDP has increased at an average annual growth rate of 3.5 percent since 1930. Above-average annual growth rates have alternated with below-average annual growth rates. During the Great Recession beginning in 2007, the annual growth rate was a negative 2.4 percent in 2009 and therefore below the zero growth line.

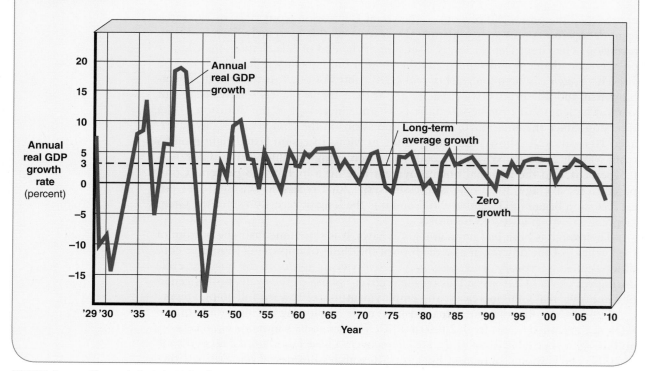

SOURCE: Bureau of Economic Analysis, National Economic Accounts, http://www.bea.gov/national/nipaweb/SelectTable.asp?Selected=Y, Table 1.1.6.

> **CONCLUSION** *We value economic growth as one of our nation's economic goals because it increases our standard of living—it creates a bigger "economic pie."*

Closer examination of Exhibit 3 reveals that the growth path of the U.S. economy over time is not a smooth, rising trend, but instead a series of year-to-year variations in real GDP growth. In 1991, for example, the economy was in recession and slipped below the zero growth line (negative growth). During the Great Recession beginning in 2007, the growth rate was again a negative 2.4 percent in 2009. In fact, in the first quarter of 2009, the economy contracted at a −6.4 percent pace, which was the worst slide in a quarter century.

CHECKPOINT

Where Are We on the Business-Cycle Roller Coaster?

Suppose the economy is in a recession and everyone is asking when the economy will recover. To find an answer to the state of the economy's health, a television reporter interviews Terrence Carter, a local car dealer. Carter says, "I do not see any recovery. The third quarter of this year we sold more cars than the second quarter, but sales in these two quarters were far below the first quarter." Is Mr. Carter correct? Are his observations consistent with the peak, recession, trough, or recovery phase of the business cycle?

Real GDP Growth Rates in Other Countries

Exhibit 4 presents real GDP growth rates for selected countries in 2009. China and India had the largest rates of growth at 8.5 and 5.4 percent, respectively. The United States was in recession with a −2.4 percent growth rate and the growth rates of other countries throughout the world were also negative.

Global Economics

Business-Cycle Indicators

In addition to changes in real GDP, the media often report several other macro variables that measure business activity and are published by the U.S. Department of Commerce in *Business Conditions Digest*. These economic *indicator* variables are classified in three categories: leading indicators, coincident indicators, and lagging indicators. Exhibit 5 lists the variables corresponding to each indicator series.

The government's chief forecasting gauge for business cycles is the index of leading indicators. Leading indicators are variables that change before real GDP changes. This index captures the headlines when there is concern over swings in the economy. The first set of 10 variables in Exhibit 5 is used to forecast the business cycle months in advance. For example, a slump ahead is signaled when declines exceed advances in the components of the leading indicators data series. But beware! The leading indicators may rise for two consecutive months and then fall for the next three consecutive months. Economists are therefore cautious and

Leading indicators

Variables that change before real GDP changes.

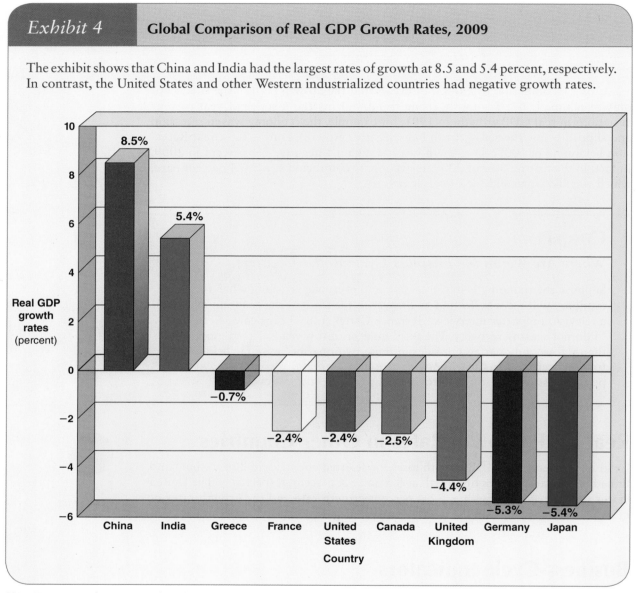

Exhibit 4   **Global Comparison of Real GDP Growth Rates, 2009**

The exhibit shows that China and India had the largest rates of growth at 8.5 and 5.4 percent, respectively. In contrast, the United States and other Western industrialized countries had negative growth rates.

SOURCE: International Monetary Fund, World Economic Outlook Database, http://www.imf.org/external/ns/cs.aspx?id=28.

wait for the leading indicators to move in a new direction for several months before forecasting a change in the cycle.

Is a recession near or when will a recession end? The Conference Board's Consumer Confidence Index is often reported in the news as a key measure of the economy's health. It is based on a survey of 5,000 households who are asked their expectations of how well the economy will perform over the next six months. Prolonged consumer pessimism can result in less consumer spending and contribute to slowing economic growth. Stated differently, persistent consumer pessimism can result in lower personal consumption expenditures (*C*) and business investment (*I*) because businesses reduce investment when consumers' purchases of their products fall.

Exhibit 5	**Business-Cycle Indicators**

Leading indicators	
Average workweek	New building permits
Unemployment claims	Stock prices
New consumer goods orders	Money supply
Delayed deliveries	Interest rates
New orders for plant and equipment	Consumer expectations

Coincident indicators	**Lagging indicators**
Nonagricultural payrolls	Unemployment rate
Personal income minus transfer payments	Duration of unemployment
Industrial production	Labor cost per unit of output
Manufacturing and trade sales	Consumer price index for services
	Commercial and industrial loans
	Consumer credit to personal income ratio
	Prime rate

The second data series of variables listed in Exhibit 5 are four **coincident indicators**. Coincident indicators are variables that change at the same time that real GDP changes. For example, as real GDP rises, economists expect employment, personal income, industrial production, and sales to rise.

The third group of variables listed in Exhibit 5 are **lagging indicators**. Lagging indicators are seven variables that change after real GDP changes. For example, the duration of unemployment is a lagging indicator. As real GDP increases, the average time workers remain unemployed does not fall until some months after the beginning of the recovery.

Coincident indicators

Variables that change at the same time that real GDP changes.

Lagging indicators

Variables that change after real GDP changes.

TOTAL SPENDING AND THE BUSINESS CYCLE

The uneven historical pattern of economic growth for the U.S. economy gives rise to the following question: What causes business cycles? The theory generally accepted by economists today is that changes in total or aggregate expenditures are the cause of variations in real GDP. Recall from the previous chapter that aggregate expenditures refer to total spending for *final goods* by households, businesses, government, and foreign buyers. Expressed as a formula:

$$GDP = C + I + G + (X - M)$$

Why do changes in total spending cause the level of GDP to change? Stated simply, if total spending increases, businesses find it profitable to increase output. When firms increase production, they use more land, labor, and capital. Hence, increased spending leads to economic growth in output, employment, and incomes. When total spending falls, businesses find it profitable to produce a lower volume of goods and avoid accumulating unsold inventory. In this case, output, employment, and incomes fall. These cutbacks, in turn, can lead to a recession.

The situation just described assumes the economy is operating below full employment. Once the economy reaches full employment, increases in total spending have no impact on real GDP. Further spending in this case will simply pull up the price level and "inflate" nominal GDP.

In subsequent chapters, much more will be explained about the causes of business cycles. Using aggregate demand and supply curves, you will learn to analyze why changes occur in national output, unemployment, and the price level.

UNEMPLOYMENT

Since the abyss of the Great Depression, a major economic goal of the United States has been to achieve a high level of employment. The Employment Act of 1946 declared it the responsibility of the federal government to use all practical means consistent with free competitive enterprise to create conditions under which all able individuals who are willing to work and seeking work will be afforded useful employment opportunities. Later, Congress amended this act with the Full Employment and Balanced Growth Act of 1978, which established specific goals for unemployment and the level of prices.

Each month the Bureau of Labor Statistics (BLS) of the U.S. Department of Labor, in conjunction with the Bureau of the Census, conducts a survey of a random sample of about 60,000 households in the United States. Each member of the household who is 16 years of age or older is asked whether he or she is employed or unemployed. If a person works at least 1 hour per week for pay or at least 15 hours per week as an unpaid worker in a family business, he or she is counted as employed. If the person is not employed, the question then is whether he or she has looked for work in the last month. If so, the person is said to be unemployed. Based on its survey data, the BLS publishes the **unemployment rate** and other employment-related statistics monthly.

The unemployment rate is the percentage of people in the **civilian labor force** who are without jobs and are actively seeking jobs. But who is actually counted as an unemployed worker, and which people belong to the labor force? Certainly, all people without jobs are not classified as unemployed. Babies, full-time students, and retired persons are not counted as unemployed. Likewise, individuals who are ill or severely disabled are not included as unemployed. And there are other groups not counted.

Turn to Exhibit 6. The *civilian labor force* is the number of people 16 years of age and over who are either employed or unemployed, excluding members of the armed forces and other groups listed in the "persons not in labor force" category. Based on survey data, the BLS computes the *civilian unemployment rate* using the following formula:

$$\text{Unemployment rate} = \frac{\text{unemployed}}{\text{civilian labor force}} \times 100$$

Unemployment rate

The percentage of people in the civilian labor force who are without jobs and are actively seeking jobs.

Civilian labor force

The number of people 16 years of age and older who are employed or who are actively seeking a job, excluding armed forces, homemakers, discouraged workers, and other persons not in the labor force.

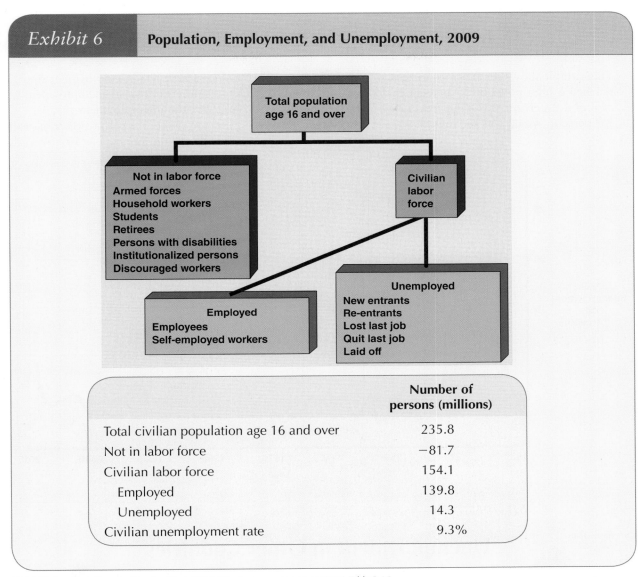

Exhibit 6   **Population, Employment, and Unemployment, 2009**

	Number of persons (millions)
Total civilian population age 16 and over	235.8
Not in labor force	−81.7
Civilian labor force	154.1
Employed	139.8
Unemployed	14.3
Civilian unemployment rate	9.3%

SOURCE: Economic Report of the President, 2010, http://www.gpoaccess.gov/eop/, Table B-35.

In 2009, the unemployment rate was

$$9.3\% = \frac{14.3 \text{ million persons}}{154.1 \text{ million persons}} \times 100$$

Exhibit 7 charts a historical record of the U.S. unemployment rate since 1929. Note that the highest unemployment rate reached was 25 percent in 1933 during the Great Depression. At the other extreme, the lowest unemployment rate we have attained was 1.2 percent in 1944. During the current recession, the unemployment rate was 9.3 percent in 2009, which was the highest annual rate since 1982.

| *Exhibit 7* | **The U.S. Unemployment Rate, 1929–2009** |

This exhibit shows fluctuations in the civilian unemployment rate since 1929. The unemployment rate reached a high point of 25 percent in 1933 during the Great Depression. The lowest unemployment rate of 1.2 percent was achieved during World War II in 1944. In 2009, the unemployment rate was 9.3 percent, which was the highest annual rate since 1982.

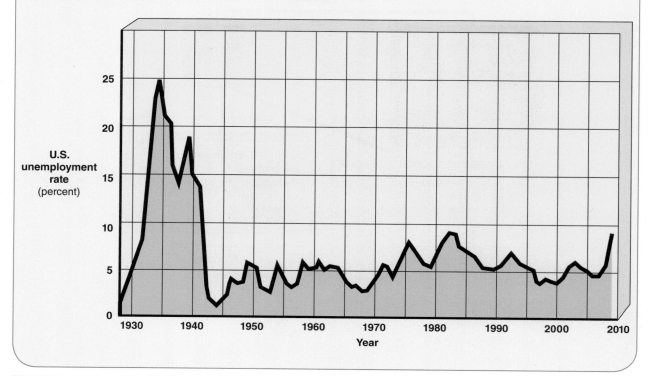

SOURCE: Economic Report of the President, 2010, http://www.gpoaccess.gov/eop/, Table B-35.

Global Economics

Unemployment in Other Countries

Exhibit 8 shows unemployment rates for selected countries in 2009. Spain and other major industrialized countries had unemployment rates higher than the United States. The U.S. unemployment rate was 9.3 percent, while France, Canada, and Japan had lower rates.

Unemployment Rate Criticisms

Discouraged worker

A person who wants to work, but who has given up searching for work because he or she believes there will be no job offers.

The unemployment rate is criticized for both understating and overstating the "true" unemployment rate. An example of *overstating* the unemployment rate occurs when respondents to the BLS survey falsely report they are seeking employment. The motivation may be that their eligibility for unemployment compensation or welfare benefits depends on actively pursuing a job. Or possibly an individual is "employed" in illegal activities.

The other side of the coin is that the official definition of unemployment *understates* the unemployment rate by not counting so-called discouraged workers.

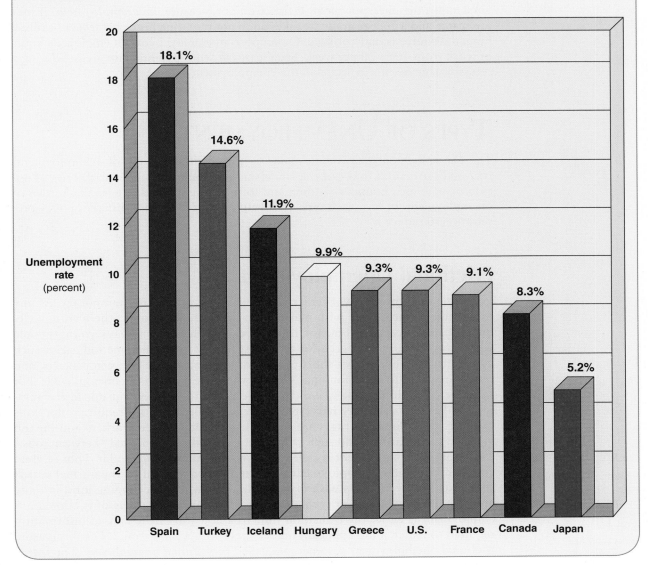

Exhibit 8 **Unemployment Rates for Selected Nations, 2009**

In 2009, the major industrialized nations shown had a higher unemployment rate than the United States. The United States had an unemployment rate of 9.3 percent, while France, Canada, and Japan had lower rates.

SOURCE: OECD Economic Outlook, No. 86, http://www.oecd.org, Annex Table 18.

A discouraged worker is a person who wants to work, but has given up searching for work because he or she believes there will be no job offers. After repeated rejections, discouraged workers often turn to their families, friends, and public welfare for support. The BLS counts a discouraged worker as anyone who has looked for work within the last 12 months, but is no longer actively looking. The BLS simply includes discouraged workers in the "not in labor force" category listed in Exhibit 6. Because the number of discouraged workers rises during a recession, the underestimation of the official unemployment rate increases during a downturn.

Another example of *understating* the unemployment rate occurs because the official BLS data include all part-time workers as fully employed. These workers are actually partially employed, and many would work full time if they could find full-time employment.

Finally, the unemployment statistics do not measure *underemployment*. If jobs are scarce and a college graduate takes a job not requiring his or her level of skills, a human resource is underutilized. Or suppose an employer cuts an employee's hours of work from 40 to 20 per week. Such losses of work potential are greater during a recession, but are not reflected in the unemployment rate.

TYPES OF UNEMPLOYMENT

The unemployment rate is determined by three different types of unemployment: *frictional*, *structural*, and *cyclical*. Understanding these conceptual categories of unemployment aids in understanding and formulating policies to ease the burden of unemployment. In fact, each type of unemployment requires a different policy prescription to reduce it.

Frictional Unemployment

For some unemployed workers, the absence of a job is only temporary. At any given time, some people with marketable skills are fired, and others voluntarily quit jobs to accept or look for new ones. And there are always young people who leave school and search for their first job. Workers in some industries such as construction experience short periods of unemployment between projects, and temporary layoffs are common. Other workers are "seasonally unemployed." For example, ski resort workers will be employed in the winter, but not in the summer, and certain crops are harvested "in season." Because jobs requiring the skills of these unemployed workers are available, the unemployed workers and the job vacancies are matched and such workers are therefore considered "between jobs." This type of unemployment is called **frictional unemployment**, and it is not of great concern. Frictional unemployment is unemployment caused by the normal search time required by workers with marketable skills who are changing jobs, initially entering the labor force, or reentering the labor force. The cause of frictional unemployment is either the transition time to a new job or the lack of information required to match a job applicant immediately with a job vacancy. For this reason, frictional unemployment is sometimes called *transitional unemployment* or *search unemployment*.

The fact that job market information is imperfect and operates with "friction" causes frictional unemployment in the economy. Because it takes time to search for the information required to match employer and employees, some workers will always be frictionally unemployed. Frictional unemployment is therefore a normal condition in an economic system permitting freedom of job choice. Improved methods of distributing job information through job listings

Frictional unemployment

Unemployment caused by the normal search time required by workers with marketable skills who are changing jobs, initially entering the labor force, reentering the labor force, or seasonally unemployed.

on the Internet help unemployed workers find jobs more quickly and reduce frictional unemployment.

Structural Unemployment

Unlike frictional unemployment, **structural unemployment** is not a short-term situation. Instead, it is long-term, or possibly permanent unemployment resulting from the nonexistence of jobs for unemployed workers. Structural unemployment is unemployment caused by a mismatch of the skills of workers who are out of work and the skills required for existing job opportunities. Note that changing jobs and lack of job information are *not* problems for structurally unemployed workers. Unlike frictionally unemployed workers who have marketable skills, structurally unemployed workers require additional education or retraining. Changes in the structure of the economy create the following three cases of structural unemployment.

> **Structural unemployment**
>
> Unemployment caused by a mismatch of the skills of workers out of work and the skills required for existing job opportunities.

First, workers may face joblessness because they lack the education or the job-related skills to perform available jobs. This type of structural unemployment particularly affects teenagers and minority groups, but other groups of workers can be affected as well. For example, environmental concerns, such as protecting the spotted owl by restricting trees from being cut, cost some loggers their jobs. Reducing such structural unemployment requires retraining loggers for new jobs as, say, forest rangers. Another example involves the "peace dividend" from the reduction in defense spending after a war. This situation creates structural unemployment for discharged military personnel who require retraining after a war for, say, teaching, nursing, or police jobs.

Second, the consuming public may decide to increase the demand for Porsches and decrease the demand for Chevrolet Corvettes. This shift in demand would cause U.S. auto workers who lose their jobs in Bowling Green, Kentucky, to become structurally unemployed. To regain employment, these unemployed autoworkers must retrain and find job openings in other industries, for example, manufacturing IBM computer printers in North Carolina.

Third, implementation of the latest technology may also increase the pool of structural unemployment in a particular industry and region. For example, the U.S. textile industry, located primarily in the South, can fight less expensive foreign textile imports by installing modern machinery. This new capital may replace textile workers. But suppose these unemployed textile workers do not wish to move to a new location where new types of jobs are available. The costs of moving, fear of the unknown, and family ties are understandable reasons for reluctance to move, and instead, the workers become structurally unemployed.

There are many causes of structural unemployment, including poor schools, new products, new technology, foreign competition, geographic differences, restricted entry into jobs, and shifts in government priorities. Because of the numerous sources of mismatching between skills and jobs, economists consider a certain level of structural unemployment inevitable. Public and private programs that train employees to fill existing job openings decrease structural unemployment. Conversely, one of the concerns about the minimum wage is that it may contribute to structural unemployment. In Exhibit 6 of Chapter 4, we demonstrated that a minimum wage set by legislation above the equilibrium wage causes unemployment. One approach intended to offset such undesirable effects of the minimum wage is a subminimum wage paid during a training period to give employers an incentive to hire unskilled workers.

Cyclical Unemployment

Cyclical unemployment

Unemployment caused by the lack of jobs during a recession.

Cyclical unemployment is directly attributable to the lack of jobs caused by the business cycle. Cyclical unemployment is unemployment caused by the lack of jobs during a recession. When real GDP falls, companies close, jobs disappear, and workers scramble for fewer available jobs. Similar to the game of musical chairs, there are not enough chairs (jobs) for the number of players (workers) in the game.

The Great Depression is a dramatic example of cyclical unemployment. There was a sudden decline in consumption, investment, government spending, and net exports. As a result of this striking fall in real GDP, the unemployment rate rose to about 25 percent (see Exhibit 7). Now notice what happened to the unemployment rate when real GDP rose sharply during World War II. The Great Recession beginning in 2007 is another example of cyclical unemployment. Falling home prices

CheckPoint

What Kind of Unemployment Did the Invention of the Wheel Cause?

But Egor, what about the effect on labor?

Did the invention of the wheel cause frictional, structural, or cyclical unemployment?

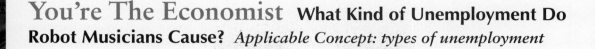

You're The Economist What Kind of Unemployment Do Robot Musicians Cause? *Applicable Concept: types of unemployment*

The following is a classic article from the late 1980s that illustrates the types of unemployment and describes a recurring labor market situation:

People looking for job security have rarely chosen the music industry. But these days, musicians say, competition from machines has removed what little stability there was. Modern machines can effectively duplicate string sections, drummers, and even horn sections, so with the exception of concerts, the jobs available to live musicians are growing fewer by the day. . . .

It is not the first time that technology has thrown a wrench into musical careers. When talking pictures helped usher in the death of vaudeville, and again, when recorded music replaced live music in radio station studios, the market for musicians took a beating from which it never fully recovered. . . . The musicians' plight is not getting universal sympathy. Some industry insiders say that the current job problems are an inevitable price of progress, and that musicians should update their skills to deal with the new instruments. . . .

But others insist that more than musicians' livelihood is at stake. Mr. Glasel, [Musicians' Union] Local 802's president, warns that unbridled computerization of music could eventually threaten the quality of music. Jobs for trumpet players, for instance, have dropped precipitously since the synthesizer managed a fair approximation of the trumpet. And without trumpet players, he asked, "where is the next generation going to get its Dizzy Gillespie?"[1]

The threat to musicians' jobs continues: The Toyota Motor Corp. unveiled its instrument-playing humanoid robots at the 2005 World Exposition. The robots played drums and horn instruments, such as trumpets and tubas. And in 2008, a humanoid robot walked on the stage, said, "Hello, everyone," lifted the baton, and conducted the Detroit Symphony Orchestra. Its timing was judged to be impeccable, but the robot conductor lacked any spur-of-the-moment emotions.

Now there is a Robot Hall of Fame at Carnegie Mellon University. The robots fall into two categories—robots from science and robots from science fiction. A panel of experts, each serving a two-year term, chooses robots in each category to be inducted into the Hall of Fame. Envelope please! The first winners were: The Unimate, the first industrial robot; the

© Image copyright Rick Lord, 2009. Used under license from Shutterstock.com

Sojourner robot from NASA's Mars Pathfinder mission; R2-D2, the "droid" from the Stars Wars films; and HAL 9000, the rogue computer from the film *2001: A Space Odyssey*.

ANALYZE THE ISSUE

1. Are the musicians experiencing frictional, structural, or cyclical unemployment? Explain.
2. What solution would you propose for the trumpet players mentioned above?

---

1. James S. Newton, "A Death Knell Sounds for Musical Jobs," *The New York Times*, March 1, 1987, sec. 3, p. 9.

and a plunge in stock prices caused households to cut back on consumption spending and in combination with a fall in business investment spending caused a negative growth rate and sharp rise in the unemployment rate to a high of 9.3 percent. To smooth out these swings in unemployment, a focus of macroeconomic policy is to moderate cyclical unemployment.

THE GOAL OF FULL EMPLOYMENT

Full employment

The situation in which an economy operates at an unemployment rate equal to the sum of the frictional and structural unemployment rates. Also called the *natural rate of unemployment.*

In this section, we take a closer look at the meaning of **full employment**, also called the *natural rate of unemployment.* Because both frictional and structural unemployment are present in good and bad times, *full employment* does not mean "zero percent unemployment." Full employment is the situation in which an economy operates at an unemployment rate equal to the sum of the frictional and structural unemployment rates. Full employment therefore is the rate of unemployment that exists without cyclical unemployment.

Unfortunately, economists cannot state with certainty what percentages of the labor force are frictionally and structurally unemployed at any particular point in time. In practice, therefore, full employment is difficult to define. Moreover, the full-employment rate of unemployment, or natural rate of unemployment, changes over time. In the 1960s, 4 percent unemployment was generally considered to represent full employment. In the 1980s, the accepted rate was 6 percent, and, currently, the consensus among economists is that the natural rate is close to 5 percent.

Several reasons are given for why full employment is not fixed. One reason is that between the early 1960s and the early 1980s, the participation of women and teenagers in the labor force increased. This change in the labor force composition increased the full-employment rate of unemployment because both women and young workers (under age 25) typically experience higher unemployment rates than men. Another frequently cited and controversial reason for the rise in the full-employment rate of unemployment is that larger unemployment compensation payments, food stamps, welfare, and Social Security benefits from the government make unemployment less painful. In the 1990s, the natural rate of unemployment declined somewhat because the entry of females and teenagers into the labor force slowed. Also, the baby boom generation has aged, and middle-aged workers have lower unemployment rates.

THE GDP GAP

GDP gap

The difference between actual real GDP and potential or full-employment real GDP.

When people in an economy are unemployed, society forfeits the production of goods and services. To determine the dollar value of how much society loses if the economy fails to reach the natural rate of unemployment, economists estimate the **GDP gap**. The GDP gap is the difference between actual real GDP and full-employment real GDP. The level of GDP that could be produced at full employment is also called *potential real GDP.* Expressed as a formula:

$$\text{GDP gap} = \text{actual real GDP} - \text{potential real GDP}$$

The GDP gap can be either positive if actual real GDP exceeds potential real GDP or negative if actual real GDP is less than potential real GDP. Because the GDP gap is calculated on the basis of the difference between GDP at the actual unemployment rate and estimated GDP at the full-employment rate of unemployment, the GDP gap measures the cost of cyclical unemployment. A positive GDP gap measures a boom in the economy when workers are employed overtime, and a negative GDP gap increases during a recession. Exhibit 9 shows the size of the GDP gap (in

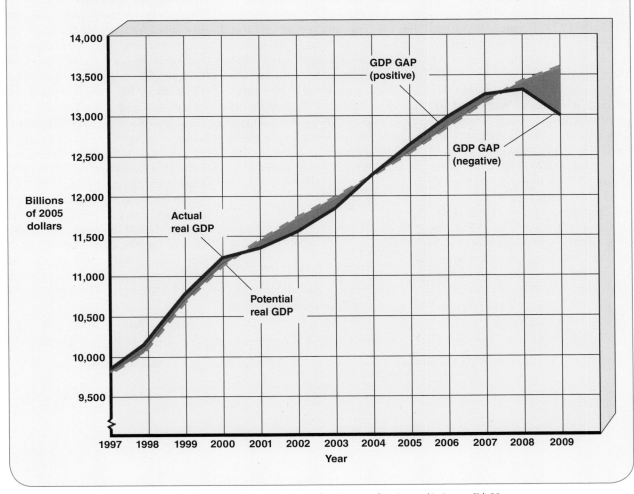

Exhibit 9   **Actual and Potential GDP, 1997–2009**

The GDP gap is the difference between actual real GDP and potential real GDP, which is based on the assumption that the economy operates at full employment. A positive GDP gap measures a boom in the economy when workers are employed overtime. Between 1997 and 2000, the U.S. economy experienced a positive GDP gap. The recession in 2001 reversed the GDP gap and the economy has operated with a negative GDP gap below its potential until 2004 when the gaps were positive through 2007. Since the recession beginning in 2007, the U. S. economy has experienced increasingly large negative GDP gaps.

SOURCE: International Monetary Fund, World Economic Outlook Database, http://www.imf.org/external/ns/cs.aspx?id=28.

You're The Economist   Brother Can You Spare a Dime?   *Applicable Concept: human costs of unemployment*

The unemployment rate does not measure the full impact of unemployment on individuals. Prolonged unemployment not only means lost wages, but it also impairs health and social relationships. The United States fought its most monstrous battle against unemployment during the Great Depression of the 1930s. Return to Exhibit 7 and note that the unemployment rate stayed at 20 percent or more from 1932 through 1935. In 1933, it reached almost 25 percent of the civilian labor force; that is, about one out of every four people who wanted to work could not. This meant 16 million Americans were out of work when our country's population was less than half its present size.[1] For comparison, at the low point of the 1990–1991 recession, about 10 million Americans were officially unemployed.

But these statistics tell only part of the horror story. Millions of workers were "discouraged workers" who had simply given up looking for work because there was no work available, and these people were not counted. People were standing in line for soup kitchens, selling apples on the street, and living in cardboard shacks. "Brother can you spare a dime?" was a common greeting. Some people jumped out of windows and others roamed the country trying valiantly to survive. John Steinbeck's great novel *The Grapes of Wrath* described millions of midwesterners who drove in caravans to California after being wiped out by drought in what became known as the Dust Bowl.

A 1992 study estimated the frightening impact of sustained unemployment that is not reflected in official unemployment data. Mary Merva, a University of Utah economist, co-authored a study of unemployment in 30 selected big cities from 1976 to 1990. This research found that a one percentage point increase in the national unemployment rate resulted in

- 6.7 percent more murders,
- 3.1 percent more deaths from stroke,
- 5.6 percent more deaths from heart disease, and
- 3.9 percent increase in suicides.[2]

Hard times during the recession of 2007 caused people to cut back on their medical care. According to a survey by the American Heart Association (AHA), 42 percent of the respondents said they trimmed health-related expenses, 32 percent skipped some preventative care such as a mammogram or annual physical, and 10 percent stopped or diminished the use of medicine for chronic conditions. And a 2009 article in *The New York Times* reported the finding in a Harvard School of Public Health survey that "workers who lost a job through no fault of their own. . . were twice as likely to report developing a new ailment like high blood pressure, diabetes or heart disease over the next year and a half, compared with people who were continuously employed."[3]

Although these estimates are subject to statistical qualifications, they underscore the notion that prolonged unemployment poses a real danger to many individuals. As people change their behavior in the face of layoffs, cutbacks, or a sudden drop in net worth, more and more Americans find themselves clinically depressed.

1. U.S. Bureau of the Census, *Historical Statistics of the United States, Colonial Times to 1957* (Washington, D.C.: U.S. Government Printing Office, 1960), Series D46–47, p. 73.
2. Robert Davis, "Recession's Cost: Lives," *USA Today*, October 16, 1992, p. 1A.
3. Roni Caryn Rabin, "Losing Job Maybe Hazardous to Health," *New York Times*, May 9, 2009, p. A11.

2005 prices) from 1997 to 2009, based on potential real GDP and actual real GDP for each of these years. Prior to the 2001 recession, the economy operated above its potential (positive GDP gap). After the 2001 recession, the economy operated below its potential (negative gap) until 2004 when the gap was positive through 2007. Since the recession beginning in 2007, the U.S. economy has experienced increasingly large negative GDP gaps. In 2009, the economy operated further below the economy's potential than at any time since 1982.

CONCLUSION *The gap between actual and potential real GDP measures the monetary losses of real goods and services to the nation from operating at less than full employment.*

Nonmonetary and Demographic Consequences of Unemployment

The burden of unemployment is more than the loss of potential output measured by the GDP gap. Unemployment also has nonmonetary costs. Some people endure unemployment pretty well because they have substantial savings to draw on, but others sink into despair. Without work, many people lose their feeling of worth. A person's self-image suffers when he or she cannot support a family and be a valuable member of society. Research has associated high unemployment with suicides, crime, mental illness, heart attacks, and other maladies. Moreover, severe unemployment causes despair, family breakups, and political unrest.

Various labor market groups share the impact of unemployment unequally. Exhibit 10 presents the unemployment rates experienced by selected demographic groups. In 2009, the overall unemployment rate was 9.3 percent, but the figures in the exhibit reveal the unequal burden by race, age, and educational attainment. First, it is interesting to note that the unemployment rate for males was greater than for females. Second, the unemployment rate for African-Americans was higher than for whites and Hispanics. Third, teenagers experienced a high unemployment rate because they are new entrants to the workforce who have little employment experience, high quit rates, and little job mobility. Again, race is a strong factor, and the unemployment rate for African-American teenagers was greater than for white teenagers. Among the explanations are discrimination; the concentration of African-Americans in the inner city, where job opportunities for less skilled (blue-collar) workers are inadequate; and the minimum wage law.

Finally, comparison of the unemployment rates in 2009 by educational attainment reveals the importance of education as an insurance policy against unemployment. Firms are much less likely to lay off a higher-skilled worker with a college education, in whom they have a greater investment in terms of training and salaries, than a worker with only a high school diploma.

Exhibit 10	Civilian Unemployment Rates by Selected Demographic Groups, 2009	
Demographic group	**Unemployment rate (percent)**	
Overall	9.3%	
Gender		
Male	10.3	
Female	8.1	
Race		
White	8.5	
Hispanic	12.1	
African-American	14.8	
Teenagers (16–19 years old)		
All	24.3	
White	21.8	
Hispanics	30.2	
African-American	39.5	
Education (25 years and over)		
Less than high school diploma	14.6	
High school graduates	9.7	
Bachelor's degree and higher	4.6	

SOURCE: Bureau of Labor Statistics, Current Population Survey, http://stats.bls.gov/cps/cpsatabs.htm, Table 1–4.

Key Concepts

Business cycle
Peak
Recession
Trough
Recovery
Economic growth

Leading indicators
Coincident indicators
Lagging indicators
Unemployment rate
Civilian labor force
Discouraged worker

Frictional unemployment
Structural unemployment
Cyclical unemployment
Full employment
GDP gap

Summary

- *Business cycles* are recurrent rises and falls in real GDP over a period of years. Business cycles vary greatly in duration and intensity. A cycle consists of four phases: peak, recession, trough, and recovery. The generally accepted theory today is that changes in the forces of demand and supply cause business cycles. A *recession* is generally defined as at least two consecutive quarters of real GDP decline. A *trough* is the turning point in national output between recession and recovery. During a *recovery*, there is an upturn in the business cycle, during which real GDP rises. A *peak* occurs when real GDP reaches its maximum level during a recovery.

Hypothetical Business Cycle

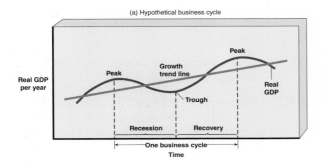

- *Economic growth* is measured by the annual percentage change in real GDP in a nation. The long-term average annual growth rate since 1930 in the United States is 3.5 percent.

- *Leading, coincident,* and *lagging indicators* are economic variables that change before, at the same time as, and after changes in real GDP, respectively.

- The *unemployment rate* is the ratio of the number of unemployed to the number in the civilian labor force multiplied by 100. The nation's **civilian labor force** consists of people who are employed plus those who are out of work, but seeking employment.

- *Discouraged workers* are a reason critics say the unemployment rate is *understated*. Discouraged workers are persons who want to work, but have given up searching for work. Another criticism of the unemployment rate is that it *overstates* unemployment because respondents can falsely report they are seeking a job.

- *Frictional, structural,* and *cyclical unemployment* are different types of unemployment. *Frictional unemployment,* including seasonal unemployment, results when workers are seeking new jobs that exist. The problem is that imperfect information prevents matching the applicants with the available jobs. *Structural unemployment* is unemployment caused by factors in the economy, including lack of skills, changes in product demand, and technological change. *Cyclical unemployment* is unemployment resulting from insufficient aggregate demand.

- *Full employment* occurs when the unemployment rate is equal to the total of the frictional and structural unemployment rates. Currently, the full-employment rate of unemployment (natural rate of unemployment) in the United States is considered to be close to 5 percent. At this rate of unemployment, the economy is producing at its maximum potential.

- The *GDP gap* is the difference between actual real GDP and full employment, or potential real GDP. Therefore, the GDP gap measures the loss of output due to cyclical unemployment.

Summary of Conclusion Statements

- We value economic growth as one of our nation's economic goals because it increases our standard of living—it creates a bigger "economic pie."

- The gap between actual and potential real GDP measures the monetary losses of real goods and services to the nation from operating at less than full employment.

Study Questions and Problems

1. What is the basic cause of the business cycle?

2. Following are real GDP figures for 10 quarters:

Quarter	Real GDP (billions of dollars)
1	$ 400
2	500
3	300
4	200
5	300
6	500
7	800
8	900
9	1,000
10	500

Plot these data points, and identify the four phases of the business cycle. Give a theory that may explain the cause of the observed business cycle. What are some of the consequences of a prolonged decline in real GDP? Is the decline in real GDP from $1,000 billion to $500 billion a recession?

3. In a given year, there are 10 million unemployed workers and 120 million employed workers in an economy. Excluding members of the armed forces and persons in institutions, and assuming these figures include only civilian workers, calculate the civilian unemployment rate.

4. Describe the relevant criteria that government statisticians use to determine whether a person is "unemployed."

5. How has the official unemployment rate been criticized for overestimating and underestimating unemployment?

6. Why is frictional unemployment inevitable in an economy characterized by imperfect job information?

7. How does structural unemployment differ from cyclical unemployment?

8. Is it reasonable to expect the unemployment rate to fall to zero for an economy? What is the relationship of frictional, structural, and cyclical unemployment to the full-employment rate of unemployment, or natural rate of unemployment?

9. In the 1960s, economists used 4 percent as their approximation for the natural rate of

unemployment. Currently, full employment is on the order of 5 percent unemployment. What is the major factor accounting for this rise?

10. Speculate on why teenage unemployment rates exceed those for the overall labor force.

11. Explain the GDP gap.

For Online Exercises, go to the Tucker Web site at www.cengage.com/economics/tucker.

CHECKPOINT ANSWERS

Where Are We on the Business-Cycle Roller Coaster?

The car dealer's sales in the first quarter conformed to the recession phase of the business cycle, and those in the second quarter to the trough. Then car sales in the third quarter were below those in the first quarter, but the increase over the second quarter indicated a recovery. If you said real GDP during a recovery can be lower than real GDP during a recession, YOU ARE CORRECT.

What Kind of Unemployment Did the Invention of the Wheel Cause?

The invention of the wheel represented a new technology for primitive people. Even in the primitive era, many workers who transported goods lost their jobs to the more efficient cart with wheels. If you said the invention of the wheel caused structural unemployment, YOU ARE CORRECT.

Practice Quiz

For an explanation of the correct answers, visit the Tucker Web site at www.cengage.com/economics/tucker.

1. The phases of a business cycle are
   a. upswing and downswing.
   b. full employment and unemployment.
   c. peak, recession, trough, and recovery.
   d. full employment, depression, expansion, and plateau.

2. The phase of a business cycle during which real GDP reaches its minimum level is the
   a. recession.
   b. depression.
   c. recovery.
   d. trough.

3. Which of the following is not a variable in the index of leading indicators?
   a. New consumer goods orders
   b. Delayed deliveries
   c. New building permits
   d. Prime rate

4. Which of the following is a coincident indicator?
   a. Personal income
   b. Industrial production
   c. Manufacturing and trade sales
   d. All of the above

5. The labor force consists of all persons
   a. 21 years of age and older.
   b. 21 years of age and older who are working.
   c. 16 years of age and older.
   d. 16 years of age and older who are working or actively seeking work.

6. People who are not working will be counted as employed if they are
   a. on vacation.
   b. absent from their job because of bad weather.

Practice Quiz Continued

c. absent from their job because of a labor dispute.
d. all of the above.

7. The number of people officially unemployed is *not* the same as the number of people who can't find a job because
   a. people who have jobs continue to look for better ones.
   b. the armed forces are included.
   c. discouraged workers are not counted.
   d. all of the above.

8. Frictional unemployment applies to
   a. workers with skills not required for existing jobs.
   b. short periods of unemployment needed to match jobs and job seekers.
   c. people who spend long periods of time out of work.
   d. unemployment related to the ups and downs of the business cycle.

9. Structural unemployment is caused by
   a. shifts in the economy that make certain job skills obsolete.
   b. temporary layoffs in industries such as construction.
   c. the impact of the business cycle on job opportunities.
   d. short-term changes in the economy.

10. Unemployment that is due to a recession is
   a. involuntary unemployment.
   b. frictional unemployment.
   c. structural unemployment.
   d. cyclical unemployment.

11. The sum of the frictional and structural unemployment rates is equal to the
   a. potential unemployment rate.
   b. actual unemployment rate.
   c. cyclical unemployment rate.
   d. full employment rate.

12. Which of the following statements is *true*?
   a. The four phases of the business cycle, in order, are peak, recovery, trough, and recession.
   b. When unemployment is rising, then real GDP is rising.

c. The economic problem typically associated with a recovery is rising unemployment.
d. Full employment exists in an economy when the unemployment rate equals the sum of frictional and structural unemployment rates.

13. Which of the following groups typically has the highest unemployment rate?
   a. White men and women as a group
   b. African-American men and women as a group
   c. Teenagers as a group
   d. Persons who completed high school

14. Which of the following statements is *true*?
   a. The GDP gap is the difference between actual real GDP and full-employment real GDP.
   b. We desire economic growth because it increases the nation's real GDP.
   c. Economic growth is measured by the annual percentage increase in a nation's real GDP.
   d. Discouraged workers are a reason critics say the unemployment rate is understated.
   e. All of the above are true.

15. The economy is considered to be at full employment when
   a. the actual rate of unemployment is less than the natural rate.
   b. the leading economic indicators are unchanged for two consecutive quarters.
   c. structural unemployment is zero.
   d. frictional plus structural unemployment is less than the natural rate.
   e. the rate of cyclical unemployment is zero.

Inflation

In addition to the goals of full employment and economic growth discussed in the previous chapter, keeping prices stable is one of the most important economic goals facing a nation. In the United States, the Great Depression of the 1930s produced profound changes in our lives. Similarly, the "Great Inflation" of the 1970s and early 1980s left memories of the miseries of inflation. In fact, every American president since Franklin Roosevelt has resolved to keep the price level stable. Politicians are aware that, as with high unemployment, voters are quick to blame any administration that fails to keep inflation rates under control.

This chapter explains what inflation is: What does it mean when a 50 percent hike in the price

of gasoline causes pain at the pump, eggs jump by 35 percent, a gallon of milk is up 23 percent, a loaf of bread climbs 16 percent, and around the world others feel the pinch of higher prices? Here you will study how the government actually measures changes in the price level and computes the rate of inflation. The chapter concludes with a discussion of the consequences and root causes of inflation. It explains who the winners are and who the losers are. For example, you will see what happened in Zimbabwe when the inflation rate reached 231,000,000 percent. After studying this chapter, you will have a much clearer understanding of why inflation is so feared.

In this chapter, you will learn to solve these economics puzzles:

- What is the inflation rate of your college education?

- Can a person's income fall even though he or she received a raise?

- What would Babe Ruth's salary be worth today?

- What is the real price of gasoline?

- Can an interest rate be negative?

- Does inflation harm everyone equally?

MEANING AND MEASUREMENT OF INFLATION

Inflation

An increase in the general (average) price level of goods and services in the economy.

Deflation

A decrease in the general (average) price level of goods and services in the economy.

After World War II, a 12-ounce bottle of Pepsi sold for 5 cents. Today, a 12-ounce can of Pepsi sells for more than 20 times that much. This is not **inflation**. Inflation is an increase in the *general* (average) price level of goods and services in the economy. Inflation's opposite is **deflation**. Deflation is a decrease in the *general* (average) price level of goods and services in the economy. Note that inflation does not mean that *all* prices of *all* products in the economy rise during a given period of time. For example, the annual percentage change in the average overall price level during the 1970s reached double digits, but the prices of pocket calculators and digital watches actually declined. The reason that the average price level rose in the 1970s was that the rising prices of Pepsi, houses, and other goods outweighed the falling prices of pocket calculators, digital watches, and other goods.

> **CONCLUSION** *Inflation is an increase in the overall average level of prices and not an increase in the price of any specific product.*

The Consumer Price Index

Consumer price index (CPI)

An index that measures changes in the average prices of consumer goods and services.

The most widely reported measure of inflation is the **consumer price index (CPI)**, which measures changes in the average prices of consumer goods and services. The CPI is sometimes called the *cost-of-living index*. It includes only consumer goods and services in order to determine how rising prices affect the income of consumers. Unlike the *GDP chain price index* explained in the previous chapter on GDP, the CPI does not consider items purchased by businesses and government.

The Bureau of Labor Statistics (BLS) of the Department of Labor prepares the CPI. Each month the bureau's "price collectors" contact retail stores, homeowners, and tenants in selected cities throughout the United States. Based on these monthly inquiries, the BLS records average prices for a "market basket" of different items purchased by the typical *urban* family. These items are included under the following categories: food, housing, apparel, transportation, medical care, entertainment, and other expenditures. Exhibit 1 presents a more detailed breakdown of these

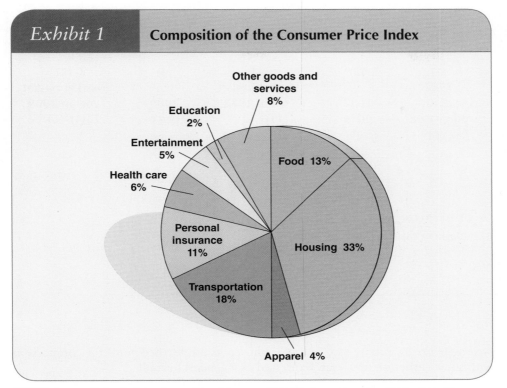

Exhibit 1	Composition of the Consumer Price Index

SOURCE: Bureau of Labor Statistics, Composition of Consumer Unit, http://www.bls.gov/cex/#tables, Table 49.

categories and shows the relative importance of each as a percentage of total expenditures. The survey reveals, for example, that 33 cents out of each consumer dollar are spent for housing and 18 cents for transportation. The composition of the market basket generally remains unchanged from one period to the next, so the CPI is called a *fixed-weight price index*. If 33 percent of consumer spending was on housing during a given base year, the assumption is that 33 percent of spending is still spent on housing in, say, 2009. Over time, particular items in the CPI change. For example, personal computers, digital cameras, and cell phones have been added. The base period is changed periodically.

How the CPI Is Computed

Exhibit 2 illustrates the basic idea behind the CPI using hypothetical data to show how this price index measures inflation. Suppose, in 1982, a typical family in the United States lived a very meager existence and purchased a market basket of only hamburgers, gasoline, and jeans. Column 1 shows the quantity purchased for each of these items, and column 2 lists the corresponding average selling price. Multiplying the price times the quantity gives the market basket cost in column 3 of each consumer product purchased in 1982. The total cost paid by our typical family for the market basket, based on 1982 prices and quantities purchased, is $245.

Years later it is 2009, and we wish to know the impact of rising prices on consumer purchases. To calculate the CPI, we determine the cost of the *same* market basket, valued at 2009 *current-year prices*, and compare this to the cost at 1982

Exhibit 2	**A Hypothetical Consumer Price Index for a Simple Economy**				

Products in consumers' market basket	(1) 1982 quantity purchased	(2) 1982 price	(3) Market basket cost in 1982 [(1)×(2)]	(4) 2009 price	(5) Market basket cost in 2009 [(1)×(4)]
Hamburgers	50	$ 0.80	$ 40	$ 1.00	$ 50
Gallons of gasoline	250	0.70	175	0.90	225
Jeans	2	15.00	30	30.00	60
			Total 1982 cost = $245		Total 2009 cost = $335

$$2009\ CPI = \frac{2009\ \text{market basket cost}}{1982\ \text{market basket cost}} \times 100$$

$$2009\ CPI = \frac{\$335}{\$245} \times 100 = 136.7$$

Base year

A year chosen as a reference point for comparison with some earlier or later year.

base-year prices. A base year is a year chosen as a reference point for comparison with some earlier or later year. Expressed as a general formula:

$$CPI = \frac{\text{cost of market basket of products at current}-\text{year}(2009)\ \text{prices}}{\text{cost of some market basket of products at base}-\text{year}(1982)\ \text{prices}} \times 100$$

As shown in Exhibit 2, the 2009 cost for our market basket example is calculated by multiplying the 2009 price for each item in column 4 times the 1982 quantity purchased in column 1. Column 5 lists the result for each item in the market basket, and the total market basket cost in 2009 is $335. The CPI value of 136.7 is computed in Exhibit 2 as the ratio of the current 2009 cost of the market basket ($335) to the cost of the same market basket in the 1982 base year ($245) multiplied by 100.

The value of the CPI in the base year is always 100 because the numerator and the denominator of the CPI formula are the same in the base year. Currently, the CPI uses 1982–1984 spending patterns as its base year. Once the BLS selects the base year and uses the market basket technique to generate the CPI numbers, the annual *inflation rate* is computed as the percentage change in the official CPI from one year to the next. Mathematically,

$$\text{Anual rate of inflation} = \frac{\text{CPI in given year} - \text{CPI in previous year}}{\text{CPI in previous year}} \times 100$$

Exhibit 3 lists actual CPI for selected years. You can use the above formula and calculate the inflation rate for any given year using the base year of 1982–1984 = 100. In 2009, for example, the CPI was 214.5, while in 2008, it was 215.3. The rate of inflation for 2009 is computed as follows:

$$-0.4\% = \frac{214.5-215.3}{215.3} \times 100$$

Exhibit 3	Consumer Price Indexes and Inflation Rates, Selected Years	
Year	CPI	Inflation rate
1931	15.2	—
1932	13.7	−9.9%
1979	72.6	—
1980	82.4	13.5
2000	172.2	—
2001	177.1	2.8
2002	179.9	1.6
2007	207.3	—
2008	215.3	2.8
2009	214.5	−0.4

SOURCE: Bureau of Labor Statistics, Consumer Price Index, http://data.bls.gov/cgi-bin/surveymost?cu

The negative inflation rate of 9.9 percent for 1932 was deflation, and the 13.5 percent inflation rate for 1980 illustrates a relatively high rate in recent U.S. history. The fall in the inflation rate from 2.8 percent to 1.6 percent between 2001 and 2002 was **disinflation**. Disinflation is a reduction in the rate of inflation. Disinflation does not mean that prices are falling; rather, it means that the rate of increases in prices is falling. Finally, the negative inflation rate of −0.4 percent in 2009 was the first U.S. deflation since 1955.

Disinflation

A reduction in the rate of inflation.

CHECKPOINT

The College Education Price Index

Suppose your *market basket* for a college education consisted of only the four items listed in the following table:

Item	2009	2010
Tuition and fees[1]	$2,500	$2,600
Room and board[2]	6,000	6,200
Books[3]	1,000	1,200
Soft drinks[4]	150	200

[1]Tuition for two semesters.
[2]Payment for nine months.
[3]Twenty books of 800 pages with full color.
[4]Three hundred 12-ounce Coca-Colas.

Using 2009 as your base year, what is the percentage change in the college education price index in 2010?

You're The Economist How Much More Does It Cost to Laugh? *Applicable Concept: consumer price index*

Are we paying bigger bucks for smaller yuks? Or is it a lower fee for more glee? Is there a bone to pick with the price of rubber chickens? Is the price of Groucho glasses raising eyebrows, the cost of *Mad* magazine driving you mad, and, well, you get the idea. Malcolm Kushner, an attorney-turned-humor consultant based in Santa Cruz, California, developed an index based on a compilation of leading humor indicators to measure price changes in things that make us laugh. Kushner created the cost-of-laughing index to track how trends in laughter affect the bottom line. He is a humor consultant who advises corporate leaders on making humor work for business professionals. For example, humor can make executives better public speakers, and laughter reduces stress and can even cure illnesses. Kushner believes humor is America's greatest asset, and his consulting business gets a lot of publicity from publication of the index. To combat rising humor costs, Kushner has established a Web site at http://www.kushnergroup.com. It organizes links to databases of funny quotes, anecdotes, one-liners, and other material for business speakers and writers.

The exhibit with the Groucho face traces annual percentage changes in the cost of laughing that Kushner has reported to the media. On an annual basis, the inflation rate for laughing remained almost flat as a pancake at about 3 percent from 2000 through 2005. Then, in 2006, the humor index took a slippery slide on a banana peel to a disinflation rate of only one-tenth of 1 percent. In 2007, the index rode a roller coaster ride up to 4.7 percent, which was the largest increase since 1999, and then down to −1.4 percent in 2009. This deflation was the first negative percent change in the index history that began in 1987.

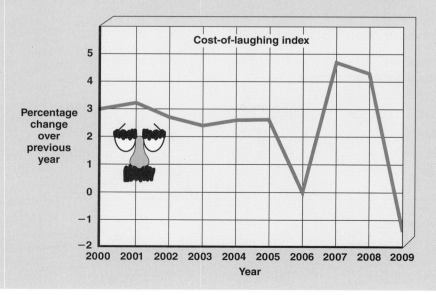

Cost-of-laughing index

Percentage change over previous year

Closer examination of the cost-of-laughing index over the years and some other items gives both smiley and sad faces. The good news in 2009 is that the price of a pink gorilla singing telegram decreased, but the bad news is that the admissions to comedy clubs rose. The major reason for more expensive humor is the price of writing a half-hour television situation comedy. Just like the CPI, Kushner's index has been criticized. Note that the fee for writing a TV sitcom dominates the index. Kushner responds to this issue by saying, "Well, I wanted the index to be truly national. The fact that this price dominates the index reflects that TV comedy shows dominate our national culture. If you can laugh for free at a sitcom, you don't need to buy a rubber chicken or go to a comedy club."

ANALYZE THE ISSUE

No question here. This one is just for fun.

Cost-of-Laughing Index

Item	2006	2007	2008	2009
Rubber chicken[1]	$ 51.00	$ 51.00	$ 51.00	$ 51.00
Groucho glasses[1]	15.00	15.00	15.00	15.00
Whoopee cushion[1]	5.40	5.40	5.40	5.40
Mad magazine[2]	3.99	3.99	4.99	4.99
Singing telegrams[3]				
Pink gorilla	125.00	150.00	250.00	150.00
Dancing chicken	125.00	150.00	250.00	150.00
Fee for writing a TV sitcom[4]	14,377.00	15,032.00	15,482.00	15,482.00
Comedy clubs[5]				
Atlanta: The Punch Line	22.00	22.50	23.00	20.00
Chicago: Second City	24.00	24.00	25.00	25.00
Houston: Laff Stop	24.65	35.00	25.00	20.00
Denver: Comedy Works	35.00	25.00	25.00	28.00
Indianapolis: Crackers Comedy	15.00	7.00	13.00	15.00
Los Angeles: Laugh Factory	17.00	20.00	20.00	20.00
New York: Comic Strip	20.00	20.00	22.00	25.00
Pittsburgh: The Funny Bone	15.00	15.00	15.00	15.00
San Francisco: Punch Line	20.00	20.00	25.00	21.00
Seattle: Comedy Underground	15.00	15.00	15.00	15.00
Total cost of humor basket	$14,910.04	$15,613.89	$16,284.39	$16,062.39
Annual inflation rate	0.1%	4.7%	4.3%	−1.4%

1. One dozen wholesale from Franco-American Novelty Company, Long Island City, New York.
2. April issue.
3. Available from Bellygrams, Manhattan, New York.
4. Minimum fee under Writers Guild of America basic agreement.
5. Admission on Saturday night.

SOURCE: Data provided by Malcolm Kushner.

History of U.S. Inflation Rates

Exhibit 4 shows how prices have changed in the United States since 1929, as measured by annual changes in the CPI. During the early years of the Great Depression, the nation experienced *deflation*, and the CPI declined at almost a double-digit rate. In contrast, the CPI reached a double-digit inflation rate during and immediately following World War II. After 1950, the inflation rate generally remained below 3 percent until the inflationary pressures from the Vietnam War in the late 1960s. In fact, the average inflation rate between 1950 and 1968 was only 2 percent. Then the inflation rate climbed to more than 10 percent in 1974, 1979, 1980, and 1981, reaching a high of 13.5 percent in 1980. During the 1973–1982 period, the average annual inflation rate was 8.8 percent. Following the 1990–1991 recession, the annual inflation rate moderated, and it averaged 2.6 percent between 1992 and 2009. In 2009, during the current recession, the inflation rate was –0.4 percent.

Exhibit 4 — The U.S. Inflation Rate, 1929–2009

During the Great Depression, the economy experienced deflation as prices plunged. During and immediately after World War II, the annual rate of inflation reached the double-digit level. After 1950, the inflation rate was generally below 3 percent until the inflationary pressures from the Vietnam War in the late 1960s. During the 1950–1968 period, the average inflation rate was only 2 percent. In contrast, the inflation rate climbed sharply to an average of 7.6 percent between 1969 and 1982. Since 1992, inflation moderated and averaged 2.6 percent annually. In 2009, during the current recession, the inflation rate was –0.4 percent.

SOURCE: Economic Report of the President, 2010, http://www.gpoaccess.gov/eop/, Table B-64.

Consumer Price Index Criticisms

Just as there is criticism of the unemployment rate, the CPI is not a perfect measure of inflation, and it has been the subject of much public debate. There are reasons for this criticism:

1. Changes in the CPI are based on a typical market basket of products that does not match the actual market basket purchased by many consumers. Suppose you spend your nominal annual income entirely on lemonade, hot dogs, and jeans. During this year, the inflation rate is 5 percent, but assume the prices of lemonade, hot dogs, and jeans actually fall. In this case, your real income will rise, and the official inflation rate based on the CPI will *overstate* the impact of inflation on your standard of living. Retired persons, for example, buy a bundle of products that differs from that of the "typical" family. Because retired persons purchase proportionally more medical services than the typical family, the inflation rate may understate the impact of inflation on older persons.

2. The BLS has difficulty adjusting the CPI for changes in *quality*. Compare a TV made in the past with a new TV. The new TV may cost more, but it is much better than the old TV. A portion of the price increase therefore reflects better quality instead of simply a higher price for the same item. If the quality of items improves, increases in the CPI *overstate* inflation. Similarly, deteriorating quality *understates* inflation. The BLS attempts to make adjustments for quality changes in automobiles, electronic equipment, and other products in the market basket, but these adjustments are difficult to determine accurately.

3. The use of a single base-year market basket ignores the law of demand. If the price of a product rises, consumers purchase substitutes, and a smaller quantity is demanded. Suppose orange growers suffer from severe frosts and the supply of oranges decreases. Consequently, the price of oranges increases sharply. According to the *law of demand*, consumers will decrease the quantity demanded of oranges and substitute consumption of, say, apples for oranges. Because the market basket does not automatically change by reducing the percentage or weight of oranges and increasing the percentage of apples, the CPI will *overstate* the impact of higher prices for oranges on the price level. To deal with this *substitution* bias problem, the BLS takes annual surveys to keep up with changing consumption patterns and correct for the fixed market basket limitations of the CPI.

CONSEQUENCES OF INFLATION

We will now turn from measuring inflation to examining its effects on people's income and wealth. Why should inflation cause concern? You will learn in this section that inflation is feared because it can significantly alter one's standard of living. You will see that inflation can create winners, who enjoy a larger slice of the national income pie, and losers, who receive a smaller slice as a result of inflation.

Inflation Shrinks Income

Economist Arthur Okun once stated, "This society is built on implicit and explicit contracts. . . . They are linked to the idea that the dollar means something. If you cannot depend on the value of the dollar, this system is undermined. People will constantly feel they've been fooled and cheated." When prices rise, people worry whether the rise in their income will keep pace with inflation. And the more quickly prices rise, the more people suffer from the stresses of inflation and its uncertainties.

Inflation tends to reduce your standard of living through declines in the purchasing power of money. The greater the rate of inflation, the greater the decline in the quantity of goods we can purchase with a given **nominal income**, or *money income*. Nominal income is the actual number of dollars received over a period of time. The source of income can be wages, salary, rent, dividends, interest, or pensions.

Nominal income does not measure your real purchasing power. Finding out if you are better or worse off over time requires converting nominal income to **real income**. Real income is the actual number of dollars received (nominal income) adjusted for changes in the CPI. Real income measures the amount of goods and services that can be purchased with one's nominal income. If the CPI increases and your nominal income remains the same, your real income (purchasing power) falls. In short, if your nominal income fails to keep pace with inflation, your standard of living falls. Suppose your nominal income in 2007 was $50,000 and the 2007 CPI value is 207.3. Your real income relative to a base year is

$$\text{Real income} = \frac{\text{nominal income}}{\text{CPI (as decimal, or CPI/100)}}$$

$$\text{2007 real income} = \frac{\$50,000}{2.07} = \$24,155$$

Now assume your nominal income rose in 2008 by 10 percent, from $50,000 to $55,000, and the CPI increases by 3.8 percent, from 207.3 to 215.3. Thus, you earn more money, but how much better off are you? To answer this question, you must compute your 2008 real income as follows:

$$\text{2008 real income} = \frac{\$55,000}{2.15} = \$25,581$$

Using the preceding two computed real-income figures, the percentage change in your real income between 2007 and 2008 was 5.9 percent ($1,426/$24,155 × 100). This means that your standard of living has risen because you have an extra $1,426 to spend on entertainment, clothes, or travel. Even though the general price level has risen, your purchasing power has increased because the percentage rise in nominal income more than offsets the rate of inflation. Instead of precisely calculating this relationship, a good approximation can be obtained through the following simple formula:

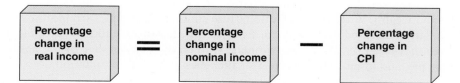

It should be noted that workers with union contracts are largely unaffected by inflation because their wages automatically increase with increases in the CPI, which is called a *cost-of-living adjustment (COLA)*. For example, under union contracts, an inflation rate of 3 percent in a given year would automatically increase wages by 3 percent.

Nominal income

The actual number of dollars received over a period of time.

Real income

The actual number of dollars received (nominal income) adjusted for changes in the CPI.

CONCLUSION *People whose nominal incomes rise faster than the rate of inflation gain purchasing power, while people whose nominal incomes do not keep pace with inflation lose purchasing power.*

Now suppose someone asks you the following question: In 1932, Babe Ruth, the New York Yankees' home run slugger, earned $80,000. How much did he earn in 2009 dollars? Economists convert a past salary into a salary today by using this formula:

$$\text{Salary in given year} = \text{salary in previous year} \times \frac{\text{CPI in given year}}{\text{CPI in previous year}}$$

$$\text{Salary in 2009 dollars} = \$80,000 \times \frac{214.5}{13.7} = \$1,252,555$$

In other words, a salary of $80,000 in 1932 was equivalent to a salary of over $1 million today.

CHECKPOINT

What Is the Real Price of Gasoline?

In 1981, consumers were shocked when the average price for gasoline reached $1.35 per gallon because only a few years previously gasoline was selling for one half this price. If the CPI in 1981 was 90.9 and the CPI in 2009 was 214.5, what is the average inflation-adjusted price in 2009 dollars?

"I've called the family together to announce that, because of inflation, I'm going to have to let two of you go."

• •

Inflation and Wealth

Wealth

The value of the stock of assets owned at some point in time.

Income is one measure of economic well-being, and **wealth** is another. Income is a flow of money earned by selling factors of production. Wealth is the value of the stock of assets owned at some point in time. Wealth includes real estate, stocks, bonds, bank accounts, life insurance policies, cash, and automobiles. A person can have a high income and little wealth, or great wealth and little income.

Inflation can benefit holders of wealth because the value of assets tends to increase as prices rise. Consider a home purchased in 2000 for $200,000. By 2009, this home might sell for $300,000. This 50 percent increase is largely a result of inflation. Also, people who own forms of wealth that increase in value faster than the inflation rate, such as real estate, are winners. (Use Exhibit 3 to calculate that the inflation rate between 2000 and 2009 was 25 percent.)

On the other hand, the impact of inflation on wealth penalizes people without it. Consider younger couples wishing to purchase a home. As prices rise, it becomes more difficult for them to buy a home or acquire other assets.

Inflation and the Real Interest Rate

Nominal interest rate

The actual rate of interest without adjustment for the inflation rate.

Real interest rate

The nominal rate of interest minus the inflation rate.

Borrowers and savers may be winners or losers, depending on the rate of inflation. Understanding how this might happen requires making a distinction between the **nominal interest rate** and the **real interest rate**. The nominal interest rate is the actual rate of interest earned over a period of time. The nominal interest rate, for example, is the interest rate specified on a loan or savings account. If you borrow $10,000 from a bank at a 10 percent annual interest rate for five years, this is more accurately called a 10 percent annual nominal interest rate. Similarly, a $10,000 certificate of deposit that yields 10 percent annual interest is said to have a 10 percent annual nominal interest rate.

The real interest rate is the nominal interest rate minus the inflation rate. The occurrence of inflation means that the real rate of interest will be less than the nominal rate. Suppose the inflation rate during the year is 5 percent. This means that a 10 percent annual nominal interest rate paid on a $10,000 loan amounts to a 5 percent *real interest rate,* and a certificate of deposit that yields 10 percent annual nominal interest also earns 5 percent *real interest.*

To understand how inflation can make those who borrow winners, suppose you receive a one-year loan from your parents to start a business. Earning a profit is not your parents' motive, and they know you will repay the loan. Their only concern is that you replace the decline in purchasing power of the money they loaned you. Both you and your parents anticipate the inflation rate will be 5 percent during the year, so the loan is made and you agree to repay the principal plus the 5 percent to offset inflation. In short, both parties assume payment of a zero real interest rate (the 5 percent nominal interest rate minus the 5 percent rate of inflation). Now consider what happens if the inflation rate is actually 10 percent during the year of the loan. The clear unintentional winner is you, the debtor, because your creditor parents are paid the principal plus 5 percent interest, but their purchasing power still falls by 5 percent because the actual inflation rate is 10 percent. Stated differently, instead of zero, the real interest rate paid on the loan was –5 percent (the 5 percent nominal interest rate minus the 10 percent rate of inflation). In real terms, your parents paid you to borrow from them.

During the late 1970s, the rate of inflation rose frequently. This forced mortgage lenders to protect themselves against declining real interest rates on their loans by offering **adjustable-rate mortgages (ARMs)** in addition to conventional fixed-rate mortgages. ARMs are home loans that adjust the nominal interest rate to changes in an index, such as rates on Treasury securities. The *subprime loan crisis* resulted from homeowners who were unable to make payments as the interest rate rose on their ARMs. This subject is discussed in more depth in the chapter on monetary policy.

A nest egg in the form of a savings account set aside for a rainy day is also affected by inflation. For example, if the interest rate on a one-year $10,000 certificate of deposit is 5 percent and the inflation rate is zero (5 percent real interest rate), the certificate holder will earn a 5 percent return on his or her savings. If the inflation rate exceeds the nominal rate of interest, the real interest rate is negative, and the saver is hurt because the interest earned does not keep pace with the inflation rate. This is the reason: Suppose, after one year, the saver withdraws the original $10,000 plus the $500 interest earned and the inflation rate during the year has been 10 percent. The real value of $10,500 adjusted for loss of purchasing power is only $9,500 [$10,000 + ($10,000 × −0.05)].

Finally, it is important to note that the nominal interest rate is never negative, but the real interest rate can be either positive or negative.

> **CONCLUSION** *When the real rate of interest is negative, lenders and savers lose because interest earned does not keep up with the inflation rate.*

DEMAND-PULL AND COST-PUSH INFLATION

Economists distinguish between two basic types of inflation, depending on whether it originates from the buyers' or the sellers' side of the market. The analysis presented in this section returns to the cause-and-effect relationship between total spending and the business cycle discussed in the previous chapter.

Demand-Pull Inflation

Perhaps the most familiar type of inflation is **demand-pull inflation**, which is a rise in the general price level resulting from an excess of total spending (demand). Demand-pull inflation is often expressed as "too much money chasing too few goods." When sellers are unable to supply all the goods and services buyers demand, sellers respond by raising prices. In short, the general price level in the economy is "pulled up" by the pressure from buyers' total expenditures.

Demand-pull inflation occurs at or close to full employment, when the economy is operating at or near full capacity. Recall that at full employment all but the frictionally and structurally unemployed are working and earning income. Therefore, total,

Adjustable-rate mortgage (ARM)

A home loan that adjusts the nominal interest rate to changes in an index rate, such as rates on Treasury securities.

Demand-pull inflation

A rise in the general price level resulting from an excess of total spending (demand).

or aggregate demand, for goods and services is high. Businesses find it profitable to expand their plants and production to meet the buyers' demand, but cannot in the short run. As a result, national output remains fixed, and prices rise as buyers try to outbid one another for the available supply of goods and services. If total spending subsides, so will the pressure on the available supply of products, and prices will not rise as rapidly or may even fall.

A word of caution: Consumers may not be the only villain in the demand-pull story. Recall that total aggregate spending includes consumer spending (C), business investment (I), government spending (G), and net exports (X − M). Even foreigners may contribute to inflation by bidding up the price of U.S. exports.

Cost-Push Inflation

Cost-push inflation

An increase in the general price level resulting from an increase in the cost of production.

An excess of total spending is not the only possible explanation for rising prices. For example, suppose the Organization of Petroleum Exporting Countries (OPEC) sharply increases the price of oil. This action means a significant increase in the cost of producing goods and services. The result could be **cost-push inflation**. Cost-push inflation is a rise in the general price level resulting from an increase in the cost of production.

The source of cost-push inflation is not always such a dramatic event as an OPEC price hike. Any sharp increase in costs to businesses can be a potential source of cost-push inflation. This means that upward pressure on prices can be caused by cost increases for labor, raw materials, construction, equipment, borrowing, and so on. Businesses can also contribute to cost-push inflation by raising prices to increase profits.

The influence of *expectations* on both demand-pull and cost-push inflation is an important consideration. Suppose buyers see prices rise and believe they should purchase that new house or car today before these items cost much more tomorrow. At or near full employment, this demand-pull results in a rise in prices. On the suppliers' side, firms might expect their production costs to rise in the future, so they raise prices in anticipation of the higher costs. The result is cost-push inflation.

Here you should take note of coming attractions. The chapter on aggregate demand and supply develops a modern macro model that you can use to analyze with more precision the factors that determine national output, employment, and the price level. In particular, the last section of this chapter applies the aggregate demand and supply model to the concepts of demand-pull and cost-push inflation. Also, the chapter on monetary policy will discuss the theory that inflation is the result of increases in the money supply in excess of increases in the production of goods and services.

Global Economics

INFLATION IN OTHER COUNTRIES

Exhibit 5 reveals that inflation rates vary widely among nations. In 2009, Congo, Ethiopia, Venezuela, and other countries experienced very high rates of inflation. In contrast, the United States, Ireland, and other countries had negative inflation rates.

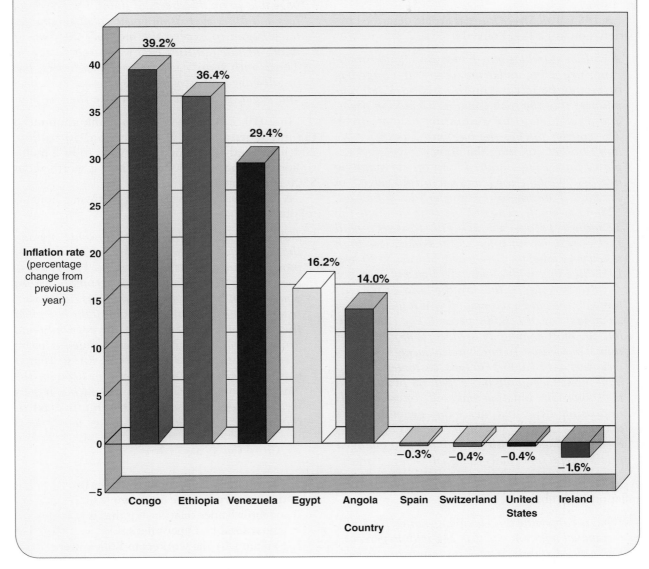

Exhibit 5 — **Annual Inflation Rates in Selected Countries, 2009**

As shown by the bars, inflation was a serious problem in 2009 for Congo, Ethiopia, Venezula, and other countries. The United States, Ireland, and other countries had negative rates.

Inflation rate (percentage change from previous year)

Country	Rate
Congo	39.2%
Ethiopia	36.4%
Venezuela	29.4%
Egypt	16.2%
Angola	14.0%
Spain	−0.3%
Switzerland	−0.4%
United States	−0.4%
Ireland	−1.6%

SOURCE: International Monetary Fund, World Economic Outlook Database, http://www.imf.org/external/pubs/ft/weo/2009/01/data/weoselgr.aspx

Inflation on a Rampage

Some people must carry a large stack of money to pay for a chocolate bar because of the disastrous consequences of **hyperinflation**. Hyperinflation is an extremely rapid rise in the general price level. There is no consensus on when a particular rate of inflation becomes "hyper." However, most economists would agree that an inflation rate

Hyperinflation

An extremely rapid rise in the general price level.

Global Economics   Who Wants to be a Trillionaire?

Applicable Concept: hyperinflation

The following are two historical examples of hyper-inflation:

A 1985 *Wall Street Journal* article described hyperinflation in La Paz, Bolivia:

A courier stumbles into Banco Boliviano Americano, struggling under the weight of a huge bag of money he is carrying on his back. He announces that the sack contains 32 million pesos, and a teller slaps on a notation to that effect. The courier pitches the bag into a corner. "We don't bother counting the money anymore," explains Max Lowes Stah, a loan officer standing nearby. "We take the client's word for what's in the bag." Pointing to the courier's load, he says, "That's a small deposit." At that moment the 32 million pesos— enough bills to stuff a mail sack—were worth only $500. Today, less than two weeks later, they are worth at least $180 less. Life's like that with quadruple-digit inflation. . . .

Prices go up by the day, the hour or the customer. If the pace continues all year it would mean an annual rate of 116,000 percent. The 1,000-peso bill, the most commonly used, costs more to print than it purchases. To purchase an average-size television set with 1,000-peso bills, customers have to haul money weighing more than 68 pounds into the showroom. Inflation makes use of credit cards impossible here, and merchants generally can't take checks, either. Restaurant owners often covered their menus with cellophane and changed prices several times daily using a dry-erase marker.[1]

A *San Franciso Chronicle* article reported on hyperinflation in Zimbabwe:

What is happening is no laughing matter. [In 2008, the annual inflation rate was 231 million percent.] For untold numbers of Zimbabweans, bread, margarine, meat and even the morning cup of tea have become unimaginable luxuries. The city suffers rolling electrical blackouts because the state cannot afford parts or technicians to fix broken *down power turbines. Mounds of uncollected garbage pile up on the streets of slums. Public-school fees and other ever-rising government surcharges have begun to exceed the monthly incomes of many urban families lucky enough to work. Those with spare cash put it not in banks, but in gilt-edged investments like bags of cornmeal and sugar, guaranteed not to lose their value.[2]*

In 2010, Zimbabwe's central bank announced the introduction of new 100 trillion, 50 trillion, 20 trillion, and 10 trillion notes. Want to be a multi-trillionaire? The new 100 trillion note is worth about $300 in U.S. currency.

A *Newsweek* article made the following thoughtful observation:

Hyperinflation is the worst economic malady that can befall a nation, wiping out the value of money, savings, assets, and thus work. It is worse even than a deep recession. Hyperinflation robs you of what you have now (savings), whereas a recession robs you of what you might have had (higher standards of living if the economy had grown). That's why it so often toppled governments and produced revolution. Recall that it was not the Great Depression that brought the Nazis to power in Germany but rather hyperinflation, which destroyed the middle class of that country by making its savings worthless.[3]

ANAYLZE THE ISSUE

1. Can you relate inflation psychosis to these excerpts? Give an example of a debtor-lender relationship that is jeopardized by hyperinflation.
2. Explain why the workers in Bolivia were striking even though wages rose at an annual rate of 1,500 percent. Do you see any connection between hyperinflation and the political system?

1. Sonia L. Nazario, "When Inflation Rate Is 116,000 Percent, Prices Change by the Hour," *The Wall Street Journal*, Feb. 7, 1985, p. 1.
2. Michale Wines, "Zimbabwe: Inflation Capitol," *San Francisco Chronicle*, May 2, 2006, p. A-2.
3. Fareed Zakaria, "Is This the End of Inflation? Turkey's Currency Crisis May Be the Last Battle in the Global War Against Hyperinflation," *Newsweek*, Mar. 19, 2001, p. 38.

of about 100 percent per year or more is hyperinflation. Runaway inflation is conducive to rapid and violent social and political change stemming from four causes.

First, individuals and businesses develop an *inflation psychosis*, causing them to buy quickly today in order to avoid paying even more tomorrow. Everyone feels pressure to spend their earnings before their purchasing power deteriorates. No matter whether you are paid once, twice, or any number of times per day, you will be eager to spend it immediately.

Second, huge unanticipated inflation jeopardizes debtor-lender contracts, such as credit cards, home mortgages, life insurance policies, pensions, bonds, and other forms of savings. For example, if nominal interest rates rise unexpectedly in response to higher inflation, borrowers find it more difficult to make their monthly payments.

Third, hyperinflation sets a **wage-price spiral** in motion. A wage-price spiral occurs in a series of steps when increases in nominal wage rates are passed on in higher prices, which, in turn, result in even higher nominal wage rates and prices. A wage-price spiral continues when management believes it can boost prices faster than the rise in labor costs. As the cost of living moves higher, however, labor must again demand even higher wage increases. Each round yields higher and higher prices as wages and prices chase each other in an upward spiral.

Fourth, because the future rate of inflation is difficult or impossible to anticipate, people turn to more speculative investments that might yield higher financial returns. To hedge against the high losses of purchasing power from hyperinflation, funds flow into gold, silver, stamps, jewels, art, antiques, and other currencies, rather than into new factories, machinery, and technological research that expand an economy's production possibilities curve.

History reveals numerous hyperinflation examples. One of the most famous occurred during the 1920s in the German Weimar Republic. Faced with huge World War I reparations payments, the Weimar government simply printed money to pay its bills. By late 1923, the annual inflation rate in Germany had reached 35,000 percent per month. Prices rose frequently, sometimes increasing in minutes, and German currency became so worthless that it was used as kindling for stoves. No one was willing to make new loans, and credit markets collapsed. Wealth was redistributed because those who were heavily in debt easily paid their debts, and people's savings were wiped out.

Finally, hyperinflation is invariably the result of a government's ill-advised decision to increase a country's money supply. Moreover, hyperinflation is not a historical relic, as illustrated in the Global Economics article.

Wage-price spiral

A situation that occurs when increases in nominal wage rates are passed on in higher prices, which, in turn, result in even higher nominal wage rates and prices.

Key Concepts

Inflation
Deflation
Consumer price index (CPI)
Base year
Disinflation
Nominal income

Real income
Wealth
Nominal interest rate
Real interest rate
Adjustable-rate mortgage (ARM)
Demand-pull inflation

Cost-push inflation
Hyperinflation
Wage-price spiral

Summary

- *Inflation* is an increase in the general (average) price level of goods and services in the economy.
- *Deflation* is a decrease in the general level of prices. During the early years of the Great Depression, there was deflation, and the CPI declined at about a double-digit rate.
- The *consumer price index (CPI)* is the most widely known price-level index. It measures the cost of purchasing a market basket of goods and services by a typical household during a time period relative to the cost of the same bundle during a base year. The annual rate of inflation is computed using the following formula:

  annual rate of inflation =
  $$\frac{\text{CPI in given year} - \text{CPI in previous year}}{\text{CPI in previous year}} \times 100$$

- *Disinflation* is a reduction in the inflation rate. This does not mean that prices were falling, only that the inflation rate fell.
- The *inflation rate* determined by the CPI is criticized because (1) it is not representative, (2) it has difficulty adjusting for quality changes, and (3) it ignores the relationship between price changes and the importance of items in the market basket.
- *Nominal income* is income measured in actual money amounts. Measuring your purchasing

power requires converting nominal income into *real income*, which is nominal income adjusted for inflation.

- The *real interest rate* is the nominal interest rate adjusted for inflation. If real interest rates are negative, lenders incur losses.
- An *adjustable-rate mortgage* is a home loan that adjusts the nominal interest rate to changes in an index rate, such as rates on Treasury securities.
- *Demand-pull inflation* is caused by pressure on prices originating from the buyers' side of the market. In contrast, *cost-push inflation* is caused by pressure on prices originating from the sellers' side of the market.
- *Hyperinflation* can seriously disrupt an economy by causing inflation psychosis, credit market collapses, a wage-price spiral, and speculation. A *wage-price spiral* occurs when increases in nominal wages cause higher prices, which, in turn, cause higher wages and prices.

Summary of Conclusion Statements

- Inflation is an increase in the overall average level of prices and not an increase in the price of any specific product.
- People whose nominal incomes rise faster than the rate of inflation gain purchasing power, while people whose nominal incomes do not keep pace with inflation lose purchasing power.
- When the real rate of interest is negative, lenders and savers lose because interest earned does not keep up with the inflation rate.

Study Questions and Problems

1. Consider this statement: "When the price of a good or service rises, the inflation rate rises." Do you agree or disagree? Explain.

2. Suppose, in the base year, a typical market basket purchased by an urban family cost $250. In Year 1, the same market basket cost $950. What is the consumer price index (CPI) for Year 1? If the same market basket cost $1,000 in Year 2, what is the CPI for Year 2? What was the Year 2 rate of inflation?

3. What are three criticisms of the CPI?

4. Suppose you earned $100,000 in a given year. Calculate your real income, assuming the CPI is 200 for this year.

5. Explain how a person's purchasing power can decline in a given year even though he or she received a salary increase.

6. Who loses from inflation? Who wins from inflation?

7. Suppose you borrow $100 from a bank at 5 percent interest for one year and the inflation rate that year is 10 percent. Was this loan advantageous to you or to the bank?

8. Suppose the annual nominal rate of interest on a bank certificate of deposit is 12 percent. What would be the effect of an inflation rate of 13 percent?

9. When the economy approaches full employment, why does demand-pull inflation become a problem?

10. How does demand-pull inflation differ from cost-push inflation?

11. Explain this statement: "If everyone expects inflation to occur, it will."

For Online Exercises, go to the Tucker Web site at www.cengage.com/economics/tucker

CHECKPOINT ANSWERS

The College Education Price Index

2009 college education price index $= \dfrac{\text{market basket cost at 2009 prices}}{\text{market basket cost at base-year (2009) prices}} \times 100$

$= \dfrac{\$9,650}{\$9.650} \times 100 = 100$

2010 college education price index $= \dfrac{\text{market basket cost at 2010 prices}}{\text{market basket cost at base-year (2009) prices}} \times 100$

$= \dfrac{\$10,200}{\$9,650} \times 100 = 105.7$

Percentage change in price level of college education $= \dfrac{105.7 - 100}{100} \times 100 = 5.7\%$

If you said the price of a college education increased 5.7 percent in 2010, **YOU ARE CORRECT.**

What Is the Real Price of Gasoline?

Average gasoline price in 2009 dollars $= \$1.35 \times \dfrac{214.5}{90.9} = \$3.19$

If you said the price of $1.35 per gallon for gasoline in 1981 was $3.19 per gallon in 2009 after adjusting for inflation over these years, **YOU ARE CORRECT.**
To update this calculation, click on the CPI Inflation Calculator at http://data.bls.gov/cgi-bin/cpicalc.pl

Practice Quiz

For an explanation of the correct answers, visit the Tucker Web site at www.cengage.com/economics/tucker.

1. Inflation is
   a. an increase in the general price level.
   b. not a concern during war.
   c. a result of high unemployment.
   d. an increase in the relative price level.

2. If the consumer price index in year *X* was 300 and the CPI in year *Y* was 315, the rate of inflation was
   a. 5 percent.
   b. 15 percent.
   c. 25 percent.
   d. 315 percent.

Practice Quiz Continued

3. Consider an economy with only two goods: bread and wine. In the base year, the typical family bought 4 loaves of bread at $2 per loaf and 2 bottles of wine for $9 per bottle. In a given year, bread cost $3 per loaf, and wine cost $10 per bottle. The CPI for the given year is
   a. 100.
   b. 123.
   c. 126.
   d. 130.

4. As shown in Exhibit 6, the rate of inflation for Year 2 is
   a. 5 percent.
   b. 10 percent.
   c. 20 percent.
   d. 25 percent.

5. As shown in Exhibit 6, the rate of inflation for Year 5 is
   a. 4.2 percent.
   b. 5 percent.
   c. 20 percent.
   d. 25 percent.

Exhibit 6	Consumer Price Index
Year	Consumer price index
1	100
2	110
3	115
4	120
5	125

6. Deflation is a (an)
   a. increase in most prices.
   b. decrease in the general price level.
   c. situation that has never occurred in U.S. history.
   d. decrease in the inflation rate.

7. Which of the following would overstate the consumer price index?
   a. Substitution bias
   b. Improving quality of products

   c. Neither (a) nor (b)
   d. Both (a) and (b)

8. Suppose a typical automobile tire cost $50 in the base year and had a useful life of 40,000 miles. Ten years later, the typical automobile tire cost $75 and had a useful life of 75,000 miles. If no adjustment is made for mileage, the CPI would
   a. underestimate inflation between the two years.
   b. overestimate inflation between the two years.
   c. accurately measure inflation between the two years.
   d. not measure inflation in this case.

9. When the inflation rate rises, the purchasing power of nominal income
   a. remains unchanged.
   b. decreases.
   c. increases.
   d. changes by the inflation rate minus one.

10. Last year the Harrison family earned $50,000. This year their income is $52,000. In an economy with an inflation rate of 5 percent, which of the following is correct?
    a. The Harrisons' nominal income and real income have both risen.
    b. The Harrisons' nominal income and real income have both fallen.
    c. The Harrisons' nominal income has fallen, and their real income has risen.
    d. The Harrisons' nominal income has risen, and their real income has fallen.

11. If the nominal rate of interest is less than the inflation rate,
    a. lenders win.
    b. savers win.
    c. the real interest rate is negative.
    d. the economy is at full employment.

12. Demand-pull inflation is caused by
    a. monopoly power.
    b. energy cost increases.
    c. tax increases.
    d. full employment.

Practice Quiz Continued

13. Cost-push inflation is due to
   a.   excess total spending.
   b.   too much money chasing too few goods.
   c.   resource cost increases.
   d.   the economy operating at full employment.

14. Suppose you place $10,000 in a retirement fund that earns a nominal interest rate of 8 percent. If you expect inflation to be 5 percent or lower, then you are expecting to earn a real interest rate of at least
   a.   1.6 percent.
   b.   3 percent.
   c.   4 percent.
   d.   5 percent.

15. Which of the following statements is *true*?
   a.   Demand-pull inflation is caused by excess total spending.
   b.   Cost-push inflation is caused by an increase in resource costs.
   c.   If nominal interest rates remain the same and the inflation rate falls, real interest rates increase.
   d.   If real interest rates are negative, lenders incur losses.
   e.   All of the above are true.

Road Map   Macroeconomic Fundamentals

This road map feature helps you tie material in the part together as you travel the Economic Way of Thinking Highway. The following are review questions listed by chapter from the previous part. The key concept in each question is given for emphasis, and each question or set of questions concludes with an interactive game to reinforce the concepts. Click on the Tucker Web site at www.cengage.com/economics/tucker, select the chapter, and play the visual causation chain game designed to make learning fun. Enjoy the cheers when correct and suffer the jeers if you miss. The correct answers to the multiple choice questions are given in Appendix C of the text.

part

3

Chapter 5. Gross Domestic Product

1. **Key Concept: Gross Domestic Product**
    Which of the following items is included in the calculation of GDP?
    a. Purchase of 100 shares of General Motors stock.
    b. Purchase of a used car.
    c. The value of a homemaker's services.
    d. Sale of Gulf War military surplus.
    e. None of the above would be included.

2. **Key Concept: Expenditure Approach**
    Using the expenditure approach, GDP equals:
    a. $C + I + G + (X - M)$.
    b. $C + I + G + (X + M)$.
    c. $C + I - G + (X - M)$.
    d. $C + I + G - (X - M)$.

3. **Key Concept: GDP Shortcomings**
    If the underground economy is sizable, then GDP will
    a. understate the economy's performance.
    b. overstate the economy's performance.
    c. fluctuate unpredictably.
    d. accurately reflect this subterranean activity.

4. **Key Concept: Real GDP**
    The equation for determining real GDP for year X is:
    a. $\dfrac{\text{nominal GDP for year } X}{\text{average nominal GDP}}$

    b. $\dfrac{\text{nominal GDP for year } X}{\text{GDP for year } X} - 100$

c. $\dfrac{\text{nominal GDP for year } X}{\text{GDP chain price index for year } X} \times 100$

d. $\dfrac{\text{nominal GDP for year } X}{\text{average family income}} \times 100$

Chapter 6. Business Cycles and Unemployment

5. **Key Concept: Business Cycle**
   A business cycle is the
   a. period of time in which expansion and contraction of economic activity are equal.
   b. period of time in which there are three phases which are: peak, depression, and recovery.
   c. recurring growth and decline in real GDP.
   d. period of time in which a business is established and ceases operations.

6. **Key Concept: Business Cycle**
   A business cycle is the period of time in which
   a. a business is established and ceases operations.
   b. there are four phases: peak, recession, trough, and recovery.
   c. the price level varies with real GDP.
   d. expansion and contraction of economic activity are equal.
   e. none of the above.

7. **Key Concept: Unemployment**
   John Steinbeck's *Cannery Row* describes a character who takes his own life because of poor job prospects. If he was an unemployed person who gave up looking for work, he would be considered:
   a. chronically unemployed.
   b. a discouraged worker.
   c. a member of the labor force.
   d. frictionally unemployed.

8. **Key Concept: Unemployment**
   Consider a broom factory that permanently closes because of foreign competition. If the broom factory's workers cannot find new jobs because their skills are no longer marketable, then they are classified as:
   a. seasonally unemployed.
   b. frictionally unemployed.
   c. structurally unemployed.
   d. cyclically unemployed.

Chapter 7. Inflation

9. Key Concept: Inflation
Inflation is measured by an increase in
a. homes, autos, and basic resources.
b. prices of all products in the economy.
c. the consumer price index (CPI).
d. none of the above.

10. Key Concept: Consumer Price Index Bias
Suppose the price of gasoline rose and consumers cut back on their use of gasoline relative to other consumer goods. This situation contributed to which bias in the consumer price index?
a. Substitution bias.
b. Transportation bias.
c. Quality bias.
d. Indexing bias.

11. Key Concept: Real Income
Real income in Year X is equal to

a. $\dfrac{\text{Year } X \text{ nominal income}}{\text{Year } X \text{ real GDP}} \times 100$

b. $\dfrac{\text{Year } X \text{ nominal income}}{\text{Year } X \text{ real output}} \times 100$

c. $\dfrac{\text{Year } X \text{ nominal income}}{\text{CPI}/100}$

d. $\text{Year } X \text{ nominal income} \times \text{CPI}$

12. Key Concept: Cost-push Inflation
Cost-push inflation is due to:
a. labor cost increases.
b. energy cost increases.
c. raw material cost increases.
d. all of the above.

Macroeconomic Theory and Policy

This part begins with two chapters that present a theoretical model originating in a book published in 1936 by British economist John Maynard Keynes. The purpose of the Keynesian model is to understand the causes and cures of the Great Depression. The next chapter explains another theoretical macro model based on aggregate demand and aggregate supply. The following chapter discusses the federal government's taxing and spending policies, and the next chapter explains actual data measures of government spending and taxation patterns. The part concludes with a chapter on hotly debated topics: federal deficits, surpluses, and the national debt.

8

The Keynesian Model

In U.S. history, the 1920s are known as the "Roaring Twenties." It was a time of optimism and prosperity. Between 1920 and 1929, real GDP rose by 42 percent. Stock prices soared year after year and made many investors rich. As business boomed, companies invested in new factories, and the U.S. economy was a job-creating machine. People bought fine clothes, had parties, and danced the popular Charleston. Then the business cycle took an abrupt downturn on October 29, 1929, Black Tuesday. The most severe recession in recent U.S. history had begun. During the Great Depression, stock prices fell. Wages fell. Real output fell. Banks failed. Businesses closed their doors, and the unemployment rate soared to 25 percent. Unemployed workers would fight over a job, sell apples on the corner to survive, and walk the streets in bewilderment.

The misery of the Great Depression created a revolution in economic thought. Prior to the Great Depression, economists recognized that over the years business downturns would interrupt the nation's prosperity, but they believed these episodes were temporary. They argued that in a short time the price system would automatically restore an economy to full employment without government intervention.

Why didn't the economy self-correct to its 1929 level of real output? What went wrong? The stage was set for a new idea offered by British economist **John Maynard Keynes** (pronounced "canes"). Keynes argued that the economy was not self-correcting and therefore could indeed remain below full employment indefinitely because of inadequate aggregate spending. Keynes's work not only explained the crash, but also offered cures requiring the government to play an active role in the economy.

Whether or not economists agree with Keynes's ideas, this famous economist still influences macroeconomics today. This chapter begins with a discussion of classical economic theory before Keynes. Then you will learn what determines the level of consumption and investment expenditures. Finally, these components form a simple Keynesian model.

In this chapter, you will learn to solve these economics puzzles:

• Why did economists believe the Great Depression was impossible?

• What are the components of the Keynesian Cross?

• Why did Keynes believe that "animal spirits" and government policy were important to maintain full employment?

INTRODUCING CLASSICAL THEORY AND THE KEYNESIAN REVOLUTION

Prior to the Great Depression of the 1930s, a group of economists known as the **classical economists** dominated economic thinking.[1] The founder of the classical school of economics was Adam Smith (discussed in the chapter on economies in transition). Macroeconomics had not developed as a separate economic theory, and classical economics was therefore based primarily on microeconomic market equilibrium theory. The classical school of economics was mainstream economics from the 1770s to the Great Depression era. The classical economists believed in the *laissez-faire* "leave it alone" theory that our economy was self-regulating and would correct itself without government interference. The classical economists believed, as you studied in Chapter 4, that the forces of supply and demand naturally achieve full employment in the economy because flexible prices (including wages and interest rates) in competitive markets bring all markets to equilibrium. After a temporary adjustment period, markets always clear because firms sell all goods and services offered for sale. In short, recessions would naturally cure themselves because the capitalistic price system would automatically restore full employment. The classical model is explained in more detail in the chapter on aggregate demand and supply.

> **CONCLUSION** *The classical economists believed that a continuing depression is impossible because markets eliminate persistent shortages or surpluses.*

The simple idea known as **Say's Law**, developed in the early 1800s by *Jean-Baptiste Say*, convinced classical economists that a prolonged depression was impossible. Say's Law is the theory that supply creates its own demand. Say's Law was the cornerstone of classical economics. Simply put, this theory states that long-term underspending is impossible because the production of goods and services (supply) generates an equal amount of total spending (demand) for these goods and services.

John Maynard Keynes

British economist (1883–1946) whose influential work offered an explanation of the Great Depression and suggested, as a cure, that the government should play an active role in the economy.

Classical economists

A group of economists whose theory dominated economic thinking from the 1770s to the Great Depression. They believed recessions would naturally cure themselves because the price system would automatically restore full employment.

Say's Law

The theory that supply creates its own demand.

---

1. The classical economists included Adam Smith, J.-B. Say, David Ricardo, John Stuart Mill, Thomas Malthus, Alfred Marshall, and others.

Recall the circular flow model explained in the chapter on GDP. Suppose a firm produces $1 worth of bread in the product market. This supply decision creates $1 of income to the household sector through the factor markets. In other words, Say's Law is a theory that a glut of unsold products causing workers to lose their jobs is a temporary problem because there is just the right amount of income in the economy to purchase all products without layoffs.

> **CONCLUSION** *In the classical view, unemployment is the result of a short-lived adjustment period in which wages and prices decline or people voluntarily choose not to work. Thus, there is a natural tendency for the economy to restore full employment over time.*

In 1936, seven years after the beginning of the Great Depression and three years before the beginning of World War II, John Maynard Keynes published *The General Theory of Employment, Interest, and Money*.[2] Keynes, a Cambridge University economist, wrote in a time of great uncertainty and instability. His book established macroeconomics as a separate field of economics and challenged the baffled classical economists by turning Say's Law upside down. Keynesian theory argues that "demand creates its own supply." Keynes explained that *aggregate expenditures* (*demand*) can be forever inadequate for an economy to achieve full employment. Aggregate expenditures are the sum of consumption (*C*), investment (*I*), government spending (*G*), and net exports (*X−M*). Aggregate expenditures are also known as *aggregate spending* and *aggregate demand*. Recall from the chapter on GDP that you learned that *C, I, G,* and (*X−M*) are national accounting categories used to calculate GDP following the expenditures approach. The remainder of this chapter is devoted to Keynes's theory for the determination of consumption and investment expenditures. The government and net exports expenditure components are developed in the next chapter.

The Consumption Function

Consumption function

The graph or table that shows the amount households spend for goods and services at different levels of disposable income.

What determines your family's spending for food, clothing, automobiles, education, and other consumer goods and services? According to Keynes, the most important factor is disposable income (personal income to spend after taxes; see Exhibit 9 in the chapter on GDP). Keynes argued it is a fundamental psychological law that if take-home pay increases, consumers increase their spending and saving. Keynes's focus on the relationship between consumption and disposable income is represented by the **consumption function**. The consumption function shows the amount households spend for goods and services at different levels of disposable income. Recall from Exhibit 2 in the chapter on GDP that consumption is the largest single component of aggregate expenditures.

Exhibit 1 provides data on real disposable income (*Y_d*) in column 1, consumption (*C*) in column 2, and saving (*S*) in column 3 for a hypothetical economy. Since

---

2. John Maynard Keynes, *The General Theory of Employment, Interest, and Money* (New York: Harcourt, Brace, and World, 1936).

Exhibit 1	Consumption Function ($Y_d = C + S$)		
(1) Real disposable income (Y_d)		**(2) Consumption (C)**	**(3) Saving (S)**
$ 0		$1.00	−$1.00
1.00		1.75	−0.75
2.00		2.50	−0.50
3.00		3.25	−0.25
4.00		4.00	0
5.00		4.75	0.25
6.00		5.50	0.50
7.00		6.25	0.75
8.00		7.00	1.00

NOTE: All amounts are in trillions of dollars per year.

households spend each dollar of real disposable income either for consumption or for saving, the formula for saving is

$$S = Y_d - C$$

From the above equation, it follows that

$$Y_d = C + S$$

Exhibit 2 charts the consumption function using the real disposable income and consumption data given in columns 1 and 2 in Exhibit 1. At low levels of disposable income, households spend more on consumer goods and services than they earn during the year. If annual real disposable income is any level below $4 trillion, households **dissave**. Dissaving is the amount by which personal consumption expenditures exceed disposable income. Negative saving, or dissaving, is financed by drawing down previously accumulated financial assets, such as savings accounts, stocks, and bonds, or by borrowing. At a real disposable income of $2 trillion per year, for example, families spend $2.5 trillion and thereby dissave $0.5 trillion.

Note that if disposable income is zero, consumption expenditures will be $1 trillion of **autonomous consumption**. Autonomous consumption is consumption that is independent of the level of disposable income. It is the amount of consumption expenditures that occur even when disposable income is zero. In the event disposable income is zero, households will dissave to satisfy basic consumption needs.

Exhibit 2 represents dissaving as the vertical distance below the consumption function to the *45-degree line*. The 45-degree line is a geometric construct that makes it easier to identify the *break-even*, or *no-saving income*, which equates aggregate real disposable income measured on the horizontal axis and consumption on the vertical axis. In our example, $C = Y_d$ at $4 trillion, where households spend every dollar earned and saving is therefore zero.

The consumption function has a positive slope because consumption spending increases with real disposable income. At higher levels beyond the break-even income,

Dissaving

The amount by which personal consumption expenditures exceed disposable income.

Autonomous consumption

Consumption that is independent of the level of disposable income.

| Exhibit 2 | The Consumption Function |

This exhibit shows the consumption function for a hypothetical economy. The break-even income is $4 trillion real disposable income, where households spend each dollar of real disposable income, $C = Y_d$, and savings are zero. Below $4 trillion, households spend more than their real disposable income by borrowing or withdrawing from past savings. Above the break-even income, households spend less than their real disposable income, and saving occurs. The marginal propensity to consume (*MPC*) is 0.75 because the slope of the consumption schedule shows that for each dollar increase in income (ΔY_d), consumption increases (ΔC) by 75 cents, and the remaining 25 cents are saved.

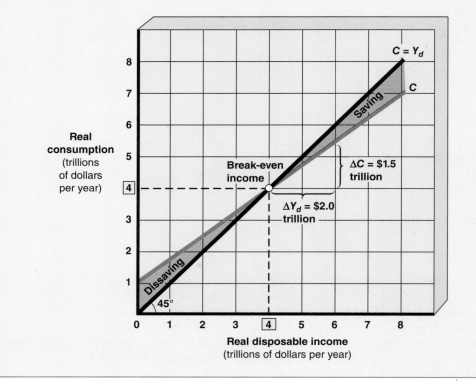

Saving

The part of disposable income households do not spend for consumer goods and services.

households earn more income than they wish to spend, and a portion of income is saved. Saving is the part of disposable income households do not spend for consumer goods and services. Savings can be in various forms, such as funds in a passbook savings account, a certificate of deposit, stocks, or bonds. In Exhibit 2, positive saving is the vertical distance above the consumption function to the 45-degree line. For example, at a disposable income of $8 trillion, households save $1 trillion.

CONCLUSION *The 45-degree line is a geometric construct. It indicates all points where aggregate real income (measured on the horizontal axis) and consumption (measured on the vertical axis) are equal. Consequently, the 45-degree line makes it easier to identify the break-even, or no-saving, income level.*

Marginal Propensities to Consume and Save

Keynes argued that as income grows, so does consumption, but by less than income. This crucial concept is called the **marginal propensity to consume (*MPC*)**. The marginal propensity to consume is "the change" or "extra" in consumption resulting from a given change in real disposable income. Stated differently, the *MPC* is the ratio of the change in consumption (ΔC) to the change in real disposable income (ΔY_d). The Greek letter Δ (delta) means "a change in." Mathematically,

$$MPC = \frac{\text{change in consumption}}{\text{change in real disposable income}} = \frac{\Delta C}{\Delta Y_d}$$

Exhibit 3 reproduces and expands the data from Exhibit 1. As shown in column 4 of Exhibit 3, the *MPC* is 0.75. This means for every dollar increase (decrease) in disposable income (ΔY_d), consumption (ΔC) increases (decreases) 75 cents. In each model developed throughout this text, we assume the *MPC* is constant for all income levels. In our numerical example, real disposable income rises by $1 trillion between each level of income listed in column 1 of Exhibit 3, and consumption rises by $0.75 trillion. Mathematically,

$$MPC = \frac{\Delta C}{\Delta Y_d} = \frac{\$0.75 \text{ trillion}}{\$1 \text{ trillion}} = 0.75$$

What do households do with an extra dollar of real disposable income if they do not spend it? There is only one other choice—they save it. The **marginal propensity to save (*MPS*)** is the change in saving resulting from a given change in

Marginal propensity to consume (*MPC*)

The change in consumption resulting from a given change in real disposable income.

Marginal propensity to save (*MPS*)

The change in saving resulting from a given change in real disposable income.

Exhibit 3	**Consumption, Saving, *MPC*, and *MPS* Data**			
(1) Real disposable income (Y_d)	**(2)** Consumption (C)	**(3)** Saving (S)	**(4)** Marginal propensity to consume (*MPC*) [$\Delta C/\Delta Y_d$ or $\Delta 2/\Delta 1$]	**(5)** Marginal propensity to save (*MPS*) [$\Delta S/\Delta Y_d$ or $\Delta 3/\Delta 1$]
$0	$1.00	−$1.00	—	—
1	1.75	−0.75	0.75	0.25
2	2.50	−0.50	0.75	0.25
3	3.25	−0.25	0.75	0.25
4	4.00	0	0.75	0.25
5	4.75	0.25	0.75	0.25
6	5.50	0.50	0.75	0.25
7	6.25	0.75	0.75	0.25
8	7.00	1.00	0.75	0.25

Note: All amounts are in trillions of dollars per year.

real disposable income. That is, the MPS is the ratio of the change in saving (ΔS) to the change in real disposable income (ΔY_d). Mathematically,

$$MPS = \frac{\text{change in saving}}{\text{change in real disposable income}} = \frac{\Delta S}{\Delta Y_d}$$

The *MPS* given in column 5 of Exhibit 3 is 0.25. Each dollar increase (decrease) in disposable income (ΔY_d) yields a rise (fall) of 25 cents in the amount of savings (ΔS). Mathematically,

$$MPS = \frac{\Delta S}{\Delta Y_d} = \frac{\$0.25 \text{ trillion}}{\$1 \text{ trillion}} = 0.25$$

As derived previously, $Y_d = C + S$, so it follows that $\Delta C + \Delta S = \Delta Y_d$. Dividing both sides of this equation by ΔY_d yields

$$\frac{\Delta C}{\Delta Y_d} + \frac{\Delta S}{\Delta Y_d} = \frac{\Delta Y_d}{\Delta Y_d}$$

or

$$MPC + MPS = 1$$

In our example, $0.75 + 0.25 = 1$, which means any change in real disposable income is divided between changes in consumption and changes in saving. Hence, if you know the *MPC*, you can calculate the *MPS* and vice versa. In addition to the consumption function, Exhibit 2 shows a graphic representation of the *MPC*. The *MPC* (slope) of the consumption function, C, between \$4 trillion and \$6 trillion is measured by dividing $\Delta C = \$1.5$ trillion (the rise) by $\Delta Y_d = \$2.0$ trillion (the run). Since the *MPC* is constant, the ratio $\Delta C/\Delta Y_d$ between any two levels of real disposable income is 0.75. As a formula:

$$\text{Slope of consumption function} = \frac{\text{rise}}{\text{run}} = \frac{\Delta C}{\Delta Y_d} = \frac{\$1.5 \text{ trillion}}{\$2.0 \text{ trillion}} = 0.75$$

The points along the consumption function, C, in Exhibit 2 can be expressed by the following equation:

$$C = a + bY_d$$

where *a* is autonomous consumption and *b* is the *MPC*, which falls between 0 and 1. Keynes used this basic equation to derive consumption (C), and it is called the Keynesian consumption function.

Using this equation,

$$C = \$1 \text{ trillion} + 0.75 \, Y_d$$

For example, at $Y_d = \$4$ trillion,

$$C = \$1 \text{ trillion} + 0.75 \, (\$4 \text{ trillion})$$
$$C = \$4 \text{ trillion}$$

Note that only at $4 trillion real disposable income does consumption equal this amount, as represented by the intersection of the *C* line and the 45-degree line. To demonstrate the relationship between the *MPC* and various levels of consumption, Exhibit 4 shows two consumption functions with the same autonomous consumption of $1 trillion, but each has a different slope. C_1 has an *MPC* of 0.50, and C_2 has a larger *MPC* of 0.75. Thus, the higher the marginal propensity to consume, the steeper the consumption function.

 Exhibit 4 | **Consumption Functions for Two Marginal Propensities to Consume**

The *MPC* is the slope of the consumption function. Here two consumption functions are shown for *MPCs* of 0.50 and 0.75. The autonomous consumption of $1 trillion is the same for both consumption functions. The higher the *MPC*, the steeper the consumption function.

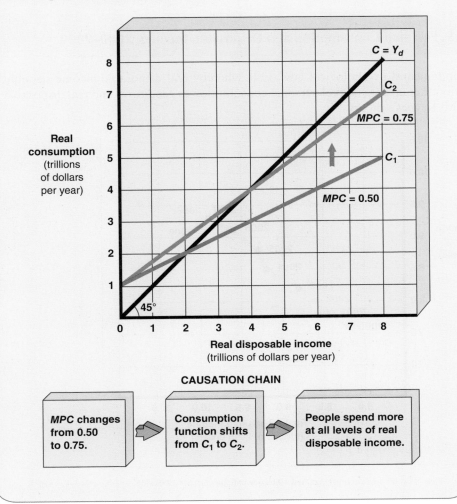

CAUSATION CHAIN

| *MPC* changes from 0.50 to 0.75. | → | Consumption function shifts from C_1 to C_2. | → | People spend more at all levels of real disposable income. |

How do changes in taxes cause movements along the consumption function? Suppose there is an income-tax cut. As a result, real disposable income (Y_d) increases and, in turn, induces an upward movement along the consumption function. An income-tax hike, on the other hand, reduces real disposable income and causes a downward movement along the consumption function.

Exhibit 5 provides recent empirical evidence that supports Keynes's theoretical consumption function. Each point in the exhibit represents a pair of values for real personal consumption spending and real disposable income in the United States for years since 2000. Note that the relationship is close to an upward-sloping linear line. As real disposable income rises, real consumption spending also rises.

CONCLUSION *There is a direct relationship between changes in real disposable income and changes in consumption.*

Exhibit 5	**U. S. Personal Consumption and Disposable Income, 2000–2009**

Keynes argued that a fundamental psychological law exists whereby real disposable income strongly influences real consumption. Actual data on real personal consumption expenditures and real disposable income are consistent with Keynes's theory.

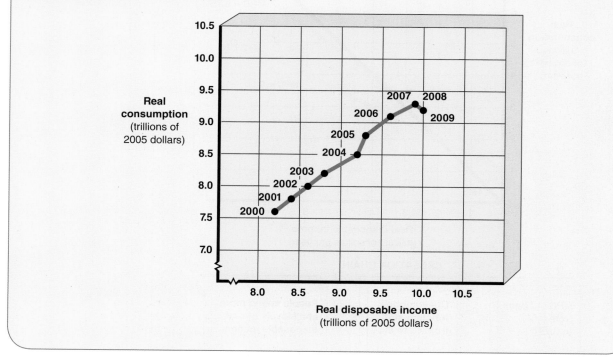

SOURCE: Bureau of Economic Research, National Economic Accounts, http://www.bea.gov/national/nipaweb/SelectTable.asp?Selected=Y.

REASONS THE CONSUMPTION FUNCTION SHIFTS

Just as nonprice factors in the market supply and demand model, such as consumer tastes and income, shift the demand curve, changes in certain *nonincome* factors cause the consumption function to shift.

CONCLUSION *A change in real disposable income is the sole cause of a movement along the consumption function. A shift or relocation in the consumption schedule occurs when a factor other than real disposable income changes.*

Exhibit 6 uses hypothetical data to illustrate this difference in terminology. The sole cause of the change in consumption spending from $3 trillion (point *A*) to $4 trillion (point *B*) along the stable consumption schedule, C_1, is a $2 trillion change in the level of real disposable income. A change in a nonincome determinant, on the other hand, can cause the consumption schedule to shift upward from $C_1 = a_1 + bY_d$ to $C_2 = a_2 + bY_d$. As a result, households spend an extra $1 trillion $(a_2 - a_1)$ at each point along C_2. This means that the level of autonomous consumption has increased by $1 trillion from $1.5 trillion to $2.5 trillion because of some influence other than current Y_d. Nonincome variables that can shift the consumption schedule include expectations, wealth, the price level, the interest rate, and the stock of durable goods.

Expectations

Consumer expectations are optimistic or pessimistic views of the future which can change consumption spending in the present. Expectations may involve the future inflation rate, the likelihood of becoming unemployed, the likelihood of receiving higher income, or the future shortage of products resulting from a war or other circumstances. Suppose households believe prices will be much higher next year and buy now, rather than paying more in the future. The effect of such expectations would be to trigger current spending and shift the consumption schedule upward. The anticipation of a recession and fears about losing jobs would make families more tightfisted in their current spending. This means an autonomous decrease in consumption, and the consumption function shifts downward.

Exhibit 6	Movement along and Shifts in the Consumption Function

The movement from real consumption spending of $3 trillion (point *A*) to $4 trillion (point *B*) along the stable consumption schedule, C_1, is a change in real consumption caused by a $2 trillion change in the level of real disposable income (Y_d). A change in a nonincome determinant causes the consumption function to shift. For example, some nonincome factors may increase autonomous consumption by $1 trillion from a_1 to a_2. As a result, the entire consumption function shifts upward from C_1 to C_2. Nonincome factors include changes in expectations, wealth, the price level, the interest rate, and the stock of durable goods.

CAUSATION CHAIN

Increase in real disposable income	⇨	Movement along the consumption function

| Change in nonincome determinant increases autonomous consumption measured by points a_1 and a_2 | ⇨ | Upward shift in the consumption function from C_1 to C_2 |

Wealth

Holding all other factors constant, the more wealth households accumulate, the more they spend at any current level of disposable income, causing the consumption function to shift upward. Wealth owned by households includes both *real* assets, such as homes, automobiles, and land and *financial* assets, including cash, savings accounts, stocks, bonds, insurance policies, and pensions. Changes in prices of stocks, real estate, and other assets affect the value of wealth and, in turn, can shift the nation's consumption function. A so-called wealth effect occurred in the 1990s when stock values rose and households increased their spending. And during the financial turmoil in 2008 the fall in stock prices and housing prices was a significant factor in depressing consumption.

Wealth effect

A shift in the consumption function caused by a change in the value of real and financial assets.

The Price Level

Any change in the general price level shifts the consumption schedule by reducing or enlarging the *purchasing power* of financial assets (wealth) with fixed nominal value. Suppose you own a $100,000 government bond or certificate of deposit. If the price level increases by, say, 10 percent, this same financial asset will buy approximately 10 percent less. Once the real value of financial wealth falls, families are poorer and spend less at any level of current disposable income. As a result, the consumption function shifts downward. The next chapter discusses this phenomenon in more detail.

The Interest Rate

The consumption schedule includes the option of borrowing to finance spending. A lower rate of interest on loans encourages consumers to borrow more, and a higher interest rate discourages consumer indebtedness. If interest rates fall, households may use more credit to finance consumer purchases. The result is a shift upward in the consumption schedule.

Stock of Durable Goods

When World War II ended, Americans had pent-up demand for many durable goods. During the war, automobiles, washing machines, refrigerators, and other goods were not produced. After the war ended, consumption exploded because people rushed out to make purchases and satisfy their long wish lists. This massive buying spree caused an upward shift in the consumption function.

INVESTMENT EXPENDITURES

According to Keynes, changes in the private-sector components of aggregate expenditures (personal consumption and investment spending) are the major cause of the business cycle. And the more volatile of these two components is investment spending. Personal consumption may be more stable than investment spending because changes in nonincome determinants of personal consumption tend to offset each other. Or maybe people are simply reluctant to change their personal consumption habits. Whatever the reason for the stability of personal consumption, Exhibit 7 demonstrates this point. Over the years, the annual growth rate of real investment has indeed fluctuated much more than real personal consumption. Recall from Exhibit 2 in the chapter on GDP that investment expenditures (gross private domestic investment) consist of spending on newly produced nonresidential structures, such as factories, equipment, changes in inventories, and residential structures.

The Investment Demand Curve

The classical economists believed that the interest rate alone determines the level of investment spending. Keynes disputed this idea. Instead, Keynes argued that expectations of future profits are the primary factor in determining investment, and the interest rate is the financing cost of any investment proposal.

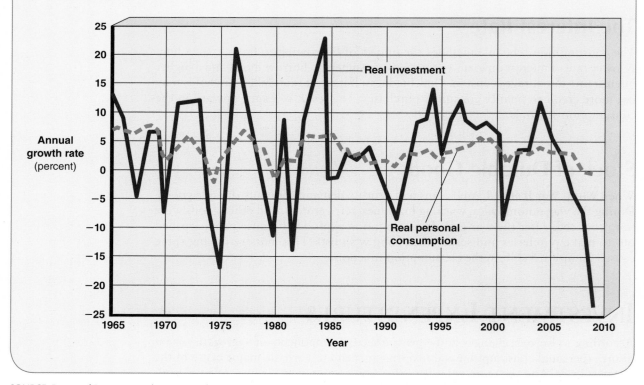

Exhibit 7   **A Comparison of the Volatility of Real Investment and Real Consumption, 1965–2009**

Real investment spending is highly volatile compared to real personal consumption. The data since 1965 confirm that the annual growth rate of real investment (gross private domestic investment) fluctuates much more than the annual growth rate of real personal consumption.

SOURCE: Bureau of Economic Analysis, National Economic Accounts, http://www.bea.gov/national/nipaweb/SelectTable.asp?Selected=Y, Table 1.1.1.

Using a micro example to illustrate the investment decision-making process, suppose a consulting firm plans to purchase a new computer program for $1,000 that will be obsolete in a year. It anticipates that the new software will increase the firm's revenue by $1,100. Thus, assuming no taxes or other expenses exist, the expected rate of return or profit is 10 percent.

Now consider the impact of the cost of borrowing funds to finance the software investment. If the interest rate is less than 10 percent, the business will earn a profit, so it will make the investment expenditure to buy the computer program. On the other hand, a rate of interest higher than 10 percent means the software investment will be a loss, so this project will not be undertaken.

Understanding a single firm's investment decision from a micro perspective allows us to develop the **investment demand curve** from the macro vantage point. The investment demand curve shows the amount businesses spend for investment goods at different possible rates of interest. Exhibit 8 expresses the interest rate as annual percentages on the vertical axis. As shown in part (a), changes in the interest rate generate movements along the firm's investment demand curve. If the interest rate falls from, say, 12 percent at point *A* to 8 percent at point *B*, an additional $5 million of real investment spending occurs because *marginal* planned projects become profitable. Stated another way, as a result of this fall in the rate of interest, the firm's real investment increases from $5 million to $10 million.

The relationship among the expected rate of profit, the interest rate, and investment follows this investment rule: *Businesses will undertake all planned investment projects for which the expected rate of profit equals or exceeds the interest rate.*

Investment demand curve

The curve that shows the amount businesses spend for investment goods at different possible rates of interest.

WHY INVESTMENT DEMAND IS UNSTABLE

Why did Keynes view investment spending as so susceptible to ups and downs? The reason is there are several volatile determinants that cause the investment demand curve to be quite unstable. In short, any factor that changes the expected rate of profit shifts the investment demand curve and thereby changes the investment component of real GDP. As shown in Exhibit 8(b), the initial investment demand curve, I_1, has shifted rightward to I_2, and at an interest rate of 8 percent, $5 million of additional investment spending occurs between points *B* and *C*. The next sections discuss major factors that can shift the investment demand curve.

Expectations

Keynes argued that swings in "animal spirits" cause volatile investment expenditures. Translated this means businesspersons are quite susceptible to moods of optimism and pessimism about future economic conditions. Their expectations about the future translate into estimates of future sales, future costs, and future profitability of investment projects. These forecasts involve a clouded crystal ball, requiring a degree of intuition or normative analysis. There are always

Exhibit 8   Movement along and a Shift in a Firm's Investment Demand

Part (a) shows that investment spending by a hypothetical business firm depends on the interest rate. Ceteris paribus, lowering the interest rate from 12 percent at point *A* to 8 percent at point *B* increases the quantity of real investment purchases from $5 million to $10 million during the year.

Keynes argued that investment spending is unstable because a change in volatile factors, such as expectations, technological change, capacity utilization, and business taxes, can shift the location of the investment demand curve. As shown in part (b), the initial investment demand curve, I_1, has shifted rightward to I_2, and at an interest rate of 8 percent, $5 million in additional investment spending occurs between points *B* and *C*.

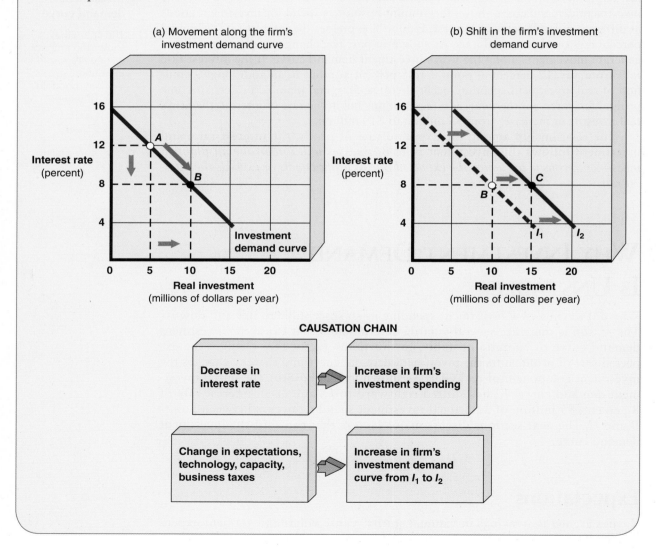

(a) Movement along the firm's investment demand curve

(b) Shift in the firm's investment demand curve

CAUSATION CHAIN

Decrease in interest rate → Increase in firm's investment spending

Change in expectations, technology, capacity, business taxes → Increase in firm's investment demand curve from I_1 to I_2

many ever-changing factors, such as government spending and tax policies, world events, population growth, and stock market conditions, that make forecasting difficult.

When a wave of pessimism becomes pervasive, businesspeople reduce their expectations for profitability at each rate of interest. Such a pessimistic attitude can become contagious and shift the investment demand curve leftward. This was the case during the Great Depression, when the outlook was dismal. At other times, such as during the 1990s, businesspersons become very optimistic and revise upward their expected rate of profit for investment at each interest rate. If so, the investment demand curve shifts rightward. Thus, Keynes viewed changes in business confidence (expectations) as a major cause of investment spending volatility.

Technological Change

Technological progress includes the introduction of new products and new ways of doing things. Robots, personal computers, fax machines, cellular phones, the Internet, and similar new inventions provide less costly ways of production. New technologies create a flurry of investment spending as firms buy the latest innovations in order to improve their production capabilities, thereby causing the investment demand curve to shift rightward.

Capacity Utilization

During the Great Depression, many businesses operated at less than 50 percent of capacity. Capacity is defined as the maximum possible output of a firm or industry. Since much of the nation's capital stock stood idle, firms had little incentive to buy more. As a result, the investment demand curve shifted far to the left. Conversely, firms may be operating their plants at a high rate of capacity utilization, and the outlook for sales growth is optimistic. In this case, there is pressure on firms to invest in new investment projects, and the investment demand curve shifts to the right.

Business Taxes

As explained earlier, changes in income taxes on individuals affect disposable income and the level of consumption. Similarly, taxes on business firms can shift the investment demand curve. Business decisions, in reality, depend on the expected *after-tax* rate of profit. An increase in business taxes therefore would lower profitability and shift the investment demand curve to the left. On the other hand, the U.S. government may wish to encourage investment by allowing, say, a *tax credit* for new investment. A 10 percent *investment tax credit* means that if ExxonMobil decides to invest $10 million in a new plant, the corporation's tax bill to the IRS will be cut by $1 million. The effect of this tax policy is that the government increases the profitability of new investment projects by 10 percent and the investment demand curve shifts to the right.

You're The Economist   Does a Stock Market Crash
Cause Recession?   *Applicable Concept: aggregate expenditures function*

The stock market soared during the "Roaring Twenties." Lavish spending was in style as people enjoyed their new wealth. Then, on October 29, 1929, Black Tuesday, the stock market crashed. During the Great Depression, banks failed, businesses closed their doors, real GDP plummeted, and unemployment soared. Over the years, much debate has occurred over whether the 1929 stock market crash was merely a symptom or a major cause of the downturn. Evidence exists that the 1929 stock market crash only reflected an economic decline already in progress. For example, months before Black Tuesday, national production had already fallen.

The argument over the impact of a stock market crash on the economy was renewed in 2001.

The National Association for Business Economics (NABE) was holding its annual meeting in the World Trade Center when disaster struck the building on September 11, 2001. "The chandeliers shook, we heard a concussive sound, and as we were herding out, we could see that one tower was burning," said Carl Tannenbaum, the chief economist of LaSalle Bank in Chicago, who was attending the meeting.[1] Just the day before a panel of NABE economists predicted slow growth for the economy, but no recession. That forecast became obsolete the moment the first plane hit. Analysts predicted a recession, and one reason was that they expected the stock market would dive as profit expectations fell. Indeed, as a result of the September terrorist attacks, the stock market suffered its worst one-week loss since the

Great Depression. In the immediate aftermath, equities losses were estimated to be an extraordinary $1.2 trillion in value.[2]

Prior to the September attacks, the Dow Jones Industrial Average had reached a high of about 11,500 in May, but it had already fallen almost 2,000 points to a low of 9,431 on September 10, 2001. During this period of time, the economy was plagued by the implosion of the dot.com companies and sharp declines in

© Image copyright Sai Yeung Chan, 2009. Used under license from Shutterstock.com

1 "Worldwide, Hope for Recovery Dims," *Business Week,* September. 24, 2001, p. 42.
2 "Economy under Siege," *Fortune,* October 15, 2001, p. 86.

Investment as an Autonomous Expenditure

Autonomous expenditure

Spending that does not vary with the current level of disposable income.

Assuming none of the above factors changes in the short run, Keynes argued that investment spending is an **autonomous expenditure**. An autonomous expenditure is spending that does not vary with the current level of disposable income. Stated simply, autonomous expenditures in the Keynesian model remain a fixed amount, regardless of the level of disposable income. Exhibit 9 shows how the rate of interest determines the aggregate level of autonomous investment for all firms in an economy, regardless of or external to the level of real disposable income. In part (a), at an interest rate of 8 percent, *all* businesses spend $1 trillion for capital goods and inventory. Part (b) shows this $1 trillion is the amount of real investment spending, no matter what the level of real disposable income. If the rate of interest is lower, investment increases, and the horizontal investment demand curve shifts vertically upward. A higher rate of interest discourages investment and shifts the horizontal investment demand curve vertically downward.

high-tech stocks. After the attacks, the stock market closed for the remainder of the week and re-opened the following Monday, September 17, 2001, with the famous statue of the Wall Street Bull decorated with American flags and the National Guard patrolling the streets. The result of trading was a huge sell-off and another loss of 1,371 points during the week. Throughout the remainder of the year, the Dow Jones Industrial Average gradually rose toward its pre-September 11 levels, closing at 10,022 on December 31, 2001. Real GDP contracted at a 1.3 percent annual rate in the third quarter of 2001, and then it rose in the final three months of 2001 by 1.7 percent, which was a surprisingly strong performance under the circumstances. The six-member panel at the National Bureau of Economic Research (NBER), which is considered the nation's arbiter of U.S. business cycles, declared in November 2001 that a recession had begun in March and ended eight months later in November of that year.

Stock market plunges are widely reported headline news. One result of these plunges is that many Americans feel poorer because of the threat to their life's savings. In only a few hours, spectacular paper losses reduce the wealth that people are counting on to pay for homes, automobiles, college tuition, or retirement. Although not all U.S. households own stock, everyone fears a steep downhill ride on the Wall Street roller coaster. If a stock market crash leads to a recession, it would cause layoffs and cuts in profit-sharing and pension funds. Businesses fear that many families will postpone buying major consumer items in case they need their cash to tide them over the difficult economic times ahead. Reluctance of consumers to spend lowers aggregate demand, and, in turn, prices and profits fall. Falling sales and anxiety about a recession may lead many business executives to postpone modernization plans. Rather than buying new factories and equipment, businesses continue with used plants and machinery, which means lower private investment spending, employment, output, and income for the overall economy.

In early October 2008, stocks fell to their lowest since the 2001 terrorist attacks. The loss followed an initial failure of the House of Representative to pass a $700 billion financial-market bailout plan discussed in more detail in the You're The Economist in the chapter on monetary policy.

ANALYZE THE ISSUE

Immediately following the attack on the United States on September 11, 2001, the stock market plunged and many observers predicted a recession. Using the consumption and investment functions, explain their predictions.

THE AGGREGATE EXPENDITURES FUNCTION

You will now use what you have learned about consumption and investment to develop a basic Keynesian model. To keep the analysis simple, visualize a private-sector domestic economy with no government sector (no taxes or government spending) and no foreign trade (net exports). Moreover, the marginal propensity to consume is 0.50, so each dollar increase in disposable income leads to an increase in consumption of 50 cents. As shown previously in Exhibit 9, investment spending depends on the expected rate of profit and interest rate and is $1 trillion regardless of the level of real disposable income.

A little drum roll please! Now we are ready to finish this chapter by tying concepts together and pointing the spotlight on an important model necessary to understand

Exhibit 9 — The Aggregate Investment Demand and Autonomous Investment Demand Curves

In part (a), the level of real investment for all firms in an economy is determined by the investment rule that all investment projects for which the expected rate of profit equals or exceeds the interest rate will be undertaken. If the interest rate is 8 percent, real autonomous investment will be $1 trillion, shown as point A on the investment demand curve, I.

In part (b), autonomous real investment expenditures are shown to be independent of the level of real disposable income per year. This means firms will spend $1 trillion regardless of the level of real disposable income per year.

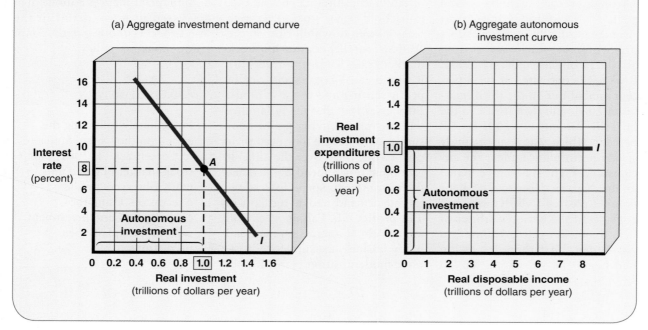

Aggregate expenditures function (AE)

The function that represents total spending in an economy at a given level of real disposable income.

Keynes's cure for the Great Depression. The table in Exhibit 10 gives various levels of real disposable income in column 1 and corresponding levels of consumption and investment in columns 2 and 3, respectively. The relationship between real disposable income and the sum of C + I listed in column 4 is called the **aggregate expenditures function (AE)**. The aggregate expenditures function is the total spending in an economy at a given level of real disposable income. The AE function is derived graphically in Exhibit 10 by summing the consumption function (C) and the investment demand curve (I) on the vertical axis at each level of disposable income on the horizontal axis. Note that the C and the C + I functions are parallel. The slope of the consumption function is determined by the MPC, as explained earlier in Exhibit 2. Then the autonomous investment of $1 trillion is added at each level of real disposable income. As a result, the consumption function, C, shifts vertically by $1 trillion to become the AE function.

The aggregate expenditures function is sometimes called the *Keynesian Cross*. Note in Exhibit 10 that the AE line begins above the 45-degree line and then *crosses*

Exhibit 10	**Aggregate Expenditures Function Data**

The aggregate expenditures function (*AE*) for a hypothetical economy begins with the consumption function (*C*). Then we add the investment demand curve (*I*) to obtain the *AE* function (*C* + *I*). Note that the *C* and *C* + *I* lines are parallel. Because *I* is assumed to be an autonomous expenditure of $1 trillion, the slope of the *C* + *I* function equals the slope (*MPC*) of the consumption function (*C*). At $6 trillion of real disposable income per year, aggregate income equals consumption plus investment, and the economy is in equilibrium.

(1) **Real disposable income (Y_d)**	(2) **Consumption (C)**	(3) **Investment (I)**	(4) **Aggregate expenditures (AE) [(C + I) or (2) + (3)]**
$0	$2.0	$1	$3.0
1	2.5	1	3.5
2	3.0	1	4.0
3	3.5	1	4.5
4	4.0	1	5.0
5	4.5	1	5.5
6	5.0	1	6.0
7	5.5	1	6.5
8	6.0	1	7.0

NOTE: All amounts are in trillions of dollars per year.

it at $6 trillion of real disposable income. The *AE* line represents only private-sector spending in our hypothetical economy. For example, if real disposable income is $1 trillion per year, then consumers spend $2.5 trillion per year, businesses spend $1 trillion for investment, and *AE* = $3.5 trillion. This means the *AE* line is above the 45-degree line and a condition of dissaving exists. As a result, aggregate spending exceeds aggregate income by $2.5 trillion. Instead, if real disposable income is $8 trillion per year and investment remains fixed at $1 trillion, the *AE* line is below the 45-degree line. This means aggregate spending is $1 trillion less than real disposable income. At $6 trillion of real disposable income per year, the economy is in macro equilibrium because aggregate income equals aggregate spending by households and firms. Looking ahead to the next chapter, the discussion will expand the Keynesian Cross model by adding additional aggregate spending components and explaining macro equilibrium. Also, the aggregate expenditures model in this chapter has been developed with disposable income on the horizontal axis as originally developed by Keynes. In the next chapter, the broader measure of real GDP will be used instead.

Key Concepts

John Maynard Keynes
Classical economists
Say's Law
Consumption function
Dissaving

Autonomous consumption
Saving
Marginal propensity to consume (*MPC*)
Marginal propensity to save (*MPS*)

Wealth effect
Investment demand curve
Autonomous expenditure
Aggregate expenditures function (*AE*)

Summary

- *Say's Law* is the classical theory that "supply creates its own demand," and therefore the Great Depression was impossible. Say's Law is the theory that the value of production generates an equal amount of income and, in turn, total spending. The classical economists rejected the argument that underconsumption is possible because they believed flexible prices, wages, and interest rates would soon establish a balance between supply and demand.

- *John Maynard Keynes* rejected the classical theory that the economy self-corrects in the long run to full employment. The key in Keynesian theory is aggregate demand, rather than the classical economists' focus on aggregate supply. Unless aggregate spending is adequate, the economy can experience prolonged and severe unemployment.

- The *consumption function* (**C**) is determined by changes in the level of disposable income. *Autonomous consumption* is consumption that occurs even if disposable income equals zero. Changes in such nonincome determinants as expectations, wealth, the price level, interest rates, and the stock of durable goods can cause shifts in the consumption function.

- The *marginal propensity to consume* (**MPC**) is the change in consumption associated with a given change in disposable income. The *MPC* tells how much of an additional dollar of disposable income households will spend for consumption.

Consumption Function

- The *marginal propensity to save* (**MPS**) is the change in saving associated with a given change in disposable income. The *MPS* measures how much of an additional dollar of disposable income households will save.

- The *investment demand curve* (**I**) shows the amount businesses spend for investment goods at different possible rates of interest. The determinants of this schedule are the expected rate of profit and rate of interest. Shifts in the investment demand curve result from changes in expectations, technology, capacity utilization, and business taxes.

Causation Chains

- An *autonomous expenditure* is spending that does not vary with the current level of disposable income. The Keynesian model applies this simplifying assumption to investment. As a result, the investment demand curve is a fixed amount determined by the rate of profit and the interest rate.
- The *aggregate expenditures function* (*AE*) shows the total spending in an economy at a given level of disposable income. Assuming investment spending is autonomous, the slope of the *AE* function is determined by the *MPC*.

Aggregate Expenditures Function

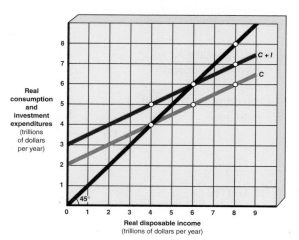

Summary of Conclusion Statements

- The classical economists believed that a continuing depression is impossible because markets eliminate persistent shortages or surpluses.
- In the classical view, unemployment is the result of a short-lived adjustment period in which wages and prices decline or people voluntarily choose not to work. Thus, there is a natural tendency for the economy to restore full employment over time.
- The 45-degree line is a geometric construct. It indicates all points where aggregate real income (measured on the horizontal axis) and consumption (measured on the vertical axis)

are equal. Consequently, the 45-degree line makes it easier to identify the break-even, or no-saving, income level.
- There is a direct relationship between changes in real disposable income and changes in consumption.
- A change in real disposable income is the sole cause of a movement along the consumption function. A shift or relocation in the consumption schedule occurs when a factor other than real disposable income changes.
- Businesses will undertake all planned investment projects for which the expected rate of profits equals or exceeds the interest rate.

Study Questions and Problems

1. Explain how the classical economists concluded that Say's Law is valid and long-term unemployment impossible.

2. Use the consumption function data below to answer the following questions:

Keynesian Consumption Function (billions of dollars per year)				
Real disposable income	Consumption	Saving	MPC	MPS
$100	$150	$____	____	____
200	200	____	____	____
300	250	____	____	____
400	300	____	____	____
500	350	____	____	____

a. Calculate the saving schedule.
b. Determine the marginal propensities to consume (MPC) and save (MPS).
c. Determine the break-even income.
d. What is the relationship between the MPC and the MPS?

3. Explain why the MPC and the MPS must always add up to one.

4. How do households "dissave"?

5. Explain how each of the following affects the consumption function:
   a. The expectation is that a prolonged recession will occur in the next year.
   b. Stock prices rise sharply.
   c. The price level rises by 10 percent.
   d. The interest rate on consumer loans rises sharply.
   e. Income taxes increase.

6. Your college is considering investing $6 million to add 10,000 seats to its football stadium. The athletic department forecasts it can sell all these extra seats each game for a ticket price of $20 per seat, and the team plays six home games per year. If the school can borrow at an interest rate of 14 percent, should the school undertake this project? What would happen if the school expected a losing season and could sell tickets for only half of the 10,000 seats?

7. Why is the investment demand curve less stable than the consumption and saving schedules? What are the basic determinants that can shift the investment demand curve?

8. Suppose most business executives expect a slowdown in the economy. How might this situation affect the economy?

9. The levels of real disposable income and aggregate expenditures for a two-sector economy (consumption and investment) are given in the following table:

Real disposable income (trillions of dollars per year)	Aggregate expenditures (trillions of dollars per year)
$0	$3.00
1	3.25
2	3.50
3	3.75
4	4.00
5	4.25
6	4.50
7	4.75
8	5.00

a. Construct a graph of the aggregate expenditures function (AE).
b. Determine the autonomous consumption, MPC, and MPS for this hypothetical economy.
c. What is the equilibrium level of real disposable income?
d. What will happen to the equilibrium level of real disposable income if autonomous investment increases?

For Online Exercises, go to the Tucker Web site at www.cengage.com/economics/tucker.

CHECKPOINT ANSWER
What's Your MPC?

Early in your career when your income is relatively low, you are likely to spend your entire income, and perhaps even dissave, just to afford necessities. During this stage of your life, your *MPC* will be close to 1. As your income increases and you have purchased the necessities, additional income can go to luxuries. If you become wealthier, you have a higher marginal propensity to save and consequently a lower marginal propensity to consume. If you said your *MPC* will probably decrease as your income increases, **YOU ARE CORRECT**.

Practice Quiz

For an explanation of the correct answers, visit the Tucker Web site at www.cengage.com/economics/tucker.

1. The French classical economist Jean-Baptiste Say transformed the equality of production and spending into a law that can be expressed as follows:
   a. The invisible hand creates its own supply.
   b. Wages always fall to the subsistence level.
   c. Supply creates its own demand.
   d. Aggregate output does not always equal consumption.

2. Autonomous consumption is
   a. positively related to the level of consumption.
   b. negatively related to the level of consumption.
   c. positively related to the level of disposable income.
   d. independent of the level of disposable income.

3. The consumption function represents the relationship between consumer expenditures and
   a. interest rates.
   b. saving.
   c. the price level.
   d. disposable income.

4. John Maynard Keynes's proposition that a dollar increase in disposable income will increase consumption, but by less than the increase in disposable income, implies a marginal propensity to consume that is
   a. greater than or equal to one.
   b. equal to one.
   c. less than one, but greater than zero.
   d. negative.

5. Above the break-even disposable income for the consumption function, which of the following occurs?
   a. Dissaving
   b. Saving
   c. Neither (a) nor (b)
   d. Both (a) and (b)

6. Which of the following changes produces an upward shift in the consumption function?
   a. An increase in consumer wealth
   b. A decrease in consumer wealth
   c. A decrease in autonomous consumption
   d. Both (b) and (c)

7. An upward shift in the consumption schedule, other things being equal, could be caused by households
   a. becoming optimistic about the state of the economy.
   b. becoming pessimistic about the state of the economy.

Practice Quiz Continued

c. expecting future income and wealth to decline.

d. doing none of the above.

8. The investment demand curve represents the relationship between business spending for investment goods and

a. GDP.

b. interest rates.

c. disposable income.

d. saving.

9. Which of the following changes produces a leftward shift in the investment demand curve?

a. A wave of optimism about future profitability

b. Technological change

c. High plant capacity utilization

d. An increase in business taxes

10. The aggregate expenditures function (*AE*) represents which of the following?

a. The consumption function only

b. Autonomous consumption only

c. The investment demand curve only

d. All three of the above combined

e. A combination of (a) and (c)

11. In Exhibit 11, what is the households' marginal propensity to consume (*MPC*)?

a. 0.50

b. 0.67

c. 0.75

d. 0.80

12. In Exhibit 11, aggregate disposable income will equal consumption plus investment (aggregate expenditures), and the economy will be in equilibrium when real disposable income is

a. $2.33 trillion.

b. $3 trillion.

c. $6 trillion.

d. $10 trillion.

13. As shown in Exhibit 12, autonomous consumption is

a. 0.

b. $1 trillion.

c. $2 trillion.

d. $3 trillion.

e. $6 trillion.

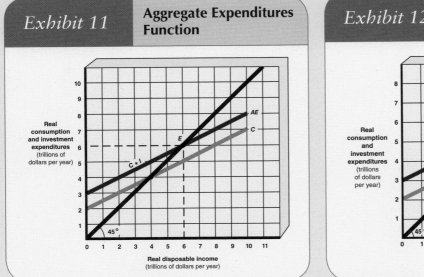

Exhibit 11   **Aggregate Expenditures Function**

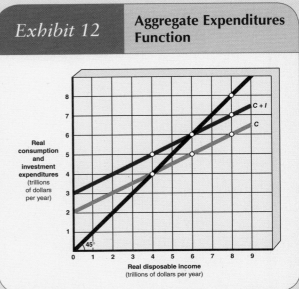

Exhibit 12   **Aggregate Expenditures Function**

Practice Quiz Continued

14. As shown in Exhibit 12, saving occurs
  a. at 0.
  b. between 0 and $4 trillion.
  c. where disposable income is greater than $4 trillion.
  d. at $2 trillion.

15. As shown in Exhibit 12, the marginal propensity to save (MPS) is
  a. 0.33.
  b. 0.50.
  c. 0.67.
  d. 0.75.

The Keynesian Model in Action

In 1935, George Bernard Shaw received a letter from John Maynard Keynes, which stated, "I believe myself to be writing a book [*The General Theory*] on economic theory which will largely revolutionize—not, I suppose, at once but in the course of the next ten years—the way the world thinks about economic problems." Indeed, Keynes's macroeconomic theory offered powerful ideas whose time had come during the Great Depression. Building on the foundation of the previous chapter, this chapter describes how Keynes conceived the economy as driven by aggregate demand that can be separated and analyzed under the individual components of consumption (*C*), investment (*I*), government spending (*G*), and net exports (*X* − *M*).

You must keep in mind that during the Great Depression era, plants had idle capacity and unemployment was massive. Under these conditions, inflation was not the problem. The Keynesian model therefore generally ignores price level changes and focuses instead on how full-employment output can be achieved by changes in aggregate expenditures.

Like adding icing to a cake, this chapter begins by adding government spending and global trade to the aggregate expenditures line in the Keynesian model developed in the previous chapter. Next, you will learn how the economy gravitates to an equilibrium where aggregate expenditures equal aggregate output. And you will look at the link between the equilibrium output and the level of employment in an economy. The analysis will make clear why Keynes argued that there is no self-correction mechanism that eventually moves the nation to the full-employment equilibrium output.

Finally, you will understand one of Keynes's most powerful ideas—the spending multiplier. At the very heart of Keynesian theory is the concept that an initial increase in aggregate spending of $1 in an economy can increase equilibrium output by more than $1. Thus, Keynesian economics offers a cure for an economy in deep recession: government policies that expand aggregate demand, raise national output, create jobs, and restore full employment.

In this chapter, you will learn to solve these economics puzzles:

- Why did Keynes reject the classical theory that "supply creates its own demand"?

- Why did Keynes argue that the government should adopt active policies, rather than allowing the price system to prevail?

- Can the Keynesian model explain an ice cream war?

ADDING GOVERNMENT AND GLOBAL TRADE TO THE KEYNESIAN MODEL

In this chapter, we continue our study of the simple economy begun in the previous chapter (Exhibit 10). Consumption and investment are not the only forms of spending. As shown earlier in the chapter on GDP (Exhibit 2), consumption and investment represent 83 percent of total spending, while government spending and net exports account for the remaining 17 percent of GDP.

Government Spending

Government spending is the second largest component of aggregate expenditures in the United States. Like investment, government spending can be considered an autonomous expenditure. The reasoning is that government spending is primarily the result of political decisions made independent of the level of national output.

Exhibit 1(a) shows hypothetical government spending as a horizontal line labeled G at $1 trillion. If government officials increase government spending, the G line shifts upward to G_1, and reduced government spending shifts the G line downward to G_2. The amount of the shift is equal to the amount of change in government spending.

Here we must pause to take special note of the change from real disposable income to real GDP on the horizontal axis of the graph. Does it make a difference? No, it makes little difference. In the previous chapter, real disposable income was used, following the theory Keynes himself developed. However, it is important to connect aggregate output and income measures. Recall from Exhibit 7 in the chapter on GDP the adjustments required to convert GDP into disposable income (Y_d). As it turns out, real disposable income is a sizable portion of real GDP. Over the last decade, real disposable income, on an average, has consistently been about 70 percent of real GDP. If we are willing to assume that real disposable income remains the same high proportion of real GDP each year, then we can substitute real GDP for real disposable income in the Keynesian model. Changes in real GDP therefore reflect changes in both real national output and real disposable income.

Exhibit 1	Autonomous Government Spending and Net Exports Curves

In part (a), government spending (G) is assumed to be determined by the political decision-making process. The autonomous government spending line, G, is therefore a horizontal line indicating that government spending is independent of the level of real GDP. An increase in government spending shifts G upward to G_1. A decrease shifts G downward to G_2.

Part (b) also shows that net exports are assumed to be independent of the level of GDP. Horizontal line $(X-M)_1$ is negative because imports exceed exports. If exports equal imports, then the net export line shifts upward to $(X-M)$. If exports exceed imports, the net exports line is represented by a positive net exports line, $(X-M)_2$.

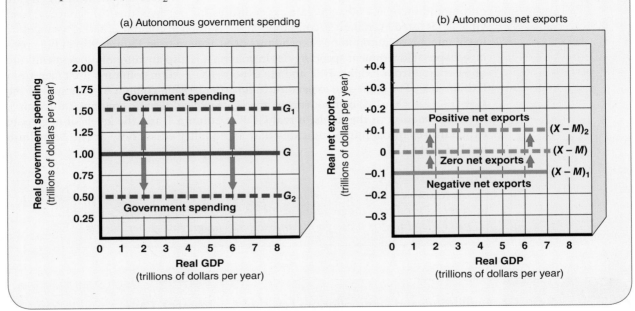

(a) Autonomous government spending

(b) Autonomous net exports

Net Exports

Like investment and government spending, exports and imports can be treated as autonomous expenditures unaffected by a nation's domestic level of real GDP. Economic conditions in the countries that buy U.S. products affect the level of our exports. On the other hand, the level of imports purchased by U.S. citizens is influenced by economic conditions in the United States. As shown in Exhibit 1(b), net exports, $(X - M)$, can be positive, zero, or negative. The level of net exports, or the $(X - M)$ line, is horizontal because net exports are assumed to be independent of the level of real GDP. Since for many years the value of imports we have purchased from foreigners has exceeded the value of exports we have been selling them, the model assumes net exports are negative at line $(X - M)_1$. If exports and imports are equal, the net exports line shifts upward to zero at line $(X - M)$. If exports exceed imports, the positive $(X - M)$ line shifts farther upward to line $(X - M)_2$.

*Global
Economics*

THE AGGREGATE EXPENDITURES MODEL

Keynes countered classical theory by developing an alternative theory that explained how a depressed economy can be stuck forever in a below-full-employment equilibrium without adequate aggregate expenditures. In this section, a simple Keynesian model is developed to explain what Keynes meant by his famous saying, "In the long run, we are all dead."

Tabular Analysis of Keynesian Equilibrium

Exhibit 2 presents data to illustrate the relationship between employment, aggregate output and income, and aggregate expenditures for our hypothetical economy. Real GDP (Y) is listed in column 1, consumption (C) is listed in column 2, and investment (I) in column 3 is an autonomous expenditure of $1 trillion from Exhibit 9(b) in the previous chapter. Government spending (G) in column 4 is also an autonomous expenditure of $1 trillion from Exhibit 1(a), and net exports ($X - M$) in column 5 are taken from Exhibit 1(b). The aggregate expenditures function (AE) in column 6 is the sum of the $C + I + G + (X - M)$ components of aggregate expenditures in columns 2 through 5.

Examination of the levels of real GDP in column 1 and the levels of aggregate expenditures in column 6 indicates that an equality exists only at the $5 trillion level of real GDP.

CONCLUSION *At the equilibrium level of real GDP, the total value of goods and services produced (aggregate output and income, Y) is precisely equal to the total spending for these goods and services (aggregate expenditures, AE).*

Exhibit 2	Equilibrium and Disequilibrium Levels of Employment, Output, and Income						
(1) Aggregate Output and Income (real GDP) (Y)	(2) Consumption (C)	(3) Investment (I)	(4) Government (G)	(5) Net Exports ($X - M$)	(6) Aggregate Expenditures (AE)	(7) Unplanned Inventory Investment Depletion (−) or Accumulation (+)	(8) Direction of Real GDP and Employment
$ 0	$0.6	$1	$1	$−0.1	$2.5	$−2.5	Increase
1.0	1.1	1	1	−0.1	3.0	−2.0	Increase
2.0	1.6	1	1	−0.1	3.5	−1.5	Increase
3.0	2.1	1	1	−0.1	4.0	−1.0	Increase
4.0	2.6	1	1	−0.1	4.5	−0.5	Increase
5.0	3.1	1	1	−0.1	5.0	0	Equilibrium
6.0	3.6	1	1	−0.1	5.5	+0.5	Decrease
7.0	4.1	1	1	−0.1	6.0	+1.0	Decrease
8.0	4.6	1	1	−0.1	6.5	+1.5	Decrease

NOTE: All amounts are in trillions of dollars per year.

All output levels other than $5 trillion are unsustainable macro disequilibrium levels. Consider what happens if businesses employ only enough workers to produce an output of $1 trillion real GDP. Business managers expect total spending to equal aggregate output at this level of production, but this does not happen. At the level of $1 trillion, aggregate expenditures of $3 trillion exceed aggregate output by an *unplanned inventory investment depletion* of $2 trillion, listed in column 7. Firms respond to this happy state of affairs by hiring more workers, expanding output, and generating additional aggregate income. As a result of this process, the economy moves toward the equilibrium of $5 trillion real GDP. Thus, the pressure of empty shelves and warehouses drives our hypothetical economy to create jobs and reduce the unemployment rate (not explicitly shown in the model).

The reverse is true for all levels of real GDP above the $5 trillion equilibrium level. Now, suppose firms hire more workers and aggregate output is $7 trillion real GDP. At the real GDP disequilibrium level of $7 trillion, *unplanned inventory investment accumulation* occurs because aggregate expenditures of $6 trillion are insufficient to purchase $7 trillion of output. The result is that unwanted inventories worth $1 trillion remain unsold on the shelves and in the warehouses of business firms. Producers react to this undesirable condition by cutting the rate of output and employment. In this case, real GDP declines toward the equilibrium level of $5 trillion, jobs are lost, and unemployment rises.

> **CONCLUSION** *Aggregate expenditures in Keynesian economics pull aggregate output either higher or lower toward equilibrium in the economy, as opposed to the classical view that aggregate output generates an equal amount of aggregate spending.*

Graphical Analysis of Keynesian Equilibrium

The tabular analysis of Keynesian theory can be presented graphically. Using the data from Exhibit 2, Exhibit 3 presents a graph measuring real aggregate expenditures on the y-axis and real GDP on the x-axis. Exhibit 3 illustrates the **aggregate expenditures model**. The aggregate expenditures model determines the equilibrium level of real GDP by the intersection of the aggregate expenditures and aggregate output (and income) curves. The 45-degree line now takes on a special significance. Each point along this line is equidistant from the horizontal and vertical axes. Therefore, each point reflects a *possible* equilibrium between real GDP aggregate output (Y) and aggregate expenditures (AE). Note that the AE line indicates aggregate expenditures along a line less steep than the 45-degree line. This is because the slope of the AE line is determined by the marginal propensity to consume (MPC), which is less than 1. Aggregate expenditures equal aggregate output at the $5 trillion real GDP level, and any other level of output is unstable. If businesses produce at some output level that is higher than equilibrium GDP, such as $7 trillion real GDP, the vertical distance between the 45-degree equilibrium line and the AE line measures an undesired inventory accumulation of $1 trillion. This leads businesses to reduce employment, and production drops downward until the economy reaches equilibrium at $5 trillion. You may have already recognized that the difference of $1 trillion between the equilibrium output (actual GDP) at point E

Aggregate expenditures model

The model that determines the equilibrium level of real GDP by the intersection of the aggregate expenditures and aggregate output (and income) curves.

Exhibit 3 — The Keynesian Aggregate Expenditures Model

Aggregate expenditures (*AE*) equal aggregate output (*Y*) at the equilibrium level of $5 trillion real GDP. Below the equilibrium level of real GDP, an undesired inventory depletion causes businesses to expand production, which pushes the economy toward equilibrium output. Above the equilibrium level of real GDP, an unintended inventory accumulation causes businesses to reduce production, which pushes the economy toward equilibrium output. In Keynesian theory, the full-employment output of $6 trillion real GDP can be reached only by shifting the *AE* curve upward until the full-capacity output of $6 trillion real GDP is reached.

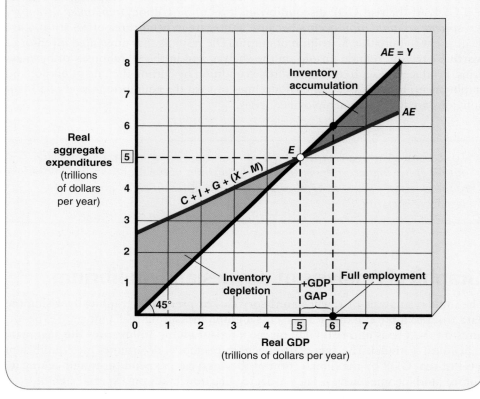

and the full-employment output (potential GDP) is a positive *GDP gap*, discussed in the chapter on business cycles and unemployment (see Exhibit 9).

Now consider the case in which businesses hire only enough workers to produce aggregate output where the *AE* line is above the 45-degree equilibrium line. Since aggregate expenditures exceed aggregate output, businesses sell more than they currently produce, which depletes their inventories. Business managers react to this excess aggregate demand condition by hiring more workers and expanding production, causing movement upward along the *AE* function toward the equilibrium level of $5 trillion real GDP.

Now it's time to pause, take a deep breath, and appreciate what you have been studying so diligently. It's a powerful idea! Exhibit 3 illustrates the basic explanation offered by Keynes for the Great Depression: *Contrary to classical theory, once an equilibrium is established between aggregate expenditures and aggregate output, there is no tendency for the economy to change, even when equilibrium is well below full employment.* The solution Keynes offered Western economies facing the Great Depression is to shift the *AE* line upward until the full-employment equilibrium is reached. Otherwise, prolonged unemployment persists indefinitely, and the economy never self-corrects. We now turn to the key idea behind changes in aggregate spending to stabilize the macro economy.

THE SPENDING MULTIPLIER EFFECT

Changes in aggregate expenditures in the Keynesian model make things happen. The crux of Keynesian macroeconomic policy depends on a change in aggregate expenditures, which is multiplied or amplified by rounds of spending and responding throughout the economy. Exhibit 4 is an enlarged version of Exhibit 3. Our analysis begins at the initial equilibrium of $5 trillion real GDP (point *E*), which is below the full-employment output level of $6 trillion real GDP. Now let's assume the government decides to increase government spending by $0.5 trillion. An increase in autonomous government spending of $0.5 trillion per year shifts the aggregate expenditures curve *vertically* upward by this amount from point *E* on AE_1 to point *a* on AE_2. This means, at the initial output of $5 trillion real GDP, aggregate demand expands by $0.5 trillion to $5.5 trillion. The initial expansion of spending causes inventories (not shown in the graph) to decline by $0.5 trillion because aggregate spending of $5.5 trillion exceeds aggregate output of $5.0 trillion real GDP. Firms respond by stepping up output by $0.5 trillion real GDP per year to replace inventories. The exhibit shows this by the move from point *a* to point *b*. Now the marginal propensity to consume enters the picture. Assuming the *MPC* is 0.50, the expansion of output from $5 trillion to $5.5 trillion puts an extra $500 billion of income into the pockets of workers. Given the *MPC* of 0.50, these workers increase spending on goods and services by $250 billion (movement from point *b* to point *c*). This expansion of consumer spending again causes inventories to decline and output, in turn, to expand by $250 billion, represented by the distance between point *c* and point *d*. This again puts extra income into workers' pockets, of which $125 billion (the distance between points *d* and *e*) is spent (*MPC* × Δ*Y* = 0.50 × $250 billion = $125 billion).

This process of spending-output-spending continues through an infinite number of rounds until output reaches the new equilibrium level of $6 trillion per year at point E_1. Thus, an initial expansion of government spending of $0.5 trillion expands equilibrium output by $1 trillion, which is twice the magnitude of the increase in government spending. Hence, the **spending multiplier** is 2. The spending multiplier is the ratio of the change in real GDP to the initial change in any component of aggregate expenditures including consumption, investment, government spending, and net exports. The formula to compute the amount of change in government spending or other aggregate expenditures required to shift equilibrium aggregate output measured by real GDP is

$$\text{Spending multiplier} = \frac{\text{change in equilibrium real GDP}}{\textit{initial} \text{ change in aggregate expenditures}}$$

In the example presented in Exhibit 4, the spending multiplier is computed as

$$\text{Spending multiplier} = \frac{\Delta Y}{\Delta G} = \frac{\$1{,}000 \text{ billion}}{\$500 \text{ billion}} = 2$$

Spending multiplier (*SM*)

The ratio of the change in real GDP to an initial change in any component of aggregate expenditures, including consumption, investment, government spending, and net exports. As a formula, the spending multiplier equals $1/(1-MPC)$ or $1/MPS$.

Exhibit 4 The Spending Multiplier Effect of a Change in Government Spending

This graph is an enlargement of the spending multiplier process beginning at the point where the economy is in equilibrium at $5 trillion. Then, an initial increase of $500 billion in government spending shifts the aggregate expenditures line up vertically from AE_1 to AE_2. After all spending-output-spending rounds are complete, a new equilibrium is restored at point E_1 with a full-employment output of $6 trillion. Thus, the $500 billion initial increase in government spending has caused a $1 trillion increase in real GDP, and the value of the multiplier is 2.

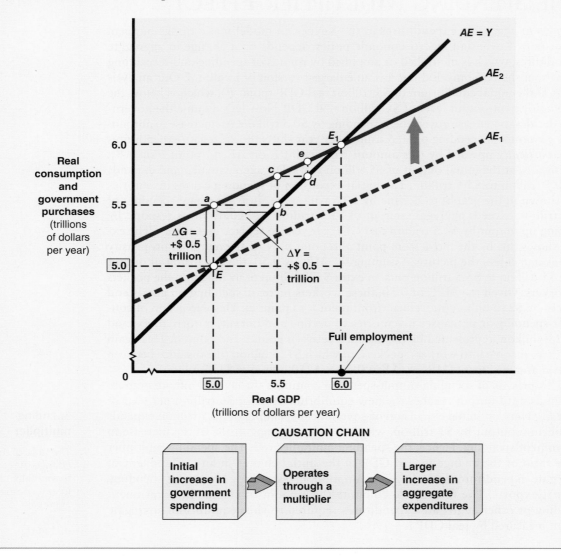

Spending Multiplier Arithmetic

The graphical presentation of the spending multiplier process should make the basic mechanics clear to you, but we need to be more specific and derive a formula. Therefore, let's pause to tackle the task of explaining in more detail the spending multiplier of 2 used in the above example. Exhibit 5 illustrates numerically the cumulative increase in aggregate expenditures resulting from a $500 billion increase in government spending. In the initial round, the government spends this amount for bridges, national defense, and so forth. Households receive this amount of income. In the second round, these households spend $250 billion (0.50 × $500 billion) on houses, cars, groceries, and other products. In the third round, the incomes of realtors, auto workers, grocers, and others are boosted by $250 billion, and they spend $125 billion (0.50 × $250 billion). These rounds of spending create income for respending in a downward spiral throughout the economy in smaller and smaller amounts until the total level of aggregate expenditures rises by an extra $1,000 billion.

CONCLUSION *Any initial change in spending by the government, households, or firms creates a chain reaction of further spending, which causes a greater cumulative change in aggregate expenditures.*

You might recognize from algebra that the spending multiplier effect is a process based on an infinite geometric series. The formula for the sum of such a series of numbers is the initial number times $1/(1 - r)$, where r is the ratio that relates the numbers. Using this formula, the sum (total spending) is calculated as $500 billion ($\Delta G$) × [1/(1 − 0.50)] = $1,000 billion. By simply defining r in the infinite series formula as MPC, the spending multiplier for aggregate demand is expressed as

$$\text{Spending multiplier} = \frac{1}{1 - MPC}$$

Exhibit 5	Spending Multiplier Effect	
Round	**Component of total spending**	**New consumption spending**
1	Government spending	$500
2	Consumption	250
3	Consumption	125
4	Consumption	63
.	.	.
.	.	.
.	.	.
All other rounds	Consumption	62
Total spending		$1,000

Note: All amounts are rounded to the nearest billion dollars per year.

Exhibit 6	**Relationship between *MPC*, *MPS*, and the Spending Multiplier**		
(1) **Marginal propensity** **to consume (*MPC*)**	**(2)** **Marginal propensity** **to save (*MPS*)**	**(3)** **Spending** **multiplier**
0.90	0.10	10
0.80	0.20	5
0.75	0.25	4
0.67	0.33	3
0.50	0.50	2
0.33	0.67	1.5

Applying this formula to our example:

$$\text{Spending multiplier} = \frac{1}{1-0.50} = \frac{1}{0.50} = 2$$

Recall from the previous chapter that *MPC* + *MPS* = 1, and therefore *MPS* = 1 − *MPC*. Hence, the above multiplier formula can be rewritten as

$$\text{Spending multiplier} = \frac{1}{MPS}$$

Applying the multiplier formula to our example:

$$\text{Spending multiplier} = \frac{1}{MPS} = \frac{1}{1-0.50} = 2$$

Since *MPS* and *MPC* are related, the size of the multiplier depends on the size of the *MPC*. What will the result be if people spend 80 percent or 33 percent of each dollar of income instead of 50 percent? If the *MPC* increases (decreases), consumers spend a larger (smaller) share of each additional dollar of output/income in each round, and the size of the multiplier increases (decreases). Exhibit 6 lists the multiplier for different values of *MPC* and *MPS*. Economists use real-world macroeconomic data to estimate a more complex multiplier than the simple multiplier formula developed in this chapter. Their estimates of the long-run real-world *MPC* range from 0.80 to 0.90. An *MPC* of 0.50 is used in the above examples for simplicity.

RECESSIONARY AND INFLATIONARY GAPS

The multiplier is important in the Keynesian model because it means that the initial change in aggregate expenditures results in an amplified change in the equilibrium level of real GDP. Such inherent instability can mean bad or good news for an economy. The bad news occurs, for example, when the multiplier amplifies small declines in total spending from, say, consumer and business manager pessimism into downturns in national output, income, and employment. The good news is that, in theory, macroeconomic policy can manage, or manipulate, the economy's performance by a relatively small initial change in aggregate expenditures.

Recessionary Gap

Using Government Spending to Close a Recessionary Gap Consider the aggregate expenditures function AE_1 in Exhibit 7. Beginning at point E_1, this hypothetical economy's initial equilibrium level is $4 trillion real GDP. The *MPC*

Exhibit 7   **A Recessionary Gap**

The hypothetical economy begins in equilibrium at point E_1, with an equilibrium output of $4 trillion real GDP. With aggregate expenditures of AE_1, real GDP will not automatically increase to the $6 trillion full-employment output. The $1 trillion deficiency in total spending required to achieve full employment is the recessionary gap measured by the vertical distance between points a and E_2. Given a multiplier of 2, an initial increase in autonomous expenditures equal to the recessionary gap works through the spending multiplier and causes the economy to move from E_1 to E_2 and achieve full employment.

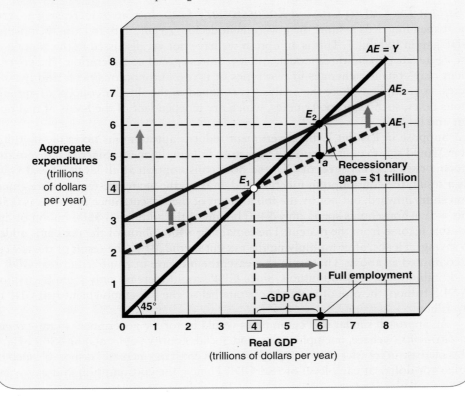

Recessionary gap

The amount by which the aggregate expenditures curve must be increased to achieve full-employment equilibrium.

is 0.50, and the spending multiplier is therefore 2. The full-employment output is $6 trillion real GDP, which means the economy faces a negative GDP gap of $2 trillion. Along the vertical line at the full-employment output level, look at the segment between point *a* on the initial AE_1 line and point E_2 on the AE_2 line, which is labeled a **recessionary gap**. A recessionary gap is the amount by which aggregate expenditures fall short of the amount required to achieve full-employment equilibrium. In our example, the recessionary gap is $1 trillion. What is the importance of the recessionary gap? The recessionary gap is the initial increase in autonomous spending required to trigger the multiplier, shift the aggregate expenditures function upward from AE_1 to AE_2, and eliminate the positive GDP gap. Stated as an expression,

Initial increase in autonomous expenditures × spending multiplier = increase in equilibrium output

Using the data in our example,

$1 trillion × 2 = $2 trillion

We now turn to the important question of how to inject an additional $1 trillion spending into the economy, cause AE_1 to shift upward to AE_2, and thereby increase the equilibrium output from $4 trillion to $6 trillion real GDP. Under Keynesian theory, when market forces do not automatically do the job, then the central government should take aggressive action and adopt policies that boost autonomous spending [C, I, G, or $(X - M)$] by an amount equal to the recessionary gap.

Using a Tax Cut to Close a Recessionary Gap Instead of increasing government spending, let's assume the government decides to cut taxes to close the positive GDP gap in Exhibit 7. This is an option we have not yet discussed in the context of the aggregate expenditures model, and it requires special consideration. The government may consider changes in two types of taxes: autonomous taxes and income taxes. For simplicity, here the analysis is confined to the simpler concept of autonomous taxes, such as property taxes, which are independent of the levels of real output and income.

Suppose in Exhibit 7 the government reduces autonomous taxes by $800 billion. Would this tax cut be enough to restore full employment? Since real disposable income rises at every level of GDP, so does consumption at all levels of real GDP. As a result, the consumption function and, in turn, the aggregate expenditures function shifts upward, but not by the full amount of the tax cut. Since the MPC is 0.50, this means households spend only $400 billion of the additional $800 billion of disposable income from the tax cut. The remaining $400 billion of the tax cut is added to savings. Hence, after multiplying the tax cut by the MPC, the result of the tax cut is computed as above. That is, in this case, the increase in equilibrium real GDP is $400 billion × 2 = $800 billion. Since GDP would increase only from $4 trillion to $4.8 trillion, the economy would operate below the full-employment real GDP of $6 trillion.

An approach similar to a cut in taxes would be for the government to raise *transfer payments* (welfare, unemployment, and Social Security payments) by $800 billion. This increase in transfer payments, holding taxes constant, increases disposable income dollar-for-dollar at each level of real GDP. Hence, the consumption and aggregate

Global Economics The Great Ice Cream War

Applicable Concept: aggregate expenditures model

The following *Wall Street Journal* article provides a rare insight into the politics of global trade, and the Analyze the Issue connects trade policy to the macro model developed in this chapter:

While many people relish American-made ice cream with deliberately foreign-sounding names, few people realize that the U.S. government declared war on ice cream imports by restricting them to less than one-tenth of one percent of U.S. consumption. With quotas so low and transportation costs high, few countries bothered to ship any ice cream at all to the United States. For example, in 1988 the United States exported hundreds of thousands of gallons of ice cream to Canada, yet Canadian ice cream was banned from the United States. Only 576 gallons was imported from New Zealand and 12 gallons from Denmark. This was not enough ice cream to stock a large grocery store on a summer Saturday.

The U.S. ice cream quotas dated back to December 31, 1970, when President Nixon decreed that future ice cream imports could not exceed 431,330 gallons a year. Why? That year, according to Deputy Secretary of Agriculture Ann Veneman, testifying before the ITC [U.S. International Trade Commission], the U.S. was hit with a "flood of imports." This so-called "flood" amounted to barely 1 percent of U.S. ice cream consumption.

How did Mr. Nixon decide to limit imports to exactly 431,330 gallons a year? Section 22 of the Agriculture Adjustment Act allowed the U.S. government to protect domestic price-support programs by restricting imports to 50 percent of the annual average imports for a representative period. Ice

© Image copyright wildarrow, 2009. Used under license from Shutterstock.com

cream imports did not begin until 1969, so the U.S. government chose 1969 and the two previous years with no ice cream imports in order to calculate a low annual average import quota for this product.

Finally, the article concluded that the U.S. government probably spent more than $1,000 in administrative expenses for each gallon of ice cream imported into the United States. The article's author concluded, "Global trade disputes are rapidly degenerating into a full employment program for government bureaucrats."

ANALYZE THE ISSUE

Assume the U.S. economy is in an inflationary gap condition. Use the Keynesian aggregate expenditures model to explain why increasing U.S. exports and restricting imports is or is not a desirable policy.

SOURCE: James Bovard, "The Great Ice Cream War," *The Wall Street Journal*, 6, 1989, p. A18.

expenditures lines shift upward by $400 billion. This initial boost in total spending is computed by multiplying the *MPC* of 0.50 times the increase of $800 billion in transfer payments. The increase in transfer payments has the same effect as an identical cut in taxes, and the equilibrium real GDP increases by $800 billion. Hence, a transfer payment is simply a cut in net taxes.

Tax multiplier

The change in aggregate expenditures (total spending) resulting from an initial change in taxes. As a formula, the tax multiplier equals 1 − spending multiplier.

Another simpler method of calculating the impact of a change in taxes is to use a **tax multiplier**. The tax multiplier is the change in aggregate expenditures (total spending) resulting from an initial change in taxes. Expressed as a formula:

$$\text{Tax multiplier} = 1 - \text{spending multiplier}$$

After you calculate the tax multiplier, multiply your answer by the amount of the tax increase or decrease in order to determine the change in aggregate expenditures. Expressed as a formula:

$$\text{Change in taxes } (\Delta T) \times \text{tax multiplier} = \text{change in aggregate expenditures}$$

Returning to the example shown in Exhibit 7, suppose we wish to calculate the tax cut required to increase real GDP by $2 trillion from $4 trillion to $6 trillion and achieve full employment. Using the tax multiplier formula:

$$\text{Tax multiplier} = 1 - 2 = -1$$
$$\Delta T \times (-1) = \$2 \text{ trillion}$$
$$\Delta T = -\$2 \text{ trillion}$$

Therefore, in this hypothetical economy, a $2 trillion tax cut will increase GDP by the $2 trillion required to achieve full employment.

CHECKPOINT

Full-Employment Output, Where Are You?

Suppose the U.S. economy is in equilibrium at $15 trillion real GDP with a recessionary gap. Given an *MPC* of 0.50, the government estimates that a tax cut of $500 billion is just enough to restore full employment. What is the full-employment real GDP target?

Inflationary Gap

Inflationary gap

The amount by which the aggregate expenditures curve must be decreased to achieve full-employment equilibrium.

Under other circumstances, an **inflationary gap** may burden an economy. An inflationary gap is the amount by which aggregate expenditures exceed the amount required to achieve full-employment equilibrium. In Exhibit 8, the inflationary gap of $1 trillion is the vertical distance between point *a* on the initial AE_1 line and point E_2 on the AE_2 line. Since the economy can produce only $4 trillion in real output, this excess aggregate demand puts upward pressure on prices as buyers compete for this limited real output. If aggregate spending declines from AE_1 to AE_2, the economy moves from an equilibrium of $6 trillion at point E_1 to the full-employment equilibrium of $4 trillion at point E_2, and the inflationary pressure cools.

Again, the Keynesian prescription is for the central government to take aggressive action and adopt policies that reduce autonomous spending [C, I, G, or (X − M)] by an amount equal to the inflationary gap. Note from the analysis in the previous section that the government could cut government spending or use a tax hike or a cut in transfer payments to reduce consumption. Stated as an expression,

Initial decrease in autonomous expenditures × spending multiplier = decrease in equilibrium output

Exhibit 8	An Inflationary Gap

The hypothetical economy begins in equilibrium at point E_1 with an equilibrium output of $6 trillion real GDP. Given an initial aggregate expenditures function of AE_1, real GDP will not self-correct to the full-employment output of $4 trillion. The $1 trillion excess of total spending over the amount required at full employment is the inflationary gap measured by the vertical distance between points a and E_2. Given a multiplier of 2, an initial decrease in autonomous expenditures of $1 trillion causes the economy to move from point E_1 to E_2, achieve full employment, and cool the upward pressure on prices.

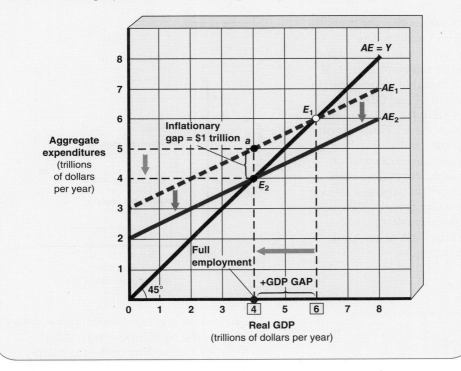

In our example, the MPC is 0.50, so the multiplier is 2. The actual real GDP of $6 trillion is greater than the potential real GDP of $4 trillion, so the negative real GDP gap is −$2 trillion. Hence,

$$-\$1 \text{ trillion} \times 2 = -\$2 \text{ trillion}$$

CHECKPOINT

How Much Spending Must Uncle Sam Cut?

Suppose the U.S. economy is troubled by inflation. The economy is in equilibrium at a real GDP of $15.5 trillion, the MPC is 0.90, and the full-employment output is $15 trillion. If the government decides to eliminate the inflationary gap by cutting government spending, what will be the size of the cut?

Key Concepts

Aggregate expenditures
model

Spending multiplier (*SM*)
Recessionary gap

Tax multiplier
Inflationary gap

Summary

- The **Keynesian theory** argues that the economy is inherently unstable and may require government intervention to control aggregate expenditures and restore full employment. If we assume that real disposable income remains the same high proportion of real GDP, then we can substitute real GDP for real disposable income in the Keynesian model. *Government spending* and *net exports* can be treated as autonomous expenditures in the Keynesian model. *Net exports* are the only component of aggregate expenditures that changes from a positive to a negative value as real GDP rises. Both exports and imports are determined by foreign or domestic income, tastes, trade restrictions, and exchange rates.

Government Spending

Net Exports

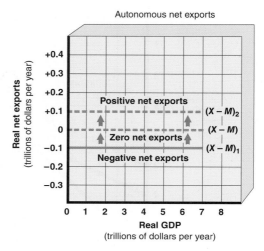

- The **Keynesian aggregate expenditures model** determines the equilibrium level of real GDP by the intersection of the aggregate expenditures and the aggregate output and income curves. Each equilibrium level in the economy is associated with a level of employment and corresponding unemployment rate. Aggregate expenditures and real GDP are equal, graphically, where the $AE = C + I + G + (X - M)$ line intersects the 45-degree line. At any output greater or lesser than the equilibrium real GDP, unintended inventory investment pressures businesses to alter aggregate output and income until equilibrium at full-employment real GDP is restored.

Keynesian Aggregate Expenditures Model

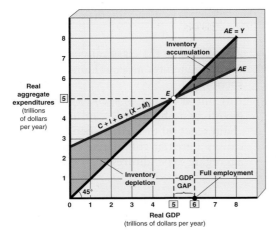

- The *spending multiplier* is the ratio of the change in equilibrium output to the initial change in any of the components of aggregate expenditures. Algebraically, the multiplier is the reciprocal of the marginal propensity to save. The multiplier effect causes the equilibrium level of real GDP to change by several times the initial change in spending.
- A *recessionary gap* is the amount by which aggregate expenditures fall short of the amount necessary for the economy to operate at full-employment real GDP. To eliminate a negative GDP gap, the Keynesian solution is to increase autonomous spending by an amount equal to the recessionary gap and operate through the multiplier to increase equilibrium output and income.

Recessionary Gap

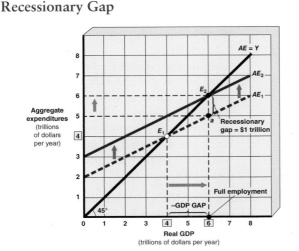

- The *tax multiplier* is the multiplier by which an initial change in taxes changes aggregate demand (total spending) after an infinite number of spending cycles. Expressed as a formula, the tax multiplier = 1 − spending multiplier.
- An *inflationary gap* is the amount by which aggregate expenditures exceed the amount necessary to establish full-employment equilibrium and indicates upward pressure on prices. To eliminate a positive GDP gap, the Keynesian solution is to decrease autonomous spending by an amount equal to the inflationary gap and operate through the multiplier to decrease equilibrium output and income.

Inflationary Gap

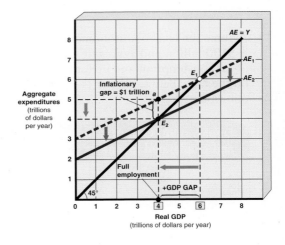

Summary of Conclusion Statements

- At the equilibrium level of real GDP, the total value of goods and services produced (aggregate output and income, Y) is precisely equal to the total spending for these goods and services (aggregate expenditures, AE).
- Aggregate expenditures in Keynesian economics pull aggregate output either higher or lower toward equilibrium in the economy,

as opposed to the classical view that aggregate output generates an equal amount of aggregate spending.

- Any initial change in spending by the government, households, or firms creates a chain reaction of further spending, which causes a greater cumulative change in aggregate expenditures.

Study Questions and Problems

1. Assume the level of autonomous investment is $100 billion and aggregate expenditures equal consumption and investment. Based on the table below, answer the following questions.

    ### Employment, Output, Consumption, and Unplanned Inventory

Possible levels of employment (millions of workers)	Real GDP (output) equals disposable income (billions of dollars)	Consumption (billions of dollars)	Unplanned inventory (billions of dollars)
40	$325	$300	$_____
45	375	325	_____
50	425	350	_____
55	475	375	_____
60	525	400	_____
65	575	425	_____
70	625	450	_____

    a. Fill in the unplanned inventory column.
    b. Determine the MPC and MPS.
    c. If this economy employs a labor force of 40 million, what will happen to this level of employment? Explain and identify the equilibrium level of output.

2. Using the data given in Question 1, what is the impact of adding net exports? Let imports equal $75 billion, and assume exports equal

$50 billion. What is the equilibrium level of employment and output?

3. Explain the determination of equilibrium real GDP by drawing an abstract graph of the aggregate expenditures model. Label the aggregate expenditures line AE and the aggregate output line AO. Explain why the interaction of AE and AO determines the Keynesian equilibrium level of real GDP.

4. Use the aggregate expenditures model to demonstrate the multiplier effect.

5. How are changes in the MPC, changes in the MPS, and the size of the multiplier related? Answer the following questions:
    a. What is the multiplier if the MPC is 0? 0.33? 0.90?
    b. Suppose the equilibrium real GDP is $100 billion and the MPC is 4/5. How much will the equilibrium output change if businesses increase their level of investment by $10 billion?
    c. Using the data given in question 5(b), what will be the change in equilibrium real GDP if the MPC equals 2/3?

6. Assume the MPC is 0.90 and autonomous investment increases by $500 billion. What will be the impact on real GDP?

7. Suppose autonomous investment increases by $100 billion and the *MPC* is 0.75.
   a. Use the following table to compute four rounds of the spending multiplier effect:

Round	Components of total spending	New consumption spending (billions of dollars)
1	Investment	$_____
2	Consumption	_____
3	Consumption	_____
4	Consumption	_____
	Total spending	_____

   b. Use the spending multiplier formula to compute the final cumulative impact on aggregate spending.

8. First, use the data given in question 1, and assume the level of autonomous investment is $50 billion. If the full-employment level of output is $525 billion, what is the equilibrium level of output and employment? Does a recessionary gap or an inflationary gap exist? Second, assume the level of autonomous investment is $150 billion. What is the equilibrium level of output and employment? Does a recessionary gap or an inflationary gap exist? Explain the consequences of an inflationary gap using the aggregate expenditures model.

9. Assume an economy is in recession with a *MPC* of 0.75 and there is a GDP gap of $100 billion. How much must government spending increase to eliminate the gap? Instead of increasing government spending by the amount you calculate, what would be the effect of the government cutting taxes by this amount?

10. Suppose the government wishes to eliminate an inflationary gap of $100 billion and the *MPC* is 0.50. How much must the government cut its spending? Instead of decreasing government spending by the amount you calculate, what would be the effect of the government increasing taxes by this amount?

For Online Exercises, go to the Tucker Web site at www.cengage.com/economics/tucker.

CHECKPOINT ANSWERS

Full-Employment Output, Where Are You?

A tax cut of $500 billion boosts consumer income by this amount. Since the *MPC* is 0.50, consumers will spend $250 billion of the tax cut and save the remaining $250 billion. To compute the impact of the rise in consumption (ΔC) on real GDP (ΔY), use this formula:

$$\Delta C \times \text{multiplier} = \Delta Y$$

where

$$\text{Multiplier} = \frac{1}{MPS} = \frac{1}{1-MPC} = \frac{1}{1-0.50} = 2$$

Thus, $250 billion $\times$ 2 = $500 billion. The increase in real GDP from the tax cut equals $500 billion, which is added to the initial equilibrium real GDP of $15 trillion to achieve full-employment output. If you said the full-employment real GDP is $15.5 trillion, **YOU ARE CORRECT.**

How Much Spending Must Uncle Sam Cut?

The GDP gap is $500 billion real GDP. To calculate the size of the government spending cut (ΔG) required to decrease real GDP (ΔY) by $500 billion, use this formula:

$$\Delta G \times \text{multiplier} = -\Delta Y$$

where

$$\text{Multiplier} = \frac{1}{MPS} = \frac{1}{1-MPC} = \frac{1}{1-0.90} = 10$$

Thus,

$$\Delta G = \frac{-\Delta Y}{\text{multiplier}} = \frac{-\$500 \text{ billion}}{10} = -\$50 \text{ billion}$$

If you said the size of the cut in government spending is $50 billion, **YOU ARE CORRECT.**

Practice Quiz

For an explanation of the correct answers, visit the Tucker Web Site at www.cengage.com/economics/tucker

1. The net exports line can be
   a. positive.
   b. negative.
   c. zero.
   d. any of the above.

2. There will be unplanned inventory investment accumulation when
   a. aggregate output (real GDP) equals aggregate expenditures.
   b. aggregate output (real GDP) exceeds aggregate expenditures.
   c. aggregate expenditures exceed aggregate output (real GDP).
   d. firms increase output.

3. John Maynard Keynes proposed that the multiplier effect can correct an economic depression. Based on this theory, an increase in equilibrium output would be created by an initial
   a. increase in investment.
   b. increase in government spending.
   c. decrease in government spending.
   d. both (a) and (b).
   e. both (a) and (c).

4. The spending multiplier is defined as
   a. 1/(1 − marginal propensity to consume).
   b. 1/(marginal propensity to consume).
   c. 1/(1 − marginal propensity to save).
   d. 1/(marginal propensity to consume + marginal propensity to save).

5. If the value of the marginal propensity to consume (MPC) is 0.50, the value of the spending multiplier is
   a. 0.50.
   b. 1.
   c. 2.
   d. 5.

6. If the marginal propensity to consume (MPC) is 0.80, the value of the spending multiplier is
   a. 2.
   b. 5.
   c. 8.
   d. 10.

7. If the marginal propensity to consume (MPC) is 0.75, a $50 billion decrease in government spending would cause equilibrium output to
   a. increase by $50 billion.
   b. decrease by $50 billion.
   c. increase by $200 billion.
   d. decrease by $200 billion.

8. If the marginal propensity to consume (MPC) is 0.90, a $100 billion increase in planned investment expenditure, other things being equal, will cause an increase in equilibrium output of
   a. $90 billion.
   b. $100 billion.
   c. $900 billion.
   d. $1,000 billion.

9. Keynes's criticism of the classical theory was that the Great Depression would not correct itself. The multiplier effect would restore an economy to full employment if
   a. government would follow a "least government is the best government" policy.
   b. government taxes were increased.
   c. government spending were increased.
   d. government spending were decreased.

10. The equilibrium level of real GDP is $1,000 billion, the full-employment level of real GDP is $1,250 billion, and the marginal propensity to consume (MPC) is 0.60. The full-employment target can be reached if government spending is
    a. increased by $60 billion.
    b. increased by $100 billion.
    c. increased by $250 billion.
    d. held constant.

11. In Exhibit 9, the spending multiplier for this economy is equal to
    a. 1⅔.
    b. 2½.
    c. 3.
    d. 5.

Practice Quiz Continued

Exhibit 9

Keynesian Aggregate Expenditures Model When the *MPC* is 3/5

Real aggregate expenditures (trillions of dollars per year)

Real GDP (trillions of dollars per year)

12. To close the recessionary gap and achieve full-employment real GDP as shown in Exhibit 9, the government should increase spending by
a. $1 trillion.
b. $1.2 trillion.
c. $2.0 trillion.
d. $2.5 trillion.

13. To close the recessionary gap and achieve full-employment real GDP as shown in Exhibit 9, the government should cut taxes by
a. $0.60 trillion.
b. $1 trillion.
c. $2 trillion.
d. $3 trillion.

14. Using the aggregate expenditures model, assume the aggregate expenditures (*AE*) line is above the 45-degree line at full-employment GDP. This vertical distance is called a (an)
a. inflationary gap.
b. recessionary gap.
c. negative GDP gap.
d. marginal propensity to consume gap.

15. Use the aggregate expenditures model and assume an economy is in equilibrium at $5 trillion, which is $250 billion below full-employment GDP. If the marginal propensity to consume (*MPC*) is 0.60, full-employment GDP can be reached if government spending
a. decreases by $60 billion.
b. decreases by $100 billion.
c. decreases by $250 billion.
d. is held constant.

10

Aggregate Demand and Supply

Classical economic theory held that the economy would bounce back to full employment as long as prices and wages were flexible. As the unemployment rate soared and remained high during the Great Depression, British economist John Maynard Keynes formulated a new theory with new policy implications. Instead of taking a wait-and-see policy until markets self-correct the economy, Keynes argued that policymakers must take action to influence aggregate spending through changes in government spending. The prescription for the Great Depression was simple: Increase government spending and jobs will be created. Faced with the current financial crisis, Keynesian management of the economy is currently being used to stabilize the U.S. and global economy. Keynes himself would be amazed at the scale and scope of what is happening. The opposition view today is based on the classical model that rejects the federal government stimulus package concept because the economy will self-correct to full employment.

In this chapter, you will use aggregate demand and supply analysis to study the business cycle. The chapter opens with a presentation of the aggregate demand curve and then the aggregate supply curve. Once these concepts are developed, the analysis shows why modern macroeconomics teaches that shifts in aggregate supply or aggregate demand can influence the price level, the equilibrium level of real GDP, and employment. For example, although Keynes was not concerned with the problem of inflation, his theory has implications for fighting demand-pull inflation. In this case, the government must cut spending or increase taxes to reduce aggregate demand. You will probably return to this chapter often because it provides the basic tools with which to organize your thinking about the macro economy.

In this chapter, you will learn to solve these economics puzzles:

- Why does the aggregate supply curve have three different segments?

- Would the greenhouse effect cause inflation, unemployment, or both?

- Was John Maynard Keynes's prescription for the Great Depression right?

THE AGGREGATE DEMAND CURVE

Here we view the collective demand for *all* goods and services, rather than the *market* demand for a particular good or service. Exhibit 1 shows the **aggregate demand curve** (*AD*), which slopes downward and to the right for a given year. The aggregate demand curve shows the level of real GDP purchased by households, businesses, government, and foreigners (net exports) at different possible price levels during a time period, ceteris paribus. Stated differently, the aggregate demand curve shows us the total dollar amount of goods and services that will be demanded in the economy at various price levels. As for the demand curve for an individual market, the lower the economywide price level, the greater the aggregate quantity demanded for real goods and services, ceteris paribus.

The downward slope of the aggregate demand curve shows that at a given level of aggregate income, people buy more goods and services at a lower average price level. While the horizontal axis in the market supply and demand model measures *physical* units, such as bushels of wheat, the horizontal axis in the aggregate demand and supply model measures the value of *final* goods and services included in real GDP. Note that the horizontal axis represents the quantity of aggregate production demanded, measured in base-year dollars. The vertical axis is an *index* of the overall price level, such as the chain price index or the CPI, rather than the price per bushel of wheat. As shown in Exhibit 1, if the price level measured by the CPI is 300 at point *A*, a real GDP of $8 trillion is demanded in a given year. If the price level is 200 at point *B*, a real GDP of $12 trillion is demanded. Note that hypothetical data is used throughout this chapter and the next unless otherwise stated.

Although the aggregate demand curve looks like a market demand curve, these concepts are different. As we move along a market demand curve, the price of related goods is assumed to be constant. But when we deal with changes in the general or average price level in an economy, this assumption is meaningless because we are using a market basket measure for *all* goods and services.

> **CONCLUSION** *The aggregate demand curve and the demand curve are not the same concept.*

Aggregate demand curve (*AD*)

The curve that shows the level of real GDP purchased by households, businesses, government, and foreigners (net exports) at different possible price levels during a time period, ceteris paribus.

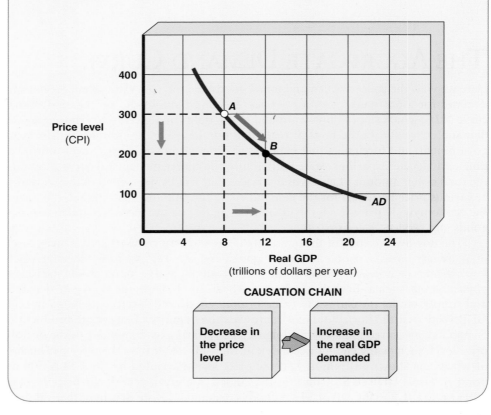

Exhibit 1   **The Aggregate Demand Curve**

The aggregate demand curve (*AD*) shows the relationship between the price level and the level of real GDP, other things being equal. The lower the price level, the larger the GDP demanded by households, businesses, government, and foreigners. If the price level is 300 at point *A*, a real GDP of $8 trillion is demanded. If the price level is 200 at point *B*, the real GDP demanded increases to $12 trillion.

REASONS FOR THE AGGREGATE DEMAND CURVE'S SHAPE

The reasons for the downward slope of an aggregate demand curve include the *real balances effect*, the *interest-rate effect*, and the *net exports effect*.

Real Balances Effect

Recall from the discussion in the chapter on inflation that cash, checking deposits, savings accounts, and certificates of deposit are examples of financial assets whose real value changes with the price level. If prices are falling, the purchasing power of households rises and they are more willing and able to spend. Suppose you have $1,000 in a checking account with which to buy 10 weeks' worth of groceries. If prices fall by 20 percent, $1,000 will now buy enough groceries for 12 weeks. This rise in your real wealth may make you more willing and able to purchase a new iPhone out of current income.

> **CONCLUSION** *Consumers spend more on goods and services when lower prices make their dollars more valuable. Therefore, the real value of money is measured by the quantity of goods and services each dollar buys.*

When inflation reduces the real value of fixed-value financial assets held by households, the result is lower consumption, and real GDP falls. The effect of the change in the price level on real consumption spending is called the **real balances effect**. The real balances effect is the impact on total spending (real GDP) caused by the inverse relationship between the price level and the real value of financial assets with fixed nominal value.

Interest-Rate Effect

The second reason why the aggregate demand curve is downward sloping involves the **interest-rate effect**. The interest-rate effect is the impact on total spending (real GDP) caused by the direct relationship between the price level and the interest rate. A key assumption of the aggregate demand curve is that the supply of money available for borrowing remains fixed. A high price level means people must take more dollars from their wallets and checking accounts in order to purchase goods and services. At a higher price level, the demand for borrowed money to buy products also increases and results in a higher cost of borrowing, that is, higher interest rates. Rising interest rates discourage households from borrowing to purchase homes, cars, and other consumer products. Similarly, at higher interest rates, businesses cut investment projects because the higher cost of borrowing diminishes the profitability of these investments. Thus, assuming fixed credit, an increase in the price level translates through higher interest rates into a lower real GDP.

Net Exports Effect

Whether American-made goods have lower prices than foreign goods is another important factor in determining the aggregate demand curve. A higher domestic price level tends to make U.S. goods more expensive than foreign goods, and imports rise because consumers substitute imported goods for domestic goods. An increase in the price of U.S. goods in foreign markets also causes U.S. exports to decline. Consequently, a rise in the domestic price level of an economy tends to increase imports, decrease exports, and thereby reduce the net exports component of real GDP. This condition is the **net exports effect**. The net exports effect is the impact on total spending (real GDP) caused by the inverse relationship between the price level and the net exports of an economy.

Exhibit 2 summarizes the three effects that explain why the aggregate demand curve in Exhibit 1 is downward sloping.

Real balances effect

The impact on total spending (real GDP) caused by the inverse relationship between the price level and the real value of financial assets with fixed nominal value.

Interest-rate effect

The impact on total spending (real GDP) caused by the direct relationship between the price level and the interest rate.

Global Economics

Net exports effect

The impact on total spending (real GDP) caused by the inverse relationship between the price level and the net exports of an economy.

Exhibit 2	Why the Aggregate Demand Curve Is Downward Sloping
Effect	**Causation chain**
Real balances effect	Price level decreases → Purchasing power rises → Wealth rises → Consumers buy more goods → Real GDP demanded increases
Interest-rate effect	Price level decreases → Purchasing power rises → Demand for fixed supply of credit falls → Interest rates fall → Businesses and households borrow and buy more goods → Real GDP demanded increases
Net exports effect	Price level decreases → U.S. goods become less expensive than foreign goods → Americans and foreigners buy more U.S. goods → Exports rise and imports fall → Real GDP demanded increases

NONPRICE-LEVEL DETERMINANTS OF AGGREGATE DEMAND

As was the case with individual demand curves, we must distinguish between *changes in real GDP demanded*, caused by changes in the price level, and *changes in aggregate demand*, caused by changes in one or more of the *nonprice-level determinants*. Once the ceteris paribus assumption is relaxed, changes in variables other than the price level cause a change in the location of the aggregate demand curve. Nonprice-level determinants include the consumption (C), investment (I), government spending (G), and net exports ($X - M$) components of aggregate expenditures explained in the chapter on GDP.

CONCLUSION *Any change in the individual components of aggregate expenditures shifts the aggregate demand curve.*

Exhibit 3 illustrates the link between an increase in expenditures and an increase in aggregate demand. Begin at point A on aggregate demand curve AD_1, with a price level of 200 and a real GDP of $12 trillion. Assume the price level remains constant at 200 and the aggregate demand curve increases from AD_1 to AD_2. Consequently, the level of real GDP rises from $12 trillion (point A) to $16 trillion (point B) at the price level of 200. The cause might be that consumers have become more optimistic about the future and their consumption expenditures (C) have risen. Or possibly an increase in business optimism has increased profit expectations, and the level of investment (I) has risen because businesses are spending more for plants and equipment. The same increase in aggregate demand could also have been caused by

Exhibit 3   A Shift in the Aggregate Demand Curve

At the price level of 200, the real GDP level is $12 trillion at point A on AD_1. An increase in one of the nonprice-level determinants of consumption (C), investment (I), government spending (G), or net exports ($X - M$) causes the level of real GDP to rise to $16 trillion at point B on AD_2. Because this effect occurs at any price level, an increase in aggregate expenditures shifts the AD curve rightward. Conversely, a decrease in aggregate expenditures shifts the AD curve leftward.

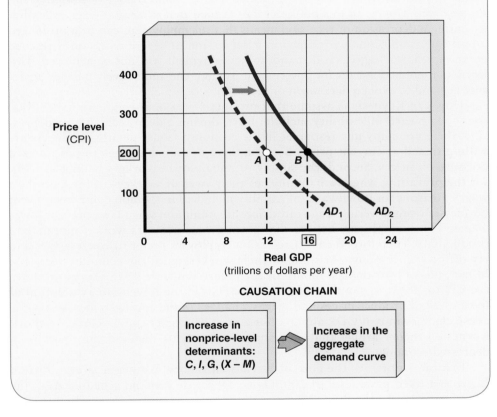

a boost in government spending (G) or a rise in net exports ($X - M$). A swing to pessimistic expectations by consumers or firms will cause the aggregate demand curve to shift leftward. A leftward shift in the aggregate demand curve may also be caused by a decrease in government spending or net exports.

THE AGGREGATE SUPPLY CURVE

Just as we must distinguish between the *aggregate* demand and *market* demand curves, the theory for a *market* supply curve does not apply directly to the *aggregate* supply curve. Keeping this condition in mind, we can define the **aggregate supply curve** (*AS*)

Aggregate supply curve (*AS*)

The curve that shows the level of real GDP produced at different possible price levels during a time period, ceteris paribus.

as the curve that shows the level of real GDP produced at different possible price levels during a time period, ceteris paribus. Stated simply, the aggregate supply curve shows us the total dollar amount of goods and services produced in an economy at various price levels. Given this general definition, we must pause to discuss two opposing views—the Keynesian horizontal aggregate supply curve and the classical vertical aggregate supply curve.

Keynesian View of Aggregate Supply

In 1936, John Maynard Keynes published *The General Theory of Employment, Interest, and Money.* In this book, Keynes argued that price and wage inflexibility during a depression or recession means that unemployment can be a prolonged affair. Unless an economy trapped in a depression or severe recession is rescued by an increase in aggregate demand, full employment will not be achieved. This Keynesian prediction calls for government to intervene and actively manage aggregate demand to avoid a depression or recession.

How can Keynesians assume that product prices and wages are fixed? Reasons for upward inflexibility include: First, during a deep recession or depression, there are many idle resources in the economy. Consequently, producers are willing to sell at current prices because there are no shortages to put upward pressure on prices. Second, the supply of unemployed workers willing to work for the prevailing wage rate diminishes the power of workers to increase their wages. Reasons for downward inflexibility include: First, union contracts prevent businesses from lowering wage rates. Second, minimum wage laws prevent lower wages. Third, employers believe that cutting wages lowers worker morale and productivity. Therefore, during a recession employers prefer to freeze wages and lay off or reduce hours for some of their workers until the economy recovers. In fact, the CPI for the last month of each recession since 1948 was at or above the CPI for the first month of the recession. Given the Keynesian assumption of fixed or rigid product prices and wages, changes in the aggregate demand curve cause changes in real GDP along a horizontal aggregate supply curve. In short, Keynesian theory argues that only shifts in aggregate demand can revitalize a depressed economy.

Exhibit 4 portrays the core of Keynesian theory. We begin at equilibrium E_1, with a fixed price level of 200. Given aggregate demand schedule AD_1, the equilibrium level of real GDP is \$8 trillion. Now government spending (G) increases, causing aggregate demand to rise from AD_1 to AD_2 and equilibrium to shift from E_1 to E_2 along the horizontal aggregate supply curve (*AS*). At E_2, the economy moves to \$12 trillion, which is closer to the full-employment GDP of \$16 trillion.

CONCLUSION *When the aggregate supply curve is horizontal and an economy is in recession below full employment, the only effects of an increase in aggregate demand are increases in real GDP and employment, while the price level does not change. Stated simply, the Keynesian view is that "demand creates its own supply."*

Exhibit 4 — The Keynesian Horizontal Aggregate Supply Curve

The increase in aggregate demand from AD_1 to AD_2 causes a new equilibrium at E_2. Given the Keynesian assumption of a fixed price level, changes in aggregate demand cause changes in real GDP along the horizontal portion of the aggregate supply curve, AS. Keynesian theory argues that only shifts in aggregate demand possess the ability to restore a depressed economy to the full-employment output.

CAUSATION CHAIN

Government spending (G) increases → Aggregate demand increases and the economy moves from E_1 to E_2 → Price level remains constant, while real GDP and employment rise

Classical View of Aggregate Supply

Prior to the Great Depression, a group of *laissez-faire* economists known as the *classical economists* dominated economic thinking. The founder of the classical school of economics was Adam Smith. Exhibit 5 uses the aggregate demand and supply model to illustrate the classical view that the aggregate supply curve, AS, is a vertical line at the full employment output of $16 trillion. The vertical shape of the classical aggregate supply curve is based on two assumptions. First, the economy normally operates at its full-employment output level. Second, the price level of products and production costs change by the same percentage, that is, proportionally, in order to maintain

Exhibit 5   The Classical Vertical Aggregate Supply Curve

Classical theory teaches that prices and wages adjust to keep the economy operating at its full-employment output of $16 trillion. A decline in aggregate demand from AD_1 to AD_2 will temporarily cause a surplus of $4 trillion, the distance from E' to E_1. Businesses respond by cutting the price level from 300 to 200. As a result, consumers increase their purchases because of the real balances effect, and wages adjust downward. Thus, classical economists predict the economy is self-correcting and will restore full employment at point E_2. E_1 and E_2 therefore represent points along a classical vertical aggregate supply curve, AS.

CAUSATION CHAIN

| Aggregate demand decreases at full employment and the economy moves from E_1 to E' | ⇒ | At E' unemployment and a surplus of unsold goods and services cause cuts in prices and wages | ⇒ | The economy moves from E' to E_2, where full employment is restored |

a full-employment level of output. This classical theory of flexible prices and wages is at odds with the Keynesian concept of sticky (inflexible) prices and wages.

Exhibit 5 illustrates why classical economists believe a market economy over time automatically self-corrects without government intervention to full employment. Following the classical scenario, the economy is initially in equilibrium at E_1, the price level is 300, real output is at its full-employment level of $16 trillion, and the aggregate demand curve AD_1 traces total spending. Now suppose private spending falls because households and businesses are pessimistic about economic conditions. This condition causes AD_1 to shift leftward to AD_2. At a price level of 300, the immediate effect is that aggregate output exceeds aggregate spending by $4 trillion ($E_1$ to E'), and unexpected inventory accumulation occurs. To eliminate unsold inventories resulting from the decrease in aggregate demand, business firms temporarily cut back on production and reduce the price level from 300 to 200.

At E', the decline in aggregate output in response to the surplus also affects prices in the factor markets. As a result of the economy moving from point E_1 to E', there is a decrease in the demand for labor, natural resources, and other inputs used to produce products. This surplus condition in the factor markets means that some workers who are willing to work are laid off and compete with those who still have jobs by reducing their wage demands. Owners of natural resources and capital likewise cut their prices.

How can the classical economists believe that prices and wages are completely flexible? The answer is contained in the *real balances effect,* explained earlier. When businesses reduce the price level from 300 to 200, the cost of living falls by the same proportion. Once the price level falls by 33 percent, a nominal or money wage rate of, say, $21 per hour will purchase 33 percent more groceries after the fall in product prices than it would before the fall. Workers will, therefore, accept a pay cut of 33 percent, or $7 per hour. Any worker who refuses the lower wage rate of $14 per hour will be replaced by an unemployed worker willing to accept the going rate.

Exhibit 5 shows an economywide proportional fall in prices and wages by the movement downward along AD_2 from E' to a new equilibrium at E_2. At E_2, the economy has self-corrected through downwardly flexible prices and wages to its full-employment level of $16 trillion worth of real GDP at the lower price level of 200. E_1 and E_2 therefore represent points along a classical vertical aggregate supply curve, AS. (The classical model is explained in more detail in the appendix to this chapter.)

CONCLUSION *When the aggregate supply curve is vertical at the full-employment GDP, the only effect over time of a change in aggregate demand is a change in the price level. Stated simply, the classical view is that "supply creates its own demand."*[1]

Although Keynes himself did not use the *AD-AS* model, we can use Exhibit 5 to distinguish between Keynes's view and the classical theory of flexible prices and wages. Keynes believed that once the demand curve has shifted from AD_1 to AD_2, the surplus (the distance from E' to E_1) will persist because he rejected price-wage downward flexibility. The economy therefore will remain at the less-than-full-employment output of $12 trillion until the aggregate demand curve shifts rightward and returns to its initial position at AD_1.

CONCLUSION *Keynesian theory rejects classical theory for an economy in recession because Keynesians argue that during a recession prices and wages do not adjust downward to restore an economy to full-employment real GDP.*

---

1. This quotation is known as Say's Law, named after the French classical economist Jean-Baptiste Say (1767–1832).

Keynesian range

The horizontal segment of the aggregate supply curve, which represents an economy in a severe recession.

Intermediate range

The rising segment of the aggregate supply curve, which represents an economy as it approaches full-employment output.

THREE RANGES OF THE AGGREGATE SUPPLY CURVE

Having studied the differing theories of the classical economists and Keynes, we will now discuss an eclectic or general view of how the shape of the aggregate supply curve varies as real GDP expands or contracts. The aggregate supply curve, *AS*, in Exhibit 6 has three quite distinct ranges or segments, labeled (1) *Keynesian range*, (2) *intermediate range*, and (3) *classical range*.

The **Keynesian range** is the horizontal segment of the aggregate supply curve, which represents an economy in a severe recession. In Exhibit 6, below real GDP Y_K, the price level remains constant as the level of real GDP rises. Between Y_K and the full-employment output of Y_F, the price level rises as the real GDP level rises. The **intermediate range** is the rising segment of the aggregate supply curve, which represents an economy approaching full-employment output. Finally, at Y_F, the level of real GDP remains constant, and only the price level rises.

Exhibit 6   The Three Ranges of the Aggregate Supply Curve

The aggregate supply curve shows the relationship between the price level and the level of real GDP supplied. It consists of three distinct ranges: (1) a Keynesian range between 0 and Y_K wherein the price level is constant for an economy in severe recession; (2) an intermediate range between Y_K and Y_F, where both the price level and the level of real GDP vary as an economy approaches full employment; and (3) a classical range, where the price level can vary, while the level of real GDP remains constant at the full-employment level of output, Y_F.

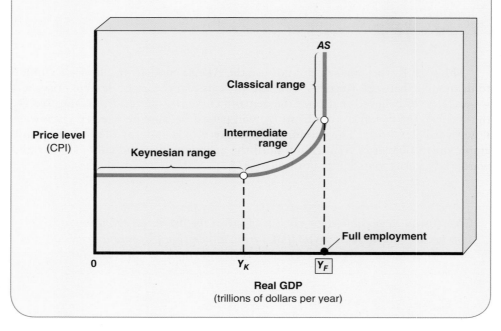

The **classical range** is the vertical segment of the aggregate supply curve, which represents an economy at full-employment output. We will now examine the rationale for each of these three quite distinct ranges.

Aggregate Demand and Aggregate Supply Macroeconomic Equilibrium

In Exhibit 7, the *macroeconomic equilibrium* level of real GDP corresponding to the point of equality, *E*, is $8 trillion, and the equilibrium price level is 200. This is the unique combination of price level and output level that equates how much people want to buy with the amount businesses want to produce and sell. Because the entire real GDP value of final products is bought and sold at the price level of 200, there is no upward or downward pressure for the macroeconomic equilibrium to change. Note that the economy shown in Exhibit 7 is operating on the edge of the Keynesian range, with a negative GDP gap of $8 trillion.

Suppose that in Exhibit 7 the level of output on the *AS* curve is below $8 trillion and the *AD* curve remains fixed. At a price level of 200, the real GDP demanded exceeds the real GDP supplied. Under such circumstances, businesses cannot fill orders quickly enough, and inventories are drawn down unexpectedly. Business managers react by hiring more workers and producing more output. Because the economy

---

Exhibit 7   The Aggregate Demand and Aggregate Supply Model

Macroeconomic equilibrium occurs where the aggregate demand curve, *AD*, and the aggregate supply curve, *AS*, intersect. In this case, equilibrium, *E*, is located at the far end of the Keynesian range, where the price level is 200 and the equilibrium output is $8 trillion. In macroeconomic equilibrium, businesses neither overestimate nor underestimate the real GDP demanded at the prevailing price level.

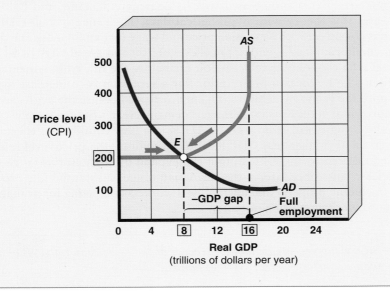

is operating in the Keynesian range, the price level remains constant at 200. The opposite scenario occurs if the level of real GDP supplied on the *AS* curve exceeds the real GDP in the intermediate range between $8 trillion and $16 trillion. In this output segment, the price level is between 200 and 400, and businesses face sales that are less than expected. In this case, unintended inventories of unsold goods pile up on the shelves, and management will lay off workers, cut back on production, and reduce prices.

This adjustment process continues until the equilibrium price level and output level are reached at point *E* and there is no upward or downward pressure for the price level to change. Here the production decisions of sellers in the economy equal the total spending decisions of buyers during the given period of time.

> **CONCLUSION** *At macroeconomic equilibrium, sellers neither overestimate nor underestimate the real GDP demanded at the prevailing price level.*

CHANGES IN THE *AD-AS* MACROECONOMIC EQUILIBRIUM

One explanation of the business cycle is that the aggregate demand curve moves along a stationary aggregate supply curve. The next step in our analysis therefore is to *shift* the aggregate demand curve along the three ranges of the aggregate supply curve and observe the impact on real GDP and the price level. As the macroeconomic equilibrium changes, the economy experiences more or fewer problems with inflation and unemployment.

Keynesian Range

Keynes's macroeconomic theory offered a powerful solution to the Great Depression. Keynes perceived the economy as driven by aggregate demand, and Exhibit 8(a) demonstrates this theory with hypothetical data. The range of real GDP below $8 trillion is consistent with Keynesian price and wage inflexibility. Assume the economy is in equilibrium at E_1, with a price level of 200 and a real GDP of $4 trillion. In this case, the economy is in recession far below the full-employment GDP of $16 trillion. The Keynesian prescription for a recession is to increase aggregate demand until the economy achieves full employment. Because the aggregate supply curve is horizontal in the Keynesian range, "demand creates its own supply." Suppose demand shifts rightward from AD_1 to AD_2 and a new equilibrium is established at E_2. Even at the higher real GDP level of $8 trillion, the price level remains at 200. Stated differently, aggregate output can expand throughout this range without raising prices. This is because, in the Keynesian range, substantial idle production capacity (including property and unemployed workers competing for available jobs) can be put to work at existing prices.

> **CONCLUSION** *As aggregate demand increases in the Keynesian range, the price level remains constant as real GDP expands.*

Exhibit 8   **Effects of Increases in Aggregate Demand**

The effect of a rightward shift in the aggregate demand curve on the price and output levels depends on the range of the aggregate supply curve in which the shift occurs. In part (a), an increase in aggregate demand causing the equilibrium to change from E_1 to E_2 in the Keynesian range will increase real GDP from $4 trillion to $8 trillion, but the price level will remain unchanged at 200.

In part (b), an increase in aggregate demand causing the equilibrium to change from E_3 to E_4 in the intermediate range will increase real GDP from $8 trillion to $12 trillion, and the price level will rise from 200 to 250.

In part (c), an increase in aggregate demand causing the equilibrium to change from E_5 to E_6 in the classical range will increase the price level from 300 to 400, but real GDP will not increase beyond the full-employment level of $16 trillion.

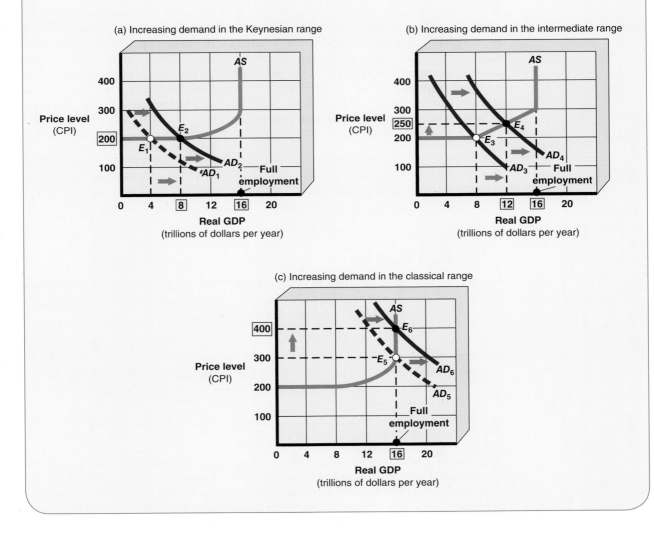

(a) Increasing demand in the Keynesian range

(b) Increasing demand in the intermediate range

(c) Increasing demand in the classical range

Intermediate Range

The intermediate range in Exhibit 8(b) is between $8 trillion and $16 trillion worth of real GDP. As output increases in the range of the aggregate supply curve near the full-employment level of output, the considerable slack in the economy disappears. Assume an economy is initially in equilibrium at E_3 and aggregate demand increases from AD_3 to AD_4. As a result, the level of real GDP rises from $8 trillion to $12 trillion, and the price level rises from 200 to 250. In this output range, several factors contribute to inflation. First, *bottlenecks* (obstacles to output flow) develop when some firms have no unused capacity and other firms operate below full capacity. Suppose the steel industry is operating at full capacity and cannot fill all its orders for steel. An inadequate supply of one resource, such as steel, can hold up auto production even though the auto industry is operating well below capacity. Consequently, the bottleneck causes firms to raise the price of steel and, in turn, autos. Second, a shortage of certain labor skills while firms are earning higher profits causes businesses to expect that labor will exert its power to obtain sizable wage increases, so businesses raise prices. Wage demands are more difficult to reject when the economy is prospering because businesses fear workers will change jobs or strike. Besides, businesses believe higher prices can be passed on to consumers quite easily because consumers expect higher prices as output expands to near full capacity. Third, as the economy approaches full employment, firms must use less productive workers and less efficient machinery. This inefficiency creates higher production costs, which are passed on to consumers in the form of higher prices.

> **CONCLUSION** *In the intermediate range, increases in aggregate demand increase both the price level and the real GDP.*

Classical Range

While inflation resulting from an outward shift in aggregate demand was no problem in the Keynesian range and only a minor problem in the intermediate range, it becomes a serious problem in the classical or vertical range.

> **CONCLUSION** *Once the economy reaches full-employment output in the classical range, additional increases in aggregate demand merely cause inflation, rather than more real GDP.*

Assume the economy shown in Exhibit 8(c) is in equilibrium at E_5, which intersects AS at the full-capacity output. Now suppose aggregate demand shifts rightward from AD_5 to AD_6. Because the aggregate supply curve AS is vertical at $16 trillion, this increase in the aggregate demand curve boosts the price level from 300 to 400, but it fails to expand real GDP. The explanation is that once the economy operates at capacity, businesses raise their prices in order to ration fully employed resources to those willing to pay the highest prices.

In summary, the *AD-AS* model presented in this chapter is a combination of the conflicting assumptions of the Keynesian and the classical theories separated by an intermediate range, which fits neither extreme precisely. Be forewarned that in later chapters you will encounter a continuing great controversy over the shape of the aggregate supply curve. Modern-day classical economists believe the entire aggregate supply curve is steep or vertical. In contrast, Keynesian economists contend that the aggregate supply curve is much flatter or horizontal.

The *AD-AS* Model for 2008–2009 during the Great Recession

Exhibit 9 uses actual data to illustrate the *AD-AS* model. At E_1, the economy in the third quarter of 2008 was operating at a CPI of 219 and a real GDP of $13.3 trillion, which was below the full-employment real GDP of $13.4 trillion. In 2008, the

Exhibit 9	**Effect of Decreases in Aggregate Demand during 2008–2009 of the Recession**

Beginning in the third quarter of 2008 at E_1 the aggregate demand curve shifted leftward from E_1 to E_2 in the fourth quarter of 2008 along the intermediate range of the aggregate supply curve, *AS*. The CPI fell from 219 to 212 and real GDP fell from $13.3 trillion to $13.1 trillion. Next, the aggregate demand curve decreased from AD_2 at E_2 to AD_3 at E_3 in the second quarter of 2009 along the Keynesian range of the aggregate supply curve. Here the price level remained constant and real GDP fell from $13.1 trillion to $12.9 trillion.

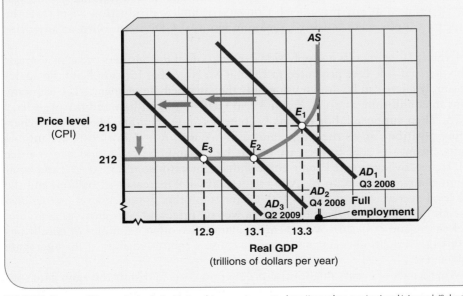

SOURCES: Bureau of Economic Analysis, National Income Accounts, http://www.bea.gov/national/nipaweb/SelectTable .asp?Selected=Y, Table 1.1.6 and Bureau of Labor Statistics, Consumer Price Index, http://data.bls.gov/cgi-bin/ surveymost?cu.

combination of home prices falling sharply and a plunge in stock prices destroyed household wealth. At the same time, new home construction fell rapidly, which decreased investment spending. Recall from the chapter on Gross Domestic Product that new residential housing is included in investment spending (I). This recessionary condition is illustrated by a movement between E_1 and E_2 caused by the aggregate demand curve decreasing from AD_1 to AD_2 along the intermediate range of the aggregate supply curve AS. At E_2, in the fourth quarter of 2008, the CPI dropped to 212, and real GDP decreased from $13.3 trillion to $13.1 trillion. Next, the aggregate demand curve decreased again from AD_2 to AD_3 in the second quarter of 2009 along the flat Keynesian range between E_2 and E_3. Here the price level remained approximately constant at 212, while real GDP declined from $13.1 trillion to $12.9 trillion. Although not shown explicitly in the exhibit, the unemployment rate rose during this period from 4.7 percent to 9.5 percent.

NONPRICE-LEVEL DETERMINANTS OF AGGREGATE SUPPLY

Our discussion so far has explained changes in real GDP supplied resulting from changes in the aggregate demand curve, given a stationary aggregate supply curve. Now we consider the situation when the aggregate demand curve is stationary and the aggregate supply curve shifts as a result of changes in one or more of the *nonprice-level determinants*. The nonprice-level factors affecting aggregate supply include resource prices (domestic and imported), technological change, taxes, subsidies, and regulations. Note that each of these factors affects production costs. At a given price level, the profit businesses make at any level of real GDP depends on production costs. If costs change, firms respond by changing their output. Lower production costs shift the aggregate supply curve rightward, indicating greater real GDP is supplied at any price level. Conversely, higher production costs shift the aggregate supply curve leftward, meaning less real GDP is supplied at any price level.

Exhibit 10 represents a supply-side explanation of the business cycle, in contrast to the demand-side case presented in Exhibit 8. (Note that for simplicity the aggregate supply curve can be drawn using only the intermediate segment.) The economy begins in equilibrium at point E_1, with real GDP at $10 trillion and the price level at 175. Then suppose labor unions become less powerful and their weaker bargaining position causes the wage rate to fall. With lower labor costs per unit of output, businesses seek to increase profits by expanding production at any price level. Hence, the aggregate supply curve shifts rightward from AS_1 to AS_2, and equilibrium changes from E_1 to E_2. As a result, real GDP increases $2 trillion, and the price level decreases from 175 to 150. Changes in other nonprice-level factors also cause an increase in aggregate supply. Lower oil prices, greater entrepreneurship, lower taxes, and reduced government regulation are other examples of conditions that lower production costs and therefore cause a rightward shift of the aggregate supply curve.

What kinds of events might raise production costs and shift the aggregate supply curve leftward? Perhaps there is war in the Persian Gulf or the Organization of Petroleum Exporting Countries (OPEC) disrupts supplies of oil, and higher energy

Exhibit 10 | A Rightward Shift in the Aggregate Supply Curve

Holding the aggregate demand curve constant, the impact on the price level and real GDP depends on whether the aggregate supply curve shifts to the right or the left. A rightward shift of the aggregate supply curve from AS_1 to AS_2 will increase real GDP from $10 trillion to $12 trillion and reduce the price level from 175 to 150.

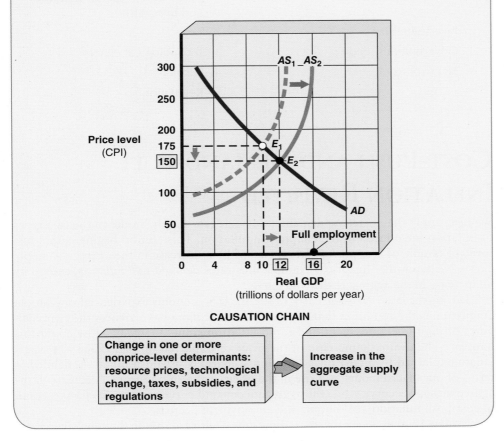

CAUSATION CHAIN

| Change in one or more nonprice-level determinants: resource prices, technological change, taxes, subsidies, and regulations | ⇨ | Increase in the aggregate supply curve |

prices spread throughout the economy. Under such a "supply shock," businesses decrease their output at any price level in response to higher production costs per unit. Similarly, larger-than-expected wage increases, higher taxes to protect the environment (see Exhibit 8(a) in Chapter 4), greater government regulation, or firms having to pay higher health insurance premiums would increase production costs and therefore shift the aggregate supply curve leftward. A leftward shift in the aggregate supply curve is discussed further in the next section.

Exhibit 11 summarizes the nonprice-level determinants of aggregate demand and supply for further study and review. In the chapter on monetary policy, you will learn how changes in the supply of money in the economy can also shift the aggregate demand curve and influence macroeconomic performance.

Exhibit 11	Summary of the Nonprice-Level Determinants of Aggregate Demand and Aggregate Supply

Nonprice-level determinants of aggregate demand (total spending)	Nonprice-level determinants of aggregate supply
1. Consumption (C)	1. Resource prices (domestic and imported)
2. Investment (I)	2. Taxes
3. Government spending (G)	3. Technological change
4. Net exports (X − M)	4. Subsidies
	5. Regulation

COST-PUSH AND DEMAND-PULL INFLATION REVISITED

We now apply the aggregate demand and aggregate supply model to the two types of inflation introduced in the chapter on inflation. This section begins with a historical example of *cost-push inflation* caused by a decrease in the aggregate supply curve. Next, another historical example illustrates *demand-pull inflation*, caused by an increase in the aggregate demand curve.

During the late 1970s and early 1980s, the U.S. economy experienced **stagflation**. Stagflation is the condition that occurs when an economy experiences the twin maladies of high unemployment and rapid inflation simultaneously. How could this happen? The dramatic increase in the price of imported oil in 1973–1974 was a villain explained by a **cost-push inflation** scenario. Cost-push inflation, defined in terms of our macro model, is a rise in the price level resulting from a decrease in the aggregate supply curve while the aggregate demand curve remains fixed. As a result of cost-push inflation, real output and employment decrease.

Exhibit 12(a) uses actual data to show how a leftward shift in the supply curve can cause stagflation. In this exhibit, aggregate demand curve *AD* and aggregate supply curve AS_{73} represent the U.S. economy in 1973. Equilibrium was at point E_1, with the price level (CPI) at 44.4 and real GDP at $4,341 billion. Then, in 1974, the impact of a major supply shock shifted the aggregate supply curve leftward from AS_{73} to AS_{74}. The explanation for this shock was the oil embargo instituted by OPEC in retaliation for U.S. support of Israel in its war with the Arabs. Assuming a stable aggregate demand curve between 1973 and 1974, the punch from the energy shock resulted in a new equilibrium at point E_2, with the 1974 CPI at 49.3. The inflation rate for 1973 was 6.2 percent and for 1974 was 11 percent [(49.3 − 44.4)/44.4] × 100. Real GDP fell from $4,341 billion in 1973 to $4,319 billion in 1974, and the unemployment rate (not shown directly in the exhibit) climbed from 4.9 percent to 5.6 percent between these two years.[2]

Stagflation

The condition that occurs when an economy experiences the twin maladies of high unemployment and rapid inflation simultaneously.

Cost-push inflation

An increase in the general price level resulting from an increase in the cost of production that causes the aggregate supply curve to shift leftward.

---

2. *Economic Report of the President, 2010,* http://www.gpoaccess.gov/eop/, Tables B-2, B-42, B-62, and B-64.

Exhibit 12   Cost-Push and Demand-Pull Inflation

Parts (a) and (b) illustrate the distinction between cost-push inflation and demand-pull inflation. Cost-push inflation is inflation that results from a decrease in the aggregate supply curve. In part (a), higher oil prices in 1973 caused the aggregate supply curve to shift leftward from AS_{73} to AS_{74}. As a result, real GDP fell from \$4,341 billion to \$4,319 billion, and the price level (CPI) rose from 44.4 to 49.3. This combination of higher price level and lower real output is called stagflation.

As shown in part (b), demand-pull inflation is inflation that results from an increase in aggregate demand beyond the Keynesian range of output. Government spending increased to fight the Vietnam War without a tax increase, causing the aggregate demand curve to shift rightward from AD_{65} to AD_{66}. Consequently, real GDP rose from \$3,191 billion to \$3,399 billion, and the price level (CPI) rose from 31.5 to 32.4.

In contrast, an outward shift in the aggregate demand curve can result in **demand-pull inflation**. Demand-pull inflation, in terms of our macro model, is a rise in the price level resulting from an increase in the aggregate demand curve while the aggregate supply curve remains fixed. Again, we can use aggregate demand and supply analysis and actual data to explain demand-pull inflation. In 1965, when the unemployment rate of 4.5 percent was close to the 4 percent natural rate of unemployment, real government spending increased sharply to fight the Vietnam War without a tax increase (an income tax surcharge was enacted in 1968). The inflation rate jumped sharply from 1.6 percent in 1965 to 2.9 percent in 1966.

Exhibit 12(b) illustrates what happened to the economy between 1965 and 1966. Suppose the economy was operating in 1965 at E_1, which is in the intermediate output range. The impact of the increase in military spending shifted the aggregate demand curve from AD_{65} to AD_{66}, and the economy moved upward

Demand-pull inflation

A rise in the general price level resulting from an excess of total spending (demand) caused by a rightward shift in the aggregate demand curve.

You're The Economist
Was John Maynard Keynes Right? *Applicable Concepts: aggregate demand and aggregate supply analysis*

In *The General Theory of Employment, Interest, and Money,* Keynes wrote:

The ideas of economists and political philosophers, both when they are right and when they are wrong, are more powerful than is commonly understood. Indeed the world is ruled by little else. Practical men, who believe themselves to be quite exempt from any intellectual influences, are usually the slaves of some defunct economist. Madmen in authority, who hear voices in the air, are distilling their frenzy from some academic scribbler of a few years back. . . . There are not many who are influenced by new theories after they are twenty-five or thirty years of age, so that the ideas which civil servants and politicians and even agitators apply to current events are not likely to be the newest.[1]

Keynes (1883–1946) is regarded as the father of modern macroeconomics. He was the son of an eminent English economist, John Neville Keynes, who was a lecturer in economics and logic at Cambridge University. Keynes was educated at Eton and Cambridge in mathematics and probability theory, but ultimately he selected the field of economics and accepted a lectureship in economics at Cambridge.

© CORBIS

Keynes was a many-faceted man who was an honored and supremely successful member of the British academic, financial, and political upper class. He amassed a $2 million personal fortune by speculating in stocks, international currencies, and commodities. (Use CPI index numbers to compute the equivalent amount in today's dollars.) In addition to making a huge fortune for himself, Keynes served as a trustee of King's College and increased its endowment over tenfold.

Keynes was a prolific scholar who is best remembered for *The General Theory,* published in 1936. This work made a convincing attack on the classical theory that capitalism would self-correct from a severe recession. Keynes based his model on the belief that increasing aggregate demand will achieve full employment, while prices and wages remain inflexible. Moreover, his bold policy prescription was for the government to raise its spending and/or reduce taxes in order to increase the economy's aggregate demand curve and put the unemployed back to work.

Price Level, Real GDP, and Unemployment Rate, 1933–1941

Year	CPI	Real GDP (billions of 2000 dollars)	Unemployment rate (percent)
1933	13.0	$ 635	24.9%
1939	13.9	951	17.2
1940	14.0	1,034	14.6
1941	14.7	1,211	9.9

SOURCES: Bureau of Labor Statistics, ftp://ftp.bls.gov/pub/special.requests/cpi/cpiai.txt, Bureau of Economic Analysis, National Economic Accounts, http://www.bea.gov/national/nipaweb/SelectTable.asp?Selected=Y, Table 1.1.6 and Economic Report of the President, 2010, http://www.gpoaccess.gov/eop/index.html, Table B-35.

ANALYZE THE ISSUE

Was Keynes correct? Based on the above data, use the aggregate demand and aggregate supply model to explain Keynes's theory that increases in aggregate demand propel an economy toward full employment.

---

1. J. M. Keynes, *The General Theory of Employment, Interest, and Money* (London: Macmillan, 1936), p. 383.

along the aggregate supply curve until it reached E_2. Holding the aggregate supply curve constant, the *AD-AS* model predicts that increasing aggregate demand at near full employment causes demand-pull inflation. As shown in Exhibit 12(b), real GDP increased from $3,191 billion in 1963 to $3,399 billion in 1966, and the CPI rose from 31.5 to 32.4. Thus, the inflation rate for 1966 was 2.9 percent [(32.4−31.5)/31.5] × 100. Corresponding to the rise in real output, the unemployment rate of 4.5 percent in 1965 fell to 3.8 percent in 1966.[3]

In summary, the aggregate supply and aggregate demand curves shift in different directions for various reasons in a given time period. These shifts in the aggregate supply and aggregate demand curves cause upswings and downswings in real GDP—the business cycle. A leftward shift in the aggregate demand curve, for example, can cause a recession. Whereas, a rightward shift of the aggregate demand curve can cause real GDP and employment to rise, and the economy recovers. A leftward shift in the aggregate supply curve can cause a downswing, and a rightward shift might cause an upswing.

> **CONCLUSION** *The business cycle is a result of shifts in the aggregate demand and aggregate supply curves.*

INCREASE IN BOTH AGGREGATE DEMAND AND AGGREGATE SUPPLY CURVES

Let the trumpets blow! Aggregate demand and supply curves will now edify you by explaining the U.S. economy from the mid-1990s through 2000. Begin in Exhibit 13 at E_1 with real GDP at $8,031 billion and the CPI at 152. As shown in the *AD-AS* model for 1995, the economy operated below full employment (5.6 percent unemployment rate, not explicitly shown). Over the next five years, the U.S. economy moved to E_2 in 2000 and experienced strong growth in real GDP (from $8,031 billion to $9,817 billion) and mild inflation (the CPI increased from 152 to 172, which is 13.1 percent, or 2.6 percent per year).

The movement from E_1 (below full employment) to E_2 (full employment) was caused by an increase in AD_{95} to AD_{00} and an increase in AS_{95} to AS_{00}. The rightward shift in the *AS* curve was the result of technological advances, such as the Internet and electronic commerce, which produced larger-than-usual increases in productivity at each possible price level. And, as shown earlier in Exhibit 9 of the chapter on business cycles and unemployment, the economy has returned to operating below its full-employment potential real GDP since the recession of 2001, and this negative GDP rose sharply during the recession beginning in 2007.

---

3. Ibid.

Exhibit 13	A Rightward Shift in the Aggregate Demand and Supply Curves

From late 1995 through 2000, the aggregate demand curve increased from AD_{95} to AD_{00}. Significant increases in productivity from technology advances shifted the aggregate supply curve from AS_{95} to AS_{00}. As a result, the U.S economy experienced strong real GDP growth to full employment with mild inflation (the CPI increased from 152 to 172).

CAUSATION CHAIN

Increase in aggregate demand and supply → Increase in real GDP → Increase in price level

CHECKPOINT

Would the Greenhouse Effect Cause Inflation, Unemployment, or Both?

You are the chair of the President's Council of Economic Advisers. There has been an extremely hot and dry summer due to a climatic change known as the greenhouse effect. As a result, crop production has fallen drastically. The president calls you to the White House to discuss the impact on the economy. Would you explain to the president that a sharp drop in U.S. crop production would cause inflation, unemployment, or both?

Key Concepts

Aggregate demand curve (*AD*)
Real balances effect
Interest-rate effect
Net exports effect

Aggregate supply curve (*AS*)
Keynesian range
Intermediate range
Classical range

Stagflation
Cost-push inflation
Demand-pull inflation

Summary

- The *aggregate demand curve* shows the level of real GDP purchased in the economy at different price levels during a period of time.
- *Reasons why the aggregate demand curve is downward sloping* include the following three effects: (1) The *real balances effect* is the impact on real GDP caused by the inverse relationship between the purchasing power of fixed-value financial assets and inflation, which causes a shift in the consumption schedule. (2) The *interest-rate effect* assumes a fixed money supply; therefore, inflation increases the demand for money. As the demand for money increases, the interest rate rises, causing consumption and investment spending to fall. (3) The *net exports effect* is the impact on real GDP caused by the inverse relationship between net exports and inflation. An increase in the U.S. price level tends to reduce U.S. exports and increase imports, and vice versa.

- The *aggregate supply curve* shows the level of real GDP that an economy will produce at different possible price levels. The shape of the aggregate supply curve depends on the flexibility of prices and wages as real GDP expands and contracts. The aggregate supply curve has three ranges: (1) The *Keynesian range* of the curve is horizontal because neither the price level nor production costs will increase or decrease when there is substantial unemployment in the economy. (2) In the *intermediate range*, both prices and costs rise as real GDP rises toward full employment. Prices and production costs rise because of bottlenecks, the stronger bargaining power of labor, and the utilization of less-productive workers and capital. (3) The *classical range* is the vertical segment of the aggregate supply curve. It coincides with the full-employment output. Because output is at its maximum, increases in aggregate demand will only cause a rise in the price level.

Shift in the Aggregate Demand Curve

Aggregate Supply Curve

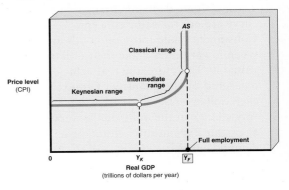

- *Aggregate demand and aggregate supply analysis* determines the equilibrium price level and the equilibrium real GDP by the intersection of the aggregate demand and aggregate supply curves. In macroeconomic equilibrium, businesses neither overestimate nor underestimate the real GDP demanded at the prevailing price level.
- *Stagflation* exists when an economy experiences inflation and unemployment simultaneously. Holding aggregate demand constant, a decrease in aggregate supply results in the unhealthy condition of a rise in the price level and a fall in real GDP and employment.
- *Cost-push inflation* is inflation that results from a decrease in the aggregate supply curve while the aggregate demand curve remains fixed. Cost-push inflation is undesirable because it is accompanied by declines in both real GDP and employment.

Cost-Push Inflation

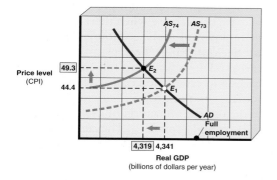

Price level (CPI)

49.3

44.4

E_2

E_1

AS_{74} AS_{73}

AD

Full employment

4,319 4,341

Real GDP
(billions of dollars per year)

- *Demand-pull inflation* is inflation that results from an increase in the aggregate demand curve in both the classical and the intermediate ranges of the aggregate supply curve, while the aggregate supply curve is fixed.

Demand-Pull Inflation

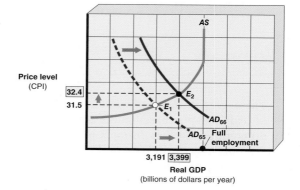

Price level (CPI)

32.4

31.5

AS

E_2

E_1

AD_{66}

AD_{65}

Full employment

3,191 3,399

Real GDP
(billions of dollars per year)

Summary of Conclusion Statements

- The aggregate demand curve and the demand curve are not the same concept.
- Consumers spend more on goods and services when lower prices make their dollars more valuable. Therefore, the real value of money is measured by the quantity of goods and services each dollar buys.
- Any change in the individual components of aggregate expenditures shifts the aggregate demand curve.
- When the aggregate supply curve is horizontal and an economy is in recession below full employment, the only effects of an increase in

aggregate demand are increases in real GDP and employment, while the price level does not change. Stated simply, the Keynesian view is that "demand creates its own supply."

- When the aggregate supply curve is vertical at the full-employment GDP, the only effect over time of a change in aggregate demand is a change in the price level. Stated simply, the classical view is that "supply creates its own demand."
- Keynesian theory rejects classical theory for an economy in recession because Keynesians argue that during a recession prices and

wages do not adjust downward to restore an economy to full-employment real GDP.

- At macroeconomic equilibrium, sellers neither overestimate nor underestimate the real GDP demanded at the prevailing price level.
- As aggregate demand increases in the Keynesian range, the price level remains constant as real GDP expands.

- In the intermediate range, increases in aggregate demand increase both the price level and the real GDP.
- Once the economy reaches full-employment output in the classical range, additional increases in aggregate demand merely cause inflation, rather than more real GDP.
- The business cycle is a result of shifts in the aggregate demand and aggregate supply curves.

Study Questions and Problems

1. Explain why the aggregate demand curve is downward sloping. How does your explanation differ from the reasons behind the downward-sloping demand curve for an individual product?

2. Explain the theory of the classical economists that flexible prices and wages ensure that the economy operates at full employment.

3. In which direction would each of the following changes in conditions cause the aggregate demand curve to shift? Explain your answers.
   a. Consumers expect an economic downturn.
   b. A new U.S. president is elected, and the profit expectations of business executives rise.
   c. The federal government increases spending for highways, bridges, and other infrastructure.
   d. The United States increases exports of wheat and other crops to Russia, Ukraine, and other former Soviet republics.

4. Identify the three ranges of the aggregate supply curve. Explain the impact of an increase in the aggregate demand curve in each segment.

5. Consider this statement: "Equilibrium GDP is the same as full employment." Do you agree or disagree? Explain.

6. Assume the aggregate demand and aggregate supply curves intersect at a price level of 100. Explain the effect of a shift in the price level to 120 and to 50.

7. In which direction would each of the following changes in conditions cause the aggregate supply curve to shift? Explain your answers.
   a. The price of gasoline increases because of a catastrophic oil spill.
   b. Labor unions and all other workers agree to a cut in wages to stimulate the economy.
   c. Power companies switch to solar power, and the price of electricity falls.
   d. The federal government increases the excise tax on gasoline in order to finance a deficit.

8. Assume an economy operates in the intermediate range of its aggregate supply curve. State the direction of shift for the aggregate demand or aggregate supply curve for each of the following changes in conditions. What is the effect on the price level? On real GDP? On employment?
   a. The price of crude oil rises significantly.
   b. Spending on national defense doubles.
   c. The costs of imported goods increase.
   d. An improvement in technology raises labor productivity.

9. What shifts in aggregate supply or aggregate demand would cause each of the following conditions for an economy?
   a. The price level rises, and real GDP rises.
   b. The price level falls, and real GDP rises.
   c. The price level falls, and real GDP falls.
   d. The price level rises, and real GDP falls.
   e. The price level falls, and real GDP remains the same.
   f. The price level remains the same, and real GDP rises.

10. Explain cost-push inflation verbally and graphically, using aggregate demand and aggregate supply analysis. Assess the impact on the price level, real GDP, and employment.

11. Explain demand-pull inflation graphically using aggregate demand and supply analysis. Assess the impact on the price level, real GDP, and employment.

For Online Exercises, go to the Tucker Web site at www.cengage.com/economics/tucker.

CHECKPOINT ANSWER

Would the Greenhouse Effect Cause Inflation, Unemployment, or Both?

A drop in food production reduces aggregate supply. The decrease in aggregate supply causes the economy to contract, while prices rise. In addition to the OPEC oil embargo between 1972 and 1974, worldwide weather conditions destroyed crops and contributed to the supply shock that caused stagflation in the U.S. economy. If you said that a severe greenhouse effect would cause both higher unemployment and inflation, **YOU ARE CORRECT.**

Practice Quiz

For an explanation of the correct answers, visit the Tucker Web Site at www.cengage.com/economics/tucker.

1. The aggregate demand curve is defined as the
   a. net national product.
   b. sum of wages, rent, interest, and profits.
   c. real GDP purchased at different possible price levels.
   d. total dollar value of household expectations.

2. When the supply of credit is fixed, an increase in the price level stimulates the demand for credit, which, in turn, reduces consumption and investment spending. This effect is called the
   a. real balances effect.
   b. interest-rate effect.
   c. net exports effect.
   d. substitution effect.

3. The real balances effect occurs because a higher price level reduces the real value of people's
   a. financial assets.
   b. wages.
   c. unpaid debt.
   d. physical investments.

4. The net exports effect is the inverse relationship between net exports and the _____ of an economy.
   a. real GDP
   b. GDP deflator
   c. price level
   d. consumption spending

5. Which of the following will shift the aggregate demand curve to the left?
   a. An increase in exports
   b. An increase in investment
   c. An increase in government spending
   d. A decrease in government spending

Practice Quiz Continued

6. Which of the following will *not* shift the aggregate demand curve to the left?
   a. Consumers become more optimistic about the future.
   b. Government spending decreases.
   c. Business optimism decreases.
   d. Consumers become pessimistic about the future.

7. The popular theory prior to the Great Depression that the economy will automatically adjust to achieve full employment is
   a. supply-side economics.
   b. Keynesian economics.
   c. classical economics.
   d. mercantilism.

8. Classical economists believed that the
   a. price system was stable.
   b. goal of full employment was impossible.
   c. price system automatically adjusts the economy to full employment in the long run.
   d. government should attempt to restore full employment.

9. Which of the following is *not* a range on the eclectic or general view of the aggregate supply curve?
   a. Classical range
   b. Keynesian range
   c. Intermediate range
   d. Monetary range

10. Macroeconomic equilibrium occurs when
    a. aggregate supply exceeds aggregate demand.
    b. the economy is at full employment.
    c. aggregate demand equals aggregate supply.
    d. aggregate demand equals the average price level.

11. Along the classical or vertical range of the aggregate supply curve, a decrease in the aggregate demand curve will decrease
    a. both the price level and real GDP.
    b. only real GDP.
    c. only the price level.
    d. neither real GDP nor the price level.

12. Other factors held constant, a decrease in resource prices will shift the aggregate
    a. demand curve leftward.
    b. demand curve rightward.
    c. supply curve leftward.
    d. supply curve rightward.

13. Assuming a fixed aggregate demand curve, a leftward shift in the aggregate supply curve causes a (an)
    a. increase in the price level and a decrease in real GDP.
    b. increase in the price level and an increase in real GDP.
    c. decrease in the price level and a decrease in real GDP.
    d. decrease in the price level and an increase in real GDP.

14. An increase in the price level caused by a rightward shift of the aggregate demand curve is called
    a. cost-push inflation.
    b. supply shock inflation.
    c. demand shock inflation.
    d. demand-pull inflation.

15. Suppose workers become pessimistic about their future employment, which causes them to save more and spend less. If the economy is on the intermediate range of the aggregate supply curve, then
    a. both real GDP and the price level will fall.
    b. real GDP will fall and the price level will rise.
    c. real GDP will rise and the price level will fall.
    d. both real GDP and the price level will rise.

10

The Self-Correcting Aggregate Demand and Supply Model

It can be argued that the economy is self-regulating. This means that over time the economy will move itself to full-employment equilibrium. Stated differently, this classical theory is based on the assumption that the economy might ebb and flow around it, but full employment is the normal condition for the economy regardless of gyrations in the price level. To understand this adjustment process, the *AD-AS* model presented in the chapter must be extended into a more complex model called the self-correcting *AD-AS* model. First, a distinction will be made between the short-run and long-run aggregate supply curves. Indeed, one of the most controversial areas of macroeconomics is the shape of the aggregate supply curve and the reasons for that shape. Second, we will explain long-run equilibrium using the self-correcting *AD-AS* model. Third, this appendix concludes by using the self-correcting *AD-AS* model to explain short-run and long-run adjustments to changes in aggregate demand.

Why the Short-Run Aggregate Supply Curve is Upward Sloping

Short-run aggregate supply curve (SRAS)

The curve that shows the level of real GDP produced at different possible price levels during a time period in which nominal incomes do not change in response to changes in the price level.

Exhibit A-1(a) shows the short-run aggregate supply curve (*SRAS*), which does not have either the perfectly flat Keynesian segment or the perfectly vertical classical segment developed in Exhibit 6 of this chapter. The short-run supply curve shows the level of real GDP produced at different possible price levels during a time period in which nominal wages and salaries (incomes) do not change in response to changes in the price level. Recall from the chapter on inflation that

$$\text{Real income} = \frac{\text{nominal income}}{\text{CPI (as decimal)}}$$

As explained by this formula, a rise in the price level measured by the CPI decreases real income, and a fall in the price level increases real income. Given the definition of the short-run aggregate supply curve, there are two reasons why one can assume nominal wages and salaries remain fixed in spite of changes in the price level:

1. **Incomplete knowledge.** In a short period of time, workers may be unaware that a change in the price level has changed their real incomes. Consequently, they

> *Exhibit A-1*   **Aggregate Supply Curves**
>
> The short-run aggregate supply curve (*SRAS*) in part (a) is based on the assumption that nominal wages and salaries are fixed based on an expected price level of 100 and full-employment real GDP of $8 trillion. An increase in the price level from 100 to 150 increases profits, real GDP, and employment, moving the economy from point *A* to point *B*. A decrease in the price level from 100 to 50 decreases profits, real GDP, and employment, moving the economy from point *A* to point *C*.
>
> The long-run aggregate supply curve (*LRAS*) in part (b) is vertical at full-employment real GDP. For example, if the price level rises from 100 at point *A* to 150 at point *B*, workers now have enough time to renegotiate higher nominal incomes by a percentage equal to the percentage increase in the price level. This flexible adjustment means that real incomes and profits remain unchanged, and the economy continues to operate at full-employment real GDP.

do not adjust their wage and salary demands according to changes in their real incomes.

2. **Fixed-wage contracts.** Unionized employees, for example, have nominal or money wages stated in their contracts. Also, many professionals receive set salaries for a year. In these cases, nominal incomes remain constant, or "sticky," for a given time period regardless of changes in the price level.

Given the assumption that changes in the prices of goods and services measured by the CPI do not in a short period of time cause changes in nominal wages, let's examine Exhibit A-1(a) and explain the *SRAS* curve's upward-sloping shape. Begin at point *A* with a CPI of 100 and observe that the economy is operating at the full-employment real GDP of $8 trillion. Also, assume that labor contracts are based on this expected price level. Now suppose the price level unexpectedly increases from 100 to 150 at point *B*. At higher prices for products, firms' revenues increase, and with nominal wages and salaries fixed, profits rise. In response, firms increase output from $8 trillion to $12 trillion, and the economy operates beyond its full-employment output. This occurs because firms increase work hours and train and hire homemakers, retirees, and unemployed workers who were not profitable at or below full-employment real GDP.

Now return to point *A* and assume the CPI falls to 50 at point *C*. In this case, the prices firms receive for their products drop while nominal wages and salaries remain fixed. As a result, firms' revenues and profits fall, and they reduce output from $8 trillion to $4 trillion real GDP. Correspondingly, employment (not shown explicitly in the model) falls below full employment.

CONCLUSION *The upward-sloping shape of the short-run aggregate supply curve (SRAS) is the result of fixed nominal wages and salaries as the price level changes.*

Why the Long-Run Aggregate Supply Curve is Vertical

Long-run aggregate supply curve (*LRAS*)

The curve that shows the level of real GDP produced at different possible price levels during a time period in which nominal incomes change by the same percentage as the price level changes.

The long-run aggregate supply curve (*LRAS*) is presented in Exhibit A-1(b). The long-run aggregate supply curve shows the level of real GDP produced at different possible price levels during a time period in which nominal incomes change by the same percentage as the price level changes. Like the classical vertical segment of the aggregate supply curve developed in Exhibit 6 of the chapter, the long-run aggregate supply curve is vertical at full-employment real GDP.

To understand why the long-run aggregate supply curve is vertical requires the assumption that sufficient time has elapsed for labor contracts to expire, so that nominal wages and salaries can be renegotiated. Stated another way, over a long enough time, workers will calculate changes in their real incomes and obtain increases in their nominal incomes to adjust proportionately to changes in purchasing power. Suppose the CPI is 100 (or in decimal, 1.0) at point *A* in Exhibit A-1(b) and the average nominal wage is $10 per hour. This means the average real wage is also $10 ($10 nominal wage divided by 1.0). But if the CPI rises to 150 at point *B*, the $10 average real wage falls to $6.67 ($10/1.5). In the long run, workers will demand and receive a new nominal wage of $15, returning their real wage to $10 ($15/1.5). Thus, both the CPI (rise from 100 to 150) and the nominal wage (rise from $10 to $15) changed by the same rate of 50 percent, and the economy moved from point *A* to point *B*, upward along the long-run aggregate supply curve. Note that because both the prices of products measured by the CPI and the nominal wage rise by the same percentage, profit margins remain unchanged in real terms, and firms have no incentive to produce either more or less than the full-employment real GDP of $8 trillion. And because this same adjustment process occurs between any two price levels along *LRAS*, the curve is vertical, and potential real GDP is independent of the price level. Regardless of rises or falls in the CPI, potential real GDP remains the same.

CONCLUSION *The vertical shape of the long-run aggregate supply curve (LRAS) is the result of nominal wages and salaries eventually changing by the same percentage as the price level changes.*

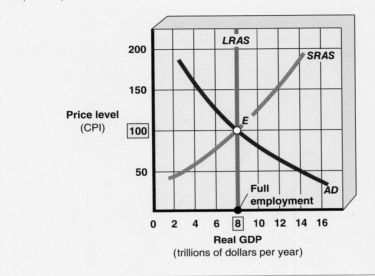

Exhibit A-2   Self-Correcting *AD-AS* Model

The short-run aggregate supply curve (*SRAS*) is based on an expected price level of 100. Point *E* shows that this equilibrium price level occurs at the intersection of the aggregate demand curve *AD*, *SRAS*, and the long-run aggregate supply curve (*LRAS*).

Equilibrium in the Self-Correcting *AD-AS* Model

Exhibit A-2 combines aggregate demand with the short-run and long-run aggregate supply curves from the previous exhibit to form the self-correcting *AD-AS* model. Equilibrium in the model occurs at point *E*, where the economy's aggregate demand curve (*AD*) intersects the vertical long-run aggregate supply curve (*LRAS*) and the short-run aggregate supply curve (*SRAS*). In long-run equilibrium, the economy's price level is 100, and full-employment real GDP is $8 trillion.

The Impact of an Increase in Aggregate Demand

Now you're ready for some actions and reactions using the model. Suppose that, beginning at point E_1 in Exhibit A-3, a change in a nonprice determinant (summarized in Exhibit 11 at the end of the chapter) causes an increase in aggregate demand from AD_1 to AD_2. For example, the shift could be the result of an increase in consumption spending (*C*), government spending (*G*), or business investment (*I*), or greater demand for U.S. exports. Regardless of the cause, the short-run effect is for the economy to move upward along $SRAS_{100}$ to the intersection with AD_2 at the temporary or short-run equilibrium point E_2 with a price level of 150. Recall that nominal incomes

Exhibit A-3   Adjustments to an Increase in Aggregate Demand

Beginning at long-run equilibrium E_1, the aggregate demand curve increases from AD_1 to AD_2. Since nominal incomes are fixed in the short run, firms raise product prices, earn higher profits, and expand output to short-run equilibrium point E_2. After enough time passes, workers increase their nominal incomes to restore their purchasing power, and the short-run supply curve shifts leftward along AD_2 to a transitional point such as E_3. As the economy moves from E_2 to E_4, profits fall, and firms cut output and employment. Eventually, long-run equilibrium is reached at E_4 with full employment restored by the self-correction process.

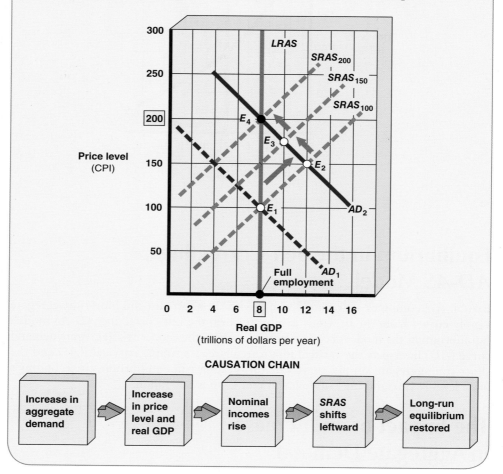

CAUSATION CHAIN

Increase in aggregate demand → Increase in price level and real GDP → Nominal incomes rise → *SRAS* shifts leftward → Long-run equilibrium restored

are fixed in the short run. Faced with higher demand, firms raise prices for products and, because the price of labor remains unchanged, firms earn higher profits and increase employment by hiring workers who were not profitable at full employment. As a result, for a short period of time, real GDP increases above the full-employment real GDP of $8 trillion to $12 trillion. However, the economy cannot produce in excess of full employment forever. What forces are at work to bring real GDP back to full-employment real GDP?

Assume time passes and labor contracts expire. The next step in the transition process at E_2 is that workers begin demanding nominal income increases that will eventually bring their real incomes back to the same real incomes established initially at E_1. Since firms are anxious to maintain their output levels, and they are competing for workers, firms meet the wage increase demands of labor. These increases in nominal incomes shift the short-run aggregate supply curve leftward, which causes an upward movement along AD_2. One of the successions of possible intermediate adjustment short-run supply curves along AD_2 is $SRAS_{150}$. This short-run intermediate adjustment is based on an expected price level of 150 determined by the intersection of $SRAS_{150}$ and $LRAS$. Although the short-run aggregate supply curve $SRAS_{150}$ intersects AD_2 at E_3, the adjustment to the increase in aggregate demand is not yet complete. Workers negotiated increases in nominal incomes based on an expected price level of 150, but the leftward shift of the short-run aggregate supply curve raised the price level to about 175 at E_3. Workers must, therefore, negotiate another round of higher nominal incomes to restore purchasing power. This process continues until long-run equilibrium is restored at E_4, where the adjustment process ends.

The long-run forecast for the price level at full employment is now 200 at point E_4. $SRAS_{100}$ has shifted leftward to $SRAS_{200}$, which intersects $LRAS$ at point E_4. As a result of the shift in the short-run aggregate supply curve from E_2 to E_4 and the corresponding increase in nominal incomes, firms' profits are cut, and they react by raising product prices, reducing employment, and reducing output. At E_4, the economy has self-adjusted to both short-run and long-run equilibrium at a price level of 200 and full-employment real GDP of $8 trillion. If there are no further shifts in aggregate demand, the economy will remain at E_4 indefinitely. Note that nominal income is higher at point E_4 than it was originally at point E_1, but real wages and salaries remain unchanged, as explained in Exhibit A-1(b).

CONCLUSION *An increase in aggregate demand in the long run causes the short-run aggregate supply curve to shift leftward because nominal incomes rise and the economy self-corrects to a higher price level at full-employment real GDP.*

The Impact of a Decrease in Aggregate Demand

Point E_1 in Exhibit A-4 begins where the sequence of events described in the previous section ends. Now, let's see what happens when the aggregate demand curve decreases from AD_1 to AD_2. The reason might be that a wave of pessimism from a stock market crash causes consumers to cut back on their spending and firms postpone buying new factories and equipment. As a result, firms find their sales and profits have declined, and they react by cutting product prices, output, and employment. Workers' nominal incomes remain fixed in the short run with contracts negotiated based on an expected price level of 200. The result of this situation is that the economy moves downward along $SRAS_{200}$ from point E_1 to short-run equilibrium point E_2. Here, the price level falls from 200 to 150, and real GDP has fallen from $8 trillion to $4 trillion.

At E_2, the economy is in a serious recession, and after, say, a year, workers will accept lower nominal wages and salaries when their contracts are renewed in order to keep their jobs in a time of poor profits and competition from unemployed workers. This willingness to accept lower nominal incomes is made easier by the realization that lower prices for goods means it costs less to maintain the workers' standard of

| Exhibit A-4 | **Adjustments to a Decrease in Aggregate Demand** |

Assume the economy is initially at long-run equilibrium point E_1 and aggregate demand decreases from AD_1 to AD_2. Nominal incomes in the short run are fixed based on an expected price level of 200. In response to the fall in aggregate demand, firms' profits decline, and they cut output and employment. As a result, the economy moves downward along $SRAS_{200}$ to temporary equilibrium at E_2. When workers lower their nominal incomes because of competition from unemployed workers, the short-run aggregate supply curve shifts downward to an intermediate point, such as E_3. As workers decrease their nominal incomes based on the new long-run expected price level of 150 at point E_3, profits rise, and firms increase output and employment. In the long run, the short-run aggregate supply curve continues to automatically adjust downward along AD_2 until it again returns to long-run equilibrium at E_4.

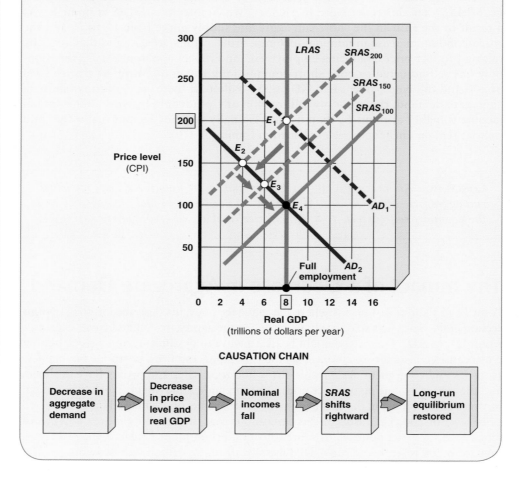

CAUSATION CHAIN

Decrease in aggregate demand ⇨ Decrease in price level and real GDP ⇨ Nominal incomes fall ⇨ SRAS shifts rightward ⇨ Long-run equilibrium restored living. As workers make a series of downward adjustments in nominal incomes, the short-run aggregate supply curve moves downward along AD_2 toward E_4. $SRAS_{150}$ illustrates one possible intermediate position corresponding to the long-run expected price level of 150 determined by the intersection of $SRAS_{150}$ and $LRAS$. However, like E_2, E_3 is not the point of long-run equilibrium. Workers negotiated decreases in nominal increases based on an expected price level of 150, but the rightward shift of the short-run aggregate supply curve has lowered the price level to about 125 at E_3. Under pressure from unemployed workers who will work for still lower real wages and salaries, workers will continue this process of adjusting their nominal incomes lower until $SRAS_{150}$ shifts rightward to point E_4.

Eventually, the long-run expected full-employment price level returns to 100 at point E_4 where the economy has self-corrected to long-run full-employment equilibrium. The result of this adjustment downward along AD_2 between E_2 and E_4 is that lower nominal incomes raise profits and firms respond by lowering prices of products, increasing employment, and increasing output so that real GDP increases from \$4 trillion to \$8 trillion. Unless aggregate demand changes, the economy will be stable at E_4 indefinitely. Finally, observe that average nominal income has decreased by the same percentage between points E_1 and E_4 as the percentage decline in the price level. Therefore, real incomes are unaffected as explained in Exhibit A-1(b).

CONCLUSION *A decrease in aggregate demand in the long run causes the short-run aggregate supply curve to shift rightward because nominal incomes fall and the economy self-corrects to a lower price level at full-employment real GDP.*

Changes in Potential Real GDP

Like the aggregate demand and short-run aggregate supply curves, the long-run aggregate supply curve also changes. As explained in Chapter 2, changes in resources and technology shift the production possibilities curve outward. We now extend this concept of economic growth to the long-run aggregate supply curve as follows:

1. *Changes in resources:* For example, the quantity of land can be increased by reclaiming land from the sea or revitalizing soil. Over time, potential real GDP increases if the full-employment number of workers increases, holding capital and technology constant. Such growth in the labor force can result from population growth. Greater quantities of plants, production lines, computers, and other forms of capital also produce increases in potential real GDP. Capital includes *human capital*, which is the accumulation of education, training, experience, and health of workers.

2. *An advance in technology:* Technological change enables firms to produce more goods from any given amount of inputs. Even with fixed quantities of labor and capital, the latest computer-age machinery increases potential GDP.

CONCLUSION *A rightward shift of the long-run aggregate supply curve represents economic growth in potential full-employment real GDP.*

Exhibit A-5	**Trend of Macro Equilibrium Price Level over Time**

Each hypothetical long-run equilibrium point shows the CPI and real GDP for a given year determined by the intersection of the aggregate demand curve, short-run aggregate supply curve, and the long-run aggregate supply curve. Over time, these curves shift, and both the price level and real GDP increase.

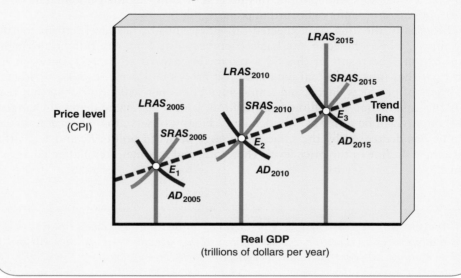

Over time, the U.S. economy typically adds resources and improves technology, and growth occurs in full-employment output. Exhibit A-5 uses basic aggregate demand and supply analysis to explain a hypothetical trend in the price level measured by the CPI between the years 2005, 2010, and 2015. The trend line connects the macro equilibrium points for each year. The following section uses real-world data to illustrate changes in the long-run aggregate supply curve over time.

Increase in the Aggregate Demand and Long-Run Aggregate Supply Curves

The self-correcting *AD-AS* model shown in Exhibit A-5 revisits Exhibit 13 in the chapter, which illustrated economic growth that occurred between 1995 and 2000 in the U.S. economy. Exhibit A-6, however, uses short-run and long-run aggregate supply curves to expand the analysis. (For simplicity, the real GDP amounts have been rounded.) In 1995, the economy operated at point E_1, with the CPI at 152 and a real GDP of $8.0 trillion. Since $LRAS_{95}$ at E_1 was estimated to be $8.3 trillion real GDP, the economy was operating below its full-employment potential with an unemployment rate of 5.6 percent (not explicitly shown in the model). Over the next five years, the U.S. economy moved to full employment at point E_3 in 2000 and experienced growth in real GDP from $8.0 trillion to $9.8 trillion.

Exhibit A-6	**A Rightward Shift in the Aggregate Demand and Long-Run Aggregate Supply Curves**

In 1995, the U.S. economy was operating at $8.0 trillion, which was below full-employment real GDP of $8.3 trillion at $LRAS_{95}$. Between 1995 and 2000, the aggregate demand curve increased from AD_{95} to AD_{00}, and the U.S economy moved upward along the short-run aggregate supply curve $SRAS_{95}$ from point E_1 to point E_2. Nominal or money incomes of workers increased, and $SRAS_{95}$ shifted leftward to $SRAS_{00}$, establishing long-run full-employment equilibrium at E_3 on long-run aggregate supply curve $LRAS_{00}$. Technological changes and capital accumulation over these years caused the rightward shift from $LRAS_{95}$ to $LRAS_{00}$, and potential real GDP grew from $8.3 trillion to $9.8 trillion.

CAUSATION CHAIN

Increase in aggregate demand and long-run supply ⇒ Increase in price level and real GDP ⇒ Nominal incomes rise ⇒ SRAS shifts leftward ⇒ Long-run equilibrium restored

The CPI increased from 152 to 175 (mild inflation), and the unemployment rate fell to 4.0 percent.

During this time period, extraordinary technological change and capital accumulation, particularly in high-tech industries, caused economic growth in potential real GDP, represented by the rightward shift in the vertical long-run supply curve from $LRAS_{95}$ to $LRAS_{00}$. The movement from E_1 below full-employment real GDP was caused by an increase in AD_{95} to AD_{00}, and a movement upward along short-run aggregate supply curve $SRAS_{95}$ to point E_2. Over time the nominal or money wage rate increased, and $SRAS_{95}$ shifted leftward to $SRAS_{00}$. At point E_3, the price level was 175 and equal to potential real GDP of $9.8 trillion.

Key Concepts

Short-run aggregate supply curve (*SRAS*)   Long-run aggregate supply curve (*LRAS*)

Summary

- The **upward-sloping shape of the short-run aggregate supply curve (*SRAS*)** is the result of fixed nominal wages and salaries as the price level changes.
- The **vertical shape of the long-run aggregate supply curve (*LRAS*)** is the result of nominal wages and salaries eventually changing by the same percentage as the price level changes.
- An **increase in aggregate demand (*AD*) in the long run** causes the short-run aggregate supply curve (*SRAS*) to shift leftward because nominal incomes rise and the economy self-corrects to a higher price level at full-employment real GDP.

- A **decrease in aggregate demand in the long run** causes the short-run aggregate supply curve (*SRAS*) to shift rightward because nominal incomes fall and the economy self-corrects to a lower price level at full-employment real GDP.
- **Economic growth in potential real GDP** is represented by a rightward shift in the long-run aggregate supply curve (*LRAS*). Shifts in *LRAS* are caused by changes in resources and advances in technology.

Study Questions and Problems

1. The economy of Tuckerland has the following aggregate demand and supply schedules, reflecting real GDP in trillions of dollars:

Price level (CPI)	Aggregate demand	Short-run aggregate supply
250	$ 4	$16
200	8	12
150	12	8
100	16	4

   a. Graph the aggregate demand curve and the short-run aggregate supply curve.
   b. What are short-run equilibrium real GDP and the price level?
   c. If Tuckerland's potential real GDP is $12 trillion, plot the long-run aggregate supply curve (*LRAS*) in the graph.

2. Using the graph from question 1 and assuming long-run equilibrium at $12 trillion, explain the impact of a 10 percent increase in workers' income.

3. Use the graph drawn in question 1 and assume the initial equilibrium is E_1. Next, assume aggregate demand increases by $4 trillion. Draw the effect on short-run equilibrium.

4. Based on the assumptions of question 3, explain verbally the impact of an increase of $4 trillion in aggregate demand on short-run equilibrium.

5. The economy shown in Exhibit A-7 is initially in equilibrium at point E_1, and the aggregate demand curve decreases from AD_1 to AD_2. Explain the long-run adjustment process.

Exhibit A-7   **Aggregate Demand and Supply Model**

6. In the first quarter of 2001, real GDP was $9.88 trillion, and the price level measured by the GDP chain price index was 101. Real GDP was approximately equal to potential GDP. In the third quarter, aggregate demand decreased to $9.83 trillion, and the price level rose to 103. Draw a graph of this recession.

For Online Exercises, go to the Tucker Web site at www.cengage.com/economics/tucker.

Practice Quiz

For an explanation of the correct answers, visit the Trucker Web site at www.cengage.com/economics/tucker.

1. An assumption for the short-run aggregate supply curve is that it is a period of time in which
   a. knowledge is complete.
   b. wages are fixed.
   c. wages are constant for under one year.
   d. prices firms charge for products are fixed.

2. The long-run aggregate supply curve is based on the assumption that
   a. both the price level and nominal incomes are fixed.
   b. prices are flexible after one year.
   c. both the price level and nominal incomes change by the same percentage.
   d. potential GDP is undetermined.

3. Graphically, long-run macro equilibrium occurs at the
   a. midpoint of the aggregate demand curve.
   b. intersection of the aggregate demand and long-run aggregate supply curves regardless of the short-run aggregate supply curve.
   c. midpoint of the long-run aggregate supply curve.
   d. intersection of the aggregate demand, short-run aggregate supply, and long-run aggregate supply curves.

4. An increase in nominal incomes of workers results in the
   a. aggregate demand curve shifting to the left.
   b. long-run aggregate supply curve shifting to the right.

Practice Quiz Continued

c. short-run aggregate supply curve shifting to the left.
d. short-run aggregate supply curve shifting to the right.

5. An increase in aggregate demand in the long run will result in ____ in full-employment real GDP and _____ in the price level.
   a. no change; an increase
   b. an increase; no change
   c. a decrease; no change
   d. no change; a decrease

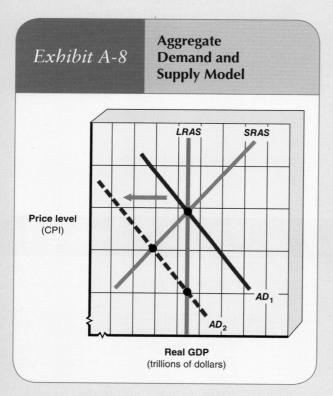

Exhibit A-8

Aggregate Demand and Supply Model

Price level (CPI)

LRAS   SRAS

AD₁

AD₂

Real GDP (trillions of dollars)

6. In Exhibit A-8, the intersection of AD_1 with SRAS indicates
   a. short-run equilibrium.
   b. long-run equilibrium.
   c. that the economy is not operating at full employment.
   d. that prices and wages are inflexible.

7. In Exhibit A-8, the intersection of AD_2 with SRAS indicates
   a. short-run equilibrium.
   b. long-run equilibrium.
   c. that the economy is operating at full employment.
   d. that prices and wages are inflexible.

8. In Exhibit A-8, the self-correcting AD-AS model argument is that competition
   a. from unemployed workers causes an increase in nominal wages and a rightward shift in SRAS.
   b. from unemployed workers causes a rightward shift in LRAS.
   c. among firms for workers increases nominal wages, and this causes a leftward shift in SRAS.
   d. among consumers causes an increase in the CPI and a rightward shift in SRAS.

9. In Exhibit A-8, the self-correcting AD-AS model theory is that in the long run the economy will
   a. remain where SRAS intersects AD_1.
   b. shift to the intersection of AD_2 and SRAS.
   c. shift to the intersection of AD_2 and LRAS.
   d. shift to the intersection of AD_2 and a new leftward-shifted SRAS.

10. In Exhibit A-8, the self-correcting AD-AS model predicts that the long-run result of the decrease from AD_1 to AD_2 will be a (an)
    a. higher price level and higher unemployment rate.
    b. lower price level and higher unemployment rate.
    c. unchanged price level and full employment.
    d. lower price level and full employment.

11. Which of the following is *most* likely to cause a leftward shift in the long-run aggregate supply curve?
    a. An increase in labor
    b. An increase in capital
    c. An advance in technology
    d. Destruction of resources

Practice Quiz Continued

12. As shown in Exhibit A-9, and assuming the aggregate demand curve shifts from AD_1 to AD_2, the full-employment level of real GDP is
  a. $12 billion.
  b. $8 billion.
  c. $150 billion.
  d. unable to be determined.

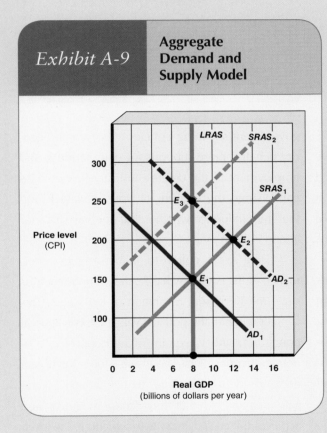

Exhibit A-9

Aggregate Demand and Supply Model

13. Given the shift of the aggregate demand curve from AD_1 to AD_2 in Exhibit A-9, the real GDP and price level (CPI) in long-run equilibrium will be
  a. $8 billion and 150.
  b. $12 billion and 200.
  c. $8 billion and 250.
  d. $8 billion and 200.

14. Beginning from long-run equilibrium at point E_1 in Exhibit A-9, the aggregate demand curve shifts to AD_2. The real GDP and price level (CPI) in short-run equilibrium will be
  a. $12 billion and 200.
  b. $8 billion and 250.
  c. $8 billion and 150.
  d. $12 billion and 250.

15. Beginning from short-run equilibrium at point E_2 in Exhibit A-9, the economy's movement to a new position of long-run equilibrium would best be described as
  a. a movement along the AD_2 curve with a shift in the $SRAS_1$ curve.
  b. a movement along the $SRAS_2$ curve with a shift in the AD_2 curve.
  c. a shift in the $LRAS$ curve to an intersection at E_1.
  d. no shift of any kind.

Fiscal Policy

In the early 1980s, under President Ronald Reagan, the federal government reduced personal income tax rates. The goal was to expand aggregate demand and boost real GDP output and employment in order to end the recession of 1980–1981. In the 1990s, a key part of President Bill Clinton's programs was to stimulate economic growth by boosting government spending on long-term investment, including highways, bridges, and education. In 2001, the United States experienced a recession and during the next two years President George W. Bush proposed and signed into law tax cuts in order to stimulate the economy. And in 2008, Americans received a $170 billion tax rebate stimulus package, followed by another $787 billion federal stimulus package under the President Obama administration in 2009 intended to jump-start the economy into recovery from the recession.

Fiscal policy is one of the major issues that touches everyone's life. Fiscal policy is the use of government spending and taxes to influence the nation's output, employment, and price level. Federal government spending policies affect Social Security benefits, price supports for dairy farmers, and employment in the defense industry. Tax policies can change the amount of your paycheck and therefore influence whether you purchase a car or attend college.

Using fiscal policy to influence the performance of the economy has been an important idea since the Keynesian revolution of the 1930s. This chapter removes the political veil and looks at fiscal policy from the viewpoint of two opposing economic theories. First, you will study Keynesian demand-side fiscal policies that "fine-tune" aggregate demand so that the economy grows and achieves full employment with a higher price level. Second, you will study supply-side fiscal policy, which gained prominence during the Reagan administration. Supply-siders view aggregate supply as far more important than aggregate demand. Their fiscal policy prescription is to increase aggregate supply so that the economy grows and achieves full employment with a lower price level.

In this chapter, you will learn to solve these economics puzzles:

- Does an increase in government spending or a tax cut of equal amount provide a greater stimulus to economic growth?

- Can Congress fight a recession without taking any action?

- How could one argue that the federal government can increase tax revenues by cutting taxes?

DISCRETIONARY FISCAL POLICY

Here we begin where the previous chapter left off, that is, discussing the use of discretionary fiscal policy, as Keynes advocated, to influence the economy's performance. Discretionary fiscal policy is the deliberate use of changes in government spending or taxes to alter aggregate demand and stabilize the economy. Exhibit 1 lists three basic types of discretionary fiscal policies and the corresponding ways in which the government can pursue each of these options. The first column of the table shows that the government can choose to increase aggregate demand by following an *expansionary* fiscal policy. The second column lists *contractionary* fiscal policy options the government can use to restrain aggregate demand.

Increasing Government Spending to Combat a Recession

Suppose the U.S. economy represented in Exhibit 2 has fallen into recession at equilibrium point E_1, where aggregate demand curve AD_1 intersects the aggregate supply curve, AS, in the near-full-employment range. The price level measured by the CPI is 210, and a real GDP gap of $1 trillion exists below the full-employment output of $14 trillion real GDP. As explained in the previous chapter (Exhibit 5), one approach the president and Congress can follow is provided by classical theory. The classical economists' prescription is to wait because the economy will self-correct

Fiscal policy

The use of government spending and taxes to influence the nation's spending, employment, and price level.

Discretionary fiscal policy

The deliberate use of changes in government spending or taxes to alter aggregate demand and stabilize the economy.

Exhibit 1	Discretionary Fiscal Policies
Expansionary fiscal policy	**Contractionary fiscal policy**
Increase government spending	Decrease government spending
Decrease taxes	Increase taxes
Increase government spending and taxes equally	Decrease government spending and taxes equally

Exhibit 2   Using Government Spending to Combat a Recession

The economy in this exhibit is in recession at equilibrium point E_1 on the intermediate range of the aggregate supply curve, AS. The price level is 210, with an output level of \$13 trillion real GDP. To reach the full-employment output of \$14 trillion in real GDP, the aggregate demand curve must be shifted to the right by \$2 trillion real GDP, measured by the horizontal distance between point E_1 on curve AD_1 and point X on curve AD_2. The necessary increase in aggregate demand from AD_1 to AD_2 can be accomplished by increased government spending. Given a spending multiplier of 2, a \$1 trillion increase in government spending brings about the required \$2 trillion rightward shift in the aggregate demand curve, and equilibrium in the economy changes from E_1 to E_2. Note that the equilibrium real GDP changes by \$1 trillion and not by the full amount by which the aggregate demand curve shifts horizontally.

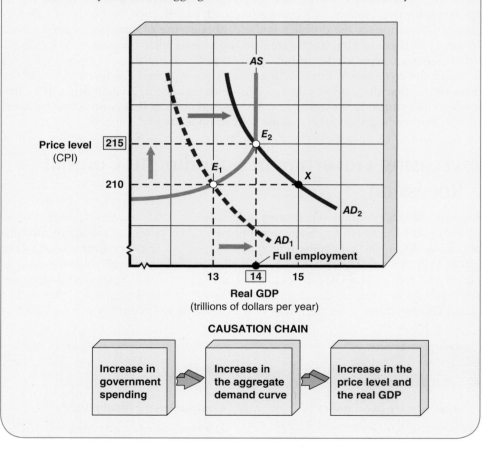

CAUSATION CHAIN

Increase in government spending ⇨ Increase in the aggregate demand curve ⇨ Increase in the price level and the real GDP

to full employment in the long run by adjusting downward along AD_1. But election time is approaching, so there is political pressure to do something about the recession now. Besides, recall Keynes's famous statement, "In the long run, we are all dead." Hence, policymakers follow Keynesian economics and decide to shift the aggregate demand curve rightward from AD_1 to AD_2 and thereby cure the recession.

How can the federal government do this? In theory, any increase in consumption (C), investment (I), or net exports (X − M) can spur aggregate demand. But these spending boosts are not directly under the government's control as is government spending (G). After all, there is always a long wish list of spending proposals for federal highways, health care, education, environmental programs, and so forth. Rather than crossing their fingers and waiting for things to happen in the long run, suppose members of Congress gladly increase government spending to boost employment now.

But just how much new government spending is required? Note that the economy is operating $1 trillion below its full-employment output, but the horizontal distance between AD_1 and AD_2 is $2 trillion. This gap between AD_1 and AD_2 is indicated by the dotted line between points E_1 and X ($15 trillion−$13 trillion). This means that the aggregate demand curve must be shifted to the right by $2 trillion. But it is not necessary to increase government spending by this amount. The following formula can be used to compute the amount of additional government spending required to shift the aggregate demand curve rightward and establish a new full-employment real GDP equilibrium:

Initial change in government spending (ΔG) × spending multiplier = change in aggregate demand (total spending)

The spending multiplier (SM) in the formula amplifies the amount of new government spending. The spending multiplier is the change in aggregate demand (total spending) resulting from an initial change in any component of aggregate demand, including consumption, investment, government spending, and net exports. Assume the value for the spending multiplier in our example is 2. The next section explains the algebra behind the spending multiplier so the example can be solved:

$$\Delta G \times 2 = \$2 \text{ trillion}$$

$$\Delta G = \$1 \text{ trillion}$$

Note that the Greek letter Δ (delta) means "a change in." Thus, it takes $1 trillion worth of new government spending to shift the aggregate demand curve to the right by $2 trillion. As described in the previous chapter (Exhibit 6), bottlenecks occur throughout the upward-sloping range of the AS curve. This means prices rise as production increases in response to greater aggregate demand. Returning to Exhibit 2, you can see that $1 trillion worth of new government spending shifts aggregate demand from AD_1 to AD_2. As a result, firms increase output upward along the aggregate supply curve, AS, and total spending moves upward along aggregate demand curve AD_2. This adjustment mechanism moves the economy to a new equilibrium at E_2, with full employment, a higher price level of 215, and a real GDP of $14 trillion per year. At point E_2, the economy experiences *demand-pull inflation*. And here is the important point: Although the aggregate demand curve has increased by $2 trillion, the equilibrium real GDP has increased by only $1 trillion from $13 to $14 trillion.

Spending Multiplier (SM)

The change in aggregate demand (total spending) resulting from an initial change in any component of aggregate expenditures, including consumption, investment, government spending, and net exports. As a formula, spending multiplier equals 1/(1−MPC) or 1/MPS.

CONCLUSION *In the intermediate segment of the aggregate supply curve, the equilibrium real GDP changes by less than the change in government spending times the spending multiplier.*

Spending Multiplier Arithmetic Revisited[1]

Marginal Propensity to Consume (*MPC*)

The change in consumption spending resulting from a given change in income.

Now let's pause to tackle the task of explaining in more detail the spending multiplier of 2 used in the above example. The spending multiplier begins with a concept called the **marginal propensity to consume** (*MPC*). The marginal propensity to consume is the change in consumption spending resulting from a given change in income. Algebraically,

$$MPC = \frac{\text{change in consumption spending}}{\text{change in income}}$$

Exhibit 3 illustrates numerically the cumulative increase in aggregate demand resulting from a $1 trillion increase in government spending. In the initial round, the government spends this amount for bridges, national defense, and so forth. Households receive this amount of income. In the second round, these households spend $500 billion (0.50 × $1 trillion, or $1,000 billion) on houses, cars, groceries, and other products. In the third round, the incomes of realtors, autoworkers, grocers, and others are boosted by $500 billion, and they spend $250 billion (0.50 × $500 billion). Each round of spending creates income for consumption respending in a downward spiral throughout the economy in smaller and smaller amounts until the total level of aggregate demand rises by an extra $2,000 billion ($2 trillion).

> **CONCLUSION** *Any initial change in spending by the government, households, or firms creates a chain reaction of further spending, which causes a greater cumulative change in aggregate demand.*

Exhibit 3	The Spending Multiplier Effect	
Round	**Component of total spending**	**New consumption spending (billions of dollars)**
1	Government spending	$1,000
2	Consumption	500
3	Consumption	250
4	Consumption	125
.	.	.
.	.	.
.	.	.
All other rounds	Consumption	125
	Total spending	$2,000

NOTE: All amounts are rounded to the nearest billion dollars per year.

---

1. This section duplicates material presented earlier in the chapters titled "The Keynesian Model" and "The Keynesian Model in Action." The reason for repeating this material is that an instructor may choose to skip the Keynesian model presented in these two chapters.

You might recognize from algebra that the spending multiplier effect is a process based on an *infinite geometric series*. The formula for the sum of such a series of numbers is the initial number times $1/(1 - r)$, where r is the ratio that relates the numbers. Using this formula, the sum (total spending) is calculated as $1 trillion $(\Delta G) \times [1/(1 - 0.50)] = \$2$ trillion. By simply defining r in the infinite series formula as MPC, the spending multiplier for aggregate demand is expressed as

$$\text{Spending multiplier} = \frac{1}{1 - MPC}$$

Applying this formula to our example:

$$\text{Spending multiplier} = \frac{1}{1 - 0.50} = \frac{1}{0.50} = 2$$

If households spend a portion of each extra dollar of income, then the remaining portion of each dollar is saved. The **marginal propensity to save** (*MPS*) is the change in saving resulting from a given change in income. Therefore:

$$MPC + MPS = 1$$

rewritten as

$$MPS = 1 - MPC$$

Hence, the above spending multiplier formula can be rewritten as

$$\text{Spending multiplier} = \frac{1}{MPS}$$

Since MPS and MPC are related, the size of the multiplier depends on the size of the MPC. What will the result be if people spend 80 percent or 33 percent of each dollar of income instead of 50 percent? If the MPC increases (decreases), consumers spend a larger (smaller) share of each additional dollar of output/income in each round, and the size of the multiplier increases (decreases). Exhibit 4 lists the multiplier for different values of MPC and MPS.

Marginal Propensity to Save (*MPS*)

The change in saving resulting from a given change in income.

Exhibit 4	Relationship between *MPC*, *MPS*, and the Spending Multiplier	
(1) Marginal propensity to consume (*MPC*)	(2) Marginal propensity to save (*MPS*)	(3) Spending multiplier
0.90	0.10	10
0.80	0.20	5
0.75	0.25	4
0.67	0.33	3
0.50	0.50	2
0.33	0.67	1.5

✓

CheckPoint

What is the MPC for Uncle Sam's Stimulus Package?

Assume the economy is in a recession, and a stimulus package of $800 billion is passed by the federal government. The administration predicts that this measure will provide a $2,400 billion boost to GDP this year because consumers will spend their extra cash on HD televisions and other items. For this amount of stimulus, what is the established value of *MPC* used in this forecast?

Cutting Taxes to Combat a Recession

Another expansionary fiscal policy intended to increase aggregate demand and restore full employment calls for the government to cut taxes. Let's return to point E_1 in Exhibit 2. As before, the problem is to shift the aggregate demand curve to the right by $2 trillion. But this time, instead of a $1 trillion increase in government spending, assume Congress votes for a $1 trillion tax cut. How does this cut in taxes affect aggregate demand? First, *disposable personal income* (take-home pay) increases by $1 trillion—the amount of the tax reduction. Second, once again assuming the *MPC* is 0.50, the increase in disposable personal income induces new consumption spending of $500 billion (0.50 × $1 trillion). Thus, a cut in taxes triggers a multiplier process similar to, but smaller than, the spending multiplier.

Exhibit 5 demonstrates that a tax reduction adds less to aggregate demand than does an equal increase in government spending. Column 1 reproduces the effect of increasing government spending by $1 trillion, and column 2 gives for comparison the effect of lowering taxes by $1 trillion. Note that the only difference between increasing government spending and cutting taxes by the same amount is the impact in the initial round. The reason is that a tax cut injects zero new spending into the economy because the government has purchased no new goods and services. The effect of a tax reduction in round 2 is that people spend a portion of the $1 trillion boost in after-tax income from the tax cut introduced in round 1. Subsequent rounds in the tax multiplier chain generate a cumulative increase in consumption expenditures that totals $1 trillion. Comparing the total changes in aggregate demand in columns 1 and 2 of Exhibit 4 leads to the following:

> **Conclusion** *A tax cut has a smaller multiplier effect on aggregate demand than an equal increase in government spending.*

Tax Multiplier

The change in aggregate demand (total spending) resulting from an initial change in taxes. As a formula, tax multiplier equals 1 − spending multiplier.

The **tax multiplier** (*TM*) can be computed by using a formula and the information from column 2 of Exhibit 5. The tax multiplier is the change in aggregate demand (total spending) resulting from an initial change in taxes. Mathematically, the tax multiplier is given by this formula:

$$\text{Tax multiplier} = 1 - \text{spending multiplier}$$

| | | Increase in aggregate demand from a | |
Round	Component of Total spending	(1) $1 trillion increase in government spending $(+\Delta G)$	(2) $1 trillion cut in taxes $(-\Delta T)$
1	Government spending	$1,000	$ 0
2	Consumption	500	500
3	Consumption	250	250
4	Consumption	125	125
.	.	.	.
.	.	.	.
.	.	.	.
All other rounds	Consumption	125	125
	Total spending	$2,000	$1,000

Exhibit 5 — **Comparison of the Spending and Tax Multipliers**

Note: All amounts are rounded to the nearest billion dollars per year.

Returning to Exhibit 2, the tax multiplier formula can be used to calculate the cumulative increase in the aggregate demand from a $1 trillion tax cut. Applying the formula given above and a spending multiplier of 2 yields a tax multiplier of -1. Note that the sign of the tax multiplier is always negative. Thus, a $1 trillion tax cut shifts the aggregate demand curve rightward by only $1 trillion and fails to restore full-employment equilibrium at point E_2. Mathematically,

Change in taxes (ΔT) $\times$ tax multiplier (TM) = change in aggregate demand (AD)

$$-\$1 \text{ trillion} \times -1 = \$1 \text{ trillion}$$

The key to the amount of real GDP growth achieved from a stimulus package depends on the size of the *MPC*. What proportion of the government spending increase or tax cut is spent for consumption? The answer means the difference between a deeper or milder recession as well as the speed of recovery. What are estimates of real-world multipliers? In Congressional testimony given in July 2008, Mark Zandi, chief economist for Moody's Economy.com, provided estimates for the one-year multiplier effect for several fiscal policy options. The spending multiplier varied from 1.36 to 1.73 for different federal government spending programs, such as food stamps, extended unemployment insurance benefits, aid to state governments, or bridges and highways. The tax multiplier also varied from 0.27 to 1.29 for different temporary tax cut plans. According to another economist, Otto Eckstein, the general estimate for the spending multiplier is 1.93 and 1.19 for the tax multiplier.

Using Fiscal Policy to Combat Inflation

So far, Keynesian expansionary fiscal policy, born of the Great Depression, has been presented as the cure for an economic downturn. Contractionary fiscal policy, on the other hand, can serve in the fight against inflation. Exhibit 6 shows an economy

---

Exhibit 6   **Using Fiscal Policy to Combat Inflation**

The economy in this exhibit is in equilibrium at point E_1 on the classical range of the aggregate supply curve, AS. The price level is 220, and the economy is operating at the full-employment output of $14 trillion real GDP. To reduce the price level to 215, the aggregate demand curve must be shifted to the left by $1 trillion, measured by the horizontal distance between point E_1 on curve AD_1 and point E' on curve AD_2. One way this can be done is by decreasing government spending. With MPC equal to 0.50, and therefore a spending multiplier of 2, a $500 billion decrease in government spending results in the needed $100 billion leftward shift in the aggregate demand curve. As a result, the economy reaches equilibrium at point E_2, and the price level falls from 220 to 215, while real output remains unchanged at full capacity.

An identical decrease in the aggregate demand curve can be obtained by a hike in taxes. A $1 trillion tax increase works through a tax multiplier of -1 and provides the needed $1 trillion decrease in the aggregate demand curve from AD_1 to AD_2.

CAUSATION CHAIN

| Decrease in government spending or increase in taxes | ⟹ | Decrease in the aggregate demand curve | ⟹ | Decrease in the price level |

operating at point E_1 on the classical range of the aggregate supply curve, *AS*. Hence, this economy is producing the full-employment output of $14 trillion real GDP, and the price level is 220. In this situation, any increase in aggregate demand only causes inflation, while real GDP remains unchanged.

Suppose Congress and the president decide to use fiscal policy to reduce the CPI from 220 to 215 because they fear the wrath of voters suffering from the consequences of inflation. Although a fall in consumption, investment, or net exports might do the job, Congress and the president may be unwilling to wait, and they prefer taking direct action by cutting government spending. Given a marginal propensity to consume of 0.50, the spending multiplier is 2. As shown by the horizontal distance between point E_1 on AD_1 and point E' on AD_2 in Exhibit 6, aggregate demand must be decreased by $1 trillion in order to shift the aggregate demand curve from AD_1 to AD_2 and establish equilibrium at E_2, with a price level of 215. Mathematically,

$$\Delta G \times 2 = -\$1 \text{ trillion}$$

$$\Delta G = -\$500 \text{ billion}$$

Using the above formula, a $500 billion cut in real government spending would cause a $1 trillion decrease in the aggregate demand curve from AD_1 to AD_2. The result is a temporary excess aggregate supply of $1 trillion, measured by the distance from E' to E_1. As explained in Exhibit 5 of the previous chapter, the economy follows classical theory and moves downward along AD_2 to a new equilibrium at E_2. Consequently, inflation cools with no change in the full-employment real GDP.

Another approach to the inflation problem would be for Congress and the president to raise taxes. Although tax increases are often considered political suicide, let's suppose Congress calculates just the correct amount of a tax hike required to reduce aggregate demand by $1 trillion. Assuming a spending multiplier of 2, the tax multiplier is −1. Therefore, a $1 trillion tax hike provides the necessary $1 trillion leftward shift in the aggregate demand curve from AD_1 to AD_2. As a result, the desired equilibrium change from E_1 to E_2 is achieved, and the price level drops from 220 to 215 at the full-employment output of $14 trillion. Mathematically,

$$\Delta T \times -1 = -\$1 \text{ trillion}$$

$$\Delta T = \$1 \text{ trillion}$$

The Balanced Budget Multiplier

The analysis of Keynesian discretionary fiscal policy presented in the previous section supposes the federal government selects a change in *either* government spending or taxes as a remedy for recession or inflation. However, a controversial fiscal policy requires the government to match, or "balance," any new spending with new taxes. Understanding the impact on the economy of this fiscal policy requires derivation of the **balanced budget multiplier**. The balanced budget multiplier is an equal change in government spending and taxes, which as shown below changes aggregate demand by the amount of the change in government spending. Expressed as a formula,

Cumulative change in aggregate demand (ΔAD)
= government spending multiplier effect
+ tax multiplier effect

Balanced budget multiplier

An equal change in government spending and taxes, which changes aggregate demand by the amount of the change in government spending.

rewritten as

$$\text{Cumulative change in aggregate demand } (\Delta AD)$$
$$= (\text{initial change in government spending} \times \text{spending multiplier})$$
$$+ (\text{initial change in taxes} \times \text{tax multiplier})$$

To see how the balanced budget multiplier works, suppose Congress enacts a $1 billion increase in government spending for highways and it finances these purchases with a $1 billion increase in gasoline taxes. Mathematically,

$$\Delta AD = \left(\$1 \text{ billion} \times \frac{1}{1-MPC} \right) + \left(\$1 \text{ billion} \times 1 - \frac{1}{1-MPC} \right)$$

$$= \left(\$1 \text{ billion} \times \frac{1}{1-0.50} \right) + \left(\$1 \text{ billion} \times 1 - \frac{1}{1-0.50} \right)$$

$$= (\$1 \text{ billion} \times 2) + (\$1 \text{ billion} \times -1)$$

$$= \$2 \text{ billion} - \$1 \text{ billion}$$

$$= \$1 \text{ billion}$$

Hence, the balanced budget multiplier is always equal to 1, and the cumulative change in aggregate demand is $1 billion—*the amount of the initial change in government spending.*

CONCLUSION *Regardless of the MPC, the net effect on the economy of an equal initial increase (decrease) in government spending and taxes is an increase (decrease) in aggregate demand equal to the initial increase (decrease) in government spending.*

CHECKPOINT

Walking the Balanced Budget Tightrope

Suppose the president proposes a $800 billion economic stimulus package intended to create jobs. A major criticism of this new spending proposal is that it is not matched by a tax increase. Assume the U.S. economy is below full employment and Congress has passed a law requiring that any increase in spending be matched or balanced by an equal increase in taxes. The *MPC* is 0.75, and aggregate demand must be increased by $1,000 billion to reach full employment. Will the economy reach full employment if Congress increases spending by $800 billion and increases taxes by the same amount?

AUTOMATIC STABILIZERS

Unlike discretionary fiscal policy, **automatic stabilizers** are policy tools built into the federal budget that help fight unemployment and inflation, while spending and tax laws remain unchanged. Automatic stabilizers are federal expenditures and tax revenues that automatically change levels in order to stabilize an economic expansion or contraction. Automatic stabilizers are sometimes referred to as *nondiscretionary fiscal policy*. Exhibit 7 illustrates the influence of automatic stabilizers on the economy. The downward-sloping line, *G*, represents federal government expenditures, including such *transfer payments* as unemployment compensation, Medicaid, and welfare. This line falls as real GDP rises. When the economy expands, unemployment falls, and government spending for unemployment compensation, welfare, and other transfer payments decreases. During a downturn, people lose their jobs, and government spending automatically increases because unemployed individuals become eligible for unemployment compensation and other transfer payments.

The direct relationship between tax revenues and real GDP is shown by the upward-sloping line, *T*. During an expansion, jobs are created, unemployment falls, and workers earn more income and therefore pay more taxes. Thus, income tax collections automatically vary directly with the growth in real GDP.

We begin the analysis of automatic stabilizers with a balanced federal budget. Federal spending, *G*, is equal to tax collections, *T*, and the economy is in equilibrium at $14 trillion real GDP. Now assume consumer optimism soars and a spending spree increases the consumption component (*C*) of total spending. As a result, the economy moves to a new equilibrium at $16 trillion real GDP. The rise in real GDP creates more jobs and higher tax collections. Consequently, taxes rise to $2 trillion on line *T*. Also, government expenditures fall to $1 trillion because fewer people are collecting transfer payments, such as unemployment compensation and welfare. As a result, the vertical distance between lines *T* and *G* represents a federal **budget surplus** of $1 trillion. A budget surplus occurs when government revenues exceed government expenditures in a given time period.

Now begin again with the economy at $14 trillion in Exhibit 7, and let's change the scenario. Assume that business managers lower their profit expectations. Their revised outlook causes business executives to become pessimistic, so they cut investment spending (*I*), causing aggregate demand to decline. The corresponding decline in real GDP from $14 trillion to $12 trillion causes tax revenues to fall from $1.5 trillion to $1 trillion on line *T*. The combined effect of the rise in government spending and the fall in taxes creates a **budget deficit**. A budget deficit occurs when government expenditures exceed government revenues in a given time period. The vertical distance between lines *G* and *T* at $12 trillion real GDP illustrates a federal budget deficit of $1 trillion.

The key feature of automatic stabilization is that it "leans against the prevailing wind." In short, changes in federal spending and taxes moderate changes in aggregate demand. Stated differently, built-in stabilizers diminish or reduce swings in real GDP. When the economy expands, the fall in government spending for transfer payments and the rise in the level of taxes result in a budget surplus. As the budget surplus grows, people send more money to Washington, which applies braking power against further increases in real GDP. When the economy contracts, the rise in government spending for transfer payments and the fall in the level of taxes yield a budget deficit. As the budget deficit grows, people receive more money from Washington to spend, which slows further decreases in real GDP.

Automatic stabilizers

Federal expenditures and tax revenues that automatically change levels in order to stabilize an economic expansion or contraction; sometimes referred to as *nondiscretionary fiscal policy*.

Budget surplus

A budget in which government revenues exceed government expenditures in a given time period.

Budget deficit

A budget in which government expenditures exceed government revenues in a given time period.

Exhibit 7   Automatic Stabilizers

Federal government spending varies inversely with real GDP and is represented by the downward-sloping line, G. Taxes, in contrast, vary directly with real GDP and are represented by the upward-sloping line, T. This means government spending for welfare and other transfer payments declines and tax collections rise as real GDP rises. Thus, if real GDP falls below $14 trillion, the budget deficit rises automatically. The size of the budget deficit is shown by the vertical distance between lines G and T. This budget deficit assists in offsetting a recession because it stimulates aggregate demand. Conversely, when real GDP rises above $14 trillion, a federal budget surplus increases automatically and assists in offsetting inflation.

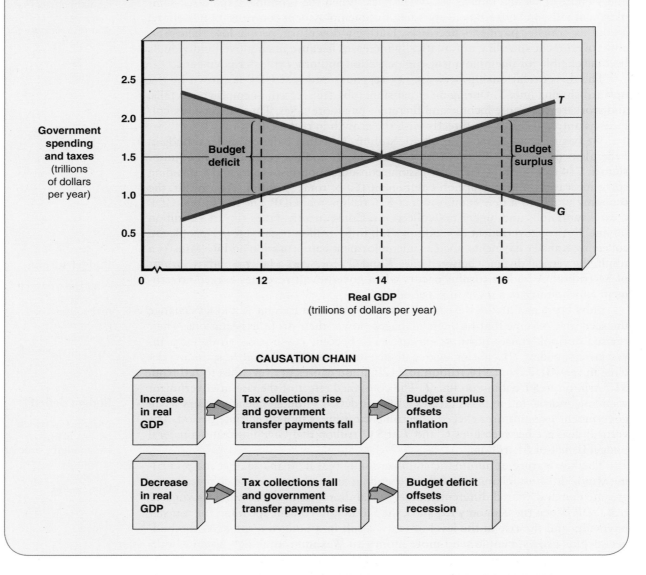

CONCLUSION *Automatic stabilizers assist in offsetting a recession when real GDP falls and in offsetting inflation when real GDP expands.*

SUPPLY-SIDE FISCAL POLICY

The focus so far has been on fiscal policy that affects the macro economy solely through the impact of government spending and taxation on aggregate demand. Supply-side economists, whose intellectual roots are in classical economics, argue that *stagflation* in the 1970s was the result of the federal government's failure to follow the theories of **supply-side fiscal policy**. Supply-side fiscal policy emphasizes government policies to increase aggregate supply in order to achieve long-run growth in real output, full employment, and a lower price level. Supply-side policies became an active economic idea with the election of Ronald Reagan as the president in 1980. As discussed in the previous chapter, the U.S. economy in the 1970s experienced high rates of both inflation and unemployment. Stagflation aroused concern about the ability of the U.S. economy to generate long-term advances in the standard of living. This set the stage for a new macroeconomic policy.

Suppose the economy is initially at E_1 in Exhibit 8(a), with a CPI of 150 and an output of $8 trillion real GDP. The economy is experiencing high unemployment, so the goal is to achieve full employment by increasing real GDP to $12 trillion. As described earlier in this chapter, the federal government might follow Keynesian expansionary fiscal policy and shift the aggregate demand curve rightward from AD_1 to AD_2. Higher government spending or lower taxes operate through the multiplier effect and cause this increase in aggregate demand. The good news from such a demand-side fiscal policy prescription is that the economy moves toward full employment, but the bad news is that the price level rises. In this case, *demand-pull inflation* would cause the price level to rise from 150 to 200.

Exhibit 8(b) represents the supply-siders' alternative to Keynesian fiscal policy. Again, suppose the economy is initially in equilibrium at E_1. Supply-side economists argue that the federal government should adopt policies that shift the aggregate supply curve rightward from AS_1 to AS_2. An increase in aggregate supply would move the economy to E_2 and achieve the full-employment level of real GDP. Under supply-side theory, there is an additional bonus to full employment. Instead of rising as in Exhibit 8(a), the price level in Exhibit 8(b) falls from 150 to 100. Comparing the two graphs in Exhibit 8, you can see that the supply-siders have a better theoretical case than proponents of demand-side fiscal policy when both inflation and unemployment are concerns.

Note the causation chain under each graph in Exhibit 8. The demand-side fiscal policy options are from column 1 of Exhibit 1 in this chapter, and the supply-side policy alternatives are similar to Exhibit 10 in the previous chapter. For supply-side economics to be effective, the government must implement policies that increase the total output that firms produce at each possible price level. An increase in aggregate supply can be accomplished by some combination of cuts in resource prices, technological advances, subsidies, and reductions in government taxes and government regulations.

Although a laundry list of supply-side policies was advocated during the Reagan administration, the most familiar policy action taken was the tax cuts implemented in 1981. By reducing tax rates on wages and profits, the Reagan administration sought to increase the aggregate supply of goods and services at any price level. However, tax cuts are a Keynesian policy intended to increase aggregate demand, so supply-siders must have a different view of the impact of tax cuts on the economy. To explain these different views of tax cuts, let's begin by stating that both Keynesians and supply-siders agree that tax cuts increase disposable personal income.

Supply-side fiscal policy

A fiscal policy that emphasizes government policies that increase aggregate supply in order to achieve long-run growth in real output, full employment, and a lower price level.

Exhibit 8 — Keynesian Demand-Side versus Supply-Side Effects

In part (a), assume an economy begins in equilibrium at point E_1, with a price level of 150 and a real GDP of $8 trillion. To boost real output and employment, Keynesian economists prescribe that the federal government raise government spending or cut taxes. By following such demand-side policies, the policymakers work through the multiplier effect and shift the aggregate demand curve from AD_1 to AD_2. As a result, the equilibrium changes to E_2, where real GDP rises to $12 trillion, but the price level also rises to 200. Hence, full employment has been achieved at the expense of higher inflation.

The initial situation for the economy at point E_1 in part (b) is identical to that shown in part (a). However, supply-siders offer a different fiscal policy prescription than the Keynesians. Using some combination of cuts in resource prices, technological advances, tax cuts, subsidies, and regulation reduction, supply-side fiscal policy shifts the aggregate supply curve from AS_1 to AS_2. As a result, the equilibrium in the economy changes to E_2, and real GDP increases to $12 trillion, just as in part (a). The advantage of the supply-side stimulus over the demand-side stimulus is that the price level falls to 100, rather than rising to 200.

In Keynesian economics, this boost in disposable personal income works through the *tax multiplier* to increase aggregate demand, as shown earlier in Exhibit 5. Supply-side economists argue instead that changes in disposable income affect the incentive to supply work, save, and invest.

Consider how a supply-side tax cut influences the labor market. Suppose supply and demand in the labor market are initially in equilibrium at point E_1 in Exhibit 9. Before a cut in personal income tax rates, the equilibrium hourly wage rate is W_1, and workers supply L_1 hours of labor per year at this wage rate. When the tax rates are cut, supply-side theory predicts the labor supply curve will shift rightward and establish a new equilibrium at E_2. The rationale is that an increase in the after-tax wage rate gives workers the incentive to work more hours per year. Those in the labor force will want to work longer hours and take fewer vacations. And because Uncle Sam takes a smaller bite out of workers' paychecks, many of those not already in the labor force will now supply their labor. As a result of the increase in the labor supply curve, the price of labor falls to W_2 per hour, and the equilibrium number of labor hours increases to L_2.

Supply-side tax cuts of the early 1980s also provided tax breaks that subsidized business investment. Tax credits were available for new equipment and plants and for research and development to encourage technological advances. The idea here was to increase the nation's productive capacity by increasing the quantity and quality of capital. Consequently, the aggregate supply curve would shift rightward because businesses have an extra after-tax profit incentive to invest and produce more at each price level.

Exhibit 9   **How Supply-Side Fiscal Policies Affect Labor Markets**

Begin with equilibrium in the labor market at point E_1. Here, the intersection of the labor supply and demand curves determines a wage rate of W_1 and L_1 hours of labor per year. By lowering tax rates, supply-side fiscal policies increase net after-tax earnings. This extra incentive causes workers to provide additional hours of labor per year. As a result, the labor supply curve increases and establishes a new equilibrium at point E_2. The new wage rate paid by employers falls to W_2, and they use more labor hours per year, L_2.

You're The Economist The Laffer Curve

Applicable Concept: supply-side fiscal policy

Supply-side economics became popular during the presidential campaign of 1980. This fiscal policy prescription gained prominence after supply-side economist Arthur Laffer, using his pen to draw on a paper napkin, explained what has come to be known as the Laffer curve to a *Wall Street Journal* journalist at a restaurant in Washington, D.C. The Laffer curve is a graph depicting the relationship between tax rates and total tax revenues. As shown in the figure, the hypothetical Laffer curve can be drawn with the federal tax rate on the horizontal axis and tax revenue on the vertical axis. The idea behind this curve is that the federal tax rate affects the incentive for people to work, save, invest, and produce, which in turn influences tax revenue. As the tax rate climbs, Laffer and other supply-siders argue that the erosion of incentives shrinks national income and total tax collections. The journalist kept the napkin and published the curve in an editorial in *The Wall Street Journal*. And a theory was born.

Here is how the Laffer curve works. Suppose the federal government sets the federal income tax rate at zero (point A). At a zero income tax rate, people have the maximum incentive to produce, and optimum national income would be earned, but there is zero tax revenue for Uncle Sam. Now assume the federal government sets the income tax rate at the opposite extreme of 100 percent (point D). At a 100 percent confiscating income tax rate, people have no reason to work, take business risks, produce, and earn income. People seek ways to reduce their tax liabilities by engaging in unreported or underground transactions or by not working at all. As a result, no tax revenue is collected by the Internal Revenue Service. Laffer compared this situation to Robin Hood and his band of merry men (the government) who robbed rich people (taxpayers) traveling through Sherwood Forest to give to the poor. Laffer posed this question, "Do you think that travelers continued to go through Sherwood Forest?" The answer is "no," and Robin Hood's "revenue" would fall.

Because the federal government does not want to collect zero tax revenue, Congress sets the federal income tax rate between zero and 100 percent. Assuming that the income tax rate is related to tax revenue as depicted in the figure, maximum tax revenue, R_{max}, is collected at a tax rate of T_{max} (point B). Laffer argued that the federal income tax rate of T (point C) in 1981 exceeded T_{max} and the result would be tax revenue of R, which is below R_{max}. In Laffer's view, reducing the federal income tax rate leads to an increase in tax revenue because people would increase their work effort, saving, and investment and would reduce

their attempts to avoid paying taxes. Thus, Laffer argued that a cut in federal income tax rates would unleash economic activity and boost tax revenues needed to reduce the federal budget deficit. President Reagan's belief in the Laffer curve was a major reason why he thought that the federal government could cut personal income tax rates and still balance the federal budget.

The Laffer curve remains a controversial part of supply-side economics. There is still considerable uncertainty about the shape of the Laffer curve and at what point B, C, or otherwise, along the curve the U.S. economy is operating. Thus, the existence and the usefulness of the Laffer curve are a matter of dispute.

ANALYZE THE ISSUE

Compare the common perception of how a tax rate cut affects tax revenues with economist Laffer's theory.

The idea of using tax cuts to shift the aggregate supply curve outward is controversial. Despite its logic, the Keynesians argue that the magnitude of any rightward shift in aggregate supply is likely to be small and occur only in the long run. They point out that it takes many years before tax cuts for business generate any change in actual plants and equipment or technological advances. Moreover, individuals can accept tax cuts with a "thank you, Uncle Sam" and not work longer or harder. Meanwhile, unless a reduction in government spending offsets the tax cuts, the effect will be a Keynesian increase in the aggregate demand curve and a higher price level. Exhibit 10 summarizes the important distinction between the supply-side and Keynesian theories on tax cut policy.

Laffer curve

A graph depicting the relationship between tax rates and total tax revenues.

Exhibit 10   **Supply-Side Effects versus Keynesian Demand-Side Effects of Tax Cuts**

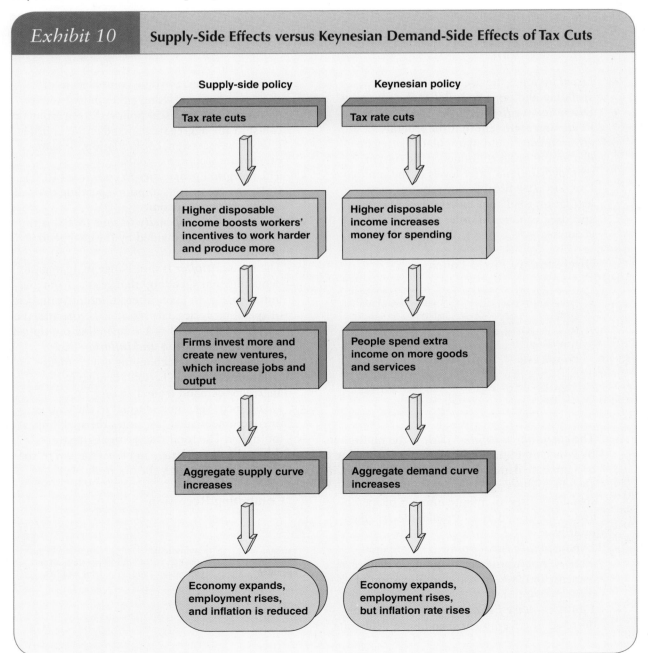

Key Concepts

Fiscal policy
Discretionary fiscal policy
Spending multiplier (*SM*)
Marginal propensity to consume
(*MPC*)

Marginal propensity to save (*MPS*)
Tax multiplier
Balanced budget multiplier
Automatic stabilizers
Budget surplus

Budget deficit
Supply-side fiscal policy
Laffer curve

Summary

- *Fiscal policy* is the use of government spending and taxes to stabilize the economy.
- *Discretionary fiscal policy* follows the Keynesian argument that the federal government should manipulate aggregate demand in order to influence the output, employment, and price levels in the economy. Discretionary fiscal policy requires new legislation to change either government spending or taxes in order to stabilize the economy.

Discretionary Fiscal Policies

Expansionary fiscal policy	Contractionary fiscal policy
Increase government spending	Decrease government spending
Decrease taxes	Increase taxes
Increase government spending and taxes equally	Decrease government spending and taxes equally

- The *spending multiplier (SM)* is the multiplier by which an initial change in one component of aggregate demand, for example, government spending, alters aggregate demand (total spending) after an infinite number of spending cycles. Expressed as a formula, the spending multiplier = $1/(1 - MPC)$.
- *Expansionary fiscal policy* is a deliberate increase in government spending, a deliberate decrease in taxes, or some combination of these two options.
- *Contractionary fiscal policy* is a deliberate decrease in government spending, a deliberate

increase in taxes, or some combination of these two options. Using either expansionary or contractionary fiscal policy, the government can shift the aggregate demand curve in order to combat recession, cool inflation, or achieve other macroeconomic goals.

- The *marginal propensity to consume (MPC)* is the change in consumption spending divided by the change in income.
- The *marginal propensity to save (MPS)* is the change in savings divided by the change in income.
- The *tax multiplier* is the change in aggregate demand (total spending) that results from an initial change in taxes after an infinite number of spending cycles. Expressed as a formula, the tax multiplier $(TM) = 1 -$ spending multiplier.
- *Combating recession and inflation* can be accomplished by changing government spending or taxes. The total change in aggregate demand from a change in government spending is equal to the change in government spending times the spending multiplier. The total change in aggregate demand from a change in taxes is equal to the change in taxes times the tax multiplier.

Combating Recession

Combating Inflation

- The *balanced budget multiplier* is not neutral. A dollar of government spending increases real GDP more than a dollar cut in taxes. Thus, even though the government does not spend more than it collects in taxes, it is still stimulating the economy.
- A *budget surplus* occurs when government revenues exceed government expenditures. A *budget deficit* occurs when government expenditures exceed government revenues.
- *Automatic stabilizers* are changes in taxes and government spending that occur automatically in response to changes in the level of real GDP. The business cycle therefore creates braking power: A *budget surplus* slows an expanding

economy; a *budget deficit* reverses a downturn in the economy.

Automatic Stabilizers

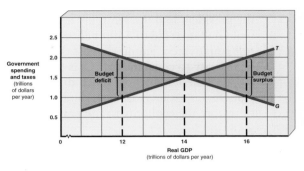

- According to *supply-side fiscal policy*, lower taxes encourage work, saving, and investment, which shift the aggregate supply curve rightward. As a result, output and employment increase without inflation.
- The *Laffer curve* represents the relationship between the income tax rate and the amount of income tax revenue collected by the government.

Summary of Conclusion Statements

- In the intermediate segment of the aggregate supply curve, the equilibrium real GDP changes by less than the change in government spending times the spending multiplier.
- Any initial change in spending by the government, households, or firms creates a chain reaction of further spending, which causes a greater cumulative change in aggregate demand.
- A tax cut has a smaller multiplier effect on aggregate demand than an equal increase in government spending.

- Regardless of the *MPC*, the net effect on the economy of an equal initial increase (decrease) in government spending and taxes is an increase (decrease) in aggregate demand equal to the initial increase (decrease) in government spending.
- Automatic stabilizers assist in offsetting a recession when real GDP falls and in offsetting inflation when real GDP expands.

Study Questions and Problems

1. Explain how discretionary fiscal policy fights recession and inflation.

2. How does each of the following affect the aggregate demand curve?
   a. Government spending increases.
   b. The amount of taxes collected decreases.

3. In each of the following cases, explain whether the fiscal policy is expansionary, contractionary, or neutral.
   a. The government decreases government spending.
   b. The government increases taxes.
   c. The government increases spending and taxes by an equal amount.

4. Why does a reduction in taxes have a smaller multiplier effect than an increase in government spending of an equal amount?

5. Suppose you are an economic adviser to the president and the economy needs a real GDP increase of $500 billion to reach full-employment equilibrium. If the marginal propensity to consume (MPC) is 0.75 and you are a Keynesian, by how much do you believe Congress must increase government spending to restore the economy to full employment?

6. Consider an economy that is operating at the full-employment level of real GDP. Assuming the MPC is 0.90, predict the effect on the economy of a $50 billion increase in government spending balanced by a $50 billion increase in taxes.

7. Why is a $100 billion increase in government spending for goods and services more expansionary than a $100 billion decrease in taxes?

8. What is the difference between discretionary fiscal policy and automatic stabilizers? How are federal budget surpluses and deficits affected by the business cycle?

9. Assume you are a supply-side economist who is an adviser to the president. If the economy is in recession, what would your fiscal policy prescription be?

10. Suppose Congress enacts a tax reform law and the average federal tax rate drops from 30 percent to 20 percent. Researchers investigate the impact of the tax cut and find that the income subject to the tax increases from $600 billion to $800 billion. The theoretical explanation is that workers have increased their work effort in response to the incentive of lower taxes. Is this a movement along the downward-sloping or the upward-sloping portion of the Laffer curve?

11. Indicate how each of the following would change either the aggregate demand curve or the aggregate supply curve.
   a. Expansionary fiscal policy
   b. Contractionary fiscal policy
   c. Supply-side economics
   d. Demand-pull inflation
   e. Cost-push inflation

For Online Exercises, go to the Tucker Web site at www.cengage.com/economics/tucker.

CHECKPOINT ANSWERS

What is the MPC for Uncle Sam's Stimulus Package?

To calculate the value of the MPC required to increase real GDP (ΔY) by $2,400 billion from an increase in government spending (ΔG) of $800 billion, use this formula:

$$\Delta G \times \text{multiplier} = \Delta Y,$$

where

$$\$800 \text{ billion} \times \text{multiplier} = \$2,400 \text{ billion}$$

Thus,

$$\text{Multiplier} = \frac{\$2,400 \text{ billion}}{\$800 \text{ billion}} = 3$$

Using Exhibit 4, if you said that the MPC is 0.67, **YOU ARE CORRECT**.

Walking the Balanced Budget Tightrope

An $800 billion increase in government spending increases aggregate demand by $3,200 billion [government spending increase × spending multiplier, where the spending multiplier = 1/(1 − MPC) = 1/0.25 = 4]. On the other hand, an $800 billion increase in taxes reduces aggregate demand by $2,400 billion (tax cut × tax multiplier, where the tax multiplier = 1 − spending multiplier = 1 − 4 = −3). Thus, the net effect of the spending multiplier and the tax multiplier is an increase in aggregate demand of $800 billion. If you said Congress has missed its goal of a $1,000 billion boost in aggregate demand by $200 billion and has not restored full employment, **YOU ARE CORRECT**.

Practice Quiz

For an explanation of the correct answers, visit the Tucker Web site at www.cengage.com/economics/tucker.

1. Contractionary fiscal policy is deliberate government action to influence aggregate demand and the level of real GDP through
   a. expanding and contracting the money supply.
   b. encouraging business to expand or contract investment.
   c. regulating net exports.
   d. decreasing government spending or increasing taxes.

2. The spending multiplier is defined as
   a. 1/(1 − marginal propensity to consume).
   b. 1/(marginal propensity to consume).
   c. 1/(1 − marginal propensity to save).
   d. 1/(marginal propensity to consume + marginal propensity to save).

3. If the marginal propensity to consume (MPC) is 0.60, the value of the spending multiplier is
   a. 0.4.
   b. 0.6.
   c. 1.5.
   d. 2.5.

4. Assume the economy is in recession and real GDP is below full employment. The marginal propensity to consume (MPC) is 0.80, and the government increases spending by $500 billion. As a result, aggregate demand will rise by
   a. zero.
   b. $2,500 billion.
   c. more than $2,500 billion.
   d. less than $2,500 billion.

5. Mathematically, the value of the tax multiplier in terms of the marginal propensity to consume (MPC) is given by the formula
   a. $MPC - 1$.
   b. $(MPC - 1)/MPC$.
   c. $1/MPC$.
   d. $1 - [1/(1 - MPC)]$.

6. Assume the marginal propensity to consume (MPC) is 0.75 and the government increases taxes by $250 billion. The aggregate demand curve will shift to the
   a. left by $1,000 billion.
   b. right by $1,000 billion.
   c. left by $750 billion.
   d. right by $750 billion.

7. If no fiscal policy changes are made, suppose the current aggregate demand curve will increase horizontally by $1,000 billion and cause inflation. If the marginal propensity to consume (MPC) is 0.80, federal policymakers could follow Keynesian economics and restrain inflation by decreasing
   a. government spending by $200 billion.
   b. taxes by $100 billion.
   c. taxes by $1,000 billion.
   d. government spending by $1,000 billion.

8. If no fiscal policy changes are implemented, suppose the future aggregate demand curve will exceed the current aggregate demand curve by $500 billion at any level of prices. Assuming the marginal propensity to consume (MPC) is 0.80, this increase in aggregate demand could be prevented by
   a. increasing government spending by $500 billion.
   b. increasing government spending by $140 billion.
   c. decreasing taxes by $40 billion.
   d. increasing taxes by $125 billion.

9. Suppose inflation is a threat because the current aggregate demand curve will increase by $600 billion at any price level. If the marginal propensity to consume (MPC) is 0.75, federal policymakers could follow Keynesian economics and restrain inflation by
   a. decreasing taxes by $600 billion.
   b. decreasing transfer payments by $200 billion.
   c. increasing taxes by $200 billion.
   d. increasing government spending by $150 billion.

10. If no fiscal policy changes are implemented, suppose the future aggregate demand curve will

Practice Quiz Continued

shift and exceed the current aggregate demand curve by $900 billion at any level of prices. Assuming the marginal propensity to consume (*MPC*) is 0.90, this increase in aggregate demand could be prevented by

a. increasing government spending by $500 billion.
b. increasing government spending by $140 billion.
c. decreasing taxes by $40 billion.
d. increasing taxes by $100 billion.

11. Which of the following is *not* an automatic stabilizer?
a. Defense spending
b. Unemployment compensation benefits
c. Personal income taxes
d. Welfare payments

12. Supply-side economics is most closely associated with
a. Karl Marx.
b. John Maynard Keynes.
c. Milton Friedman.
d. Ronald Reagan.

13. Which of the following statements is *true*?
a. A reduction in tax rates along the downward-sloping portion of the Laffer curve would increase tax revenues.
b. According to supply-side fiscal policy, lower tax rates would shift the aggregate demand curve to the right, expanding the economy and creating some inflation.

c. The presence of automatic stabilizers tends to destabilize the economy.
d. To combat inflation, Keynesians recommend lower taxes and greater government spending.

14. The sum of the marginal propensity to consume (*MPC*) and the marginal propensity to save (*MPS*) always equals
a. 1.
b. 0.
c. the interest rate.
d. the marginal propensity to invest (*MPI*).

15. The marginal propensity to save is
a. the change in saving induced by a change in consumption.
b. (change in S) / (change in Y).
c. $1 - MPC / MPC$.
d. (change in $Y - bY$) / (change in Y).
e. $1 - MPC$.

The Public Sector

In the early 1980s, President Ronald Reagan adopted the Laffer curve theory that the federal government could cut tax rates and increase tax revenues. Critics said the result would be lower tax revenues. During the 2000 campaign for the Republican presidential nomination, Steve Forbes continued his attempt to win support for a flat tax, and George W. Bush advocated cutting individual marginal tax rates. However, President Bill Clinton said cutting taxes was not a good idea because ensuring the integrity of Social Security should come first. Between 2001 and 2004, President George W. Bush signed laws that provided for phased-in cuts in the marginal tax rates, and increased spending for the war in Iraq and homeland defense. Critics argued that changing the tax structure while increasing spending would worsen the long-term federal budget outlook. And in 2009, grassroots "Tea Parties" were conducted across the nation to protest a too-large federal government that is spending large amounts on economic stimulus packages to deal with the recession.

These events illustrate the persistent real-world controversy surrounding fiscal policy. The previous chapter presented the theory behind fiscal policy. In this chapter, you will examine the practice of fiscal policy. Here, the facts of taxation and government expenditures are clearly presented and placed in perspective. You can check, for example, the trend in federal taxes and expenditures during the Obama administration and compare these figures to those of other countries. And you will discover why the government uses different types of taxes and tax rates.

The final section of the chapter challenges the economic role of the public sector. Here you will learn a theory called *public choice*, which examines public sector decisions of politicians, government bureaucrats, voters, and special-interest groups.

In this chapter, you will learn to solve these economics puzzles:

- How does the tax burden in the United States compare to other countries?

- How does the Social Security tax favor the upper-income worker?

- Is a flat tax fair?

- Should we replace the income tax with a national sales tax or a flat tax?

GOVERNMENT SIZE AND GROWTH

Government expenditures

Federal, state, and local government outlays for goods and services, including transfer payments.

How big is the public sector in the United States? If we look at Exhibit 1, we see total **government expenditures** or outlays—including those of federal, state, and local governments—as a percentage of GDP for the 1929–2009 period. When we refer to *government expenditures*, we refer to more than the *government consumption expenditures and investment* (G) account used by national income accountants to calculate GDP (see Exhibit 3 in the chapter on GDP). Government expenditures, or outlays, equal government purchases plus *transfer payments*. Recall from the chapter on GDP that the government national income account (G) includes federal government spending for defense, highways, and education. Transfer payments, not in (G), include payments to persons entitled to welfare, Social Security, and unemployment benefits.

As shown in Exhibit 1, total government expenditures skyrocketed as a percentage of GDP during World War II and then took a sharp plunge, but not to previous peacetime levels. Since 1950, total government expenditures grew from about one-quarter of GDP to about one-third beginning in 1975 and remained at this level until total expenditures increased sharply in 2009 during the Great Recession to a record 39 percent of GDP. The other side of the coin is that today the private sector's share of national output is approximately 61 percent of GDP. Issues concerning federal government spending and financing its debt are discussed in the next chapter.

Government Expenditures Patterns

Exhibit 2 shows program categories for federal government expenditures for 1970 and 2009. The largest category by far in the federal budget for 2009 was a category called *income security*. "Security" means these payments provide income to the elderly or disadvantaged, including Social Security, Medicare, unemployment compensation, public assistance (welfare), federal retirement, and disability benefits. These entitlements are transfer payments in the form of either direct cash payments or in-kind transfers that redistribute income among persons. In 2009, 44 percent of income security expenditures were spent for Social Security and 28 percent for Medicare.

The second largest category of federal government expenditures in 2009 was national defense. Note that the percentage of the federal budget spent for defense declined from 40 percent in 1970 to 19 percent in 2009, while income security ("safety net") expenditures grew from 22 percent in 1970 to 47 percent in 2009.

Exhibit 1	The Growth of Government Expenditures as a Percentage of GDP in the United States, 1929–2009

The graph shows the growth of the federal, state, and local governments as measured by government expenditures for goods and services as a percentage of GDP since 1929. Expenditures rose dramatically during World War II and fell dramatically after the war, but not to previous peacetime levels. Taking account of all government outlays, including transfer payments, the government sector has grown from about one-quarter of GDP in 1950 to about one-third of GDP beginning in 1975 and remained at this level until total government expenditures increased sharply in 2009 during the Great Recession to a record 39 percent of GDP.

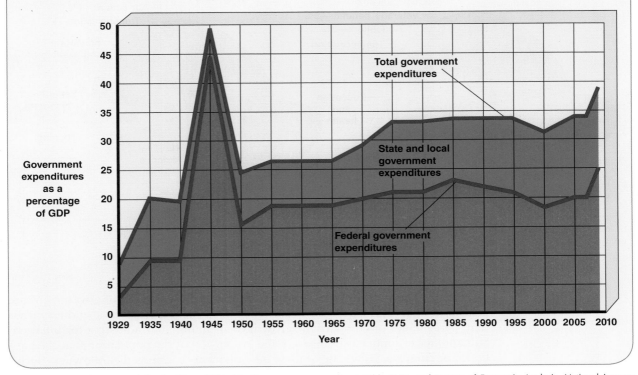

SOURCES: Economic Report of the President, 2010, http://www.gpoaccess.gov/eop/, Table B-79; and Bureau of Economic Analysis, National Income Accounts, http://www.bea.gov/national/nipaweb/SelectTable.asp?Selected=Y, Tables 1.1.5 and 3.3.

Hence, with a boost from an end to the Cold War, the dominant trend in federal government spending between 1970 and 2009 was an increase in the redistribution-of-income role of the federal government and a decrease in the portion of the budget spent for defense.

Federal expenditures for education and health were in third place in 2009, housing in fourth place, and net interest on the federal debt was in fifth place. Net interest paid is the interest on federal government borrowings minus the interest earned on federal government loans, and in 2009 this category of the budget was 5 percent. Thus, the federal government spent about the same proportion of the budget on financing its debt as on international affairs, veterans' benefits, and agriculture combined.

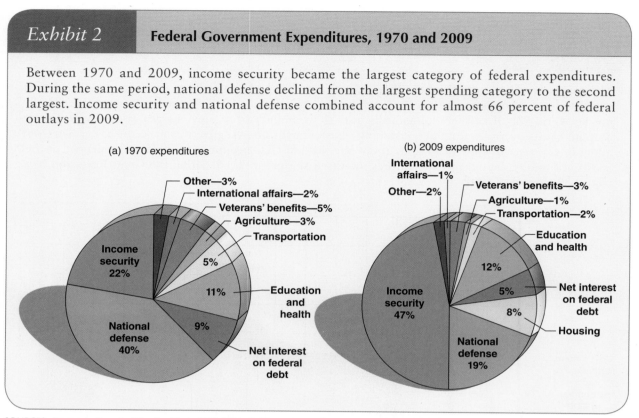

Exhibit 2   **Federal Government Expenditures, 1970 and 2009**

Between 1970 and 2009, income security became the largest category of federal expenditures. During the same period, national defense declined from the largest spending category to the second largest. Income security and national defense combined account for almost 66 percent of federal outlays in 2009.

(a) 1970 expenditures

- Other—3%
- International affairs—2%
- Veterans' benefits—5%
- Agriculture—3%
- Transportation
- Income security 22%
- 5%
- 11% — Education and health
- National defense 40%
- 9%
- Net interest on federal debt

(b) 2009 expenditures

- International affairs—1%
- Other—2%
- Veterans' benefits—3%
- Agriculture—1%
- Transportation—2%
- Education and health
- Income security 47%
- 12%
- 5% — Net interest on federal debt
- 8%
- Housing
- National defense 19%

SOURCES: Economic Report of the President, 1975, Table C-65, p. 325; and Economic Report of the President, 2010, http://www.gpoaccess.gov/eop/, Table B-81.

Finally, you need to be aware that the size and the growth of government are measured in several ways. We could study *absolute* government spending rather than percentages or compare the growth of spending after adjusting for inflation. Still another technique is to measure the proportion of the population that the public sector employs. Using any of these measurements confirms the following conclusion reached from Exhibit 1:

CONCLUSION *The government's share of total economic activity has generally increased since World War II ended in 1945. Most of the growth in combined government expenditures as a percentage of GDP reflects rapidly growing federal government transfer programs.*

Global Economics

Government Expenditures in Other Countries

In 2009, U.S. government spending for all levels as a percentage of GDP was lower than other advanced industrial countries. As shown in Exhibit 3, the governments of Sweden, France, Germany, and other countries spent a higher percentage of their GDPs than the federal, state, and local governments of the United States.

| Exhibit 3 | Government Expenditures in Other Countries, 2009 |

In 2009, the U.S. government was less of a spender than other advanced industrial countries. As shown in this exhibit, the governments of Sweden, France, Germany, and other countries spent a higher percentage of their GDPs than the federal, state, and local governments of the United States.

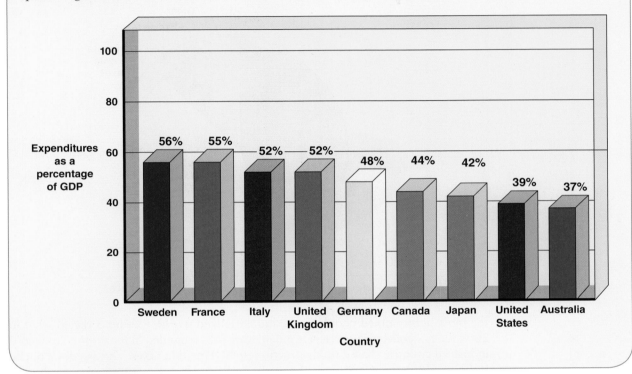

SOURCE: *OECD Economic Outlook* No. 84, December 2009, http://www.oecd.org, Annex Table 25.

FINANCING GOVERNMENT BUDGETS

Where does the federal government obtain the funds to finance its outlays? Exhibit 4 tells the story. We find that the largest revenue source in 2009 was individual income taxes (44 percent), followed closely by social insurance taxes (42 percent), which include payroll taxes paid by employers and employees for Social Security, workers' compensation, and unemployment insurance. The third best revenue getter was corporate income taxes (7 percent). An *excise tax* is a sales tax on the purchase of a particular good or service. Excise taxes contributed 3 percent of total tax receipts. The "Other" category includes receipts from such taxes as customs duties, estate taxes, and gift taxes.

The Tax Burden in Other Countries

Before turning our attention in the next section to the criteria for selecting which tax to impose, we must ask how burdensome overall taxation in the United States is. It may surprise you to learn that by international standards U.S. citizens are among

*Global
Economics*

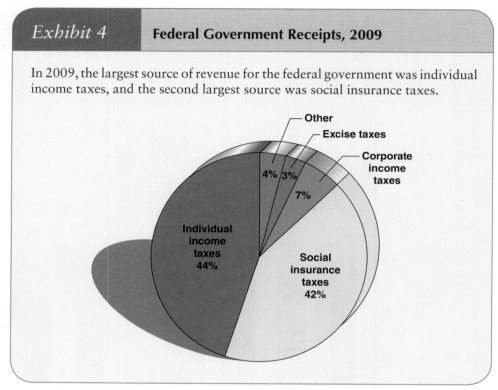

Exhibit 4   Federal Government Receipts, 2009

In 2009, the largest source of revenue for the federal government was individual income taxes, and the second largest source was social insurance taxes.

- Other
- Excise taxes
- Corporate income taxes

4% 3%

7%

Individual income taxes 44%

Social insurance taxes 42%

SOURCES: *Economic Report of the President*, 2010, http://www.gpoaccess.gov/eop/, Table B-81.

the most lightly taxed people in the industrialized world. Exhibit 5 reveals that in 2009 the tax collector was clearly much more heavy-handed in most other advanced industrial countries based on the fraction of GDP paid in taxes. The Swedes, French, Italians, Germans, Canadians, Spanish, and British, for example, pay far higher taxes as a percentage of GDP than Americans. It should be noted that countries that tax more heavily also are expected to provide more public services compared to the United States.

Another way to study the burden of taxation in the United States is to observe how it has changed over time. Exhibit 6 charts the growth of taxes as a percentage of GDP in the United States since 1929. Total government taxes, including federal, state, and local taxes, climbed from 11 percent of GDP in 1929 to their highest level of 34 percent in 2000, and then fell to 29 percent in 2009. The exhibit also shows that in 2000 federal taxes as a percentage of GDP rose to a post–World War II high of 21 percent before falling to about 15 percent in 2009.

THE ART OF TAXATION

Jean-Baptiste Colbert, finance minister to King Louis XIV of France, once said, "The art of taxation consists of so plucking the goose as to obtain the largest amount of feathers while promoting the smallest amount of hissing." Each year with great zeal, members of Congress and other policymakers debate various ways of raising revenue without causing too much "hissing." As you will learn, the task is difficult because each kind of tax has a different characteristic. Government must decide

| Exhibit 5 | The Tax Burden in Selected Countries, 2009 |

Americans were more lightly taxed in 2009 than the citizens of other advanced industrial countries. For example, the Swedes, French, Italians, Germans, Canadians, Spanish, and British pay higher taxes as a percentage of GDP.

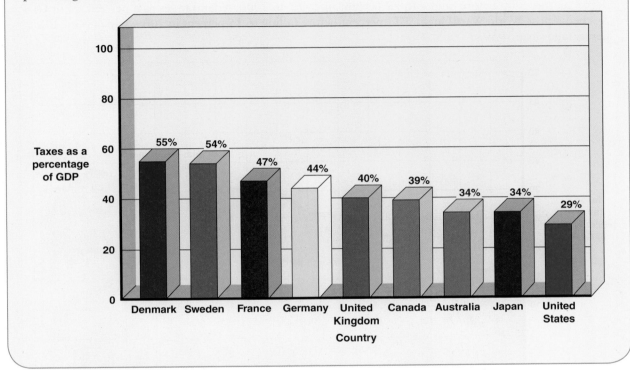

SOURCE: *OECD Economic Outlook* No. 84, December 2009, http://www.oecd.org, Annex Table 26, page 2.

which tax is "appropriate" based on two basic philosophies of fairness—benefits received and ability to pay.

The Benefits-Received Principle

What standard or guideline can we use to be sure everyone pays his or her "fair" share of taxes? One possibility is the benefits-received principle of taxation, which is the concept that those who benefit from government expenditures should pay the taxes that finance their benefits. The gasoline tax is an example of a tax that follows the *benefits-received principle*. The number of gallons of gasoline bought is a measure of the amount of highway services used, and the more gallons purchased, the greater the tax paid. Applying benefit-cost analysis, voters will approve additional highways only if the benefits they receive exceed the costs in gasoline taxes they must pay for highway construction and repairs.

Although the benefits-received principle of taxation is applicable to a private good like gasoline, the nature of *public goods* often makes it impossible to apply this principle. Recall from Chapter 4 that national defense is a public good, which

Benefits-received principle

The concept that those who benefit from government expenditures should pay the taxes that finance their benefits.

Exhibit 6

The Growth of Taxes as a Percentage of GDP in the United States, 1929–2009

The graph shows the growth in federal, state, and local government taxes as a percentage of GDP since 1929. Total government taxes climbed from about 11 percent of GDP in 1929 to their highest level of 34 percent in 2000 before falling to 29 percent in 2009. In 2000, federal taxes as a percentage of GDP reached a post-World War II high of 21 percent before falling to 15 percent in 2009, which is the lowest percentage since 1950.

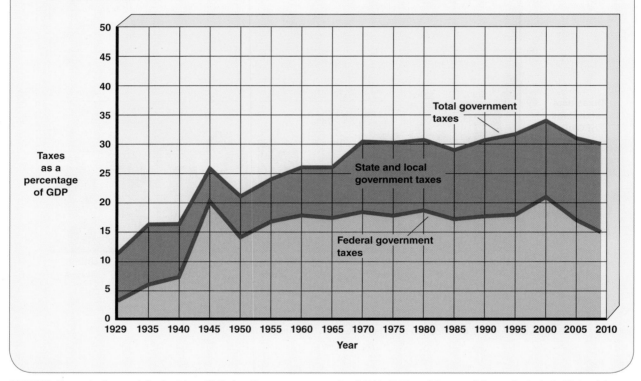

SOURCES: Economic Report of the President, 2010, http://www.gpoaccess.gov/eop/, Table B-79; and Bureau of Economic Analysis, National Income Accounts, http://www.bea.gov/national/nipaweb/SelectTable.asp?Selected=Y, Tables 1.1.5 and 3.3.

users collectively consume. So how can we separate those who benefit from national defense and make them pay? We cannot, and there are other goods and services for which the benefits-received principle is inconsistent with societal goals. It would be foolish, for example, to ask families receiving food stamps to pay all the taxes required to finance their welfare benefits.

The Ability-to-Pay Principle

A second popular principle of fairness in taxation sharply contrasts with the benefits-received principle. The **ability-to-pay principle** of taxation is the concept that those who have higher incomes can afford to pay a greater proportion of their income in taxes, regardless of benefits received. Under this tax philosophy, the rich may send their children to private schools or use private hospitals, but they should

Ability-to-pay principle

The concept that those who have higher incomes can afford to pay a greater proportion of their income in taxes, regardless of benefits received.

bear a heavier tax burden because they are better able to pay. How could there possibly be a problem with such an approach? An individual who earns $200,000 per year should pay X more taxes than an individual who earns only $10,000 per year. The difficulty lies in determining exactly how much more the higher-income individual should pay in taxes to ensure he or she is paying a "fair" amount. Unfortunately, no scientific method can measure precisely what one's "ability" to pay taxes means in dollars or percentage of income. Nevertheless, in the U.S. economy, the ability-to-pay principle dominates the benefits-received principle.

Where is the money I gave you last year?

Progressive, Regressive, and Proportional Taxes

As we have seen, governments raise revenues from various taxes, such as income taxes, sales taxes, excise taxes, and property taxes. For purposes of analysis, economists classify each of these taxes into three types of taxation—*progressive, regressive,* and *proportional*. The focus of these three classifications is the relationship between changes in the tax rates and increases or decreases in income. Income is the tax base because people pay taxes out of income, even though a tax is levied on property, such as land, buildings, automobiles, or furniture.

Progressive Taxes   Following the ability-to-pay principle, individual and corporate income taxes are **progressive taxes**. A progressive tax charges a higher percentage of income as income rises. For example, if a person earning $10,000 a year pays $1,500 in taxes, the average tax rate is 15 percent. If another person earns $100,000 a year and pays $28,000 in taxes, the average tax rate is 28 percent. This tax rate progressivity is the principle behind the federal and state income tax systems. Exhibit 8 illustrates the progressive nature of the federal income tax for a single person filing a 2009 tax return.

Column 1 of Exhibit 7 lists the *taxable income* tax brackets. Taxable income is gross income minus the personal exemption and the standard deduction.

Progressive tax

A tax that charges a higher percentage of income as income rises.

Exhibit 7	Federal Individual Income Tax Rate Schedule for a Single Taxpayer, 2009					
(1) Taxable income		(2)	(3) Average tax rate [(2)/(1)]	(4) Change in taxable income	(5) Change in tax	(6) Marginal tax rate [(5)/(4)]
Over	But not over	Tax*				
$ 0	$ 8,350	$ 835	10%	$ 8,350	$ 835	10%
8,350	33,950	4,675	14	25,600	3,840	15
33,950	82,250	16,750	20	48,300	12,075	25
82,250	171,550	41,754	24	89,300	25,004	28
171,550	372,950	108,216	29	201,400	66,462	33
372,950	...	...	...	...	...	35

*Tax calculated at the top of the taxable income brackets.
SOURCE: Internal Revenue Service, Publication 17, Your Federal Income Tax, 2009, http://www.irs.gov/publications/index.html, Tax Rate Schedules, p. 277.

Average tax rate

The tax divided by the income.

The personal exemption and the standard deduction are adjusted each year so inflation does not push taxpayers into higher tax brackets. Column 2 shows the tax bill that a taxpayer at the upper income of each of the five lowest taxable income brackets must pay, and the figures in column 3 are the corresponding average tax rates. The average tax rate is the tax divided by the income:

$$\text{Average tax rate} = \frac{\text{total tax due}}{\text{total taxable income}}$$

Thus, at a taxable income of $33,950, the average tax rate is 14 percent ($4,675 divided by $33,950), and at $82,250, it is 20 percent ($16,750 divided by $82,250). A taxable income of over $372,950 is included to represent the upper-income bracket. As these figures indicate, our federal individual income tax is a progressive tax because the average tax rate rises as income increases.

Marginal tax rate

The fraction of additional income paid in taxes.

Another key tax rate measure is the marginal tax rate, which is the fraction of additional income paid in taxes. The marginal tax rate formula is expressed as

$$\text{Marginal tax rate} = \frac{\text{change in taxes due}}{\text{change in taxable income}}$$

Column 6 in Exhibit 7 computes the marginal tax rate for each federal tax bracket in the table. You can comprehend the marginal tax rate by observing in column 1 that when taxable income rises from $8,350 to $33,950 in the second lowest tax bracket, the tax rises from $835 to $4,675 in column 2. Column 4 reports this change in taxable income, and column 5 shows the change in the tax. The marginal tax rate in column 6 is therefore 15 percent ($3,840 divided by $25,600). Apply the same analysis when taxable income increases by $48,300 from $33,950 to $82,250 in the next bracket. An additional $12,075 is added to the $4,675 tax bill, so the marginal tax rate on this extra income is 25 percent ($12,075 divided by $48,300). Similar computations provide the marginal tax rates for the remaining taxable income brackets. The marginal tax rate is important because it determines how much a taxpayer's tax bill changes as his or her income rises or falls within each tax bracket.

Regressive Taxes   A tax can also be a **regressive tax**. A regressive tax charges a lower percentage of income as income rises. Suppose Mutt, who is earning $10,000 a year, pays a tax of $5,000, and Jeff, who earns $100,000 a year, pays $10,000 in taxes. Although Jeff pays twice the absolute amount, this would be regressive taxation because richer Jeff pays an average tax rate of 10 percent and poorer Mutt suffers a 50 percent tax bite. Such a tax runs afoul of the ability-to-pay principle of taxation.

> **Regressive tax**
>
> A tax that charges a lower percentage of income as income rises.

We will now demonstrate that sales and excise taxes are regressive taxes. Assume that there is a 5 percent sales tax on all purchases and that the Jones family earned $80,000 during the last year, while the Jefferson family earned $20,000. A sales tax is regressive because the richer Jones family will spend a smaller portion of their income to buy food, clothing, and other consumption items. The Joneses, with an $80,000 income, can afford to spend $40,000 on groceries and clothes and save the rest, while the Jeffersons, with a $20,000 income, spend their entire income to feed and clothe their family. Because each family pays a 5 percent sales tax, the lower-income Jeffersons pay sales taxes of $1,000 (0.05 × $20,000), or 1/20 of their income. The higher-income Joneses, on the other hand, pay sales taxes of $2,000 (0.05 × $40,000), or only 1/40 of their income. Although the richer Jones family pays twice the amount of sales tax to the tax collector, the sales tax is regressive because their average tax rate is lower than the Jefferson family's tax rate.

In practice, an example of a regressive tax is the Social Security payroll tax, FICA. The payroll tax works like this: A fixed percentage of 12.4 percent is levied on each worker's earnings. The tax is divided equally between employers and employees. This means that an employee with a gross monthly wage of, say, $1,000 will have $62 (6.2 percent of $1,000) deducted from his or her check by the employer. In turn, the employer adds $62 and sends $124 to the government.

Payroll taxes are regressive for two reasons. First, only wages and salaries are subject to this tax, while other sources of income, such as interest and dividends, are not. Because wealthy individuals typically receive a larger portion of their income from sources other than wages and salaries than do lower-income individuals, the wealthy pay a smaller fraction of their total income in payroll taxes. Second, earnings above a certain level are exempt from the Social Security tax. Thus, the *marginal tax rate* above a given threshold level is zero. In 2009, this level was $106,800 for wage and salary income subject to Social Security tax. Hence, any additional dollars earned above this figure add no additional taxes, and the average tax rate falls. On the other hand, there is no wage base limit for the Medicare tax. It is noteworthy that one idea for reforming Social Security is to adjust or remove the limit on income subject to Social Security tax.

Finally, property taxes are also considered regressive for two reasons. First, property owners add this tax to the rent paid by tenants who generally are lower-income persons. Second, property taxes are a higher percentage of income for poor families than rich families because the poor spend a much greater proportion of their incomes for housing.

Proportional tax

A tax that charges
the same percentage
of income,
regardless of the size
of income. Also
called a *flat-tax rate*
or simply a *flat tax*.

Proportional Taxes There continues to be considerable interest in simplifying the federal progressive income tax by substituting a **proportional tax**, also called a *flat tax*. A proportional tax charges the same percentage of income, regardless of the size of income. For example, one way to reform the federal progressive tax rate system would be to eliminate all deductions, exemptions, and loopholes and simply apply the same tax rate, say, 17 percent of income to everyone. Such a reform is illustrated in Exhibit 8. This would avoid the "hissing" from taxpayers who would no longer require legions of accountants and lawyers to file their tax returns. Actually, most flat-tax proposals are not truly proportional because they exempt income below some level and are therefore somewhat progressive. Also, it is debatable that a 17 percent flat tax would raise enough revenue.

Let's look at whether the flat tax satisfies the benefits-received principle and the ability-to-pay principle. First, the flat tax does not necessarily relate to the benefits received from any particular government goods or services. Second, consider a 17 percent tax that collects $17,000 from Ms. "Rich," who is earning $100,000 a year, and $1,700 from Mr. "Poor," who is earning $10,000 a year. Both taxpayers pay the same proportional 17 percent of their incomes, but the $1,700 tax is thought to

Exhibit 8   **The Progressive Income Tax versus a Flat Tax**

The taxable income tax brackets for 2009 are drawn from Exhibit 7. In contrast to the "stair step" tax rates, a flat tax would charge a single rate of, say, 17 percent. This reform proposal is controversial and is discussed in the You're The Economist, "Is It Time to Trash the 1040s?"

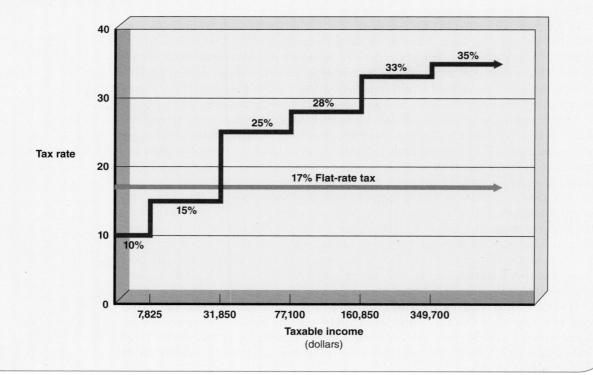

represent a much greater sacrifice to Mr. Poor than does the $17,000 tax paid by Ms. Rich. After paying her taxes, Ms. Rich can still live comfortably, but Mr. Poor complains that he desperately needed the $1,700 to buy groceries for his family. To be fair, one can argue that the $17,000 paid by Ms. Rich is not enough based on the ability-to-pay principle.

Reforming the Tax System

The Supreme Court declared the personal income tax unconstitutional in 1895. This changed in 1913 when the states ratified the Sixteenth Amendment to the Constitution, granting Congress the power to levy taxes on income. The federal income tax was an inconsequential source of revenue until World War II, but since then it has remained a major source. Currently, 41 states have income taxes, and personal income taxes may become an increasingly important source of state and local revenues in years to come.

Over the years, Congress has enacted various reforms of the federal tax system. The Tax Reform Act of 1986, for example, marked the first time Congress has completely rewritten the Federal Tax Code since 1954. This law removed millions of households from the tax rolls by roughly doubling the personal exemption allowed for each taxpayer and his or her dependents. Before the tax law changed, there were 15 marginal tax brackets for individuals, ranging from 11 to 50 percent. The Tax Reform Act of 1986 reduced the number of tax brackets to only four. Most taxpayers are in the lower brackets so the loss in tax revenue that resulted from lowering the individual tax rates was offset by raising taxes on corporations and closing numerous tax loopholes. Consistent with the two key taxation objectives, the intention of this major revision of the federal income tax law was to improve efficiency and to make the system fairer by shifting more of the tax burden to corporations. As shown in Exhibits 7 and 8, there are currently six tax brackets, and critics argue that another tax reform act is long overdue. The You're The Economist titled "Is It Time to Trash the 1040s?" discusses ideas to reform the current federal tax system.

PUBLIC CHOICE THEORY

James Buchanan, who won the 1986 Nobel Prize in economics, is the founder of a body of economic literature called **public choice theory**. Public choice theory is the analysis of the government's decision-making process for allocating resources. Recall from Chapter 4 that private-market failure is the reason for government intervention in markets. The theory of public choice considers how well the government performs when it replaces or regulates a private market. Rather than operating as the market mechanism to allocate resources, the government is a nonmarket, political decision-making force. Instead of behaving as private-interest buyers or sellers in the marketplace, actors in the political system have complex incentives in their roles as elected officials, bureaucrats, special-interest lobbyists, and voters.

Buchanan and other public choice theorists raise the fundamental issue of how well a democratic society can make efficient economic decisions. The basic principle of public choice theory is that politicians follow their own self-interest and seek to maximize their reelection chances, rather than promoting the best interests of society. Thus, a major contribution of Buchanan has been to link self-interest motivation

Public choice theory

The analysis of the government's decision-making process for allocating resources.

You're The Economist Is It Time to Trash the 1040s?

Applicable Concepts: flat tax, national sales tax and value-added tax (VAT).

Two controversial fundamental tax reform ideas are often hot news topics. One proposal is the flat tax discussed earlier in this chapter, and the other is a national sales tax. The flat tax is favored by former presidential candidate and publisher Steve Forbes. It would grant a personal exemption of about $36,000 for a typical family and then tax income above this amount at 17 percent with no deductions. As stated by recent presidential candidate John McCain, the argument for a flat tax is that it would allow people to file their tax returns on a postcard and reduce the number of tax cheats. McCain proposed that the flat tax would be optional to the current tax system.

The flat-tax plan described above creates serious political problems by eliminating taxes on income from dividends, interest, capital gains, and inheritances. Also, eliminating deductions and credits would face strong opposition from the public. For example, eliminating the mortgage interest deduction and exemptions for health care and charity would be a difficult political battle. And there is the fairness question. People at the lower end of the current system of six progressive rates could face a tax increase while upper-income people would get the biggest tax break. The counterargument is that under the current tax system many millionaires pay nothing because they shelter their income. Under a flat-tax scheme, they would lose deductions and credits.

A national retail sales tax is another tax reform proposal. In 2008, Mike Huckabee, Republican candidate for president, made this idea central to his campaign. A consumption tax could eliminate all federal income taxes entirely (personal, corporate, and Social Security) and tax only consumer purchases at a given percentage, say, 30 percent. Like the flat tax, loopholes would be eliminated, and tax collection would become so simple that the federal government could save billions of dollars by cutting or eliminating the IRS. Taxpayers would save because they no longer need to hire accountants and lawyers to prepare their complicated 1040 tax returns. Also, the tax base would broaden because, while not everyone earns income, almost everyone makes purchases.

Critics of a national sales tax argue that retail businesses would have the added burden of being tax collectors for the federal government, and the IRS would still be required to ensure that taxes are collected on billions of sales transactions. Moreover, huge price increases from the national sales tax would lead to "black market" transactions. The counterargument is that this problem would be no worse than current income tax evasion, and a sales tax indirectly taxes participants in illegal markets when they spend their income in legal markets. Also, a sales tax is regressive because the poor spend a greater share of their income on food, housing, and other necessities. To offset this problem, sales tax advocates propose subsidy checks paid up to some level of income. Critics also point out that retired people who pay little or no federal income tax will not welcome paying a national sales tax.

Recently there has been debate on using a Value-Added Tax (VAT) that is popular in Europe and many other countries. VAT is a consumption tax levied at each state of production. Suppose a vendor buys apples from a farmer to sell at a market. The vendor's VAT is based on a percentage of the difference (value added) between the cost the vendor paid and the sales price customers pay. Customers who buy the apples bear the VAT cost built into the price of the apples they purchase.

ANALYZE THE ISSUE

Assume the federal government replaces the federal income tax with a national sales tax on all consumption expenditures. Analyze the impact of this tax change on taxation efficiency and equity. Note that the federal government already collects a nationwide consumption tax through excise taxes on gasoline, liquor, and tobacco.

to government officials just as Adam Smith earlier identified the pursuit of self-interest as the motivation for consumers and producers. In short, individuals within any government agency or institution will act analogously to their private-sector counterparts; they will give first priority to improving their own earnings, working conditions, and status, rather than to being altruistic.

Given this introduction to the subject, let's consider a few public choice theories that explain why the public sector, like the private sector, may also "fail."

Majority-Rule Problem

To evaluate choices, economists often use a technique called benefit-cost analysis. Benefit-cost analysis is the comparison of the additional rewards and costs of an economic alternative. If a firm is considering producing a new product, its benefit ("carrots") will be the extra revenue earned from selling the product. The firm's cost ("sticks") is the opportunity cost of using resources to make the product. How many units of the product should the firm manufacture?

Benefit-cost analysis

The comparison of the additional rewards and costs of an economic alternative.

> **CONCLUSION** *Rationally, a profit-maximizing firm follows the marginal rule and produces additional units so long as the marginal benefit exceeds the marginal cost.*

The basic rule of benefit-cost analysis is that undertaking a program whose cost exceeds its benefit is an inefficient waste of resources. In the competitive market system, undertaking projects that yield benefits greater than costs is a sure bet. In the long run, any firm that does not follow the benefit-cost rule will either go out of business or switch to producing products that yield benefits equal to or greater than their costs. Majority-rule voting, however, can result in the approval of projects whose costs outweigh their benefits. Exhibit 9 illustrates how an inefficient economic decision can result from the ballot box.

As shown in Exhibit 9, suppose Bob, Juan, and Theresa are the only voters in a mini-society that is considering whether to add two publicly financed park projects, *A* and *B*. The total cost to taxpayers of either park project is $300, and the marginal cost of park *A* or park *B* to each taxpayer is an additional tax of $100 (columns 2 and 5). Next, assume each taxpayer determines his or her additional dollar value

Exhibit 9	Majority-Rule Benefit-Cost Analysis of Two Park Projects					
	Park project A			**Park project B**		
(1) Voter	**(2)** Marginal cost (taxes)	**(3)** Marginal benefit	**(4)** Vote	**(5)** Marginal cost (taxes)	**(6)** Marginal benefit	**(7)** Vote
Bob	$100	$ 0	No	$100	$ 90	No
Juan	100	101	Yes	100	90	No
Theresa	100	101	Yes	100	301	Yes
Total	$300	$202	Passes	$300	$481	Fails

derived from the benefits of park projects *A* and *B* (columns 3 and 6). Assuming each person applies marginal analysis, each will follow the *marginal rule* and vote for a project only if his or her benefit exceeds the cost of the $100 tax. Consider park project *A*. This project is worth $0 to Bob, $101 to Juan, and $101 to Theresa, and this means two Yes votes and one No vote: The majority votes for park *A* (column 4). This decision would not happen in the business world. The Disney company, for example, would rationally reject such a project because the total of all consumers' marginal benefits is only $202, which is less than its $300 marginal cost.

The important point here is that majority-rule voting can make the correct benefit-cost marginal analysis, but it can also lead to a rejection of projects with marginal total benefits that exceed marginal costs. Suppose park project *B* costs $300 as well, and Bob's benefits are $90, Juan's $90, and Theresa's $301 (column 6). The total of all marginal benefits from constructing park *B* is $481, and this project would be undertaken in a private-sector market. But because only Theresa's benefits exceed the marginal $100 tax, park project *B* in the political arena receives only one Yes vote against two No votes and fails.

Why is there a distinction between political majority voting and benefit-cost analysis? The reason is that dollars can measure the intensity of voter preferences and "one-person, one-vote" does not. A count of ballots can determine whether a proposal passes or fails, but this count may not be proportional to the dollar strength of benefits among the individual voters.

Special-Interest Group Effect

In addition to benefit-cost errors from majority voting, special-interest groups can create government support for programs with costs outweighing their benefits. The *special-interest effect* occurs when the government approves programs that benefit only a small group within society, but society as a whole pays the costs. The influence of special-interest groups is indeed a constant problem for effective government because the benefits of government programs to certain small groups are great and the costs are relatively insignificant to each taxpayer. For example, let's assume the benefits of support prices for dairy farmers are $100 million. Because of the size of these benefits to dairy farmers, this special-interest group can well afford to hire professional lobbyists and donate a million dollars or so to the reelection campaigns of politicians voting for dairy price supports.

In addition to the incentive of financial support from special interests, politicians can also engage in *logrolling*. Logrolling is the political practice of trading votes of support for legislated programs. Politician A says to politician B, "You vote for my dairy price support bill, and I will vote for your tobacco price support bill."

But who pays for these large benefits to special-interest groups? Taxpayers do, of course, but the extra tax burden per taxpayer is very low. Although Congress may enact a $200 million program to favor, say, a few defense contractors, this expenditure costs 100 million taxpayers only $2 per taxpayer. Because in a free society it is relatively easy to organize special-interest constituencies and lobby politicians to spread the cost, it is little wonder that spending programs are popular. Moreover, the small cost of each pet program per taxpayer means there is little reward for a single voter to learn the details of the many special-interest legislation proposals.

Rational Voter Ignorance

Politicians, appointed officials, and bureaucrats constitute the supply side of the political marketplace. The demand side of the political market consists of special-interest groups and voters who are subject to what economists call rational ignorance. Rational ignorance is a voter's decision that the benefit of becoming informed about an issue is not worth the cost. A frequent charge in elections is that the candidates are not talking about the issues. One explanation is that the candidates realize that a sizable portion of the voters will make a calculated decision not to judge the candidates based on in-depth knowledge of their positions on a wide range of issues. Instead of going to the trouble of reading position papers and doing research, many voters choose their candidates based simply on party affiliation or on how the candidate appears on television. This approach is rational if the perceived extra effort required to be better informed exceeds the marginal benefit of knowing more about the candidate.

> **Rational ignorance**
>
> The voter's choice to remain uninformed because the marginal cost of obtaining information is higher than the marginal benefit from knowing it.

    The principle of rational ignorance also explains why eligible voters fail to vote on election day. A popular explanation is that low voter participation results from apathy among potential voters, but the decision can be an exercise in practical benefit-cost analysis. Nonvoters presumably perceive that the opportunity cost of going to the polls outweighs the benefit gained from any of the candidates or issues on the ballot. Moreover, nonvoters perceive that one extra vote is unlikely to change the outcome.

    Public choice theorists argue that one reason benefits are difficult to measure is that the voter confronts an *indivisible* public service. In a grocery store, the consumer can decide to spend so much on apples, oranges, and other *divisible* items, but voting involves candidates who take stands on many issues. The point is that voting does not allow the voter to pick and choose among the candidate's good and bad positions. Most voters, in short, must "buy" a confusing mixture of "wants" and "unwants" that are difficult to interpret as a benefit.

Bureaucratic Inefficiency

The bureaucracy is the body of nonelected officials and administrators who operate government agencies. As government grows, one of the concerns is that the bureaucracy may become more powerful than the executive, legislative, and judicial branches. Public choice theory also considers how bureaucratic behavior affects economic decision making. One principle is that the government bureaucracy tends to be inefficient because of the absence of the profit motive.

    What happens when a government agency performs poorly? First, there is no competition from other producers to take away market share. There are no shareholders demanding reform when profits are falling because taxpayers are a poor substitute for stockholder pressure. Second, the typical government response each year is to request a larger budget. Without profits as a measure of performance, the tendency is to use the size of an agency's budget and staff as an indicator of success. In brief, the basic incentive structure of government agencies encourages inefficient management because, unlike the market system, there is a lack of incentive to be cost-conscious or creative. Instead, the hallmark of the bureaucrat is to be extremely cautious and make all decisions "by the book." Such behavior may maximize prestige and security, but it usually fails to minimize costs.

Shortsightedness Effect

Finally, it can be argued that democracy has a bias toward programs offering clear benefits and hidden costs. The reason is that political officeholders must run for reelection after a relatively short period of two to six years. Given this reality, politicians tend to favor proposals providing immediate benefits, with future generations paying most of the costs. Conversely, they reject programs that have easily identifiable short-run high costs, but offer benefits only after a decade. Hence, the essence of the hidden costs bias or *shortsightedness effect* is that both voters and politicians suffer from a short time horizon. Such a myopic view of either future costs or future benefits can cause an irrational acceptance of a program, even though long-run costs exceed short-run benefits, or an irrational rejection of a program with long-run benefits that outweigh short-run costs.

CHECKPOINT

What Does Public Choice Say about a Budget Deficit?

In 2002, the situation switched from a few years in which the federal government spent less than it collected in taxes to spending more than tax revenues (discussed in the next chapter). James Buchanan predicted over 30 years ago that growing government deficits would be inevitable. He maintained that government officials would increase spending for their constituents in order to gain votes. Furthermore, politicians would shy away from tax increases for fear of alienating voters. The net effect would be deficits. Was Buchanan's prediction based on the rational ignorance effect, government inefficiency, or the shortsightedness effect?

Key Concepts

Government expenditures
Benefits-received principle
Ability-to-pay principle
Progressive tax

Average tax rate
Marginal tax rate
Regressive tax
Proportional or flat tax

Public choice theory
Benefit-cost analysis
Rational ignorance

Summary

- *Government expenditures*, including transfer payments, have grown from about one-quarter of GDP in 1950 to about 40 percent of GDP today.

Government Expenditures

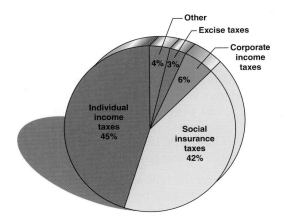

- *Federal tax revenues* are collected primarily from individual income taxes and social insurance taxes.

Federal Tax Revenues

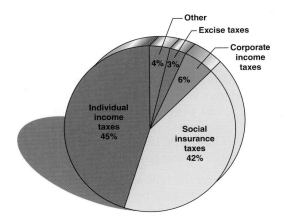

- The *taxation burden*, measured by taxes as a percentage of GDP, is lighter in the United States than in many other advanced industrial countries.

Taxation Burden

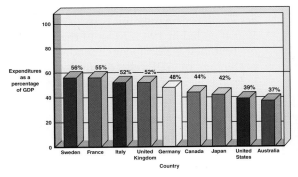

- **Total tax revenues** amounted to about 11 percent of GDP in 1929 and reached the highest level of close to 34 percent in 2000 before falling to 29 percent in 2009. Federal taxes take a larger share of GDP than state and local governments.

Total Tax Revenues

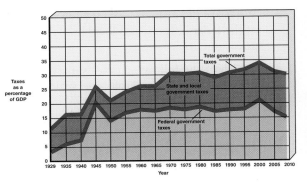

- The ***benefits-received principle*** and the **ability-to-pay principle** are two basic philosophies of taxation fairness. The gasoline tax is a classic example of the benefits-received principle because users of the highways pay the gasoline tax. Progressive income taxes follow the ability-to-pay principle because there is a direct relationship between the average tax rate and income size. Sales, excise, property, and flat-rate taxes violate this principle because each results in a greater burden on the poor than on the rich.
- ***Public choice theory*** reveals the government's decision-making process. For example, government failure can occur for any of the following reasons: (1) majority voting may not follow benefit-cost analysis; (2) special-interest groups can obtain large benefits and spread their costs over many taxpayers; (3) rational voter ignorance means a sizable portion of the voters will decide not to make informed judgments; (4) bureaucratic behavior may not lead to cost-effective decisions; and (5) politicians suffer from a short time horizon, leading to a bias toward hiding the costs of programs.

Summary of Conclusion Statements

- The government's share of total economic activity has generally increased since World War II ended in 1945. Most of the growth in combined government expenditures as a percentage of GDP reflects rapidly growing federal government transfer programs.
- Rationally, a profit-maximizing firm follows the marginal rule and produces additional units so long as the marginal benefit exceeds the marginal cost.

Study Questions and Problems

1. Explain why federal, state, and local expenditures account for more than 30 percent of GDP, but total government spending (G in GDP) is only about 20 percent of GDP.

2. Identify the major differences between federal government outlays and spending by state and local governments.

3. What are the primary tax revenue sources at the federal, state, and local levels of government?

4. Which of the following taxes satisfy the benefits-received principle, and which satisfy the ability-to-pay principle?
   a. Gasoline tax
   b. Federal income tax
   c. Tax on Social Security benefits

5. What is the difference between the marginal tax rate and the average tax rate?

6. Explain why a 5 percent sales tax on gasoline is regressive.

7. Ms. Jones has a taxable income of $30,000, and she must pay $3,000 in taxes. Mr. Smith has a taxable income of $60,000. How much tax must Mr. Smith pay for the tax system to be
   a. progressive?
   b. regressive?
   c. proportional?

8. Explain why each of the following taxes is progressive or regressive:
   a. A $1 per pack federal excise tax on cigarettes
   b. The federal individual income tax
   c. The federal payroll tax

9. Complete the following table, which describes the sales tax paid by individuals at various income levels. Indicate whether the tax is progressive, proportional, or regressive.

Income	Total Spending	Sales Tax Paid	Sales Tax Paid as a Percentage of Income
$ 1,000	$ 1,000	$ 100	_____%
5,000	3,500	350	_____
10,000	6,000	600	_____
100,000	40,000	4,000	_____

Income	Tax Paid	Average Tax Rate	Marginal Tax Rate
$ 0	$ 0	0%	0%
100	10	_____	_____
200	30	_____	_____
300	60	_____	_____
400	100	_____	_____
500	150	_____	_____

10. Calculate the average and the marginal tax rates in the following table, and indicate whether the tax is progressive, proportional, or regressive. What observation can you make concerning the relationship between marginal and average tax rates?

11. Compare "dollar voting" in private markets with "majority voting" in the political decision-making system.

For Online Exercises, go to the Tucker Web site at www.cengage.com/economics/tucker.

CHECKPOINT ANSWER

What Does Public Choice Say about a Budget Deficit?

The government uses the deficit to finance clear short-term benefits with little attention to long-term consequences. If you said public choice predicts that government officials will emphasize near-term benefits to gain votes (the shortsightedness effect), **YOU ARE CORRECT.**

Practice Quiz

For an explanation of the correct answers, visit the Tucker Web site at www.cengage.com/economics/tucker.

1. Since 1975, total government expenditures as a percentage of GDP in the United States have
   a. grown from one-third to about 40 percent.
   b. remained fairly constant at about one-third.
   c. grown from one-fourth to one-half.
   d. grown from one-quarter to one-third.

2. Which of the following accounted for the second largest percentage of total federal government expenditures in 2009?
   a. Income security
   b. National defense
   c. Interest on the national debt
   d. Education and health

3. Which of the following contributed the largest percentage of total federal government expenditures in 2009?
   a. Interest on the national debt
   b. Education and health
   c. National defense
   d. Income security

4. Which of the following countries devotes about the same percentage of its GDP to taxes as the United States?
   a. Sweden
   b. Italy
   c. United Kingdom
   d. Japan

Practice Quiz Continued

5. "The poor should not pay income taxes." This statement reflects which of the following principles of taxation?
   a. Fairness of contribution
   b. Benefits-received
   c. Inexpensive-to-collect
   d. Ability-to-pay

6. Some cities finance their airports with a departure tax: Every person leaving the city by plane is charged a small fixed dollar amount that is used to help pay for building and running the airport. The departure tax follows the
   a. benefits-received principle.
   b. ability-to-pay principle.
   c. flat-rate principle.
   d. public-choice principle.

7. Which of the following statements is *true*?
   a. The most important source of tax revenue for the federal government is individual income taxes.
   b. The taxation burden, measured by taxes as a percentage of GDP, is lighter in the United States than in most other advanced industrial countries.
   c. Both (a) and (b) are true.
   d. Neither (a) nor (b) are true.

8. Which of the following statements is *true*?
   a. A sales tax on food is a regressive tax.
   b. The largest source of federal government tax revenue is individual income taxes.
   c. The largest source of state and local government tax revenue is sales taxes.
   d. All of the above are true.

9. A tax that is structured so that people with higher incomes pay a larger percentage of their incomes for the tax than do people with smaller incomes is called a (an)
   a. income tax.
   b. regressive tax.
   c. property tax.
   d. progressive tax.

10. Generally, most economists feel that a _____ type of income tax is a fairer way to raise government revenue than a sales tax.
    a. regressive
    b. proportional
    c. flat-rate
    d. progressive

11. The federal personal income tax is an example of a (an)
    a. excise tax.
    b. proportional tax.
    c. progressive tax.
    d. regressive tax.

12. A 5 percent sales tax on food is an example of a
    a. flat tax.
    b. progressive tax.
    c. proportional tax.
    d. regressive tax.

13. Margaret pays a local income tax of 2 percent, regardless of the size of her income. This tax is
    a. proportional.
    b. regressive.
    c. progressive.
    d. a mix of (a) and (b).

14. Which of the following statements relating to public choice is *true*?
    a. A low voter turnout may result when voters perceive that the marginal cost of voting exceeds its marginal benefit.
    b. If the marginal cost of voting exceeds its marginal benefit, the vote is unimportant.
    c. Special-interest groups always cause the will of a majority to be imposed on a minority.
    d. All of the above are true.

15. According to the shortsightedness effect, politicians tend to favor projects with
    a. short-run benefits and short-run costs.
    b. short-run benefits and long-run costs.
    c. long-run benefits and short-run costs.
    d. long-run benefits and long-run costs.

chapter 13

Federal Deficits, Surpluses, and the National Debt

The U.S. government has been in the red almost continuously since the Revolutionary War forced the Continental Congress to borrow money. The only exception was a brief interlude more than a century and a half ago when our government was debt-free. In December 1834, President Andrew Jackson proudly reported to Congress what he considered to be a major accomplishment of his administration. By New Year's Day of 1835, the federal government would succeed in paying off the national debt. It was Jackson's second term as president. Since the close of the War of 1812, the country had experienced tremendous growth, and revenues flowed into the U.S. Treasury from import tariffs and the sale of public land. By early 1836, the nation had been out of debt for two years, and there was a budget surplus of $37 million. The dilemma in those days was how to use the surplus. In 1836, Congress simply decided to divide all but $5 million of the surplus among the states. Then the financial panic of 1837 caused the government to plunge into debt again, where it remains today and for the foreseeable future.

Unlike Andrew Jackson, Abraham Lincoln in his 1864 Annual Message to Congress expressed no concern for paying off the national debt. Lincoln stated:

> *The great advantage of citizens being creditors as well as debtors, with relation to the public debt, is obvious. Men can readily perceive that they cannot be much oppressed by a debt which they owe to themselves.*

In 2009, federal government borrowing to cover its budget deficits had accumulated a national debt of about $12 trillion. To the average citizen, this is an incomprehensible amount of money for even the government to owe. Perhaps the best way to picture this sea of red ink is that your individual share is over $39,000 and rising.

In this chapter, you will learn to solve these economics puzzles:

- Can Uncle Sam go bankrupt?

- How does the national debt of the United States compare to the debt of other countries?

- Are we passing the debt burden to our children?

- Who owns the national debt?

THE FEDERAL BUDGET BALANCING ACT

What will happen next? Like a high-wire performer swinging one way and then another while the crowd below gazes transfixed, the public in the late 1990s and early 2000s watched the federal budget sway back and forth between deficits and surpluses. As you learned in the preceding chapter on fiscal policy, a federal budget deficit occurs whenever the government spends more than it collects in taxes. The accumulation of these budget deficits over the years is the origin of the national debt. When the federal government has a surplus in its budget, some or all of the surplus can be used to retire the national debt, and it decreases. Here you will take a closer look at the actual budgetary process that creates and finances our national debt.

The Federal Budgetary Process

In theory, Keynesian discretionary fiscal policy requires that legislation be enacted to change government spending or taxes in order to shift the aggregate demand curve represented in the *AD-AS* model. In practice, the federal budgetary process, which determines the level of spending and taxation, is not so orderly. The annual "battle of the budget" on Capitol Hill involves political decisions on how much the government plans to spend and where the money will come from to finance these outlays. Wrangling takes place between all sorts of camps: the president versus Congress, Republicans versus Democrats, national security versus economic equality, price stability versus full employment, health care versus tax cuts, and so on. Given the complexities of world events, special-interest groups, volatile public opinion, and political ambitions that complicate the budget process, it is no wonder actual fiscal policy often ignores textbook macroeconomics.

The following brief look at the federal budgetary process shows how Congress and the president make federal spending and tax decisions each year:

Stage 1: Formation of the Budget Between February and December, federal agencies develop and submit their budget requests for the upcoming fiscal year to the Office of Management and Budget (OMB). (The government's fiscal year begins on October 1 and ends on September 30, so the budgetary process begins in the preceding calendar year.) The Pentagon argues for more defense spending, the Department of Transportation for more highway funds, and so on. The OMB reviews each

Exhibit 1	**Major Steps in the Federal Budgetary Process**

The first step in the federal budgetary process is the OMB's formation of the budget based on requests from all federal agencies. The second step is the president's transmittal of the administration's budget to Congress. In the third step, Congress passes a budget resolution that sets targets for spending, taxes, and the deficit or surplus. In the final step, Congress passes the budget, consisting of specific spending and tax bills. When the president signs the spending and revenue bills, the federal government has its actual budget.

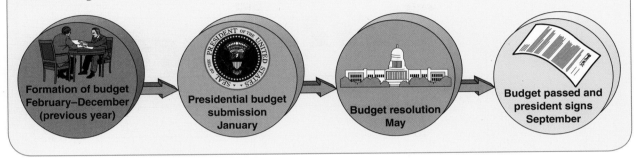

Formation of budget February–December (previous year) → **Presidential budget submission January** → **Budget resolution May** → **Budget passed and president signs September**

agency's request. After receiving advice from the president, officials from cabinet departments, the Council of Economic Advisors (CEA), and the Treasury, the OMB compiles all the proposals into a budget recommendation. Applying the administration's goals, the OMB sends the proposed budget to the president by December.

Stage 2: Presidential Budget Submission
In January, nine months before the new fiscal year begins on October 1, the president submits the proposed budget to Congress. The official title is *The Budget of the United States*. This unveiling of the administration's budget is always big news. Does the president recommend that less money be spent for defense and more for education? Is there an increase in the Social Security payroll tax or the income tax? And how large is the national debt? Is there a budget deficit or a budget surplus?

Stage 3: Budget Resolution
After the president submits the budget in January, Congress takes the lead in the budgetary process. The president's budget now becomes the starting point for congressional consideration. The Congressional Budget Office (CBO) employs a professional staff who advise Congress on the budget much the way the OMB advises the president. The CBO analyzes the budget by February and reports its evaluation at budget committee hearings in both the House of Representatives and the Senate. After debate, in May Congress approves an overall budget outline called the *budget resolution*, which sets target levels for spending, tax revenues, and the budget deficit or surplus.

Stage 4: Budget Passed
Throughout the summer and supposedly ending by October 1, Congress and the president debate while congressional committees and subcommittees prepare specific spending and tax law bills. The budget resolution is supposed to guide the spending and revenue decisions of these committees. After Congress

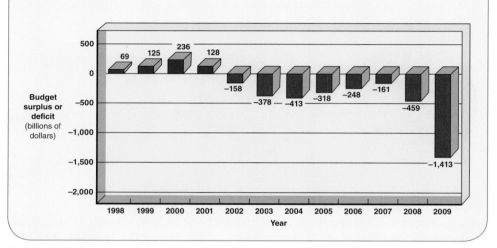

Exhibit 2   **U.S. Federal Budget Surpluses and Deficits, 1998–2009**

During 1998 through 2001, the annual federal government budget was in surplus each year. After the recession of 2001, these surpluses disappeared and deficits appeared, exploding to $1.4 trillion in 2009.

SOURCE: Economic Report of the President, 2010, http://www.gpoacess.gov/eop/, Table B-78.

passes and the president signs the spending and revenue bills, the federal government has its actual budget for spending and tax collection.

As summarized in Exhibit 1, the budgetary process seems orderly enough, but in practice it does not work so smoothly. The process can, and often does, go astray. One problem is that Congress does not necessarily follow its own rules. The budget bills are not always passed on time, and when that happens, the fiscal year starts without a budget. Then federal agencies must operate on the basis of *continuing resolutions*, which means each agency operates as it did the previous year until spending bills are approved. In some years, Congress even fails to pass a continuing resolution, and the federal government must shut down and workers stay home until Congress approves the necessary funds.

Financing the National Debt

Over the years, the federal government budget experiences imbalances. A budget deficit occurs when federal expenditures, including spending for final goods plus transfer payments, exceed tax revenues collected. A surplus occurs when the government collects more in taxes than it spends. For example, for four years between 1998 and 2001 budget surpluses existed, as discussed in the next You're The Economist feature. As shown in Exhibit 2, deficits returned after the 2001 recession, and following the recession beginning in 2007, deficits reached record highs. In 2009, a record-breaking federal deficit was about $1.4 trillion.

What happens when the government overspends, and the U.S. Treasury must borrow to finance the difference between expenditures and revenues? The answer to that is the U.S. Treasury borrows by selling Treasury bills (T-bills), notes, and bonds promising to make specified interest payments and to repay the loaned funds on a given date. These government securities are IOUs of the federal government. They are considered a safe haven for idle funds and are purchased by Federal Reserve banks, government agencies, private banks, corporations, individual U.S. citizens, and foreigners. If you own a U.S. government savings bond, for example, you have loaned your funds to the federal government. The stock of these federal government IOUs accumulated over the years is called the *gross public debt, federal debt,* or *national debt.* The national debt is the total amount owed by the federal government to owners of government securities. There are national debt clocks on the Internet and in several cities around the United States that display the amount of money owed by the federal government.

Note that the national debt does not include state and local governments' debt. Also, as mentioned above, the national debt does include U.S. Treasury securities purchased by various federal agencies, such as the Social Security trust fund. Currently, the Social Security trust fund collects more in taxes than it pays out in retirement benefits, and it lends the extra money to the federal government for spending. In fact, federal budget deficits would be significantly higher, or budget surpluses would be significantly lower, without federal government borrowing from this trust fund. If we subtract the portion of the national debt held by all government agencies (what the federal government owes to itself), we can compute the **net public debt**. Beware! Confusion sometimes occurs when the media use the term *public debt* without specifying whether the reference is to "gross" or "net" public debt.

Before proceeding, let's pause and explain the Social Security trust fund in a little more detail. A misconception is that the Social Security Administration (SSA) collects the annual Social Security surpluses and stacks the cash with reserve cash from previous surpluses in a vault, or special checking account. If the trust fund were to be in deficit as the baby boomers retire and the ratio of workers paying into the system to people drawing benefits shrinks, then the SSA will open the vault and/or write a check to draw on trust fund reserves to pay its obligations.

Here is what really happens to Social Security tax dollars. When excess Social Security taxes are collected by the SSA, these surplus funds must, by law, be immediately withdrawn and given to the Treasury, which, in turn, issues "nonmarketable" interest-bearing Treasury bonds to the SSA. The Treasury then spends this money on welfare, roads, tax cuts, defense, or whatever the federal government decides. On the other hand, if the trust fund cannot pay for retirees' needs, then the SSA will ask the Treasury to redeem its bonds for cash to pay benefits. In this situation, where will the Treasury get the money to repay the SSA? It will either print it, borrow it, levy additional taxes, or cut benefits. In short, the full faith and credit of the U.S. federal government promises to pay itself enough money when needed to pay for Social Security.

> **National debt**
>
> The total amount owed by the federal government to owners of government securities.

> **Net public debt**
>
> National debt minus all government interagency borrowing.

CONCLUSION *The national debt includes the Social Security trust fund and, as a result, federal budget deficits are reduced or budget surpluses are raised.*

The Rise and Fall of Federal Budget Surpluses and Deficits

Here we will examine in more detail influences affecting recent federal budget surpluses and deficits. Restraint on federal spending began with the 1990 Budget Enforcement Act (BEA), which set spending caps on broad areas of discretionary spending. The BEA also required that any proposal to increase spending or decrease tax revenues over agreed limits had to be offset by an equal amount of tax revenue increases or new spending cuts. This pay-as-you-go legislation is called a "PayGo" rule. In 1993, Congress passed the Deficit Reduction Act, which increased tax revenues. This act took into account the ability-to-pay principle by increasing the highest marginal tax rate for individuals and raising the corporate income tax rate. It also increased the federal tax on gasoline. A gasoline tax offers the extra benefit of reducing the quantity of energy demanded and conforms to the benefits-received principle. However, a gasoline tax suffers from the problem of being regressive.

The spending caps combined with tax increases and a growing high-employment economy driven by technological advances, for example, the Internet, transformed federal budget deficits into surpluses during the late 1990s. Exhibit 3(a) shows federal expenditures and tax revenues expressed as a percentage of GDP. The difference between these two curves represents the federal deficit or surplus, also expressed as a percentage of GDP. Between 1991 and 2000, federal government expenditures as a percentage of GDP declined from 22.3 percent to 18.4 percent of GDP, and federal government tax revenues as a percentage of GDP crept steadily upward from 17.8 percent to 20.8 percent of GDP. The result of these changes in tax and spending percentages of GDP was four years of federal surpluses from 1998 to 2001. However, in 2002 the PayGo budget rule expired and from 2002 through today, the federal budget has returned to red ink deficits.

After the recession beginning in 2007, the deficit surged to historic highs when in 2009 federal expenditures climbed sharply to 25 percent of GDP, while tax revenues plummeted to a record low of only 15 percent of GDP. Recall from the automatic stabilizers explained in the previous chapter that during a recession government expenditures rise for transfer payments when people lose jobs and tax revenues decline from individuals and companies making less money. Moreover, these unprecedented deficit figures flow from the Wall Street bailout and economic stimulus bill, which sharply increased federal government spending relative to tax collections.

Exhibit 3(b) provides an alternate graph of the federal budget deficit or surplus as a percentage of GDP. During President Reagan's first term in the early 1980s, the combined effect of recession, a military spending buildup, and a cut in income taxes caused a rise in the deficit to 5 percent of GDP. During the 1990–1991 recession, the deficit as a percentage of GDP again reached close to 5 percent. However, during the latest recession in 2009, the federal deficit soared to a record high since World War II of 9.9 percent of GDP. It is interesting to note that during the Great Depression, federal deficits were unimpressive by today's standards. As a share of GDP, Roosevelt's New Deal deficits (stimulus package) peaked at 5.9 percent of GDP in 1934. It is also noteworthy that in 2010 President Obama requested and the Senate passed a new PayGo law. But there are 50 programs whose spending is exempt from this law, including Social Security, veterans, trust funds, and emergency spending, such as a jobs bill or unemployment benefits.

Exhibit 3	**Federal Expenditures, Revenues, and Deficits as a Percentage of GDP, 1990–2009**

Part (a) shows that after the 1990–1991 recession, federal government expenditures as a percentage of GDP declined until 2000, while federal government tax revenues rose steadily. The results were federal surpluses between 1998 and 2001. After the recession beginning in 2007, the deficit reached a record high when expenditures rose to 21 percent of GDP in 2009, and tax revenues plummeted to only 15 percent of GDP.

Part (b) focuses on the federal deficit or surplus as a percentage of GDP. In 1992, the federal deficit as a percentage of GDP was about 5 percent. After reaching a budget surplus peak of 2.4 percent in 2000, the federal budget deficit soared to a historic high of 9.9 percent of GDP in 2009.

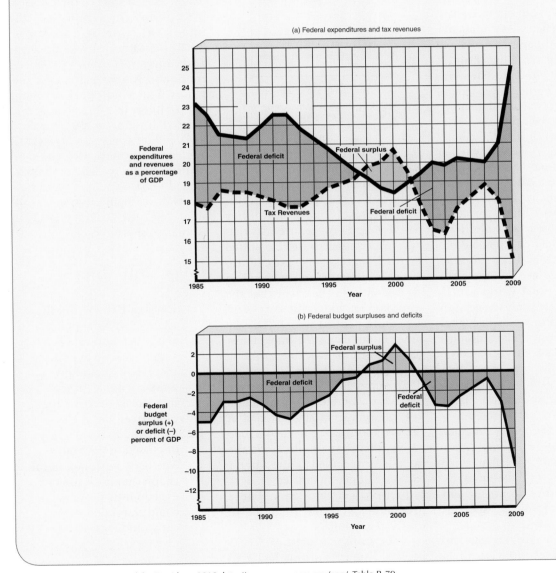

SOURCE: Economic Report of the President, 2010, http://www.gpoaccess.gov/eop/, Table B-79.

As unprecedented deficit figures flow during the current deep recession, it is hard to believe that for four years the federal budget was in surplus. After a one-year small budget surplus in 1969, it took 29 contentious years to eliminate federal budget deficits. And then surpluses occurred between 1998 and 2001, as shown in Exhibits 2 and 3, before becoming today what seems to be a historic relic. These federal budget surpluses aroused as much controversy in their time as deficits do in their years. In short, the hotly contested debate involved whether the surplus should be saved, spent, or devoted to tax cuts. The case for tax cuts and smaller government is based on the view that a surplus is the result of excess tax collections. Proponents of tax cuts pointed out that in 2000 federal tax revenues as a percentage of GDP were the highest since during World War II. Moreover, tax rate cuts would spur the economy and result in higher future tax revenues. The argument for spending a surplus is based on "unmet needs." Instead of tax cuts, the surplus could be used to finance spending for defense, public infrastructure, research and development, and social programs such as education or health care. Also, a large proportion of American households pay no income taxes. Tax cuts therefore do not benefit people who are not prosperous enough to pay taxes.

An alternative to tax cuts and spending increases is paying down

Federal budget deficit projections
(billions of dollars)

SOURCE: Office of Management and Budget, http://www.whitehouse.gov/omb/budget/overview/, Table 5.1.

the national debt. Former Federal Reserve Chairman Alan Greenspan supported this approach. He said Congress faced the quandary of trying to establish fiscal policy based on long-range forecasts that may prove inaccurate. He stated that if Congress cuts taxes, it also has to be prepared to cut spending significantly in the event that the forecasts on which the cuts were based are proved wrong. On the other hand, using the budget surplus to fund "irrevocable spending programs" would be "the worst of all outcomes." Testifying before the Senate Budget Committee in 2001, Greenspan suggested that the proposed tax cut bill include provisions that would limit the tax cuts if specified future targets for the budget surpluses or debt reduction were not met. These provisions were not included in the 2001 tax bill.

The outcome of the "Great Federal Budget Surplus Debate"

was that President George W. Bush signed a $1.35 trillion tax cut bill in 2001 spread over 10 years. It was the largest and most widespread tax cut since the 1980s, during Ronald Reagan's presidency. And in spite of the tax cuts, the outlook for surpluses in the future was optimistic. In August 2001, the Office of Management and Budget (OMB) projected continuously growing budget surpluses that would peak at about $400 billion in 2007. The actual federal budget in 2007 was a $162 billion deficit, and the OMB has since dramatically changed its projections to deficits that exploded to $1.4 trillion in 2009. As actual deficit figures become available, check the accuracy of OMB estimates reported here.

ANALYZE THE ISSUE

1. Refer to Exhibit 8 in the chapter on fiscal policy. Using demand-side and supply-side fiscal policy theories, explain how a tax cut could either increase or decrease the price level.
2. Using the Laffer curve discussed in the You're The Economist box in the chapter on fiscal policy, explain how proponents could claim that the tax cut would increase tax revenues.

Debt Ceiling

The debt ceiling is a method for curbing the national debt. A debt ceiling is a legislated legal limit on the national debt. This means that the federal government cannot legally allow a budget deficit to raise the national debt beyond the ceiling. It works like the credit limit on your charge card. When you reach the limit, you cannot charge any more and you must pay cash. When the federal government hits the debt limit, it cannot borrow any more to supplement its cash from taxes and other sources. What usually happens when the budget pushes against the debt ceiling is that the federal government raises its own ceiling to accommodate the budget deficit. Raising the debt ceiling often provokes a fiery political debate over government spending. Failure to raise the debt ceiling means no money for the government to pay its bills, meet its payroll, or pay interest due on the national debt. In 1990, Congress rejected President George H. W. Bush's spending plan, and the government shut down throughout the three-day Columbus Day weekend. Most workers were off for the holiday, and few government agencies were affected. In 2009, a provision of the stimulus bill raised the U.S. debt ceiling in order to allow the record budget deficit described in the previous section.

Debt ceiling

A legislated legal limit on the national debt.

Budget Surpluses and Deficits in Other Countries

Exhibit 4 shows numerous countries with government budget deficits as a percentage of GDP in 2009. While Norway had a budget surplus of 9.6 percent of GDP, Ireland, the United Kingdom, Greece, and Iceland had deficit percentages greater than the U.S. deficit percentage of 9.9 percent of GDP.

Global Economics

WHY WORRY OVER THE NATIONAL DEBT?

In 2009, Greece was in financial crisis with a national debt-to-GDP ratio of 115 percent and budget deficit of 12.7 percent. Fearing default on Greece's debt, creditors demanded solutions. In response, Greece cut civil service salaries, froze pensions, and enacted new taxes on a long list of items including fuel, cigarettes, alcohol, jewelry, leather goods, yachts, private jets, and high-end automobiles. As this text is written in 2010, Greece has accepted an international bail out package and there are fears that this crisis could spread.

As shown in Exhibit 5(a), the result of the accumulation of federal deficits in the United States is that the national debt is rising at a rapid rate. The national debt crossed $1 trillion in 1982. And it took 14 years before adding another $4 trillion and reaching the $5 trillion mark in 1996. In 2006, we were at the $8 trillion milestone; however, rather than 14 years, it required a mere 4 years to accelerate the national debt by $4 trillion to $12 trillion.

What are some major causes of the rising national debt? Observe in Exhibit 5(a) the increase in the debt during World War II. In wartime, the government must

Exhibit 4	A Global Comparison of Government Surpluses and Deficits as a Percentage of GDP, 2009

In 2009, Norway had a budget surplus of 9.6 percent of GDP. Other nations, such as Ireland, the United Kingdom, Greece, and Iceland had budget deficits greater than the U.S. deficit of 9.9% of GDP.

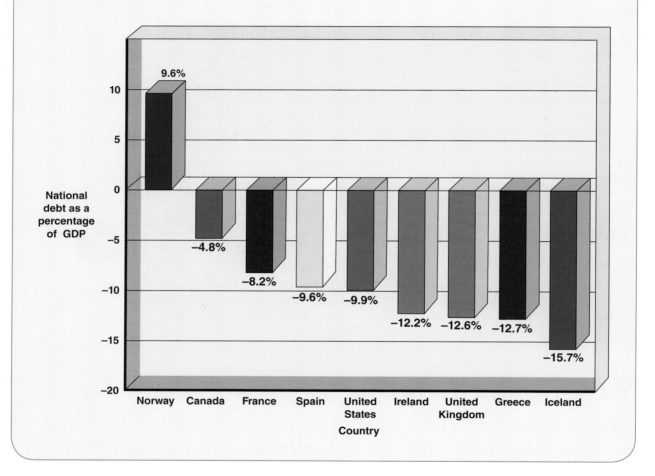

increase military expenditures sharply and escalate the national debt. Recession also causes the national debt to rise dramatically. Cyclical downturns like the 1930s, 1974–1975, 1981–1982, 1990–1991, 2001, and 2007 also cause the debt to rise rapidly because a decline in real GDP automatically increases the budget deficit due to lower tax collections and greater spending for unemployment compensation and welfare. Currently, as a result of the bailout plans and stimulus spending to boost troubled credit markets, the federal government is financing these plans with government borrowing that has caused a rise in the federal deficit, debt ceiling, and the national debt.

Exhibit 5   The National Debt, 1930–2009

In part (a), we see that the federal debt has skyrocketed since 1980. A concern is that sooner or later the U.S. government will be bankrupt. The counterargument is shown in part (b). The national debt as a percentage of GDP has declined since the end of World War II, when it reached a peak of about 120 percent. After 1980, the federal debt as a percentage of GDP increased, and has risen sharply to a historic high of about 83 percent, which is back to its level of 1951.

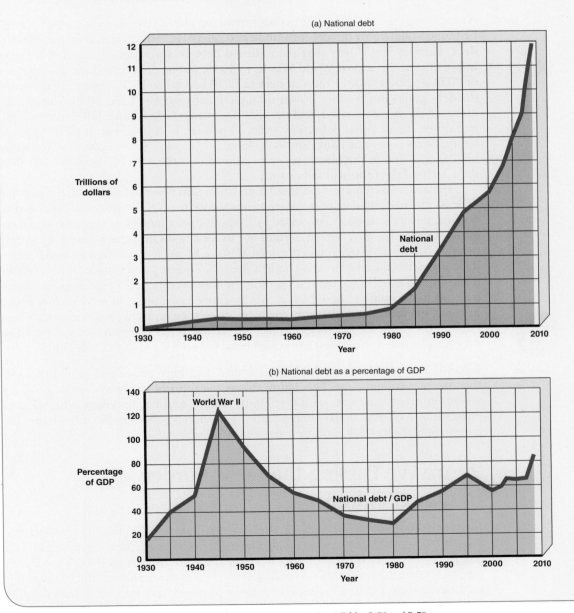

SOURCE: Economic Report of the President, 2010, http://www.gpoaccess.gov/eop/, Tables B-78 and B-79.

Politicians and nonpoliticians alike often speak of the gloom and doom of the national debt. Should we lose sleep over it? To find out, we'll consider three controversial questions:

1. Can Uncle Sam Go Bankrupt?

Reasons to Worry If households and firms persistently operate in the red, as the federal government does, they will sooner or later go bankrupt. How long can a national debt continue to rise before the U.S. government is broke?

Reasons Not to Worry Whether private or public debt is the issue, debt must be judged relative to the debtor's ability to repay the principal and interest on the debt. Exhibit 5(b) shows that the national debt as a percentage of GDP is lower today than at the end of World War II. In 1945, public debt was about 120 percent of GDP, and by 1980 the ratio of debt to GDP had fallen to 33 percent. This means the debt grew considerably slower than GDP between 1945 and 1980. Since 1980, however, the trend reversed, and the debt has grown faster than GDP. Between 1980 and 2009, the national debt grew from 33 percent to 83 percent of GDP. Still, the United States was not bankrupt in 1945 or 1951 when the ratio was at the same level as in 2009. In the future, it can be argued that the debt will grow slower than the GDP and the ratio will fall again.

There is an even more important point: Uncle Sam never has to pay off the national debt. At the maturity date on a government security, the U.S. Treasury has the constitutional authority to collect taxes levied by Congress, print money, or refinance its obligations. Suppose the government decides not to raise taxes or cause inflation by simply printing money, so it refinances the debt. When a $1 million government bond comes due, as described earlier in this chapter, the U.S. Treasury can simply "roll over" the debt. This financial trade expression means a borrower (here the federal government) pays off its $1 million bond that reaches maturity by issuing a new $1 million bond. In short, the federal government refinances its debt by replacing old bonds with new bonds. This means the federal government never has to pay off the national debt. These debts can be rolled over forever, provided bond buyers have faith in Uncle Sam.

Global Economics

Global Perspective on National Debt Exhibit 6 provides a global perspective on the national debt. This figure shows the ratio of national debt to GDP for several industrialized nations. Japan, Italy, Greece, and Belgium have a higher debt in relation to GDP than the United States. The United States, on the other hand, has a national debt-to-GDP ratio over five times as large as the Australia ratio.

2. Are We Passing the Debt Burden to Our Children?

Reasons to Worry The fear is that interest payments to finance the national debt will swallow an enormous helping of the federal government's budget pie. This means future generations will pay more of their tax dollars to the government's creditors and have less to spend for highways, health care, defense, and other public sector programs. Exhibit 7 shows net interest payments as a percentage of GDP. The net interest payment was only about 1.5 percent of GDP right after World War II, but it increased dramatically after the mid-1970s to more than 3 percent in 1990. Since 1990, the interest payment burden declined to 1.3 percent of GDP in 2009.

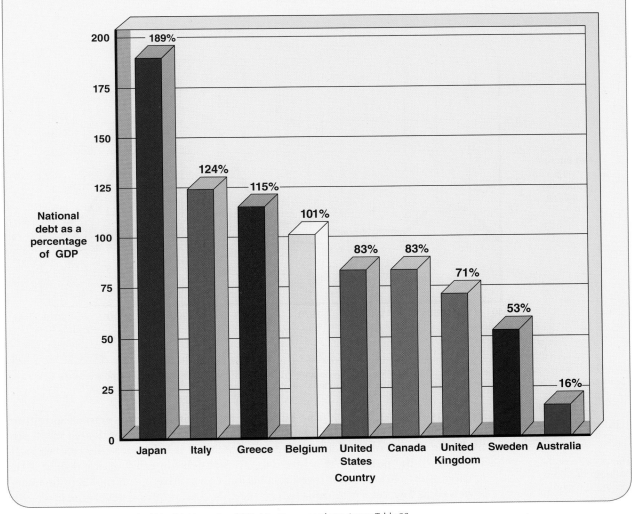

Exhibit 6 | **A Global Comparison of National Debt Ratios, 2009**

This exhibit shows estimated ratios of national debt to GDP in 2009 for selected industrialized countries. Japan, Italy, Greece, and Belgium have higher national debt-to-GDP ratios compared to the United States. On the other hand, the United States has a debt ratio five times as large as Australia.

National debt as a percentage of GDP

Country	
Japan	189%
Italy	124%
Greece	115%
Belgium	101%
United States	83%
Canada	83%
United Kingdom	71%
Sweden	53%
Australia	16%

SOURCE: *OECD Economic Outlook* No. 84, November 2009, http://www.oecd.org, Annex Table 32.

CHECKPOINT

What's Behind the National Debt?

Suppose the federal government has balanced budgets each year and the entire national debt comes due. How could the federal government pay off the national debt without refinancing, raising taxes, or printing money?

Exhibit 7

Federal Net Interest as a Percentage of GDP, 1940–2009

Some fear that interest payments on the national debt will swallow an enormous portion of the federal budget. The exhibit shows that the net interest payment as a proportion of GDP was only about 1.5 percent after World War II. In the 1980s and early 1990s, however, the interest rate burden increased dramatically. Since 1990, it declined to 1.3 percent in 2009.

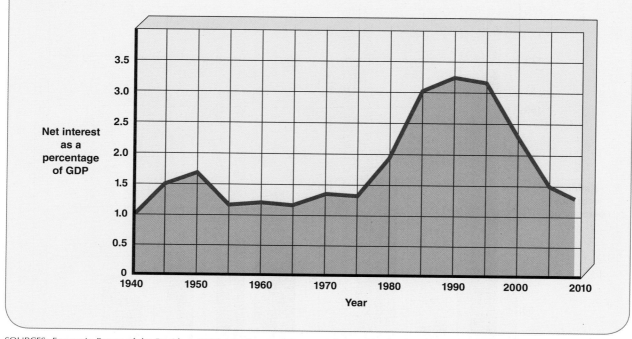

SOURCES: Economic Report of the President, 2010, http://www.gpoaccess.gov/eop/, Tables B-1 and B-80 and Bureau of Economic Analysis, National Economic Accounts, http://www.bea.gov/national/nipaweb/SelectTable.asp?Selected=Y, Table 1.1.

Internal national debt

The portion of the national debt owed to a nation's own citizens.

External national debt

The portion of the national debt owed to foreign citizens.

Reasons Not to Worry The burden of the national debt on present and future generations depends on who owns the accumulated national debt. Stated more precisely, the burden of the debt depends on whether it is held internally or externally. The bulk of the public debt is **internal national debt**. Internal national debt is the portion of the national debt owed to a nation's own citizens. Internal debt financing is viewed as "we owe it to ourselves." One U.S. citizen buys a government security and lends Uncle Sam the money to pay the interest and principal on a maturing government security held by another U.S. citizen. Although this redistribution of income and wealth does indeed favor bondholders, who are typically upper-income individuals, transferring dollars between U.S. citizens does not alter the overall purchasing power in the U.S. economy.

Those on the "not to worry" side of this issue also concede that an **external national debt** is a concern. External national debt is the portion of the national debt owed to foreign citizens. Financing the external national debt means interest and principal payments are transfers of money from U.S. citizens to other nations. If foreign governments, banks, corporations, and individual investors hold part of the national debt, the "we owe it to ourselves" argument is weakened. Exhibit 8 shows who owns

Exhibit 8	**Ownership of the National Debt, 2009**

In 2009, 43 percent of the national debt was held by the public sector, including federal, state, and local governments and Federal Reserve banks. The private sector, including individuals, banks, corporations, and insurance companies, held 29 percent, and foreigners owned the remaining 28 percent.

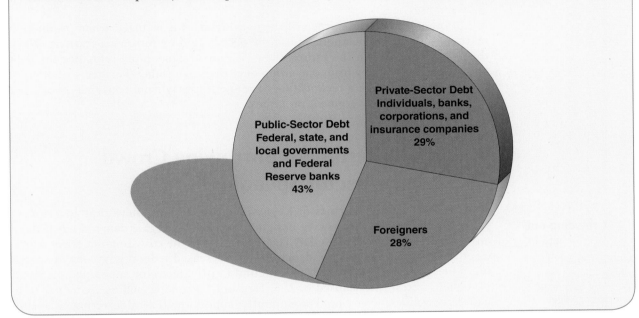

SOURCE: Economic Report of the President, 2010, http://www.gpoaccess.gov/eop/, Table B-89.

the securities the U.S. Treasury has issued. In 2009, foreigners owned 28 percent of the total national debt. The largest foreign holder of the debt was China with 6 percent of the total national debt, and next was Japan with 5 percent. Forty-three percent was held by the federal, state, and local governments, primarily by federal agencies such as the U.S. Treasury, the Social Security Administration, and Federal Reserve banks. The Federal Reserve is an independent government agency, as explained in the next chapter. The private sector, consisting of individuals, banks, corporations, and insurance companies, held 29 percent of the national debt. The debt held by the private sector and government entities constitutes the internal national debt.

Although 72 percent of the national debt was internal, the 28 percent of total U.S. debt that is external debt is not necessarily undesirable. Foreign investment in the United States supplements domestic saving. Borrowing from abroad can prevent the higher interest rates that would exist if the U.S. Treasury relied only on domestic savers to purchase federal government securities. A lower interest rate increases U.S. investment and consumer spending, causing the aggregate demand curve to shift rightward.

If we do not need to worry about shifting the burden to future generations, can the current generation escape the debt burden? The answer is *No*. During World War II, for example, the United States operated at full employment along its *production possibilities curve*. As illustrated earlier in Exhibit 2 of Chapter 2, people at that time in history were forced to trade off consumer goods production for military goods production. Because massive amounts of resources were diverted to fight World War II, people at that time were forced to give up private consumption of houses, cars, refrigerators, and so on. After the war was over, resources were again devoted to producing more consumer goods and fewer military goods. The same analysis can be used today. At full employment, the burden of the national debt on the current generation is the opportunity cost of private-sector goods and services forgone because land, labor, and capital are used to produce public-sector goods and services.

In other words, the burden of the national debt is incurred when production takes place; it is not postponed until the debt is paid by future generations. When the debt comes due in the future, the government can simply refinance the debt and redistribute money from one group of citizens to another. This redistribution of income does not cause a reallocation of resources away from consumer goods and services in favor of government programs.

3. Does Government Borrowing Crowd Out Private-Sector Spending?

Crowding-out effect

A reduction in private-sector spending as a result of federal budget deficits financed by U.S. Treasury borrowing. When federal government borrowing increases interest rates, the result is lower consumption by households and lower investment spending by businesses.

Reasons to Worry Critics of Keynesian fiscal policy believe that government spending financed by borrowing designed to boost aggregate demand has little, if any, effect on growth of real GDP. The reason is that the crowding-out effect dampens the stimulus to aggregate demand from increased federal government spending. The crowding-out effect is a reduction in private-sector spending as a result of higher interest rates caused by U.S. Treasury borrowing (selling securities) to finance government spending. For example, suppose the federal government spends and borrows, rather than collecting taxes, to finance new health care programs. In this case, the size of the national debt rises, and interest rates are pushed up in loan markets. Interest rates rise because the federal government competes with private borrowers for available savings, and less credit is available to consumers and business borrowers. The result of this crowding-out effect is lower consumption $(-\Delta C)$ and business investment $(-\Delta I)$, which offset the boost in aggregate demand $(+\Delta AD)$ from increased government spending $(+\Delta G)$ operating through the spending multiplier.

The crowding-out effect contradicts the theory, explained in the previous Reasons Not to Worry section, that future generations do not bear some of today's debt burden. Recall from Chapter 2 that current investment spending increases living standards in the future by shifting the production possibilities curve outward (Exhibit 5 in Chapter 2). If federal borrowing crowds out private investment in plants and equipment, future generations will have a smaller possible productive capacity.

The *AD-AS* model will help you understand the crowding-out concept. Exhibit 9 reproduces the situation in which government spending is used to combat a recession, depicted earlier in Exhibit 2 of the chapter on fiscal policy. Begin at E_1, with an equilibrium GDP of $13 trillion, and assume the government increases its spending and uses the spending multiplier to shift the aggregate demand curve rightward from AD_1 to AD_2. Following Keynesian theory, there is zero crowding out, and the economy achieves full employment at equilibrium point E_2, corresponding to real GDP of $14 trillion. Critics of Keynesian theory, however, argue that crowding out occurs. The result of expansionary fiscal policy is not E_2, but some equilibrium

Exhibit 9   Zero, Partial, and Complete Crowding Out

Beginning at equilibrium E_1, the federal government borrows to finance a deficit created by expansionary fiscal policy. Keynesian theory predicts zero crowding out, which means that an increase in government spending operates through the spending multiplier to shift aggregate demand from AD_1 to AD_2. If crowding out is zero, consumption and investment spending are unaffected by the increase in government spending financed by borrowing. Partial crowding out occurs when a decrease in private spending partially offsets the multiplier effect from an increase in deficit-financed government spending. Partial crowding out results in a shift only from AD_1 to AD'_2 and an equilibrium at E'_2, rather than E_2. If crowding out is complete, a decrease in private spending completely offsets the increase in government spending financed by debt. In this case, the aggregate demand curve remains at AD_1, and the economy remains at E_1.

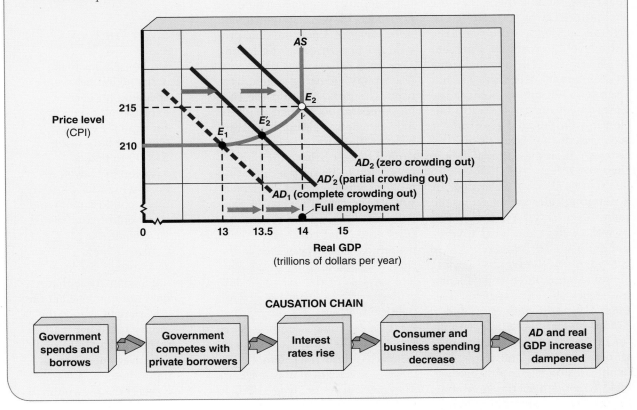

point along the AS line between E_1 and E_2. For example, a fall in private expenditures might partially offset the government spending stimulus. With incomplete crowding out, the aggregate demand curve increases only to AD'_2 because of the decline in consumption and investment. The economy therefore moves to E'_2 at a real GDP of $13.5 trillion and does not achieve full employment at E_2. Or crowding out can completely offset the multiplier effect of increased government spending. The fall in private expenditures by consumers and businesses can result in no change in aggregate demand curve AD_1. In this case, the economy remains at E_1,

You're The Economist   How Real Is Uncle Sam's Debt?   *Applicable Concepts: national debt and federal deficit*

Perhaps the national debt and federal budget deficits are really not so large and threatening. For example, it can be argued that we should use real rather than nominal values to report the national debt—similar to using real GDP to report economic growth. Suppose the national debt rises from $10 trillion to $10.3 trillion and the price level increases by 3 percent in a given year. The nominal value of the national debt therefore has risen by $300 billion because the government must issue $300 billion in newly issued government securities due to higher prices, and real growth in the national debt is therefore zero.

Critics also warn that federal accounting rules are an economic policy disaster. Private businesses, as well as state and local governments, use two budgets. One is the *operating budget*, which includes salaries, interest payments, and other current expenses. The second type of budget, called a *capital budget*, includes spending for investment items, such as machines, buildings, and roads. Expenditures on the capital budget yield benefits over time and may be paid for by long-term borrowing. The federal government does not use a capital budget. Capital budgeting allows spreading the cost of long-lasting assets over future years. For example, the federal budget makes no distinction between the rental cost of a federal office building and the cost of constructing a new federal office building to replace rented office space. However, payments on borrowing for a new building provide the benefit of a long-lasting asset that offsets rent payments. If a capital budgeting system were used, the public would see that most federal borrowing really finances assets yielding long-term benefits. In short, proponents of a capital budget believe the public's focus should be on the operating budget, which gives a truer measure of the federal deficit. Opponents of changing the accounting rules argue that controversial expenditures would be placed in the capital budget in order to manipulate the size of the deficit or surplus in the operating budget for political reasons.

Finally, some economists argue for other numerical adjustments that show the federal deficit or surplus is really not as it seems. They say it is not the federal deficit or surplus that really matters, but the combined deficits or surpluses of federal, state, and local governments. When state and local governments run budget surpluses, these surpluses are a source of savings in financial markets that adds to federal surpluses or offsets federal borrowing to finance its deficit.

with unemployment unaffected by expansionary policy. Meanwhile, the deficit required to finance extra government spending increases the national debt.

Reasons Not to Worry The crowding-out effect is controversial. Keynesian economists counter critics by saying that any crowding-out effect is small or non-existent. Instead, at below full-employment real GDP, their counterargument is the crowding-in effect. For example, government capital spending for highways, dams, universities, and infrastructure financed by borrowing might offset any decline in private investment. Another Keynesian argument is that consumers and business-persons may believe that federal spending is "just what the doctor ordered" for an ailing economy. Federal borrowing incurred to finance the new spending would boost consumption and therefore increase aggregate demand. The reason is because holders of Treasury bills, notes, and bonds feel richer. As a result of their greater wealth, consumers spend more now and plan to spend more in the future. Such a blush of optimism may also raise the profit expectations of business managers, and they may increase investment spending. The effect of increased private-sector spending could nullify some or all of the crowding-out effect, which would otherwise offset the boost in aggregate demand from increased government spending. Hence, as explained in the graphical analysis in Exhibit 9, the spending multiplier shifts the aggregate demand curve from AD_1 to AD_2, with zero crowding out.

Finally, both sides of the debate agree that complete crowding out occurs in one situation. Suppose the economy is operating at full employment (point E_2). This is comparable to being on the economy's production possibilities curve. If the government shifts the aggregate demand curve rightward by increasing spending or cutting taxes, the result will be higher prices and a replacement of private sector output with public sector output.

CONCLUSION *Crowding out is complete if the economy is at full employment, but debatable at less than full employment.*

Crowding-in effect

An increase in private-sector spending as a result of federal budget deficits financed by U.S. Treasury borrowing. At less than full employment, consumers hold more Treasury securities and this additional wealth causes them to spend more. Business investment spending increases because of optimistic profit expectations.

Key Concepts

National debt
Net public debt
Debt ceiling

Internal national debt
External national debt
Crowding-out effect

Crowding-in effect

Summary

- The *national debt* is the dollar amount that the federal government owes holders of government securities. It is the cumulative sum of past deficits. The U.S. Treasury issues government securities to finance the deficits. The debt has increased sharply since 1980.

National Debt

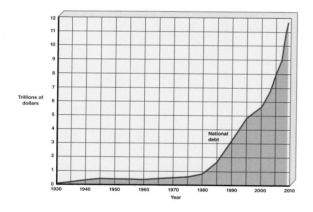

- The *net public debt* is the national debt minus all government interagency borrowing (the debt that the federal government owes to itself).
- A *debt ceiling* is a method used to restrict the growth of the national debt.
- *Internal national debt* is the percentage of the national debt a nation owes to its own citizens. In 2009, 72 percent of the national debt was internally held by individuals, banks, corporations, insurance companies, and government entities. The "we owe it to ourselves" argument over the debt is that U.S. citizens own the bulk of the U.S. national debt. *External national debt* is a burden because it is the portion of the national debt a nation owes to foreigners. The interest paid

on external debt transfers purchasing power to other nations. In 2009, 28 percent of the national debt was external.

Internal and External National Debt

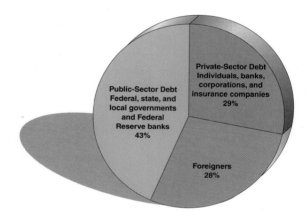

- The *burden of the debt debate* involves controversial questions:
  1. *Can Uncle Sam Go Bankrupt?* The U.S. government will not go bankrupt because it never has to pay off its debt. When government securities mature, the U.S. Treasury can refinance, or roll over, the debt by issuing new securities.
  2. *Are We Passing the Debt Burden to Our Children?* One side of this argument is that the burden of the debt falls only on the current generation when the tradeoff between public-sector goods and private-sector goods along the production possibilities curve occurs. In short, when resources are used to make missiles today, citizens are forced to give up, say, airplane production in the current period and not

later. The counterargument is that there is a sizable external national debt that transfers purchasing power to foreigners.

3. ***Does Government Borrowing Crowd Out Private-Sector Spending?*** The ***crowding-out effect*** is a burden of the national debt that occurs when the government borrows to finance its deficit, causing the interest rate to rise. As the interest rate rises, consumption and business investment fall. If crowding out occurs, reduced private spending completely or partially offsets the multiplier effect of increased government spending. As a result, the expected magnitude of the rightward shift in the aggregate demand curve is partially or completely offset.

Opponents believe in the ***crowding-in effect***. In this view, government capital spending for highways, dams, universities, and infrastructure offsets any decline in business investment from crowding out.

Zero, Partial, and Complete Crowding Out

Summary of Conclusion Statements

- The national debt includes the Social Security trust fund and, as a result, federal budget deficits are reduced or budget surpluses are raised.

- Crowding out is complete if the economy is at full employment, but it is debatable at less than full employment.

Study Questions and Problems

1. Explain the relationship between budget deficits and the national debt.

2. Discuss various ways of measuring the size of the national debt.

3. Explain this statement: "The national debt is like taking money out of your left pocket and putting it into your right pocket."

4. Explain this statement: "The most unlikely problem of the national debt is that the government will go bankrupt."

5. Suppose the percentage of the federal debt owned by foreigners increases sharply. Would this trend concern you? Why or why not?

6. Explain the theory that crowding out can weaken or nullify the effect of expansionary fiscal policy financed by federal government borrowing.

7. Suppose the federal government has no national debt and spends $100 billion, while raising only $50 billion in taxes.
   a. What amount of government bonds will the U.S. Treasury issue to finance the deficit?
   b. Next year, assume tax revenues remain at $50 billion. If the government pays a 10 percent rate of interest, add the debt-servicing interest payment to the government's $100 billion expenditure for goods and services the second year.
   c. For the second year, compute the deficit, the amount of new debt issued, and the new national debt.

8. Suppose the media report that the federal deficit this year is $200 billion. The national debt was $5,000 billion last year, and it is $5,200 billion this year. The price level this year is 3 percent higher than it was last year. What is the real deficit?

9. During the presidential campaign of 1932 in the depth of the Great Depression, candidates Herbert Hoover and Franklin D. Roosevelt both advocated reducing the budget deficit, using tax hikes and/or expenditure reductions. Evaluate this fiscal policy.

10. Consider this statement: "Our grandchildren may not suffer the entire burden of a federal deficit." Do you agree or disagree? Explain.

11. Suppose you are the economic policy adviser to the president and are asked what should be done to eliminate a federal deficit. What would you recommend?

For Online Exercises, go to the Tucker Web site at www.cengage.com/economics/tucker.

CHECKPOINT ANSWER
What's Behind the National Debt?

Every item owned by the federal government, including the White House, office buildings, tanks, and computers, is an asset standing behind the national debt. If you said the assets of the federal government could be sold to pay off the national debt, **YOU ARE CORRECT.**

Practice Quiz

For an explanation of the correct answers, visit the Tucker Web site at www.cengage.com/economics/tucker.

1. During 1998–2001, federal government budget deficits
   a. were completely removed.
   b. dropped significantly from a high of $300 billion.
   c. remained fairly stable at about $150 billion per year.
   d. exceeded $200 billion in each year.

2. The federal government finances a budget by
   a. taxing businesses and households.
   b. selling Treasury securities.
   c. printing more money.
   d. reducing its purchases of goods and services.

3. In 2009, the national debt was approximately
   a. $60 billion.
   b. $600 billion.
   c. $12 trillion.
   d. $20 trillion.

4. The national debt to GDP ratio in 2009
   a. was about seven times its size in 1982.
   b. was twice as large in 2000.
   c. was approximately the same size in 1945.
   d. was approximately the same size in 1951.

5. Which of the following countries has the smallest national debt as a percentage of GDP in 2009?
   a. Italy
   b. Canada
   c. Australia
   d. Japan
   e. France

Practice Quiz Continued

6. Which of the following is *true*?
   a. The national debt's size increased sharply after 1980.
   b. The national debt increases in size whenever the federal government has a budget deficit.
   c. The national debt as a percentage of GDP is currently about the same size as it was in the late 1950s.
   d. All of the above are true.

7. In 2009, approximately what percentage of the U.S. national debt was owed to foreigners?
   a. 2.5 percent
   b. 30 percent
   c. 20 percent
   d. 60 percent

8. Which of the following own a portion of the national debt?
   a. Federal, state, and local governments
   b. Private U.S. citizens
   c. Banks
   d. Foreigners
   e. All of the above

9. The portion of the U.S. national debt held by foreigners
   a. represents a burden because it transfers purchasing power from U.S. taxpayers to other countries.
   b. is an accounting entry that represents no real burden.
   c. decreased as a proportion of the total debt during the 2000s.
   d. has been constant for many decades.

10. Which of the following statements about crowding out is *true*?
    a. It is caused by a budget surplus.
    b. It is not caused by a budget deficit.
    c. It cannot completely offset the multiplier effect of deficit government spending.
    d. It affects interest rates and, in turn, consumption and investment spending.

11. Which of the following statements about crowding out is *true*?
    a. It can completely offset the multiplier.
    b. It is caused by a budget deficit.
    c. It is not caused by a budget surplus.
    d. All of the above are true.

12. "Crowding in" refers to federal government deficits
    a. used for public infrastructure, which will offset any decline in business investment.
    b. which reduce private business and consumption spending.
    c. which reduce future rates of economic growth.
    d. all of the above.

13. When measured as a percentage of GDP, the U.S. national debt reached its highest levels as a result of
    a. World War II.
    b. the Vietnam War.
    c. the Reagan defense buildup and tax cuts.
    d. the Bush economic recovery program.

14. The national debt is unlikely to cause national bankruptcy because the
    a. national debt can be refinanced by issuing new bonds.
    b. interest on the public debt equals GDP.
    c. national debt cannot be shifted to future generations for repayment.
    d. federal government cannot repudiate the outstanding national debt.

15. Supply-side economists argue that less government spending
    a. will contract the productive side of the economy.
    b. will result in more crowding out.
    c. causes higher rates of unemployment and inflation.
    d. would cause interest rates to increase dramatically.
    e. would make more investment capital available at lower rates of interest to the private sector.

Road Map   Macroeconomic theory and policy issues

part

4

This road map feature helps you tie material in the part together as you travel the Economic Way of Thinking Highway. The following are review questions listed by chapter from the previous part. The key concept in each question is given for emphasis, and each question or set of questions concludes with an interactive game to reinforce the concepts. Click on the Tucker Web site at www.cengage.com/economics/tucker, select the chapter, and play the visual causation chain game designed to make learning fun. Enjoy the cheers when correct and suffer the jeers if you miss. The correct answers for the multiple-choice questions are given in Appendix C of the text.

Chapter 8. The Keynesian Model

1. **Key Concept: Consumption function**
   The consumption function will shift for all of the following reasons except
   a. a change in a household's real assets.
   b. a change in interest rates.
   c. expectations of price changes.
   d. changes in a household's disposable incomes.
   e. changes in taxation policy.

   Causation Chain Game
   Movement Along and Shifts in the Consumption Function—Exhibit 6

2. **Key Concept: Investment demand curve**
   Which of the following will increase investment spending?
   a. More optimistic business expectations
   b. An increase in interest rates
   c. An increase in business taxes
   d. A decrease in capacity utilization
   e. All of the above

   Causation Chain Game
   Movement Along and Shifts in a Firm's Investment Demand—Exhibit 8

Chapter 9. The Keynesian Model in Action

3. **Key Concept: Spending multiplier**
   The ratio of the change in GDP to an initial change in aggregate expenditures
   (*AE*) is the
   a. spending multiplier.
   b. permanent income rate.
   c. marginal expenditure rate.
   d. marginal propensity to consume.

   Causation Chain Game
   The Multiplier Effect and Government Spending—Exhibit 4

Chapter 10. Aggregate Demand and Supply

4. **Key Concept: Aggregate demand curve**
   Which of the following is *not* a reason for the downward slope of an aggregate
   demand curve?
   a. Real balance effect
   b. Real interest-rate effect
   c. Net exports effect
   d. All of the above are reasons.

   Causation Chain Game
   The Aggregate Demand Curve—Exhibit 1

5. **Key Concept: Aggregate demand curve**
   Which of the following could *not* be expected to shift the aggregate demand
   curve?
   a. Net exports fall.
   b. Consumption spending decreases.
   c. An increase in government spending.
   d. A change in real GDP.

   Causation Chain Game
   A Shift in the Aggregate Demand Curve—Exhibit 3

6. **Key Concept: Aggregate supply curve**
   The horizontal segment of the aggregate supply curve
   a. shows that real GDP can increase only by affecting the economy's price
      level.
   b. shows that real GDP can increase without affecting the economy's price
      level.
   c. depicts a positive relationship between real GDP and the price level.
   d. depicts a negative relationship between real GDP and the price level.
   e. marks the full-employment level of real GDP.

   Causation Chain Game
   The Keynesian Horizontal Aggregate Supply Curve—Exhibit 4

Chapter 13. Federal Deficits, Surpluses, and the National Debt

15. Key Concept: Federal budget process
If Congress fails to pass a budget before the fiscal year starts, then federal agencies may continue to operate only if Congress has passed a
a. balanced budget amendment.
b. deficit reduction plan.
c. conference resolution.
d. continuing resolution.

Causation Chain Game
Major Steps in the Federal Budgetary Process—Exhibit 1

Money, Banking, and Monetary Policy

© Getty Images

S tudents often find the material in these chapters the most interesting in their principles course because the topic is *money.* The first chapter begins the discussion of money with basic definitions and a description of the Federal Reserve System. Of special interest is a feature on the history of money in the colonies. The next chapter explains how the banking system and the Federal Reserve influence the supply of money. The following chapter compares different macroeconomic theories and concludes with a discussion of monetary policy in the Great Depression, and the current financial crisis. The final chapter in this part explores additional macro theories based on expectations.

Money and the Federal Reserve System

As the lyrics of the old song go, "Money makes the world go round, the world go round, the world go round." Recall the circular flow model presented in the chapter on GDP. Households exchange *money* for goods and services in the product markets, and firms exchange *money* for resources in the factor markets. In short, money affects the way an economy works. In the chapter on aggregate demand and supply and the chapter on fiscal policy presented earlier in the text, the *AD-AS* model was developed without explicitly discussing money. In this chapter, and throughout this part, money takes center stage.

Exactly what is money? The answer may surprise you. Imagine yourself on the small South Pacific island of Yap. You are surrounded by exotic fowl, crystal-clear lagoons, delicious fruits, and sunny skies. Now suppose while leisurely strolling along the beach one evening, you suddenly discover a beautiful bamboo hut for sale. As you

will discover in this chapter, to pay for your dream hut, you must roll a 5-foot-diameter stone to the area of the island designated as the "bank."

We begin our discussion of money with the three functions money serves. Next, we identify the components of three different definitions of the money supply used in the United States. The remainder of the chapter describes the organization and services of the Federal Reserve System, our nation's central bank. Also, we discuss the Monetary Control Act of 1980 and its relationship to the savings and loan crisis of the 1980s and early 1990s that predated the current banking crisis. Beginning in this chapter and in the next three chapters, you will learn how the Federal Reserve System controls the stock of money in the economy. Then, using the *AD-AS* model, you will learn how variations in the stock of money in the economy affect total spending, unemployment, and prices.

In this chapter, you will learn to solve these economics puzzles:

• Why do nations use money?

• Is "plastic money" really money?

• What does a Federal Reserve bank do?

WHAT MAKES MONEY *MONEY*?

Can exchange occur in an economy without money? It certainly can, using a trading system called **barter**. Barter is the direct exchange of one good or service for another good or service, rather than for money. The problem with barter is that it requires a *coincidence of wants*. Imagine for a moment that dollars and coins are worthless. Farmer Brown needs shoes, so he takes his bushels of wheat to the shoe store and offers to barter wheat for shoes. Unfortunately, the store owner refuses to barter because she wants to trade shoes for pencils, toothpaste, and coffee. Undaunted, Farmer Brown spends more time and effort to find Mr. Jones, who has pencils, toothpaste, and coffee he will trade for bushels of wheat. Although Farmer Brown's luck has improved, he and Mr. Jones must agree on the terms of exchange. Exactly how many pounds of coffee, for example, is a bushel of wheat worth? Assuming this exchange is worked out, Farmer Brown must spend more time returning to the shoe store and negotiating the terms of an exchange of pencils, coffee, and toothpaste for shoes.

Barter

The direct exchange of one good or service for another good or service, rather than for money.

> **CONCLUSION** *The use of money simplifies and therefore increases market transactions. Money also prevents wasting time that can be devoted to production, thereby promoting economic growth by increasing a nation's production possibilities.*

The Three Functions of Money

Suppose citizens of the planet of Starcom want to replace their barter system and must decide what to use for money. Assuming this planet is fortunate enough to have economists, they would explain that anything, regardless of its value, can serve as money if it conforms to the following definition. **Money** is anything that serves as a medium of exchange, unit of account, and store of value. Money is not limited to dimes, quarters, and dollar bills. Notice that "anything" meeting the three tests is a candidate to serve as money. This explains why precious metals, beaver skins, wampum (shells strung in belts), and cigarettes have all served as money. Let's discuss each of the three functions money serves.

Money

Anything that serves as a medium of exchange, unit of account, and store of value.

Money as a Medium of Exchange In a simple society, barter is a way for participants to exchange goods and services in order to satisfy wants. Barter, however, requires wasting time in the process of exchange that people could use for productive work. If the goal is to increase the volume of transactions and live in a modern economy, the most important function of money is to serve as a **medium of exchange**. Medium of exchange is the primary function of money to be widely accepted in exchange for goods and services. Money removes the problem of coincidence of wants because everyone is willing to accept money in payment, rather than goods and services. You give up two $20 bills in exchange for a ticket to see a rock concert. Because money serves as generalized purchasing power, all in society know that no one will refuse to trade their products for money. In short, money increases trade by providing a much more convenient method of exchange than a cumbersome barter system.

A fascinating question is whether people will find digital cash a more convenient means of payment. Each year more people avoid using checks, paper currency, or coins by transferring funds electronically from their accounts via various Internet-based and other systems. In fact, it is possible that widespread adoption of privately issued digital cash will ultimately replace government-issued currency. Vending and copy machines on many college campuses already accept plastic stored-value cards. Someday vending machines everywhere are likely to have smart card readers that accept electronic money.

Money as a Unit of Account How does a wheat farmer know whether a bushel of wheat is worth one, two, or more pairs of shoes? How does a family compare its income to expenses or a business know whether it is making a profit? Government must be able to measure tax revenues collected and program expenditures made. And GDP is the *money* value of final goods and services used to compare the national output of the United States to, say, Japan's output. In each of these examples, money serves as a **unit of account**. Without money, we face the difficult task of, say, pricing pizzas in terms of other goods. Unit of account is the function of money to provide a common measurement of the relative value of goods and services. Without dollars, there is no common denominator. We must therefore decide if one pizza equals a box of pencils, 20 oranges equals one quart of milk, and so forth. Now let's compare the value of two items using money. If the price of one pizza is $10 and the price of a movie ticket is $5, then the value of one pizza equals two movie tickets. In the United States, the monetary unit is the dollar; in Japan, it is the yen; Mexico has its peso; and so on.

Money as a Store of Value Can you save shrimp for months and then exchange them for some product? You could, but not without the extra expense of freezing the shrimp. Money, on the other hand, serves as a **store of value** in exchange for some item in the future. Store of value is the ability of money to hold value over time. You can bury money in your backyard or store it under your mattress for months or years and not worry about it spoiling. Stated differently, money allows us to synchronize our income more precisely with expenditures. However, recall from the chapter on inflation that hyperinflation can destroy money's store-of-value function and, in turn, its medium-of-exchange function.

Medium of exchange

The primary function of money to be widely accepted in exchange for goods and services.

Unit of account

The function of money to provide a common measurement of the relative value of goods and services.

Store of value

The ability of money to hold value over time.

> **CONCLUSION** *Money is a useful mechanism for transforming income in the present into future purchases.*

The key property of money is that it is completely *liquid*. This means that money is immediately available to spend in exchange for goods and services without any additional expense. Money is more liquid than real assets (real estate or gold) or paper assets (stocks or bonds). These assets also serve as stores of value, but liquidating (selling) them often involves expenses, such as brokerage fees, and time delays.

> **CONCLUSION** *Money is the most liquid form of wealth because it can be spent directly in the marketplace.*

Are Credit Cards Money?

Credit cards, such as Visa, MasterCard, and American Express, are often called "plastic money," but are these cards really money? Let's test credit cards for the three functions of money. First, because credit cards are widely accepted, they serve as a means of payment in an exchange for goods or services.

Second, the credit card statement, and not the card itself, serves as a unit of account. One of the advantages of credit cards is that you receive a statement listing the exact price in dollars paid for each item you charged. Your credit card statement clearly records the dollar amount you spent for gasoline, a dinner, or a trip.

But credit cards clearly fail to meet the store-of-value criterion and are therefore *not* money. The word *credit* means receiving money today to buy products in return for a promise to pay in the future. A credit card represents only a prearranged short-term loan up to a certain limit. If the credit card company goes out of business or for any reason decides not to honor your card, it is worthless. Hence, credit cards do not store value and are *not* money. If credit cards were money, you would be indifferent between receiving $1,000 in cash and an equal dollar increase in your credit limit.

> **CHECKPOINT**
>
> *Are Debit Cards Money?*
>
> Debit cards are used to pay for purchases, and the money is automatically deducted from the user's bank account. Are debit cards money?

OTHER DESIRABLE PROPERTIES OF MONEY

Once something has passed the three basic requirements to serve as money, there are additional hurdles to clear. First, an important consideration is *scarcity*. Money must be scarce, but not too scarce. Sand, for example, could theoretically serve as money, but sand is a poor choice because people can easily gather a bucketful to pay

On the tiny South Pacific island of Yap, life is easy, but the currency is hard as a rock. For nearly 2,000 years, the Yapese have used large stone wheels to pay for major purchases, such as land, canoes, and permission to marry. The people of Yap have been using stone money ever since a Yapese warrior named Anagumang used canoes to bring the huge stones over the sea in ancient times from limestone caverns on neighboring Palau. Inspired by the moon, he fashioned the stones into large circles, and the rest is history. The stone's value remained high because of the difficulty and hazards involved in obtaining them over the rough seas.

Yap is a U.S. trust territory, and the dollar is used in grocery stores and gas stations, but reliance on stone money continues. Buying property with stones is "much easier than buying it with U.S. dollars," says John Chodad, who purchased a building lot with a 30-inch stone wheel. "We don't know the value of the U.S. dollar."[1] However, stone wheels don't make good pocket money, so Yapese use other forms of currency, such as beer for small transactions. Besides stone wheels and beer, the Yapese sometimes spend gaw, consisting of necklaces of stone beads strung together around a whale's tooth. They also buy things with yar, a currency made from large seashells, but these are small change.

Stone disks may change ownership during marriage, transfer of land title, or other exchanges. Yapese lean the stone wheels against their houses or prop up rows of them in village "banks." Most of the stones are smaller in diameter, but some are as much as 12 feet in diameter. Each has a hole in the center so it can be slipped onto the trunk of a fallen betelnut tree and carried. It takes 20 men to lift some wheels. Rather than risk a broken stone—or their backs—Yapese leave the larger stones where they are and make a mental accounting that the ownership has been transferred. There are some decided advantages to using massive stones for money. They are in short supply, difficult to steal, pose formidable obstacles to counterfeiting, and serve as a tourist attraction.

ANALYZE THE ISSUE

1. Explain how Yap's large stones pass the three tests in the definition of money.
2. Briefly discuss Yap's large stones in terms of other desirable properties of money.

---

1. Art Pine, "Fixed Assets, Or: Why a Loan in Yap Is Hard to Roll Over," *The Wall Street Journal*, March. 29, 1984, p. 1.

their bills. A Picasso painting would also be undesirable as money. Because there are so few for circulation, people would have to resort to barter.

Counterfeiting threatens the scarcity of money. Advances in computer graphics, scanners, and color copiers were allowing counterfeiters to win their ongoing battle with the U.S. Secret Service. In reponse, new bills were issued with a polymer security thread running through them. The larger off-center portraits on the bills allow for a watermark next to the portrait that is visible from both sides against a light.

CONCLUSION *The supply of money must be great enough to meet ordinary transaction needs, but not be so plentiful that it becomes worthless.*

Second, money should be *portable* and *divisible*. That is, people should be able to reach into their pockets and make change to buy items at various prices. Statues of George Washington might be attractive money, but they would be difficult to carry and make change. Finally, money must be *uniform*. An ounce of gold is an ounce of gold. The quality differences of beaver skins and seashells, on the other hand, complicate using these items for money. Each exchange would involve the extra trouble of buyers and sellers arguing over which skins or shells are better or worse.

WHAT STANDS BEHIND OUR MONEY?

Historically, early forms of money played two roles. If, for example, a ruler declared beans as money, you could spend them or sell them in the marketplace. Precious metals, tobacco, cows, and other tangible goods are examples of commodity money. Commodity money is anything that serves as money while having market value in other uses. This means that money itself has intrinsic worth (the market value of the material). For example, money can be pure gold or silver, both of which are valuable for nonmoney uses, such as making jewelry and serving other industrial purposes.

Commodity money

Anything that serves as money while having market value in other uses.

Today, U.S. paper money and coins are no longer backed by gold or silver. Our paper money was exchangeable for gold or silver until 1934. As a result of the Great Depression, people rapidly tried to get rid of their paper money. The U.S. Treasury's stock of gold dropped so low that Congress passed a law in 1934 that prevented anyone from exchanging gold for $5 and larger bills. Later, in 1963, Congress removed the right to exchange $1 bills for silver. And in the mid-1960s, zinc, copper, and nickel replaced silver in coins.

The important consideration for money is acceptability. The acceptability of a dollar is due in no small degree to the fact that Uncle Sam decrees it to be **fiat money**. Fiat money is money accepted by law, and not because of its redeemability or intrinsic value. A dollar bill contains only about three cents worth of paper, printing inks, and other materials. A quarter contains maybe 10 cents worth of nickel and copper. Pull out a dollar bill and look at it closely. In the upper left corner on the front side is small print that proclaims, "THIS NOTE IS LEGAL TENDER FOR ALL DEBTS, PUBLIC AND PRIVATE." This means that your paper money is fiat money. Also notice that nowhere on the note is there any promise to redeem it for gold, silver, or anything else.

Fiat money

Money accepted by law and not because of its redeemability or intrinsic value.

> **CONCLUSION** *An item's ability to serve as money does not depend on its own market value or the backing of precious metal.*

MONEY SUPPLY DEFINITIONS

Now that you understand the basic definition of money, we turn to exactly what constitutes the money supply of the U.S. economy. There is disagreement over the answer to this question because some economists define the money supply more narrowly than others. The following sections examine the methods used to measure the money supply, officially called M1 and M2.

M1: The Most Narrowly Defined Money Supply

M1

The narrowest definition of the money supply. It includes currency and checkable deposits.

M1 is the narrowest definition of the money supply. This money definition measures purchasing power immediately available to the public without borrowing or having to give notice. Specifically, M1 measures the currency, and checkable deposits held by the public at a given time, such as a given day, month, or year. M1 does not include the money held by the government, Federal Reserve banks, or depository institutions. Expressed as a formula:

$$M1 = \text{currency} + \text{checkable deposits}$$

Exhibit 1 shows the components of M1 and M2 money supply definitions based on daily averages during December 2009.

Currency

Money, including coins and paper money.

Currency Currency includes coins and paper money, officially called Federal Reserve notes, that the public holds for immediate spending. The purpose of

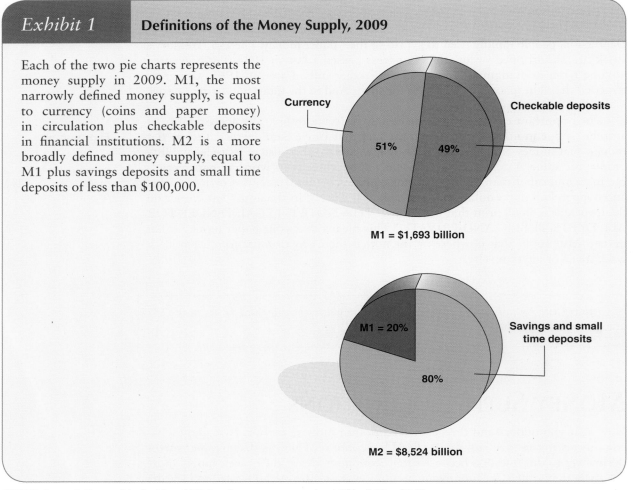

Exhibit 1 **Definitions of the Money Supply, 2009**

Each of the two pie charts represents the money supply in 2009. M1, the most narrowly defined money supply, is equal to currency (coins and paper money) in circulation plus checkable deposits in financial institutions. M2 is a more broadly defined money supply, equal to M1 plus savings deposits and small time deposits of less than $100,000.

Currency 51%   Checkable deposits 49%

M1 = $1,693 billion

M1 = 20%   Savings and small time deposits 80%

M2 = $8,524 billion

SOURCE: Economic Report of the President, 2010, http://www.gpoaccess.gov/eop/, Tables B-69 and B-70.

currency is to enable us to make small purchases. Currency represents 51 percent of M1.

Checkable Deposits   Most "big ticket" purchases are paid for with checks or credit cards (which are not money), rather than currency. Checks eliminate trips to the bank, and they are safer than cash. If lost or stolen, checks and credit cards can be replaced at little cost—money cannot. Exhibit 1 shows that a major share of M1 consists of checkable deposits. Checkable deposits are the total of checking account balances in financial institutions that are convertible to currency "on demand" by writing a check without advance notice. A checking account balance is a bookkeeping entry, often called a *demand deposit* because it can be converted into cash "on demand." Before the 1980s, only commercial banks could legally provide demand deposits. However, the law changed with the passage of the Depository Institutions Deregulation and Monetary Control Act of 1980. (This act will be discussed later in the chapter.) Today, checking accounts are available from many different financial institutions, such as savings and loan associations, credit unions, and mutual savings banks. For example, many people hold deposits in negotiable order of withdrawal (NOW) accounts or automatic transfer of savings (ATS) accounts, which serve as interest-bearing checking accounts. NOW and ATS accounts permit depositors to spend their deposits without a trip to the bank to withdraw funds. In 2009, 49 percent of M1 was checkable deposits.

> **Checkable deposits**
>
> The total of checking account balances in financial institutions convertible to currency "on demand" when a check is written without advance notice.

M2: Adding Near Monies to M1

M2 is a broader measure of the money supply because it equals M1 plus *near money*. M1 is considered by many economists to be too narrow because it does not include near money accounts that can be used to purchase goods and services. These include passbook savings accounts, money market mutual funds, and time deposits of less than $100,000. Near monies are interest-bearing deposits easily converted into spendable funds. Written as a formula:

$$M2 = M1 + \text{near monies}$$

rewritten as

$$M2 = M1 + \text{savings deposits} + \text{small time deposits of less than } \$100,000$$

> **M2**
>
> The definition of the money supply that equals M1 plus near monies, such as savings deposits and small time deposits of less than $100,000.

Savings Deposits   As shown in Exhibit 1, M1 was about one-fifth of M2 in 2009, with savings deposits and small time deposits constituting the remainder of M2. Savings deposits are interest-bearing accounts that can be easily withdrawn. These deposits include passbook savings accounts, money market mutual funds, and other types of interest-bearing deposits with commercial banks, mutual savings banks, savings and loan associations, and credit unions.

Small Time Deposits   There is a distinction between a *checkable deposit* and a *time deposit*. A time deposit is an interest-bearing account in a financial institution that requires a withdrawal notice or must remain on deposit for a specified period unless an early withdrawal penalty is paid. Certificates of deposit (CDs) are deposits

History of Money in the Colonies

The early colonists left behind their well-developed money system in Europe. North American Indians accepted wampum as money, which are beads of polished shells strung in belts. Soon, a group of settlers learned to counterfeit wampum, and it lost its value. As a result, the main method of trading with the Indians was to barter. Later, trade developed with the West Indies, and Spanish coins called "pieces of eight" were circulated widely. Colonists often cut these coins into pieces to make change. Half of a coin became known as "four bits." A quarter part of the coin was referred to as "two bits." The first English colony to mint its own coins was Massachusetts in 1652. A striking pine tree was engraved on these coins called shillings. Other coins such as a six-pence and three-pence were also produced at a mint in Boston. Several other

colonies followed by authorizing their own coin issues.

The first national coin of the United States was issued in 1787 when Congress approved a one-cent copper coin. One side was decorated with a chain of 13 links encircling the words, "We Are One." The other side had a sundial,

for a specified time, with a penalty charged for early withdrawal. Where is the line drawn between a small and a large time deposit? The answer is that time deposits of less than $100,000 are "small" and therefore are included in M2.

> **CONCLUSION** *M1 is more liquid than M2.*

To simplify the discussion throughout the remainder of this text, we will be referring to M1 when we discuss the money supply. However, one can argue that M2, or another measurement of the money supply, may be the best definition. Actually, the boundary lines for any definition of money are somewhat arbitrary.

Federal Reserve System

The 12 Central banks that service banks and other financial institutions within each of the Federal Reserve districts; popularly called the Fed.

THE FEDERAL RESERVE SYSTEM

Who controls the money supply in the United States? The answer is the **Federal Reserve System**, popularly called the "Fed." The Fed is the central banker for the nation and provides banking services to commercial banks, other financial institutions, and the federal government. The Fed regulates, supervises, and is responsible for policies concerning money. Congress and the president consult with the Fed to control the size of the money supply and thereby influence the economy's performance.

the noonday sun, and the Latin word "*fugo*," meaning "time flies." Later, this coin became known as the Franklin cent, although there is no evidence that Benjamin Franklin played any role in its design.

In 1792, Congress established a mint in Philadelphia. It manufactured copper cents and half-cents about the size of today's quarters and nickels. In 1794, silver half-dimes and half-dollars increased the variety of available coins. The next year gold eagles ($10) and half-eagles ($5) appeared. The motto "*E Pluribus Unum*" ("out of many, one") was first used on the half-eagle in 1795. The next year America's first quarters and dimes were issued.

The first paper money in the Americas was printed in 1690. Massachusetts soldiers returned to the colony from fighting the French in Quebec, where they had unsuccessfully laid siege to the city. The colony had no precious metal to pay the soldiers. Hundreds of soldiers threatened mutiny, and the colony decided it must issue bills of credit, which were simply pieces of paper promising to pay the soldiers. Other colonies followed this example and printed their own paper money. Soon paper money was being widely circulated.

In 1775, the need to finance the American Revolution forced the Continental Congress to issue paper money called "continentals," but so much was issued that it rapidly lost its value. George Washington complained, "A wagon load of money will scarcely purchase a wagon load of provisions." This statement is today shortened to the phrase "not worth a continental."

Other major nations have central banks, such as the Bank of England, the Bank of Japan, and the European Central Bank. The movement in the United States to establish a central banking system gained strength early in the twentieth century as a series of bank failures resulted in the Panic of 1907. In that year, stock prices fell, many businesses and banks failed, and millions of depositors lost their savings. The prescription for preventing financial panic was for the government to establish more centralized control over banks. This desire for more safety in banking led to the creation of the Federal Reserve System by the Federal Reserve Act of 1913 during the administration of President Woodrow Wilson. No longer would the supply of money in the economy be determined by individual banks.

The Fed's Organizational Chart

The *Federal Reserve System* is an independent agency of the federal government. Congress is responsible for overseeing the Fed, but does not interfere with its day-to-day decisions. The chairman of the Fed reports to Congress twice each year and often coordinates its actions with the U.S. Treasury and the president. Although the Fed enjoys independent status, its independence can be revoked. If the Fed were to pursue policies contrary to the interests of the nation, Congress could abolish the Fed.

The Federal Reserve System consists of 12 central banks that service banks and other financial institutions within each of the Federal Reserve districts. Each Federal Reserve bank serves as a central banker for the private banks in its region.

Exhibit 2   The Twelve Federal Reserve Districts

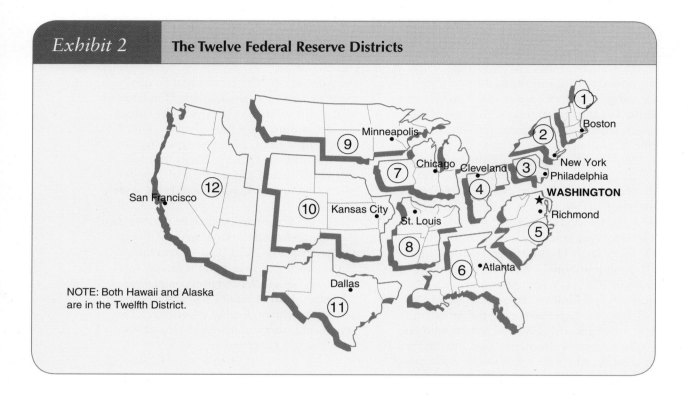

NOTE: Both Hawaii and Alaska are in the Twelfth District.

Board of Governors of the Federal Reserve System

The seven members appointed by the president and confirmed by the U.S. Senate who serve for one nonrenewable 14-year term. Their responsibility is to supervise and control the money supply and the banking system of the United States.

Ben Bernanke, Chairman of the Board of Governors of the Federal Reserve System

The United States is the only nation in the world to have 12 separate regional banks instead of a single central bank. In fact, the Fed's structure is the result of a compromise between the traditionalists, who favored a single central bank, and the populists, who distrusted concentration of financial power in the hands of a few. In addition, 25 Federal Reserve branch banks are located throughout the country. The map in Exhibit 2 shows the 12 Federal Reserve districts.

The organizational chart of the Federal Reserve System, given in Exhibit 3, shows that the **Board of Governors**, located in Washington, D.C., administers the system. The Board of Governors is made up of seven members, appointed by the president and confirmed by the U.S. Senate, who serve for one nonrenewable 14-year term. Their responsibility is to supervise and control the money supply and the banking system of the United States. Fourteen-year terms for Fed governors create autonomy and insulate the Fed from short-term politics. These terms are staggered so one term expires every two years. This staggering of terms prevents a president from stacking the board with members favoring the incumbent party's political interests. A president usually makes two appointments in a one-term presidency and four appointments in a two-term presidency. The president designates one member of the Board of Governors to serve as chairman for a four-year term. The chairman is the principal spokesperson for the Fed and has considerable power over policy decisions. In fact, it is often argued that the Fed's chairman is the most powerful individual in the United States next to the president. The current chairman is Ben Bernanke, who was appointed by President George W. Bush.

The Federal Reserve System receives no funding from Congress. This creates financial autonomy for the Fed by removing the fear of congressional review of its budget. Then where does the Fed get funds to operate? Recall from Exhibit 7 of

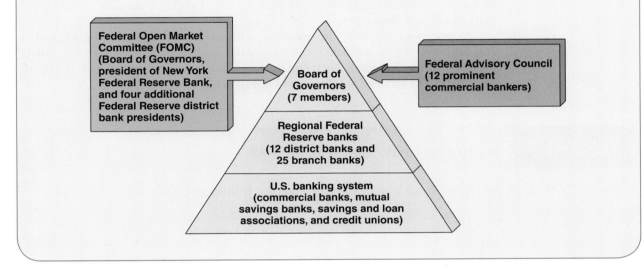

Exhibit 3 **The Organization of the Federal Reserve System**

The Federal Open Market Committee (FOMC) and the Federal Advisory Council assist the Federal Reserve System's Board of Governors. The 12 regional Federal Reserve district banks and their 25 branches implement broad policies affecting the money supply.

Federal Open Market Committee (FOMC) (Board of Governors, president of New York Federal Reserve Bank, and four additional Federal Reserve district bank presidents)

Board of Governors (7 members)

Federal Advisory Council (12 prominent commercial bankers)

Regional Federal Reserve banks (12 district banks and 25 branch banks)

U.S. banking system (commercial banks, mutual savings banks, savings and loan associations, and credit unions)

the previous chapter that the Fed holds government securities issued by the U.S. Treasury. The Fed earns interest income from the government securities it holds and the loans it makes to depository institutions. Because the Fed returns any profits to the Treasury, it is motivated to adopt policies to promote the economy's well-being, rather than earning a profit. Moreover, the Board of Governors does not take orders from the president or any other politician. Thus, the Board of Governors is the independent, self-supporting authority of the Federal Reserve System.

On the left side of the organizational chart in Exhibit 3 is the very important **Federal Open Market Committee (FOMC)**. The FOMC directs the buying and selling of U.S. government securities, which are major instruments for controlling the money supply. The FOMC consists of the seven members of the Board of Governors, the president of the New York Federal Reserve Bank, and the presidents of four other Federal Reserve district banks. The FOMC meets to discuss trends in inflation, unemployment, growth rates, and other macro data. FOMC members express their opinions on implementing various monetary policies and then issue policy statements known as *FOMC directives*. A directive, for example, might set the operation of the Fed to stimulate or restrain M1 in order to influence employment. The next two chapters explain the tools of monetary policy in more detail.

As shown on the right side of the chart, the *Federal Advisory Council* consists of 12 prominent commercial bankers. Each of the 12 Federal Reserve district banks selects one member each year. The council meets periodically to advise the Board of Governors.

Finally, at the bottom of the organizational chart is the remainder of the Federal Reserve System, consisting of only about 3,000 member banks of the

Federal Open Market Committee (FOMC)

The Federal Reserve's committee that directs the buying and selling of U.S. government securities, which are major instruments for controlling the money supply. The FOMC consists of the seven members of the Federal Reserve's Board of Governors, the president of the New York Federal Reserve Bank, and the presidents of four other Federal Reserve district banks.

approximately 7,000 commercial banks in the United States. Although these 3,000 Fed member banks represent only about one-third of U.S. banks, they have about 70 percent of all U.S. bank deposits. A sure sign of Fed membership is the word *National* in a bank's name. The U.S. comptroller of the currency charters national banks, and they are required to be Fed members. Banks that do not have "National" in their title can also be Fed members. States can also charter banks, and these state banks have the option of joining the Federal Reserve. Less than 20 percent of state banks choose to join the Fed. Exhibit 4 shows the top 10 U.S. banks based on their assets.

Nonmember depository institutions, including many commercial banks, savings and loan associations (S&Ls), savings banks, and credit unions, are not official members of the Fed team. They are, however, influenced by and depend on the Fed for a variety of services, which we will now discuss.

Exhibit 4   **Top 10 Banks in the United States, 2009**

The top 10 banks in the United States include Bank of America, JPMorgan Chase, and Wells Fargo.

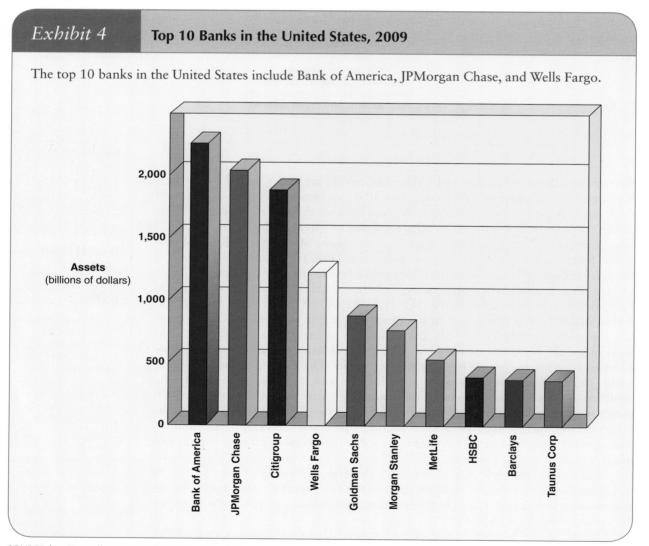

SOURCE: http://www.ffiec.gov/nicpubweb/nicweb/Top50Form.aspx.

WHAT A FEDERAL RESERVE BANK DOES

The typical bank customer never enters the doors of a Federal Reserve district bank or one of its branch banks. The reason is that the Fed does not offer the public checking accounts, savings accounts, or any of the services provided by commercial banks. Instead, the Federal Reserve serves as a "banker's bank." Following are brief descriptions of some of the principal functions of the Federal Reserve.

Controlling the Money Supply

The primary role of the Fed is to control the nation's money supply. The mechanics of Fed control over the money supply are explained in the next two chapters. To most people, this is a wondrously mysterious process. So that you do not suffer in complete suspense, here is a sneak preview: The Fed has three policy tools, or levers, it can use to change the stock of money in the banking system. The potential macro outcome of changes in the money supply is to affect total spending and therefore real GDP, employment, and the price level.

Clearing Checks

Because most people and businesses use checks to pay for goods and services, check clearing is an important function. Suppose you live in Virginia and have a checking account with a bank in that state. While on vacation in California, you purchase tickets to Disneyland with a check for $200. Disneyland accepts your check and then deposits it in its business checking account in a California bank. This bank must collect payment for your check and does so by giving the check to the Federal Reserve bank in San Francisco. From there, your check is sent to the Federal Reserve bank in Richmond. At each stop along its journey, the check earns a black stamp mark on the back. Finally, the process ends when $200 is subtracted from your personal checking account. Banks in which checks are deposited have their Fed accounts credited, and banks on which checks are written have their accounts debited. The Fed clearinghouse process is much speedier than depending on the movement of a check between commercial banks.

The 1946 film, **It's a Wonderful Life**, is based on a fractional reserve banking system without the FDIC.

Supervising and Regulating Banks

The Fed examines banks' books, sets limits for loans, approves bank mergers, and works with the **Federal Deposit Insurance Corporation (FDIC)**. The FDIC is a government agency established by Congress in 1933 to insure commercial bank deposits up to a specified limit. Congress created the FDIC in response to the huge number of bank failures during the Great Depression and set the insurance limit at $25,000. If the government provides a safety net, people are less likely to panic and withdraw their funds from banks during a period of economic uncertainty. When deposits are insured and a bank fails, the government stands ready to pay depositors or transfer their deposits to a solvent bank. Banks that are members of the Fed are members of the FDIC. State agencies supervise state-chartered banks that are not members of either the Federal Reserve System or the FDIC. To shore up confidence

Federal Deposit Insurance Corporation (FDIC)

A government agency established in 1933 to insure commercial bank deposits up to a specified limit.

in the U.S. banking system in the wake of bank failures in 2008, the $700 billion U.S. financial industry rescue law raised the FDIC coverage of bank deposits to $250,000 per customer from $100,000 through 2013.

Maintaining and Circulating Currency

Recall that the M1 money supply consists of currency (coins and Federal Reserve notes) and checkable deposits. Note that the Fed does *not* print currency—it *maintains* and *circulates* money. All Federal Reserve notes are printed at the U.S. Bureau of Engraving and Printing's facilities in Washington, D.C., and Fort Worth, Texas. The Treasury mints and issues all coins. Coins are made at U.S. mints located in Philadelphia and Denver. The bureau and the mints ship new notes and coins to the Federal Reserve banks for circulation. Much of this money is printed or minted simply to replace worn-out bills and coins. Another use of new currency is to meet public demand. Suppose it is the holiday season and banks need more paper money and coins to meet their customers' shopping needs. The Federal Reserve must be ready to ship extra money from its large vaults by armored truck.

Protecting Consumers

Since 1968, the Federal Reserve has played a role in protecting consumers by enforcing statutes enacted by Congress. Perhaps the most important is the *Equal Credit Opportunity Act*, which prohibits discrimination based on race, color, gender, marital status, religion, or national origin in the extension of credit. It also gives married women the right to establish credit histories in their own names. The Federal Reserve receives and tries to resolve consumer complaints against banks.

Maintaining Federal Government Checking Accounts and Gold

The Fed is also Uncle Sam's bank. The U.S. Treasury has the Fed handle its checking account. From this account, the federal government pays for such expenses as federal employees' salaries, Social Security, tax refunds, veterans' benefits, defense, and highways.

Finally, it is interesting to note that the New York Federal Reserve District Bank holds one of the oldest forms of money—*gold*. This gold belongs mainly to foreign governments and is one of the largest accumulations of this precious metal in the world. Viewing a Federal Reserve bank's vault is not something that most tourists typically have on their list of things to do, but I strongly recommend this tour.

The gold vault at the New York Federal Reserve Bank is nearly half the length of a football field and filled with steel and concrete walls several yards thick. Most cells contain the gold of only one nation, and only a few bank employees know the identities of the owners. When trade occurs between two countries, payment between the parties can be made by transferring gold bars from one compartment to another. Note that the Fed and the monetary system of the Yapese have a similarity. Recall from the Global Economics box that in Yap large stone wheels are not moved; rather they just change ownership.

THE U.S. BANKING REVOLUTION

Prior to the 1980s, the U.S. banking system was simpler. It consisted of many commercial banks authorized by law to offer checking accounts. Then there were the other financial institutions, the so-called thrifts, which included S&Ls, mutual savings banks, and credit unions. The thrifts by law were permitted to accept only savings deposits with no checking privileges. The commercial banks, on the other hand, could not pay interest on checkable deposits. Moreover, a "maximum interest rate allowed by law" limited competition among commercial banks and other financial institutions. As will be explained momentarily, this relatively tranquil U.S. banking structure changed dramatically, and the stage was set for a fascinating banking "horror story."

The Monetary Control Act of 1980

A significant law affecting the U.S. banking system is the Depository Institutions Deregulation and Monetary Control Act of 1980, commonly called the **Monetary Control Act**. This law gave the Federal Reserve System greater control over nonmember banks and made all financial institutions more competitive. The act's four major provisions are the following:

1. *The authority of the Fed over nonmember depository institutions was increased.* Before the Monetary Control Act, less than half the banks in the United States were members of the Fed and subject to its direct control. Under the act's provisions, the Federal Reserve sets uniform reserve requirements for *all* commercial banks, including state and national banks, S&Ls, and credit unions with checking accounts.

2. *All depository institutions are able to borrow loan reserves from Federal Reserve banks.* This practice, called *discounting*, will be explained in the next chapter. Banks also have access to check clearing and other services of the Fed.

3. *The act allows commercial banks, thrifts, money market mutual funds, stock brokerage firms, and retailers to offer a wide variety of banking services.* For example, commercial banks and other financial institutions can pay unrestricted interest rates on checking accounts. Also, S&Ls and other financial institutions can offer checking accounts. Federal credit unions are authorized to make residential real estate loans, and other major corporations can offer traditional banking services.

4. *The act eliminated all interest rate ceilings.* Before this act, S&Ls were allowed to pay depositors a slightly higher interest rate on passbook savings deposits than those paid by commercial banks. The Monetary Control Act removed this advantage of S&Ls over other financial institutions competing for depositors.

Finally, the movement toward deregulation, which blurred the distinctions between financial institutions, continued in 1999 when the *Financial Services Modernization Act* was signed into law. This sweeping measure lifted Depression-era barriers and allows banks, securities firms, and insurance companies to merge and sell each other's products.

Monetary Control Act

A law, formally titled the Depository Institutions Deregulation and Monetary Control Act of 1980, that gave the Federal Reserve System greater control over nonmember banks and made all financial institutions more competitive.

The case of Lincoln Savings and Loan is a classic example of what went wrong during one of the worst financial crises in U.S. history. In 1984, the Securities and Exchange Commission charged Charles Keating, Jr., with fraud in an Ohio loan scam, but regulators later allowed him to buy Lincoln Savings and Loan in California. Keating hired a staff to carry out his wishes and paid them and his relatives millions. Keating was also generous with politicians in Washington, D.C. Allegedly, five U.S. senators received $1.5 million in campaign contributions from Keating to influence regulators.

Where did Keating's money come from? It came from Lincoln Savings depositors and, ultimately, from taxpayers because the federal government insures deposits of failed S&Ls. When Keating took over Lincoln, it was a healthy S&L with assets of $1.1 billion. But because of deregulation mandated by the Monetary Control Act and other legislation and the lack of enforcement of regulations under the new laws, many S&Ls plunged into high-risk, but potentially highly profitable, ventures. Keating therefore took Lincoln out of sound home mortgage loans and into speculation in Arizona hotels costing $500,000 per room to build, raw land for golf courses, shopping centers, junk bonds, and currency futures.

In 1987, after it was already too late, California regulators became alarmed at the way Lincoln operated and asked the FBI and the FSLIC to take over Lincoln. Keating responded by contacting his friends in Washington, and the regulatory process moved at a snail's pace. Years passed before the government finally closed Lincoln and informed the public that their deposits were not safe in this S&L. During the time regulators were deciding what action to take, it is estimated that Lincoln cost taxpayers another $1 billion. Ultimately, the collapse of Lincoln cost U.S. taxpayers about $3 billion, making it the most expensive S&L failure of all.

Keating and other S&L entrepreneurs say they did nothing wrong. After all, Congress and federal regulators encouraged, or did not discourage, S&Ls to compete by borrowing funds at high interest rates and making risky, but potentially highly profitable, investments. If oil prices and land values fall unexpectedly and loans fail, this is simply the way a market economy works and not the fault of risk-prone wheeler-dealers like Keating.

In 1993, a federal judge sentenced Keating to 12½ years in prison for swindling small investors. The sentence ran concurrently with a 10-year state prison sentence. The judge also ordered Keating to pay $122.4 million in restitution to the government for losses caused by sham property sales. However, the government has been unable to locate any

© Elena Elisseeva, 2008/Used under license from Shutterstock.com.

significant assets. Keating served four years and nine months.

ANALYZE THE ISSUE

Critics of federal banking policy argue that deposit insurance is a key reason for banking failures. The banks enjoy a "heads I win, tails the government loses" proposition. Several possible reforms of deposit insurance have been suggested. For example, the limit on insured deposits can be raised, reduced, or eliminated. Do you think a change in deposit insurance would prevent bank failures?

The Savings and Loan Crises

Before the current financial crisis discussed in the chapter on monetary policy, the savings and loan crises of the 1980s and early 1990s was one of the worst U.S. financial crises since the Great Depression. After the Monetary Control Act removed interest rate ceilings on deposits, competition for customers forced S&Ls to pay higher interest rates on short-term deposits. Unlike the banks, however, S&Ls were earning their income from long-term mortgages at fixed interest rates below the rate required to keep or attract new deposits. The resulting losses enticed the S&Ls to forsake home mortgage loans, which they knew best, and seek high-interest, but riskier, commercial and consumer loans. Unfortunately, these risky higher-interest loans resulted in defaults and more losses. If conditions were not bad enough, lower oil prices depressed the oil-based state economies in Texas, Louisiana, and Oklahoma.

The Federal Savings and Loan Insurance Corporation (FSLIC) was the agency that insured deposits in S&Ls, similar to how the FDIC insures bank deposits. The magnitude of the losses exceeded the insurance fund's ability to pay depositors, and Congress placed the FSLIC's deposit-insurance fund under the FDIC's control. To close or sell ailing S&Ls and protect depositors, Congress enacted the Thrift Bailout Bill in 1989. One provision of this act created the Resolution Trust Corporation (RTC) to carry out a massive federal bailout of failed institutions. The RTC bought the assets and deposits of failed S&Ls and sold them to offset the cost borne by taxpayers. The RTC closed in 1995, and the ultimate cost to taxpayers totaled $125 billion!

Key Concepts

Barter
Money
Medium of exchange
Unit of account
Store of value
Commodity money
Fiat money

M1, M2
Currency
Checkable deposits
Federal Reserve System
Board of Governors of the
    Federal Reserve System

Federal Open Market
    Committee (FOMC)
Federal Deposit
    Insurance Corporation
    (FDIC)
Monetary Control Act

Summary

- *Money* can be anything that meets these three tests. Money must serve as (1) a medium of exchange, (2) a unit of account, and (3) a store of value. Money facilitates more efficient exchange than barter. Other desirable properties of money include scarcity, portability, divisibility, and uniformity.
- *Medium of exchange* is the most important function of money. This means that money is widely accepted in payment for goods and services.
- *Unit of account* is another important function of money. Money is used to measure relative values by serving as a common yardstick for valuing goods and services.
- *Store of value* is the ability of money to hold its value over time. Money is said to be highly *liquid*, which means it is readily usable in exchange.
- *Credit cards* are not money. Credit cards represent a short-term loan and therefore fail as a store of value.
- *Commodity money* is money that has a marketable value, such as gold and silver. Today, the United States uses *fiat money*, which must be accepted by law, but is not convertible into gold, silver, or any commodity.
- *M1* is the narrowest definition of the money supply, which equals currency plus checkable deposits. *M2* is a broader definition of the money supply, which equals M1 plus *near monies*, such as savings deposits and small time deposits.

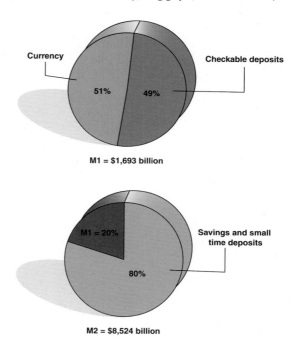

Definitions of Money Supply (M1 and M2)

Currency — 51%   Checkable deposits — 49%

M1 = $1,693 billion

M1 = 20%   Savings and small time deposits — 80%

M2 = $8,524 billion

- The *Federal Reserve System*, our central bank, was established in 1913. The Fed consists of 12 Federal Reserve district banks with 25 branches. The *Board of Governors* is the Fed's governing body. The *Federal Open Market Committee* (FOMC) directs the buying and selling of U.S. government securities, which is a key method of controlling the money supply.

- Basic *Federal Reserve bank functions* are (1) controlling the money supply, (2) clearing checks, (3) supervising and regulating banking, (4) maintaining and circulating currency, (5) protecting consumers, and (6) maintaining the federal government's checking accounts and gold.
- The *Monetary Control Act of 1980* revolutionized U.S. banking by expanding

the authority of the Federal Reserve System to all financial institutions. In addition, this law increased competition by blurring the distinctions between commercial banks, thrift institutions, and even nonfinancial institutions.

Summary of Conclusion Statements

- The use of money simplifies and therefore increases market transactions. Money also prevents wasting time that can be devoted to production, thereby promoting economic growth by increasing a nation's production possibilities.
- Money is a useful mechanism for transforming income in the present into future purchases.
- Money is the most liquid form of wealth because it can be spent directly in the marketplace.

- The supply of money must be great enough to meet ordinary transaction needs, but not be so plentiful that it becomes worthless.
- An item's ability to serve as money does not depend on its own market value or the backing of precious metal.
- M1 is more liquid than M2.

Study Questions and Problems

1. Discuss this statement: "A man with a million dollars who is lost in the desert learns the meaning of money."
2. Could each of the following items potentially serve as money? Consider each as (1) a medium of exchange, (2) a unit of account, and (3) a store of value.
   a. Visa credit card
   b. Federal Reserve note
   c. Dog
   d. Beer mug
3. Consider each of the items in question 2 in terms of scarcity, portability, divisibility, and uniformity.
4. What backs the U.S. dollar? Include the distinction between commodity money and fiat money in your answer.

5. What are the components of the most narrowly defined money supply in the United States?
6. Distinguish between M1 and M2. What are near monies?
7. What is the major purpose of the Federal Reserve System? What is the major responsibility of the Board of Governors and the Federal Open Market Committee?
8. Should the Fed be independent or a government agency subordinate to Congress and the president?
9. Which banks must be insured by the FDIC? Which banks can choose not to be insured by the FDIC?
10. Briefly discuss the importance of the Depository Institutions Deregulation and Monetary Control Act of 1980.

For Online Exercises, go to the Tucker Web site at www.cengage.com/economics/tucker.

CHECKPOINT ANSWER

Are Debit Cards Money?

Debit cards serve as a means of payment, and debit card statements serve as a unit of account. Finally, unlike credit cards, debit cards serve as a store of value because they are a means of accessing checkable deposits and not an extension of credit. If you said debit cards are money because they serve all three functions required for money, **YOU ARE CORRECT.**

Practice Quiz

For an explanation of the correct answers, visit the Tucker Web site at www.cengage.com/economics/tucker.

1. Which of the following is a problem with barter?
   a. Individuals will not exchange goods.
   b. Individuals' wants must coincide in order for there to be exchange.
   c. Goods can be exchanged, but services cannot.
   d. None of the above is a problem.

2. Which of the following is *not* a characteristic of money?
   a. It provides a way to measure the relative value of goods and services.
   b. It is always backed by something of high intrinsic value, such as gold or silver.
   c. It is generally acceptable as a medium of exchange.
   d. It allows for saving and borrowing.

3. Which of the following is *not* a store of value?
   a. Dollar
   b. Money market mutual fund share
   c. Checking account balance
   d. Credit card

4. The easier it is to convert an asset directly into goods and services without loss, the
   a. less secure it is.
   b. more secure it is.
   c. more liquid it is.
   d. less liquid it is.

5. M1 refers to
   a. the most narrowly defined money supply.
   b. currency held by the public plus checking account balances.
   c. the smallest dollar amount of the money supply definitions.
   d. all of the above.

6. The M1 definition of the money supply consists of
   a. coins and currency in circulation.
   b. coins and currency in circulation and checkable deposits.
   c. Federal Reserve notes, gold certificates, and checkable deposits.
   d. Federal Reserve notes and bank loans.

7. Which of the following items is *not* included when computing M1?
   a. Coins in circulation
   b. Currency in circulation
   c. Savings accounts
   d. Checking account entries

8. Which of the following is part of the M2 definition of the money supply, but not part of M1?
   a. Checkable deposits
   b. Currency held in banks
   c. Currency in circulation
   d. Money market mutual fund shares

9. Which of the following is *not* part of M1?
   a. Checking accounts
   b. Coins

Practice Quiz Continued

    c.   Credit cards
    d.   Paper currency

10. Which definition of the money supply includes credit cards, or "plastic money"?
    a.   M1
    b.   M2
    c.   Both (a) and (b)
    d.   Neither (a) nor (b)

11. Which of these institutions has the responsibility to control the money supply?
    a.   Commercial banks
    b.   Congress
    c.   U.S. Treasury Department
    d.   Federal Reserve System

12. Which of the following is *not* one of the functions of the Federal Reserve?
    a.   Clearing checks
    b.   Printing currency
    c.   Supervising and regulating banks
    d.   Controlling the money supply

13. Which of the following is in charge of the buying and selling of government securities by the Fed?
    a.   The president
    b.   Federal Open Market Committee (FOMC)
    c.   Congress
    d.   None of the above

14. The major protection against sudden mass attempts to withdraw cash from banks is the
    a.   Federal Reserve.
    b.   Consumer Protection Act.
    c.   deposit insurance provided by the FDIC.
    d.   gold and silver backing the dollar.

15. Which of the following is *not* part of the Federal Reserve System?
    a.   Council of Economic Advisers
    b.   Board of Governors
    c.   Federal Open Market Committee
    d.   12 Federal Reserve District Banks
    e.   Federal Advisory Council

chapter 15

Money Creation

It has been said that the most important person in Washington, D.C. is the chair of the Federal Reserve because he or she can influence the money supply and therefore the performance of the economy. This chapter builds on your knowledge of money and the Federal Reserve System gained in the previous chapter. You will discover that the Federal Reserve (the Fed) and the banks work together to determine the money supply. The chapter begins with a brief history of the evolution of banking. Then we examine the mechanics of how banks create money in a simplified system during a normal economy. This remarkable process depends on the ability of banks to amplify checkable deposits by generating a spiral of new loans and, in turn, deposits for new spending in the economy. Finally, the Fed's toolkit swings open and we discuss the three tools used by the Fed to change the money supply.

A common misconception is that banks (including savings and loans and other depository institutions) accept deposits and make loans, and that's about the end of the story. But there is another very important chapter to tell. Banking transactions expand or contract the money supply. Without minting coins or using the printing presses to make paper money, your local bank and other banks can create money; that is, banks can increase the money supply (M1).

The reason people do not understand money creation is that they think the federal government controls the money supply by turning the printing presses on and off. As explained in the previous chapter, this notion is only partly true because money consists primarily of bookkeeping entries, rather than pieces of paper and coins. Consequently, writing checks, using an automatic teller machine, and getting a loan affect the size of the checkable deposits component of the money supply.

In this chapter, you will learn to solve these economics puzzles:

- Exactly how is money created in the economy? That is, how does the money supply increase?

- What are the major tools the Federal Reserve uses to control the supply of money?

- Why is there nothing "federal" about the federal funds rate?

MONEY CREATION BEGINS

In the Middle Ages, gold was the money of choice in most European nations. One of the problems with gold is that it is a heavy commodity, which makes it difficult to use in transactions or to hide from thieves. The medieval solution was to keep it safely deposited with the people who worked with gold, called *goldsmiths*. This demand for their services inspired goldsmith entrepreneurs to become the founders of modern-day banking.

The goldsmiths sat on their benches with ledgers close by and recorded the amounts of gold placed in their vaults. In fact, the word *bank* is derived from the Italian word for bench, which is *banco*. After assessing the purity of the gold, a goldsmith issued a receipt to the customer for the amount of gold deposited. In return, the goldsmith collected a service charge, just as you pay today for services at your bank. Anyone who possessed the receipt and presented it to the goldsmith could make a withdrawal for the amount of gold written on the receipt.

With these gold receipts in circulation, people began paying their debts with these pieces of paper, rather than actually exchanging gold. Thus, goldsmith receipts became paper money. At first, the goldsmiths were very conservative and issued receipts exactly equal to the amount of gold stored in their vaults. However, some shrewd goldsmiths observed that net withdrawals in any period were only a *fraction* of all the gold "on reserve." This observation produced a powerful idea. Goldsmiths discovered that they could make loans for more gold than they actually held in their vaults. As a result, goldsmiths made extra profit from interest on loans, and borrowers had more money for spending in their hands.

HOW A SINGLE BANK CREATES MONEY

The medieval goldsmiths were the first to practice fractional reserve banking. Modern fractional reserve banking is a system in which banks keep only a percentage of their deposits on reserve as vault cash and deposits at the Fed. In a 100 percent reserve banking system, banks would be unable to create money by making loans. However, as you will learn momentarily, holding less than 100 percent on reserve allows banks to make loans and, in turn, to create money in the economy.

Fractional reserve banking

A system in which banks keep only a percentage of their deposits on reserve as vault cash and deposits at the Fed.

Banker Bookkeeping

We begin our exploration of how the fractional reserve banking system operates in the United States by looking at the balance sheet of a single bank, Typical Bank. A balance sheet is a statement of the assets and liabilities of a bank at a given point in time. Balance sheets are called *T-accounts*. The hypothetical T-account of Typical Bank in Balance Sheet 1 lists only major categories and omits details to keep things simple.

On the right side of the balance sheet are the bank's *liabilities*. Liabilities are the amounts the bank owes to others. In our example, the only liabilities are *checkable deposits*, or demand deposits. Note that checkable deposits are assets on the customers' personal balance sheets, but they are debt obligations of Typical Bank. If a depositor writes a check against his or her checking account, the bank must pay this amount. Therefore, checkable deposits are liabilities to the bank.

On the left side of the balance sheet, we see Typical Bank's *assets*. Assets are amounts the bank owns. In our example, these assets consist of **required reserves**, *excess reserves*, and *loans*. Required reserves are the minimum balance that the Fed requires a bank to hold in vault cash or on deposit with the Fed. Note that the Fed is a Scrooge and pays no interest on reserves held with the Fed. And because reserves earn no return, Typical Bank will maximize profits by trying to keep only the minimum amount possible in required reserves.

The **required reserve ratio** determines the minimum required reserves. The required reserve ratio is the percentage of deposits that the Fed requires a bank to hold in vault cash or on deposit with the Fed. Here we assume that the Fed's required reserve ratio is 10 percent. Thus, the bank must have required reserves of $5 million (10 percent of $50 million). This leaves Typical Bank with $45 million in loans that provide profit to the bank.

Exhibit 1 shows that the actual required reserve ratio depends on the level of a bank's checkable deposits. Note that the Fed requires a lower percentage for a smaller bank. In the real world, Typical Bank's required reserve ratio would be 3 percent if its checkable deposits were between $10.7 million and $55.2 million.

Typical Bank has zero **excess reserves** so far in our analysis. Excess reserves are potential loan balances held in vault cash or on deposit with the Fed in excess of required reserves. We will see shortly that excess reserves play a starring role in the

---

Required reserves

The minimum balance that the Fed requires a bank to hold in vault cash or on deposit with the Fed.

Required reserve ratio

The percentage of deposits that the Fed requires a bank to hold in vault cash or on deposit with the Fed.

Excess reserves

Potential loan balances held in vault cash or on deposit with the Fed in excess of required reserves.

Typical Bank

Balance Sheet 1

Assets		Liabilities	
Required reserves	$ 5 million	Checkable deposits	$50 million
Excess reserves	0		
Loans	45 million		
Total	$50 million	Total	$50 million

NOTE: The Fed requires the bank to keep 10 percent of its checkable deposits in reserves. Holding $5 million in required reserves, the bank has zero excess reserves and $45 million in loans to earn profit.

Exhibit 1	Required Reserve Ratio of the Federal Reserve
Type of deposit	**Required Reserve Ratio**
Checkable deposits	
$10.7–$55.2 million	3%
Over $55.2 million	10%

SOURCE: Federal Reserve Bank, Reserve Requirements, http://www.federalreserve.gov/monetarypolicy/reservereq.htm.

banking system's ability to change the money supply. The relationship between reserves accounts can be expressed as follows:

$$\text{Total reserves} = \text{required reserves} + \text{excess reserves}$$

or

$$\text{Excess reserves} = \text{total reserves} - \text{required reserves}$$

The final entry on the asset side of Typical Bank's balance sheet is loans, which are interest-earning assets of the bank. Loans are bank assets because they represent outstanding credit payable to the bank. In a fractional reserve banking system, the bank uses balances not held in reserves to earn income. In our example, loan officers have written loans totaling $45 million. Finally, note that Typical Bank's assets equal its liabilities. As you will see momentarily, any change on one side of the T-account must be accompanied by an equal amount of change on the other side of the balance sheet.

Step One: Accepting a New Deposit

You are now prepared to see how a bank creates money. Assume the required reserve ratio is 10 percent and one of Best National Bank's depositors, Brad Rich, takes $100,000 in cash from under his mattress and deposits it in his checking account. Balance Sheet 2 records this change by increasing the bank's checkable deposits on the liability side by $100,000. Brad's deposit is a liability of the bank because Brad could change his mind and withdraw his money. On the asset side, Brad's deposit increases assets because the bank has an extra $90,000 to lend after setting aside the proper amount of required reserves. Balance Sheet 2 shows that total reserves are divided between required reserves of $10,000 (10 percent of the deposit) and excess reserves of $90,000 (90 percent of the deposit). Thus, the bank's assets and liabilities remain equal when Brad makes his deposit.

Before proceeding, we must pause to make an important point. Depositing coins or paper currency in a bank has no initial effect on the money supply (M1). Recall from the previous chapter that M1 includes currency in circulation. Therefore, the transfer of $100,000 in cash from the mattress to the bank creates no money because M1 already counts this amount. Moreover, the money supply would *not* have increased had Brad Rich's initial $100,000 deposit been a check written on another bank. In this case, an increase in the assets and liabilities of Best National Bank by $100,000 would simply decrease the assets and liabilities of the other bank by $100,000. Recall that M1 also includes checkable deposits.

CONCLUSION *Transferring currency to a bank and moving deposits from one bank to another do not affect the money supply (M1).*

Best National Bank

Balance Sheet 2

Assets		Liabilities		Change in M1
Required reserves	+$ 10,000	Brad Rich account	+$100,000	0
Excess reserves	+ 90,000			
Total	$100,000	Total	$100,000	

STEP 1: Brad Rich deposits $100,000 in cash, which increases checkable deposits. The Fed requires the bank to keep 10 percent of its new deposit in required reserves, so this account is credited with $10,000. The remaining 90 percent is excess reserves of $90,000. There is no effect on the money supply.

Step Two: Making a Loan

So far, M1 has not changed, as shown in Balance Sheet 2, because Brad has simply taken $100,000 in currency and transferred it to a checkable deposit. Stated differently, the public holds the same $100,000 for spending, and only the form has changed from cash to a checkable deposit. In step two, the actual money creation process occurs. The profit motive provides the incentive for bank officials not to let $90,000 from a new deposit sit languishing in excess reserves. Instead, Best National Bank is eager to make loans and earn a profit by charging interest. Suppose, coincidentally, that Connie Jones walks in with a big smile, asking for a $90,000 loan to purchase equipment for her health spa. Connie has a fine credit record, so the bank accepts Connie's note (IOU) agreeing to repay the loan. As shown in Balance Sheet 3, three entries on the assets side have changed. First, the loan to Connie Jones boosts the loans account to $90,000. Second, the bank must increase required reserves by $9,000 because of the $90,000 increase in checkable deposits on the liabilities side. (Recall that required reserves are 10 percent of checkable deposits.) Third, transferring $9,000 from excess reserves to required reserves

Best National Bank

Balance Sheet 3

Assets		Liabilities		Change in M1
Required reserves	$ 19,000	Brad Rich account	$100,000	
Excess reserves	81,000	Connie Jones account	+90,000	+$90,000
Loans	+90,000			
Total	$190,000	Total	$190,000	

STEP 2: The bank loans Connie Jones $90,000 by crediting her checking account with this amount. A corresponding $90,000 balance is added to the loan account. The result is an increase in the money supply of $90,000.

reduces the bank's excess reserves from $90,000 to $81,000. Total reserves remain at $100,000 in both Balance Sheet 2 and Balance Sheet 3.

The corresponding entry on the liabilities side of the balance sheet is the bread and butter of money creation. Checkable deposits have increased by $90,000 to $190,000. The reason is that the bank issued a check in Connie's name drawn on a checking account in the bank. Thus, Best National Bank has performed money magic with this transaction. Look what happened to the $100,000 deposited by Brad Rich. It has generated a new $90,000 *loan*, which promptly added this amount to checkable deposits and therefore increased the money supply by $90,000.

CONCLUSION *When a bank makes a loan, it creates deposits, and the money supply increases by the amount of the loan because the money supply includes checkable deposits.*

Before proceeding further, you need to pause and take a breath. After resting, take particular notice of the impact of these transactions on the money supply. In step one, Brad's initial deposit did not change M1. But in step two, M1 increased by $90,000 when Best National Bank created money out of thin air by making the loan to Connie Jones. Now Connie has more money in her checking account than she did before, and no one else has less. Connie can now use this money to buy goods and services.

Step Three: Clearing the Loan Check

Now Connie Jones can use her new money to purchase equipment for her spa. Suppose Connie buys equipment for her business from Better Health Spa and writes a check for $90,000 drawn on Best National Bank. The owner of Better Health Spa then deposits the check in the firm's account at Yazoo National Bank. Yazoo National will send the check to its Federal Reserve district bank for collection. Recall that each bank maintains reserves at the Fed. The Fed clears the check by debiting the reserve account of Best National Bank and crediting the reserve account of Yazoo National Bank. The Fed then returns the check to Best National Bank, and this bank reduces Connie Jones's checking account by $90,000. As shown in Balance Sheet 4, Connie Jones's checking account falls to zero, and Best National Bank's liabilities are reduced by $90,000. On the asset side of the balance sheet, required reserves decrease by $9,000, and excess reserves return to zero. Now that all the dust has settled, Best National Bank has required reserves of $10,000 and an IOU for $90,000. Note that this check-clearing process in step three has no effect on M1. The $90,000 increase in M1 created by Best National Bank's loan to Connie remains on deposit at Yazoo National Bank in Better Health Spa's checking accounts.

Finally, if Brad Rich withdraws $100,000 in cash from Best National Bank, the process described above operates in reverse. The result is a $90,000 decline (destruction) in the money supply.

Best National Bank

Balance Sheet 4

Assets		Liabilities		Change in M1
Required reserves	$ 10,000	Brad Rich account	$100,000	0
Excess reserves	0	Connie Jones account	0	
Loans	90,000			
Total	$100,000	Total	$100,000	

STEP 3: Connie Jones pays Better Health Spa with a $90,000 check drawn on Best National Bank. Better Health Spa deposits the check in Yazoo National Bank, which collects from Best National Bank. The result is a debit to Connie's account and her bank's reserves accounts.

MULTIPLIER EXPANSION OF MONEY BY THE BANKING SYSTEM

The process of money creation (loans) does not stop at the doors of Best National Bank. Just like the spending multiplier from the chapter on fiscal policy, there is a money multiplier process. Let's continue our story by following the effect on Yazoo National after Better Health Spa deposits $90,000 from Connie Jones. As shown in Balance Sheet 5, Yazoo National's checkable deposits increase by $90,000. Given a required reserve ratio of 10 percent, Yazoo National Bank must keep $9,000 in required reserves, and the remaining $81,000 goes into excess reserves.

Yazoo National's loan officer now has $81,000 in additional excess reserves to lend and thus create additional checkable deposits, excess reserves, and eventually

Yazoo National Bank

Balance Sheet 5

Assets		Liabilities	
Required reserves	+$ 9,000	Better Health Spa account	+ $90,000
Excess reserves	+81,000		
Total	$90,000	Total	$90,000

NOTE: Given a required reserve ratio of 10 percent, Better Health Spa's deposit of $90,000 from Connie Jones creates $81,000 in additional excess reserves that the bank can lend, and thus create additional checkable deposits.

		Increase in Checkable Deposits	Increase in Required Reserves	Increase in Excess Reserves
Round	**Bank**			
1	Best National Bank	$ 100,000	$ 10,000	$ 90,000
2	Yazoo National Bank	90,000	9,000	81,000
3	Bank A	81,000	8,100	72,900
4	Bank B	72,900	7,290	65,610
5	Bank C	65,610	6,561	59,049
6	Bank D	59,049	5,905	53,144
7	Bank E	53,144	5,314	47,830
.	.	.	.	.
.	.	.	.	.
.	.	.	.	.
Total all other banks		478,297	47,830	430,467
Total increase		$1,000,000	$100,000	$900,000

Exhibit 2 — Expansion of the Money Supply

NOTE: A $100,000 cash deposit in Best National Bank creates $900,000 in new deposits in other banks. Each round creates excess reserves, which are loaned to a customer who deposits the loan check in another bank in the next round.

loans in other banks. Exhibit 2 presents the expansion of the money supply created when Brad Rich makes his initial $100,000 deposit and then banks make loans that are deposited in other banks.

In Exhibit 2, we see that, lo and behold, an initial deposit of $100,000 in Best National Bank can eventually create a $900,000 increase in the money supply (M1). This is because Brad Rich's initial $100,000 deposit eventually creates total excess reserves of $900,000, which are available for new loans and, in turn, new deposits in different banks. As this process continues, each bank accepts smaller and smaller increases in checkable deposits because 10 percent of each deposit is held as required reserves. As shown in Exhibit 2, the banking system as a whole can create new checkable deposits of $900,000, equal to the total of newly created excess reserves in individual banks. Note that the initial $100,000 was from cash already counted in M1, and so it is not counted in the expansion of the money supply.

The Money Multiplier

Fortunately, we do not need to calculate all the individual bank transactions listed in Exhibit 2 in order to derive the change in the money supply initiated by a deposit or withdrawal. Instead, we can use the **money multiplier**, or *deposit multiplier*. The money multiplier gives the *maximum* change in the money supply (checkable deposits)

Money multiplier

The maximum change in the money supply (checkable deposits) due to an initial change in the excess reserves banks hold. The money multiplier is equal to 1 divided by the required reserve ratio.

due to an initial change in the excess reserves held by banks.[1] The money multiplier is equal to 1 divided by the required reserve ratio. Expressed as a formula:

$$\text{Money multiplier} = \frac{1}{\text{required reserve ratio}} = \frac{1}{1/10} = 10$$

The actual change in the money supply is computed by the following formula:

Actual money supply change = initial change in excess reserves (ER) × money multiplier (MM)

Symbolically, using the data in Exhibit 2,

$$\Delta M1 = \Delta ER \times MM$$
$$\$900,000 = \$90,000 \times 10$$

The Real-World Money Multiplier

In reality, for several reasons, the size of the money multiplier can be considerably smaller than our handy little formula indicates. First, Connie Jones, or any customer along the money creation process, can decide to put a portion of the loan in her pocket, rather than writing a check to Better Health Spa for the full amount of the loan. Money outside the banking system in someone's wallet or purse or underneath the mattress is a cash leakage, which reduces the value of the money multiplier.

Second, the size of the money multiplier falls when banks do not use all their excess reserves to make loans. Perhaps a financial crisis causes many people to lose confidence in the banking system, and they make large deposit account withdrawals. As a result, banks hold their excess reserves. Or some banks can hold excess reserves because they lack enough "worthy" loan applications. This is the situation under the current credit crunch described in the You're The Economist feature in the next chapter. In short, banks are very cautious to make new loans because they are suffering from holding bad mortgage loans.

CONCLUSION *When banks decide to retain excess reserves, the money multiplier will be smaller.*

Monetary policy

The Federal Reserve's use of open market operations, changes in the discount rate, and changes in the required reserve ratio to change the money supply (M1).

HOW MONETARY POLICY CREATES MONEY

The previous chapter explained that the principal function of the Fed is to control the money supply using three policy tools or levers. The Fed's use of these tools to influence the economy is more precisely called **monetary policy**. Monetary policy is the Federal Reserve's use of open market operations, changes in the discount rate,

---

1. The money multiplier (*MM*) is the sum of the infinite geometric progression $1 + (1 - r) + (1 - r)^2 + (1 - r)^3 + \ldots + (1 - r)^\infty$, where r equals the required reserve ratio.

and changes in the required reserve ratio to change the money supply (M1). Using these three tools, or levers, of monetary policy, the Fed can limit or expand deposit creation by the banks and thereby change the money supply.

Open Market Operations

You have seen how decisions of the public—including those of Brad Rich, Connie Jones, and Better Health Spa—worked through the banking system and increased M1. In this section, you will build on this foundation by learning how the Fed can expand or contract the money supply. We begin with the aggregated Balance Sheet 6 of the 12 Federal Reserve banks of the Federal Reserve System. Total assets of the Fed on February 24, 2010 were $2,289 billion. The majority of these assets ($776 billion) were held in U.S. government securities in the form of Treasury bills, Treasury notes, and Treasury bonds, and loans to banks were $101 billion. This contrasts with commercial banks, which hold most of their assets in loans. Finally, the other assets of the Fed include high-grade mortgage-backed securities purchased from banks in order to help stabilize the banking system during the current financial crisis.

The major liability of the Fed was $892 billion worth of Federal Reserve notes—paper currency. This is in contrast to the major liability of commercial banks, which is checkable deposits. As explained in the previous chapter, the Fed issues, but does not actually print, Federal Reserve notes. Instead, the Fed decides how much to issue and then calls the Bureau of Engraving and Printing to order new batches of $10, $20, $50, and $100 bills, which the Fed sends to the banks in armored trucks.

Another important liability of the Fed is the deposits of banks and the U.S. Treasury totaling $1,272. The Fed therefore serves as a bank for these banks and the Treasury. Note that these bank deposits include the required reserve deposits discussed at the beginning of the chapter. Finally, total liabilities and net worth equaled total assets of $2,289 billion. Some details of the balance sheet are intentionally omitted.

Recall the Federal Open Market Committee (FOMC) introduced in the previous chapter. The FOMC, as its name implies, determines the money supply through **open market operations**. Open market operations are the buying and selling of government securities by the Federal Reserve System. The New York Federal Reserve Bank's trading desk executes these orders. Suppose the FOMC decides to increase the money supply and instructs the New York Fed trading desk to *buy* $100,000

Open market operations

The buying and selling of government securities by the Federal Reserve System.

Federal Reserve System

Balance Sheet 6
February 24, 2010 (billions of dollars)

Assets		Liabilities	
U.S. government securities	$ 776	Federal Reserve notes	$ 892
Loans to banks	101	Deposits	1,272
Other assets	1,412	Other liabilities and net worth	125
Total assets	$2,289	Total liabilities and net worth	$2,289

SOURCE: Federal Reserve Board, Factors Affecting Reserve Balances, http://www.federalreserve.gov/releases/h41/Current/.

worth of 90-day U.S. Treasury bills (called T-bills).[2] The Fed contacts securities dealers in the private sector for competitive bids. Suppose the Fed accepts the lowest bid, buys $100,000 worth of T-bills, and pays the dealer with a check drawn against itself. As shown in Balance Sheet 7, the Fed's assets increase by $100,000 worth of U.S. government IOUs. Once the securities dealer deposits the Fed's check in the firm's account at Best National Bank, the bank will send the $100,000 check back to the Fed. When the Fed receives the check, it will increase Best National's reserves account at the Fed by this amount. The Fed therefore increases its liabilities by $100,000, and M1 increases immediately by $100,000 because the security dealer's checking account increases at Best National Bank. Like a magician waving a magic wand, the Fed has created new money: The initial $100,000 checkable deposit and excess reserves for loans. Given a 10 percent reserve requirement, Best National Bank's required reserves increase by $10,000, and its excess reserves increase by $90,000. Therefore, the money supply will potentially increase by $1 million (the $100,000 initial increase in M1 when the Fed buys the security multiplied by the money multiplier of 10). Note that unlike the example shown previously in Exhibit 2 involving an initial $100,000 cash deposit already counted in M1, here the initial deposit was created by the Fed and therefore not already counted in M1. Expressed as a formula:

Actual money supply change = initial checkable deposit (*CD*) + (initial change in excess reserves × money multiplier)

$$\Delta M1 = \Delta CD + (\Delta ER \times MM)$$
$$\$1,000,000 = \$100,000 + (\$90,000 \times 10)$$

The process goes into reverse if the FOMC directs the New York Fed trading desk to *sell* U.S. government securities for the Fed's portfolio. As shown in Balance Sheet 8, the goal of the Fed is to decrease the money supply by selling, say, $100,000 in Treasury bonds from the asset side of its balance sheet. In this case, the Fed accepts the best offer from a securities dealer. Again, assume the securities dealer's $100,000 check payable to the Fed is written on the firm's account with Best National Bank. When the Fed accepts the check, it reduces the reserves recorded on the liabilities side

Federal Reserve Bank

Balance Sheet 7		
Assets	**Liabilities**	**Initial change in M1**
U.S. government securities +$100,000	Reserves of Best National Bank +$100,000	+$100,000

NOTE: To increase the money supply, the Fed conducted open market operations by purchasing $100,000 in government securities. The Fed pays a securities dealer with a Fed check, which the dealer deposits in its bank. The initial change in the money supply is an increase of $100,000.

---

2. The U.S. Treasury issues T-bills in minimum denominations of $10,000. These marketable obligations of the federal government mature in three months, six months, or one year and are used to finance the budget deficit, as explained in the chapter on this topic. The Treasury sells three-month bills at weekly auctions and six-month and one-year bills less often.

Federal Reserve Bank

Balance Sheet 8

Assets	Liabilities	Initial change in M1
U.S. government securities −$100,000	Reserves of Best National Bank −$100,000	−$100,000

NOTE: To decrease the money supply, the Fed conducted open market operations by selling $100,000 in government securities. The Fed accepts a securities dealer's check drawn on the dealer's bank. The initial change in the money supply is a decrease of $100,000.

of Balance Sheet 8, and Best National Bank reduces the checkable deposits account of the securities dealer. By subtracting $100,000 from Best National Bank's reserves, the Fed decreases M1 initially by $100,000. Again, the Fed has waved its magic wand and extinguished money in the banking system. Given a 10 percent reserve requirement, the money supply can potentially fall by $1 million (the $100,000 initial decrease in M1 when the Fed sells the security multiplied by the money multiplier of 10).

Another way to study open market operations is to look at a typical day at the trading desk located at the Federal Reserve Bank of New York. The manager of the trading desk starts the day by studying estimates of excess reserves in the banking system. If excess reserves are low, few banks have funds to lend. High excess reserves mean many banks can make loans. After collecting this information and other data, the manager looks at the directive from the FOMC and formulates the day's "game plan." Then the manager makes conference calls to several members of the FOMC for approval. With their blessing, the manager has traders in the trading room call dealers who trade in government securities for price quotations. The open market operation has two alternative objectives: purchase or sell government securities.

> **CONCLUSION** *A purchase of government securities by the Fed injects reserves into the banking system and increases the money supply. A sale of government securities by the Fed reduces reserves in the banking system and decreases the money supply.*

Exhibit 3 illustrates the Federal Reserve's open market operations.

CHECKPOINT

Who Has More Dollar Creation Power?

You find a $1,000 bill hidden beneath the floorboards in your house and decide to deposit it in your checking account. On the same day, the Fed decides to buy $1,000 in government securities from your bank. Assuming a 10 percent reserve requirement, which of these actions creates more money in the economy?

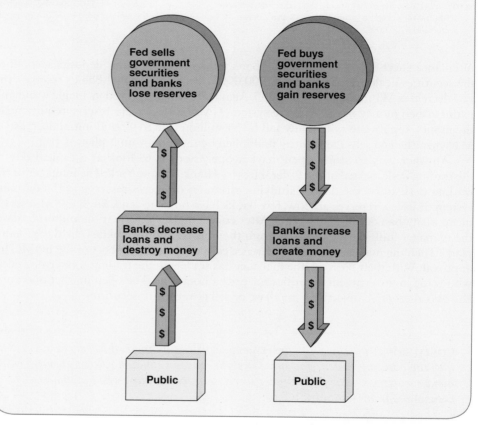

Exhibit 3 | Open Market Operations

When the Fed buys government securities from dealers, it increases the reserves of the banks. Banks can use these reserves to make loans, which operate through the money multiplier to expand the money supply. When the Fed sells government securities to dealers, it decreases the reserves of the banks. Thus, the banks' capacity to lend diminishes, and as a consequence, the money supply decreases.

Fed sells government securities and banks lose reserves

Fed buys government securities and banks gain reserves

Banks decrease loans and destroy money

Banks increase loans and create money

Public

Public

The Discount Rate

So far, money creation in the banking system depends on excess reserves acquired from new checkable deposits. Actually, the Fed itself provides another option for banks to obtain reserves through its *discount window*. This is a department within each of the Federal Reserve district banks and not an actual window. Suppose Best National Bank has no excess reserves and Brad Rich does not walk in with a deposit. Also assume the Fed does not purchase government securities and pay a dealer with a check deposited in Best National Bank. Now enters Connie Jones, who asks for a loan. In this situation, the bank has no money to lend, but it can borrow reserves from the Fed for a short period and pay the **discount rate**. The discount rate is the interest rate the Fed charges on loans of reserves to banks. All banks and other depository

Discount rate

The interest rate the Fed charges on loans of reserves to banks.

institutions have the privilege of occasionally borrowing at the Fed to cover reserve deficiencies. Changes in the discount rate often signal the Fed's monetary policy direction and therefore can affect the public's expectations about the economy. A lower discount rate encourages banks to borrow reserves and make loans.

> **CONCLUSION** *A higher discount rate discourages banks from borrowing reserves and making loans. If the Fed wants to expand the money supply, it reduces the discount rate. If the objective is to contract the money supply, the Fed raises the discount rate.*

Banks wanting to expand their reserves in order to seek profitable loan opportunities can also turn to the federal funds market. The federal funds market is a private market in which banks lend reserves to each other for less than 24 hours. The word *federal* does not mean it is a government market. It simply means this is an economywide or national market. In this market, a bank short of reserves can borrow some reserves from another bank. Using the interbank loan market, Best National Bank can borrow excess reserves from Yazoo National and pay the federal funds rate. The federal funds rate is the interest rate banks charge for overnight loans of reserves to other banks. Reserves borrowed in the federal funds market have no effect on the money supply because such borrowing simply moves reserves from one bank to another. Note that most banks borrow money to meet their reserve requirements primarily through the federal funds market and not the discount window. Also, the federal funds rate is a primary barometer of Fed policy reported in the media. The following You're The Economist provides further explanation of the federal funds rate.

Federal funds market

A private market in which banks lend reserves to each other for less than 24 hours.

Federal funds rate

The interest rate banks charge for overnight loans of reserves to other banks.

The Required Reserve Ratio

Under the Monetary Control Act of 1980, discussed in the preceding chapter, the Fed can set reserve requirements by law for all banks and savings and loan associations. By changing the required reserve ratio, the Fed can change banks' excess reserves and therefore banks' lending ability. This is potentially a powerful policy lever. Recall that the money multiplier equals 1 divided by the required reserve ratio. Suppose the Fed is concerned about inflation, so it wants to restrain the money supply and thereby dampen aggregate demand in the economy. If the Fed increases the required reserve ratio, the effect is to reduce excess reserves and generate a smaller change in the money supply because the money supply multiplier is smaller. For example, a required reserve ratio of 10 percent yields a money multiplier of 10 (1/0.10). If the Fed increases the ratio to 20 percent, the money multiplier falls to 5 (1/0.20).

> **CONCLUSION** *There is an inverse relationship between the size of the required reserve ratio and the money multiplier.*

Raising the required reserve ratio can sharply reduce the lending power of banks. Consider an initial increase in excess reserves of $10 billion in the banking

You're The Economist   How Does the FOMC Really Work?   *Applicable Concept: monetary policy*

The Federal Open Market Committee (FOMC), which is the Fed's most powerful monetary policy making group, meets eight times a year at the Federal Reserve in Washington, D.C. Often it seems that the whole world is watching for the results. Before the meeting, board members are given three books prepared by the Fed staff. The "Green Book" forecasts aggregate demand and various prices based on a variety of equations and the assumptions that monetary policy does or does not change. The "Blue Book" might discuss as many as three monetary policy options, the rationale for each option, and the impact of each option on the economy. There is also a "Beige Book," published eight times per year, that gathers anecdotal information on current economic conditions obtained from interviews with key businesspersons, economists, bankers, and other sources.

The meeting begins at precisely 9:00 a.m. with a discussion of foreign currency operations and domestic open market operations illustrated with colorful graphics. Next, the staff presents their analysis of recent developments and forecasts for the economy laid out in the Green Book. Then each board member around the impressive 27-foot oval mahogany table expresses their views about the analyses, except for the chair, who may choose not to participate in this round. Now, it's coffee time and everyone relaxes beneath a 23-foot ceiling with a 1,000-pound chandelier.

After the coffee break, the staff discusses each policy op-

tion from the Blue Book without recommending a particular option. Generally, three options are presented. Option A is always a decline in interest rates, Option B is always no change in interest rates, and Option C is always an increase. After the staff presentation, board members politely discuss the policy options, but with an important difference. In this policy round, the chair goes first. He leads the discussion and advocates a policy decision. After other board members express

system when the required reserve ratio is 10 percent. The potential value of loans (deposits) is $100 billion ($10 billion of excess reserves × 10). Now assume the Fed raises the required reserve ratio to 20 percent. The potential value of loans (deposits) falls to $50 billion ($10 billion of excess reserves × 5).

> **CONCLUSION** *If the Fed wishes to increase the money supply, it decreases the required reserve ratio. If the objective is to decrease the money supply, the Fed increases the required reserve ratio. In reality, changing the required reserve ratio is considered a heavy-handed approach that is an infrequently used tool of monetary policy.*

Exhibit 4 presents a summary of the impact of monetary policy tools.

The Fed used all three of its monetary policy tools to increase the money supply and battle the 1990–1991 recession. In the fall of 1990, the Fed recognized the economy was slipping into a recession, so it purchased federal government securities to inject new reserves into the banking system. The discount rate was lowered eight their views, the chair summarizes the consensus and reads a draft of the Directive to be voted on. The Directive gives instructions to the Fed's staff on how to conduct open market operations until the next FOMC meeting. For example, the New York Fed's trading desk may be instructed to increase the money supply in the range of 1 to 5 percent and lower interest rates by buying 90-day U.S. Treasury bills. After discussion, board members vote on the Directive, with the chair voting first and the decision going to the majority. The chair is always expected to be on the winning side.

The Directive is sent to the New York Fed's trading desk, and soon about four dozen bond dealers receive the Fed's call. If there is a change in policy, it will be announced at 2:15 that afternoon. To maintain confidentiality, minutes of the meeting will become available the Thursday following the next meeting. A full transcript of the meeting will not be available for five years.

The Fed now communicates its changes in monetary policy by announcing changes in its targets for the federal funds rate. Recall that the Fed does not set this interest rate, but it can influence the rate through open market operations. If the Fed buys bonds, the supply of excess reserves in the banking system increases, and the rate falls. If the Fed sells bonds, the supply of excess reserves in the banking system decreases, and the rate increases. As a result, interest rates in general are influenced. In 2001, the Fed was fighting against a recession. To accomplish this goal, the Fed cut the federal funds rate 11 times, the most since the last recession in 1990–1991. The next chapter explains in more detail the link between changes in the interest rate and changes in other key macro measures. In 2002 and 2003, the Fed again cut the federal funds rate target to support economic recovery. Between 2004 and 2006, the Fed became concerned about inflation and increased the federal funds

rate 17 times. When measuring inflation, the Fed pays closest attention to the *core* CPI—the CPI excluding food and fuel—because it is less volatile than the total CPI inflation rate. In 2007, the Fed changed its focus again because it became concerned that a housing slump and credit crunch would slow the economy, and it cut this key rate for the first time in four years. In 2008, the Fed continued cutting the federal funds rate until it reached a record low of zero to 0.25 percent in 2009.

ANALYZE THE ISSUE

What happened at the last FOMC meeting? Would you like to send the Fed your comments on monetary policy? Visit **http://www.federalreserve.gov/fomc/default.htm**.

Exhibit 4	The Effect of Monetary Policy Tools on the Money Supply		
Type of Monetary Policy	**Monetary Policy Action**	**Mechanism**	**Change in the Money Supply**
Expansionary	Open market operations purchase	Reserves increase	Increases
Contractionary	Open market operations sale	Reserves decrease	Decreases
Expansionary	Discount rate decreases	Borrowing reserves becomes cheaper	Increases
Contractionary	Discount rate increases	Borrowing reserves becomes costlier	Decreases
Expansionary	Required reserve ratio decreases	Money multiplier increases	Increases
Contractionary	Required reserve ratio increases	Money multiplier decreases	Decreases

times between the end of 1990 and early 1992. In early 1992, the reserve require-ment on demand deposits was also lowered from 12 percent to 10 percent. In 2002, the Fed responded to the 2001 recession by using open market purchases of secu-rities to increase the money supply, and it decreased the discount rate numerous times. These responses by the Fed eased the negative effects of the terrorist attacks and the recession.

During the current recession beginning in 2007, the Fed again followed expan-sionary monetary policy and used open market purchases to sharply increase the money supply and decrease interest rates by dropping the federal funds rate to a his-toric low of about zero percent. Moreover, the Fed reduced its reserve requirement and dramatically expanded its scope in response to the loss in confidence among lenders and panic sweeping financial markets that resulted in the flow of credit fall-ing sharply. Using Depression-era emergency powers, the Fed took the radical step of becoming a "lender of last resort" source of short-term loans for a wide range of in-stitutions other than banks. For example, the Fed provided funds to bail out Fannie Mae (the Federal National Mortgage Association) and Freddie Mac (the Federal Home Mortgage Corporation), which backed about half of the nation's mortgage loans, and the Fed provided loans for AIG, the huge insurance firm, because it was simply too large to fail. For more details on monetary policy, read the You're The Economist titled "How Does the FOMC Really Work?"

MONETARY POLICY SHORTCOMINGS

Monetary policy, like fiscal policy, has its limitations. The Fed's control over the money supply is imperfect for the following reasons.

Money Multiplier Inaccuracy

If the Fed is to manage the money supply, it must know the size of the money multi-plier so that it can forecast the increase in the money supply resulting from a change in excess reserves. The value of the money multiplier, however, can be uncertain and subject to decisions independent of the Fed. As explained earlier in the chapter, the public's decision to hold cash and the willingness of banks to make loans affect the total expansion from an initial change in excess reserves. These decisions vary with conditions of prosperity and recession. When the business cycle is in an upturn, banks are very willing to use their excess reserves for making loans, and the money supply expands. During a downturn, bankers are less willing to use their excess re-serves for making loans, and the money supply tends to contract.

Which Money Definition Should the Fed Control?

As discussed in the previous chapter, there are different definitions of the money supply. What if the Fed masterfully controls M1, but the public transfers more of its deposits to M2? For example, banks can pay higher interest and attract more cus-tomers to invest in certificates of deposit. Consequently, the Fed might respond by focusing on M2 instead of M1. In fact, in recent years, the Fed has focused more on M2 than M1 because M2 more closely correlates with changes in GDP.

Lags in Monetary Policy versus Fiscal Policy

Fiscal policy does not happen instantaneously, and neither does monetary policy. Like fiscal policy, monetary policy is subject to time lags. First, an *inside lag* exists between the time a policy change is needed and the time the Fed identifies the problem and decides which policy tool to use. The inside lag is fairly short because financial data are available daily, data on inflation and unemployment monthly, and data on real GDP within three months. Once the Fed has the data, it can quickly decide which policy changes are needed and make appropriate adjustments. The inside lag for monetary policy is shorter than for fiscal policy because fiscal policy is usually the result of a long political budget process.

Second, there is an *outside lag* between the time a policy decision is made and the time the policy change has its effect on the economy. This lag refers to the length of time it takes the money multiplier or spending multiplier to have its full effect on aggregate demand and, in turn, employment, the price level, and real GDP.

Now it's time to answer an important question: Who is the hare and who is the tortoise in the race to the finish line of stabilizing the economy? In the popular version of this story, the hare is much faster, but goofs off along the way and eventually loses to the tortoise at the finish line. In our economics story, however, the Fed is the hare and wins easily over fiscal policy (the tortoise). Although computer model estimates differ widely, the total lag (inside plus outside lags) for monetary policy can be 3 to 12 months. In contrast, the total lag for fiscal policy is not less than a year, and a total lag of three years is quite possible.

Key Concepts

Fractional reserve banking
Required reserves
Required reserve ratio
Excess reserves

Money multiplier
Monetary policy
Open market operations

Discount rate
Federal funds market
Federal funds rate

Summary

- *Fractional reserve banking*, the basis of banking today, originated with the goldsmiths in the Middle Ages. Because depository institutions (banks) are not required to keep all their deposits in vault cash or with the Federal Reserve, banks create money by making loans.
- *Required reserves* are the minimum balance that the Fed requires a bank to hold in vault cash or on deposit with the Fed. The percentage of deposits that must be held as required reserves is called the **required reserve ratio.**
- *Excess reserves* exist when a bank has more reserves than required. Excess reserves allow a bank to create money by exchanging loans for deposits. The money supply is reduced when excess reserves are reduced and loans are repaid.
- The *money multiplier* is used to calculate the maximum change (positive or negative) in checkable deposits (money supply) due to a change in excess reserves. As a formula:

$$\text{Money multiplier} = \frac{1}{\text{required reserve ratio}}$$

The actual change is computed as

> Money multiplier
> × initial change in excess reserves =
> money supply change

- *Monetary policy* is action taken by the Fed to change the money supply. The Fed uses three basic tools: (1) *open market operations*, (2) *changes in the discount rate*, and (3) *changes in the required reserve ratio*.

- *Open market operations* are the buying and selling of government securities by the Fed through its trading desk at the New York Federal Reserve Bank. **Buying government securities** creates extra bank reserves and loans, thereby *expanding* the money supply. **Selling government securities** reduces bank reserves and loans, thereby *contracting* the money supply.

Open Market Operations

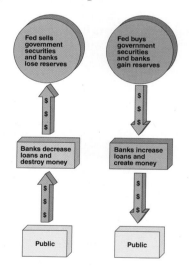

- *Changes in the discount rate* occur when the Fed changes the rate of interest it charges on loans of reserves to banks. Lowering the discount rate makes it easier for banks to borrow reserves from the Fed and expands the money supply. Raising the discount rate discourages banks from borrowing reserves from the Fed and contracts the money supply.

- *Changes in the required reserve ratio* and the size of the money multiplier are *inversely* related. Thus, if the Fed decreases the required reserve ratio, the money multiplier and money supply increase. If the Fed increases the required reserve ratio, the money multiplier and money supply decrease.

- *Monetary policy limitations* include the following: (1) The size or value of the money multiplier can vary. (2) The Fed might control M1, but the public can shift funds to the M2 money supply definition. (3) Time lags occur.

Summary of Conclusion Statements

- Transferring currency to a bank and moving deposits from one bank to another do not affect the money supply (M1).
- When a bank makes a loan, it creates deposits, and the money supply increases by the amount of the loan because the money supply includes checkable deposits.
- When banks decide to retain excess reserves, the money multiplier will be smaller.
- A purchase of government securities by the Fed injects reserves into the banking system and increases the money supply. A sale of government securities by the Fed reduces reserves in the banking system and decreases the money supply.

- A higher discount rate discourages banks from borrowing reserves and making loans. If the Fed wants to expand the money supply, it reduces the discount rate. If the objective is to contract the money supply, the Fed raises the discount rate.
- There is an inverse relationship between the size of the required reserve ratio and the money multiplier.
- If the Fed wishes to increase the money supply, it decreases the required reserve ratio. If the objective is to decrease the money supply, the Fed increases the required reserve ratio. In reality, changing the required reserve ratio is considered a heavy-handed approach, so it is an infrequently used tool of monetary policy.

Study Questions and Problems

1. Relate Shakespeare's admonition "Neither a borrower nor a lender be" to the goldsmiths' evolutionary use of fractional reserve banking.

2. If you deposit a $20 bill into a checking account and your bank has a 10 percent reserve requirement, by how much will the bank's excess reserves rise?

3. Consider this statement: "Banks do not create money because this is the Fed's responsibility." Do you agree or disagree? Explain.

4. In what form does a bank hold its required reserves? Assume the Fed has a 20 percent required reserve ratio. What amount of checkable deposits can be supported by $10 million in required reserves?

5. Suppose you deposit your paycheck drawn on another bank. Explain the impact on the money supply.

6. Suppose you remove $1,000 from under your mattress and deposit it in First National Bank. Using a balance sheet, show the impact of your deposit on the bank's assets and liabilities. If the required reserve ratio is 10 percent, what is the maximum amount the bank can loan from this deposit?

7. Suppose it is the holiday season and you withdraw $1,000 from your account at First National Bank to purchase presents. Using a balance sheet, show the impact on this bank's assets and liabilities. If the required reserve

ratio is 20 percent, what is the impact on the bank's loans?

8. Suppose the Federal Reserve's trading desk buys $500,000 in T-bills from a securities dealer who then deposits the Fed's check in Best National Bank. Use a balance sheet to show the impact on the bank's loans. Consider the money multiplier and assume the required reserve ratio is 10 percent. What is the maximum increase in the money supply that can result from this open market transaction?

9. Assume the required reserve ratio is 10 percent and a bank's excess reserves are $50 million. Explain why checkable deposits resulting from new loans based on excess reserves are not likely to generate the maximum of $500 million.

10. Briefly describe the effect on the money supply of the following monetary policies:
    a. The Fed purchases $20 million worth of U.S. Treasury bonds.
    b. The Fed increases the discount rate.
    c. The Fed decreases the discount rate.
    d. The Fed sells $40 million worth of U.S. T-bills.
    e. The Fed decreases the required reserve ratio.

11. What are some problems faced by the Fed in controlling the money supply?

For Online Exercises, go to the Tucker Web site at www.cengage.com/economics/tucker.

CHECKPOINT ANSWER
Who Has More Dollar Creation Power?

Your action adds $1,000 to your bank's liabilities. Also, assets in the form of required reserves increase by $100 (0.10 × $1,000). This means excess reserves increase by $900, allowing the bank to make this amount of new loans. When the Fed buys $1,000 in government securities, the bank again receives $1,000 in reserves. But the Fed's transaction does not change the bank's liabilities; therefore, the full $1,000 can go into loans. Comparing the effect on the total money supply, the money multiplier effect shows a $9,000 addition to the money supply from your action and a $10,000 addition from the Fed's action. If you said the Fed's action creates more money, **YOU ARE CORRECT.**

Practice Quiz

For an explanation of the correct answers, visit the Tucker Web site at www.cengage.com/economics/tucker.

1. If a bank has total deposits of $100,000 with $10,000 set aside to meet reserve requirements of the Fed, its required reserve ratio is
    a. $10,000.
    b. 10 percent.
    c. 0.1 percent.
    d. 1 percent.

2. Assume a simplified banking system in which all banks are subject to a uniform required reserve ratio of 30 percent and checkable deposits are the only form of money. A bank that receives a new deposit of $10,000 is able to extend new loans up to a maximum of
    a. $3,000.
    b. $7,000.
    c. $10,000.
    d. $30,000.

Practice Quiz Continued

3. The Best National Bank operates with a 10 percent required reserve ratio. One day a depositor withdraws $400 from his or her checking account at the bank. As a result, the bank's excess reserves
a. fall by $400.
b. fall by $360.
c. rise by $40.
d. rise by $400.

4. If an increase of $100 in excess reserves in a simplified banking system can lead to a total expansion in bank deposits of $400, the required reserve ratio must be
a. 40 percent.
b. 400 percent.
c. 25 percent.
d. 4 percent.
e. 2.5 percent.

5. In a simplified banking system in which all banks are subject to a 25 percent required reserve ratio, a $1,000 open market sale by the Fed would cause the money supply to
a. increase by $1,000.
b. decrease by $1,000.
c. decrease by $4,000.
d. increase by $4,000.

6. In a simplified banking system in which all banks are subject to a 20 percent required reserve ratio, a $1,000 open market purchase by the Fed would cause the money supply to
a. increase by $100.
b. decrease by $200.
c. decrease by $5,000.
d. increase by $5,000.

7. The cost to a member bank of borrowing from the Federal Reserve is measured by the
a. reserve requirement.
b. price of securities in the open market.
c. discount rate.
d. yield on government bonds.

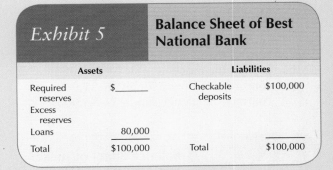

	Balance Sheet of Best National Bank

Exhibit 5

Assets		Liabilities	
Required reserves	$_____	Checkable deposits	$100,000
Excess reserves			
Loans	80,000		
Total	$100,000	Total	$100,000

8. The required reserve ratio in Exhibit 5 is
a. 10 percent.
b. 15 percent.
c. 20 percent.
d. 25 percent.

9. If the bank in Exhibit 5 received $100,000 in new deposits, its addition to required reserves would be
a. $10,000.
b. $20,000.
c. $30,000.
d. $40,000.

10. Suppose Brad Jones deposits $1,000 in the bank shown in Exhibit 5. The result would be
a. a $200 increase in excess reserves.
b. a $200 increase in required reserves.
c. a $1,200 increase in required reserves.
d. zero change in required reserves.

11. If all banks in the system were identical to Best National Bank in Exhibit 5, the money multiplier would be
a. 5.
b. 10.
c. 15.
d. 20.

Practice Quiz Continued

12. Assume all banks in the system are identical to Best National Bank in Exhibit 5. A $1,000 open market sale by the Fed would
    a. expand the money supply by $1,000.
    b. expand the money supply by $15,000.
    c. contract the money supply by $1,000.
    d. contract the money supply by $5,000.

Exhibit 6	Balance Sheet of Tucker National Bank		
Assets		**Liabilities**	
Required reserves	$_____	Checkable deposits	$100,000
Excess reserves	50,000		
Loans	70,000		
Total	$100,000	Total	$100,000

13. The required reserve ratio in Exhibit 6 is
    a. 10 percent.
    b. 15 percent.
    c. 20 percent.
    d. 25 percent.

14. In Exhibit 6, the bank could
    a. extend new loans by $5,000.
    b. extend new loans by $20,000.
    c. call in $5,000 existing loans.
    d. call in $20,000 existing loans.

15. If all banks in the system shown in Exhibit 6 were identical to Tucker National Bank, the money multiplier for the system would be
    a. 4.
    b. 5.
    c. 10.
    d. 25.

Monetary Policy

Vladimir Lenin, the first communist leader of the Soviet Union, once said the best way to destroy a nation is to destroy its money. Adolf Hitler had the same idea. During World War II, he planned to counterfeit British currency and drop it from planes flying over England. Both cases illustrate that the amount of money in circulation matters. A sudden increase in the quantity of money can render a nation's money valueless. As a consequence, people must resort to barter and waste time making direct exchanges of goods and services, rather than being productive.

The previous two chapters provided the prerequisites for understanding the market for money. You have learned two definitions for the money supply, how the banking system creates money, and how the Fed can control the money supply. Here you will begin by studying the demand for and the supply of money and how they interact to determine the rate of interest. Then we add to this story

by linking changes in the money supply to the aggregate demand and aggregate supply model. Using this tool of analysis, you will understand how changes in the demand for money affect interest rates and, in turn, real GDP, employment, and prices.

The first half of this chapter explores how Keynesian economists view the relationship between monetary policy and the economy. The second half of the chapter presents the opposing view of the monetarists. This debate is a clash between two radically different perspectives over the channels through which monetary policy influences the economy. This ideologically charged confrontation is important to the United States' future and is still far from resolved. The chapter concludes with two You're The Economists that allow you to analyze the Keynesian and monetarist views applied to the current financial crisis and the Great Depression.

In this chapter, you will learn to solve these economics puzzles:

- Why do people wish to hold money balances?

- What is a monetary policy transmission mechanism?

- Why would a Nobel laureate economist suggest replacing the Federal Reserve with an intelligent horse?

THE KEYNESIAN VIEW OF THE ROLE OF MONEY

The Demand for Money

Why do people hold (demand) currency and checkable deposits (M1), rather than putting their money to work in stocks, bonds, real estate, or other nonmoney forms of wealth? Because money yields no direct return, people (including businesses) who hold cash or checking account balances incur an *opportunity cost* of forgone interest or profits on the amount of money held. So what are the benefits of holding money? Why would people hold money and thereby forgo earning interest payments? John Maynard Keynes, in his 1936 book *The General Theory of Employment, Interest, and Money*, gave three important motives for doing so: transactions demand, precautionary demand, and speculative demand.

Transactions demand for money

The stock of money people hold to pay everyday predictable expenses.

Transactions Demand for Money The first motive to hold money is the transactions demand. The transactions demand for money is the stock of money people hold to pay everyday predictable expenses. The desire to have "walking around money" to make quick and easy purchases is the principal reason for holding money. Students, for example, have a good idea of how much money they will spend on rent, groceries, utilities, gasoline, and other routine purchases. A business can also predict its payroll, utility bill, supply bills, and other routine expenses. Without enough cash, the public must suffer forgone interest and possibly withdrawal penalties as a result of converting their stocks, bonds, or certificates of deposit into currency or checkable deposits in order to make transactions.

Precautionary demand for money

The stock of money people hold to pay unpredictable expenses.

Precautionary Demand for Money In addition to holding money for ordinary expected purchases, people have a second motive to hold money, called the precautionary demand. The precautionary demand for money is the stock of money people hold to pay unpredictable expenses. This is the "mattress money" people hold to guard against those proverbial rainy days. For example, your car might break down, or your income may drop unexpectedly. Similarly, a business might experience unexpected repair expenses or lower-than-anticipated cash receipts from sales. Because of unforeseen events that could prevent people from paying their bills on time, people hold precautionary balances. This affords the peace of mind that

420

unexpected payments can be made without having to cash in interest-bearing financial assets or to borrow.

Speculative Demand for Money The third motive for holding money is the speculative demand. The **speculative demand for money** is the stock of money people hold to take advantage of expected future changes in the price of bonds, stocks, or other nonmoney financial assets. In addition to the transactions and precautionary motives, individuals and businesses demand "betting money" to speculate, or guess, whether the prices of alternative assets will rise or fall. This desire to take advantage of profit-making opportunities when the prices of nonmoney assets fall is the driving force behind the speculative demand. When the interest rate is high, people buy, say, IBM 30-year bonds because the opportunity cost of holding money is the high forgone interest earned on these nonmoney assets. When the interest rate is low, people hold more money because there is less opportunity cost in forgone interest earned on investing in bonds. Suppose the interest rate on IBM 30-year bonds is low. If so, people decide to hold more of their money in the bank and *speculate* that soon the interest rate will climb higher.

> **CONCLUSION** *As the interest rate falls, the opportunity cost of holding money falls, and people increase their speculative balances.*

The Demand for Money Curve The three motives for holding money combine to create a **demand for money curve**, which represents the quantity of money people hold at different possible interest rates, ceteris paribus. As shown in Exhibit 1, people increase their money balances when interest rates fall. The reason is that many people move their money out of, for example, money market mutual funds and into checkable deposits (M1).

> **CONCLUSION** *There is an inverse relationship between the quantity of money demanded and the interest rate.*

What determines the shape of the demand for money curve? Let's start with the transactions and the precautionary demands for money. These money balances are computed as a given proportion of real GDP. Suppose real GDP is $5,000 billion and people wish to hold, say, 10 percent for transactions and precautionary purposes. This means the first $500 billion read along the horizontal axis in Exhibit 1 are held to make purchases and handle unforeseen events.

Now consider the impact of changes in the interest rate on the speculative demand for money. As the interest rate falls, people add larger speculative balances to their transactions and precautionary balances. For example, when the rate is 8 percent per year, the total quantity of money demanded at point *A* is $1,000 billion, of which $500 billion are speculative balances. If the interest rate is 4 percent, the total quantity of money demanded increases to $1,500 billion at point *B*, of which $1,000 billion are speculative balances. Therefore, the demand for money curve, labeled *MD*, looks much like any other demand curve.

Speculative demand for money

The stock of money people hold to take advantage of expected future changes in the price of bonds, stocks, or other nonmoney financial assets.

Demand for money curve

A curve representing the quantity of money that people hold at different possible interest rates, ceteris paribus.

CONCLUSION *The speculative demand for money at possible interest rates gives the demand for money curve its downward slope.*

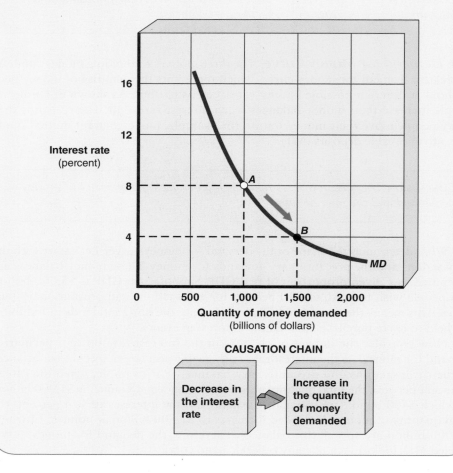

| *Exhibit 1* | **The Demand for Money Curve** |

Assume the level of real GDP is $5,000 billion. Also assume households and businesses demand to hold 10 percent of real GDP ($500 billion) for transactions and precautionary balances. The speculative demand for money varies inversely with the interest rate. At an interest rate of 8 percent, the quantity of money demanded (M1) is $1,000 billion (point *A*), calculated as the sum of transactions and precautionary demand ($500 billion) and speculative demand ($500 billion). At a lower interest rate, a greater total quantity of money is demanded because the opportunity cost of holding money is lower.

Interest rate
(percent)

16

12

8 ---- *A*

4 ---- *B*

MD

0   500   1,000   1,500   2,000

Quantity of money demanded
(billions of dollars)

CAUSATION CHAIN

Decrease in the interest rate ⟹ Increase in the quantity of money demanded

The Equilibrium Interest Rate

We are now ready to form the money market and determine the equilibrium interest rate by putting the demand for money and the supply of money together. In Exhibit 2, the money demand curve (*MD*) is identical to that in Exhibit 1.

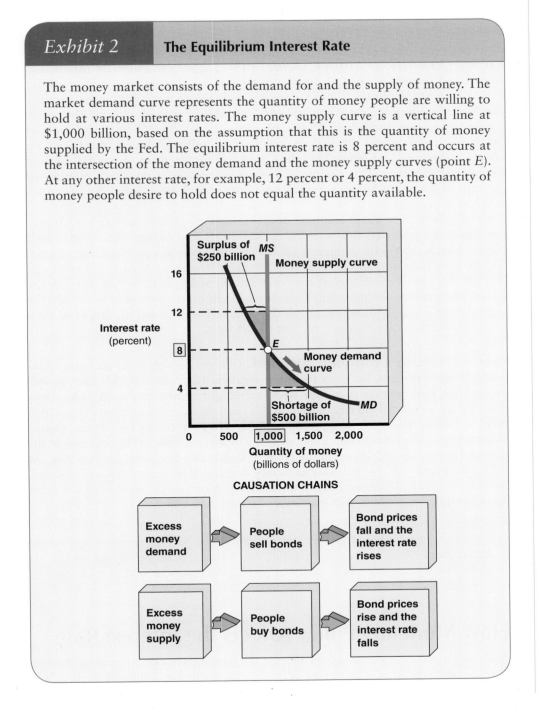

Exhibit 2   **The Equilibrium Interest Rate**

The money market consists of the demand for and the supply of money. The market demand curve represents the quantity of money people are willing to hold at various interest rates. The money supply curve is a vertical line at $1,000 billion, based on the assumption that this is the quantity of money supplied by the Fed. The equilibrium interest rate is 8 percent and occurs at the intersection of the money demand and the money supply curves (point *E*). At any other interest rate, for example, 12 percent or 4 percent, the quantity of money people desire to hold does not equal the quantity available.

The supply of money curve (*MS*) is a vertical line because the $1,000 billion quantity of money supplied does not respond to changes in the interest rate. The reason is that our model assumes the Fed has used its tools to set the money supply at this quantity of money regardless of the interest rate.

At point *E*, the equilibrium interest rate is 8 percent, determined by the intersection of the demand for money curve and the vertical supply of money curve. People wish to hold exactly the amount of money in circulation, and, therefore, there is neither upward nor downward pressure on the interest rate.

Excess Quantity of Money Demanded Suppose the interest rate in Exhibit 2 is 4 percent instead of 8 percent. Such a low opportunity cost of money means that people desire to hold a greater quantity of money than the quantity supplied. To eliminate this shortage of $500 billion, individuals and businesses adjust their asset portfolios. They seek more money by selling their bonds or other nonmoney assets. When many sell or try to sell their bonds, there is an increase in the supply of bonds for sale. Consequently, the price of bonds falls, and the interest rate rises. This rise in the interest rate ceases at the equilibrium interest rate of 8 percent because people are content with their portfolio of money and bonds at point *E*.

Here we need to pause and look at an example to understand what is happening. Suppose Apple pays 4 percent on its $1,000 30-year bonds. This means Apple pays a bondholder $40 in interest each year and promises to repay the original $1,000 price (face amount) at the end of 30 years. However, a holder of these bonds can sell them before maturity at a market-determined price. If bondholders desire to hold more money than is supplied, they will sell more of these bonds. Then the increase in the supply of bonds causes the price of bonds to fall to, say, $500. As a result, the interest rate rises to 8 percent ($40/$500).

Excess Quantity of Money Supplied The story reverses for any rate of interest above 8 percent. Let's say the interest rate is 12 percent. In this case, people are holding more money than they wish. Stated differently, they wish to hold less money than is currently in circulation. In this case, the quantity of money demanded is $250 billion less than the quantity supplied. To correct this imbalance, people will move out of cash and checkable deposits by buying bonds. This increase in the demand for bonds will drive up the price of bonds and lower the interest rate. As the interest rate falls, the quantity of money demanded increases as people become more willing to hold money. Finally, the money market reaches equilibrium at point *E*, and people are content with their mix of money and bonds.

CONCLUSION *There is an inverse relationship between bond prices and the interest rate that enables the money market to achieve equilibrium.*

How Monetary Policy Affects the Interest Rate

Assuming a stationary demand for money, the equilibrium rate of interest changes in response to changes in monetary policy. As we learned in Exhibit 4 of the previous chapter, the Federal Reserve can alter the money supply through open market operations, changes in the required reserve ratio, or changes in the discount rate. In this section, you will see that the Fed's power to change the money supply can also alter the equilibrium rate of interest.

Increasing the Money Supply   Exhibit 3(a) shows how increasing the money supply will cause the equilibrium rate of interest to fall. Our analysis begins at point E_1, with the money supply at $1,000 billion, which is equal to the quantity of money demanded, and with the equilibrium interest rate at 12 percent. Now suppose the Fed increases the money supply to $1,500 billion by buying government securities in the open market. The impact of the Fed's expansionary monetary policy is to create a $500 billion surplus of money at the prevailing 12 percent interest rate.

Exhibit 3	**The Effect of Changes in the Money Supply**

In part (a), the Federal Reserve increases the money supply from $1,000 billion ($MS_1$) to $1,500 billion ($MS_2$). At the initial interest rate of 12 percent (point E_1), there is an excess of $500 billion beyond the amount people wish to hold. They react by buying bonds, and the interest rate falls until it reaches a new lower equilibrium interest rate at 8 percent (point E_2).

The reverse happens in part (b). The Fed decreases the money supply from $1,500 billion ($MS_1$) to $1,000 billion ($MS_2$). Beginning at 8 percent (point E_1), people wish to hold $500 billion more than is available. This shortage disappears when people sell their bonds. As the price of bonds falls, the interest rate rises to the new higher equilibrium interest rate of 12 percent at point E_2.

How will people react to this excess money in their pockets or checking accounts? Money becomes a "hot potato," and people buy bonds. The rush to purchase bonds drives the price of bonds higher and the interest rate lower. As the interest rate falls, people are *willing* to hold larger money balances. Or, stated differently, the quantity of money demanded increases until the new equilibrium at E_2 is reached. At the lower interest rate of 8 percent, the opportunity cost of holding money is also lower, and the imbalance between the money demand and money supply curves disappears.

Decreasing the Money Supply Exhibit 3(b) illustrates how the Fed can put upward pressure on the interest rate with contractionary monetary policy. Beginning at point E_1, the money market is in equilibrium at an interest rate of 8 percent. This time the Fed shrinks the money supply by selling government securities through its trading desk, raising the required reserve ratio, or raising the discount rate. As a result, the money supply decreases from \$1,500 billion to \$1,000 billion. At the initial equilibrium interest rate of 8 percent, this decrease in the money supply causes a shortage of \$500 billion.

Individuals and businesses wish to hold more money than is available. How can the public put more money in their pockets and checking accounts? They can sell their bonds for cash. This selling pressure lowers bond prices, causing the rate of interest to rise. At point E_2, the upward pressure on the interest rate stops. Once the equilibrium interest rate reaches 12 percent, people willingly hold the \$1,000 billion money supply.

CHECKPOINT

What Does the Money Supply Curve Look Like When the Fed Targets the Federal Funds Rate?

Suppose the Fed has a policy of adjusting the money supply to achieve interest rate targets. For example, the Fed might set a 6 percent target federal funds rate. If an increase in the demand for money boosts the federal funds rate above 6 percent, the Fed adjusts the money supply until the 6 percent interest rate is restored. Under such a monetary policy, is the supply of money curve vertical, horizontal, or upward sloping with respect to the federal funds rate?

How Monetary Policy Affects Prices, Output, and Employment

The next step in our journey is to understand how monetary policy alters the macro economy. Here you should pause and study Exhibit 4. This exhibit illustrates the causation chain linking monetary policy and economic performance.

CONCLUSION *In the Keynesian model, changes in the supply of money affect interest rates. In turn, interest rates affect investment spending, aggregate demand, and, finally, real GDP, employment, and prices.*

Exhibit 4	**The Keynesian Monetary Policy Transmission Mechanism**

Keynesians focus on how changes in the money supply affect interest rates and investment spending. In turn, aggregate demand shifts and affects prices, real GDP, and employment.

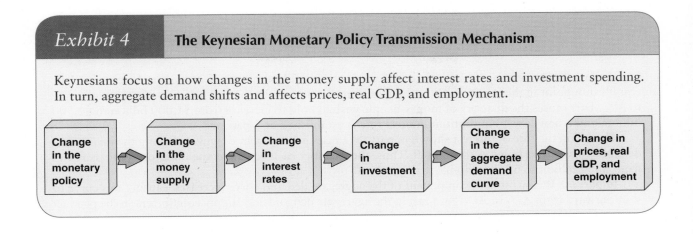

The Impact of Monetary Policy Using the AD-AS Model

How do changes in the rate of interest affect aggregate demand? Begin with Exhibit 5(a), which is identical to Exhibit 3(a) and represents the money market. As explained earlier, we assume that the Fed increases the money supply from $1,000 billion ($MS_1$) to $1,500 billion ($MS_2$) and the equilibrium interest rate falls from 12 percent to 8 percent. In part (b), we can see that the falling rate of interest causes an increase in the quantity of investment spending from $800 billion to $850 billion per year. Stated another way, there is a movement downward along the *investment demand curve* (*I*), which you recall from the chapter on GDP is a component of total spending or aggregate demand. The investment demand curve shows the amount businesses spend for investment goods at different possible interest rates.

The classical economists believed that the interest rate alone determines the level of investment spending. Keynes disputed this idea. Instead, Keynes argued that the expectation of future profits is the primary factor determining investment and the interest rate is the financing cost of any investment proposal. Using a micro example to illustrate the investment decision-making process, suppose a consulting firm plans to purchase a new computer program for $1,000 that will be obsolete in a year. The firm anticipates the new software will increase its revenue by $1,100. Thus, assuming no taxes and other expenses, the expected rate of return or profit is 10 percent.

Now consider the impact of the cost of borrowing funds to finance the software investment. If the interest rate is less than 10 percent, the business will earn a profit, and it will make the investment expenditure to obtain the computer program. On the other hand, a rate of interest higher than 10 percent means the software investment will be a loss, so this purchase will not be made. The expected rate of the profit-interest rate-investment relationship follows this rule: *Businesses will undertake all investment projects for which the expected rate of profit equals or exceeds the interest rate.*

Exhibit 5(c) uses the fiscal policy aggregate demand and aggregate supply analysis developed earlier. Begin at point E_1, with a real GDP per year of $13 trillion and a price level of 210. Now consider the link to the change in the money supply. The increase in investment resulting from the fall in the interest rate works through the *spending multiplier* and shifts the aggregate demand curve rightward from AD_1 to AD_2. At the new equilibrium point, E_2, the level of real GDP rises from $13 trillion to $14 trillion, and full employment is achieved. In addition, the price level

Exhibit 5   The Effect of Expansionary Monetary Policy on Aggregate Demand

In part (a), the money supply is initially MS_1, and the equilibrium rate of interest is 12 percent. The equilibrium point in the money market changes from E_1 to E_2 when the Fed increases the money supply to MS_2. This causes the quantity of money people wish to hold to increase from \$1,000 billion to \$1,500 billion, and a new lower equilibrium interest rate is established at 8 percent.

The fall in the rate of interest shown in part (b) causes a movement downward along the investment demand curve from point A to point B. Thus, the quantity of investment spending per year increases from \$800 billion to \$850 billion.

In part (c), the investment component of the aggregate demand curve increases, causing this curve to shift outward from AD_1 to AD_2. As a result, the aggregate demand and supply equilibrium in the product market changes from E_1 to E_2, and the real GDP gap is eliminated. The price level also changes from 210 to 215.

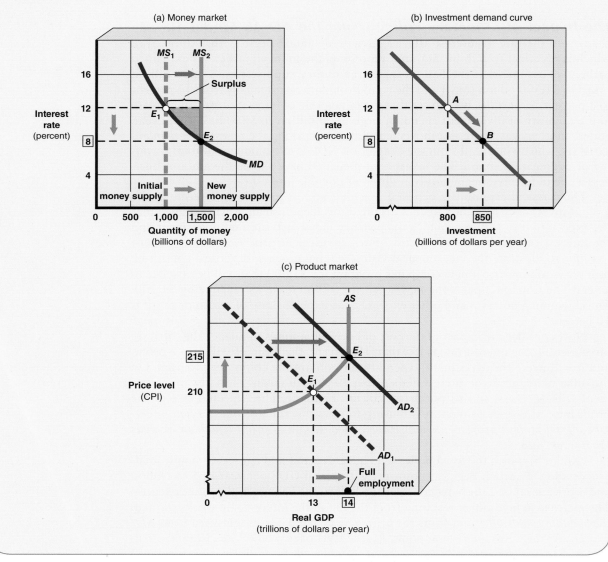

rises from 210 to 215. Exhibit 5(a) also demonstrates the effect of a contractionary monetary policy. In this case, assume the economy is initially at E_2, and the money supply shifts inward from MS_2 to MS_1, causing the equilibrium rate of interest to rise from 8 percent to 12 percent. The Fed's "tight" money policy causes the level of investment spending to fall from $850 billion to $800 billion, which, in turn, decreases the equilibrium level of real GDP per year from $14 trillion to $13 trillion. As a result, the unemployment rate rises, and the inflation rate falls because the price level falls from 215 to 210.

THE MONETARIST VIEW OF THE ROLE OF MONEY

The Monetarist Transmission Mechanism

Monetarists believe Keynesians suffer from the delusion that monetary policy operates only indirectly, causing changes in the interest rate before affecting aggregate demand and then prices, real GDP, and employment. The opposing school of economic thought, called **monetarism**, challenges this view. Monetarism is the theory that changes in the money supply directly determine changes in prices, real GDP, and employment. Exhibit 6 illustrates the monetarist transmission mechanism. Comparison of this figure with Exhibit 4 shows that the monetarist model omits the Keynesian interest rate-investment linkage.

Monetarism

The theory that changes in the money supply directly determine changes in prices, real GDP, and employment.

The Equation of Exchange Monetarists put the spotlight on the money supply. They argue that to predict the condition of the economy, you simply look at the money supply. If it expands too much, higher rates of inflation will be the forecast. If it contracts too much, unemployment lines will lengthen. Monetarism has its intellectual roots in classical economics, introduced in the chapter on aggregate demand and supply. Monetarists proudly wear *laissez faire* on their sleeves and believe the price system is the macro economy's best friend. To understand monetarism,

Exhibit 6	**The Monetarist Monetary Policy Transmission Mechanism**

Monetarists believe that changes in the money supply directly cause changes in the aggregate demand curve and thereby changes in prices, real GDP, and employment.

Equation of exchange

An accounting identity that states the money supply times the velocity of money equals total spending.

Velocity of money

The average number of times per year a dollar of the money supply is spent on final goods and services.

we begin with the **equation of exchange** developed by the classical economists in the nineteenth century. The equation of exchange is an accounting identity that states the money supply times the velocity of money equals total spending. Expressed as a formula, the equation of exchange is written as

$$MV = PQ$$

Let's begin with the left side of the equation ($M \times V$). M is the money supply (more precisely M1) in circulation, and V represents the **velocity of money**. The velocity of money is the average number of times per year a dollar of the money supply is spent on final goods and services. Assume you have one crisp $20 bill and this is the only money in an ultrasimple economy. Suppose you spend this money on a pizza and soda at Zeno's Pizza Hut. Once Mr. Zeno puts your money in his pocket, he decides to buy an economics book and learn how the views of Keynesians and monetarists differ. And so, Mr. Zeno buys the book at the Wise Professor Book Store for exactly $20. At this point, both Mr. Zeno and Ms. Wise have sold $20 worth of goods. Thus, a single $20 bill has financed $40 worth of total spending. And as long as this $20 bill passes from hand to hand during, say, one year, the value of sales will increase. For example, assume the $20 travels from hand to hand 5 times. This means the velocity of money is 5, and the equation of exchange is expressed as

$$\$20 \times 5 = \$100$$

The equation of exchange is an *identity*—true by definition—that expresses the fact that the value of what people spend is equal to, or exchanged for, what they buy. What people buy is nominal GDP, or ($P \times Q$). Recall that nominal, or money, GDP is equal to the average selling price during the year (P) multiplied by the quantity of actual output of final goods and services (Q). In our simple economy, total spending equals $100. Note that the identity between MV and PQ does not say what happens to either P or Q if MV increases. Although we know by how much the total value of output (PQ) increases, we do not know whether the price level (P) or the quantity of output (Q) or both increase.

Consider a more realistic example. Suppose that nominal GDP last year was $5 trillion and M1 was $1 trillion. How many times did each dollar of the money supply have to be spent to generate this level of total spending in the economy? Using the equation of exchange,

$$M \times V = P \times Q$$
$$\$1 \text{ trillion} \times V = \$5 \text{ trillion}$$
$$V = 5$$

Thus, each dollar was spent an average of 5 times per year.

The Quantity Theory of Money

The equation of exchange is converted from an *identity* to a *theory* by making certain assumptions. The classical economists became the forerunners of modern-day monetarists by arguing that the velocity of money (V) and real output (Q) are fairly constant. The classical economists viewed V as constant because people's habits of holding a certain quantity of money, and therefore the number of times a dollar is spent, are slow to change. Recall from the chapter on aggregate demand and supply that classical economists believed in price and wage flexibility. Hence, they believed the economy would automatically adjust to long-run full-employment output (Q).

Because V and Q are constant by assumption, we have one of the oldest theories of inflation, called the **quantity theory of money**. The quantity theory of money states that changes in the money supply are directly related to changes in the price level. Monetary policy based on the quantity theory of money therefore directly affects the price level. To illustrate, we will modify the equation of exchange by putting a bar (–) over V and over Q to indicate they are fixed or constant in value:

$$M \times \bar{V} = P \times \bar{Q}$$

What if the money supply doubles? The price level also doubles. Or, if the Fed cuts the money supply in half, then the price level is also cut in half. Meanwhile, real output of goods and services, Q, remains unchanged.

> **CONCLUSION** *According to the quantity theory of money, any change in the money supply must lead to a proportional change in the price level.*

In short, monetarists say the cause of inflation is "too much money chasing too few goods." The quantity theory of money denies any role for nonmonetary factors, such as supply shocks from a hike in oil prices, which cause cost-push inflation [see Exhibit 11(a) in the chapter on aggregate demand and supply]. Moreover, this theory ignores the impact of fiscal policy changes in taxation and spending on the price level.

What do the data reveal about the link between changes in the money supply and changes in the rate of inflation? Although the relationship does not exist for all years, the evidence supports the general conclusion that sustained levels of higher growth in the money supply correspond to increases in the inflation rate. For example, when the money supply growth rate was low and averaged 1.5 percent between 1953 and 1962, the inflation rate averaged 1.3 percent. During 1973–1982, the money supply grew at a higher average rate of 6.7 percent, and the average inflation rate rose to 8.8 percent. More recently, between 1994 and 2007, the money supply increased at a lower average rate of 1.5 percent, and the average inflation rate dropped to 2.5 percent. In 2009, the money supply grew 15.9 percent. If high growth rates of the money supply are sustained, the concern is that the inflation rate will rise.

Modern Monetarism Today's monetarists have changed the assumptions of the classical quantity theory of money. The evidence indicates that velocity is not constant and the economy does not always operate at full employment. Although M and P are correlated, they do not change proportionally. *Monetarists argue that although velocity is not unchanging, it is nevertheless predictable.* Suppose the predicted velocity of money is 5 and the money supply increases by $100 billion this year. Monetarists would predict that nominal GDP will increase by about $500 billion ($\Delta M \times V$). [The circumflex (^) indicates velocity is predicted.] If the economy is far below full employment, most of the rise in total spending will be in real output. If the economy is near full employment, much of the increase will be in rising prices.

Quantity theory of money

The theory that changes in the money supply are directly related to changes in the price level.

Monetarists refute the Keynesian view that the rate of interest is so important. Instead, the monetarist view is often expressed in the famous single-minded statement that "money does matter." Instead of working through the rate of interest to affect investment and, in turn, the economy, changes in the money supply directly determine economic performance.

> **CONCLUSION** *To avoid inflation and unemployment, the monetarists' prescription is to be sure that the money supply is at the proper level.*

Fixed Money Target Monetarism gained credibility in the late 1950s and 1960s, led by Professor Milton Friedman at the University of Chicago. The monetarists have an answer for how to make sure the economy grows at the right rate: Instead of risking policy errors, forget about the rate of interest and follow a steady, predictable monetary policy. Recall from the chapter on money creation that there are limitations on the Fed's ability to control the money supply because of the independent actions of households, firms, banks, and the U.S. Treasury. Monetarists would stop the Fed from tinkering with the money supply, missing the target, and making the economy worse, rather than better. Instead, they say the money supply should expand at the same rate as the potential growth rate in real GDP. That is, it should increase somewhere between 3 percent and 5 percent per year. The Fed should therefore pick a rate and stick to it, even if unexpected changes in velocity cause short periods of inflation or unemployment. This is called following a *monetary rule*. Monetarists argue that their "straitjacket" approach would reduce the intensity and duration of unemployment and inflation by eliminating the monetarists' public enemy number one—the Fed's discretion to change the money supply. A Keynesian once summarized the fixed money supply approach as "Don't do something, just stand there."

> **CONCLUSION** *Monetarists advocate that the Federal Reserve increase the money supply by a constant percentage each year.*

How Stable Is Velocity? How stable, or predictable, is the velocity of money? This is a critical question in the Keynesian-monetarist debate. Keynesians do not accept the monetarists' argument that over long periods of time velocity is stable and predictable. Hence, a change in the money supply can lead to a much larger or smaller change in GDP than the monetarists would predict. As shown in Exhibit 7, Keynesians are quick to point out the turbulent variations in velocity. Velocity gyrated up and down during the 1980s, early 1990s, and years after 2001. Monetarists counter by pointing to the evidence that during the periods of 1960–1981 and 1993–2000 velocity generally rose along a quite predictable or steady annual rate and trend line.

Keynesians focus on short-run variations in *V* that accompany any long-run velocity growth rate. They therefore argue that following a monetary rule is folly. Suppose the money supply increases at a constant rate, but velocity is greater than

| Exhibit 7 | **The Velocity of Money, 1960–2009** |

The velocity of money (*V*) equals GDP divided by the supply of money (M1). Keynesians argue that velocity is not stable. During the 1980s, early 1990s, and years after 2001, velocity became quite unpredictable. Monetarists believe velocity is stable over the long term and point to the periods of 1960–1981 and 1993–2000. During these years, velocity rose along a predictable annual rate trend line.

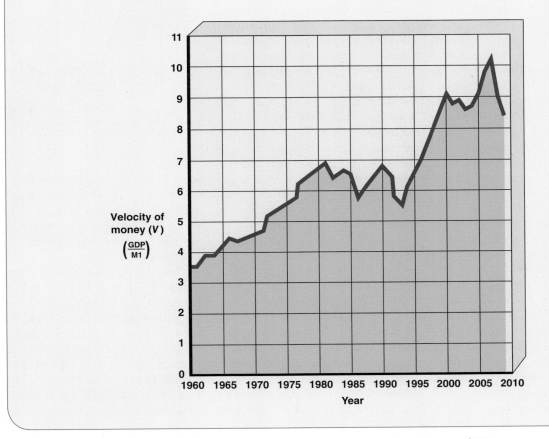

SOURCE: Economic Report of the President, 1980 and 2010, http://www.gpoaccess.gov/eop/, Tables B-52, B-1, and B-69.

expected. This means that total spending (aggregate demand) will be greater than predicted, causing inflation. Lower-than-predicted velocity results in unemployment because total spending is less-than-expected, which causes the economy to expand too little. The Keynesians believe that the Federal Reserve must be free to change the money supply to offset unexpected changes in velocity. Monetarists counter that the Fed *cannot* predict short-run variations in *V*, so its "quick-fix" changes in the money supply will often be wrong. This is why monetarists advocate that the Fed follow a monetary rule. Keynesians are willing to accept occasional policy errors and reject this idea in favor of maintaining Fed flexibility to change the money supply in order to affect interest rates, aggregate demand, and the economy.

You're The Economist   America's Housing Market Bubble
Busts   *Applicable Concept: monetarism*

The story of the worst collapse of the housing market and the most serious financial crisis since the Great Depression is filled with villains and no action hero to sweep down from the sky and save the day. It is an Alice in Wonderland story with plenty of blame to go around: homeowners who bought a Trojan horse, rampant speculation, predatory lenders, slick Wall Street operators, greedy CEOs, lax regulators, and debatable Fed policy. Perhaps a phrase by Alan Greenspan, former Fed chairman, called "The Maestro," best described the bust of the housing market bubble when he said, "How do we know when irrational exuberance has unduly escalated asset values?"

The stage was set for the housing crisis by the Fed's response to the recession of 2001. The annual change in the money supply jumped sharply upward from −3.1 percent in 2000 to an 8.7 percent increase in 2001.[1] And, as shown in the above exhibit, the Fed decreased interest rates sharply after 2001 and kept them historically low in order to boost aggregate demand and prevent another recession. Then in 2004, Greenspan addressed the Credit Union Association and said, "American consumers might benefit if lenders provided greater mortgage product alternatives to the traditional fixed rate mortgage." And as if following the Fed chairman's advice, adjustable rate mortgages (ARMs) became the loan of choice for subprime borrowers who have poor or less than ideal credit scores. Mailboxes were stuffed with offers to borrow 100 percent or more of a home's value with zero down. Television shows advertised the idea that anyone could make it rich in real estate, and housing became a speculative game. Payments and "teaser" interest rates were held artificially low for the first few years of the loan and then they would jump sharply upward. Forget worrying about not affording the home, your income would not be checked following a "no document" lending practice. In fact, some loans

were made to people who were no longer living. Thus, using risky ARMs, banks lent billions of dollars to home buyers who could not pay the bank when the payments and interest rates rose.

Faced with accumulating portfolios of risky debt, banks and mortgage companies sold these risky mortgages to New York investment firms such as Bear Stearns (acquired by JP Morgan Chase with financial backing from the Fed) and Merrill Lynch, who pooled them with other securities. These packages, often called collateralized debt

SOURCE: FRB Federal Open Market Committee, http://www.federalreserve.gov/fomc/fundsrate.htm.

---

1. Economic Report of the President 2010, http://www.gpoaccess.gov/eop/, Table B-69.

CheckPoint
A Horse of Which Color?

A famous economist once proposed replacing the Fed with an intelligent horse. Each New Year's Day, the horse would stand in front of Fed headquarters to answer monetary policy questions. Reporters would ask, "What is going to happen to the money supply this year?" The horse would tap its hoof four times, and the next day headlines would read "Fed to Once Again Increase the Money Supply 4 Percent." Is this famous economist a Keynesian or a monetarist?

obligations or CDOs, were sold to customers around the world—a process called "securitization." And this securitization occurred with the blessing of ratings agencies such as Standard & Poor's who actually did not know how to evaluate the risk of these securities. With each of these transactions, large fees were collected, and in short, consummation of the deal was the criterion and not validity of the assessment of risk.

Expansion of the housing market bubble was based on an assumption by all the players that the party would never end and real estate prices would always go up. However, beginning in the summer of 2005, subprime foreclosures rose and home prices dropped as people's payments rose under their ARMs. Also, once the value of homes fell below the loan value, people could not refinance loans to get lower payments. When people walked away from their mortgages, Wall Street and foreign investors were stuck with bad loans in their CDOs to write off, CEOs were fired, and many real estate executives were indicted for mortgage fraud. As a result, lenders greatly tightened their lending standards to avoid further risky

loans, and a credit crunch made home financing difficult to obtain.

In 2008, the Fed announced that it would allow Wall Street investment firms to receive emergency loans and exchange risky investments for Treasury securities. Also, the Housing and Economic Recovery Act of 2008 was passed that allowed some borrowers to refinance their mortgages with new fixed-rate loans backed by a federal guarantee, and it provided grants for state and local governments in the hardest-hit communities to buy foreclosed property. It also included a tax credit for first-time home buyers who buy housing that is unoccupied. And the Treasury Department was given authority to bail out or take over Fannie Mae and Freddie Mac, the troubled government-created firms that fund the vast majority of mortgage loans in the United States.

In addition, a massive $700 billion bailout plan was enacted in 2008 that gave the Treasury the authority under TARP (Troubled Assets Recovery Program) to buy and resell bad mortgage debt from financial institutions. But TARP changed its original purpose because it was very difficult to determine the price that the government

should pay for the risky assets. Consequently, TARP changed its plan and spent over half of its funds to invest government capital into banks by buying preferred stock with a 5 percent rate of return, which is the equivalent of a loan to the bank. Also, the federal government decided to take partial ownership in private U.S. banks until they regain stability and increase lending. Participating banks must curtail executive bonuses and other perks. Moreover, Congress has promised the biggest changes in regulation of financial companies since the 1930s. Meanwhile, the final price tag to the taxpayers for this financial crisis is unknowable.

ANALYZE THE ISSUE

In support of the Fed's monetary policy prior to the deflation of the home prices bubble, one can argue that the reality is that increasing the money supply and low-interest rates were required to sustain expansion. Based on the Monetarist school of thought, criticize the Fed's policy.

A COMPARISON OF MACROECONOMIC VIEWS

By now, your head is probably spinning with dueling schools of economic thought. The debate among the classicals, Keynesians, and monetarists can be quite confusing. This chapter has presented differences in monetary policy between these schools. To refresh your memory and complete the discussion, this section presents a brief review of key differences in fiscal policy introduced in earlier chapters. Exhibit 8 gives a thumbnail summary of the key differences between the three camps. Note the similarity between the classical and the monetarist schools.

Subprime mortgage loan

A home loan made to borrowers with an above-average risk of default.

435

Exhibit 8	**Comparison of Macroeconomic Theories**		
Issue	**Classical**	**Keynesian**	**Monetarist**
	Adam Smith	**John Maynard Keynes**	**Milton Friedman**
Stability of economy	Stable in long run at full employment	Inherently unstable at less than full employment	Stable in long run at full employment
Price-wage flexibility	Yes	No	Yes
Velocity of money	Stable	Unstable	Predictable
Cause of inflation	Excess money supply	Excess aggregate demand	Excess money supply
Causes of unemployment	Short-run price and wage adjustment	Inadequate aggregate demand	Short-run price and wage adjustment
Effect of monetary policy	Changes aggregate demand and prices	Changes interest rate, which changes investment and real GDP	Changes aggregate demand and prices
Effect of fiscal policy	Not necessary	Spending multiplier changes aggregate demand	No effect because of crowding-out effect

Classical Economics

As discussed in the chapter on aggregate demand and supply, the dominant school of economic thought before the Great Depression was classical economics. The basic theory of the classical economists, introduced by Adam Smith in *The Wealth of Nations* and followed by the eighteenth and nineteenth-century economists, was that a market-directed economy will automatically correct itself to full employment. Consequently, there is no need for fiscal policy designed to restore full employment.

Recall that a key assumption of classical theory is that, given time to adjust, prices and wages will decrease to ensure the economy operates at full employment. A decrease in the aggregate demand curve causes a temporary surplus, which, in turn, causes businesses to cut prices, and, in turn, causes more goods to be purchased because of the real balances effect. As a result, wages adjust downward, and employment rises. Classical economists therefore view the economy as operating in the long run along a vertical aggregate supply curve originating at the full-employment real GDP.

Keynesian Economics

The Great Depression challenged the classical prescription to wait until markets adjust and full employment is automatically restored. As the unemployment rate rose to 24.9 percent in 1933, people asked how long it would take for the market mechanism to adjust. John Maynard Keynes responded with his famous saying, "In the long run we are all dead." Keynes, in his book *The General Theory*, attacked classical theory and in the process revolutionized macroeconomic thought.

As explained in the chapter on fiscal policy, using fiscal policy to affect aggregate demand is a cornerstone of Keynesian economics. While Keynesians believe monetary policy is often not very powerful, especially during a downturn, they regard fiscal policy as their "top banana." However, Keynesians recognize that one of the potential problems of fiscal policy is the *crowding-out effect*. As shown earlier in Exhibit 9 of the chapter on federal deficits and the national debt, financing a federal deficit by borrowing competes with private borrowers for funds. Given a fixed money supply, the extra demand from the federal government to finance its deficit causes the interest rate to rise. As a result, businesses cut back on investment spending and offset the expected increase in aggregate demand. The Keynesian view, however, is that the investment demand curve is not very sensitive to changes in the interest rate, and therefore only a relatively small amount of investment spending will be crowded out. Thus, the decline in investment only slightly counteracts or offsets an increase in aggregate demand created by a deficit.

> **CONCLUSION** *Keynesians view the shape of the investment demand curve as rather steep or vertical, so the crowding-out effect is insignificant.*

Monetarism

Monetarists are iconoclasts because they attack the belief in the ability of either the Fed or the federal government to stabilize the economy. They argue that fiscal policy is an essentially useless tool that has little or no impact on output or employment because of a total crowding-out effect. Suppose the money supply remains fixed and the federal government borrows to finance its deficit. The intended goal is to increase aggregate demand and restore full employment. According to the monetarists, financing the deficit will drive up the interest rate and crowd out a substantial, not a small, amount of investment spending. The reason is that the monetarists view the investment demand curve as sensitive to changes in the interest rate; therefore, greater amounts of investment spending will be crowded out. As a result, the net effect is no increase in aggregate demand and no reduction in unemployment.

> **CONCLUSION** *Monetarists view the shape of the investment demand curve as less steep or relatively flat, so the crowding-out effect is significant.*

You're The Economist Monetary Policy during the
Great Depression *Applicable Concept: Keynesians versus monetarists*

Monetarists and Keynesians still debate the causes of the Great Depression. Monetarists Milton Friedman and Anna Schwartz, in their book *A Monetary History of the United States*, argued that the Great Depression was caused by the decline in the money supply, as shown in Exhibit 9(a).

During the 1920s, the money supply expanded steadily, and prices were generally stable. In response to the great stock market crash of 1929, bank failures, falling real GDP, and rising unemployment, the Fed changed its monetary policy. Through the Great Depression years from 1929 to 1933, M1 declined by 27 percent. Assuming velocity is relatively constant, how will a sharp reduction in the quantity of money in circulation affect the economy? Monetarists predict a reduction in prices, output, and employment. Between 1929 and 1933, the price level declined by 24 percent. In addition to deflation, real GDP was 27 percent lower in 1933 than in 1929. Unemployment rose

from 3.2 percent in 1929 to 24.9 percent in 1933. Friedman and Schwartz argued that the ineptness of the Fed's monetary policy during the Great Depression caused the trough in the business cycle to be more severe and sustained.

The Great Depression was indeed not the Fed's finest hour. What should the Fed have done? Friedman and Schwartz argued that the Fed should have used open market operations to increase the money supply. Thus, they concluded that the Fed was to blame for not pursuing an expansionary policy, which would have reduced the severity and duration of the contraction. As shown in part (b), this was not the case for the Great Recession of 2007. From the beginning, the Fed followed an expansionary policy and sharply increased the money supply.

Finally, although the emphasis here is monetary policy, parts (c) and (d) contrast fiscal policy during the two periods using the federal deficit as a percentage of GDP. During the Great Depression, there was a slight budget surplus

until 1931 when the budget turned into a slight budget deficit before reaching a deficit of 5.9 percent of GDP in 1934. In contrast, fiscal policy was more expansionary by running deficits from the beginning of the recession in 2007 to an estimated 10.6 percent of GDP in 2010.

ANALYZE THE ISSUE

1. Explain why monetarists believe the Fed should have expanded the money supply during the Great Depression.
2. The Keynesians challenge the Friedman-Schwartz monetarists' monetary policy cure for the Great Depression. Use the *AD-AS* model to explain the Keynesian view. (Hint: Your answer must include the investment demand curve.)

SOURCE: Milton Friedman and Anna J. Schwartz, *A Monetary History of the United States, 1867–1960* (Princeton, N.J.: Princeton University Press, 1963).

Although the monetarists do not trust the Federal Reserve to use discretionary monetary policy, they are quick to point out that only money is important. Changes in the money supply, the basic lever of monetary policy, have a powerful impact. Instead of ineffectual government deficit spending to cure unemployment, an increase in the money supply would definitely stimulate the economy based on the quantity theory of money. In short, changes in the money supply directly result in changes in real GDP.

Exhibit 9 | **The Great Depression Economic Data, 1929–1934, Compared to the Great Recession of 2007**

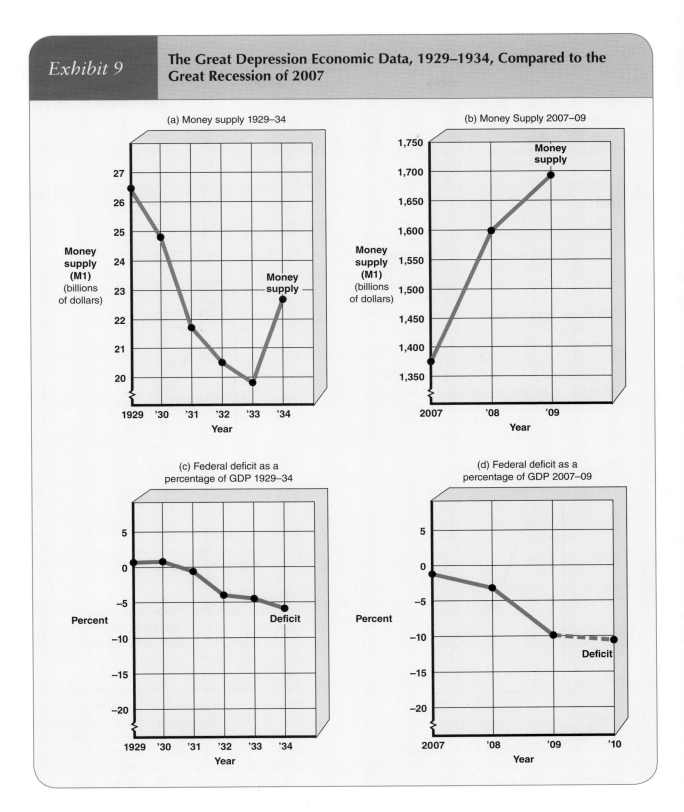

(a) Money supply 1929–34

(b) Money Supply 2007–09

(c) Federal deficit as a percentage of GDP 1929–34

(d) Federal deficit as a percentage of GDP 2007–09

Key Concepts

Transactions demand for money
Precautionary demand for money
Speculative demand for money
Demand for money curve

Monetarism
Equation of exchange
Velocity of money
Quantity theory of money

Adjustable rate
    mortgage (ARM)
Subprime mortgage
    loan

Summary

- The *demand for money* in the Keynesian view consists of three reasons why people hold money: (1) *Transactions demand* is money held to pay for everyday predictable expenses. (2) *Precautionary demand* is money held to pay unpredictable expenses. (3) *Speculative demand* is money held to take advantage of price changes in nonmoney assets.
- The *demand for money curve* shows the quantity of money people wish to hold at various rates of interest. As the interest rate rises, the quantity of money demanded is less than when the interest rate is lower.

Demand for Money Curve

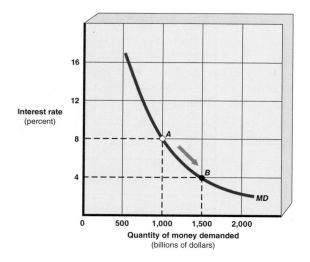

- The *equilibrium interest rate* is determined in the money market by the intersection of the demand for money and the supply of money curves. The money supply (M1), which is determined by the Fed, is represented by a vertical line.

The Equilibrium Interest Rate

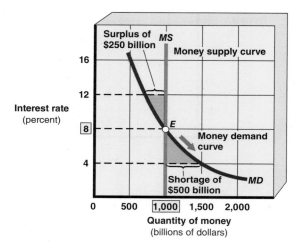

- An *excess quantity of money demanded* causes households and businesses to increase their money balances by selling bonds. This causes the price of bonds to fall, thus driving up the interest rate.
- An *excess quantity of money supplied* causes households and businesses to reduce their money balances by purchasing bonds. The effect is to cause the price of bonds to rise, and, thereby, the rate of interest falls.
- The *Keynesian view of the monetary policy transmission mechanism* operates as follows: First, the Fed uses its policy tools to change the money supply. Second, changes in the money supply change the equilibrium interest rate, which affects investment spending. Finally, a change in investment changes aggregate demand and determines the level of prices, real GDP, and employment.

- *Monetarism* is the simpler view that changes in monetary policy directly change aggregate demand, and thereby prices, real GDP, and employment. Thus, monetarists focus on the money supply, rather than on the rate of interest.
- The *equation of exchange* is an accounting identity that is the foundation of monetarism. The equation ($MV = PQ$) states that the money supply multiplied by the *velocity of money* is equal to the price level multiplied by real output. The velocity of money is the number of times each dollar is spent during a year. Keynesians view velocity as volatile, but monetarists disagree.
- The *quantity theory of money* is a monetarist argument that the velocity of money (V) and the output (Q) variables in the equation of exchange are relatively constant. Given this assumption, changes in the money supply yield proportional changes in the price level. The monetarist solution to inept Fed tinkering with the money supply that causes inflation or recession is to have the Fed simply pick a rate of growth in the money supply that is consistent with real GDP growth and stick to it.
- *Keynesians' and monetarists' views on fiscal policy* are also different. Keynesians believe the investment demand curve is relatively vertical, and monetarists view it as relatively flat. Monetarists assert that the *crowding-out effect* is large and, therefore, fiscal policy is ineffective. Keynesians argue that the crowding-out effect is small and that fiscal policy is effective.

Summary of Conclusion Statements

- As the interest rate falls, the opportunity cost of holding money falls, and people increase their speculative balances.
- There is an inverse relationship between the quantity of money demanded and the interest rate.
- The speculative demand for money at possible interest rates gives the demand for money curve its downward slope.
- There is an inverse relationship between bond prices and the interest rate that enables the money market to achieve equilibrium.
- In the Keynesian model, changes in the supply of money affect interest rates. In turn, interest rates affect investment spending, aggregate demand, and, finally, real GDP, employment, and prices.

- According to the quantity theory of money, any change in the money supply must lead to a proportional change in the price level.
- To avoid inflation and unemployment, the monetarists' prescription is to be sure that the money supply is at the proper level.
- Monetarists advocate that the Federal Reserve increase the money supply by a constant percentage each year.
- Keynesians view the shape of the investment demand curve as rather steep or vertical, so the crowding-out effect is insignificant.
- Monetarists view the shape of the investment demand curve as less steep or relatively flat, so the crowding-out effect is significant.

Study Questions and Problems

1. How much money do you keep in cash or checkable deposits on a typical day? Under the following conditions, would you increase or decrease your demand for money? Also identify whether the condition affects your transactions demand, precautionary demand, or speculative demand.
   a. Your salary doubles.
   b. The rate of interest on bonds and other assets falls.

appendix to chapter

16 Policy Disputes Using the Self-Correcting Aggregate Demand and Supply Model

In the appendix to the chapter on aggregate demand and supply, the classical self-correcting aggregate demand and supply model was explained without disagreement. Expansionary and contractionary fiscal policy was discussed in the chapter on fiscal policy, and this chapter explained monetary policy. In this appendix, we combine these topics and examine contrasting fiscal and monetary policies using the self-correcting model.

THE CLASSICAL VERSUS KEYNESIAN VIEWS OF EXPANSIONARY POLICY

The Keynesian activist approach rejects classical nonintervention policy to stabilize the economy using discretionary fiscal policy or activist monetary policy. Exhibit A-1 illustrates opposing theories for restoring an economy in recession to full employment. In both parts (a) and (b), the economy starts with a real GDP of $8 trillion and a price level of 150 at macro equilibrium E_1. Since full-employment real GDP is $12 trillion, the recessionary gap equals $4 trillion. In part (a), the economy closes the gap through the self-correction process. The key classical assumption is that nominal wages are flexible and fall as a result of competition among unemployed workers for jobs. Over time, the result is that the short-term aggregate supply curve ($SRAS_1$) shifts rightward to $SRAS_2$ and the economy automatically adjusts to long-run macro full-employment equilibrium at E_2 with a price level of 100.

Part (b) illustrates the opposing Keynesian theory. This view argues that nominal wages are fixed in the short run. In contrast to the self-correction model, Keynesians advocate using discretionary fiscal policy in which the federal government manages the aggregate demand curve (AD) by increasing government spending or cutting taxes. Both of these policy options work through the multiplier process and increase AD_1 to AD_2. The result is that the economy achieves full employment at macro equilibrium point E_2 where the price level is 200.

Activist monetary policy can also stabilize the economy. The Federal Reserve can increase the money supply, which lowers the interest rate, and in response,

446

Exhibit A-1 — Opposing Anti-Recession Theories

Part (a) illustrates classical theory, which advocates noninterventionist fiscal and monetary policy. The classical assumption is that nominal wages are flexible. At point E_1, unemployed workers compete for jobs, and the wage rate falls causing the short-run aggregate supply curve to shift from $SRAS_1$ to $SRAS_2$. Full employment is therefore automatically restored at point E_2.

In part (b), Keynesian policy advocates interventionist fiscal and monetary policy. Discretionary fiscal policy increases government spending or cuts taxes to increase the aggregate demand curve from AD_1 to AD_2. Discretionary monetary policy would increase the money supply to increase AD_1 to AD_2.

business investment spending increases. As a result, AD_1 shifts to AD_2 in part (b) of Exhibit A-1, and full employment is restored at E_2.

Note that both approaches in parts (a) and (b) restore full-employment real GDP; however, the impact on the price level is quite different. If classical theory is correct, the price level falls from 150 to 100. In contrast, if Keynesian theory is correct, the price level rises from 150 to 200, resulting in a higher inflation rate.

CONCLUSION *The classical approach to a recession is to let market forces shift the short-run aggregate supply curve rightward and restore the economy to full employment. The opposing Keynesian approach to cure a recession is to use discretionary fiscal and monetary policy to increase aggregate demand and achieve full-employment real GDP.*

CLASSICAL VERSUS KEYNESIAN VIEWS OF CONTRACTIONARY POLICY

Exhibit A-2 shows alternative theories for closing an inflationary gap. The classical nonintervention policy relies on competition between firms in response to a shortage of labor. In parts (a) and (b), the economy is at macro equilibrium at point E_1 where the price level is 150 and real GDP is $16 trillion. There is an inflationary gap of $4 trillion greater than the potential real GDP of $12 trillion. In part (a), classical theory assumes flexible wages, so nominal wages rise, causing the $SRAS_1$ to shift upward to $SRAS_2$, and the economy reaches full-employment real GDP at point E_2 with a price level of 200.

In part (b), Keynesian contractionary policy aims at decreasing AD_1 to AD_2 using cuts in government spending or tax hikes. Working through the multiplier process, the inflationary gap is eliminated, and the economy moves from point E_1 to E_2 where the price level falls from 150 to 100 and full-employment real GDP of $12 trillion is achieved.

Exhibit A-2	Opposing Anti-Inflation Theories

In part (a), the classical assumption is that at point E_1 firms face a labor shortage and their competition for available workers drives up the nominal wage rate. Under a noninterventionist policy, the short-run aggregate supply curve shifts leftward from $SRAS_1$ to $SRAS_2$, and the economy is automatically restored to full employment at E_2.

Part (b) shows the effect of Keynesian contractionary policy. Discretionary fiscal policy decreases government spending or increases taxes to shift the aggregate demand curve leftward from AD_1 to AD_2. Discretionary monetary policy would decrease the money supply to decrease AD_1 to AD_2.

Monetary policy can also be used to shift the aggregate demand curve leftward. In this case, the Federal Reserve could follow a contractionary policy and decrease the money supply, resulting in a higher interest rate, and firms respond by decreasing their investment spending. Consequently, AD_1 decreases to AD_2, and full-employment real GDP is reached at E_2.

As shown in the previous exhibit, opposing theories have different impacts on the price level. In part (a) of Exhibit A-2, the classical approach leads to an increase in the price level from 150 to 200. In contrast, the Keynesian approach yields a decrease in the price level from 150 to 100.

CONCLUSION *The classical approach to an inflationary gap is to let market forces shift the short-run aggregate supply curve leftward and restore the economy to full employment. The opposing Keynesian approach to cure inflation uses discretionary fiscal and monetary policy to decrease aggregate demand and achieve full-employment real GDP.*

Summary

- The *Keynesian prescription for a recession* rejects the classical assumption that wages are flexible and will fall, causing the short-run aggregate supply curve to shift downward and restore full-employment GDP. Instead, Keynesians support expansionary fiscal and monetary policy to increase aggregate demand and return the economy to the natural rate of unemployment.

- The *Keynesian cure for inflation* also rejects the classical assumption that wages are flexible and will rise, causing the short-run aggregate supply curve to shift upward and restore full-employment GDP. In contrast, Keynesian theory advocates contractionary fiscal and monetary policy to decrease aggregate demand and achieve full-employment macro equilibrium.

Summary of Conclusion Statements

- The classical approach to a recession is to let market forces shift the short-run aggregate supply curve rightward and restore the economy to full employment. The opposing Keynesian approach to cure a recession is to use discretionary fiscal and monetary policy to increase aggregate demand and achieve full-employment real GDP.

- The classical approach to an inflationary gap is to let market forces shift the short-run aggregate supply curve leftward and restore the economy to full employment. The opposing Keynesian approach to cure inflation uses discretionary fiscal and monetary policy to decrease aggregate demand and achieve full-employment real GDP.

Practice Quiz

For an explanation of the correct answers, visit the Tucker Web site at www.cengage.com/economics/tucker.

1. Assume the economy is experiencing a recessionary gap. Classical economists would support which of the following policies?
   a. Contractionary
   b. Expansionary
   c. Noninterventionist
   d. Fixed wage

2. Assume the economy is in short-run equilibrium at a real GDP below its potential real GDP. According to classical self-correction theory, which of the following policies should be followed?
   a. The Federal Reserve should increase the money supply.
   b. The federal government should increase spending.

   c. The federal government should cut taxes.
   d. None of the above.

3. Assuming the economy is in a recession, classical economists predict that
   a. wages will remain fixed.
   b. monetary policy will sell government securities.
   c. higher wages will shift the short-run aggregate supply curve leftward.
   d. lower wages will shift the short-run aggregate supply curve rightward.

4. Assume the economy is operating at a real GDP below full-employment real GDP. Keynesian economists would prescribe which of the following policies?
   a. Noninterventionist
   b. Fixed rule

Practice Quiz Continued

c. Contractionary
d. Expansionary

5. Assume the economy is in short-run equilibrium at a real GDP above its potential real GDP. According to Keynesian theory, which of the following policies should be followed?
    a. The Federal Reserve should use open market operations and buy U.S. government securities.
    b. The Federal Reserve should follow a fixed rule.
    c. The federal government should cut taxes.
    d. Fiscal policy and monetary policy should be contractionary.

6. Assume the economy is experiencing an inflationary gap. Keynesian economists would believe that
    a. wages will remain inflexible.
    b. the federal government should decrease spending to shift the aggregate demand curve leftward.
    c. the Federal Reserve should lower the interest rate.
    d. the federal government should increase spending to shift the aggregate demand curve rightward.

The Phillips Curve and Expectations Theory

This chapter explores the Phillips curve, expectations theory, and incomes policies (wage and price controls). The Phillips curve traces the relationship between two of the greatest problems of economies everywhere—inflation and unemployment. One of the most fascinating puzzles in economics is whether a stable tradeoff exists between these two economic evils. If true, policymakers face a dilemma described by the old saying "Inside each solution there is another problem looking to work its way out." If policymakers reduce the unemployment rate, the inflation rate worsens. Or, if they reduce the inflation rate, the unemployment rate rises. In the 1960s, most economists and policymakers thought the way to achieve a particular inflation-unemployment point on the Phillips curve menu was to use Keynesian demand-management policies.

Just as the reality of the Great Depression refuted classical theory, the Great Stagflations of the 1970s and early 1980s challenged the Phillips curve and Keynesian policies. To explain how varying rates of inflation can occur at the same rate of unemployment, we explore two competing ways of thinking called *adaptive expectations* and *rational expectations*. Both of these theories are attacks on the Keynesians who urge the government to interfere with the market economy in order to achieve full employment.

The chapter begins with a discussion of the Phillips curve and why both expectations camps believe there is no permanent inflation-unemployment tradeoff. In the last part of this chapter, you will see what happens when policymakers fight inflation using policies to control wages and prices (incomes), rather than monetary and fiscal policies.

In this chapter, you will learn to solve these economics puzzles:

- Why might expansionary fiscal and monetary policies be useless in the long run?

- If the Fed is independent, why would the money supply increase before a presidential election?

- Can economic theory explain pop quizzes?

- Can wearing a button reduce inflation?

THE PHILLIPS CURVE

In a celebrated article published in 1958, Australian economist A. W. Phillips of the London School of Economics plotted data on unemployment rates and the rate of change in wage rates between 1861 and 1957 in the United Kingdom.[1] Phillips showed there was a remarkably stable inverse relationship between changes in money wages and the unemployment rate. Economists have since extended this concept to the following definition of the Phillips curve. The Phillips curve is a curve showing an inverse relationship between the inflation rate and the unemployment rate. The reason it is acceptable to use the inflation rate, rather than the change in wages, is that wages are the main component of prices. At low rates of unemployment, labor has the market power to push up wages and, in turn, prices. When many workers are pounding the pavement eager for jobs, labor lacks bargaining power to ask for raises. As a result, the upward pressure on prices eases.

Phillips curve

A curve showing an inverse relationship between the inflation rate and the unemployment rate.

The Phillips Curve in Theory

Exhibit 1 shows the relationship between the *AD-AS* model developed earlier and the Phillips curve. In part (a), we assume that the aggregate supply curve, *AS*, is stationary. Thus, points *A–D* represent possible equilibrium points depending on the location of the aggregate demand curve. As the aggregate demand curve increases from AD_1 to AD_4, real GDP rises from $6.0 trillion to $6.6 trillion, more workers are employed, and the price level (CPI) rises from 100 to 112. The astute reader will recognize from the chapter on aggregate demand and supply that we are discussing *demand-pull inflation*.

The inverse relationship between the price level and unemployment in part (a) determines the shape of the Phillips curve in part (b). Points *A–D* in both figures correspond. If the economy operates at point *A*, the annual rate of inflation is zero, and the unemployment rate is 8 percent. If the economy is at point *B*, the annual rate of inflation is 4 percent, and the unemployment rate is 5 percent. Similarly, points *C* and *D* correspond in both graphs. Note that below point *A*, the price level is below 100 and the economy experiences deflation.

1. A. W. Phillips, "The Relation between Unemployment and the Rate of Change in Money Wage Rates in the United Kingdom, 1861–1957," *Economica* 25 (November 1958): pp 283–299.

Exhibit 1	**The Theoretical Relationship between Changes in Aggregate Demand and the Phillips Curve**

In part (a), the aggregate demand curve shifts upward, while the aggregate supply curve remains stationary. The result is a series of equilibrium points *A–D*. As aggregate demand rises along the *AS* curve, the price level (CPI), real GDP, and employment increase. Points *A–D* in parts (a) and (b) correspond. An increase in aggregate demand from AD_1 to AD_4 causes the unemployment rate to fall, but the inflation rate rises. Thus, the increase in aggregate demand results in a movement upward along the Phillips curve.

CONCLUSION *Changes in aggregate demand cause a movement along a stationary Phillips curve.*

The Phillips Curve in Practice

So far so good. If the world works this way, policymakers must choose from a menu of inflation rate and unemployment rate combinations along the Phillips curve. Do we want *X* percent less unemployment with an opportunity cost of *Y* percent more inflation? Early studies verified the Phillips curve for the U.S. economy in the 1960s. As shown in Exhibit 2, the data fit the Phillips curve very well. Based on this evidence, most economists, including Nobel laureates Paul Samuelson and Robert Solow of MIT, believed the Phillips curve was stable. Policymakers might choose low inflation and high unemployment, as in 1961. Or they may prefer higher inflation and lower unemployment, as, for example, in 1969. And the most popular way in the 1960s to

Exhibit 2	The Phillips Curve for the United States in the 1960s

The figure plots the inflation rate and unemployment rate combinations for the period 1960–1969. A freehand curve drawn through the points conforms very well to the Phillips curve.

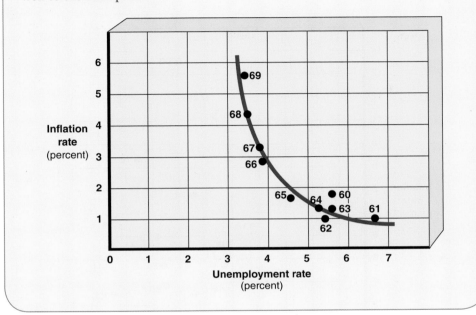

SOURCE: Economic Report of the President, 2010, http://www.gpoaccess.gov/eop/, Tables B-35 and B-64.

reach a particular point on the Phillips curve was to "fine tune" the economy using Keynesian demand-management policies.

Then, just as policymakers and economists became comfortable with the Phillips curve, the dream turned into a nightmare. As shown in Exhibit 3, the points for 1970–1990 show the Phillips curve in chaos. The pattern disappeared, and many points moved far above and to the right of the 1960s data. At higher unemployment rates, the corresponding inflation rate was much higher than the Phillips curve predicted. For example, look at the years 1975, 1979, 1980, and 1981. These data reflect bouts with stagflation, which occurred in the 1970s and early 1980s. Recall from Exhibit 12(a) in the chapter on aggregate demand and supply that *cost-push inflation* is the result of a leftward shift of the aggregate supply curve. In the Great Stagflations of 1973–1974 and 1979–1980, the influence of such "supply shocks" as soaring oil prices pushed up production costs and shifted the economy's aggregate supply curve inward. Thus, the Phillips curve theory was in shambles as the nation simultaneously experienced both high inflation and high unemployment. Policymakers therefore turned their focus from the Phillips curve, based on tradeoffs, to a "misery index," which added the inflation and unemployment rates.

| Exhibit 3 | Inflation and Unemployment Rates for the United States, 1970–1990 |

By 1990, the Phillips curve became unstable. Clearly, many points have been established upward and to the right. The inflation rate therefore can be much higher at any unemployment rate than the Phillips curve of the 1960s predicted.

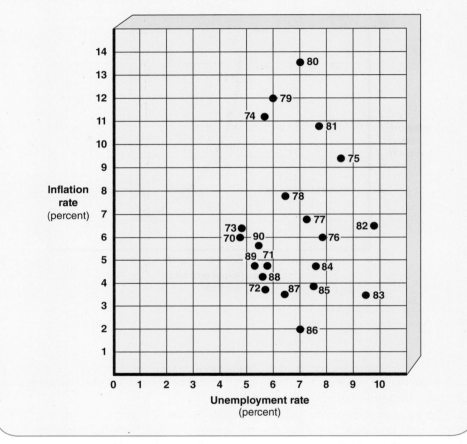

SOURCE: Economic Report of the President, 2010, http://www.gpoaccess.gov/eop/, Tables B-35 and B-64.

THE LONG-RUN PHILLIPS CURVE

The simple idea of a stable tradeoff between unemployment and inflation was an overnight sensation in the 1960s. By the early 1970s, the Phillips curve was becoming a "has-been." Since Keynesian demand-management policies generate the curve, it will come as no surprise that monetarists such as Milton Friedman and Edmund S. Phelps always believed the Phillips curve was just a transitory, short-run relationship. In the mid-1960s, they suggested that the unemployment rate and the rate of inflation are unrelated in the long run. As shown in Exhibit 4, the challengers argued that after a few years the Phillips curve is a vertical line. As explained below, this monetarist view is also debatable.

Exhibit 4 — The Short-Run and Long-Run Phillips Curves

Beginning at point A, the economy is operating at the 6 percent natural rate of unemployment. The actual and anticipated inflation rates are 3 percent. An increase in aggregate demand temporarily causes the inflation rate to rise to 6 percent. Under adaptive expectations theory, real wages fall, profits rise, and more workers are employed. The unemployment rate falls to 4 percent, and the economy moves along the short-run Phillips curve PC_1 to point B. Over time, workers demand and get nominal wage rate hikes, and profits fall. Workers lose their jobs, and the unemployment rate returns to 6 percent at point C on the short-run Phillips curve PC_2. This process will repeat each time expansionary policy attempts to reduce unemployment below the natural rate. The long-run Phillips curve is therefore a vertical line at the natural rate of unemployment. This suggests that Keynesian expansionary policies create only inflation over time.

Under rational expectations theory, workers do not rely only on recent experience. They adjust their nominal wages quickly in proportion to changes in prices. Expansionary policy will move the economy directly upward along the long-run Phillips curve.

CAUSATION CHAINS

Short-run adaptive expectations theory

Aggregate demand increases → Inflation rate rises, real wages fall, and profits rise → Unemployment rate falls

Long-run adaptive expectations theory

Inflation rate is constant at higher rate, workers' nominal wage rate rises, and profits fall → Unemployment rate is restored to full employment

Rational expectations theory

Aggregate demand increases → Inflation rate rises and nominal wages adjust quickly to equal inflation rate → Inflation rate rises on vertical line at full employment

Natural Rate Hypothesis

If the Phillips curve is vertical in the long run, there are profound implications for macroeconomic policy. Expansionary monetary and fiscal policies can at best produce a short-lived lowering of unemployment. This is the so-called **natural rate hypothesis**. The natural rate hypothesis argues that the economy will self-correct to the natural rate of unemployment. The long-run Phillips curve is therefore a vertical line at the natural rate of unemployment. Recall from the chapter on business cycles and unemployment that the natural rate of unemployment, or the full-employment unemployment rate, is equal to the sum of the frictional and structural unemployment rates. In Exhibit 4, the natural rate of unemployment is 6 percent. Two versions of expectations theory explain the natural rate model. We begin our analysis using *adaptive expectations theory* and then turn to the more recent *rational expectations theory*.

Natural rate hypothesis

The hypothesis that argues the economy will self-correct to the natural rate of unemployment. The long-run Phillips curve is therefore a vertical line at the natural rate of unemployment.

Adaptive Expectations Theory

To explain the reasoning behind the natural rate hypothesis, let us begin in Exhibit 4 with the economy operating at point *A*, with a 3 percent inflation rate and a 6 percent unemployment rate. Assume the inflation rate has been 3 percent in recent years and this trend is expected to continue. Based on this recent 3 percent rise in the CPI, collective bargaining agreements call for hourly nominal or money wages of $10.00 this year and $10.30 next year. Now suppose an election is approaching and the president and Congress strive to make voters happy by reducing the unemployment rate to 4 percent. Or perhaps policymakers incorrectly believe 4 percent is the natural rate of unemployment. Regardless of the reason for setting this goal, suppose the new expansionary fiscal policy shifts the aggregate demand curve upward along the aggregate supply curve and the economy moves unexpectedly from point *A* this year to point *B* the next year.

Keynesians declare "mission accomplished" when the economy moves up the short-run Phillips curve PC_1 from point *A* to point *B*. This unexpected change brings good news to businesses. Based on an expected inflation rate of 3 percent, employers agreed to pay real wages of $10.00 at point *B*. However, if the inflation rate rises unexpectedly to 6 percent, real wages fall to $9.72 as prices rise.[2] With cheaper labor costs in real terms, profits increase, more workers are hired, real GDP expands, and the unemployment rate drops to 4 percent.

So far, Keynesians and monetarists agree that policymakers and businesses are running the race like the hare and the workers are acting like the tortoise. But monetarists do not believe workers are caught flat-footed as time passes. Workers soon realize that higher prices have eroded their purchasing power. Consequently, they demand an extra 3 percent raise in the nominal wage rate so that their real wages can be restored to the level prior to the unexpected rise in the inflation rate from 3 to 6 percent. When workers get their raise to offset the higher cost-of-living, business profits decline, and some workers are laid off until the unemployment rate returns to 6 percent at point *C*. At point *C*, the unemployment rate is right back where it began before the government unsystematically changed its fiscal policy, but

---

2. Assume the price level at point *A* is 100 and the price level rises to 106 at point *B*. The real wage is computed as the nominal wage multiplied by the initial price level divided by the new price level. Thus, the real wage rate at point *B* is equal to $10.30 × (100/106) = $9.72. If the price level had risen to 103, as expected, the real wage at point *B* would equal $10.30 × (100/103) = $10.00.

the inflation rate has risen from 3 to 6 percent. Keynesians, on the other hand, believe nominal wages are fixed because workers do not demand and get an extra 3 percent rise in nominal wages. In the Keynesian view, demand stimulus reduced unemployment in exchange for the higher inflation rate, and the economy remains at point *B* and does not automatically move in time to point *C*.

Our story describes a *wage-price spiral,* defined in the chapter on inflation, and we need a theory to explain how people form their inflationary expectations. The reason the economy moved from point *A* to point *B* is based on **adaptive expectations theory**. Adaptive expectations theory is the concept that people believe the best indicator of the future is recent information. As a result, people persistently underestimate inflation when it is accelerating and overestimate it while it is slowing down. Adaptive expectations theory assumes ignorance of future events, including changes in fiscal and monetary policies. People learn from recent experience and gradually adjust their anticipated inflation rate to the actual inflation rate. This means that at point *C* workers expect a higher rate of inflation at any unemployment rate because last year the actual rate of inflation was 6 percent. Unions therefore expect a 6 percent rate of inflation and are no longer satisfied with a contract with less than a 6 percent increase in the nominal wage rate, since anything less would mean a cut in real wages. Thus, workers *adapt* their expectations to 6 percent instead of 3 percent, and the short-run Phillips curve shifts outward from PC_1 to PC_2 in Exhibit 4. In other words, the economy moves from point *A* to point *C* on the vertical long-run Phillips curve. If policymakers follow a contractionary policy, adaptive expectations operate in reverse, and the inflation rate declines (see You're The Economist: The Political Business Cycle).

Suppose policymakers figure expansionary policy worked last time, so why not try it again? So they take another stab at creating jobs by stimulating aggregate demand. This time the economy will ride up the new short-run Phillips curve PC_2 from point *C* to point *D*, and the whole process will repeat. When the actual inflation rate rises from 6 to 9 percent, nominal wage increases will be a step slow in catching up with price hikes. In time, workers will demand and get a nominal wage hike, which restores their real wage rate, and the economy will reach point *E*. Faced with the new short-run Phillips curve PC_3, the government will cause an inflation rate of 12 percent at point *F* if it persists in trying to achieve 4 percent unemployment. Eventually, nominal wages will rise (reducing profits), some workers will lose their jobs, and the economy will move from point *F* to point *G*.

> **Adaptive expectations theory**
>
> The concept that people believe the best indicator of the future is recent information. As a result, people persistently underestimate inflation when it is accelerating and overestimate it while it is slowing down.

CONCLUSION *According to adaptive expectations theory, expansionary monetary and fiscal policies to reduce the unemployment rate are useless in the long run. After a short-run reduction in unemployment, the economy will self-correct to the natural rate of unemployment, but at a higher inflation rate. Thus, there is no long-run tradeoff between inflation and unemployment.*

The Long-Run Phillips Curve and the Labor Market

We can now give one explanation for the tendency of the inflation-unemployment points shown earlier in Exhibit 3 to shift upward to the right in the 1970s and early 1980s. Demand stimulus policies in the 1960s caught people by surprise, and there

You're The Economist The Political Business Cycle

Applicable Concept: adaptive expectations

The basic ideal of Keynesian economics is that the government uses monetary and fiscal policies to stabilize the economy. On the other hand, the government may be diabolical and deliberately cause business cycles. The **political business cycle** is therefore Keynesianism in reverse. A political business cycle is a business cycle caused by policymakers to improve politicians' reelection chances.

A basic assumption of the political business cycle model is that democratic government causes business cycles. This theory views politics as by nature a short-run game. The rational self-interest goal of politicians is to maximize votes today and worry about tomorrow when tomorrow comes. This means a politician who faces an election must act now and not later. Voters are also short-sighted and want good news now, rather than promises of long-term solutions. If people want jobs, for example, the politicians who seek reelection will use expansionary policies to create jobs. The political process will therefore gladly force a lower unemployment rate now in exchange for a higher inflation rate in the future. The politician who

commits the sin of truth and tells the voters a "quick fix" is harmful will probably taste defeat.

Given the realities of politics, politicians may find it easier to let the Fed stimulate the economy. Expansionary fiscal policy requires Congress to approve tax cuts or spending increases. Since members of Congress belong to opposing parties, each side has an incentive to prevent the other party from taking credit for legislation. Even if a bill eventually passes, it may be too late for the election. Fiscal policy takes considerable time to implement and actually affect the economy and, in turn, the voters.

If the Fed is independent, why would the Fed be willing to create political business cycles? Recall that the president appoints the Fed chair and members of the Board of Governors. Thus, the Fed is a semiseparate branch of government and often wishes to avoid conflict with Congress or the president. If the Fed is willing to stimulate aggregate demand before an election, incumbent politicians will benefit at the expense of their opponents. Once the election is over, the Fed will slow down the economy to reduce the inflation rate.

Then the concern becomes recession until the next election looms and the Fed stimulates the economy again. Meanwhile, politicians can blame the Fed for driving up prices or starting the downturn.

Exhibit 5 reveals that the money supply has generally been on the rise before presidential elections. In 1964, 1968, 1972, 1976, 1980 (slight), 1988, 1992, and 2008 the money supply rose before the presidential election and then fell after the presidential election. The 1984, 1996, 2000, and 2004 elections were exceptions.

ANALYZE THE ISSUE

Based on adaptive expectations theory, assume an expansionary monetary policy has moved the economy to point C in Exhibit 4. Now suppose the election is over and inflation concerns policymakers, so the Fed applies the brakes to monetary policy. Use this diagram to explain the short-run and long-run effects of a contractionary monetary policy.

Political business cycle

A business cycle caused by policymakers to improve politicians' reelection chances.

was a movement upward along a short-run Phillips curve. As inflation worsened during the 1970s and the early 1980s, adaptive expectations caused the short-run Phillips curves to shift outward. As the inflation rate dropped sharply during the late 1980s, people's inflationary expectations adapted in the downward direction, and the short-run Phillips curve shifted inward. Moreover, as discussed in the chapter on business cycles and unemployment, economists estimated that the *natural rate of unemployment* increased from the 1960s to the 1980s. Recall that the natural rate

| *Exhibit 5* | **Money Supply Growth and Presidential Elections, 1960–2008** |

Since 1960, the money supply has often increased prior to presidential elections. The 1984, 1996, 2000, and 2004 elections were exceptions.

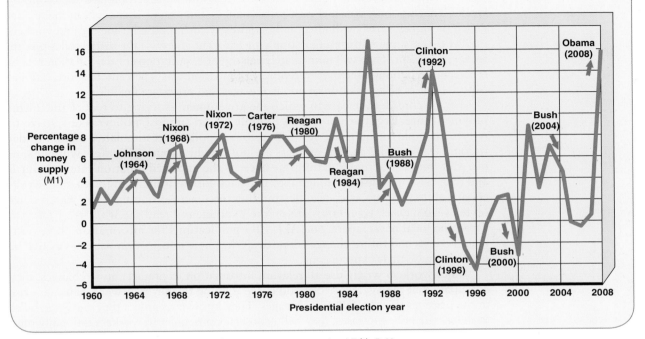

SOURCES: Economic Report of the President, 2010, http://www.gpoaccess.gov/eop/, Table B-69.

of unemployment is the full-employment unemployment rate at which the economy operates at capacity (potential GDP). This means the vertical long-run Phillips curve intersecting each short-run Phillips curve shifted to the right. The explanation, in part, is because women and teenagers became a larger percentage of the labor force, and these groups of workers often experience higher rates of unemployment. It is also argued that the following measures might reduce the natural rate of unemployment: revising unemployment compensation, changing the minimum wage law, providing better education and training, improving information on available jobs, removing discrimination, and reducing the monopoly power of unions and businesses.

THE THEORY OF RATIONAL EXPECTATIONS

Whether expectations are formed "adaptively" or "rationally" is a hotly contested debate among economists. In the mid-1970s, Robert Lucas of the University of Chicago (1995 Nobel Laureate) is generally credited with introducing the **theory of rational expectations**, which is the competing view that adaptive expectations theory is too simplistic. Rational expectations theory is the belief that people use all available

Rational expectations theory

The belief that people use all available information to predict the future, including the future impact of predictable expansionary monetary and fiscal policies. Predictable expansionary macroeconomic policies can therefore be negated by immediately flexible wages and prices when businesses and workers anticipate the effects of these policies on the economy.

information to predict the future, including future monetary and fiscal policies. Hands-on discretionary macroeconomic policies intended to stabilize the economy can therefore be negated when businesses and workers anticipate the effects of these policies on the economy. According to the rational expectations hypothesis, people do not simply think inflation will be about the same next year as last year. Although everyone's crystal ball is clouded, people are intelligent and informed on how the economy works. They not only consider past price changes, but also how changes in the federal deficit or money supply will affect inflation next year. Suppose businesses and workers predict that a surge in the money supply or a tax cut will raise the actual inflation rate to, say, 6 percent. They will immediately raise their expectations of the inflation rate to 6 percent even though the most recent rate of inflation was 3 percent. In short, rational expectationists believe that both nominal wages and prices are flexible.

Let's reconsider the case in which the government is trying to reduce the unemployment rate. Begin at point *A* in Exhibit 4, and suppose policymakers strive to reduce unemployment, using new expansionary policies to stimulate demand. Under rational expectations theory, workers are not caught napping. Workers will not simply wait until the actual inflation rate exceeds the expected inflation rate at point *B* and then ask for a raise. Although they may lack formal training in forecasting, workers are quite sophisticated in understanding the macro economy. They watch news on television, check economic data on the Internet, and read the *Wall Street Journal*, *Time*, the local newspapers, and AFL-CIO publications for information on government policies and future changes in prices. When new information becomes available, workers revise their expectations.

Since workers wisely use all relevant information to predict future changes, they anticipate that the aggregate demand curve is going to shift rightward, causing a rise in the price level and a fall in real wages. They know that unless they get wage hikes to match the price increases, they will be losers. Consequently, workers rationally raise their nominal wage demands without a time lag so that no gap between the actual and expected rates of inflation occurs. In fact, many collective bargaining agreements contain escalator clauses, providing automatic nominal wage increases as the price level rises. Assuming that workers correctly anticipate the inflation rate, real wages remain unchanged because nominal wages and prices rise proportionately. This means the temporary increase in profits, real GDP, and employment does *not* happen as predicted by adaptive expectationists. In short, rational expectationists refute the short-run Phillips curves drawn in Exhibit 4. There would be, for example, no decrease in unemployment from 6 percent (point *A*) to 4 percent (point *B*). Instead, the only movement in the inflation rate is directly from 3 percent (point *A*) to 6 percent (point *C*). This means higher anticipated inflation is added without delay to current nominal wages and prices, which generates a vertical Phillips curve along such points as *A, C, E,* and *G*.

> **CONCLUSION** *According to rational expectations theory, expansionary monetary and fiscal policies used to reduce unemployment are not only useless, but also harmful because the only result is higher inflation.*

On the brighter side, rational expectations theory argues that a credible "stay the course" contractionary fiscal and monetary policy can quickly cool inflation without increasing unemployment. Suppose the economy is at the natural rate of unemployment and the Fed decreases the money supply to lower the rate of inflation. Workers analyze available information on the future impact of the Fed's action from AFL-CIO economists and other sources. They are convinced that policymakers are committed to decreasing aggregate demand until the price level recedes. Armed with this analysis, workers are not surprised, and they reduce their nominal wages as prices fall. In this case, there is no short-run Phillips curve. Contrary to adaptive expectations, inflation can be cured without recession, since workers are not caught off-guard.

Keynesians reject rational expectations theory because they argue that prices and wages are "sticky" downward (see Exhibit 4 of the chapter on aggregate demand and supply). On the other hand, the classical economists believed that the economy automatically adjusts after short-run delays to full employment in the long run. But in the rational expectations model, not so! There is no short run. Nevertheless, because the theory of rational expectations is similar to the self-correction model of the classical economists, rational expectationists are called *new classical* economists.

> **CONCLUSION** *According to rational expectations theory, flexible wages and prices adjust immediately to negated predictable monetary and fiscal policy changes, so the economy's self-correction mechanism will restore the natural rate of unemployment. Therefore, discretionary policies should be abandoned and fixed-rule, stable policies to achieve constant money supply growth and a balanced federal budget are therefore the best way to lower the inflation rate.*

CHECKPOINT

Does Rational Expectations Theory Work in the Classroom?

An economics professor is considering improving class attendance and preparation by giving pop quizzes. Two approaches are being considered: (1) If rational expectations theory operates in the classroom, should the professor give pop quizzes on days when homework is due or (2) keep it a secret and give pop quizzes randomly?

APPLYING THE *AD–AS* MODEL TO THE GREAT EXPECTATIONS DEBATE

The distinction between adaptive expectations and rational expectations can be analyzed using the aggregate demand-aggregate supply model presented in Exhibit 6. Assume the economy is currently in equilibrium at point E_1, with a full-employment output of $6 trillion. Now suppose the Fed pursues an expansionary monetary policy designed to create jobs and further reduce unemployment. Hence, the aggregate demand curve shifts rightward from AD_1 to AD_2 along the short-run aggregate supply curve $SRAS_1$. Based on adaptive expectations theory, a monetarist urges the Fed to leave the economy alone. The monetarist's prediction is that the economy will move from equilibrium at E_1 to E_2, causing real GDP to rise from the potential GDP of $6 trillion to the GDP of $6.5 trillion. Recall from Exhibit 9 of the chapter on

Exhibit 6 **Adaptive Expectations versus Rational Expectations**

Suppose policymakers use expansionary policies to increase the aggregate demand curve from AD_1 to AD_2. Adaptive expectations theory argues that labor adjusts nominal wages sluggishly. As a result, the path of the economy is E_1 to E_2 to E_3 with a temporary increase in real GDP to $6.5 trillion and lower unemployment at point E_2. The theory of rational expectations is the competing view that the expansionary policy used to increase the aggregate demand curve from AD_1 to AD_2 is anticipated. Workers anticipate that the price level (CPI) will rise to 110, so they increase their nominal wages without a period of adjustment. As a result, the aggregate supply curve shifts from $SRAS_1$ to $SRAS_2$, causing the economy to move directly from equilibrium point E_1 to point E_3. The result of Keynesian expansionary policies under both theories is that inflation becomes worse and there is no effect on real GDP or employment.

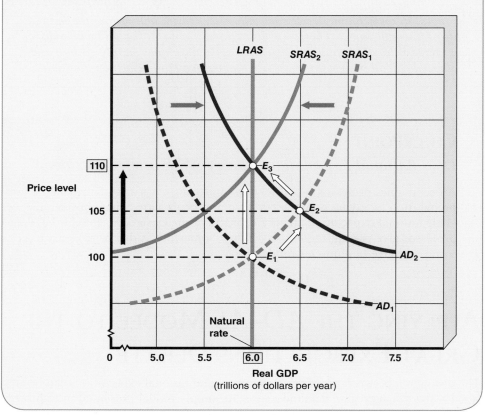

business cycles and unemployment that this condition in the economy is a positive GDP gap of $0.5 trillion. In addition, the price level (CPI) increases from 100 to 105. Eventually, at equilibrium E_2, with unemployment below the natural rate, workers are no longer "caught off-guard" and demand higher nominal wages to offset the rise in prices. As a result, production costs rise, causing the short-run aggregate supply curve to shift leftward from $SRAS_1$ to $SRAS_2$; and, therefore, a new equilibrium is established at E_3. This response drives up the unemployment rate to the natural rate as real output returns to the initial level of $6 trillion. However, Fed activism has not had a neutral effect on the price level because it has risen from the initial level of 100 to 110. The monetarist's prediction is therefore higher inflation and no impact on employment and real GDP in the long run.

A rational expectationist sees events differently. Most people are not "fooled." They are able to rationally predict the consequences of expansionary monetary policies. People anticipate that the economy will move from point E_1 to point E_3, the price level will rise from 100 to 110, and real GDP will not change. Consequently, businesses and workers do not stumble around in the dark, unable to see what the actual inflation rate is going to be. They know, or *anticipate*, that the inflation rate is going to rise 10 percent, and they react immediately by raising prices and wages 10 percent. Since prices and wages increase quickly and proportionately, rational expectations theory predicts a direct path of change in the economy's equilibrium from E_1 to E_3. Stated differently, if firms and workers formulate expectations rationally, any impact of stimulative monetary policy is nullified. Under rational expectations theory, only *unanticipated* or *surprise* policies can influence output and employment. But monetary and fiscal policies based on surprises are not practical.

If workers foresee inflation and prevent erosion of their real wages by demanding and receiving nominal wage raises in advance, aggregate supply is the vertical curve, *LRAS*. When real wages remain unchanged, there is no incentive for businesses to alter production as prices rise. If rational expectations theory is correct, the economy does not enjoy the short-lived pleasure of lower unemployment at point E_2, as predicted by adaptive expectations theory.

INCOMES POLICY

Suppose we accept the power of unions and businesses to raise wages and prices as inevitable. Let's also assume Milton Friedman is correct that discretionary monetary and fiscal policies are useless or counterproductive. Then what approach is left to fight inflation? There is another way, used in the past, which is a collection of regulatory policies called incomes policies. Incomes policies are federal government policies designed to affect the real incomes of workers by controlling nominal wages and prices. Such policies include presidential jawboning, wage-price guidelines, and wage-price controls.

Presidential Jawboning

The mildest form of incomes policies is jawboning. Jawboning is oratory intended to pressure unions and businesses to reduce wage and price increases. The government attempts to prevent or roll back wage and price hikes by appealing to labor and business leaders. The most spectacular success with this technique occurred in 1962. President John F. Kennedy called major U.S. steel manufacturers and convinced them to rescind their price increases. But President Kennedy jawboned with a club in hand. He threatened to sell government stockpiles of steel at lower prices. The president also informed the firms that those failing to cooperate would lose government contracts to firms that would lower prices. President Lyndon Johnson followed Kennedy's example

Incomes policies

Federal government policies designed to affect the real incomes of workers by controlling nominal wages and prices. Such policies include presidential jawboning, wage-price guidelines, and wage-price controls.

Jawboning

Oratory intended to pressure unions and businesses to reduce wage and price increases.

and jawboned even more. Then there was the "Blow the Whistle" program under President Richard Nixon. An official agency was established to monitor unwarranted price increases and publicly announce violators of the national interest.

Most economists argue that firms raise prices when changes in demand or cost make it profitable to do so. Jawboning may do a little good for a while, but over time it is a blunt weapon against inflation.

Wage and Price Guidelines

Wage and price guidelines

Voluntary standards set by the government for "permissible" wage and price increases.

A more formal policy to cool down the inflation rate is to establish **wage and price guidelines**. Wage and price guidelines are voluntary standards set by the government for "permissible" wage and price increases. The Truman and Eisenhower administrations made unsystematic attempts to discourage business and labor from raising prices and wages. But the first systematic wage and price guideline program was initiated during the Kennedy administration, and this approach was also used during the Johnson and Carter administrations. For example, the Carter administration asked labor unions to limit their wage increases to 7 percent. Violators were identified in hopes that adverse publicity would force the unions to comply. Without any enforcement mechanism, the dominant view among economists is that guidelines accomplish little against self-interest.

Wage and Price Controls

Wage and price controls

Legal restrictions on wage and price increases. Violations can result in fines and imprisonment.

When guidelines have the force of law, the economy moves to a mandatory system of wage and price controls. Wage and price controls are legal restrictions on wage and price increases. Violations can result in fines and imprisonment. Once people believe wages and prices are under control by law, the good news is that they expect lower prices. The bad news is that controls are government interference with market supply and demand.

As discussed in Chapter 4, a ceiling price established below the equilibrium price will cause shortages in markets (see Exhibit 5 in Chapter 4). This usually means rationing of such scarce items as gasoline. When price is not allowed to serve as the rationing device, consumers must incur higher opportunity costs by waiting in long lines for gasoline. This happened in 1979, when the government imposed a price ceiling on gasoline. Another rationing device is government ration coupons that give the right to buy a good. Ration coupons were used for many goods during World War II. Shortages also lead to *black markets*, which are illegal markets for goods at unregulated prices. To enforce the system requires a government bureaucracy at taxpayers' expense.

Long lines for products, ration coupons, and black markets are not popular. This explains why wage and price controls appear primarily during war and rarely in peacetime. The United States has imposed wage and price controls during World War II, the Korean War, and most recently during the Nixon administration. President Nixon hoped to combat high inflationary expectations built up during the Vietnam War. The inflation rate from 1969 to 1971 averaged 5.2 percent, an alarming rate in those days. The plan was to control inflation and then fight unemployment, which averaged 4.8 percent over the same period. The first phase of the attack was a 90-day freeze on wages and prices in August 1971. A 15-member

You're The Economist   Ford's Whip Inflation Now (WIN)
Button   *Applicable Concept: incomes policies*

The most interesting historical artifact of the fight against inflation is gathering dust in the White House attic. In October 1974, President Gerald Ford proposed the "WIN" button to a joint session of Congress. The idea was that Americans would wear their "Whip Inflation Now" buttons, and this would break the wage-price spiral. The WIN button represented an appeal to patriotism that would discourage businesses and labor from raising prices and wages.

The logical question is, what circumstances drove the president of the United States to use a button against inflation? We will begin the story in 1971, when the Nixon administration approved wage and price controls to cool inflationary expectations. Beginning in 1972, bad crops caused food prices to soar, and the OPEC oil embargo boosted the price of crude oil. These supply shocks boosted the inflation rate from 3.2 percent in 1972 to 6.2 percent in 1973. Clearly, the wage and price control program was falling apart before controls ended in 1974.

Following the demand-management prescription against inflation, the Fed raised the discount rate in late 1973. Federal Reserve Chair Arthur Burns stated that the Fed must follow a contractionary monetary policy for years to come. Despite the Fed's restrictive policy, the inflation rate rose to an annual rate of about 14 percent in early 1974. By late 1974, the unemployment rate had risen to 6 percent, but policymakers remained committed to anti-inflation policies. The Fed raised the discount rate again in the fall of 1974, and President Ford called an economic summit meeting. The outcome of the summit was a resolve to stick to the battle plan and beat inflation before turning to the worsening unemployment problem. Aiming for public support, President Ford unveiled the WIN button, accompanied by a tax surcharge and federal spending ceiling proposals. While the fight against inflation preoccupied policymakers, the unemployment rate rose from 5.6 percent in 1974 to 8.5 percent in 1975. The percentage change in real GDP between 1974 and 1975 was –0.6 percent, and recession suddenly replaced inflation as the number one enemy. In response, Congress approved a $22.8 billion tax cut bill in 1975, and the Fed increased the money supply. In 1974, the inflation rate was 11.0 percent, and in 1975, the inflation rate was still at the high rate of 9.1 percent.

What caused this puzzling twist in stabilization policy to deal with stagflation? Many economists explain this turn of events by the absence of a conceptual framework to understand the effects of supply shocks on the aggregate supply curve. Instead, policymakers tried to shift the aggregate demand curve back and forth while asking people to wear a WIN button.

ANALYZE THE ISSUE

Assume the economy is in equilibrium at full employment and the public anticipates restrictive monetary and fiscal policies, including WIN buttons, which decrease aggregate demand in order to combat inflation. Use the *AD-AS* model depicted in Exhibit 6 to explain the new classical predictions of the impact on the price level, real GDP, and the unemployment rate.

Pay Board and a 7-member Price Commission administered the controls. For three months businesses could not raise prices, wages were frozen, and landlords could not charge higher rents. The intent was to give inflationary expectations a shock treatment. Then the freeze lifted, and wage and price controls were established to limit increases between 1971 and 1974. The bottom line is that in 1971 the inflation rate was 4.4 percent. In 1973, the inflation rate climbed to 6.2 percent. When the

| *Exhibit 7* | **How Different Macroeconomic Models Cure Inflation** |

School of thought
Monetarism

Milton Friedman

Inflation prescription
Monetarists see the cause of inflation as "too much money chasing too few goods," based on the quantity of money theory ($MV = PQ$). To cure inflation, they would cut the money supply and force the Fed to stick to a fixed money supply growth rate. In the short run, the unemployment rate will rise, but in the long run, it self-corrects to the natural rate.

School of thought
Keynesianism

John Maynard Keynes

Inflation prescription
Keynesians believe in using contractionary fiscal and monetary policies to cool an overheated economy. To decrease aggregate demand, they advocate that the government use tax hikes and/ or spending cuts. The Fed should reduce the money supply and cause the rate of interest to rise. The opportunity cost of reducing inflation is greater unemployment. Keynesians also believe that incomes policies are effective.

School of thought
Supply-side economics

Arthur Laffer

Inflation prescription
Supply-siders view the cause of inflation as "not enough goods." Their approach is to increase aggregate supply by cuts in marginal tax rates, government regulations, and import barriers. The effect provides incentives to work, invest, and expand production capacity. Thus, both the inflation rate and the unemployment rate fall.

School of thought
New classical school

Robert Lucas

Inflation prescription
The theory of rational expectations asserts that the public must be convinced that policymakers will stick to restrictive and persistent fiscal and monetary policies. If policymakers have credibility, the inflation rate will be anticipated and quickly fall without a rise in unemployment.

experiment with controls ended in 1974, the inflation rate rose to 11 percent. During the same period, the unemployment rate remained between 5 and 6 percent. Obviously, controls did not slay the inflation dragon, although some economists have argued that controls made the dragon less fierce.

In 1968, the Council of Economic Advisers eloquently stated the opinion of most economists on wage and price controls:

> *While such controls may be necessary under conditions of an all-out war, it would be folly to consider them as a solution to inflationary pressures that accompany high employment under any other circumstance. . . . Although such controls may be unfortunately popular when they are in effect, the appeal quickly disappears once people live under them.*[3]

The majority view is that controls destroy the efficient allocation of resources provided by the price system and intrude on economic freedom. Defenders of controls believe this is a small price to pay.

CHECKPOINT

Can Wage and Price Controls Cure Stagflation?

Suppose war in the Persian Gulf destroyed much of the world's oil reserves. As a result, the U.S. economy is experiencing a bout of stagflation. You are a member of Congress, and a bill is introduced to fight the problems of high inflation and high unemployment by imposing wage and price controls. Using the *AD-AS* model, will you vote in favor of controls to cure stagflation by freezing the price level? [Hint: Look at Exhibit 5 of Chapter 4 and Exhibit 12(a) in the chapter on aggregate demand and supply.]

HOW DIFFERENT MACROECONOMIC THEORIES ATTACK INFLATION

If incomes policies do not cure an overheated economy during peacetime, policymakers must decide which macroeconomic school "hat" to wear. Exhibit 7 gives a brief description of how four basic macroeconomic models deal with inflation. Recall the monetarist view presented in the previous chapter and supply-side economics explained in the chapter on fiscal policy.

---

3. *Annual Report of the Council of Economic Advisers* (Washington, D.C.: Government Printing Office, 1968), p. 119.

Key Concepts

Phillips curve
Natural rate hypothesis
Adaptive expectations theory

Political business cycle
Rational expectations theory
Incomes policies

Jawboning
Wage and price guidelines
Wage and price controls

Summary

- The *Phillips curve* shows a stable inverse relationship between the inflation rate and the unemployment rate. If policymakers reduce inflation, unemployment increases, and vice versa. During the 1960s, the curve closely fit the inflation and unemployment rates in the United States. Since 1970, the Phillips curve has not conformed to the stable inflation-unemployment tradeoff pattern of the 1960s.

The Phillips Curve for the United States in the 1960s

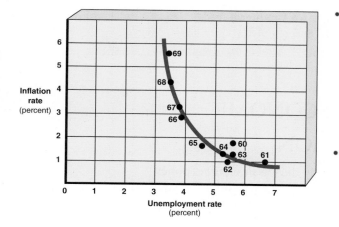

- The *natural rate hypothesis* argues that the economy self-corrects to the natural rate of unemployment. Over time, changes in the rate of inflation are fully anticipated, and prices and wages rise or fall proportionately. As a result, the long-run Phillips curve is a vertical line at the natural rate of unemployment. Thus, Keynesian demand-management policies ultimately cause only higher or lower inflation,

and the natural rate of unemployment remains unchanged.

- *Adaptive expectations theory* is the proposition that people base their economic forecasts on recent past information, rather than future information. Once the government causes the inflation rate to rise or fall, people adapt their inflationary expectations to the current inflation rate. The result is a short-run Phillips curve that intersects the vertical long-run Phillips curve. Over time, the economy self-corrects to the natural rate of unemployment.

- The *political business cycle* is a business cycle created by the incentive for politicians to manipulate the economy to get reelected. Using expansionary policies, officeholders can stimulate the economy before an election. Unemployment falls, and the price level rises. After the election, the strategy is to contract the economy to fight inflation and unemployment rises.

- *Rational expectations theory* argues that it is naive to believe that people change their inflationary expectations based only on the current inflation rate. Rational expectationists belong to the new classical school. Assuming the impact of government policy is predictable, people immediately anticipate higher or lower inflation. Workers quickly change their nominal wages as businesses change prices. Consequently, inflation worsens or improves, and unemployment remains unchanged at the natural rate. Thus, there is no short-run Phillips curve, and the vertical long-run Phillips curve is identical to adaptive expectations theory.

- *Incomes policies* are a variety of federal government programs aimed at directly controlling wages and prices. Incomes policies include jawboning, wage-price guidelines, and wage-price controls. Over time, incomes policies tend to be ineffective.

- *Wage and price controls* are legal restrictions on wages and prices. Most economists do not favor wage and price controls in peacetime. Such controls are expensive to administer, destroy efficiency, and intrude on economic freedom.

Summary of Conclusion Statements

- Changes in aggregate demand cause a movement along a stationary Phillips curve.
- According to adaptive expectations theory, expansionary monetary and fiscal policies to reduce the unemployment rate are useless in the long run. After a short-run reduction in unemployment, the economy will self-correct to the natural rate of unemployment, but at a higher inflation rate. Thus, there is no long-run tradeoff between inflation and unemployment.
- According to rational expectations theory, if people are not surprised by monetary and fiscal policy changes, the economy's self-correction mechanism will restore the natural rate of unemployment. Preannounced, stable policies to achieve low and constant money supply growth and a balanced federal budget are therefore the best way to lower the inflation rate.

- According to rational expectations theory, expansionary monetary and fiscal policies used to reduce unemployment are not only useless, but also harmful because the only result is higher inflation.
- According to rational expectations theory, flexible wages and prices adjust immediately to negate predictable monetary and fiscal policy changes, so the economy's self-correction mechanism will restore the natural rate of unemployment. Therefore, discretionary policies should be abandoned and fixed-rule, stable policies to achieve constant money supply growth and a balanced federal budget are therefore the best way to lower the inflation rate.

Study Questions and Problems

1. What is a Phillips curve? Assuming the economy's aggregate supply curve is stable, how would an increase in aggregate demand affect the unemployment rate and the inflation rate?

2. What were the inflation rate and the unemployment rate last year? Do these rates lie on a Phillips curve?

3. What happened in the 1970s and early 1980s to cast doubt on the Phillips curve?

4. Suppose you flipped an honest coin 10 times and heads came up 8 times. You are about to toss the coin another 10 times. Using adaptive expectations, how many heads do you expect?

Based on rational expectations, how many heads do you expect?

5. According to adaptive expectations, what happens to the inflation rate and the unemployment rate in the following situations?
   a. Initially, the economy is operating at the natural rate of 6 percent unemployment. The anticipated rate of inflation is 6 percent, and the actual rate is also 6 percent.
   b. In the next period, there is an unexpected rise in the inflation rate to 10 percent.
   c. In the next period, there is an unexpected rise in the inflation rate to 12 percent.

6. Explain what happens under adaptive expectations theory when monetary and fiscal policymakers use expansionary policy to achieve an unemployment rate below the natural rate.

7. Keynesians believe monetary and fiscal policymakers should stabilize the business cycle. Compare the political business cycle to Keynesian policy objectives.

8. Use Exhibit 8 to answer the questions below.
   a. Which points represent the natural unemployment rate?
   b. Which points represent an unemployment rate below the natural unemployment rate?
   c. Which points represent an unemployment rate above the natural unemployment rate?
   d. Explain points A and D on the graph.
   e. Explain points B and C on the graph.
   f. Explain points E and F on the graph.
   g. Why is curve PC_2 to the right of curve PC_1?

9. Based on rational expectations theory, what happens to the inflation rate and the unemployment rate in the following situations?
   a. Initially, the economy is operating at the natural unemployment rate of 4 percent, and the inflation rate is also 4 percent. People correctly anticipate that an increase in the money supply will increase the inflation rate to 6 percent next year.

Exhibit 8   Long-Run and Short-Run Phillips Curve

   b. In the next period, people correctly forecast that a tax cut will cause the inflation rate to rise to 8 percent.
   c. In the next period, they anticipate that the Fed's hike in the discount rate will cause the inflation rate to fall to 4 percent.

For Online Exercises, go to the Tucker Web site at www.cengage.com/economics/tucker.

CHECKPOINT ANSWERS
Does Rational Expectations Theory Work in the Classroom?

Under rational expectations, if the students know what is going to happen, they will use this information to negate the policy. If pop quizzes are given on the same day homework is due, the rational students will be certain to attend class on those days and take cuts on other days. If quizzes are random, quiz dates are unknown, so there is always a chance that missing a class may mean missing a quiz. If you said the professor will keep pop quizzes a secret and give them randomly, **YOU ARE CORRECT.**

Can Wage and Price Controls Cure Stagflation?

Assume the economy begins in equilibrium at E_1 in Exhibit 9 and an oil shock causes the economy to move to a new equilibrium at E_2. Without wage and price controls, the price level increases from 150 to 200, and real GDP decreases from $4 trillion to $3 trillion. Now assume laws keep the price level frozen at 150. This means firms cannot raise prices to meet higher costs, so under controls they are forced to lay off more workers and cut production even further. The economy's equilibrium moves from E_2 to E_3, and real GDP is $2 trillion, rather than $3 trillion, causing unemployment to climb even higher.

Using wage and price controls to fight inflation would cause an even more severe decrease in real GDP; therefore, unemployment is greater than would otherwise be the case. If you voted *no* on the wage and price controls bill because they cause greater shortages and a deeper recession, **YOU ARE CORRECT.**

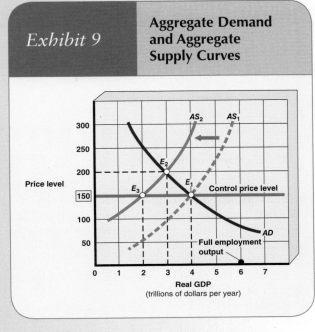

Exhibit 9 **Aggregate Demand and Aggregate Supply Curves**

Practice Quiz

For an explanation of the correct answers, visit the Tucker Web site at www.cengage.com/economics/tucker.

1. The Phillips curve depicts the relationship between the
   a. unemployment rate and the change in GDP.
   b. inflation rate and the interest rate.
   c. level of investment spending and the interest rate.
   d. inflation rate and the unemployment rate.

2. A difficulty in using the Phillips curve as a policy menu is
   a. that the natural rate of unemployment does not exist.
   b. that the curve does not remain in one position.
   c. deciding between monetary and fiscal policies.
   d. that Democrats choose one point on the curve and Republicans choose another point.

3. Since the 1970s, the
   a. Phillips curve has not been stable.
   b. inflation rate and the unemployment rate have been about equal.
   c. Phillips curve has proven to be a reliable model to guide public policy.
   d. relationship between the inflation rate and the unemployment rate moved in a counterclockwise direction.

4. According to the natural rate hypothesis,
   a. the Phillips curve is quite flat, so a large reduction in employment can be achieved without inflation.
   b. workers adapt their wage demands to inflation only after a considerable time lag.
   c. the Phillips curve is vertical in the long run at full employment.
   d. workers cannot anticipate the inflationary effects of expansionary public policies.

Practice Quiz Continued

5. Adaptive expectations theory
   a. argues that the best indicator of the future is recent information.
   b. underestimates inflation when it is accelerating.
   c. overestimates inflation when it is slowing down.
   d. does none of the above.
   e. does all of the above.

6. The conclusion of adaptive expectations theory is that expansionary monetary and fiscal policies intended to reduce the unemployment rate are
   a. effective in the long run.
   b. effective in the short run.
   c. unnecessary and cause inflation in the long run.
   d. necessary and reduce inflation in the long run.

7. Most macroeconomic policy changes, say the rational expectations theorists, are
   a. unpredictable.
   b. predictable.
   c. slow to take place.
   d. irrational.

8. Rational expectations theorists advise the federal government to
   a. change policy often.
   b. pursue stable policies.
   c. do the opposite of what the public expects.
   d. ignore future economic predictions.

9. Suppose the government shown in Exhibit 10 uses contractionary monetary policy to reduce inflation from 9 to 6 percent. If people have *adaptive* expectations, then
   a. the economy will remain stuck at point E_1.
   b. the natural rate will permanently increase to 8 percent.
   c. unemployment will rise to 8 percent in the short run.
   d. unemployment will remain at 6 percent as the inflation rate falls.

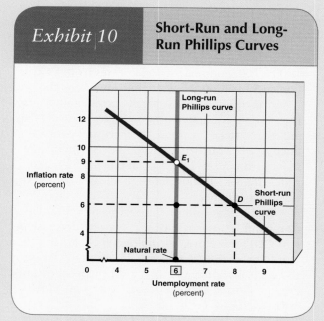

Exhibit 10 — Short-Run and Long-Run Phillips Curves

10. Suppose the government shown in Exhibit 10 uses contractionary monetary policy to reduce inflation from 9 to 6 percent. If people have *rational* expectations, then
    a. the economy will remain stuck at point E_1.
    b. the natural rate will permanently increase to 8 percent.
    c. unemployment will rise to 8 percent in the short run.
    d. unemployment will remain at 6 percent as the inflation rate falls.

11. Voluntary wage-price restraints are known as
    a. wage-price controls.
    b. price rollbacks.
    c. wage-price guidelines.
    d. anti-inflation commitments.

Practice Quiz Continued

12. Which of the following government policies is an incomes policy?
   a.   A reduction in welfare expenditures
   b.   The publication of a list of guidelines suggesting maximum wage and price increases
   c.   An increase in the money supply
   d.   All of the above

13. As shown in Exhibit 11, if people behave according to adaptive expectations theory, an increase in the aggregate demand curve from AD_1 to AD_2 will cause the price level to move
   a.   directly from 100 to 110 and then remain at 110.
   b.   directly from 100 to 105 and then remain at 105.
   c.   from 100 to 105 initially and then eventually move back to 100.
   d.   from 100 to 105 initially and then eventually move to 110.

14. As shown in Exhibit 11, if people behave according to rational expectations theory, an increase in the aggregate demand curve from AD_1 to AD_2 will cause the economy to move
   a.   directly from E_1 to E_3 and then remain at E_3.
   b.   directly from E_1 to E_2 and then remain at E_2.
   c.   from E_1 to E_2 initially and then eventually move back to E_1.
   d.   from E_1 to E_2 initially and then eventually move to E_3.

15. As shown in Exhibit 11, if people behave according to rational expectations theory, an increase in the aggregate demand curve from AD_1 to AD_2 will cause
   a.   labor to adjust nominal wages sluggishly.
   b.   the aggregate supply curve to remain at $SRAS_1$.
   c.   the price level to eventually rise from 100 to 110.
   d.   none of the above.

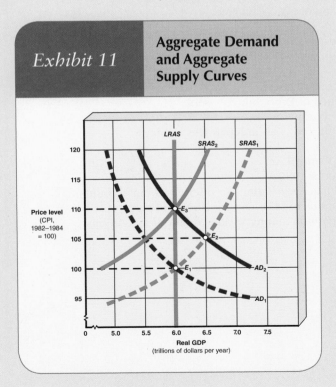

Exhibit 11

Aggregate Demand and Aggregate Supply Curves

Road Map — Money, Banking, and Monetary Policy

part 5

This road map feature helps you tie material in the part together as you travel the Economic Way of Thinking Highway. The following are review questions listed by chapter from the previous part. The key concept in each question is given for emphasis, and each question or set of questions concludes with an interactive game to reinforce the concepts. Click on the Tucker Web site at www.cengage.com/economics/tucker, select the chapter, and play the visual causation chain game designed to make learning fun. Enjoy the cheers when correct and suffer the jeers if you miss. The correct answers to the multiple-choice questions are given in Appendix C of the text.

Chapter 14. Money and the Federal Reserve System

1. **Key Concept: Money supply definitions**
   Suppose you transfer $1,000 from your checking account to your savings account. How does this action affect the M1 and M2 money supplies?
   a. M1 and M2 are both unchanged.
   b. M1 falls by $1,000, and M2 rises by $1,000.
   c. M1 is unchanged, and M2 rises by $1,000.
   d. M1 falls by $1,000, and M2 is unchanged.

2. **Key Concept: Federal Reserve System**
   Which of the following groups oversees and administers the Federal Reserve System?
   a. The House of Representatives
   b. The President's Council of Economic Advisers
   c. The U.S. Treasury Department
   d. None of the above; the Fed is an independent agency.

3. **Key Concept: Monetary Control Act**
   The Monetary Control Act of 1980
   a. allowed savings and loan associations to offer checking accounts.
   b. allowed more institutions to offer checking account services.
   c. created greater competition among various financial institutions.
   d. all of the above.
   e. none of the above.

Chapter 15. Money Creation

4. **Key Concept: Open market operations**
   When the Fed sells government securities, it
   a. lowers the cost of borrowing from the Fed, encouraging banks to make loans to the general public.
   b. raises the cost of borrowing from the Fed, discouraging banks from making loans to the general public.
   c. increases the amount of excess reserves that banks hold, encouraging them to make loans to the general public.
   d. increases the amount of excess reserves that banks hold, discouraging them from making loans to the general public.
   e. decreases the amount of excess reserves that banks hold, discouraging them from making loans to the general public.

5. **Key Concept: Open market operations**
   When the Fed buys government securities, it
   a. lowers the cost of borrowing from the Fed, encouraging banks to make loans to the general public.
   b. raises the cost of borrowing from the Fed, discouraging banks from making loans to the general public.
   c. increases the amount of excess reserves that banks hold, encouraging them to make loans to the general public.
   d. increases the amount of excess reserves that banks hold, discouraging them from making loans to the general public.
   e. decreases the amount of excess reserves that banks hold, discouraging them from making loans to the general public.

Causation Chain Game
Open Market Operations—Exhibit 3

Chapter 16. Monetary Policy

6. **Key Concept: Money demand curve**
   In a two-asset economy with money and T-bills, the quantity of money that people will want to hold, other things being equal, can be expected to
   a. decrease as real GDP increases.
   b. increase as the interest rate decreases.
   c. increase as the interest rate increases.
   d. all of the above.

Causation Chain Game
Demand for Money Curve—Exhibit 1

7. **Key Concept: Equilibrium interest rate**

Assume the Fed decreases the money supply and the demand for money curve is fixed. In response, people will

   a. sell bonds, thus driving up the interest rate.
   b. buy bonds, thus driving down the interest rate.
   c. buy bonds, thus driving up the interest rate.
   d. sell bonds, thus driving down the interest rate.

8. **Key Concept: Equilibrium interest rate**

Assume a fixed demand for money curve and the Fed increases the money supply. In response, people will

   a. sell bonds, thus driving up the interest rate.
   b. sell bonds, thus driving down the interest rate.
   c. buy bonds, thus driving up the interest rate.
   d. buy bonds, thus driving down the interest rate.

Causation Chain Game
The Equilibrium Interest Rate—Exhibit 2

9. **Key Concept: Change in money supply**

Assume the demand for money curve is stationary and the Fed increases the money supply. The result is that people

   a. increase the supply of bonds, thus driving up the interest rate.
   b. increase the supply of bonds, thus driving down the interest rate.
   c. increase the demand for bonds, thus driving up the interest rate.
   d. increase the demand for bonds, thus driving down the interest rate.

10. **Key Concept: Change in money supply**

Assume a fixed demand for money curve and the Fed decreases the money supply. In response, people will

   a. sell bonds, thus driving up the interest rate.
   b. sell bonds, thus driving down the interest rate.
   c. buy bonds, thus driving up the interest rate.
   d. buy bonds, thus driving down the interest rate.

Causation Chain Game
The Effect of Changes in the Money Supply—Exhibit 3

11. **Key Concept: Keynesian Transmission Mechanism**

The Keynesian cause-and-effect sequence predicts that a decrease in the money supply will cause interest rates to

   a. fall, boosting investment and shifting the *AD* curve rightward, leading to an increase in real GDP.
   b. fall, boosting investment and shifting the *AD* curve rightward, leading to a decrease in real GDP.
   c. rise, cutting investment and shifting the *AD* curve rightward, leading to an increase in real GDP.

    d.   rise, boosting investment and shifting the *AD* curve rightward, leading to an increase in real GDP.

    e.   rise, cutting investment and shifting the *AD* curve leftward, leading to a decrease in real GDP.

Causation Chain Game
The Keynesian Monetary Policy Transmission Mechanism—Exhibit 4

12. Key Concept: Monetarists Transmission Mechanism
Most monetarists favor
    a.   frequent changes in the growth rate of the money supply to avoid inflation.
    b.   placing the Federal Reserve under the Treasury.
    c.   a steady, gradual shrinkage of the money supply.
    d.   a constant increase in the money supply year after year equal to the potential annual growth rate in real GDP.

Causation Chain Game
The Monetarist Policy Transmission Mechanism—Exhibit 6

Chapter 17. The Phillips Curve and Expectations Theory

13. Key Concept: Adaptive expectations
According to adaptive expectations theory, expansionary monetary and fiscal policies to reduce the unemployment rate are
    a.   useless in the long run.
    b.   useless in the short run.
    c.   ineffective on the price level.
    d.   none of the above.

14. Key Concept: Rational expectations
The belief that the government can do absolutely nothing in either the short run or the long run to reduce the unemployment rate, because people will anticipate the government's actions, is held by the
    a.   rational expectations school.
    b.   neo-Keynesian school.
    c.   classical school.
    d.   supply-side school.
    e.   Keynesian school.

Causation Chain Game
The Short-Run and Long-Run Phillips Curve—Exhibit 4

The International Economy

© Getty Images

The final part of this text is devoted to global topics. The first chapter explains the importance of free trade and the mechanics of trade bookkeeping and exchange rates. Here you will find a feature on the birth of the euro. The second chapter takes a historical look at the theoretical debate over capitalism and the transition of Cuba, Russia, and China toward this system. In the opposite direction, there is a discussion of nationalization in the United States. The final chapter provides comparisons of advanced and developing countries. The chapter concludes with the fascinating economic success story of Hong Kong.

International Trade and Finance

Just imagine your life without world trade. For openers, you could not eat bananas from Honduras or chocolate from Nigerian cocoa beans. Nor could you sip French wine, Colombian coffee, or Indian tea. Also forget about driving a Japanese motorcycle or automobile. In addition, you could not buy Italian shoes and most DVDs, televisions, fax machines, and personal computers because they are foreign made. Taking your vacation in London would also be ruled out if there were no world trade. And the list goes on and on, so the point is clear. World trade is important because it gives consumers more power by expanding their choices. Today, the speed of transportation and communication means producers must compete on a global basis for the favor of consumers.

Trade is often highly controversial. Regardless of whether it is a World Trade Organization (WTO) meeting or a G8 summit meeting, trade talks face protesters in the streets complaining that globalization has triggered a crisis in the world, such as global warming, poverty, soaring oil prices, or food shortages. And in the United States, outsourcing jobs to lower paid workers overseas continues to be a hotly debated issue.

The first part of this chapter explains the theoretical reason why countries should specialize in producing certain goods and then trade them for imports. Also, you will study arguments for and against the United States protecting itself from "unfair" trade practices by other countries. In the second part of the chapter, you will learn how nations pay each other for world trade. Here you will explore international bookkeeping and discover how supply and demand forces determine that, for example, 1 dollar is worth 100 yen.

In this chapter, you will learn to solve these economics puzzles:

- How does Babe Ruth's decision not to remain a pitcher illustrate an important principle in global trade?

- Is there a valid argument for trade protectionism?

- Should the United States return to the gold standard?

WHY NATIONS NEED TRADE

Exhibit 1 reveals which regions are our major trading partners (exports plus imports). Leading the list of nations is Canada, our largest trading partner, followed by China, Mexico, and Japan. Leading U.S. exports are chemicals, machinery, agricultural products, computers, and automobiles. Major imports include petroleum, cars, trucks, clothing, and electronics. Why does a nation even bother to trade with the rest of the world? Does it seem strange for the United States to import goods it could produce for itself? Indeed, why doesn't the United States become self-sufficient by growing all its own food, including bananas, sugar, and coffee, making all its own cars, and prohibiting sales of all foreign goods? This section explains why specialization and trade are a nation's keys to a higher standard of living.

Exhibit 1	U.S. Trading Partners, 2009

In 2009, Canada, China, Mexico, and Japan accounted for 37 percent of U.S. trade (exports plus imports).

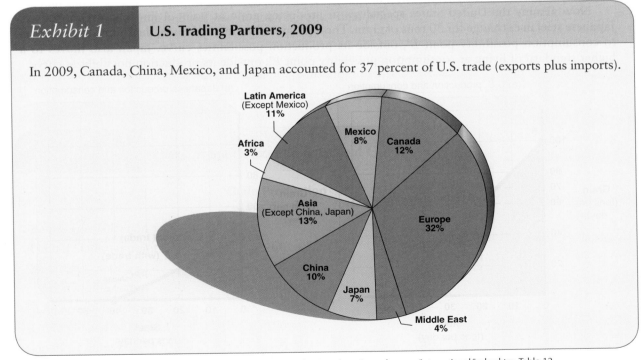

SOURCE: Bureau of Economic Analysis, U.S. International Transactions by Area, http://www.bea.gov/international/index.htm, Table 12.

Specialization with Trade

Now let's return to Exhibit 2 and demonstrate how world trade benefits countries. Suppose the United States agrees to specialize in grain production at point *A* and to import 20 tons of Japanese steel in exchange for 30 tons of its grain output. Does the United States gain from trade? The answer is Yes. At point *A*, the United States produces 100 tons of grain per day. Subtracting the 30 tons of grain traded to Japan leaves the United States with 70 tons of its own grain production to consume. In return for grain, Japan unloads 20 tons of steel on U.S. shores. Hence, specialization and trade allow the United States to move from point *A* to point *B'*, which is a consumption possibility *outside* its production possibilities curve in Exhibit 2(a). At point *B'*, the United States consumes the same amount of steel and 10 more tons of grain compared to point *B* (without trade).

Japan also has an incentive to specialize by moving its production mix from point *E* to point *F*. With trade, Japan's consumption will be at point *E'*. At point *E'*, Japan has as much grain to consume as it had at point *E*, plus 10 more tons of steel. After trading 20 tons of the 40 tons of steel produced at point *F* for grain, Japan can still consume 20 tons of steel from its production, rather than only 10 tons of steel at point *E*. Thus, point *E'* is a consumption possibility that lies *outside* Japan's production possibilities curve.

> **CONCLUSION** *Global trade allows a country to consume a combination of goods that exceeds its production possibilities curve.*

COMPARATIVE AND ABSOLUTE ADVANTAGE

Why did the United States decide to produce and export grain instead of steel? Why did Japan choose to produce steel, rather than grain? Here you study the economic principle that determines specialization and trade.

Comparative Advantage

Engaging in world trade permits countries to escape the prison of their own production possibilities curves by producing bread, cars, or whatever goods they make best. The decision of the United States to specialize in and export grain and the decision of Japan to specialize in and export steel are based on **comparative advantage**. Comparative advantage is the ability of a country to produce a good at a lower opportunity cost than another country. Continuing our earlier example, we can calculate opportunity costs for the two countries and use comparative advantage to determine which country should specialize in grain and which in steel. For the United States, the opportunity cost of producing 50 tons of steel is 100 tons of grain not produced, so 1 ton of steel costs 2 tons of grain. For Japan, the opportunity cost of producing 40 tons of steel is 40 tons of grain, so 1 ton of steel costs 1 ton of

Comparative advantage

The ability of a country to produce a good at a lower opportunity cost than another country.

grain. Japan's steel is therefore cheaper in terms of grain forgone. This means Japan has a comparative advantage in steel production because it must give up less grain to produce steel than the United States. Stated differently, the opportunity cost of steel production is lower in Japan than in the United States.

The other side of the coin is to measure the cost of grain in terms of steel. For the United States, 1 ton of grain costs 1/2 ton of steel. For Japan, 1 ton of grain costs 1 ton of steel. The United States has a comparative advantage in grain because its opportunity cost in terms of steel forgone is lower. Thus, the United States should specialize in grain because it is more efficient in grain production. Japan, on the other hand, is relatively more efficient at producing steel and should specialize in this product.

> **CONCLUSION** *Comparative advantage refers to the relative opportunity costs between different countries of producing the same goods. World output and consumption are maximized when each country specializes in producing and trading goods for which it has a comparative advantage.*

Absolute Advantage

So far, a country's production and global trade decisions depend on comparing what a country gives up to produce more of a good. It is important to note that comparative advantage is based on opportunity costs, regardless of the absolute costs of resources used in production. We have not considered how much labor, land, or capital either the United States or Japan uses to produce a ton of grain or steel. For example, Japan might have an absolute advantage in producing *both* grain and steel. Absolute advantage is the ability of a country to produce a good using fewer resources than another country. In our example, Japan might use fewer resources per ton to produce grain and steel than the United States. Maybe the Japanese work harder or are more skilled. In short, the Japanese may be more productive producers, but their absolute advantage does not matter in specialization and world trade decisions. If the United States has a comparative advantage in grain, it should specialize in grain even if Japan can produce both grain and steel with fewer resources.

Absolute advantage

The ability of a country to produce a good using fewer resources than another country.

Perhaps another example will clarify the difference between absolute advantage and comparative advantage. When Babe Ruth played for the New York Yankees, he was the best hitter and the best pitcher, not only on the team, but in all of major league baseball. In fact, before Ruth was traded to the Yankees and switched to the outfield, he was the best left-handed pitcher in the American League for a few seasons with the Boston Red Sox. His final record was 99-46. In other words, he had an *absolute advantage* in both hitting and throwing the baseball. Stated differently, Babe Ruth could produce the same home runs as any other teammate with fewer times at bat. The problem was that if he pitched, he would bat fewer times because pitchers need rest after pitching. The coaches decided that the Babe had a *comparative advantage* in hitting. A few pitchers on the team could pitch almost as well as Babe, but no one could touch his hitting. In terms of opportunity costs, the Yankees would lose fewer games if Babe specialized in hitting.

FREE TRADE VERSUS PROTECTIONISM

Free trade

The flow of goods between countries without restrictions or special taxes.

Protectionism

The government's use of embargoes, tariffs, quotas, and other restrictions to protect domestic producers from foreign competition.

Embargo

A law that bars trade with another country.

Tariff

A tax on an import.

In theory, global trade should be based on comparative advantage and free trade. Free trade is the flow of goods between countries without restrictions or special taxes. In practice, despite the advice of economists, every nation protects its own domestic producers to some degree from foreign competition. Behind these barriers to trade are special interest groups whose jobs and incomes are threatened, so they clamor to the government for protectionism. Protectionism is the government's use of embargoes, tariffs, quotas, and other restrictions to protect domestic producers from foreign competition.

Embargo

Embargoes are the strongest limit on trade. An embargo is a law that bars trade with another country. For example, the United States and other nations in the world imposed an arms embargo on Iraq in response to its invasion of Kuwait in 1990. The United States also maintains embargoes against Iran, Cuba, and North Korea.

Tariff

Tariffs are the most popular and visible measures used to discourage trade. A tariff is a tax on an import. Tariffs are also called customs duties. Suppose the United States imposes a tariff of 2.9 percent on autos. If a foreign car costs $40,000, the amount of the tariff equals $1,160 ($40,000 × 0.029), and the U.S. price, including the tariff, is $41,160. The current U.S. tariff code specifies tariffs on nearly 70 percent of U.S. imports. A tariff can be based on weight, volume, or number of units, or it can be *ad valorem* (figured as a percentage of the price). The average U.S. tariff is less than 5 percent, but individual tariffs vary widely. Tariffs are imposed to reduce imports by raising import prices and to generate revenues for the U.S. Treasury. Exhibit 4 shows the trend of the average tariff rate since 1930.

During the worldwide depression of the 1930s, when one nation raised its tariffs to protect its industries, other nations retaliated by raising their tariffs. Under the Smoot-Hawley tariffs of the 1930s, the average tariff in the United States reached a peak of 20 percent. Durable imports, which were one-third of imports, were subject to an unbelievable tariff rate of 60 percent. In 1947, most of the world's industrialized nations mutually agreed to end the tariff wars by signing the *General Agreement on Tariffs and Trade (GATT)*. Since then, GATT nations have met periodically to negotiate lower tariff rates. GATT agreements have significantly reduced tariffs over the years among member nations. In the 1994 *Uruguay round*, member nations signed a GATT agreement that decreased tariffs and reduced other trade barriers. The most divisive element

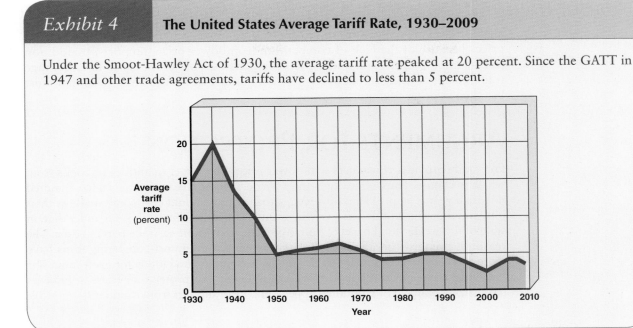

Exhibit 4   **The United States Average Tariff Rate, 1930–2009**

Under the Smoot-Hawley Act of 1930, the average tariff rate peaked at 20 percent. Since the GATT in 1947 and other trade agreements, tariffs have declined to less than 5 percent.

SOURCES: Economic Report of the President, 1989, http://www.gpoaccess.gov/eop/, p. 151; United States International Trade Commission, The Economic Effect of Significant U.S. Import Restraints, June 2002, p. 146, http://www.USITC.gov/, and Trade Profiles, http://stat.wto.org/CountryProfiles/US_e.htm.

of this agreement was the creation in 1995 of the Geneva-based **World Trade Organization (WTO)** to enforce rulings in global trade disputes. The WTO has 150 members and a standing appellate body to render final decisions regarding disputes between WTO members. Critics fear that the WTO might be far more likely to rule in favor of other countries in their trade disputes with the United States. Some people argue that the WTO is unaccountable, and these critics reject free trade and globalization.

To illustrate an interesting case, the United States imposed tariffs in 2002 on steel imports to protect jobs in the struggling U.S. steel industry against foreign competition. The WTO ruled these tariffs were illegal, and countries in Europe and Asia prepared a list of retaliatory tariffs. These levies targeted products such as citrus fruit grown in Florida and apparel produced in southern states crucial to President Bush's reelection. Meanwhile, U.S. automakers and other steel-consuming industries complained because the tariffs increased their costs. Facing these threats, the United States removed the tariffs on steel imports in 2003. It is interesting to compare this case to the Global Economics Feature titled World Trade Slips on Banana Peel.

Quota

Another way to limit foreign competition is to impose a **quota**. A quota is a limit on the quantity of a good that may be imported in a given time period. For example, the United States may allow 10 million tons of sugar to be imported over a one-year period. Once this quantity is reached, no more sugar can be imported for the year. About 12 percent of U.S. imports are subject to import quotas. Examples include import quotas on sugar, dairy products, textiles, steel, and even ice cream. Quotas can limit imports from all foreign suppliers or from specific countries. In 2005, for example, global quotas were lifted from Chinese imports. The United States and

World Trade Organization (WTO)

An international organization of member countries that oversees international trade agreements and rules on trade disputes.

Quota

A limit on the quantity of a good that may be imported in a given time period.

other European countries demanded quotas to protect their countries from Chinese textiles. Critics argue that, like all barriers to trade, quotas invite nations to retaliate with their own measures to restrict trade, and consumers are harmed by higher prices because of the lack of competition from lower-priced imports. In addition to embargoes, tariffs, and quotas, some nations use subtler measures to discourage trade, such as setting up an overwhelming number of bureaucratic steps that must be taken in order to import a product.

ARGUMENTS FOR PROTECTION

Free trade provides consumers with lower prices and larger quantities of goods from which to choose. Thus, removing import barriers might save each family a few hundred dollars a year. The problem, however, is that imports could cost some workers their jobs and thousands of dollars per year from lost income. Thus, it is no wonder that, in spite of the greater total benefits from free trade to consumers, trade barriers exist. The reason is primarily because workers and owners from import-competing firms have more at stake than consumers, so they go to Washington and lobby for protection. The following are some of the most popular arguments for protection. These arguments have strong political or emotional appeal, but weak support from economists.

Infant Industry Argument

As the name suggests, the *infant industry argument* is that a new domestic industry needs protection because it is not yet ready to compete with established foreign competitors. An infant industry is in a formative stage and must bear high start-up costs to train an entire workforce, develop new technology, establish marketing channels, and reach economies of scale. With time to grow and protection, an infant industry can reduce costs and "catch up" with established foreign firms.

Economists ask where one draws the arbitrary line between an "infant" and a "grown-up" industry. It is also difficult to make a convincing case for protecting an infant industry in a developed country, such as the United States, where industries are well established. The infant industry argument, however, may have some validity for less-developed countries. Yet, even for these countries, there is a danger. Once protection is granted, the new industry will not experience the competitive pressures necessary to encourage reasonably quick growth and participation in world trade. Also, once an industry is given protection, it is difficult to take it away.

National Security Argument

Another common argument is that defense-related industries must be protected with embargoes, tariffs, and quotas to ensure national security. By protecting critical defense industries, a nation will not be dependent on foreign countries for the essential defense-related goods it needs to defend itself in wartime. The *national defense argument* has been used to protect a long list of industries, including petrochemicals, munitions, steel, and rubber.

This argument gained validity during the War of 1812. Great Britain, the main trading partner of the United States, became an enemy that blockaded our coast. Today, this argument makes less sense for the United States. The government stockpiles missiles, sophisticated electronics, petroleum, and most goods needed in wartime.

Employment Argument

The *employment argument* suggests that restricting imports increases domestic jobs in protected industries. According to this protectionist argument, the sale of an imported good comes at the expense of its domestically produced counterpart. Lower domestic output therefore leads to higher domestic unemployment than would otherwise be the case.

It is true that protectionism can increase output and save jobs in some industries at home. Ignored, however, are the higher prices paid by consumers because protectionism reduces competition between domestic goods and imported goods. In addition, there are employment reduction effects to consider. For example, suppose a strict quota is imposed on steel imported into our nation. Reduced foreign competition allows U.S. steelmakers to charge higher prices for their steel. As a result, prices rise and sales fall for cars and other products using steel, causing production and employment to fall in these industries. Thus, the import quota on steel may save jobs in the steel industry but at the expense of more jobs lost in the steel-consuming industries. Also, by selling U.S. imports, foreigners earn dollars that they can use to buy U.S. exports. Import quotas cause foreigners to have fewer dollars to spend on U.S. exports, resulting in a decrease in employment in U.S. export industries. In short, protectionism may cause a net reduction in the nation's total employment.

Cheap Foreign Labor Argument

Another often heard popular claim is the *cheap labor argument*. It goes something like this: "How can we compete with such unfair competition? Labor costs $10 an hour in the United States, and firms in many developing countries pay only $1 an hour. Without protection against outsourcing our jobs, U.S. wages will be driven down, and our standard of living will fall."

A major flaw in this argument is that it neglects the reason for the difference in the wage rates between countries. A U.S. worker has more education, training, capital, and access to advanced technology. Therefore, if U.S. workers produce more output per hour than workers in another country, U.S. workers will earn higher wages without a competitive disadvantage. Suppose textile workers in the United States are paid $10 per hour. If a U.S. worker takes 1 hour to produce a rug, the labor cost per rug is $10. Now suppose a worker in India earns $1 per hour, but requires 20 hours to produce a rug on a handloom. In this case, the labor cost per rug is $20. Although the wage rate is 10 times higher in the United States, U.S. productivity is 20 times higher because a U.S. worker can produce 20 rugs in 20 hours, while the worker in India produces only 1 rug in the same amount of time.

Sometimes U.S. companies move their operations to foreign countries where labor is cheaper. Such moves are not always successful because the savings from paying foreign workers a lower wage rate are offset by lower productivity. Other disadvantages of foreign operations include greater transportation costs to U.S. markets and political instability.

FREE TRADE AGREEMENTS

The trend in recent years has been for nations to negotiate a reduction in trade barriers. In 1993, Congress approved the *North American Free Trade Agreement* (*NAFTA*), which linked the United States to its first- and third-largest trading partners, Canada and Mexico. Under NAFTA, which became effective January 1, 1994,

Global Economics World Trade Slips on Banana Peel

Applicable Concept: protectionism

Growing bananas for European markets was a multibillion-dollar bright spot for Latin America's struggling economies. In fact, about half of this region's banana exports traditionally were sold to Europe. Then, in 1993, the European Union (EU) adopted a package of quotas and tariffs aimed at cutting Europe's banana imports from Latin America. The purpose of these restrictions was to give trade preference to 66 banana-growing former colonies of European nations in Africa, the Caribbean, and the Pacific. Ignored was the fact that growers in Latin America grow higher-quality bananas at half the cost of EU-favored growers because of their low labor costs and flat tropical land near port cities.[1]

In 1999, the World Trade Organization (WTO) ruled that the EU was discriminating in favor of European companies importing the fruit and the WTO imposed $191.4 million per year in punitive tariffs on European goods. This was the first time in the four years the WTO had been in existence that such

retaliation had been approved, and only the second time going back to its predecessor, the General Agreement on Tariffs and Trade. When the EU failed to comply with the WTO findings, the United States enforced its WTO rights by imposing increased duties on EU imports, including goods ranging from cashmere sweaters and Italian handbags to sheep's milk cheese, British biscuits, and German coffeemakers. The effect of the U.S. sanctions was to double the wholesale prices of these items. Denmark and the Netherlands were exempt from the U.S. tariffs because they were the only nations that voted against the EU banana rules.

Critics charged that the United States was pushing the case for political reasons. American companies, including Chiquita Brands International and Dole Food Company, grow most of their bananas in Latin America. With America's trade deficit running at a record level, U.S. trade experts also argued that the United States had little choice but to act against

---

1. James Brooke, "Forbidden Fruit in Europe: Latin Bananas Face Hurdles," *New York Times*, April 5, 1993, p. A1.

tariffs were phased out, and other impediments to trade and investment were eliminated among the three nations. For example, elimination of trade restrictions allows the United States to supply Mexico with more U.S. goods and to boost U.S. jobs. On the other hand, NAFTA was expected to raise Mexico's wages and standard of living by increasing Mexican exports to the United States. Note that NAFTA made no changes in restrictions on labor movement, and workers must enter the United States under a limited immigration quota or illegally. The success of NAFTA remains controversial. At the conclusion of this chapter, we will use data to examine its impact.

The United States and other countries are considering other free trade agreements. In Europe, 27 nations have joined the *European Union (EU)*, which is dedicated to removing all trade barriers within Europe and thereby creating a single European economy almost as large as the U.S. economy. See the Birth of the Euro box insert in this chapter.

The *Asian-Pacific Economic Cooperation (APEC)* was formed in 1989 and today has 21 member nations, including China, Hong Kong, Russia, Japan, and Mexico. This organization is based on a nonbinding agreement to reduce trade barriers between member nations.

In 2003, trade ministers from 34 nations met in Miami to create a plan for the world's largest free-trade area that would tear down trade barriers from Alaska to Argentina. The Free Trade Area of the Americas (FTAA) would span the Western Hemisphere except Cuba. In 2005, the *Central American Free Trade Agreement* the EU for failing to abide by the WTO's ruling. Moreover, with increasing voices in the United States questioning the wisdom of global trade and globalization, it was important that the WTO prove that it could arbitrate these disputes.

In 2001, it appeared that the banana dispute might be resolved. The EU agreed to increase market access for U.S. banana distributors, and the United States lifted its retaliatory duties on EU products. The agreement also provided that the United States could reimpose the duties if the EU did not complete its phased-in reductions in restrictions on banana imports.[2]

And the banana story just kept "slipping along."

European Union anti-fraud officials say that illegal banana trafficking is proving more lucrative than that in cocaine. A recently exposed scheme saw Italian banana importers use false licences to pay greatly reduced customs duties on non-quota fruit. The fraud netted smugglers hundreds of millions of euros over a two-year period. Italian public prosecutor, Fabio Scavone, says more is being made from simple customs fraud than from serious crimes such as narcotics trafficking.[3]

And in 2004, Latin American growers again complained that the EU was discriminating against their bananas in favor of producers from African and Caribbean countries. Under the 2001 WTO ruling, the EU was compelled to replace its complex quota and tariff system on bananas with a tariff-only regime. So the EU placed a 176 euro tariff per ton on Latin American suppliers to get into the EU market, while bananas from African and Caribbean countries can export up to 775,000 tons duty-free. A memorandum issued by the Swedish government attacked the "considerable overprice" European consumers pay for banana protection.[4] The banana war continued in 2008 when a WTO dispute panel ruled for the third time that the EU tariff/quota banana regime was unfair.

ANALYZE THE ISSUE

Make an argument in favor of the European import restrictions. Make an argument against this plan.

---

2. "U.S. Lifts Sanctions in Banana War," *Food Institute Report,* July 9, 2001, p. 9.
3. "Banana Scam Beats Cocaine," *Australian Business Intelligence,* July 24, 2002.
4. "Bananas: Commission Proposes New Import Tariff at Euro 230 a Ton," *European Report,* Oct. 30, 2004, p. 506.

(*CAFTA*) extended the free-trade zone to six Central American countries that signed, including Costa Rica, Guatemala, El Salvador, Honduras, Nicaragua, and Dominican Republic. The success or failure of CAFTA will have an impact on future negotiation for FTAA.

Critics are concerned that regional free trade accords will make global agreements increasingly difficult to achieve. Some fear that trading blocs may erect new barriers, creating "Fortress North America," "Fortress Europe," and similar impediments to the worldwide reduction of trade barriers.

THE BALANCE OF PAYMENTS

When trade occurs between the United States and other nations, many types of financial transactions are recorded in a summary called the **balance of payments**. The balance of payments is a bookkeeping record of all the international transactions between a country and other countries during a given period of time. This summary is the best way to understand interactions between economies because it records the value of a nation's spending inflows and outflows made by individuals, firms, and governments. Exhibit 5 presents a simplified U.S. balance of payments for 2009.

Balance of payments

A bookkeeping record of all the international transactions between a country and other countries during a given period of time.

Birth of the Euro

In 1958, several European nations formed a Common Market to eliminate trade restrictions among member countries. The Common Market called for gradual removal of tariffs and import quotas on goods traded among member nations. Later the name was changed to the *European Economic Community (EEC)*, and it is now called the *European Union (EU)*. This organization established a common system of tariffs for imports from nonmember nations and created common policies for economic matters of joint concern, such as agriculture and transportation. The EU now comprises the 27 nations listed in the table.

In 1999, 11 European countries, joined later by Greece, followed the United States as an example and united in the *European Economic and Monetary Union, (EMU)*. In the United States, 50 states are linked with a common currency, and the Federal Reserve serves as the central bank by conducting monetary policy for the nation. Among the states, trade, labor, and investment enjoy freedom of movement. In 2002, the EMU members replaced

© Image copyright Matt Trommer, 2009. Used under license from Shutterstock.com

their national currencies with a single currency, the euro. The objective was to remove exchange rate fluctuations that impede cross-border transactions. This is why the U.S. Congress created a national currency in 1863 to replace state and private bank currencies.

The EU faces many unanswered questions. Unlike the states of the United States, the EU's member nations do not share a common language or government. This makes maintaining common macro policies difficult. France, for example, might seek to control inflation, while

Note the pluses and minuses in the table. A transaction that is a payment to the United States is entered as a positive amount. A payment by the United States to another country is entered with a minus sign. As our discussion unfolds, you will learn that the balance of payments provides much useful information.

Current Account

Balance of trade

The value of a nation's imports subtracted from its exports. Balance of trade can be given in terms of goods, services, or goods and services.

The first section of the balance of payments is the *current account*, which includes trade in goods and services. The most widely reported part of the current account is the **balance of trade**, also called the trade balance. The balance of trade is the value of a nation's imports subtracted from its exports, and it can be expressed in terms of goods, services, or goods and services. As shown in lines 1–2, the United States had a goods or merchandise (cars, computers) *balance of trade deficit* of –$518 billion in 2009. A trade deficit occurs when the value of a country's imports exceeds the value of its exports. When a nation has a trade deficit, it is called an *unfavorable balance of trade* because more is spent for imports than is earned from exports. Recall that net exports can have a positive (favorable) or negative (unfavorable) effect on GDP = $C + I + G + (X - M)$.

Exhibit 6 charts the annual balance of trade for the United States from 1975 through 2009. Observe that the United States experienced a *balance of trade surplus*

Germany has reducing unemployment as its highest priority. Coordinating monetary policy among EU nations is also difficult. Although the EU has established the *European Central Bank* headquartered in Frankfurt, Germany, with sole authority over the supply of euros, the central banks of member nations still function. But these national central banks operate similar to the district banks of the Federal Reserve System in the United States. Only time will tell whether EU nations will perform better with a single currency than with separate national currencies. It is possible that the euro could become a strong alternative to the U.S. dollar as a key currency for the global financial systems. Currently, the United Kingdom, Denmark, and Sweden still use their own currencies.

European Union (EU) Members

Austria	Finland	Lativia	Romania
Belgium	France	Lithuania	Slovakia
Bulgaria	Germany	Luxembourg	Slovenia
Cyprus	Greece	Malta	Spain
Czech Republic	Hungary	Netherlands	Sweden
Denmark	Ireland	Poland	United Kingdom
Estonia	Italy	Portugal	

in 1975. A trade surplus arises when the value of a country's merchandise exports is greater than the value of its merchandise imports. This is called a *favorable balance of trade* because the United States earned more from exports than it spent for imports. Since 1975, however, sizable trade deficits have occurred. These trade deficits have attracted much attention because in part they reflect the popularity of foreign goods and the lack of competitiveness of goods "Made in U.S.A." In 2001, the U.S. trade deficit narrowed slightly due to the recession and then an upward trend continued. In 2008, the U.S. trade deficits reached the record-breaking level of over $800 billion due in part to the rising price of oil imports. Between 2001 and 2008, the price per barrel grew steadily until reaching a peak in 2008, and the U.S. trade deficit with OPEC countries grew from $40 billion to $179 billion. Also, our trade deficit with China tripled over the same time period from $83 billion to $268 billion. During 2009, oil import prices plunged sharply, the United States experienced deflation, and U.S. trade deficits with OPEC countries and China fell. These factors contributed to the fall in the U.S. balance of trade in 2009.

Lines 3–6 of the current account in Exhibit 5 list ways other than goods to move dollars back and forth between the United States and other countries. Services include insurance, banking, transportation, and tourism. For example, a Japanese tourist who pays a hotel bill in Hawaii buys an export of services, which is a plus or credit to our current account (line 3). Similarly, an American visitor to foreign lands

Exhibit 5	U.S. Balance of Payments, 2009 (billions of dollars)

Type of Transaction	
Current account	
1. Goods exports	$ +1,045
2. Goods imports	−1,563
Trade balance (lines 1–2)	−518
3. Service exports	+509
4. Service imports	−371
5. Investment income (net)	+89
6. Unilateral transfers (net)	−130
Current account balance (lines 1-6)	−421
Capital account	
7. U.S. capital inflow	+435
8. U.S. capital outflow	−237
Capital account balance (lines 7–8)	+198
9. Statistical discrepancy	+223
Net balance (lines 1–9)	0

SOURCE: Bureau of Economic Analysis, click on "Detailed Estimates" for U.S. International Transactions, http://www.bea.gov/international /index.htm, Table 1.

buys an import of services, which is a minus or debit to our services and therefore a minus to our current account (line 4). Income flowing back from U.S. investments abroad, such as plants, real estate, and securities, is a payment for use of the services of U.S. capital. Foreign countries also receive income flowing from the services of their capital owned in the United States. In 2009, line 5 of the table reports a net flow of $89 billion to the United States.

Finally, we consider line 6, unilateral transfers. This category includes gifts made by our government, charitable organizations, or private individuals to other governments or private parties elsewhere in the world. For example, this item includes U.S. foreign aid to other nations. Similar unilateral transfers into the United States must be subtracted to determine the *net* unilateral transfers. Net unilateral transfers for the United States were −$130 billion in 2009.

Adding lines 1–6 gives the current account balance deficit of −$421 billion in 2009. This deficit means that foreigners sent us more goods and services than we sent to them. Because the current account balance includes *both* goods and services, it is a broader measure than the trade balance. Since 1982, the trend in the current account balance has followed the swing into the red shown by the goods trade balance in Exhibit 6.

Capital Account

The second section of the balance of payments is the *capital account*, which records payment flows for financial capital, such as real estate, corporate stocks, bonds, government securities, and other debt instruments. For example, when Chinese investors

Exhibit 6	**U.S. Balance of Trade, 1975–2009 (billions of dollars)**

Since 1975, the United States has experienced trade deficits, in which the value of goods imports has exceeded the value of goods exports. These goods trade deficits attract much attention because in part they reflect the popularity of foreign goods in the United States. During the recession in 2001, the U.S. trade deficit narrowed briefly before continuing an upward trend. The deficits continued to grow until reaching an all-time high of over $800 billion in 2008. In 2009, falling oil prices and other factors contributed to a sharp fall in the U.S. balance of trade.

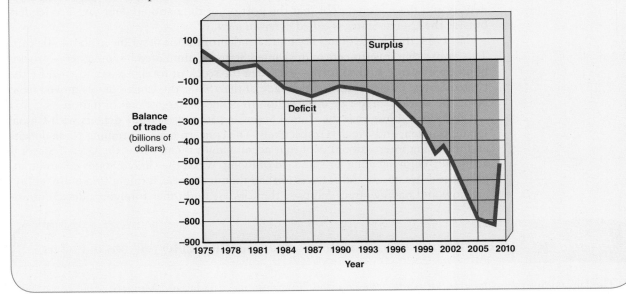

SOURCE: Bureau of Economic Analysis, click on "Detailed Estimates" for U.S. International Transactions, http://www.bea.gov/international/index, Table 1.

buy U.S. Treasury bills, or Japanese investors purchase farmland in Hawaii, there is an inflow of dollars into the United States. As Exhibit 5 shows, foreigners made payments of $435 billion to our capital account (line 7). This exceeded the –$237 billion outflow (line 8) from the United States to purchase foreign-owned financial capital.

An important feature of the capital account is that the United States finances any deficit in its current account through this account. The capital account balance in 2009 was $198 billion. This surplus indicates that there was more foreign investment in U.S. assets than U.S. investment in foreign assets during this year.

> **CONCLUSION** *A current account deficit is financed by a capital account surplus.*

The current account deficit should equal the capital account surplus, but line 9 in the exhibit reveals that the balance of payments is not perfect. The capital account balance does not exactly offset the current account balance. Hence, a credit amount is simply recorded as a statistical discrepancy; therefore, the balance of payments always balances, or equals zero.

The International Debt of the United States

If each nation's balance of payments is always zero, why is there so much talk about a U.S. balance of payments problem? The problem is with the *composition* of the balance of payments. Suppose the United States runs a $500 billion deficit in its current account. This means that the current account deficit must be financed by a net annual capital inflow in the capital account of $500 billion. That is, foreign lenders, such as banks and businesses, must purchase U.S. assets and grant loans to the United States that on balance equal $500 billion. For example, a Chinese bank could buy U.S. Treasury bonds. Recall from Exhibit 7 in the chapter on federal deficits and the national debt that the portion of the national debt owed to lenders outside the United States is called *external debt*.

In 1984, the United States became a net debtor for the first time in about 70 years. This means that investments in the United States accumulated by foreigners—stocks, bonds, real estate, and so forth—exceeded the stock of foreign assets owned by the United States. In fact, during the decade of the 1980s, the United States moved from being the world's largest creditor nation to being the largest debtor nation.

Exhibit 7 shows that the United States has its largest trade deficits with China, Japan, Canada, and Mexico respectively. The concern over continuing trade deficits and the rising international debt that accompanies them is that the United States is artificially enjoying a higher standard of living. When the United States continues to purchase more goods and services abroad than it exports, it might find itself "enjoying now and paying later." Suppose the Chinese and other foreigners decide not to

| *Exhibit 7* | **U.S. Balance of Trade with Selected Countries, 2009 (billions of dollars)** |

The United States has its greatest trade deficits with China, Japan, Canada, and Mexico.

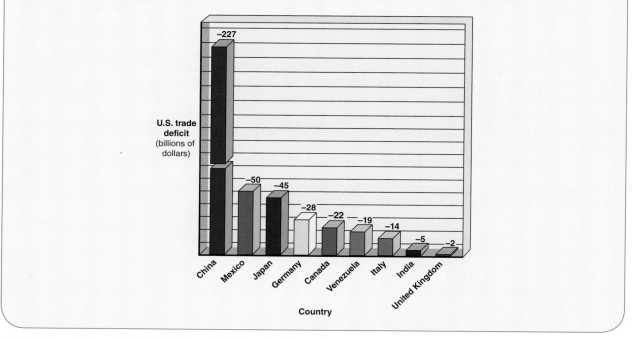

SOURCE: Bureau of Economic Analysis, U.S. International Transactions by Area, http://www.bea.gov/international/index.htm, Table 12.

make new U.S. investments and loans. In this case, the United States will be forced to eliminate its trade deficit by bringing exports and imports into balance. In fact, if other countries not only refuse to provide new capital inflows, but also decide to liquidate their investments, the United States would be forced to run a trade surplus. Stated differently, we would be forced to tighten our belts and accept a lower standard of living. How a change in foreign willingness to purchase U.S. assets also affects the international value of the dollar is the topic to which we now turn.

CheckPoint

Should Everyone Keep a Balance of Payments?

Nations keep balances of payments and calculate accounts such as their merchandise trade deficit or surplus. If nations need these accounts, the 50 states should also maintain balances of payments to manage their economies. Or should they? What about cities?

Exchange Rates

Each transaction recorded in the balance of payments requires an exchange of one country's currency for that of another. Suppose you buy a Japanese car made in Japan, say, a Mazda. Mazda wants to be paid in yen and not dollars, so dollars must be traded for yen. On the other hand, suppose Pink Panther Airline Company in France purchases an airplane from Boeing in the United States. Pink Panther has euros to pay the bill, but Boeing wants dollars. Consequently, euros must be exchanged for dollars.

The critical question for Mazda, Pink Panther, Boeing, and everyone involved in world trade is, "What is the **exchange rate**?" The exchange rate is the number of units of one nation's currency that equals one unit of another nation's currency. For example, assume 1.81 dollars can be exchanged for 1 British pound. This means the exchange rate is 1.81 dollars = 1 pound. Alternatively, the exchange rate can be expressed as a reciprocal. Dividing 1 British pound by 1.81 dollars gives 0.552 pounds per dollar. Now suppose you are visiting England and want to buy a T-shirt with a price tag of 10 pounds. Knowing the exchange rate tells you the T-shirt costs $18.10 (10 pounds × $1.81/pound).

Exchange rate

The number of units of one nation's currency that equals one unit of another nation's currency.

CONCLUSION *An exchange rate can be expressed as a reciprocal.*

Supply and Demand for Foreign Exchange

The exchange rate for dollars, or any nation's currency, is determined by global forces of supply and demand. For example, consider the exchange rate of yen to dollars, shown in Exhibit 8. Like the price and the quantity of any good traded in markets, the quantity of dollars exchanged is measured on the horizontal axis, and the price per unit is measured on the vertical axis. In this case, the price per unit is the value of the U.S. dollar expressed as the number of yen per dollar.

Exhibit 8   The Supply of and Demand for Dollars

The number of Japanese yen per dollar in the foreign exchange market is determined by the demand for dollars by Japanese citizens and the supply of dollars by U.S. citizens. The equilibrium exchange rate is 100 yen per dollar, and the equilibrium quantity is $300 million per day.

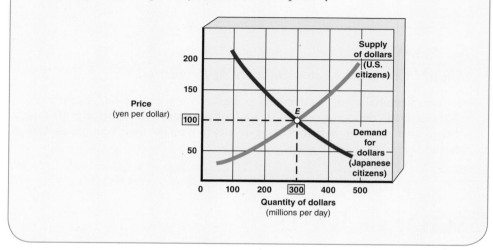

The demand for dollars in the world currency market comes from Japanese individuals, corporations, and governments that want to buy U.S. exports. Because the Japanese buyers must pay for U.S. exports with dollars, they *demand* to exchange their yen for dollars. As expected, the demand curve for dollars or any foreign currency is downward sloping. A decline in the number of yen per dollar means that one yen buys a larger portion of a dollar. This means U.S. goods and investment opportunities are less expensive to Japanese buyers because they must pay fewer yen for each dollar. Thus, as the yen price of dollars decreases, the quantity of dollars demanded by the Japanese to purchase Fords, stocks, land, and other U.S. products and investments increases. For example, suppose a CD recording of the hottest rock group has a $20 price tag. If the exchange rate is 200 yen to the dollar, a Japanese importer would pay 4,000 yen. If the price of dollars to Japanese buyers falls to 100 yen each, the same $20 CD will cost Japanese importers only 2,000 yen. This lower price causes Japanese buyers to increase their orders, which, in turn, increases the quantity of dollars demanded.

The supply curve of dollars is upward sloping. This curve shows the amount of dollars offered for exchange at various yen prices per dollar in the world currency exchange market. Similar to the demand for dollars, the supply of dollars in this market flows from individuals, corporations, and governments in the United States that want to buy Mazdas, stocks, land, and other products and investments from Japan. Because U.S. citizens must pay for the Japanese goods and services in yen, they must exchange dollars for yen. An example will illustrate why the supply curve of dollars slopes upward. Suppose a Nikon camera sells for 100,000 yen in Tokyo and the exchange rate is 100 yen per dollar or 0.01 dollar per yen ($1/100 yen). Therefore, the camera costs an American tourist $1,000. Now assume the exchange rate rises to 250 yen per dollar or 0.004 dollar per yen ($1/250 yen). The camera will now cost the American buyer only $400. Because the prices of the Nikon camera and other Japanese products fall when the number of yen per dollar rises, Americans respond by purchasing more Japanese imports, which, in turn, increases the quantity of dollars supplied.

The foreign exchange market in Exhibit 8 is in equilibrium at an exchange rate of 100 yen for $1. As you learned in Chapter 3, if the exchange rate is above equilibrium, there will be a surplus of dollars in the world currency market. Citizens of the United States are supplying more dollars than the Japanese demand, and the exchange rate falls. On the other hand, below equilibrium, there will be a shortage of dollars in the world currency market. In this case, the Japanese are demanding more dollars than Americans supply, and the exchange rate rises.

Shifts in Supply and Demand for Foreign Exchange

For most of the years between World War II and 1971, currency exchange rates were *fixed*. Exchange rates were based primarily on gold. For example, the German mark was fixed at about 25 cents. The dollar was worth 1/35 of an ounce of gold, and 4 German marks were worth 1/35 of an ounce of gold. Therefore, 1 dollar equaled 4 marks, or 25 cents equaled 1 mark. In 1971, Western nations agreed to stop fixing their exchange rates and to allow their currencies to *float* according to the forces of supply and demand. Exhibit 9 illustrates that these rates can fluctuate widely. For example, in 1980, 1 dollar was worth about 230 Japanese yen. After gyrating up and down over the years, the exchange rate hit a postwar low of 93 yen per dollar in 2009.

Exhibit 9	**Changes in the Yen-per-Dollar Exchange Rate, 1980–2009**

Today, most economies are on a system of flexible exchange rates. As the demand and supply curves for currencies change, exchange rates change. In 1980, 1 dollar was worth about 230 Japanese yen. By 2009, the exchange rate had dropped to a postwar low of 93 yen per dollar.

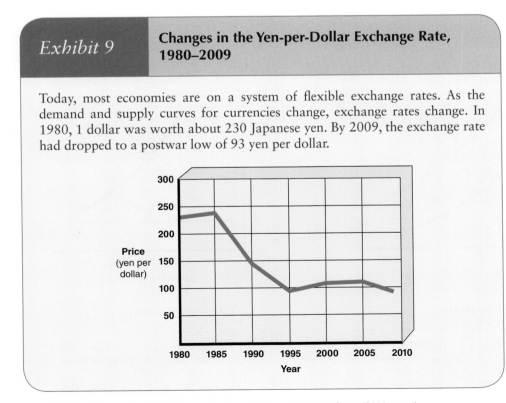

SOURCE: Federal Reserve Statistical Release, http://www.federalreserve.gov/releases/G5A/current/.

Recall from Chapter 3 that the equilibrium price for products changes in response to shifts in the supply and demand curves. The same supply and demand analysis applies to equilibrium exchange rates for foreign currency. There are four important sources of shifts in the supply and demand curves for foreign exchange. Let's consider each in turn.

Tastes and Preferences Exhibit 10(a) illustrates one important factor that causes the demand for foreign currencies to shift. Suppose the Japanese lose their "taste" for tobacco, U.S. government bonds, and other U.S. products and investment opportunities. This decline in the popularity of U.S. products in Japan decreases the demand for dollars at each possible exchange rate, and the demand curve shifts leftward from D_1 to D_2. This change causes the equilibrium exchange rate to fall from 150 yen to the dollar at E_1 to 100 yen to the dollar at E_2. Because the number of yen to the dollar declines, the dollar is said to *depreciate* or become *weaker*. **Depreciation of currency** is a fall in the price of one currency relative to another.

Depreciation of currency

A fall in the price of one currency relative to another.

Exhibit 10   **Changes in the Supply and Demand Curves for Dollars**

In part (a), U.S. exports become less popular in Japan. This change in tastes for U.S. products and investments decreases the demand for dollars, and the demand curve shifts leftward from D_1 to D_2. As a result, the equilibrium exchange rate falls from 150 yen to the dollar at E_1 to 100 yen to the dollar at E_2.

Part (b) assumes U.S. citizens are influenced by the "Buy American" idea. In this case, our demand for Japanese imports decreases, and U.S. citizens supply fewer dollars to the foreign currency market. The result is that the supply curve shifts leftward from S_1 to S_2, and the equilibrium exchange rate rises from 100 yen per dollar at E_1 to 150 yen per dollar at E_2.

What happens to the exchange rate if the "Buy American" idea changes our tastes and the demand for Japanese imports decreases? In this case, U.S. citizens supply fewer dollars at any possible exchange rate, and the supply curve in Exhibit 10(b) shifts leftward from S_1 to S_2. As a result, the equilibrium exchange rate rises from 100 yen to the dollar at E_1 to 150 yen to the dollar at E_2. Because the number of yen per dollar rises, the dollar is said to *appreciate* or become *stronger*. Appreciation of currency is a rise in the price of one currency relative to another.

Appreciation of currency

A rise in the price of one currency relative to another.

Relative Incomes   Assume income in the United States rises, while income in Japan remains unchanged. As a result, U.S. citizens buy more domestic products and more Japanese imports. The results are a rightward shift in the supply curve for dollars and a decrease in the equilibrium exchange rate. Paradoxically, growth of U.S. income leads to the dollar depreciating, or becoming weaker, against the Japanese yen.

CONCLUSION *An expansion in relative U.S. income causes a depreciation of the dollar.*

Relative Price Levels   Now we consider a more complex case, in which a change in a factor causes a change in both the supply and the demand curves for dollars. Assume the foreign exchange rate begins in equilibrium at 100 yen per dollar, as shown at point E_1 in Exhibit 11. Now assume the price level increases in Japan, but remains constant in the United States. The Japanese therefore want to buy more U.S. exports because they have become cheaper relative to Japanese products. This willingness of the Japanese to buy U.S. goods and services shifts the demand curve for dollars rightward from D_1 to D_2. In addition, U.S. products are cheaper for U.S. citizens compared to Japanese imports. As a result, the willingness to import from Japan is reduced at each exchange rate, which means the supply curve of dollars decreases from S_1 to S_2. The result of the shifts in both the demand and the supply curves for dollars is to establish a new equilibrium at point E_2, and the exchange rate reaches 200 yen per dollar.

CONCLUSION *A rise in a trading partner's relative price level causes the dollar to appreciate.*

Relative Real Interest Rates   Changes in relative real (inflation-adjusted) interest rates can have an important effect on the exchange rate. Suppose real interest rates in the United States rise, while those in Japan remain constant. To take advantage of more attractive yields, Japanese investors buy an increased amount of bonds and other interest-bearing securities issued by private and government borrowers in the United States. This change increases the demand for dollars, which increases the equilibrium exchange rate of yen to the dollar, causing the dollar to appreciate (or the yen to depreciate).

There can also be an effect on the supply of dollars. When real interest rates rise in the United States, our citizens purchase fewer Japanese securities. Hence, they offer fewer dollars at each possible exchange rate, and the supply curve for dollars shifts leftward. As a result, the equilibrium exchange rate increases, and the dollar appreciates from changes in both the demand for and the supply of dollars.

Exhibit 11   **The Impact of Relative Price Level Changes on Exchange Rates**

Begin at E_1, with the exchange rate equal to 100 yen per dollar. Assume prices in Japan rise relative to those in the United States. As a result, the demand for dollars increases, and the supply of dollars decreases. The new equilibrium is at E_2 when the dollar appreciates (rises in value) to 200 yen per dollar.

The Impact of Exchange Rate Fluctuations

Now it is time to stop for a minute, take a breath, and draw some important conclusions. As you have just learned, exchange rates between most major currencies are flexible. Instead of being pegged to gold or another fixed standard, their value is determined by the laws of supply and demand. Consequently, shifts in supply and demand create a weaker or a stronger dollar. But it should be noted that exchange rates do not fluctuate with total freedom. Governments often buy and sell currencies to prevent wide swings in exchange rates. In summary, the strength or weakness of any nation's currency has a profound impact on its economy.

A weak dollar is a "mixed blessing." Ironically, a weak dollar makes U.S. producers happy because they can sell their less expensive exports to foreign buyers. As export sales rise, jobs are created in the United States. On the other hand, a weak dollar makes foreign producers and domestic consumers unhappy because the prices of Japanese cars, French wine, and Italian shoes are higher. As U.S. imports fall, jobs are lost in foreign countries.

> **CONCLUSION** *When the dollar is weak or depreciates, U.S. goods and services cost foreign consumers less, so they buy more U.S. exports. At the same time, a weak dollar means foreign goods and services cost U.S. consumers more, so they buy fewer imports.*

A strong dollar is also a "mixed blessing." A strong dollar makes our major trading partners happy because the prices of Japanese cars, French wine, and Italian shoes are lower. A strong dollar, contrary to the implication of the term, makes U.S. producers unhappy because their exports are more expensive and related jobs decline. Conversely, a strong dollar makes foreign producers happy because the prices of their goods and services are lower, causing U.S. imports to rise.

> **CONCLUSION** *When the dollar is strong or appreciates, U.S. goods and services cost foreign consumers more, so they buy fewer U.S. exports. At the same time, a strong dollar means foreign goods and services cost U.S. consumers less, so they buy more foreign imports.*

Finally, as promised earlier in this chapter, we return to the discussion of NAFTA in order to illustrate the impact of this free trade agreement and the effect of a strong dollar. Recall that in January 1994, NAFTA began a gradual phaseout of tariffs and other trade barriers. Exhibit 12 provides trade data for the United States

Exhibit 12   U.S. Trade Balances with Mexico, 1993–2009

Year	U.S. Exports to Mexico (billions of dollars)	U.S. Imports from Mexico (billions of dollars)	Exchange Rate (pesos per dollar)	U.S. Trade Surplus (+) or Deficit (−) (billions of dollars)
1993	$ 42	$ 40	3.12	$ +2
1995	46	63	6.45	−17
1997	71	87	7.92	−16
1999	87	111	9.55	−24
2001	101	132	9.34	−31
2003	97	139	10.79	−42
2005	120	173	10.89	−53
2007	136	214	10.93	−78
2009	129	179	13.50	−50

SOURCES: Bureau of Economic Analysis, U.S. International Transactions by Area, http://www.bea.gov/international/index.htm, Table 12 and Federal Reserve Statistical Release, http://www.federalreserve.gov/releases/G5A/current/.

Global Economics   Return to the Yellow Brick Road?

Applicable Concept: exchange rates

Gold is always a fascinating story: *The Wonderful Wizard of Oz* was first published in 1900 and this children's tale has been interpreted as an allegory for political and economic events of the 1890s. For example, the Yellow Brick Road represents the gold standard, Oz in the title is an abbreviation for ounce, Dorothy is the naive public, Emerald City symbolizes Washington, D.C., the Tin Woodman represents the industrial worker, the Scarecrow is the farmer, and the Cyclone is a metaphor for a political revolution. In the end, Dorothy discovers magical powers in her *silver* shoes (changed to ruby in the 1939 film) to find her way home and not the fallacy of the Yellow Brick Road. Although the author of the story, L. Frank Baum, never stated it was his intention, it can be argued that the issue of the story concerns the election of 1896. Democratic presidential nominee William Jennings Bryan (the Cowardly Lion) supported fixing the value of the dollar to both gold and silver (bimetallism), but Republican William McKinley (the Wicked Witch) advocated using only the gold standard. Since McKinley won, the United States remained on the Yellow Brick Road.[1]

The United States adopted the gold standard in 1873 and until the 1930s, most industrial countries were on the gold standard. The gold standard served as an international monetary system in which currencies were defined in terms of gold. Under the gold standard, a nation with a balance of payments deficit was required to ship gold to other nations to finance the deficit. Hence, a large excess of imports over exports meant a corresponding outflow of gold from a nation. As a result, that nation's money supply decreased, which, in turn, reduced the aggregate demand for goods and services. Lower domestic demand led to falling prices, lower production, and fewer jobs. In contrast, a nation with a balance of payments surplus would experience an inflow of gold and the opposite effects. In this case, the nation's money supply increased, and its aggregate demand for goods and services rose. Higher aggregate spending, in turn, boosted employment and the price level. In short, the gold standard meant that governments could not control their money supplies and thereby conduct monetary policy.

The gold standard worked fairly well as a fixed exchange rate system so long as nations did not face sudden or severe swings in flows from their stocks of gold. The Great Depression marked the beginning of the end of the gold standard. Nations faced with trade deficits and high unemployment began going off the gold standard, rather than contracting their money supplies by following the gold standard.

In 1933, President Franklin D. Roosevelt took the United States off the gold standard and ordered all 1933 gold double eagle coins already manufactured to be melted down and not circulated. Through a long twisted story worthy of a Sherlock Holmes mystery novel involving the Smithsonian Institution,

---

1. Bradley A. Hansen, "The Fable of the Allegory," *Journal of Economic Education*, Summer 2002, pp. 254–264.

and Mexico for the years surrounding NAFTA. As the exhibit shows, both exports and imports of goods increased sharply after NAFTA. On the other hand, a small U.S. trade surplus of $2 billion with Mexico in 1993 turned into a huge trade deficit of $50 billion in 2009.

Before blaming this trade deficit entirely on NAFTA, you must note that the exchange rate rose from 3.12 to 13.50 pesos per dollar. Since 1995, the peso was the former king of Egypt, the Treasury Department, the Justice Department, the U.S. Mint, and a long list of intriguing supporting characters, one 1933 double eagle surfaced and was sold for $7.59 million in 2002. This was double the previous record for a coin.

Once the Allies felt certain they would win World War II, the finance ministers of Western nations met in 1944 at Bretton Woods, New Hampshire, to establish a new international monetary system. The new system was based on fixed exchange rates and an international central bank called the *International Monetary Fund (IMF)*. The IMF makes loans to countries faced with short-term balance of payments problems. Under this system, nations were expected to maintain fixed exchange rates within a narrow range. In the 1960s and early 1970s, the Bretton Woods system became strained as conditions changed. In the 1960s, inflation rates in the United States rose relative to those in other countries, causing U.S. exports to become more expensive and U.S. imports to become less expensive. This situation increased the supply of dollars abroad and caused an increasing surplus of dollars, thus putting downward pressure on the exchange rate. Monetary authorities in the United States worried that central banks would demand gold for their dollars, the U.S. gold stock would diminish sharply, and the declining money supply would adversely affect the economy.

Something had to give, and it did. In August 1971, President Richard Nixon announced that the United States would no longer honor its obligation to sell gold at $35 an ounce. By 1973, the gold standard was dead, and most of our trading partners were letting the forces of supply and demand determine exchange rates.

Today, some people advocate returning to the gold standard. These gold buffs do not trust the government to control the money supply without the discipline of a gold standard. They argue that if governments have the freedom to print money, political pressures will sooner or later cause them to increase the money supply too much and let inflation rage.

One argument against the gold standard is that no one can control the supply of gold. Big gold discoveries can cause inflation and have done so in the past. On the other hand, slow growth in the stock of mined gold can lead to slow economic growth and a loss of jobs. Governments therefore are unlikely to return to the gold standard because it would mean turning monetary policy over to uncontrollable swings in the stock of gold.

ANALYZE THE ISSUE

Return to Exhibit 8, and assume the equilibrium exchange rate is 150 yen per dollar and the equilibrium quantity is $300 million. Redraw this figure, and place a horizontal line through the equilibrium exchange rate to represent a fixed exchange rate. Now use this figure to explain why a country would abandon the gold standard.

devalued and the stronger dollar has put the price of U.S. goods out of reach for many Mexican consumers. This is one reason U.S. exports to Mexico have been lower than they would have been otherwise. At the same time, Mexican goods became less expensive for U.S. consumers, so U.S. imports from Mexico have risen.

Key Concepts

Comparative advantage
Absolute advantage
Free trade
Protectionism
Embargo

Tariff
World Trade Organization (WTO)
Quota
Balance of payments

Balance of trade
Exchange rate
Depreciation of currency
Appreciation of currency

Summary

- **Comparative advantage** is a principle that allows nations to gain from trade. Comparative advantage means that each nation *specializes* in a product for which its opportunity cost is lower in terms of the production of another product, and then nations trade. When nations follow this principle, they gain. The reason is that world output increases, and each nation ends up with a higher standard of living by consuming more goods and services than would be possible without specialization and trade.

Comparative Advantage

(b) Japanese production and consumption

(a) U.S. production and consumption

- **Free trade** benefits a nation as a whole, but individuals may lose jobs and incomes because of the competition from foreign goods and services.
- **Protectionism** is a government's use of embargoes, tariffs, quotas, and other methods to impose barriers intended to both reduce imports and protect particular domestic industries. *Embargoes* prohibit the import or export of particular goods. *Tariffs* discourage imports by making them more expensive. *Quotas* limit the quantity of imports or exports of certain goods. These trade barriers often result primarily from domestic groups that exert political pressure on government in order to gain from these barriers.

- The *balance of payments* is a summary bookkeeping record of all the international transactions a country makes during a year. It is divided into different accounts, including the *current account*, the *capital account*, and the *statistical discrepancy*. The current account summarizes all transactions in currently produced goods and services. The overall balance of payments is always zero after an adjustment for the statistical discrepancy.
- The *balance of trade* measures only goods (not services) that a nation exports and imports. A balance of trade can be in deficit or in surplus. The balance of trade is the most widely reported and largest part of the current account. Since 1975, the United States has experienced balance of trade deficits.

Balance of Trade

- An *exchange rate* is the price of one nation's currency in terms of another nation's currency. Foreigners who wish to purchase U.S. goods, services, and financial assets demand dollars.

The supply of dollars reflects the desire of U.S. citizens to purchase foreign goods, services, and financial assets. The intersection of the supply and demand curves for dollars determines the number of units of a foreign currency per dollar.

Exchange Rate

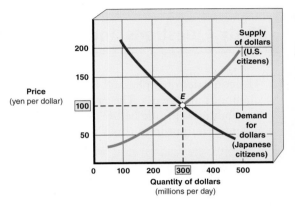

- *Shifts in supply and demand for foreign exchange* result from changes in such factors as tastes, relative price levels, relative real interest rates, and relative income levels.
- *Depreciation of currency* occurs when one currency becomes worth fewer units of another currency. If a currency depreciates, it becomes weaker. Depreciation of a nation's currency increases its exports and decreases its imports.
- *Appreciation of currency* occurs when one currency becomes worth more units of another currency. If a currency appreciates, it becomes stronger. Appreciation of a nation's currency decreases its exports and increases its imports.

Summary of Conclusion Statements

- When countries specialize, total world output increases, and, therefore, the potential for greater total world consumption also increases.
- Global trade allows a country to consume a combination of goods that exceeds its production possibilities curve.
- Comparative advantage refers to the relative opportunity costs between different countries

of producing the same goods. World output and consumption are maximized when each country specializes in producing and trading goods for which it has a comparative advantage.
- A current account deficit is financed by a capital account surplus.
- An exchange rate can be expressed as a reciprocal.

- An expansion in relative U.S. income causes a depreciation of the dollar.
- A rise in a trading partner's relative price level causes the dollar to appreciate.
- When the dollar is weak or depreciates, U.S. goods and services cost foreign consumers less, so they buy more U.S. exports. At the same time, a weak dollar means foreign goods and services cost U.S. consumers more, so they buy fewer imports.
- When the dollar is strong or appreciates, U.S. goods and services cost foreign consumers more, so they buy fewer U.S. exports. At the same time, a strong dollar means foreign goods and services cost U.S. consumers less, so they buy more foreign imports.

Study Questions and Problems

1. The countries of Alpha and Beta produce diamonds and pearls. The production possibilities schedule below describes their potential output in tons per year:

Points on Production Possibilities Curve	Alpha		Beta	
	Diamonds	Pearls	Diamonds	Pearls
A	150	0	90	0
B	100	25	60	60
C	50	50	30	120
D	0	75	0	180

Using the data in the table, answer the following questions:
   a. What is the opportunity cost of diamonds for each country?
   b. What is the opportunity cost of pearls for each country?
   c. In which good does Alpha have a comparative advantage?
   d. In which good does Beta have a comparative advantage?
   e. Suppose Alpha is producing and consuming at point B on its production possibilities curve and Beta is producing and consuming at point C on its production possibilities curve. Use a table such as Exhibit 3 to explain why both nations would benefit if they specialize.
   f. Draw a graph, and use it to explain how Alpha and Beta benefit if they specialize and Alpha agrees to trade 50 tons of diamonds to Beta and Alpha receives 50 tons of pearls in exchange.

2. Bill can paint either two walls or one window frame in one hour. In the same time, Frank can paint either three walls or two window frames. To minimize the time spent painting, who should specialize in painting walls, and who should specialize in painting window frames?

3. Consider this statement: "The principles of specialization and trade according to comparative advantage among nations also apply to states in the United States." Do you agree or disagree? Explain.

4. Would the U.S. government gain any advantage from using tariffs or quotas to restrict imports?

5. Suppose the United States passed a law stating that we would not purchase imports from any country that imposed any trade restrictions on our exports. Who would benefit and who would lose from such retaliation?

6. Now consider question 5 in terms of the law's impact on domestic producers that export goods. Does this policy adversely affect domestic producers that export goods?

7. Consider this statement: "Unrestricted foreign trade costs domestic jobs." Do you agree or disagree? Explain.

8. Do you support a constitutional amendment to prohibit the federal government from imposing any trade barriers, such as tariffs and quotas, except in case of war or national emergency? Why or why not?

9. Discuss this statement: "Because each nation's balance of payments equals zero, it follows that there is actually no significance to a balance of payments deficit or surplus."

10. For each of the following situations, indicate the direction of the shift in the supply

curve or the demand curve for dollars, the factor causing the change, and the resulting movement of the equilibrium exchange rate for the dollar in terms of foreign currency:

a. American-made cars become more popular overseas.

b. The United States experiences a recession, while other nations enjoy economic growth.

c. Inflation rates accelerate in the United States, while inflation rates remain constant in other nations.

d. Real interest rates in the United States rise, while real interest rates abroad remain constant.

e. The Japanese put quotas and high tariffs on all imports from the United States.

f. Tourism from the United States increases sharply because of a fare war among airlines.

11. The following table summarizes the supply and the demand for euros:

	U.S. Dollars per Euro				
	$0.05	$0.10	$0.15	$0.20	$0.25
Quantity demanded (per day)	500	400	300	200	100
Quantity supplied (per day)	100	200	300	400	500

Using the above table:

a. Graph the supply and demand curves for euros.

b. Determine the equilibrium exchange rate.

c. Determine what the effect of a fixed exchange rate at $0.10 per euro would be.

For Online Exercises, go to the Tucker Web site at www.cengage.com/economics/tucker.

Checkpoint Answers

Do Nations with an Advantage Always Trade?

In the United States, the opportunity cost of producing 1 calculator is 100 towels. In Costa Rica, opportunity cost of producing 1 calculator is 100 towels. If you said, because the opportunity cost is the same for each nation, specialization and trade would not boost total output, and therefore Costa Rica would not trade these products, **YOU ARE CORRECT.**

Should Everyone Keep a Balance of Payments?

The principal purpose of the balance of payments is to keep track of payments of national currencies. Because states and cities within the same nation use the same national currency, payments for goods and services traded between these parties do not represent a loss (outflow) or gain (inflow). If you said only nations need to use the balance of payments to account for flows of foreign currency across national boundaries, **YOU ARE CORRECT.**

Practice Quiz

For an explanation of the correct answers, visit the Tucker Web site at www.cengage.com/economics/tucker.

1. With trade, the production possibilities for two nations lie
   a. outside their consumption possibilities.
   b. inside their consumption possibilities.
   c. at a point equal to the world production possibilities curve.
   d. none of the above.

2. Free trade theory suggests that when trade takes place
   a. both nations will be worse off.
   b. one nation must gain at the other nation's expense.

Practice Quiz Continued

c. both nations will be better off.

d. one nation will gain and the other nation will be neither better nor worse off.

3. Which of the following is *true* when two countries specialize according to their comparative advantage?

a. It is possible to increase their total output of all goods.

b. It is possible to increase their total output of some goods only if both countries are industrialized.

c. One country is likely to gain from trade, while the other loses.

d. None of the above is true.

4. According to the theory of comparative advantage, a country should produce and

a. import goods in which it has an absolute advantage.

b. export goods in which it has an absolute advantage.

c. import goods in which it has a comparative advantage.

d. export goods in which it has a comparative advantage.

5. In Exhibit 13, which country has the comparative advantage in the production of potatoes?

a. The United States because it requires fewer resources to produce potatoes

b. The United States because it has the lower opportunity cost of potatoes

c. Ireland because it requires fewer resources to produce potatoes

d. Ireland because it has the lower opportunity cost of potatoes

6. In Exhibit 13, the opportunity cost of wheat is

a. 1/3 ton of potatoes in the United States and 1/2 ton of potatoes in Ireland.

b. 2 tons of potatoes in the United States and 1 1/2 tons of potatoes in Ireland.

c. 8 tons of potatoes in the United States and 4 tons of potatoes in Ireland.

d. 1/2 ton of potatoes in the United States and 2/3 ton of potatoes in Ireland.

7. In Exhibit 13, the opportunity cost of potatoes is

a. 1/2 ton of wheat in the United States and 2/3 ton of wheat in Ireland.

b. 2 tons of wheat in the United States and 1 1/2 tons of wheat in Ireland.

c. 16 tons of wheat in the United States and 6 tons of wheat in Ireland.

d. 3 tons of wheat in the United States and 2 tons of wheat in Ireland.

8. If the countries in Exhibit 13 follow the principle of comparative advantage, the United States should

a. buy all of its potatoes from Ireland.

b. buy all of its wheat from Ireland.

c. buy all of its potatoes and wheat from Ireland.

d. produce both potatoes and wheat and not trade with Ireland.

9. A tariff increases

a. the quantity of imports.

b. the ability of foreign goods to compete with domestic goods.

c. the prices of imports to domestic buyers.

d. all of the above.

10. The infant industry argument for protectionism is based on which of the following views?

a. Foreign buyers will absorb all of the output of domestic producers in a new industry.

b. The growth of an industry that is new to a nation will be too rapid unless trade restrictions are imposed.

c. Firms in a newly developing domestic industry will have difficulty growing if they face strong competition from established foreign firms.

d. It is based on none of the above.

Exhibit 13	Potatoes and Wheat Output (tons per hour)	
Country	Potatoes	Wheat
United States	1	3
Ireland	1	2

Practice Quiz Continued

11. The figure that results when goods imports are subtracted from goods exports is
    a. the capital account balance.
    b. the balance of trade.
    c. the current account balance.
    d. always less than zero.

12. Which of the following international accounts records payments for exports and imports of goods, military transactions, foreign travel, investment income, and foreign gifts?
    a. The capital account
    b. The merchandise account
    c. The current account
    d. The official reserve account

13. Which of the following international accounts records the purchase and sale of financial assets and real estate between the United States and other nations?
    a. The balance of trade account
    b. The current account
    c. The capital account
    d. The balance of payments account

14. If a Japanese radio priced at 2,000 yen can be purchased for $10, the exchange rate is
    a. 200 yen per dollar.
    b. 20 yen per dollar.
    c. 20 dollars per yen.
    d. none of the above.

15. The United States
    a. was on a fixed exchange rate system prior to late 1971, but now is on a flexible exchange rate system.
    b. has been on a fixed exchange rate system since 1945.
    c. has been on a flexible exchange rate system since 1945.
    d. was on a flexible exchange rate system prior to late 1983, but now is on a fixed exchange rate system.

16. Suppose the exchange rate changes so that fewer Japanese yen are required to buy a dollar. We would conclude that
    a. the Japanese yen has depreciated in value.
    b. U.S. citizens will buy fewer Japanese imports.

    c. Japanese will demand fewer U.S. exports.
    d. none of the above will occur.

17. Which of the following would cause a decrease in the demand for euros by those holding U.S. dollars?
    a. Inflation in France, but not in the United States
    b. Inflation in the United States, but not in France
    c. An increase in the real rate of interest on investments in France above the real rate of interest on investments in the United States
    d. None of the above

18. An increase in the equilibrium price of a nation's money could be caused by a (an)
    a. decrease in the supply of money curve.
    b. decrease in the demand for money curve.
    c. increase in the supply of money curve.
    d. increase in the quantity of money demanded.

19. If the dollar appreciates (becomes stronger), this causes
    a. the relative price of U.S. goods to increase for foreigners.
    b. the relative price of foreign goods to decrease for Americans.
    c. U.S. exports to fall and U.S. imports to rise.
    d. a balance of trade deficit for the United States.
    e. all of the above to occur.

20. Which of the following would cause the U.S. dollar to depreciate against the Japanese yen?
    a. Greater popularity of U.S. exports in Japan
    b. A higher price level in Japan
    c. Higher real interest rates in the United States
    d. Higher incomes in the United States

Economies in Transition

The inherent vice of capitalism is the unequal sharing of blessings. The inherent virtue of communism is the equal sharing of miseries.

—Winston Churchill

The emergence of the market system in Russia, China, and other countries continues while leaders of these countries that used to be devoted followers of Marxist ideology now say they believe that capitalism, private property, and profit are ideas superior to the communist system. The failure of communism and the transformation toward a market system is personified by the success of McDonald's in Russia and Wal-Mart in China. Today, Russia and other countries continue to experience economic problems during their restructuring, but the commitment to free-market reforms remains. And in 2009, the media reported the astonishing news that the United States was nationalizing banks and General Motors. What caused this astonishing turn of events?

To understand how the pieces of the global economic puzzle fit together, this chapter begins with a discussion of the three basic types of economies. Then you will examine the pros and cons of the "isms"—capitalism, socialism, and communism. Here you will explore the worldwide clash between the ideas of Adam Smith and Karl Marx and study their current influence on economic systems. Finally, you will examine economic reforms in Cuba, Russia, and China.

In this chapter, you will learn to solve these economics puzzles:

• Why did drivers in the former Soviet Union remove the windshield wipers and side mirrors whenever they parked their cars?

• What did Adam Smith mean when he said that an "invisible hand" promotes the public interest?

• If the Soviet Union was foolish to run its economy on five-year plans, why do universities, businesses, and governments in a capitalistic economy plan?

Basic Types of Economic Systems

North Korea and South Korea share the same language and historical background. However, South Korea today is a modern economy and people starve in North Korea. This difference relates to their differing economic systems. An **economic system** consists of the organizations and methods used to determine what goods and services are produced, how they are produced, and for whom they are produced. As explained earlier in Chapter 2, scarcity forces each economic system to decide what combination of goods to produce, how to produce such goods, and who gets the output once produced. The decision-making process involves interaction among many aspects of a nation's culture, such as its laws, form of government, ethics, religions, and customs. Economist Robert L. Heilbroner established a simple way to look at the basic methods society can employ. Each economic system can be classified into one of three basic types: (1) *traditional*, (2) *command*, and (3) *market*.

Economic system

The organizations and methods used to determine what goods and services are produced, how they are produced, and for whom they are produced.

The Traditional Economy

Why does England have a king or queen? Tradition is the answer. Historically, the traditional economy has been a common system for making economic decisions. The traditional economy is a system that answers the *What, How,* and *For Whom* questions the way they have always been answered. People in this type of society learn that copying the previous generation allows them to feel accepted. Anyone who changes ways of doing things asks for trouble from others. This is because people in such a society believe that what was good yesterday, and years ago, must still be a good idea today.

Although most traditional economies have switched to keep pace with modern economic trends, traditional systems are used today, for example, by the Ainu of Japan, the native people of Brazil's rain forest, the pygmies of Central Africa, and the Amish of Pennsylvania. In these societies, the way past generations decided what crops are planted, how they are harvested, and to whom they are distributed remains unchanged over time. People perform their jobs in the manner established by their ancestors. The Amish are well known for rejecting tractors and using horse-drawn plows. Interestingly, the Amish reject Social Security because their society voluntarily redistributes wealth to members who are needy.

Traditional economy

A system that answers the *What, How,* and *For Whom* questions the way they always have been answered.

The Traditional Economy's Strengths and Weaknesses

The benefit of the traditional approach is that it minimizes friction among members because relatively little is disputed. Consequently, people in this system may cooperate more freely with one another. In today's industrial world, the Amish and other traditional economies appear very satisfied with their relatively uncomplicated systems. However, critics argue that the traditional system restricts individual initiative and therefore does not lead to the production of advanced goods, new technology, and economic growth.

The Command Economy

Command economy

A system that answers the *What*, *How*, and *For Whom* questions by central authority.

In a **command economy**, a dictator or group of central planners makes economic decisions for society. In this system, the *What*, *How*, and *For Whom* questions are answered by planners with central authority. The former Soviet Union and China in the past and Cuba, North Korea, and Burma today are examples of nations with command economies using national economic plans implemented through powerful government committees. Politically selected committees decide on everything, including the number, color, size, quality, and price of autos, brooms, sweaters, and tanks. The state owns the factors of production and dictates answers to the three basic economic questions. The authorities might decide to produce modern weapons instead of schools, or they might decide to devote resources to building huge monuments like the pyramids, built by the rulers of ancient Egypt to honor their dead kings and queens.

In the old Soviet economy, for example, the three basic economic questions were answered by a central planning agency called the *Gosplan*. Following the policies of the political authority (the Politburo), the Gosplan set production quotas and prices for farms, factories, mines, housing construction, medical care, and other producing units. What should the cows be fed? If it is hay, how much land can be used to grow it? How much milk should the cows give? How many people will be dairy farmers? What wages should a dairy farmer earn? Should milk be given to everyone, to a few, or to any persons chosen by the leaders? If there was a shortage of goods in the shops, then goods would be rationed through queuing. The Gosplan tried to make all these decisions. Today, in Russia and the other former Soviet republics, the Gosplan is a distant memory of the discarded Soviet command system.

The pyramid shown in Exhibit 1 represents the command economy. At the top of the pyramid is a supremely powerful group of central planners, such as the old Soviet Gosplan. That agency established production targets and prices for goods and services. Then the Gosplan transmitted this information to a second layer of specialized state planning agencies. One of these specialized government bureaucracies purchased raw materials, another agency established fashion trends, another set prices, and another government bureaucracy made decisions based on employment and wages.

Production objectives were transmitted from the upper authority layers to the individual producing units, represented by the third layer of the pyramid in Exhibit 1. These producers supplied goods and services to the consumers, as commanded by the central authorities. The bottom portion of the pyramid illustrates the distribution, according to the master plan, of output to consuming units of individuals and households.

Exhibit 1   **The Command Economy Pyramid**

The principal feature of a command economy is the central planning board at the top, which transmits economic decisions down to the various producing and consuming units below. This process begins with an overall plan from a supreme planning board, such as the old Soviet Gosplan. The Gosplan established production targets and was the ultimate authority over a layer of specialized planning agencies, which authorized capital expansion, raw material purchases, prices, wages, and all other production decisions for individual producing units. Finally, the factories, farms, mines, and other producers distributed the specified output to consumers according to the approved master plan.

The Command Economy's Strengths and Weaknesses

Believe it or not, the command system can be defended. Proponents argue that economic change occurs much faster than in a traditional economy. This is one reason those dissatisfied with a traditional society might advocate establishment of a command system. The central authorities can ignore custom and order new ways of doing things. Another reason for adopting a command economy is the controversial belief that the government will provide economic security and equity. It is alleged that central authorities ensure that everyone is provided food, clothing, shelter, and medical care regardless of their ability to contribute to society.

The absolute power of central authorities to make right decisions is also the power to be absolutely wrong. Often the planners do not set production goals accurately, and either shortages or surpluses of goods and services are the result. For example, at one point the planners miscalculated and produced too few windshield wipers and side mirrors for Soviet cars. Faced with shortages of these parts, Soviet drivers removed windshield wipers and side mirrors whenever they parked their cars to prevent theft. On the other hand, the Gosplan allocated some collective farms far more fertilizer than they could use. To receive the same amount of fertilizer again the next year, farmers simply burned the excess fertilizer. As a result of such decision-making errors, people waited in long lines or stole goods. How does any decision-making group really know how many windshield wipers to produce each year and how much workers making them should earn?

Because profit is not the motive of producers in a command economy, quality and variety of goods also suffer. If the Gosplan ordered a state enterprise to produce 400,000 side mirrors for cars, for example, producers had little incentive to make the extra effort required to create a quality product in a variety of styles. The easiest way to meet the goal was to produce a low-quality product in one style regardless of consumer demand.

Exhibit 2 illustrates how the pricing policy of central planners causes shortages. The demand curve for side mirrors conforms to the law of demand. At lower prices in rubles, the quantity demanded increases. The supply curve is fixed at 400,000 side mirrors because it is set by the central planners and is therefore unresponsive to price variations.

Suppose one of the principal goals of the command economy is to keep the price low. To reach this goal, the central planners set the price of side mirrors at 20 rubles, which is below the equilibrium price of 40 rubles. At 20 rubles, more people can afford a side mirror than at the equilibrium price set by an uncontrolled marketplace. The consequence of this lower price set by the planners is a shortage. The quantity demanded at 20 rubles is 800,000 side mirrors, and the quantity supplied is only 400,000 mirrors. Thus, the model explains why side mirrors disappeared from stores long before many who were willing to buy them could do so.

The same graphical analysis applies to centrally planned rental prices for apartments. The central planners in the former Soviet Union set rents below the equilibrium rental prices for apartments. As the model predicts, low rents resulted in a shortage of housing. Meanwhile, the planners promised that improvements in housing would come in time.

> **CONCLUSION** *When central planners set prices below equilibrium for goods and services, they create shortages, which mean long lines, empty shelves, and black markets.*[1]

The Market Economy and the Ideas of Adam Smith

Market economy

An economic system that answers the *What, How,* and *For Whom* questions using prices determined by the interaction of the forces of supply and demand.

In a **market economy**, neither customs nor a single person or group of central planners answers the three basic economic questions facing society. The market economy is an economic system that answers the *What, How,* and *For Whom* questions using prices determined by the interaction of the forces of supply and demand. One of the first people to explain the power of a market economy was the Scottish economist Adam Smith. In the same year that the American colonies declared their political independence, Smith's *An Inquiry into the Nature and Causes of the Wealth of Nations* presented the blueprint for employing markets to improve economic performance. Smith spent over 10 years observing the real world and writing about how nations could best improve their material well-being. He concluded that the answer

---

1. Recall from Exhibit 5 of Chapter 4 that a black market is an illegal market that emerges when a price ceiling is imposed in a free market.

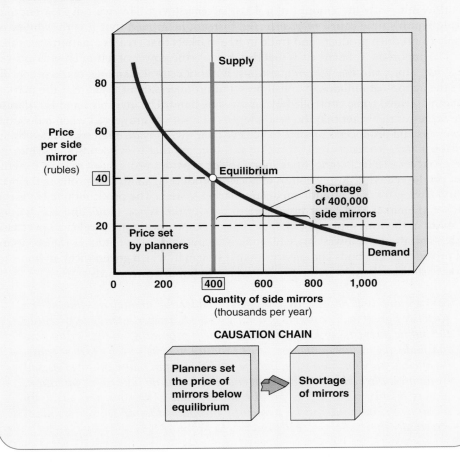

Exhibit 2 | **Central Planners Fixing Prices**

The central planners' goal is to keep prices low, so they set the price of a side mirror for a car at 20 rubles, which is below the market-determined equilibrium price of 40 rubles. At the set price, however, the quantity demanded is 800,000 side mirrors per year. Also set by the planners, the quantity supplied is 400,000 per year. Thus, the shortage at the government-established price is 400,000 side mirrors per year. As a result, long lines form to buy side mirrors, and black markets appear.

CAUSATION CHAIN

Planners set the price of mirrors below equilibrium → Shortage of mirrors

was to use free markets because this mechanism provides the incentive for everyone to follow his or her *self-interest*.

Adam Smith is the *father of modern economics*. He intended to write a book that would influence popular opinion and, unlike many famous works, his book was an immediate success.

The basic philosophy of his book is "the best government is the least government." This belief is known as *laissez faire*, a French expression meaning "allow to act." As Smith stated, the role of the government should be limited to providing

Prints & Photographs Division,
Library of Congress, LC-USZ62-1740

Adam Smith (1723-1790) The father of modern economics, who wrote *The Wealth of Nations* published in 1776.

national defense, providing education, maintaining infrastructure, enforcing contracts, and little else. Smith also advocated free trade among nations and rejected the idea that nations should impose trade barriers.

During Smith's lifetime, European nations such as England, France, and Spain intervened to control economic activities. In *The Wealth of Nations*, he argued that economic freedoms are "natural rights" necessary for the dignity of humankind. He believed that free competition among people who follow their self-interest would best benefit society because markets free of government interference produce the greatest output of goods and services possible. As noted above, Smith was an advocate of free international trade and asked the question implied in the full title of his book: Why are some nations richer than others? He explained that the source of any nation's wealth is not really the amount of gold or silver it owns. This was an idea popular during Smith's time called *mercantilism*. Instead, he argued that it is the ability of people to produce products and trade in free markets that creates a nation's wealth.

The importance of markets is that they harness the power of self-interest to answer the *What*, *How*, and *For Whom* questions. Without central planning, markets coordinate the actions of millions of consumers and producers. Smith said that the market economy seemed to be controlled by an **invisible hand**. The invisible hand is a phrase that expresses the belief that the best interests of a society are served when individual consumers and producers compete to achieve their own private interests. Guided by an invisible hand, producers must compete with one another to win consumers' money. The *profit motive* in a competitive marketplace provides profits as a reward for efficient producers, while losses punish inefficient producers. Smith saw profit as the necessary driving force in an individualistic market system. The profit motive leads the butcher, the baker, and other producers to answer the *What*, *How*, and *For Whom* questions at the lowest prices. Consumers also compete with one another to purchase the best goods at the lowest price. Competition automatically regulates the economy and provides more goods and services than a system in which government attempts to accomplish the same task in the *public interest*. In Smith's own words:

> *Every individual necessarily labours to render the annual revenue of the society as great as he can. He generally, indeed, neither intends to promote the public interest, nor knows how much he is promoting it. By ... directing that industry in such a manner as its produce may be of the greatest value, he intends only his own gain, and he is in this, as in many other cases, led by an invisible hand to promote an end which was no part of his intention. Nor is it always the worse for the society that it was no part of it. By pursuing his own interest he frequently promotes that of the society more effectually than when he really intends to promote it.*[2]

Invisible hand

A phrase that expresses the belief that the best interests of a society are served when individual consumers and producers compete to achieve their own private interests.

The Market Economy's Strengths and Weaknesses

In a market system, if consumers want Beanie Babies, they can buy them because sellers seek to profit from the sale of Beanie Babies. No single person or central planning board makes a formal decision to shift resources and tell firms how to produce what many might view as a frivolous product. Because no central body or set of customs interferes, the market system provides a wide variety of goods and services that buyers and sellers exchange at the lowest prices.

---

2. Adam Smith, *An Inquiry into the Nature and Causes of the Wealth of Nations* (1776; reprint, New York: Random House, 1937), p. 423.

> **CONCLUSION** *A market economy answers the What to produce and How to produce questions very effectively.*

Those who attack the market economy point out the market failure problems of lack of competition, externalities, public goods, and income inequality, discussed in Chapter 4. For example, critics contend that competition among buyers and sellers results in people who are very wealthy and people who are very poor. In a market economy, output is divided in favor of people who earn higher incomes and own property. Some people will dine on caviar in a fine restaurant, while others will wander the street and beg for food and shelter. Supporters of the market system argue that this inequality of income must exist to give people incentives or rewards for the value of their contributions to others.

The Mixed Economy

In the real world, no nation is a pure traditional, command, or market economy. Even primitive tribes employ a few markets in their system. For example, members of a tribe may exchange shells for animal skins. In China, the government allows many private shops and farms to operate in free markets. Although the United States is best described as a market economy, it is also a blend of the other two systems. As mentioned earlier, the Amish operate a well-known traditional economy in our nation. The draft during wartime is an example of a command economy in which the government obtains involuntary labor. In addition, taxes "commanded" from taxpayers fund government programs, such as national defense and Social Security. If the economic systems of most nations do not perfectly fit one of the basic definitions, what term best describes their economies? A more appropriate description is that most countries employ a blend of the basic types of economic systems, broadly called a mixed economy. A mixed economy is a system that answers the *What*, *How*, and *For Whom* questions through a mixture of traditional, command, and market systems.

The traditional, command, and market economies can exist in a wide variety of political situations. For instance, the United States and Japan are politically "free" societies in which the market system flourishes. But China uses the market system to a limited degree in spite of its lack of political freedom. Moreover, some of the Western democracies engage in central economic planning. French officials representing government, business, and labor meet annually to discuss economic goals for industry for the next five-year period, but compliance is voluntary. In Japan, a government agency called the *Ministry of Economy, Trade and Industry (METI)* engages in long-term planning. One of the goals of the METI is to encourage exports so that Japan can earn the foreign currencies it needs to pay for oil and other resources.

THE "ISMS"

What type of economic system will a society choose to answer the *What*, *How*, and *For Whom* questions? We could call most economies "mixed," but this would be too imprecise. In the real world, economic systems are labeled with various forms of the popular "isms"—capitalism, socialism, and communism—which are based on the basic types of systems.

Mixed economy

An economic system that answers the *What*, *How*, and *For Whom* questions through a mixture of traditional, command, and market systems.

Suppose we discover life on a new planet and the chief of their society learns of the successful economy of the United States and summons an economist to learn the secret. Sitting at the head of a huge oval table, the chief addresses the adviser seated at the other end saying, "Our economic system depends on tradition and command. It works, but not nearly so well as the U.S. economy. Our men and women lead a highly tradition-bound way of life. Men farm and hunt like their forefathers. Women work only in the home and care for children following the role approved by their elders. There is no confusion over how things are done, and there is no chaos over what work, or what output will be produced. People are simply assigned jobs by their leaders and told how much to produce. Likewise, people are told to work on community projects for our planet's benefit. If anyone refuses to follow instructions, they are shunned or banished. Tell me, how could there possibly be a better way to organize our economy?" The economist confidently responds, "Yes, there is definitely a better way. Replace tradition and command systems with the 'invisible hand' of the market system. This idea was explained long ago by a scholar named Adam Smith, the father of modern economics."

The chief is puzzled. "I have never heard of Adam Smith or the market economy. In a nutshell, explain to me how it differs from our system."

"Very well," says the economist. "In a market economy, each person is allowed to decide for himself or herself what to do based on price signals."

The chief is horrified and takes umbrage. "But what happens when they do not choose correctly? Let's talk about something specific, like computer production. Unless we designate people to make computers, how do we know the right number will select this job? What if women want to work in this industry? Who decides how much these workers should be paid and how many computers should be produced to satisfy the demand for them?"

"You may rest assured," says the economist. "Using prices determined in markets free from intervention will answer all your questions better than if leaders try to control everything."

The chief interrupts triumphantly. "Do you really expect me to believe that without instructions from the leaders, too few or too many products will not be bought and sold?"

"Ah, exactly!" the economist quickly answers. "The market will automatically do all these wonderful things. People will be more motivated by their own rational self-interest than by tradition or central authority. In short, the system runs itself."

"The economy runs without my leaders' directions!" says the chief. "That's absurd, and you have wasted my time. I thought you had a meaningful proposal. Good day!"

ANALYZE THE ISSUE

1. Describe how a traditional or a command system would make employment and production decisions compared to a market system.
2. Why might the leader find a market system inconceivable? Is it possible for economic activities not based on self-interest to take place in a market economy?

SOURCE: Adapted from Robert L. Heilbroner, *The Making of Economic Society*, 1993.

Capitalism

An economic system characterized by private ownership of resources and markets.

Capitalism

The popular term for the market economy discussed previously is capitalism. **Capitalism** is an economic system characterized by private ownership of resources and markets. *Capitalism* is also called the *free enterprise system*. Regardless of its political system, a capitalist economic system must possess two characteristics: (1) private ownership of resources and (2) decentralized decision making using markets.

Private Ownership Ownership of resources determines to a great degree who makes the *What*, *How*, and *For Whom* decisions. In a capitalist system, resources are primarily *privately* owned and controlled by individuals and firms, rather than having property rights be *publicly* held by government on behalf of society. In the United States, most capital resources are privately owned, but the term *capitalism* is somewhat confusing because it stresses private ownership of factories, raw materials, farms, and other forms of *capital* even though public ownership of land exists as well.

Decentralized Decision Making This characteristic of capitalism allows buyers and sellers to exchange goods in markets without government involvement. A capitalist system operates on the principle of **consumer sovereignty**. Consumer sovereignty is the freedom of consumers to cast their dollar votes to buy, or not to buy, at prices determined in competitive markets. As a result, consumer spending determines what goods and services firms produce. In a capitalist system, most allocative decisions are coordinated by consumers and producers interacting through markets and making their own decisions guided by Adam Smith's invisible hand. Friedrich von Hayek, an Austrian economist who was a 1974 recipient of the Nobel Prize and author of *The Road to Serfdom*, argued that political and economic freedoms are inseparable.

In the real world, many U.S. markets are not perfectly open or free markets with the consumer as sovereign. For example, consumers cannot buy illegal drugs or body organs. In Chapter 4, you learned that the U.S. government sets minimum prices (support prices) for wheat, milk, cheese, and other products. These markets are free only if the market price is above the support price. Similarly, the minimum-wage law forces employers to pay a wage above some dollar amount per hour regardless of market conditions.

Consumer sovereignty

The freedom of consumers to cast their dollar votes to buy, or not to buy, at prices determined in competitive markets.

CONCLUSION *No nation in the world precisely fits the two criteria for capitalism; however, the United States comes close.*

Capitalism's Strengths and Weaknesses

One of the major strengths of capitalism is its capacity to achieve *economic efficiency* because competition and the profit motive force production at the lowest cost. Another strength of pure capitalism is *economic freedom* because economic power is widely dispersed. Individual consumers, producers, and workers are free to make decisions based on their own self-interest. Economist Milton Friedman makes a related point: Private ownership limits the power of government to deny goods, services, or jobs to its adversaries.

Critics of capitalism cite several shortcomings. First, capitalism tends toward an unequal distribution of income. This inequality of income among citizens results for several reasons. Private ownership of capital and the other factors of production can cause these factors to become concentrated in the hands of a few individuals or firms. Also, people do not have equal labor skills, and the marketplace rewards those with greater skills. These inequalities may be perpetuated because the rich can provide better education, legal aid, political platforms, and wealth to their heirs. Second, pure capitalism is criticized for its failure to protect the environment. The pursuit of profit and self-interest can take precedence over damage or pollution to the air, rivers, lakes, and streams. Recall the graphical model used in Chapter 4 to illustrate the socially unacceptable impact of producers who pollute the environment.

Socialism

The idea of socialism has existed for thousands of years. Its basis is the command system. **Socialism** is an economic system characterized by government ownership of resources and centralized decision making. Socialism is also called *command socialism*. Under a socialist economy, a command system owns and controls in the *public interest* the major industries, such as steel, electricity, and agriculture. However, some free markets can exist in farming, retail trade, and certain service areas. Just as no pure capitalist system exists in the real world, none of the socialist countries in the world today practices pure socialism. In fact, there are as many variants of socialism as there are countries called socialist.

Before discussing socialism further, you must realize that socialism is an economic system, and politics should not be confused with economics. Great Britain, France, and Italy have representative democracies, but many of their major industries are or have been nationalized. In the United States, the federal government owns and operates the Tennessee Valley Authority (TVA), the National Aeronautics and Space Administration (NASA), and the U.S. Postal Service, while at the same time allowing private utilities and mail service firms to operate.

The Ideas of Karl Marx

Despite the transition to capitalism in Russia and Eastern Europe, socialism still prevails in China, Cuba, and many less-developed countries. The theory for socialism and *communism* can be traced to Karl Marx. Marx was a nineteenth-century German philosopher, revolutionary, and economist. Unlike other economists of the time who followed Adam Smith, Marx rejected the concept of a society operating through private interest and profit.

Karl Marx was born in Germany, the son of a lawyer. He was an outstanding student at Berlin University. In 1841, after receiving a doctorate in philosophy, he turned to journalism. In 1843, Marx married the daughter of a wealthy family and moved to Paris, but his political activities forced him to leave Paris for England. From the age of 31, he lived and wrote his books in London. In London, Marx lived an impoverished life while he and his lifelong friend Friedrich Engels wrote the *Communist Manifesto*, published in 1848. A massive work followed, titled *Das Kapital*, which was published in three volumes in 1867, 1884, and 1885.

These two works made Karl Marx the most influential economist in the history of socialism. In fact, he devoted his entire life to a revolt against capitalism. As Marx read *The Wealth of Nations*, he saw profits as unjust payments to owners of firms—the capitalists. Marx predicted that the market system would destroy itself because wealthy owners would go too far and exploit workers because unrelenting greed for profits would lead the owners to pay starvation wages. Moreover, the owners would force laborers to work in unsafe conditions, and many would not have a job at all.

Marx believed that private ownership and exploitation would produce a nation driven by a class struggle between a few "haves" and many "have-nots." As he

---

Socialism

An economic system characterized by government ownership of resources and centralized decision making.

© Photos.com/Jupiter Images

Karl Marx (1818-1883) His Criticism of capitalism advanced communism. He wrote *Communist Manifesto* and *Das Kapital*.

stated in the *Communist Manifesto*, "The history of all existing society is the history of class struggle. Freeman and slave, patrician and plebeian, lord and serf, guildmaster and journeyman, in a word, oppressor and oppressed."[3] In Marx's vision, capitalists were the modern-day oppressors, and the workers were the oppressed proletariat. Someday, Marx predicted, the workers would rise up in a spontaneous bloody revolution against a system benefiting only the owners of capital. Marx believed **communism** to be the ideal system, which would evolve in stages from capitalism through socialism. Communism is a stateless, classless economic system in which all the factors of production are owned by the workers and people share in production according to their needs. This is the highest form of socialism toward which the revolution should strive.

Under communism, no private property exists to encourage self-interest. There is no struggle between classes of people, and everyone cooperates. In fact, there is no reason to commit crime, and police, lawyers, and courts are unnecessary. Strangely, Marx surpassed Adam Smith in advocating a system with little central government. Marx believed that those who work hard, or are more skilled, will be public spirited. Any "haves" will give voluntarily to "have-nots" until everyone has exactly the same material well-being. In Marx's own words, people would be motivated by the principle "from each according to his ability, to each according to his need." World peace would evolve as nation after nation accepted cooperation and rejected profits and competition. Under the idealized society of communism, there would be no state. No central authority would be necessary to pursue the interests of the people.

Today, we call the economic systems that existed in the former Soviet Union and Eastern Europe, and still exist in China, Cuba, and other countries, *communist*. However, the definition for *socialism* given in this chapter more accurately describes their real-world economic systems. Actually, no nation has achieved the ideal communist society described by Marx, nor has capitalism self-destructed as he predicted. The 1917 communist revolution in Russia did not fit Marx's theory. At that time, Russia was an underdeveloped country, rather than an industrial country filled with greedy capitalists who exploited workers.

Characteristics of Socialism

Regardless of a society's political system, a socialist economy has two basic characteristics: (1) public ownership and (2) centralized decision making.

Public Ownership Under socialism, the government owns most of the factors of production, including factories, farms, mines, and natural resources. Agriculture in the old Soviet Union illustrates how even this real-world socialist country deviated from total public ownership. In the Soviet Union, there were three rather distinct forms of agriculture: state farms, collective farms, and private plots. In both the state farm and the collective-farm sectors, central planning authorities determined prices and outputs. In contrast, the government allowed those holding small private plots on peasant farms to operate primarily in free markets that determined price and output levels. Reforms now allow farmers to buy land, tractors, trucks, and other resources from the state. If these reforms continue, they will dramatically end the collectivization of agriculture begun under Josef Stalin.

> **Communism**
>
> A stateless, classless economic system in which all the factors of production are owned by the workers, and people share in production according to their needs. In Marx's view, this is the highest form of socialism toward which the revolution should strive.

---

3. Karl Marx and Friedrich Engels, *The Communist Manifesto* (New York: International Press, 1848), p. 31.

Centralized Decision Making Instead of the pursuit of *private interest*, the motivation of pure socialism is the *public interest* of the whole society. For instance, a factory manager cannot decide to raise or lower prices to obtain maximum profits for the factory. Regardless of inventory levels or the opportunity to raise prices, the planners will not permit this action. Instead of exploiting the ups and downs of the market, the goal of the socialist system is to make centralized decisions that protect workers and consumers from decentralized market decisions. Critics argue that the main objective of this centralization is to perpetuate the personal dictatorships of leaders such as Stalin in the old Soviet Union and Fidel Castro in Cuba.

Before the open market reforms, Soviet planners altered earnings to attract workers into certain occupations and achieve planned goals. For example, if space projects needed more engineers, then the state raised the earnings of engineers until the target number of people entered the engineering profession.

As shown earlier in Exhibit 2, central planners in the Soviet Union also manipulated consumer prices. If consumers desired more cars than were available, the authorities increased the price of cars. If people wished to purchase less of an item than was available, planners lowered prices. The problem was that this decision process took time. And while the market awaited its orders from the Soviet planners, excess inventories of some items accumulated, and consumers stood in line for cheap products that never seemed to be available. There was an old Soviet saying, "If you see a line, get in it. Whatever it is, it's scarce, and you will not see it tomorrow."

The Soviet factory system did not adhere completely to the command system. The government rewarded successful managers with bonuses that could be substantial. Better apartments, nice vacations, and medals were incentives for outstanding performance. Under economic reforms, plant managers now make decisions based on profitability instead of centralized controls.

CHECKPOINT

To Plan or Not to Plan—That Is the Question

You make plans. You planned to go to college. You plan which career to follow. You plan to get married, and so on. Businesses plan. They plan to hire employees, expand their plants, increase profits, and so forth. Because individuals and businesses plan in a market economy, there is really no difference between our system and a command economy. Or is there?

Socialism's Strengths and Weaknesses

Proponents of the socialism model argue that this system is superior in achieving an equitable distribution of income. This is because government ownership of capital and other resources prevents a few individuals or groups from acquiring a disproportionate share of the nation's wealth. Also, supporters argue that rapid economic growth is achieved when planners have the power to direct more resources to producing capital goods and fewer resources to producing consumer goods (see Exhibit 5 of Chapter 2).

National goals may seem to be easily formulated and pursued under state directives, but there are problems. For example, proponents of such an economy can claim there is no unemployment because the government assigns all workers a job and allocates resources to complete their production goals. However, economic inefficiency results because the government often uses many workers to perform work requiring only one or two workers. Critics also point out that the absence of the profit motive discourages entrepreneurship and innovation and thus suppresses economic growth.

Socialism is particularly vulnerable to the charge that it ignores the goal of economic freedom and instead creates a privileged class of government bureaucrats who assume the role of "capitalists." Central planners are the key translators of information about consumer preferences and production capabilities flowing to millions of economic units. This complex and cumbersome process is subject to errors and unresponsiveness to the wants of the majority of the population. Critics also question whether the distribution of income under socialism is more equitable than under capitalism. In the socialist system, "perks" for government officials, nepotism, and the illegal use of markets create disparities in income.

COMPARING ECONOMIC SYSTEMS

In reality, all nations operate economic systems that blend capitalism and socialism. Exhibit 3 presents a continuum that attempts to place countries between the two extremes of pure socialism on the left and pure capitalism on the right. Economies characterized by a high degree of both private ownership and market allocation are closest to pure capitalism. Hong Kong (now part of China), Japan, the United States, and Canada fall at the capitalism end of the line. Conversely, economies characterized by much government ownership of resources and central planning are closest to pure socialism. North Korea and Cuba fall close to the pure socialism end of the spectrum, with China and Russia further away from pure socialism.

Exhibit 3	**A Classification of Economic Systems**

No nation has an economic system that is pure socialism or pure capitalism. All nations mix government ownership and reliance on markets. North Korea and Cuba are closest to pure socialism, while Hong Kong comes closest to pure capitalism. Other real-world economies are placed between these two extremes on the basis of their use of government ownership versus markets.

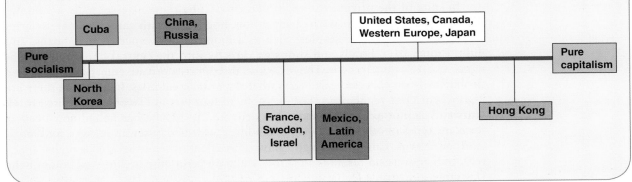

ECONOMIES IN TRANSITION

By the early 1990s, the centrally planned economies in the old Soviet Union and Eastern Europe had collapsed. After more than 70 years in the Soviet Union and over 40 years in Eastern Europe and China, the failed communist economies made a startling switch to embrace capitalism. Faced with severe shortages of food, housing, cars, and other consumer goods, communism could no longer claim better living standards for its citizens. The following is a brief discussion of reforms aimed at introducing market power into the economic systems of Cuba, Russia, and China.

Cuba

Cuba often experiences daily power blackouts, fuel shortages, housing shortages, and other economic hardships. But regardless of its economic woes, Cuba remains wedded to the communist system. Nevertheless, the collapse of Soviet bloc aid coupled with the effects of the U.S. trade embargo have forced Fidel Castro and the country's new leader, Raul Castro, die-hard Marxists, to reluctantly adopt limited free market reforms. To earn foreign exchange, the dollar has been legalized, and the Cuban government has poured capital into tourism by building several new state-owned hotels and restoring historic sections of Havana. Interestingly, Cuba operates special medical tourist hospitals that treat foreigners and diplomats, while excluding Cubans. Cuba has also set up quasi-state enterprises that accept only hard currency. Because few Cubans have dollars or other hard currency, many are earning it by turning to illegal schemes, such as driving gypsy cabs, engaging in prostitution, or selling Cuba's famous cigars and coffee on the black market. Other Cubans have abandoned state jobs and opened small businesses under these new rules. However, these small-scale businesses cannot employ anyone beyond the family of the owner. Also, spare rooms in houses can be rented, and artisans can sell their work to tourists. In addition, state farm enterprises have been broken into worker-owned units, and the government allows farmers to sell produce leftover after they have met the state's quota. As a result of this free market, some farmers have become venture capitalists, and more food, and a greater variety of food are becoming available. In 2008, a series of changes opened access to cell phones, computers, and DVD players. Cubans are now also allowed to patronize tourist hotels. However, such luxuries are prohibitive for most Cubans. And in 2009, to improve its woeful transportation system, Cuban owners of classic American cars were recruited by the government to apply for taxi licenses and set their own fares subject to price floors.

In spite of the private enterprise reforms, Cuba remains essentially a communist system. Workers receive free education, housing, health care, low state salaries in pesos, and rations of staples, such as a monthly allowance of rice, beans, and milk. Profits from hotels and shops go directly into the central bank and help finance Castro's government. The state also discourages private enterprises by taxing them heavily on expected earnings, rather than on actual sales. In addition, there are highly restrictive regulations. For example, restaurants in Havana are limited to 12 seats and cannot expand regardless of demand. And Cuba has halted new licenses for some types of self-employment, including jewelers, mousetrap makers, and magicians or clowns. Currently, Hugo Chavez, president of Venezuela, is using his country's tremendous oil reserves to throw Cuba an economic lifeline and counter the U.S. embargo against Cuba.

Russia

In 1991, communist rule ended in Russia. To function efficiently, markets must offer incentives, so workers, the public, and even foreign investors were permitted to buy state property. This meant individuals could own the factors of production and earn profits. Such market incentives were a dagger thrust into the heart of a system previously devoted to rejecting capitalism. A key reform for Russia was to allow supply and demand to set higher prices for basic consumer goods. As shown earlier in Exhibit 2, without central planners, when prices rise to their equilibrium level, the quantity supplied increases and the quantity demanded decreases. At the beginning of 1992, the Russian government removed direct government price controls on most market goods. As the model predicts, average prices rose, leaping 1,735 percent in 1992, and a greater variety of goods started appearing on the shelves. Although workers had to pay more for basic consumer goods, they could at least find goods to buy.

Since 1992, Russia has established an independent central bank and implemented anti-inflationary monetary policies. Cities throughout Russia now have restaurants, megamalls, decent hotels, and streets choked with foreign cars. Russian entrepreneurial spirit and acceptance of it in society is in an embryonic stage, and corruption, including the legal system, is a frequent way of life. Today, Russia's economy is heavily dependent on oil and natural gas exports. Russia holds the world's largest natural gas reserves, and the eighth largest oil reserves. Although Russia is far from a successful market economy, the nation is struggling to achieve an amazing economic transition. Russian privatization plans are being implemented and steps are continuing to create a dynamic economy embracing capitalism. And *Forbes* magazine reports that there are now over 30 billionaires who reside in Russia.

The People's Republic of China

Unlike Russia, China has sought economic reform under the direction of its Communist Party. Fundamental economic reforms began in China after the death of Mao Zedong in 1976. Much of this reform was due to the leadership of Deng Xiaoping. Mao was devoted to the egalitarian ideal of communist ideology. Under his rule, thoughts of self-interest were counterrevolutionary, and photographs of Marx, Lenin, and Mao hung on every street corner and in every office and factory. Deng shifted priorities by increasing production of consumer goods and steering China toward becoming a global economic power. And the results have been dramatic. International trade expanded from less than 1 percent of U.S. trade in 1975 to 10 percent in 2009, and the label "Made in China" is common throughout the world. China joined the WTO in 2001 and agreed to open some markets closed to foreigners. China's real GDP growth rate averaged 9.8 percent between 2001 and 2009, making it the world's fastest-growing economy.

To make China an industrial power in the twenty-first century, Chinese planners introduced a two-tier system for industry and agriculture in 1978. Each farm and state enterprise was given a contract to produce a quota. Any amount produced over the quota could be sold in an open market. The Chinese government also encouraged the formation of nonstate enterprises owned jointly by managers and their workforces and special economic zones open to foreign investment. In other words, a blend of capitalism and socialism would provide the incentives needed to increase output. As Deng Xiaoping explained, "It doesn't matter whether the cat is black or

Global Economics China's Quest for Free Market Reform *Applicable Concept: comparative economic systems*

For more than 2,000 years, China had a "self-reliance" policy that caused its economy to lag far behind advanced economies. After 1949, the communists under Chairman Mao Zedong abolished private property, executed landlords, and put farmers to work in collectives where members shared equally. These reforms are referred to as *The Great Leap Forward*, which in reality became *The Great Leap Backward*. Without the self-interest motive, communal property created low incentives to work that resulted in widespread famine and millions of deaths. After the death of Mao Zedong in 1976, China adopted new economic reforms that are continuing to transform one of the poorest economies in the world into one of the fastest growing. Under this reform system, households operate in a mixed world of state controls and free markets. A two-track pricing system still exists for some key goods and services, such as coal, petroleum, steel, transportation, and agriculture. The rural economy is central to China's economic reforms. In the past, when farmers worked collectively in people's communes, the government told the farmers what to produce and how much to produce. They could sell their products only to the state at a price fixed by the government, rather than in markets. A so-called household contract responsibility system was created as a

Gavin Heller/Jupiter images

reform to assign land owned by the state to farmers. The farmers must pay an annual share of their profits to the government, and the state does not cover losses. Farmers, however, have the authority to decide what to produce and the price at which to sell in open markets. As a result, both farmers and consumers are noticeably better off because everyone can find and afford more food.

As farming productivity rose sharply, fewer farmers were needed to work on the land, and this surplus labor moved into emerging township and village nonstate enterprises. These enterprises were

white as long as it catches mice." These reforms worked, leading to huge increases in farm and industrial output in the 1980s. In fact, some peasant farmers became the wealthiest people in China. After Deng's death in the mid-1990s, leadership of China passed to leaders who continued the policy of free market reforms. Today, forests of glossy skyscrapers, expressways, upscale apartments, and enormous shopping malls in Beijing, Shanghai, and other cities attest to the market-oriented reforms begun years ago. And life in China's fast lane now includes the opportunity of dining at Kentucky Fried Chicken and McDonald's restaurants located in cities throughout the country. Also, despite government censorship, China has the largest number of Internet users in the world. (See Global Economics: China's Quest for Free Market Reform.)

Today, China is a huge nation transforming itself swiftly into a powerful player in the global economy. U.S. exporters are overjoyed at the prospect of selling products to over a billion Chinese consumers. For example, swarms of bicyclists once synonymous with urban China are being pushed off the road by consumers who now can afford cars and trucks. Rolls-Royce and Bentley, the ultra-luxury cars, have expanded into China, and it is estimated that by 2030 China will have more cars mostly in light industry and owned collectively by townships or villages. As a result, the composition of rural output has changed. When the reforms began in the late 1970s, farming accounted for 70 percent of the total output and industry for 20 percent. Currently, the structure of the economy has changed dramatically. In 2009, agriculture accounted for only 11 percent of GDP and industry's share had risen to 49 percent.[1]

A 1993 article in the *Boston Globe* provides an interesting observation on China's economic transformation:

> *Stuffing the genie back into the bottle might prove difficult. The flood of money has created a bubble, particularly in stocks and property, making some people in China very rich, very fast. The China Daily, China's official English-language newspaper, recently heralded the existence of 1 million millionaires. . . . These millionaires, many of whom just five years ago were still wearing Mao outfits and following the party's socialist dictates, now sport stylish Western-style suits with the label ostentatiously left on the cuff.*[2]

A 2001 *Time* article described China's controversial womb police, who have spent two decades attempting to control the nation's population by fining citizens with more than one child. They have succeeded remarkably well. Today, the average Chinese woman has two children, compared with six 30 years ago. "For all the bad press, China has achieved the impossible," says Sven Burmester, the U.N. Population Fund representative in Beijing. "The country has solved its population problem." In fact, China's population will actually start declining in 2042, according to U.N. projections.[3]

At the sixteenth Communist Party Congress in 2003, President Hu Jintao and Communist Party leaders announced "another turning point and a new starting point in China's reform process." A key debate concerned reforms that would move China closer to capitalism including the first-ever guarantee of private property under communist rule.[4] In 2009, *Forbes* reported that China has 28 billionaires, and Rupert Hoogewerf, CEO of *Hurun Report*, says China's recent surge in mega-wealth is "comparable to the U.S. at the end of the 19th century, when you had the Rockefellers and Carnegies."

ANALYZE THE ISSUE

1. Why would China abandon the goal of income equality and shift from a centrally planned system to a more market-oriented economy?
2. Which groups in China are likely to resist the reforms?

1. The World Bank, Key Development Data & Statistics, http://web.worldbank.org/.
2. Maggie Farley, "China's Economic Boom Energizing Inflation," *Boston Globe*, Aug. 13, 1993, p. 1A.
3. "China's Lifestyle Choice: Changes to the Famous One-Child Policy Miss the Point," *Time*, Aug. 6, 2001, p. 32.
4. Joe McDonald, "China Debates Private Property," *Sun News*, Oct. 12, 2003, p. 14A.

on the road than the United States. Also, more Chinese are traveling by air. Consequently, the Chinese are buying more Boeing airplanes and American-made cars. The other side of the coin is the threat of what goods the industrious Chinese workers, with increasing training and foreign investment, might produce and sell abroad. For example, China manufactures most of the world's copiers, microwave ovens, DVD players, and shoes. A ballooning U.S. trade deficit with China is often cited as evidence that China is not playing fair, and the political rhetoric has intensified on both sides of the issue. Other countries fear that China will eliminate their export business with the United States. Moreover, there is concern that lowering trade barriers under free trade agreements will increase Chinese imports into domestic markets and eliminate jobs. In 2007, one Chinese-made product after another was removed from U.S. shelves, for example, lethal pet food, toxic toothpaste, and other contaminated products. This prompted calls for more stringent safety regulations for imports.

Currently, China's leaders are dealing with an economy that is experiencing overheating. Factories suffer electricity shortages, while ports and railways cannot handle all the cargo flowing in and out of the country. China is consuming huge quantities of crude oil, copper, steel, and aluminum. Moreover, there is discontent over labor issues, pollution, and income inequality. While some dig through trash bins, there are now wealthy private business owners. Despite the unease, China remains a market of great profit and promise as it continues its transition from a communist command economy to capitalism. In 2008, China announced the largest stimulus package in its history to counter the impact of the global economic downturn. And the debate continues over whether China, a socialist economy, is a strategic trading partner or an emerging rival that will dominate the world economy.

PRIVATIZATION VERSUS NATIONALIZATION

Privatization

is the process of turning a government enterprise into a private enterprise.

Nationalization

is the act of transforming a private enterprise's assets into government ownership.

The above discussions of Cuba, Russia, and China provide examples of **privatization**. Privatization is the process of turning a government enterprise into a private enterprise. It is the opposite of **nationalization**, which is the act of transforming a private enterprise's assets into government ownership. The motives for nationalization are political as well as economic. Proponents believe that government ownership enables the state on behalf of the people to exercise more effective control and equitable redistribution of wealth and income. Critics argue that government ownership suppresses incentives, entrepreneurship, and private investment that are essential for an enterprise to prosper. During a financial crisis, the argument in favor of nationalization is that a brief period of nationalization is needed to prevent the largest corporations and banks from a downward spiral that affects the entire economy. This is the "too big to fail" argument.

In recent years, Venezuelan President Hugo Chavez has received much press coverage for nationalizing a list of industries including oil, cement, and steel, and ordering the army to take over all rice processing and packaging plants. Chavez stated in a 2007 speech in Caracas, "We're heading toward socialism, and nothing and no one can prevent it."

The United States also has a history of nationalization—most of which was temporary. But one that has endured: Amtrak is a government-owned corporation created in 1971 after railroads had petitioned repeatedly to abandon unprofitable passenger service. As discussed at the conclusion of the chapter on Money and the Federal Reserve System, the Resolution Trust Corporation (RTC) was established in 1989 to take over more than 1,000 failed savings and loans institutions with bad loans and foreclosed homes. After fulfilling its mission to sell the assets of these S&Ls, the RTC was closed in 1995. The current financial crisis has generated several nationalizations that only in the future will it be known if they are temporary. General Motors provides a prime case. With GM facing bankruptcy in 2009, the U.S. government replaced the CEO and took a 60 percent controlling share, with Canada a 12.5 percent share, United Auto Workers (UAW) 17.5 percent, and bondholders ending up with the remaining 10 percent. Existing stockholders were given zero shares. Will GM emerge to become successful and nationalization be given credit, or will the reverse be the result?

Key Concepts

Economic system

Traditional economy

Command economy

Market economy

Invisible hand

Mixed economy

Capitalism

Consumer sovereignty

Socialism

Communism

Privatization

Nationalization

Summary

- An *economic system* is the set of established procedures by which a society answers the *What, How,* and *For Whom* to produce questions.
- *Three basic types of economic systems* are the traditional, command, and market systems. The *traditional system* makes decisions according to custom, and the *command system,* shown in the figure below, answers the three economic questions through some powerful central authority. In contrast, the *market system* uses the impersonal mechanism of the interaction of buyers and sellers in markets to answer the *What, How,* and *For Whom* questions.

Command Economy

- *Capitalism* is an economic system in which the factors of production are privately owned and economic choices are made by consumers and firms in markets. As prescribed by Adam Smith, government plays an extremely limited role, and self-interest is the driving force, held in check, or regulated, by competition.
- *Consumer sovereignty* is the freedom of consumers to determine the types and quantities of products that are produced in an economy by choosing to buy or not to buy.
- *Socialism* is an economic system in which the government owns the factors of production. The central authorities make the myriad of society's economic decisions according to a national plan. The collective good, or public interest, is the intended guiding force behind the central planners' decisions.
- *Communism* is an economic system envisioned by Karl Marx to be an ideal society in which the workers own all the factors of production. Marx believed that workers who work hard will be public spirited and voluntarily redistribute income to those who are less productive. Such a communist nation described by Marx does not exist.
- *Privatization* is the process of turning a government enterprise into a private enterprise. It is the opposite of *nationalization,* which is the act of transforming a private enterprise's assets into government ownership.

Summary of Conclusion Statements

- When central planners set prices below equilibrium for goods and services, they create shortages, which mean long lines, empty shelves, and black markets.
- A market economy answers the *What* to produce and *How* to produce questions very effectively.

- No nation in the world precisely fits the two criteria for capitalism; however, the United States comes close.

Study Questions and Problems

1. Give an example of how a nation's culture affects its economic system.

2. Explain the advantages and the disadvantages of any two of the three basic types of economic systems.

3. Suppose a national program of free housing for the elderly is paid for by a sizable increase in income taxes. Explain a tradeoff that might occur between economic security and efficiency.

4. "The schools are not in the business of pleasing parents and students, and they cannot be allowed to set their own agendas. Their agendas are set by politicians, administrators, and various constituencies that hold the keys to political power. The public system is built to see to it that the schools do what their government wants them to do—that

they conform to the higher-order values their governors seek to impose."[4] Relate this statement to Exhibit 1.

5. Suppose you are a farmer. Explain why you would be motivated to work in traditional, command, and market economies.

6. Karl Marx believed the market system was doomed. Why do you think he was right or wrong?

7. If all real-world economies are mixed economies, why is the U.S. economy described as capitalist, while the Cuban economy is described as communist?

8. Suppose you are a factory manager. Describe how you might reach production goals under a system of pure capitalism and under a system of pure socialism.

For Online Exercises, go to the Tucker Web site at www.cengage.com/economics/tucker.

---

4. John Chubb and Terry More, *Politics, Markets, and the Nation's Public Schools* (Washington, D.C.: Brookings Institution, 1990), p. 38.

CHECKPOINT ANSWER

To Plan or Not to Plan—That Is the Question

When an individual or a business plans in a market economy, other individuals are free to make and follow their own plans. Suppose Hewlett-Packard decides to produce X number of laser printers and sell them at a certain price. The decision does not prohibit IBM from producing Y number of laser printers and selling them for less than Hewlett-Packard's printers. If either firm makes a mistake, only that firm suffers, and other industries are for the most part unaffected. Under a command system, a central economic plan would be made for all laser printer manufacturers. If the central planners order the wrong quantity or quality, there could be major harm to other industries and society. If you said there is a major difference between individual planning and central planning for all society, YOU ARE CORRECT.

Practice Quiz

For an explanation of the correct answers, visit the Tucker Web site at www.cengage.com/economics/tucker.

1. The economic system in which all of the basic decisions are made through a centralized authority, such as a government agency, is termed a
   a. market economy.
   b. capitalistic economy.
   c. command economy.
   d. traditional economy.

2. Command economies typically suffer from
   a. unemployment, but not underemployment.
   b. neither unemployment nor underemployment.
   c. both unemployment and underemployment.
   d. underemployment, but not unemployment.

3. Adam Smith stated that the role of government in society should be to
   a. provide defense.
   b. enforce contracts.
   c. do absolutely nothing.
   d. do both (a) and (b).

4. When making economic decisions, Adam Smith urged society to
   a. follow the principle of self-interest.
   b. follow the principle of public interest.
   c. transfer wealth according to need.
   d. provide equal income for all citizens.

5. The doctrine of *laissez faire*
   a. advocates an economic system with extensive government intervention and little individual decision making.
   b. was advocated by Adam Smith in his book *The Wealth of Nations*.
   c. was advocated by Karl Marx in his book *Das Kapital*.
   d. is described by none of the above.

6. In Adam Smith's competitive market economy, the question of what goods to produce is determined by the
   a. "invisible hand" of the price system.
   b. "invisible hand" of government.
   c. "visible hand" of public interest.
   d. "visible hand" of laws and regulations.

7. Adam Smith wrote that the
   a. economic problems of eighteenth-century England were caused by free markets.
   b. government should control the economy with an "invisible hand."
   c. pursuit of private self-interest promotes the public interest in a market economy.
   d. public or collective interest is not promoted by people pursuing their self-interest.

Practice Quiz Continued

8. Adam Smith, in his book *The Wealth of Nations*, advocated
   a. socialism.
   b. an economy guided by an "invisible hand."
   c. government control of the "invisible hand."
   d. the adoption of mercantilism.

9. The economic system in which private individuals own the factors of production is
   a. a planned economy.
   b. capitalism.
   c. collectivism.
   d. socialism.

10. Which of the following is *not* a basic characteristic of capitalism?
    a. Economic decisions occur in markets.
    b. Factors of production are privately owned.
    c. Income is distributed on the basis of need.
    d. Businesses make their own product and price decisions.

11. According to Karl Marx, under capitalism,
    a. profits would be shared fairly.
    b. incomes would be distributed equally.
    c. workers would be exploited and revolt against owners of capital.
    d. workers would actually own the factors of production.

12. Karl Marx predicted which of the following?
    a. The market system would self-destruct.
    b. The "haves" would revolt against the "have-nots."
    c. The wealthy were entitled to profits as their reward for risk taking.
    d. None of the above

13. How many nations in the world today operate totally according to Karl Marx's theory of communism?
    a. None
    b. Several
    c. Only the United States
    d. Many

14. In Marx's ideal communist society, the state
    a. actively promotes income equality.
    b. follows the doctrine of *laissez faire*.
    c. owns resources and conducts planning.
    d. does not exist.

15. Karl Marx was a (an)
    a. nineteenth-century German philosopher.
    b. eighteenth-century Russian economist.
    c. fourteenth-century Polish banker.
    d. nineteenth-century Russian journalist.

chapter 20

Growth and the Less-Developed Countries

How would your life be different if you lived in Rwanda or Haiti instead of the United States? It is unlikely that anyone in your family would have a telephone or a car. You surely would not own a personal computer or an iPod. You would not have new clothes and be enrolled in a college or university studying economics. You would not be going out to restaurants or movies. You would be fortunate to have shoes and one full meal each day. You would receive little or no medical care and live in unsanitary surroundings. Hunger, disease, and squalor would engulf you. In fact, the World Bank estimates that over 20 percent of people in developing countries survive on less than $1 per day.

It is exceedingly difficult for Americans to grasp that one-fifth of the world's population lives at such a meager subsistence level. This chapter's important task is unraveling the secrets of economic growth and development. Why do some countries prosper while others decline?

At different times in history, Egypt, China, Italy, and Greece were highly developed by the standards of their time. On the other hand, at one time the United States was a struggling, relatively poor country on the path to becoming a rich country. Its growth came in three stages: First, was the agricultural stage. Then came the manufacturing stage when industries such as railroads, steel, and automobiles were driving forces toward economic growth. And, finally, there has been a shift toward service industries. This is the U.S. success story, but it is not the only road countries can follow to lift themselves from the misery of poverty.

COMPARING DEVELOPED AND LESS-DEVELOPED COUNTRIES

Income disparity exists not only among families within the United States but also among nations. In this section, the great inequality of income between the families of nations will be used to classify nations as rich or poor.

Classifying Countries by GDP per Capita

There are about 225 countries in the world. Exhibit 1 shows a ranking of selected countries from high to low **GDP per capita**. GDP per capita is the value of final goods produced (GDP) divided by the total population. Although any system of defining rich versus poor countries is arbitrary, GDP per capita or average GDP is a fundamental measure of a country's economic well-being. At the top of the income ladder are 27 developed countries called the **industrially advanced countries (IACs)**. Industrially advanced countries are high-income nations that have market economies based on large stocks of technologically advanced capital and well-educated labor. The United States, Canada, Australia, New Zealand, Japan, and most of the countries of Western Europe are IACs. Excluded from the IACs are countries with high incomes whose economies are based on oil under the sand, and not on widespread industrial development. The United Arab Emirates is an example of such a country.

Countries of the world other than IACs are classified as underdeveloped or **less-developed countries (LDCs)**. Less-developed countries are nations without large stocks of technologically advanced capital and well-educated labor. Their economies are based on agriculture, as in most countries of Africa, Asia, and Latin America. Most of the world's population live in LDCs and share widespread poverty.

A closer examination of Exhibit 1 reveals that the differences in living standards between the IACs and LDCs are enormous. For example, the GDP per capita in the United States was $46,025 greater than the average income in Ethiopia. Stated differently, the 2009 average income in the United States was about 111 times larger than the average income in Ethiopia ($46,443/$418). What a difference! Imagine trying to live on only $418 for a year in the United States. You probably would not survive.

Exhibit 2 compares GDP per capita for IACs to LDCs by regions of the world for 2009. The average citizen in the IACs enjoyed an income of $41,623, which was 42 times that of the average citizen in South Asia ($41,623/$986). South Asia includes countries such as Afghanistan, Bagladesh, and Pakistan. The exhibit also reveals that the greatest concentrations of world poverty are located in the rural

GDP per capita

The value of final goods produced (GDP) divided by the total population.

Industrially advanced countries (IACs)

High-income nations that have market economies based on large stocks of technologically advanced capital and well-educated labor. The United States, Canada, Australia, New Zealand, Japan, and most of the countries of Western Europe are IACs.

Less-developed countries (LDCs)

Nations without large stocks of technologically advanced capital and well-educated labor. LDCs are economies based on agriculture, such as most countries of Africa, Asia, and Latin America.

Exhibit 1	Annual GDP per Capita for Selected Countries, 2009		
Country	**GDP per capita**	**Country**	**GDP per capita**
Industrially Advanced Countries (IACs)			
Luxembourg	$94,418	Germany	39,442
Norway	76,692	Canada	39,217
Switzerland	66,127	United Kingdom	35,728
Denmark	55,942	Italy	34,955
Ireland	51,129	Singapore	34,346
Netherlands	47,042	Spain	31,142
United States	46,443	Greece	30,305
Finland	45,876	Israel	29,672
Austria	45,091	Hong Kong	29,559
Australia	45,090	New Zealand	25,354
Sweden	43,147	Portugal	20,655
Belgium	42,965	South Korea	16,450
France	42,091	Taiwan	15,373
Japan	39,573		
Less-Developed Countries (LDCs)			
Russia	8,874	Ukraine	2,538
Chile	8,853	Georgia	2,496
Turkey	8,427	Egypt	2,450
Mexico	8,040	Indonesia	2,224
Brazil	7,737	Bolivia	1,716
Romania	7,503	Vietnam	1,052
Panama	7,145	India	1,033
South Africa	5,635	Pakistan	1,017
Iran	4,477	Haiti	772
Thailand	3,973	Bangladesh	559
Jordan	3,766	Rwanda	512
China	3,566	Mozambique	456
Morocco	2,847	Ethiopia	418

SOURCE: International Monetary Fund, World Economic Outlook Database, http://www.imf.org/external/ns/cs.aspx?id=28.

areas of South Asia and Sub-Saharan Africa. The East Asia and Pacific region has many countries characterized by bleak and pervasive poverty, but there are notable exceptions, nicknamed the "Four Tigers" of East Asia—Hong Kong, Singapore, South Korea, and Taiwan. These Pacific Rim countries are newly industrialized economies, which we discuss at the end of this chapter.

| Exhibit 2 | **Average GDP per Capita for IACs and LDCs by Region, 2009** |

This exhibit shows average GDP per capita by regions of the world for 2009. The differences between the rich, industrially advanced countries (IACs) and the poor, less-developed countries (LDCs) in the various regions of the world are enormous. For example, the average citizen in the IACs had an income 42 times that of the average citizen in the LDCs of South Asia.

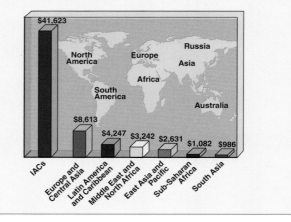

SOURCE: World Bank Group, Key Development Data & Statistics, http://www.worldbank.org/.

Problems with GDP per Capita Comparisons

Several problems are associated with using GDP per capita to compare rich versus poor countries. First, there is a measurement problem because countries tabulate GDP with differing degrees of accuracy. LDCs in general do not use sophisticated methods of gathering and processing GDP and population data. For example, in countries whose economies are based largely on agriculture, a family is more likely to produce goods and services outside the price system. In LDCs, families often grow their own food, make their own clothes, and build their own homes. Estimating the value of this output at market prices is difficult.

CONCLUSION *LDCs' GDP per capita is subject to greater measurement errors than data for IACs.*

Second, GDP per capita comparisons among countries can be misleading because they ignore the relative income distribution. Some countries have very high per capita incomes, yet most of the income goes to just a few wealthy families. The United Arab Emirates' GDP per capita is higher than that of several IACs. However, the United Arab Emirates earns its income from oil exports, and its income is actually distributed disproportionately to a relatively small number of wealthy families.

CONCLUSION *GDP per capita comparisons among nations can be misleading because GDP per capita does not measure income distribution.*

Third, GDP per capita comparisons between nations are subject to conversion problems. Making these data comparisons requires converting one nation's currency, say, Japan's yen, into a common currency, the U.S. dollar. Because, as explained in the chapter on international trade and finance, the value of a country's currency can rise or fall for many reasons, the true value of a nation's output can be distorted. For example, during a given year, one government might maintain an artificially high exchange rate and another government might not.

> **CONCLUSION** *A conversion problem may widen or narrow the GDP per capita gap between nations because the fluctuations in exchange rates do not reflect actual differences in the value of goods and services produced.*

Quality-of-Life Measures of Development

GDP per capita measures market transactions, but this measure does not give a complete picture of differences in living standards among nations. Exhibit 3 presents other selected socioeconomic indicators of the quality of life. These are variables such as life expectancy at birth, infant mortality rate, literacy rate, per capita energy consumption, and economic freedom ranking. Take a close look at the statistics in Exhibit 3. These data reflect the dimensions of poverty in many of the LDCs. For example, a person born in Japan has a life expectancy that is much longer than a person born in Mozambique, and the infant mortality rate is dramatically higher in Mozambique. Per capita energy consumption measures the use of nonhuman energy to perform work. In IACs, most work is done by machines, and in LDCs, virtually all work is done by people. For example, the average American uses 7,768 kilograms of (oil-equivalent) energy per year, while the average person in Mozambique

Exhibit 3	Quality-of-Life Indicators for Selected Countries, 2009					
	(1)	(2)	(3)	(4)	(5)	(6)
Country	**GDP per capita**	**Life expectancy at birth (years)**	**Infant mortality rate[1]**	**Literacy rate[2]**	**Per capita energy consumption[3]**	**Economic freedom rank[4]**
United States	$46,443	78	8%	99%	7,768	8
Japan	39,573	83	4	99	4,129	27
China	3,566	73	22	81	1,433	93
Egypt	2,450	71	36	71	843	75
India	1,033	65	72	61	510	77
Bangladesh	559	64	61	43	161	108
Mozambique	456	42	168	48	420	116

1. Per 1,000 live births.
2. Percentage age 15 and over who can read and write.
3. Kilograms of oil equivalent.
4. The Fraser Institute.

SOURCES: The CIA World Factbook, https://www.cia.gov/library/publications/the-world-factbook/index.html, World Bank Group, Key Development Data & Statistics, http://www.worldbank.org/ , The Fraser Institute, http://www.freetheworld.com.

uses only 420 kilograms. Finally, it is interesting to note that GDP per capita and other quality-of-life indicators are related to the ranking in economic freedom.

How good an indicator of the quality of life is GDP per capita? Exhibit 3 reflects the principle that lower GDP per capita is highly correlated with measures of the quality of life.

> **CONCLUSION** *In general, GDP per capita is highly correlated with alternative measures of quality of life.*

ECONOMIC GROWTH AND DEVELOPMENT AROUND THE WORLD

Economic growth and development are major goals of IACs and LDCs. People all over the world strive for a higher quality of life for their generation and future generations. However, growth is closer to a life-or-death situation for many LDCs, such as Bangladesh and Mozambique.

Economic growth and economic development are somewhat different, but related, concepts. As shown in Exhibit 4, recall from Chapter 2 that economic growth is the ability of an economy to produce greater levels of output, represented by an outward shift of its production possibilities curve (*PPC*). Thus, economic growth is defined on a *quantitative* basis using the percentage change in GDP per capita. When a nation's GDP rises more rapidly than its population, GDP per capita rises, and the nation experiences economic growth. Conversely, if GDP expands less than the population of a nation, GDP per capita falls, and the nation experiences negative economic growth.

Economic development is a broader concept that is more *qualitative* in nature. Economic development encompasses improvement in the quality of life, including economic growth in the production of goods and services. In short, continuous economic growth is necessary for economic development, but economic growth is not the only consideration. For example, as explained earlier, GDP per capita does not measure the distribution of income or the political environment that provides the legal, monetary, education, and transportation structures necessary for economic growth.

Economic growth and development involve a complex process that is determined by several interrelated factors. Like the performance of an NBA basketball team, success depends on the joint effort of team players, and one or two weak players can greatly reduce overall performance. However, there is no precise formula for winning. If your team has a player like former NBA great Michael Jordan, it can win even with a few weak players. The remainder of this section examines the key factors, or players, that operate together to produce a nation's economic well-being.

Endowment of Natural Resources

Most of the LDCs have comparatively limited bases of natural resources, including mineral deposits and arable land resources. In these countries, most of the available land is used for agricultural production, and clearing tropical forests to obtain more land can cause soil erosion. Also, tropical climates prevail in Central and South America, Africa, the Indian subcontinent, and Southeast Asia. The hot, humid climate in these regions is conducive to weed and insect infestations that plague agriculture.

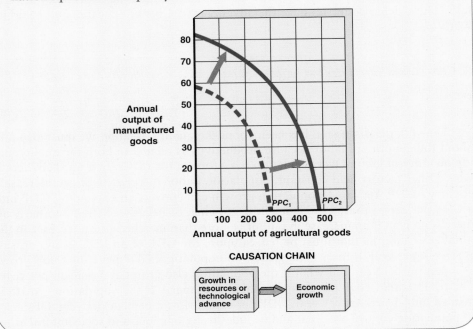

Exhibit 4 — Economic Growth

The economy begins with the capacity to produce combinations along production possibilities curve PPC_1. Growth in the resource base or technological advance shifts the production possibilities curve outward from PPC_1 to PPC_2. Points along PPC_2 represent new production possibilities that were previously impossible. The distance that the curve shifts represents an increase in the nation's productive capacity.

CAUSATION CHAIN

Growth in resources or technological advance → Economic growth

Although a narrow base of resources does pose a barrier to economic growth and development, no single conclusion can be drawn. For example, how have Hong Kong, Japan, and Israel achieved high standards of living in spite of limited natural resource bases? Each has practically no minerals, little fertile land, and no domestic sources of energy. Nonetheless, these economies have become prosperous. In contrast, Argentina, Venezuela, and Brazil have abundant fertile land and minerals. Yet these and other countries have been growing slowly or not at all. Venezuela, for example, is one of the most oil-rich countries in the world. Ghana, Kenya, and Bolivia are also resource-rich countries that are poor, with little or no economic growth.

CONCLUSION *Natural resource endowment can promote economic growth, but a country can develop without a large natural resource base.*

Investment in Human Resources

A low level of human capital can also present a barrier to economic growth and development. Recall that human capital is the education, training, experience, and health that improve the knowledge and skills of workers to produce goods and services. In most of the LDCs, investment in human capital is much less than in the IACs. Look back at column 4 in Exhibit 3. Consider how the literacy rate falls for the poorer countries. A country with a lower literacy rate has less ability to educate its labor force and create a basic foundation for economic growth. In fact, often the skills of workers in the poor countries are suited primarily to agriculture, rather than being appropriate for a wide range of industries and economic growth. Further complicating matters is a "brain drain" problem because the best educated and trained workers of poor countries pursue their education in wealthier countries. Column 2 of Exhibit 3 also gives a measure of health among countries with varying levels of GDP per capita. As the GDP per capita falls, the life expectancy at birth falls. Thus, richer countries have the advantage of a better educated and healthier workforce.

CONCLUSION *Investment in human capital generally results in increases in GDP per capita.*

Thus far, the discussion has been about the quality of labor. We must also talk about the quantity of labor because productivity is related to both the quality and the quantity of labor. Overpopulation is a problem for LDCs. In a nutshell, here is why: Other factors held constant, population (labor force) growth can increase a country's GDP. Yet rapid population growth can convert an expanding GDP into a GDP per capita that is stagnant, slow growing, or negative. Stated another way, there is no gain if an increase in output is more than matched by an increase in the number of mouths that must be fed. Suppose the GDP of an LDC grows at, say, 3 percent per year. If there is no growth in population, GDP per capita also grows at 3 percent per year. But what if the population also grows at 3 percent per year? The result is that GDP per capita remains unchanged. If the population growth is instead only 1 percent per year, GDP per capita rises 2 percent per year. Obstacles to population control are great and include strong religious and sociocultural arguments against birth control programs.

CONCLUSION *Rapid population growth combined with low human capital investment explains why many countries are LDCs.*

CHECKPOINT

Does Rapid Growth Mean a Country is Catching Up?

Suppose country Alpha has a production possibilities curve closer to the origin than the curve for country Beta. Now assume Alpha experiences a 3 percent growth rate in GDP for 10 years and Beta experiences a 6 percent growth rate in GDP for 10 years. At the end of five years, which of the following is the best prediction for the standard of living? (1) Alpha's residents are better off. (2) Beta's residents are better off. (3) Which country's residents are better off cannot be determined.

Accumulation of Capital

It did not take long for Robinson Crusoe on a deserted island to invest in a net in order to catch more fish than he could catch with his hands. Similarly, farmers working with modern tractors can cultivate more acres than farmers working with horse-drawn plows. Recall from Chapter 1 that capital in economics means factories, tractors, trucks, roads, computers, irrigation systems, electricity-generating facilities, and other human-made goods used to produce goods and services.

LDCs suffer from a critical shortage of capital. A family in Somalia owns little in the way of tools except a wooden plow. To make matters worse, roads are terrible, there are few plants generating electricity, and telephone lines are scarce. As shown in Exhibit 5, recall from Chapter 2 that a high-investment country can shift its production possibilities curve outward, but investment in capital goods is not a "free lunch." When more resources are used to produce more factories and machines, there is an opportunity cost of fewer resources available for the production of current consumer goods. This means that LDCs are often caught in a **vicious circle of poverty**. A vicious circle of poverty is the trap in which countries are poor and cannot afford to save. And low savings translate into low investment. Low investment results in low productivity, which, in turn, keeps incomes low. Any savings that do exist among higher-income persons in poor LDCs are often invested in IACs. This phenomenon is often called "capital flight." These wealthy individuals are afraid to save in their own countries because they fear that their governments may be overthrown and their savings could be lost.

The United States and other nations have attempted to provide LDCs with foreign aid so that they might grow. These countries desperately need more factories

Vicious circle of poverty

The trap in which countries are poor because they cannot afford to save and invest, but they cannot save and invest because they are poor.

> ### Exhibit 5   Alpha's and Beta's Present and Future Production Possibilities Curves
>
> In part (a), each year Alpha produces only enough capital (K_a) to replace existing capital that is worn out. Without greater capital and assuming other resources remain fixed, Alpha is unable to shift its production possibilities curve outward. In part (b), each year Beta produces K_b capital, which is more than the amount required to replenish its depreciated capital. In 2010, this expanded capital provides Beta with the extra production capacity to shift its production possibilities curve to the right. If Beta chooses point B on its curve, it has the production capacity to increase the amount of consumer goods from C_b to C_c without producing fewer capital goods.

Infrastructure	and **infrastructure.** Infrastructure is capital goods usually provided by the govern-

Infrastructure

Capital goods usually provided by the government, including highways, bridges, waste and water systems, and airports.

and **infrastructure.** Infrastructure is capital goods usually provided by the government, including highways, bridges, waste and water systems, and airports. Unfortunately, the amount of capital given to the LDCs is relatively small, and, as explained above, workers in the LDCs lack the skills necessary to use the most modern forms of capital. More specifically, LDCs face a major obstacle to capital accumulation because of the lack of entrepreneurs to assume the risks of capital formation.

The trap in which countries are poor because they cannot afford to save and invest, but they cannot save and invest because they are poor.

> **CONCLUSION** *There is a significant positive relationship between investment and economic growth and development.*

Technological Progress

As explained earlier in Chapter 2, holding natural resources, labor, and capital constant, advancing the body of knowledge applied to production shifts the production possibilities curve of a country. In fact, technological advances have been at the heart of economic growth and development in recent history. During the last 250 years, brainpower has invented new power-driven machines, advanced communication devices, new energy sources, and countless ways to produce more output with the same resources. How have innovative products improved your productivity? Consider, to name just a few products, the impact of CD-ROMs, fax machines, DVDs, personal computers, word processing software, cell phone photography, and the Internet. In contrast, in many poor countries, waterwheels still bring water to the surface, cloth is woven on handlooms, and oxcarts are the major means of transportation. Consequently, large inputs of human effort are used relative to capital resources.

The United States and other IACs have provided the world with an abundant accumulation of technological knowledge that might be adopted by those LDCs without the resources to undertake the required cost of research and development. However, the results of this transfer process have been mixed. For example, countries such as China, Hong Kong, Singapore, Taiwan, South Korea, and Japan have surely achieved rapid growth in part from the benefit of technological borrowing. Currently, Russia and other Eastern European nations are attempting to apply existing technological knowledge to boost their rates of growth.

The other side of the coin is that much available technology is not suited to LDCs. The old saying "You need to learn to walk before you can run" often applies to the LDCs. For example, small farms of most LDCs are not suited for much of the agricultural technology developed for IACs' large farms. And how many factories in the LDCs are ready to use the most modern robotics in the production process? Stated differently, LDCs need appropriate technology, rather than necessarily the latest technology.

> **CONCLUSION** *Many LDCs continue to experience low growth rates even though IACs have developed advanced technologies that the world can utilize.*

Political Environment

The discussion above leads to the generalization that in order for LDCs to achieve economic growth and development, they must wisely use natural resources, invest

Exhibit 7 | **The Effect of External Financing on an LDC's Production Possibilities Curve**

The poor country of Alpha is initially operating at point A on production possibilities curve PPC_1, with only enough capital (K_a) to replace depreciation. If C_a is the consumption level of subsistence, Alpha's economy cannot grow by reducing consumption. An inflow of external funds from abroad permits the LDC to increase its capital from K_a to K_b and its production possibilities curve shifts outward to PPC_2. At PPC_2, Alpha is able to increase its production of consumer goods from C_a to C_b.

There is a way out of the trap using external sources. Now assume Alpha receives an inflow of funds from abroad and buys capital goods that increase its rate of investment from K_a to K_b. At K_b, the rate of capital formation exceeds the value of capital depreciated, and Alpha's production possibilities curve shifts rightward to PPC_2. Economic growth made possible by external investment means Alpha can improve its standard of living by increasing its consumption level from C_a at point A on PPC_1 to C_b at point B on PPC_2.

Foreign Private Investment

Many countries' development benefits from private-sector foreign investment from private investors. For example, Microsoft might finance construction of a plant in the Philippines to manufacture software, or Bank of America may make loans to the government of Haiti. These large multinational corporations and commercial banks supply scarce capital to the LDCs. A multinational corporation is a firm with headquarters in one country and one or more branch plants in other countries. Multinational firms often seek new investment opportunities in LDCs because these poor countries offer abundant supplies of low-wage labor and raw materials. But the political environment in the LDCs must be conducive to investment. Multinational corporations often become the largest employers, largest taxpayers, and largest exporters in the LDCs.

Foreign Aid

About 1 percent of the U.S. federal budget is spent on **foreign aid**. Foreign aid is the transfer of money or resources from one government to another with no repayment required. These transfers may be made as outright grants, technical assistance, or food supplies. Foreign aid flows from country to country through governments and voluntary agencies, such as the Red Cross, CARE, and Church World Relief. The United States distributes most of its official development assistance through the **Agency for International Development (AID)**, established in 1961. The AID is the agency of the U.S. State Department that is in charge of U.S. aid to foreign countries.

One reason that countries like the United States provide foreign aid to LDCs is the belief that it is a moral responsibility of richer countries to share their wealth with poorer countries. A second reason is that it is in the best economic interest of the IACs to help the LDCs. When these countries become more prosperous, the IACs have more markets for their exports, and thereby all countries benefit from trade.

The LDCs often complain that foreign aid comes with too many economic and political strings attached. Loans are often offered on a "take it or leave it" basis, tied to policies other than basic trade policies, such as human rights, politics, or the military. Consequently, many LDCs argue for "trade, not aid." If the IACs would simply buy more goods from the LDCs, the LDCs could use their gains in export earnings to purchase more capital and other resources needed for growth. Many people in the United States feel that most foreign aid is a waste of money because it is misused by the recipient countries. This belief has caused Congress to grow increasingly reluctant to send taxpayers' money abroad except in the clearest cases of need or for reasons of national security.

Foreign Loans

A third source of external funds that can be used to finance LDCs' domestic investment is loans from abroad. Governments, international organizations, and private banks all make loans to LDCs. Like foreign private investment and foreign aid, loans give LDCs the opportunity to shift their production possibilities curves outward. There are various types of loan sources for LDCs. Bilateral loans are made directly from one country to another. The principal agent for official U.S. bilateral loans is the U.S. Agency for International Development, introduced earlier.

One prominent multilateral lending agency is the **World Bank**. The 186-member World Bank is the lending agency affiliated with the United Nations that makes long-term low-interest loans and provides technical assistance to LDCs. Loans are made only after a planning period lasting a year or more. The World Bank was established in 1944 by major nations meeting in Bretton Woods, New Hampshire. Its first charge was to assist with reconstruction after World War II. Today, the World Bank is located in Washington, D.C., and its main purpose is to channel funds from rich countries to poor countries. Voting shares are in proportion to the money provided by the members. The World Bank makes "last resort" loans to LDCs that are limited to financing basic infrastructure projects, such as schools, health centers, dams, irrigation systems, and transportation facilities, for which private financing is not available. In addition, the World Bank helps LDCs get loans from private lenders by insuring the loans. Thus, the poor countries are able to complete projects and use the economic returns to pay off the lender with interest.

The World Bank is not the only multilateral lending agency making loans to LDCs. The World Bank's partner institution is the **International Monetary Fund (IMF)**. The International Monetary Fund is the lending agency that makes short-term conditional

Global Economics   Hong Kong: A Crouching Pacific Rim Tiger   *Applicable Concept: newly industrialized economies*

As the map shows, the Pacific Rim economies are located along an arc extending from Japan and South Korea in the north to New Zealand in the south. The Four Tigers of East Asia are Hong Kong, Singapore, South Korea, and Taiwan. These "miracle economies" have often experienced higher economic growth rates, lower inflation rates, and lower unemployment rates than many long-established advanced countries.

Hong Kong is a great success story. When Adam Smith published his famous book, *The Wealth of Nations*, in 1776, Hong Kong was little more than a small barren rock island void of natural resources except fish. Today, Hong Kong is a bustling model of free enterprise in spite of the fact that seven million inhabitants are crowded into only about 400 square miles— one of the highest population densities in the world.

What is the reason for Hong Kong's success? Following the doctrine of Adam Smith, this economy is a paragon of *laissez faire*. Hong Kong has among the lowest individual and corporate income tax rates in the world and almost no legal restrictions on business. It has no capital gains tax, no interest tax, no sales tax, and no withholding tax. Hong Kong has become the largest banking center in the Pacific region after Tokyo. International trade is also largely unrestricted, and Hong Kong depends to a large extent on trade through its magnificent harbor for its economic success. Tariffs on imported goods are low, and Hong Kong is known as a safe-haven warehouse and trading center, with little or no interference from the government.

Hong Kong has proved that industrious people and entrepreneurs working hard on a crowded island with minimum regulations and open trade can improve their living standard without natural resources. Nevertheless, Hong Kong faces economic and political uncertainty. Under a 99-year lease signed in 1898, the United Kingdom transferred Hong Kong to the People's Republic of China in 1997. Will China allow Hong Kong to continue to follow Adam Smith's *laissez-faire* philosophy, resulting in high growth rates, or will Hong Kong change direction? It is anyone's guess. So far China has not tampered with Hong

Kong's *laissez-faire* economy, and its economic freedom ranking is higher than any country in the world.[1]

Recessions in the United States affect the global economy, and Hong Kong is no exception. Hong Kong's GDP growth depends heavily on exports. If, for example, U.S. consumers cut back on purchasing electronic devices, then Hong Kong's growth rate declines. After a 8 percent growth rate in 2000, the fall-off in global demand triggered by the 2001 recession in the United States slowed Hong Kong's real GDP growth rate to only 0.5 percent. Between 2004 and 2007, Hong Kong's growth rate recovered to an average of 7.3 percent, and this East Asian tiger was leaping forward and roaring again. However, as a result of the current financial crisis, Hong Kong slipped into recession in 2009 with a growth rate of −3.6 percent. So Hong Kong is a "crouching Tiger" waiting to leap forward and roar again in the future. The map compares 2009 data for the Four Tigers of East Asia.

ANALYZE THE ISSUE

One of the keys to Hong Kong's success is its free trade policy. Why is this so important for a developing country? What would be the effect of Hong Kong attempting to protect its domestic industries by raising tariffs and following other protectionist trade policies?

---

1. Frazer Institute, http://www.freetheworld.com/.

low-interest loans to developing countries. The IMF was also established at Bretton Woods in 1944. Its purpose is to help countries overcome short-run financial difficulties. Typically, the IMF makes conditional loans that require the debtor countries to implement fiscal and monetary policies that will alleviate balance-of-payments deficit problems and promote noninflationary economic growth. The 186-member IMF is not a charitable institution. It operates like a credit union with funding quotas that earn interest on the loans. The United States is the IMF's largest shareholder and thus has effective veto power over IMF decisions.

In recent years, the IMF has performed a major role in providing short-term loans to developing countries and to economies making the transition to capitalism. In the late 1990s, the IMF provided multibillion-dollar bailouts to Russia, several Asian countries, Brazil, and other countries experiencing economic turmoil. In 2010, the IMF and some the EU countries made a rescue loan to debt-plagued Greece with the condition of deep cutbacks in government spending and tax hikes. Critics argue that as long as governments believe the IMF will bail them out, they will fail to correct their own problems. IMF supporters counter that if the IMF does not intervene, troubled economies will default on outstanding loans and cause a worldwide ripple effect. Critics respond that a flood of low-cost short-term loans from the IMF encourages bad government policies and excessive risk taking by banks. Consequently, a bailout in a crisis generates new financial crises and reduces world economic growth.

Finally, private banks also engage in lending to LDCs. Until the 1970s, LDCs borrowed primarily from the World Bank and foreign governments. In the 1970s, private banks began to lend to both governments and private firms in LDCs. During the 1980s, the news was full of stories that some U.S. banks had made so many risky loans to LDCs that default on these loans would lead to the failure of one major U.S. bank after another. As the story goes, "If you can't repay the bank for your car loan, you're in trouble. If a government can't repay the bank a billion dollars, the bank's in trouble."

In the late 1980s, the debt crisis was avoided by (1) writing off some of the loans, (2) lowering the interest rate of remaining loans, and (3) lending LDCs more money to pay interest on their debt. The U.S. government, other Western governments, and the IMF were active in these solutions. Was this a case of "throwing good money after bad" because many loans would never be repaid? The answer is No. Easing the debt burden salvaged some payments and was in the best interest of both rich and poor countries because a fresh start encouraged trade. Nevertheless, the huge outstanding debts of some LDCs make another debt crisis a lingering possibility. In 2005, the wealthiest countries (G8) reached a groundbreaking agreement to eliminate the debt of some of the world's most impoverished countries. In the wake of the recent global financial crisis, IMF lending to LDCs rose sharply in 2008, in addition to financial analysis to policymakers.

CHECKPOINT

Is the Minimum Wage an Antipoverty Solution for Poor Countries?

Imagine you are an economic adviser to the president of a poor LDC. The president is seeking policies to promote economic growth and a higher standard of living for citizens of this country. You are asked whether adopting a minimum wage equal to the average of the IACs' average hourly wages would achieve these goals. Recall the discussion of the minimum wage from Chapter 4 and evaluate this policy.

Key Concepts

GDP per capita
Industrially advanced
　countries (IACs)
Less-developed countries
　(LDCs)

Vicious circle of poverty
Infrastructure
Foreign aid
Agency for International
　Development (AID)

World Bank
International Monetary
　Fund (IMF)

Summary

- *GDP per capita* provides a general index of a country's standard of living. Countries with low GDP per capita and slow growth in GDP per capita are less able to satisfy basic needs for food, shelter, clothing, education, and health.
- *Industrially advanced countries (IACs)* are countries with high GDP per capita and output is produced by technologically advanced capital. Countries that have high incomes without widespread industrial development, such as the oil-rich Arab countries, are not included in the IAC list.
- *Less-developed countries (LDCs)* are countries with low production per person. In these countries, output is produced without large amounts of technologically advanced capital and well-educated labor. The LDCs account for about three-fourths of the world's population.
- The *Four Tigers of the Pacific Rim* are Hong Kong, Singapore, South Korea, and Taiwan. These newly industrialized countries have achieved high growth rates and standards of living.
- *GDP per capita comparisons* are subject to four problems: (1) the accuracy of LDC data is questionable, (2) GDP per capita ignores income distribution, (3) fluctuations in exchange rates affect GDP per capita gaps between countries, and (4) there is no adjustment for cost-of-living differences between countries.

- *Economic growth* and *economic development* are related, but somewhat different concepts. Economic growth is measured quantitatively by GDP per capita, while economic development is a broader concept. In addition to GDP per capita, economic development includes quality-of-life measures, such as life expectancy at birth, adult literacy rate, and per capita energy consumption. Economic growth and development are the result of a complex process that is determined by five major factors: (1) natural resources, (2) human resources, (3) capital, (4) technological progress, and (5) the political environment. There is no single correct strategy for economic development, and a lack of strength in one or more of the five areas does not prevent growth.
- The *vicious circle of poverty* is a trap in which an LDC is too poor to save and therefore it cannot invest and shift its production possibilities curve outward. As a result, the LDC remains poor. One way for a poor country to gain savings, invest, and grow is to use funds from external sources such as foreign private investment, foreign aid, and foreign loans. Borrowing by many LDCs led to the debt crisis of the 1980s, which was resolved by writing off and restructuring the loans.

Summary of Conclusion Statements

- LDCs' GDP per capita is subject to greater measurement errors than data for IACs.
- GDP per capita comparisons among nations can be misleading because GDP per capita does not measure income distribution.
- A conversion problem may widen or narrow the GDP per capita gap between nations because the fluctuations in exchange rates do not reflect actual differences in the value of goods and services produced.
- In general, GDP per capita is highly correlated with alternative measures of quality of life.
- Natural resource endowment can promote economic growth, but a country can develop without a large natural resource base.
- Investment in human capital generally results in increases in GDP per capita.

- Rapid population growth combined with low human capital investment explains why many countries are LDCs.
- There is a significant positive relationship between investment and economic growth and development.
- Many LDCs continue to experience low growth rates even though IACs have developed advanced technologies that the world can utilize.
- Exchange rate controls artificially set by government above the market exchange rates reduce the volume of both exports and imports (international trade).
- There is no single strategy for economic growth and development.

Study Questions and Problems

1. What is the difference between industrially advanced countries (IACs) and less-developed countries (LDCs)? List five IACs and five LDCs.

2. Explain why GDP per capita comparisons among nations are not a perfect measure of differences in economic well-being.

3. Assume you are given the following data for country Alpha and country Beta:

Country	GDP per capita
Alpha	$25,000
Beta	$15,000

   a. Based on the GDP per capita data given above, in which country would you prefer to live?
   b. Now assume you are given the following additional quality-of-life data. In which country would you prefer to reside?

Country	Life expectancy at birth (years)	Daily per capita calorie supply	Per capita energy consumption*
Alpha	65	2,500	3,000
Beta	70	3,000	4,000

*Kilograms of oil equivalent.

4. What is the difference between economic development and economic growth? Give examples of how each of these concepts can be measured.

5. Do you agree with the argument that the rich nations are getting richer and the poor nations are getting poorer? Is this an oversimplification? Explain.

6. Explain why it is so difficult for poor LDCs to generate investment in capital in order to increase productivity and growth and therefore improve their standard of living.

7. Why is the quest for economic growth and development complicated?

8. Indicate whether each of the following is associated with a high or low level of economic growth and development:

	High	Low
a. Overpopulation		
b. Highly skilled labor		
c. High savings rate		
d. Political stability		
e. Low capital accumulation		
f. Advanced technology		
g. Highly developed infrastructure		
h. High proportion of agriculture		
i. High degree of income inequality		

9. Without external financing from foreign private investment, foreign aid, and foreign loans, poor countries are caught in the vicious circle of poverty. Explain. How does external financing help poor countries achieve economic growth and development?

10. What are some of the problems for LDCs of accepting foreign aid?

11. Why would an LDC argue for "trade, not aid"?

12. Explain the differences among the Agency for International Development (AID), the World Bank, and the International Monetary Fund (IMF).

For Online Exercises, go to the Tucker Web site at www.cengage.com/economics/tucker.

CHECKPOINT ANSWERS

Does Rapid Growth Mean a Country Is Catching Up?

GDP growth alone does not measure the standard of living. You must also consider population. Even though Beta experienced a greater GDP growth rate, its GDP per capita might be less than Alpha's because its population growth rate is greater. Of course, the reverse is also possible, but without population data, we cannot say. If you said which country's people are better off cannot be determined because the GDP must be divided by the population to measure the average standard of living, **YOU ARE CORRECT**.

Is the Minimum Wage an Antipoverty Solution for Poor Countries?

An important source of foreign investment for LDCs is multinational corporations that locate plants and other facilities in these countries. LDCs compete with each other for the economic growth and development benefits that these multinational corporations can provide. For an LDC to win the competition, it must offer political stability, adequate infrastructure, a favorable business climate, and a cheap labor force. If you said you would not support the president's proposal to raise the minimum wage because it would place the LDC at a competitive disadvantage in the labor market, thereby reducing foreign private investment and growth, **YOU ARE CORRECT**.

Practice Quiz

For an explanation of the correct answers, visit the Tucker Web site at www.cengage.com/economics/tucker.

1. An LDC is defined as a country
   a. without large stocks of advanced capital.
   b. without well-educated labor.
   c. with low GDP per capita.
   d. that is described by all of the above.

2. According to the definition given in the chapter, which of the following is *not* an LDC?
   a. India
   b. Egypt
   c. China
   d. Ireland

3. Which of the following is *true* when making GDP per capita comparisons among nations?
   a. The GDP per capita is subject to greater measurement errors for LDCs compared to IACs.
   b. The GDP per capita does not measure income distribution.
   c. The GDP per capita is subject to fluctuations from changes in exchange rates.
   d. All of the above are true.

4. LDCs are characterized by
   a. high life expectancy.
   b. high adult literacy.
   c. high infant mortality.
   d. all of the above.
   e. none of the above.

5. According to the classification in the text, which of the following is *not* an IAC?
   a. United Arab Emirates
   b. Israel
   c. Hong Kong
   d. Greece

6. When the government fixes the exchange rate above market exchange rates,
   a. international trade falls.
   b. the infrastructure improves.
   c. real GDP per capita rises.
   d. the vicious circle of poverty is broken.

7. Which of the following statements is *true*?
   a. An LDC is a country with a low GDP per capita, low levels of capital, and uneducated workers.
   b. The vicious circle of poverty exists because GDP must rise before people can save and invest.
   c. LDCs are characterized by rapid population growth and low levels of investment in human capital.
   d. All of the above are true.

8. An outward shift of the production possibilities curve represents
   a. economic growth.
   b. a decline in economic development.
   c. a decrease in human capital.
   d. a decrease in resources.

9. Which of the following problems do LDCs face?
   a. Low per capita income and high GDP growth rate
   b. Low population growth and low per capita income
   c. Rapid population growth and low human capital
   d. Low per capita income and high saving rate

10. Which of the following *best* defines the vicious circle of poverty?
    a. The GDP per capita must rise before people can save and invest.
    b. People cannot save while capital accumulates.
    c. Increased GDP per capita relates to lower population growth.
    d. Poverty, saving, and investment are related like a circle.

11. Which of the following is infrastructure?
    a. International Harvester tractor plant
    b. Waste and water system provided by government
    c. US Airways airplane
    d. Service of postal workers

Practice Quiz Continued

12. Economic growth and development in LDCs are low because many of them lack
   a.   capital investment.
   b.   technological progress.
   c.   a favorable political environment.
   d.   all of the above.
   e.   none of the above.

13. Which of the following makes short-term conditional low-interest loans to developing countries?
   a.   Agency for International Development (AID)
   b.   World Bank
   c.   International Monetary Fund (IMF)
   d.   New International Economic Order (NIEO)

14. Which of the following groups makes long-term low-interest loans to less-developed countries (LDCs)?
   a.   Agency for International Development (AID)
   b.   New International Economic Order (NIEO)

   c.   International Monetary Fund (IMF)
   d.   World Bank

15. In order for Ethiopia to increase its future economic growth, it must choose a point that is
   a.   below its production possibilities curve.
   b.   further along on its production possibilities curve toward the capital goods axis.
   c.   further along on its production possibilities curve toward the consumption goods axis.
   d.   further along on its production possibilities curve away from the population axis.
   e.   above its production possibilities curve.

Road Map The International Economy

This road map feature helps you tie material in the part together as you travel the Economic Way of Thinking Highway. The following are review questions listed by chapter from the previous part. The key concept in each question is given for emphasis, and each question or set of questions concludes with an interactive game to reinforce the concepts. Click on the Tucker Web site at www.cengage.com/economics/tucker, select the chapter, and play the visual causation chain game designed to make learning fun. Enjoy the cheers when correct and suffer the jeers if you miss. The correct answers for the multiple-choice questions are given in Appendix C of the text.

part 6

Chapter 18. International Trade and Finance

1. **Key Concept: Exchange rate changes**
    Which of the following would cause the U.S. demand curve for Japanese yen to shift to the right?
    a. An increase in the U.S. inflation rate compared to the rate in Japan
    b. A higher real rate of interest on investments in Japan than on investments in the United States
    c. The popularity of Japanese products increases in the United States
    d. All of the above

2. **Key Concept: Exchange rate changes**
    Which of the following would cause the supply of dollars curve in the United States to shift to the right?
    a. Japanese imports become less popular.
    b. The value of the dollar falls.
    c. The supply of dollars decreases.
    d. Japanese imports become more popular.

Causation Chain Game
Changes in Supply and Demand Curves for Dollars—Exhibit 10

3. **Key Concept: Impact of relative price level changes**
    An increase in inflation in the United States relative to the rate in France would make
    a. U.S. goods relatively less expensive in the United States and in France.
    b. French goods relatively less expensive in the United States and U.S. goods relatively more expensive in France.
    c. French goods relatively more expensive in the United States and in France.
    d. French goods relatively more expensive in the United States and U.S. goods relatively less expensive in France.

4. **Key Concept: Impact of relative price level changes**
   If the Japanese price level falls relative to the price level in the United States, then
   a. Japanese buy less U.S. exports.
   b. the demand for dollars decreases.
   c. the supply of dollars increases.
   d. the value of the dollar falls.
   e. all of the above are true.

   Causation Chain Game
   The Impact of Relative Price Level Changes on Exchange Rates—Exhibit 11

Chapter 19. Economies in Transition

5. **Key Concept: Command economy**
   Which of the following statements is *true* about a command economy?
   a. Shortages occur because of complexities in the planning process.
   b. Planners determine what, how many, and for whom goods and services are to be produced.
   c. Planners often allocate goods and services through a rationing system.
   d. The quality of produced goods and services tends to be inferior.
   e. All of the above are true.

6. **Key Concept: Command economy**
   Which of the following statements *best* describes the role played by prices in a command economy such as the former Soviet Union?
   a. Prices were used to allocate resources.
   b. Prices played the same role as in a market economy.
   c. Prices were used to ration final goods and services but not to allocate resources.
   d. None of the above statements is descriptive.

   Causation Chain Game
   Central Planners Fixing Prices—Exhibit 2

Chapter 20. Growth and the Less-Developed Countries

7. **Key Concept: Economic growth**
   An outward shift of an economy's production possibilities curve is caused by an
   a. increase in capital.
   b. increase in labor.
   c. advance in technology.
   d. all of the above are true.

8. **Key Concept: Economic growth**
    Which of the following is *correct*?
    a. Economic development is more quantitative than economic growth.
    b. A country cannot achieve economic growth with a limited base of natural resources.
    c. Infrastructure is capital provided by the private sector.
    d. All of the above are true.
    e. All of the above are false.

Causation Chain Game
Economic Growth—Exhibit 4

9. **Key Concept: Achieving economic growth**
    Which of the following can be a barrier to an LDC's economic growth and development?
    a. Low population growth
    b. A low level of human capital
    c. Faster capital accumulation
    d. More infrastructure

10. **Key Concept: Economic growth and development**
    To grow and prosper, less-developed countries must *not*
    a. invest in human capital.
    b. build a strong infrastructure.
    c. shift resources out of the production of consumer goods and into the production of capital goods.
    d. shift resources out of the production of capital goods and into the production of consumer goods.
    e. improve the quality of the water supply.

Causation Chain Game
The Effect of External Financing on an LDC's Production Possibilities Curve—Exhibit 7

Answers to Odd-Numbered Study Questions and Problems*

Chapter 1 Introducing the Economic Way of Thinking

1. A poor nation with many people who lack food, clothing, and shelter certainly experiences wants beyond the availability of goods and services to satisfy these unfulfilled wants. On the other hand, no wealthy nation has all the resources necessary to produce everything everyone in the nation wishes to have. Even if you had $1 million and were completely satisfied with your share of goods and services, other desires would be unfulfilled. There is never enough time to accomplish all the things that you can imagine would be worthwhile.

3. a. capital

5. a. microeconomic issue
   b. macroeconomic issue
   c. microeconomic issue
   d. macroeconomic issue

7. The real world is full of complexities that make it difficult to understand and predict the relationships between variables. For example, the relationship between changes in the price of gasoline and changes in consumption of gasoline requires abstraction from the reality that such variables as the fuel economy of cars and weather conditions often change at the same time as the price of gasoline.

9. The two events are associated, and the first event (cut in military spending) is the cause of the second event (higher unemployment in the defense industry). The point is that association does not necessarily mean causation, but it might.

11. d. statement of normative economics

---

*Note: Answers to even-numbered questions are in the Instructor's Manual

Appendix to Chapter 1 Applying Graphs to Economics

1. a. The probability of living is *inversely* related to age. This model could be affected by improvements in diet, better health care, reductions in hazards to health in the workplace, or changes in the speed limit.

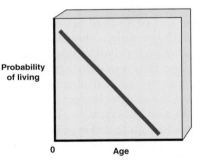

b. Annual income and years of formal education are *directly* related. This relationship might be influenced by changes in such human characteristics as intelligence, motivation, ability, and family background. An example of an institutional change that could affect this relationship over a number of years is the draft.

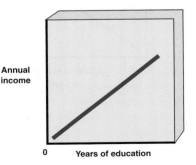

c. Inches of snow and sales of bathing suits are *inversely* related. The weather forecast and the price of travel to sunny vacation spots can affect this relationship.

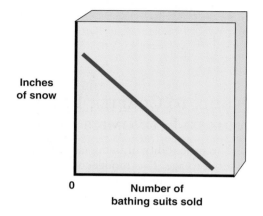

d. Most alumni and students will argue that the number of football games won is *directly* related to the athletic budget. They reason that winning football games is great advertising and results in increased attendance, contributions, and enrollment that, in turn, increase the athletic budget. Success in football can also be related to other factors, such as school size, age and type of institution, number and income of alumni, and quality of the faculty and administrators.

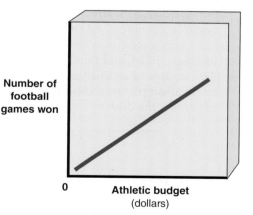

CHAPTER 2 PRODUCTION POSSIBILITIES, OPPORTUNITY COST, AND ECONOMIC GROWTH

1. Because the wants of individuals and society exceed the goods and services available to satisfy these desires, choices must be made. The consumption possibilities of an individual with a fixed income are limited, and as a result, additional consumption of one item necessarily precludes an expenditure on another next-best choice. The forgone alternative is called the opportunity cost, and this concept also applies to societal decisions. If society allocates resources to the production of guns, then those same resources cannot be used at the same time to make butter.

3. Regardless of the price of a lunch, economic resources—and, labor, and capital—are used to produce the lunch. These scarce resources are no longer available to produce other goods and services.

5. Using marginal analysis, students weigh the benefits of attending college against the costs. There is an incentive to attend college when the benefits (improved job opportunities, income, intellectual improvement, social life, and so on) outweigh the opportunity costs.

7.

Flower boxes	Opportunity cost (pies forgone)
0	
1	4 (30 − 26)
2	5 (26 − 21)
3	6 (21 − 15)
4	7 (15 − 8)
5	8 (8 − 0)

9. Movements along the curve are efficient points and conform to the well-known "free lunch" statement. However, inefficient points are exceptions because it is possible to produce more of one output without producing less of another output.

11.

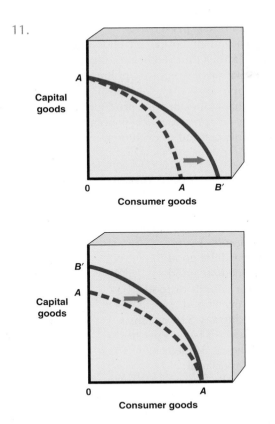

Chapter 3 Market Demand and Supply

1. If people buy a good or service because they associate higher quality with higher price, this is a violation of the ceteris paribus assumption. An increase in the quantity demanded results only from a decrease in price. Quality and other nonprice determinants of demand, such as tastes and preferences and the price of related goods, are held constant in the model.

3. a. Demand for cars decreases; oil and cars are *complements*.
   b. Demand for insulation increases; oil and home insulation are *substitutes*.
   c. Demand for coal increases; oil and coal are *substitutes*.
   d. Demand for tires decreases; oil and tires are *complements*.

5. One reason that the demand curve for word processing software shifted to the right might be that people desire new, higher-quality output features. The supply curve can shift to the right when new technology makes it possible to offer more software for sale at different prices.

7. a. Demand shifts to the right.
   b. Supply shifts to the left.
   c. Supply shifts to the right.
   d. Demand shifts to the right.
   e. Demand shifts to the right.
   f. Supply of corn shifts to the left.

9. a. The supply of CD players shifts rightward.
   b. The demand for CD players is unaffected.
   c. The equilibrium price falls, and the equilibrium quantity increases.
   d. The demand for CDs increases because of the fall in the price of CD players (a complementary good).

11. The number of seats (quantity supplied) remains constant, but the demand curve shifts because tastes and preferences change according to the importance of each game. Although demand changes, the price is a fixed amount, and to manage a shortage, colleges and universities use amount of contributions, number of years as a contributor, or some other rationing device.

Appendix to Chapter 3 Consumer Surplus, Producer Surplus, and Market Efficiency

1. $80

3.

Price	$30	$15
Consumer surplus	$80	$105
Producer surplus	$25	$5
Total surplus	$105	$110

The lower price results in higher total surplus because in this case the rise in consumer surplus exceeds fall in producer surplus.

CHAPTER 4 MARKETS IN ACTION

1.

a. The equilibrium price is $6.00 per gallon, and the equilibrium quantity is 300 million gallons per month. The price system will restore the market's $6.00 per gallon price because either a surplus will drive prices down or a shortage will drive prices up.

b. The support price results in a persistent surplus of 200 million gallons of milk per month, which the government purchases with taxpayers' money. Consequently, taxpayers who do not drink milk are still paying for milk. The purpose of the support price is to bolster the incomes of dairy farmers.

c. The ceiling price will result in a persistent shortage of 200 million gallons of milk per month, but 200 million gallons are purchased by consumers at the low price of $4.00 per gallon. The shortage places a burden on the government to ration milk in order to be fair and to prevent black markets. The government's goal is to keep the price of milk below the equilibrium price of $6.00 per gallon, which would be set by a free market.

3. The labor market can be divided into two separate markets, one for skilled union workers and one for unskilled workers. If the minimum wage is above the equilibrium wage rate and is raised, the effect will be to increase the demand for, and the wage of, skilled union workers because the two groups are substitutes.

5. The equilibrium price rises.

7. The government can reduce emissions by (a) regulations that require smoke-abatement equipment or (b) imposing pollution taxes that shift supply leftward.

9. Pure public goods are not produced in sufficient quantities by private markets because there is no feasible method to exclude free riders.

CHAPTER 5 GROSS DOMESTIC PRODUCT

1. a. final service
   b. final good
   c. intermediate good
   d. intermediate good

3.
3 million pounds of food × $1 per pound	= $3 million
50,000 shirts × $20 per shirt	= 1 million
20 houses × $50,000 per house	= 1 million
50,000 hours of medical services × $20 per hour	= 1 million
1 automobile plant × $1 million per plant	= 1 million
2 tanks × $500,000 per tank	= 1 million
Total value of output	= $8 million

5. Capital is not excluded from being a final good. A final good is a finished good purchased by an ultimate user and not for resale. The ultimate user is the warehouse, so the sale would be included in GDP and there would be no double-counting problem.

7. Using the expenditure approach, net exports are exports minus imports. If the expenditures by foreigners for U.S. products exceed the expenditures by U.S. citizens for foreign products, net exports will be a positive contribution to GDP. If foreigners spend less for U.S. products than U.S. citizens spend for foreign products, GDP is reduced. Net exports are used by national income accountants because actual consumption, investment, and government spending figures reported to the U.S. Department of Commerce do not exclude the amount of expenditures for imports.

9. NI = GDP – depreciation
   $4,007 = $4,486 – $479

   The depreciation charge is not a measure of newly produced output. It is an estimate, subject to error, of the value of capital worn out in the production of final goods and services. Errors in the capital consumption allowance overstate or understate GDP.

11. When the price level is rising, nominal GDP overstates the rate of change between years. Dividing nominal GDP by the GDP chain price index results in real GDP by removing the distortion from inflation. Comparison of real GDP changes between years reflects only changes in the market value of all final products and not changes in the price level.

13. GDP does not tell the mix of output in two nations, say, between military and consumer goods. GDP also does not reveal whether GDP is more equally distributed in one nation compared to another.

Chapter 6 Business Cycles and Unemployment

1. The generally accepted theory of business cycles is that they are the result of changes in the level of total spending, or aggregate demand. Total spending includes spending for final goods by households, businesses, government, and foreign buyers. Expressed as a formula, GDP = C + I + G + (X − M).

3. **Civilian unemployment rate**

$$= \frac{\text{unemployed}}{\text{civilian labor force}} \times 100$$

where the civilian labor force = unemployed + employed. Therefore,

$$7.7\% = \frac{10 \text{ million persons}}{130 \text{ million persons}} \times 100$$

5. The official unemployment rate is overstated when respondents to the BLS falsely report that they are seeking employment. The unemployment rate is understated when *discouraged workers* who want to work have given up searching for a job.

7. Structural unemployment occurs when those seeking jobs do not possess the skills necessary to fill the available jobs. Cyclical unemployment is caused by deficient total spending.

9. The increasing participation of women and teenagers in the labor force has increased the rate of unemployment. Women take more time

out of the labor force than do men for child-bearing and child rearing.

11. The GDP gap is the difference between potential real GDP and actual real GDP. Because potential real GDP is estimated on the basis of the full-employment rate of unemployment, the GDP gap measures the cost of *cyclical* unemployment in terms of real GDP.

Chapter 7 Inflation

1. This statement is incorrect. The price of a single good or service can rise while the average price of all goods and services falls. In short, the inflation rate rises when the average price of consumer goods and services rises.

3. First, the CPI is based on a typical market basket purchased by the urban family. Any group not buying the same market basket, such as retired persons, is not experiencing the price changes measured by changes in the CPI. Second, the CPI fails to adjust for quality changes. Third, the CPI ignores the law of demand and the substitution effect as prices of products change.

5. If the percentage increase in the CPI exceeds the salary increase, a person's purchasing power declines in a given year.

7. The loan is advantageous to you because the real interest rate is −5 percent (5 percent nominal interest rate minus 10 percent inflation). In one year, you must repay $105. If prices rise by 10 percent during the year, the real value of the $105 will be only $95. Therefore, you have borrowed $100 worth of purchasing power and are repaying $95 worth of purchasing power.

9. At full employment, the economy operates at full capacity and produces the maximum output of goods and services. As buyers try to outbid one another for the fixed supply of goods and services, prices rise rapidly.

11. If buyers think prices will be higher tomorrow, they may buy products today and cause demand-pull inflation. If businesses believe prices for inputs will be higher in the future, many will raise prices today and cause cost-push inflation.

Chapter 8 The Keynesian Model

1. Classical economists argued that underconsumption and unemployment could not exist in the long run because of price-wage flexibility. Unsold merchandise would force firms to compete and lower product prices, and unemployed workers would accept a lower wage rate.

3. Consumers have only two options for any extra disposable income they receive. The MPC and MPS must add up to one because the portion of extra income that is not spent must be saved.

5. a. The consumption schedule downshifts, and the saving schedule downshifts.
   b. The consumption schedule upshifts, and the saving schedule downshifts.
   c. The consumption schedule downshifts, and the saving schedule upshifts.
   d. The consumption schedule downshifts, and the saving schedule downshifts.
   e. Both the consumption and the saving schedules downshift.

7. Changes in the nonincome determinants of the consumption and saving schedules tend to offset each other, and people are reluctant to change their consumption and saving habits. On the other hand, Keynes considered the volatility of businesses' decisions to invest as a major cause of the business cycle. The potentially unstable determinants of investment spending include expectations, technological change, the stock of capital goods, and business taxes.

9. a.

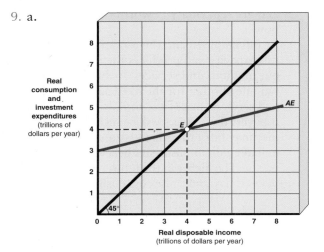

Real consumption and investment expenditures (trillions of dollars per year) / Real disposable income (trillions of dollars per year)

b. The autonomous consumption is $3 trillion, and the $MPC = 0.25$. Note that each $1 trillion increase in real disposable income results in a $0.25 trillion increase in aggregate expenditures. Since $MPS = (1 - MPC)$, $MPS = (1 - 0.25) = 0.75$.

c. The equilibrium level of real disposable income equals $4 trillion where the AE line intersects the 45° line.

d. An increase in autonomous investment adds new spending by businesses at each level of aggregate spending. The AE line would therefore shift upward, and the equilibrium level of real disposable income increases.

Chapter 9 The Keynesian Model in Action

1.

Employment, Output, Consumption, and Unplanned Inventory			
Possible levels of employment (millions)	Real GDP (output) equals disposable income (billions of dollars)	Consumption (billions of dollars)	Unplanned inventory (billions of dollars)
40	325	300	−75
45	375	325	−50
50	425	350	−25
55	475	375	0
60	525	400	25
65	575	425	50
70	625	450	75

a. Answers are given in the above table.

b. $$MPC = \frac{\text{change in consumption}}{\text{change in disposable income}}$$
$$= \frac{\$25 \text{ billion}}{\$50 \text{ billion}} = \frac{1}{2} = 0.50$$
since $MPS = 1 - MPC = 1 - 0.50 = 0.50$

c. At an employment level of 40 million workers, $75 million in unplanned inventory investment encourages businesses to expand output, and GDP increases toward the equilibrium real GDP of $475 billion.

3.

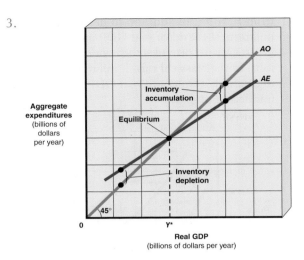

The aggregate expenditures (*AE*) line intersects the aggregate output (*AO*) line at the equilibrium level of real GDP, *Y**. Below *Y**, an unplanned inventory depletion causes businesses to expand output, which pushes the economy toward equilibrium output. Above *Y**, an unintended inventory accumulation pushes the economy toward *Y** by pressuring businesses to reduce production.

5. $$\text{Multiplier} = \frac{1}{1 - MPC} = \frac{1}{MPS}$$

The greater the *MPC*, the smaller the *MPS* and the greater the size of the multiplier.

a. 1, 1.5, 10

b. $Y = M \times I = 5 \times \$10\text{ billion} = \$50\text{ billion}$

c. $Y = M \times I = 3 \times \$10\text{ billion} = \$30\text{ billion}$

7. a.

Round	Components of total spending	New consumption spending (billions of dollars)
1	Investment	$100
2	Consumption	75
3	Consumption	56
4	Consumption	42
	Total spending	$273

b. The spending multiplier is

$$\frac{1}{(1 - MPC)} = \frac{1}{(1 - 0.75)} = \frac{1}{0.25} = 4$$

Therefore, change in investment spending × spending multiplier = change in aggregate spending ($100 billion × 4 = $400 billion).

Note: This problem demonstrates how useful the spending multiplier formula is because it avoids working through individual steps in the multiplier process.

9. **Spending multiplier**

$$= \frac{\text{change in GDP}}{\text{change in government spending}} = \frac{\Delta Y}{\Delta G}$$

Since *MPC* = 0.75,

$$\text{Spending multiplier} = \frac{1}{(1 - MPC)} = \frac{1}{0.25} = 4$$

rewritten as

$$4 = \frac{\$100\text{ billion}}{\Delta G}$$

Therefore,

$$\Delta G = \frac{\$100\text{ billion}}{4} = \$25\text{ billion}$$

Given that the *MPC* is 0.75, this means households spend only $18.75 billion of the additional $25 billion of disposable income from the tax cut. Therefore,

$$\Delta C \times \text{spending multiplier} = \text{change in GDP}$$
$$\$18.75\text{ billion} \times 4 = \$75\text{ billion}$$

Because GDP must increase by $100 billion, a tax cut of $25 billion would not be enough to restore full-employment GDP.

CHAPTER 10 AGGREGATE DEMAND AND SUPPLY

1. There are three reasons why the aggregate demand curve is downward sloping:

a. The *real balances effect* means that a lower price level increases the purchasing power of money and other financial assets. The result is an increase in consumption, which increases the quantity of real GDP demanded.

b. The *interest-rate effect* assumes a fixed money supply, and, therefore, a lower price level reduces the demand for borrowing and the interest rate. The lower rate of interest increases spending for consumption and investment.

c. The *net exports effect* encourages foreign customers to buy more of an economy's domestic exports relative to its domestic purchases of imports when the price level falls. An increase in net exports increases aggregate expenditures.

Rationales for the downward-sloping demand curve for an individual market are the income effect, the substitution effect, and the law of diminishing marginal utility, which are quite different from the three effects that determine the aggregate demand curve.

3. a. A leftward shift occurs because of a decrease in the consumption schedule.
   b. A rightward shift occurs because of an increase in autonomous investment spending.
   c. A rightward shift occurs because of an increase in government spending.
   d. A rightward shift occurs because of an increase in net exports.

5. This statement may not be correct. The equilibrium GDP is not necessarily the same as the full-employment GDP. Equilibrium GDP refers to the equality between the aggregate demand and the aggregate supply curves, which does not necessarily equal the full capacity of the economy to produce goods and services.

7. a. leftward because of an increase in resource prices
   b. rightward because of a decrease in resource prices
   c. rightward because technological change reduces the cost of production
   d. leftward because an increase in taxes means the price must cover the tax at each possible quantity supplied

9. a. Aggregate demand increases.
   b. Aggregate supply increases.
   c. Aggregate demand decreases.
   d. Aggregate supply decreases.
   e. Aggregate demand decreases along the classical range.
   f. Aggregate demand increases along the Keynesian range.

11. Assuming the aggregate supply curve remains constant, a rightward shift of the aggregate demand curve from AD_1 to AD_2 in the upward-sloping or the vertical range of the aggregate supply curve causes the price level to rise from P_1 to P_2. In addition to demand-pull inflation, the level of real GDP increases from Q_1 to Q_2 and provides the economy with new jobs. In the classical range, inflation is the only undesirable result, and real GDP remains unaffected at Q_2.

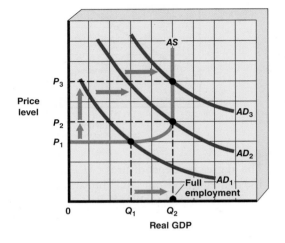

APPENDIX TO CHAPTER 10 THE SELF-CORRECTING AGGREGATE DEMAND AND SUPPLY MODEL

1. a.–c.

(trillions of dollars per year)

3.

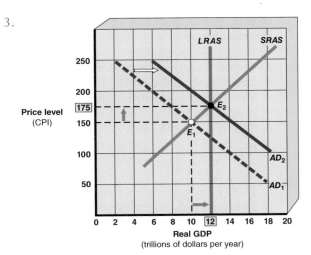

5. Nominal incomes of workers in the short run are fixed. In response to the fall in aggregate demand, firms' profits decline, and they cut output and employment. As a result, the economy moves downward along *SRAS* to temporary equilibrium at E_2. When workers lower their nominal incomes because of competition from unemployed workers, the short-run aggregate supply curve shifts rightward to E_3 and returns to long-run equilibrium. Profits rise and firms increase output and employment while the price level falls.

$$\Delta G \times SM = \Delta AD$$
$$\Delta G \times 4 = \$500 \text{ billion}$$
$$\Delta G = \$125 \text{ billion}$$

The government must increase government spending by \$125 billion in order to eliminate the GDP gap.

7. The tax multiplier equals the spending multiplier minus 1. Thus, the impact of the expansion in government spending exceeds the impact of an equal amount of tax cut.

9. As a supply-side economist, you would argue that the location of the aggregate supply curve is related to the tax rates. Ceteris paribus, if the tax rates are cut, there will be strong incentives for workers to supply more work, households to save more, and businesses to invest more in capital goods. Thus, cutting tax rates shifts the aggregate supply curve rightward, the level of real GDP rises, and the price level falls.

11. a. rightward shift in the aggregate demand curve
    b. leftward shift in the aggregate demand curve
    c. rightward shift in the aggregate supply curve
    d. rightward shift in the aggregate demand curve
    e. leftward shift in the aggregate supply curve

Chapter 11 Fiscal Policy

1. *Expansionary* fiscal policy refers to increasing government spending and/or decreasing taxes in order to increase aggregate demand and eliminate a GDP gap. *Contractionary* fiscal policy is designed to cool inflation by decreasing aggregate demand. This result is accomplished by decreasing government spending and/or increasing taxes.

3. a. contractionary fiscal policy
   b. contractionary fiscal policy
   c. expansionary fiscal policy

5. The spending multiplier is

$$\frac{1}{1 - MPC} = \frac{1}{0.25} = \frac{1}{1/4} = 4$$

The spending multiplier (*SM*) times the change in government spending (ΔG) equals the change in aggregate demand (ΔAD). Therefore,

Chapter 12 The Public Sector

1. Transfer payments account for the difference between total government expenditures, or outlays, and total government spending. Transfers do not "use up" resources; they reallocate purchasing power by collecting taxes from one group and paying benefits to other groups.

3. The primary sources are individual income taxes at the federal level, sales and excise taxes at the state level, and property taxes at the local level.

5. The marginal tax rate is the percentage of additional income paid in taxes. The average tax rate is the amount of taxes paid as a percentage of income.

7. a. more than \$6,000
   b. less than \$6,000
   c. \$6,000

9. Sales tax paid as a percentage of income:
10%
7%
6%
4%
Because the sales tax paid as a percentage of income falls as income rises, the tax is regressive.

11. A profit-maximizing firm follows the marginal rule that units will be produced so long as the marginal benefit exceeds or equals the marginal cost. Dollars can measure the intensity of benefits in relation to costs. A "one-person, one-vote" system does not necessarily measure benefits in proportion to the dollar value of benefits among individual voters. Thus, a majority of voters can approve projects for which costs exceed benefits and reject projects for which benefits exceed costs.

CHAPTER 13 FEDERAL DEFICITS, SURPLUSES, AND THE NATIONAL DEBT

1. The national debt is the sum of past federal budget deficits. When budget deficits are large, the national debt increases at a rapid rate. When budget deficits are small, the national debt increases at a lower rate.

3. The statement makes the argument that most of the debt is internal national debt that one U.S. citizen owes to another U.S. citizen. Suppose the federal government finances a deficit by having the Treasury sell government bonds to one group of U.S. citizens, thereby increasing the national debt. When the bonds mature, the government can pay the interest and principal by issuing new government bonds (rolling over the debt) to another group of U.S. citizens. This argument ignores the income distribution problem that results because interest payments go largely to those who are better off financially.

5. When the government makes interest payments on internally held debt, the money remains in the hands of U.S. citizens. External debt is very different. Repayment of interest and principal to foreigners withdraws pur-

chasing power from U.S. citizens in favor of citizens abroad.

7. a. In year one, the federal deficit begins at $50 billion, and the U.S. Treasury issues $50 billion worth of bonds to finance the deficit.
   b. The next year the federal government must pay interest of $5 billion to service the debt ($50 billion bonds $\times$ 0.10 interest rate). Adding the interest payment to the $100 billion spent for goods and services yields a $105 billion expenditure in year two.
   c. For the second year, the deficit is $55 billion ($105 billion in expenditures $-$ $50 billion in taxes), and the U.S. Treasury borrows this amount by issuing new bonds. The new national debt is $105 billion, consisting of the $50 billion in bonds issued in the first year and the $55 billion in bonds issued in the second year.

9. During a depression, tax hikes and/or expenditure cuts would only reduce aggregate demand and, in turn, real GDP, jobs, and income. Because the economy is operating in the Keynesian segment of the aggregate demand curve, this fiscal policy would have no impact on the price level.

11. This answer should be logical and supported by a thoughtful explanation. For example, the federal deficit might be the result of a recession and you argue that the deficit is correct fiscal policy. When the recession ends, the deficit will decline. Other arguments include some combinations of cutting spending or increasing taxes.

CHAPTER 14 MONEY AND THE FEDERAL RESERVE SYSTEM

1. Money is worthless in and of itself. The value of money is to serve as a medium of exchange, a unit of account, and a store of value.

3. a. The quantity of credit cards can be controlled. Credit cards are portable, divisible, and uniform in quality.

b. The quantity of Federal Reserve notes is controlled by the U.S. government. These notes are portable, divisible, and uniform in quality.

c. The quantity of dogs is difficult to control. Dogs are not very portable or divisible, and they are certainly not uniform.

d. The quantity of beer mugs can be controlled. Beer mugs are not very portable or divisible, but they could be made fairly uniform.

5. The narrowest definition of money in the United States is M1. M1 = currency (coins + paper bills) + checkable deposits.

7. The Fed's most important function is to regulate the U.S. money supply. The *Board of Governors* is composed of seven persons who have the responsibility to supervise and control the money supply and the U.S. banking system. The *Federal Open Market Committee (FOMC)* controls the money supply by directing the buying and selling of U.S. government securities.

9. Banks that belong to the Fed must join the FDIC. Banks chartered by the states may affiliate with the FDIC. There are relatively few nonmember, noninsured state banks.

CHAPTER 15 MONEY CREATION

1. At first, the goldsmiths followed Shakespeare's advice and gave receipts only for gold on deposit in their vaults. They then realized that at any given time new deposits were coming in that could offset old deposits people were drawing down. The conclusion is that banking does not require a 100 percent required reserve ratio. Therefore, loans can be made, which stimulate the economy.

3. Banks can and do create money by granting loans to borrowers. These loans are deposited in customers' checking accounts, and, therefore, banks are participants in the money supply creation process.

5. There is no impact on the money supply. A check deposited in bank *A*, drawn on bank *B*, increases deposits, reserves, and lending at bank *A*. However, bank *B* experiences an equal reduction in deposits, reserves, and lending.

7.

First National Bank			
Balance Sheet			
Assets		**Liabilities**	
Reserves	−$1,000	Checkable deposits	−$1,000
Required	−$100		
Excess	−$900		
Total assets	−$1,000	Total liabilities	−$1,000

Negative excess reserves mean that loans must be reduced by $1,000.

9. Some customers may hold cash, rather than writing a check for the full amount of the loan. Some banks may hold excess reserves, rather than using these funds to make loans.

11. The decision of the public to hold cash and the willingness of banks to use excess reserves for loans affect the money multiplier. Variations in the money multiplier can cause unexpected changes in the money supply. Nonbanks can make loans and offer other financial services that are not under the direct control of the Federal Reserve. Finally, the public can decide to transfer funds from M1 to M2 or other definitions of the money supply.

CHAPTER 16 MONETARY POLICY

1. a. Transactions and precautionary balances increase.
b. Speculative balances decrease.
c. Transactions and precautionary balances decrease.
d. Speculative balances increase.
e. Transactions and precautionary balances decrease.

3.

Bond price	Interest rate
$ 800	10%
1,000	8
2,000	4

There is an inverse relationship between the price of a bond and the interest rate.

5. a. The price level declines slightly. Real GDP and employment fall substantially.
   b. The price level, real GDP, and employment rise.
   c. The price level declines slightly. Real GDP and employment fall substantially.

7. In the monetarist view, the velocity of money, V, and the output, Q, variables in the equation of exchange are constant. Therefore, the quantity theory of money is stated as

$$M \times V = P \times Q$$

Given this equation, changes in the money supply, M1, yield proportionate changes in the price level, P.

9. In the Keynesian view, an increase in the money supply decreases the interest rate and causes investment spending, which increases aggregate demand through the multiplier effect and causes demand-pull inflation. In the monetarist view, money supply growth gives people more money to spend. This direct increase in aggregate demand causes demand-pull inflation.

11. Under such conditions, the Keynesian view is correct. The Fed would have no influence on investment because changes in the interest rate failed to alter the quantity of investment goods demanded.

CHAPTER 17 THE PHILLIPS CURVE AND EXPECTATIONS THEORY

1. The Phillips curve is an inverse relationship between the inflation rate and the unemployment rate. The increase in aggregate demand would cause the inflation rate to increase and the unemployment rate to decrease.

3. In the 1970s and early 1980s, the economy experienced supply shocks from skyrocketing oil and food prices. The result was a leftward shift in the aggregate supply curve and stagflation.

5. a. The inflation rate is 6 percent, and the unemployment rate is 6 percent.
   b. The inflation rate rises to 10 percent, and the employment rate falls in the short run.

In the long run, the unemployment rate returns to 6 percent.

   c. The inflation rate rises to 12 percent, and the unemployment rate falls in the short run. In the long run, the unemployment rate returns to 6 percent.

7. The economy is stimulated prior to an election, and there is a boom. After the election, the strategy is to contract the economy, causing recession until the next election approaches. Thus, political policies are counter to Keynesian policies because political policies cause the business cycle instead of stabilizing it.

9. a. Both prices and nominal wages will rise immediately, causing the inflation rate to rise from 4 percent to 6 percent. The unemployment rate remains unchanged at the 4 percent natural rate.
   b. Both prices and nominal wages will rise immediately, causing the inflation rate to rise from 6 percent to 8 percent. The unemployment rate remains unchanged at the 4 percent natural rate.
   c. Both prices and nominal wages will fall immediately, causing the inflation rate to fall from 8 percent to 4 percent. The unemployment rate remains unchanged at the 4 percent natural rate.

CHAPTER 18 INTERNATIONAL TRADE AND FINANCE

1. a. In Alpha, the opportunity cost of producing 1 ton of diamonds is 1/2 ton of pearls. In Beta, the opportunity cost of producing 1 ton of diamonds is 2 tons of pearls.
   b. In Alpha, the opportunity cost of producing 1 ton of pearls is 2 tons of diamonds. In Beta, the opportunity cost of producing 1 ton of pearls is 1/2 ton of diamonds.
   c. Because Alpha can produce diamonds at a lower opportunity cost than Beta can, Alpha has a comparative advantage in the production of diamonds.
   d. Because Beta can produce pearls at a lower opportunity cost than Alpha can, Beta has a comparative advantage in the production of pearls.

e.

	Diamonds (tons per year)	Pearls (tons per year)
Before specialization		
Alpha (at point *B*)	100	25
Beta (at point *C*)	30	120
Total output	130	145
After specialization		
Alpha (at point *A*)	150	0
Beta (at point *D*)	0	180
Total output	150	180

As shown in the above table, specialization in each country increases total world output per year by 20 tons of diamonds and 35 tons of pearls.

f.

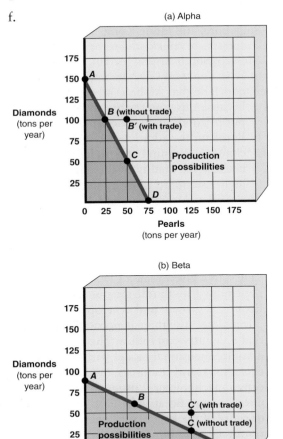

(a) Alpha

(b) Beta

Without trade, Alpha produces and consumes 100 tons of diamonds and 25 tons of pearls at point *B* on its production possibilities curve. Without trade, Beta produces and consumes 30 tons of diamonds and 120 tons of pearls (point *C*). Now assume Alpha specializes in producing diamonds at point *A* and imports 50 tons of pearls in exchange for 50 tons of diamonds. Through specialization and trade, Alpha moves its consumption possibility to point *B'*, outside its production possibilities curve.

3. The principle of specialization and trade according to comparative advantage applies to both nations and states in the United States. For example, Florida grows oranges, and Idaho grows potatoes. Trade between these states, just like trade between nations, increases the consumption possibilities.

5. U.S. industries (and their workers) that compete with restricted imports would benefit. Consumers would lose from the reduced supply of imported goods from which to choose and from higher prices for domestic products, resulting from lack of competition from imports.

7. Although some domestic jobs may be lost, new ones are created by international trade. Stated differently, the economy as a whole gains when nations specialize and trade according to the law of comparative advantage, but imports will cost jobs in some specific industries.

9. Although each nation's balance of payments equals zero, its current and capital account balances usually do not equal zero. For example, a current account deficit means a nation purchased more in imports than it sold in exports. On the other hand, this nation's capital account must have a surplus to offset the current account deficit. This means that foreigners are buying more domestic capital (capital inflow) than domestic citizens are buying foreign capital (capital outflow). Thus, net ownership of domestic capital stock is in favor of foreigners.

11. a.

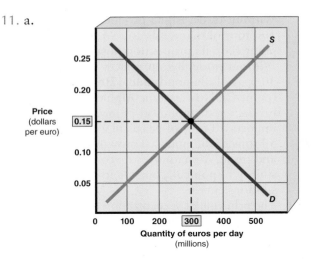

b. $0.15 per euro
c. An excess quantity of 200 million euros would be demanded.

CHAPTER 19 ECONOMIES IN TRANSITION

1. Americans prefer large cars and canned soup. Europeans predominantly buy small cars and dry soup. The role of women and minorities in the workplace is an excellent example of how culture relates to the labor factor of production.
3. Such a program would provide additional economic security for the elderly, but higher taxes could reduce the incentive to work, and economic efficiency might be reduced.
5. In a traditional agricultural system, a benefit would be that members of society would cooperate by helping to build barns, harvest, and so on. Under the command system, worrying about errors and crop failures would be minimized because the state makes the decisions and everyone in society has a basic income. In a market economy, a bumper crop would mean large profits and the capacity to improve one's standard of living.
7. Because most economies are mixed systems, this term is too broad to be very descriptive. The terms *capitalism* and *communism* are more definitive concerning the role of private ownership, market allocations, and decentralized decision making. Embracing a market-oriented system means a transfer of power from the command bureaucracy to consumers. Markets are incompatible with the principle that socialist citizens are supposed to be concerned with the collective interest.

CHAPTER 20 GROWTH AND THE LESS-DEVELOPED COUNTRIES

1. The difference between IACs and LDCs is based on GDP per capita. This classification is somewhat arbitrary. A country with a high GDP per capita and narrow industrial development based on oil, such as the United Arab Emirates, is excluded from the IAC list. There are 27 economies listed in the text as IACs, including Switzerland, Japan, the United States, Singapore, and Hong Kong. The following countries are considered to be LDCs: Argentina, Mexico, South Africa, Jordan, and Bangladesh.
3. a. Based only on GDP per capita, you would conclude that Alpha is a better place to live because this country produces a greater output of goods and services per person.
   b. Based on the additional evidence, you would change your mind and prefer to live in Beta because the quality-of-life data indicate a higher standard of living in this country.
5. The average growth rate of GDP per capita for IACs exceeds the GDP per capita growth rate for LDCs. This evidence is consistent with the argument. The argument is oversimplified because there is considerable diversity among the LDCs. In a given year, a LDC may have a GDP per capita growth rate greater than many IACs.
7. Economic growth and development are complicated because there is no single prescription that a country can follow. The chapter presents a multidimensional model with five basic categories: natural resources, human resources, capital, technological progress, and political environment. Because an LDC is weak in one or more of the key factors, such as natural resources, does not necessarily mean that the LDC cannot achieve economic success.
9. Because they are poor countries with low GDP per capita, they lack domestic savings to invest in capital; and lacking investment, they remain poor. The rich in these poor countries often put their savings abroad because of the fear

of political instability. An inflow of external funds from abroad permits the LDC to increase its capital without reducing its consumption and to shift its production possibilities curve outward.

11. Poor countries are too poor to save enough to finance domestic capital formation. International trade is a way LDCs can generate savings from abroad. Exports provide the LDCs with foreign exchange to pay for imports of capital stock that is necessary for economic growth and development.

Appendix

B Answers to Practice Quizzes

CHAPTER 1 INTRODUCING THE ECONOMIC WAY OF THINKING

1. c 2. d 3. c 4. c 5. a 6. a 7. a 8. a 9. a
10. c 11. a 12. b 13. c 14. d 15. d

APPENDIX TO CHAPTER 1 APPLYING GRAPHS TO ECONOMICS

1. d 2. d 3. a 4. d 5. d 6. c 7. c 8. c 9. d
10. d 11. d 12. b

CHAPTER 2 PRODUCTION POSSIBILITIES, OPPORTUNITY COST, AND ECONOMIC GROWTH

1. c 2. a 3. c 4. c 5. b 6. c 7. c 8. e 9. a
10. c 11. b 12. d 13. e 14. c 15. a

CHAPTER 3 MARKET DEMAND AND SUPPLY

1. e 2. a 3. b 4. b 5. a 6. b 7. c 8. b
9. c 10. b 11. c 12. c 13. d 14. d 15. c
16. d 17. d 18. c 19. d 20. d

APPENDIX TO CHAPTER 3 CONSUMER SURPLUS, PRODUCER SURPLUS, AND MARKET EFFICIENCY

1. c 2. b 3. d 4. e 5. d 6. d 7. b 8. d
9. a 10. b

CHAPTER 4 MARKETS IN ACTION

1. a 2. a 3. c 4. d 5. d 6. d 7. c 8. b
9. a 10. b 11. c 12. a 13. c 14. d 15. d

CHAPTER 5 GROSS DOMESTIC PRODUCT

1. d 2. a 3. a 4. e 5. d 6. d 7. c 8. d
9. b 10. d 11. b 12. b 13. c 14. d 15. e

CHAPTER 6 BUSINESS CYCLES AND UNEMPLOYMENT

1. c 2. d 3. d 4. d 5. d 6. d 7. c 8. b
9. a 10. d 11. d 12. d 13. c 14. e 15. e

CHAPTER 7 INFLATION

1. a 2. a 3. b 4. b 5. a 6. b 7. d 8. b
9. b 10. d 11. c 12. d 13. c 14. b 15. e

CHAPTER 8 THE KEYNESIAN MODEL

1. c 2. d 3. d 4. c 5. b 6. a 7. a 8. b
9. d 10. d 11. a 12. c 13. c 14. c 15. b

CHAPTER 9 THE KEYNESIAN MODEL IN ACTION

1. d 2. b 3. d 4. a 5. c 6. b 7. d 8. d
9. c 10. b 11. b 12. b 13. c 14. a 15. b

CHAPTER 10 AGGREGATE DEMAND AND SUPPLY

1. c 2. b 3. a 4. c 5. d 6. a 7. c 8. c
9. d 10. c 11. c 12. d 13. a 14. d 15. a

APPENDIX TO CHAPTER 10 THE SELF-CORRECTING AGGREGATE DEMAND AND SUPPLY MODEL

1. b 2. c 3. d 4. c 5. a 6. b 7. a 8. a
9. c 10. d 11. d 12. b 13. c 14. a 15. a

CHAPTER 11 FISCAL POLICY

1. d 2. a 3. d 4. b 5. d 6. c 7. a 8. d
9. c 10. d 11. a 12. d 13. a 14. a 15. e

CHAPTER 12 THE PUBLIC SECTOR

1. a 2. b 3. d 4. d 5. d 6. a 7. c 8. d
9. d 10. d 11. c 12. d 13. a 14. a 15. b

CHAPTER 13 FEDERAL DEFICITS, SURPLUSES, AND THE NATIONAL DEBT

1. a 2. b 3. c 4. d 5. c 6. d 7. b 8. e
9. a 10. d 11. d 12. a 13. a 14. a 15. e

CHAPTER 14 MONEY AND THE FEDERAL RESERVE SYSTEM

1. b 2. b 3. d 4. c 5. d 6. b 7. c 8. d
9. c 10. d 11. d 12. b 13. b 14. c 15. a

CHAPTER 15 MONEY CREATION

1. b 2. b 3. b 4. c 5. c 6. d 7. c 8. c
9. b 10. b 11. a 12. d 13. d 14. a 15. a

CHAPTER 16 MONETARY POLICY

1. d 2. b 3. d 4. a 5. a 6. d 7. c 8. d
9. d 10. c 11. b 12. a 13. b 14. c 15. d

APPENDIX TO CHAPTER 16 POLICY DISPUTES USING THE SELF-CORRECTING AGGREGATE DEMAND AND SUPPLY MODEL

1. c 2. d 3. d 4. d 5. d 6. b

CHAPTER 17 THE PHILLIPS CURVE AND EXPECTATIONS THEORY

1. d 2. b 3. a 4. c 5. e 6. c 7. b 8. c
9. c 10. d 11. c 12. b 13. d 14. a 15. d

CHAPTER 18 INTERNATIONAL TRADE AND FINANCE

1. b 2. c 3. a 4. d 5. d 6. a 7. d 8. a
9. c 10. c 11. b 12. c 13. c 14. a 15. a
16. b 17. a 18. a 19. e 20. d

CHAPTER 19 ECONOMIES IN TRANSITION

1. c 2. d 3. d 4. a 5. b 6. a 7. c 8. b
9. b 10. c 11. c 12. a 13. a 14. d 15. a

CHAPTER 20 GROWTH AND THE LESS-DEVELOPED COUNTRIES

1. d 2. d 3. d 4. c 5. a 6. a 7. d 8. a
9. c 10. a 11. b 12. d 13. c 14. d 15. b

Appendix

C Answers to Road Map Questions

PART 1

1. e 2. c 3. c 4. d 5. a 6. e 7. d 8. d
9. d 10. b

PART 2

1. b 2. c 3. a 4. a 5. d 6. d 7. d 8. c
9. c 10. c 11. b 12. a 13. c

PART 3

1. e 2. a 3. a 4. c 5. c 6. b 7. b 8. d
9. a 10. a 11. c 12. d

PART 4

1. d 2. a 3. a 4. d 5. d 6. b 7. c 8. e
9. b 10. a 11. a 12. d 13. b 14. e 15. d

PART 5

1. d 2. d 3. d 4. e 5. c 6. b 7. a 8. d
9. d 10. a 11. e 12. d 13. a 14. a

PART 6

1. d 2. d 3. b 4. e 5. e 6. c 7. d 8. e
9. b 10. d

Q

Quality-of-life measures, 541–542
Quantity, and equilibrium price, 80
Quantity demanded, changes in, 61–63, 83
Quantity supplied, changes in, 70–73, 84
Quantity theory of money, 430–431, 441
Quota, 489–490, 508

R

Racial bias. *See also* Discrimination
Rational expectations theory, 458, 461–465, 470
Rational voter ignorance, 339
Reagan, Ronald
    federal budget and, 350, 352
    fiscal policy and, 323
    supply-side fiscal policy, 313
    taxes, 300, 313
Real balances effect, 260–261, 262, 267, 281
Real consumption, 222
Real GDP. *See also* Gross domestic product (GDP)
    definition, 152
    internationally, 163–164
    in Keynesian equilibrium, 240
    nominal GDP, 147–150
    price level and unemployment, 278
Real income, 192, 200
Real interest rate, 194–195, 200
Real investment, 222
Recession
    fiscal policy and, 318
    government spending, 301–303
    Great Recession of 2007, 160–161, 163, 273–274, 300, 324–325, 350, 391, 434, 438–439
    introduction to, 159–160
    post-World War II, 161
    tax cuts, 306–307
Recessionary gap, 247–250, 253
Recession of 2008-2009, 273–274
Recovery, 159–160, 161
Regressive taxes, 333

Regulation
    pollution, 114–115
    price ceilings, 105–107, 119
Related goods, 66, 68
Relative incomes, 503
Relative price levels, 503
Relative real interest rates, 503
Renewable resources, 4
Rental income, 138, 139
Rent controls, 105–107
Required reserve ratio, 398–399, 409–412, 414, 415
Required reserves, 398, 414
Resolution Trust Corporation (RTC), 391, 532
Resources, 16
    changes in, 44
    definition, 3–5
    human, 543–544
    nonrenewable, 4
    prices of, 74, 76, 77, 128
Rinehart, James R., 78
The Road to Serfdom (Hayek), 523
"Roaring Twenties", 210, 226
Roosevelt, Franklin D., 183, 350, 506
Russia, 141, 527, 529, 552
Ruth, Babe, 487

S

Salaries, 15
Samuelson, Paul, 454
San Francisco Chronicle, 198
Saving, 214
Savings and loan crisis, 390–391
Savings deposits, 381
Say, Jean-Baptiste, 211
Say's Law, 211, 231
Scarce resources, 3–5
Scarcity, 3, 5–6, 16, 36, 377
School vouchers, 116–117
Schwartz, Anna, 438
Schwarzenegger, Arnold, 13
Search unemployment, 170
Secondhand transactions, 131
Secret Service, U.S., 378
Securities and Exchange Commission (SEC), 390

Self-correcting aggregate demand-aggregate supply model, 286–295
    changes in potential real GDP, 293–294
    decrease in aggregate demand, 291–293
    equilibrium in, 289
    increase in aggregate demand, 289–291
    increase in aggregate demand and long-run aggregate supply curves, 294–295
    long-run aggregate supply curve (LRAS), 288
    short-run aggregate supply curve (SRAS), 286–288
Self-interest, 519
"Self-reliance" policy, 530
Sellers, 74, 76, 128
September 11, 2001, terror attacks, 226
Services, 135
Shaw, George Bernard, 12, 237
Shortage, 80
Short-run aggregate supply curve (SRAS), 286–288, 289, 296
Shortsightedness effect, 340
Singapore, 539, 551, 553
Slope of a curve, 26–27
Slope of a straight line, 24–25
Small time deposits, 381
Smith, Adam
    as father of modern economics, 519
    founder of classical economic theory, 211, 265
    market economy, 518–521
    overview of, 436
    The Wealth of Nations, 111, 518, 520, 524
Smith, Frederick W., 45
Smithsonian Institution, 45
Smoot-Hawley Act of 1930, 488–489
Sneakers, demand for, 79, 81
Socialism, 524–527, 533
Social Security contributions, 147
Social Security trust fund, 349
Solow, Robert, 454
South Korea, 539, 551, 553